D0002270

BEYOND PICTURE BOOKS

BEYOND PICTURE BOOKS™
A GUIDE TO FIRST READERS

SECOND EDITION

BARBARA BARSTOW

JUDITH RIGGLE

R.R. BOWKER®
A Reed Reference Publishing Company
New Providence, New Jersey

Published by R. R. Bowker,
a Reed Reference Publishing Company
Copyright © 1995 by Reed Elsevier Inc.
All rights reserved
Printed and bound in the United States of America
Bowker® is a registered trademark of Reed Reference Publishing,
a division of Reed Elsevier Inc. Beyond Picture Books™ is a trademark
of Reed Reference Publishing, a division of Reed Elsevier Inc.

Library of Congress Cataloging-in-Publication Data

Barstow, Barbara.
    Beyond picture books : a guide to first readers / Barbara Barstow.
    Judith Riggle. — 2nd ed.
        p.   cm.
    Includes index.
    ISBN 0-8352-3519-X
    1. Children—United States—Books and reading.   2. Children's
literature—Bibliography.   3. Children's libraries—United States—
Book lists.   I. Riggle, Judith.   II. Title.
Z1037.B278   1995
[PN1009.A1]
011.62—dc20   94–49731
                                                              CIP

ISBN 0 - 8352 - 3519 - X

9 780835 235198

CONTENTS

PREFACE

First readers are defined here as books intended for children at a first or second grade level (occasionally third) that have a recognizable format and generally belong to a series. The standard format for a first reader has large print, short sentences, a limited amount of print per page, and usually at least one illustration on each double-page spread. The vocabulary can be, but is not always, controlled and is generally limited to sight words, words of few syllables, and a familiar spoken vocabulary.

The following criteria were used to select books for inclusion in this bibliography. The book had to be well-written, contain accurate information, have stories or subjects of interest to children in the primary grades, and have illustrations that complement the text and are attractive to children. Both in- and out-of-print books are included here. Excluded were books that had a very limited vocabulary but seemed more suitable to toddlers than first or second graders and books that were too sophisticated for first or second graders in spite of their format or vocabulary.

In locating the books for the first edition of this bibliography, the collections of five Cuyahoga County Public Library (CCPL) branches were used: Berea, Brook Park, Fairview Park, Middleburg Heights, and North Olmsted. The collections at four other Ohio libraries were also extensively used: Cleveland Public Library; Lakewood Public Library; Avon Lake Public Library; and Boulevard Elementary School, Shaker Heights; as well as many other state libraries via interlibrary loan. For titles that might have been missed, reference was made to publishers' catalogs, *The Elementary School Library Collection, The Children's Catalog,* and a computer printout of all first readers maintained at Maple Heights Regional Library of CCPL. Since that time titles included in CCPL materials examination meetings were a chief source.

From the 2,495 titles in the Annotated Bibliography, a list of 200 Outstanding First Readers has been selected. These outstanding titles were chosen on the basis of exceptional language and treatment of subject. This list includes both old and new titles, some standard in most library collections. All in print titles were verified in *Children's Books in Print 1994–95.*

The Annotated Bibliography is arranged alphabetically by author surname. Each title has been assigned an entry number. Where applicable each annotation contains the following information: title, illustrator, publisher, date of publication, out-of-print (o.p.) status, paperback data (publisher, if different from hardbound edition; date), ISBN (not given for o.p. titles), subjects, reading category, and a brief annotation.

One ISBN number has been used for each title that is still in print. Wherever possible the trade ISBN has been used; however, in instances where that is o.p. the library edition ISBN is used. When both the library binding and trade editions are o.p., the paperback edition ISBN is used. The annotations are short, give a brief plot synopsis, occasionally provide critical information, and offer a few words about the illustrations.

The most challenging task continues to be the selection of meaningful subject headings. The *Sears List of Subject Headings*, 10th edition, provided the first and most useful source. Library of Congress subject headings from the copyright pages of more recent titles were also helpful. In addition we relied on our experience with patron requests to create subject headings; for example, "Babies, new" rather than just "Babies."

Probably the most controversial part of this bibliography was the assignment of reading levels. Researchers have consistently questioned the reliability of the available tests (for example, Fry and Spache), and for many of the same reasons we do too. The formulas used for testing readability do not take into consideration the sophistication of the information with which they are dealing, do not guarantee comprehension of information, have not been based on real statistical investigations of children and their reading, and do not consider cultural differences in language usage. Further, research has shown that sections of books can vary greatly in reading level. This was noticed when, for the first edition, we used what we found to be the best computer readability program for Spache—Minnesota Educational Computing Corporation's 1982 program for the Apple IIe. Three 100-word passages chosen at random from the beginning, middle, and end of each book were entered into the computer and then evaluated by the readability program. Reading levels varied according to which passages were entered and the judgment of the person entering the passages in dividing compound sentences; in punctuation, especially in poetry; or in designating a word like astronaut as "known" to a reader.

For this second edition, readability formulas were not used. We instead evaluated and compared many first readers, noticing a distinct pattern in format. The intention is that the reading level assignments be used in the most general way to identify books on the low, middle, and high range of difficulty for children beginning to read. The objective is to *encourage* children to read by providing access to quality material within their reach and by helping children *stretch* their skill, not stifling their interest. Reading Level A usually has sentences with three to five single-syllable, easily recognizable words and the text is often in large print. For these books the illustrations generally take up two-thirds of each page. In assigning books to Reading Level B, we looked for a balance between text and illustrations, more complex sentences, and more descriptors, phrases, and multi-syllabic words. In Reading Level C illustrative material is frequently reduced to alternating pages, there is more text, sentences are frequently compound, and vocabulary is more difficult.

There is a large body of fine literature classified as "first readers." Outstanding writers of books for older children like Jane Yolen, Virginia Hamilton, Eleanor Coerr, William Sleator, Marjorie Weinman Sharmat, and Betsy Byars write creatively for this age level. Outstanding picture book writers and illustrators such as Russell Hoban, Pat Hutchins, Arnold Lobel, Aliki, Lillian Hoban, Ann Rockwell, Marc Simont, Steven Kellogg, and Tomie dePaola also share or shared their talents with this group. The language these writers use is simple but natural, nonpatronizing, varied, and inventive. Their nonfiction is accurate, clear, and makes complex subjects surprisingly understandable. Much of the nonfiction might be useful for newly literate adults wanting to explore a field of interest. The illustrations offer a visual extension of the text, often in a humorous way, and provide a bridge between profusely illustrated picture books and the books for upper elementary school children.

The first edition of *Beyond Picture Books* contained 1,610 titles. This total has grown to 2,495 with this second edition; however, the net gain is more that 885 new titles as many that appeared in the first edition were deleted for various reasons. We recognize that there may be omissions in our list and would welcome suggestions for books to include in a future edition.

OUTSTANDING FIRST READERS

The following is a selected list of 200 outstanding first readers. This list is a mix of old and new titles, fiction and nonfiction, all currently in-print according to *Children's Books in Print, 1994–95* and all worthy of purchase for school or public library collections. Many of what we considered to be the very best first readers were out-of-print and therefore ineligible for this list. All of these books are well-written, contain accurate information when dealing with nonfiction subjects, are of interest to primary age children, and have attractive illustrations that complement the text. No attempt was made to present a balanced list of fiction and nonfiction works or of first, second, and third grade books. For books in a series like those of Arnold Lobel's Frog and Toad series and Cynthia Rylant's Henry and Mudge series, only one title is listed.

Agell, Charlotte
  Sailor's Book
Alexander, Sue
  World Famous Muriel and the Magic Mystery
Aliki
  Communication
  The King's Day: Louis XIV of France
  My Feet
Arnosky, Jim
  Crinkelroot's Guide to Knowing the Trees
Baker, Betty
  The Turkey Girl
Bang, Molly G.
  Wiley and the Hairy Man
Benchley, Nathaniel
  George the Drummer Boy
Berenstain, Stan, and Berenstain, Jan
  The Berenstain Bears and the Spooky Old Tree

Berger, Melvin
  Look Out for Turtles
Berger, Melvin, and Berger, Gilda
  The Whole World in Your Hands
Boegehold, Betty
  Horse Called Starfire
Bonsall, Crosby
  And I Mean It, Stanley
  Mine's the Best
  Tell Me Some More
Brandenberg, Franz
  Aunt Nina and Her Nephews and Nieces
Branley, Franklin M.
  The Big Dipper
  Shooting Stars
Brenner, Barbara
  A Dog I Know
  Wagon Wheels
Bulla, Clyde Robert
  Daniel's Duck
Bunting, Eve

Big Red Barn

Calder, S. J.
If You Were a Cat

Carlson, Nancy
Harriet and Walt

Cazet, Denys
Saturday

Chenery, Janet
Toad Hunt

Chorao, Kay
Oink and Pearl

Christian, Mary B.
Penrod's Party

Coerr, Eleanor
Chang's Paper Pony

Cole, Joanna
Bony-Legs
The Magic School Bus: At the Waterworks
Plants in Winter

Coville, Bruce, and Coville, Katherine
Sarah's Unicorn

Cromie, William J.
Steven and the Green Turtle

Delton, Judy
A Birthday Bike for Brimhall

dePaola, Tomie
Cloud Book

Dorros, Arthur
Follow the Water from Brook to Ocean
Me and My Shadow

Eastman, Philip D.
Are You My Mother?

Ehrlich, Amy
Leo, Zack and Emmie Together Again

Fisher, Aileen
The House of a Mouse

Florian, Douglas
A Potter

Frasier, Debra
On the Day You Were Born

Freedman, Russell

Dinosaurs and Their Young

Frith, Michael K.
I'll Teach My Dog 100 Words

Fritz, Jean
Surprising Myself

Gackenbach, Dick
Hound and Bear

Gage, Wilson
Down in the Boondocks

Gauch, Patricia L.
Aaron and the Green Mountain Boys

Gibbons, Gail
Stargazers

Greene, Carol
John Philip Sousa: The March King
Margaret Wise Brown: Author of Goodnight Moon

Haddad, Helen R.
Truck and Loader

Hall, Katy, and Eisenberg, Lisa
Snakey Riddles

Heilbroner, Joan
This Is the House Where Jack Lives

Heller, Ruth
Merry-Go-Round: A Book About Nouns

Himmelman, John
The Day-Off Machine

Hoban, Lillian
Arthur's Prize Reader

Hoff, Syd
Danny and the Dinosaur

Holl, Adelaide
Small Bear's Name Hunt

Holland, Marion
Big Ball of String

Hopkins, Lee Bennett
Good Books, Good Times!

Hopkins, Lee Bennett, ed.
Questions
Weather

Howe, James

Newman, Nanette
That Dog!
O'Connor, Jane
*EEK! Stories to Make You
Shriek*
Molly the Brave and Me
Oppenheim, Joanne
The Show-and-Tell Frog
Orgel, Doris, and Schecter, Ellen
The Flower of Sheba
Otto, Carolyn
I Can Tell by Touching
Palacios, Argentina
*A Christmas Surprise for
Chabelita*
*Viva Mexico! A Story of Benito
Juarez and Cinco de Mayo*
Palmer, Helen M.
A Fish Out of Water
Parish, Peggy
Amelia Bedelia
Scruffy
Penner, Lucille Recht
Dinosaur Babies
Petersen, P. J.
The Fireplug Is First Base
Pfeffer, Wendy
From Tadpole to Frog
Pilkey, Dav
*A Friend for Dragon: Dragon's
First Tale*
Platt, Kin
Big Max
Pomerantz, Charlotte
The Outside Dog
Porte, Barbara Ann
Harry Gets and Uncle
Powell, E. Sandy
Rats
Prager, Annabelle
The Spooky Halloween Party
Prelutsky, Jack
It's Halloween
Rabinowitz, Sandy
How I Trained My Colt

Random House
*The Random House Book of
Easy-to-Read Stories*
Reit, Seymour
*Things That Go: A Traveling
Alphabet*
Retan, Walter
Armies of Ants
Robbins, Ken
*Make Me a Peanut Butter
Sandwich and a Glass of Milk*
Robins, Joan
Addie's Bad Day
Robinson, Fay, ed.
*A Frog Inside My Hat: A First
Book of Poems*
Roop, Peter, and Roop, Connie
Keep the Lights Burning, Abbie
Rosen, Sidney
Where Does the Moon Go?
Ross, Pat
*M and M and the Halloween
Monster*
Rubin, Mark
The Orchestra
Ryder Joanne
Hello, First Grade
White Bear, Ice Bear
Rylant, Cynthia
*Henry and Mudge Take the Big
Test: The Tenth Book of Their
Adventures*
*Mr. Putter and Tabby Pour the
Tea*
Sandin, Joan
The Long Way Westward
Schick, Eleanor
Home Alone
Schulman, Janet
The Big Hello
Schultz, Walter A.
Will and Orv
Schwartz, Alvin
*Busy Buzzing Bumblebees and
Other Tongue Twisters*

ANNOTATED BIBLIOGRAPHY

A

Abisch, Roz

1 *Do You Know What Time It Is?* Ill. by
Boche Kaplan. Prentice-Hall, 1968, o.p.
SUBJECTS: Clocks; Concepts—Time; Science.
RL C.
Information about telling time is followed by
instructions for making a clock with which to
practice. The information is clearly and logically presented, and the illustrations contribute well to the story.

Adams, Florence

2 *Mushy Eggs*. Ill. by Marilyn Hirsch.
Putnam, 1973, o.p. SUBJECTS: Baby-sitting—
Fiction; Family life—Fiction; Parents,
working—Fiction. RL C.
The new baby-sitter is nice and bakes good
cookies, but cannot make the mushy eggs like
the boys' previous baby-sitter, their beloved
Fanny. Homely details warm this tale of special relationships.

Adler, David A.

3 *The Carsick Zebra and Other Animal
Riddles*. Ill. by Tomie dePaola. Holiday
House, 1983; Bantam, pap., 1985. ISBN 0-
8234-0479-X. SUBJECTS: Animals—Fiction;
Jokes and riddles. RL B.
Wordplay employing familiar situations and
animals is used in an extremely inventive
manner. Line drawings are of humorous animals.

4 *My Dog and the Birthday Mystery*. Ill. by
Dick Gackenbach. Holiday House, hb and
pap., 1987. ISBN 0-8234-0632-6. SERIES: First

Mystery. SUBJECTS: Animals—Dogs—Fiction;
Birthdays—Fiction; Mystery and detective
stories. RL A.
Jennie's friends, having arranged a surprise
party for her birthday, trick her into working
on a mystery that leads her to the party. The
story is accompanied by pictures with red,
orange, yellow, and gray washes with black
outlining.

5 *My Dog and the Green Sock Mystery*. Ill. by
Dick Gackenbach. Holiday House, 1986.
ISBN 0-8234-0590-7. SERIES: First Mystery.
SUBJECTS: Animals—Dogs—Fiction; Mystery
and detective stories. RL B.
Jennie's astute observations and My Dog's contributions help locate Andy's missing belongings. Characteristic mishaps of childhood add
humor and warmth to the tale. My Dog, curious and appealingly shaggy, is the focus of the
ink drawings.

6 *My Dog and the Knock Knock Mystery*. Ill.
by Marsha Winborn. Holiday House, 1985,
o.p. SERIES: First Mystery. SUBJECTS:
Animals—Dogs—Fiction; Mystery and
detective stories. RL B.
This gently humorous mystery is solved with
the intuitive help of My Dog. A slightly sick
shaggy white pup lying on marbleized avocado
grass surrounded by the remains of the apples
he has consumed—in the course of duty—is
typically appealing.

7 *Redwoods Are the Tallest Trees in the World*.
Ill. by Kazue Mizumura. HarperCollins,
1978, o.p. SERIES: Let's-Read-and-Find-Out
Science Books. SUBJECTS: Nature; Plants—
Trees; Science. RL C.
The size and growth of redwoods are contrast-
ed with more familiar trees. Brown and green
watercolors are fairly dull.

Adler, David A. (cont.)

8 *The Twisted Witch and Other Spooky Riddles*. Ill. by Victoria Chess. Holiday House, 1985; Bantam, pap., 1986. ISBN 0-8234-0571-0. SUBJECTS: Holidays—Halloween—Fiction; Jokes and riddles. RL C.

Riddles include topics such as witches. Illustrations are in gray and black.

Agell, Charlotte

9 *Sailor's Book*. Ill. by author. Firefly, 1991, o.p. SUBJECTS: Mythical creatures—Dragons—Fiction; Poetry. RL A.

Gentle, rhythmic extended simile about the sea as a dragon, whose breath is the clouds, whose waves are the scales, and whose eye is the sun. Illustrations are in textured turquoise, deep purple, and orange washes.

Ahlberg, Allan

10 *Dinosaur Dreams*. Ill. by Andre Amstutz. Greenwillow, 1991. ISBN 0-688-09955-6. SERIES: Funnybones. SUBJECTS: Cumulative tales; Dinosaurs—Fiction; Dreams—Fiction. RL B.

A slim story about the coordinated dinosaur dreams of little and big skeleton and their skeleton dog. Readers who are familiar with the characters will enjoy the text and the striking colorful graphic illustrations against a black background.

11 *The Ghost Train*. Ill. by Andre Amstutz. Putnam, 1992. ISBN 0-688-11435-0. SERIES: Funnybones. SUBJECTS: Cumulative tales; Ghosts—Fiction; Trains—Fiction. RL A.

A baby crying in the night scares the skeletons, witches, and monsters on a midnight train adventure. The striking graphic illustrations use bright colors on a black ground.

12 *Mystery Tour*. Ill. by Andre Amstutz. Greenwillow, 1991. ISBN 0-688-09957-2. SERIES: Funnybones. SUBJECTS: Cumulative tales; Mystery and detective stories; Visual perception. RL B.

Friendly skeletons—one large and one small—drive on a mystery tour to identify silhouettes: a baby in a crib, a train, a teddy in a tent. The illustrator's vivid graphic colors against a black background are well suited to a nighttime mystery adventure.

13 *The Pet Shop*. Ill. by Andre Amstutz. Greenwillow, 1990. ISBN 0-688-09905-X. SERIES: Funnybones. SUBJECTS: Humorous stories; Pets—Fiction. RL A.

Tired of their dog's digging holes and barking, the skeletons trade him in for a series of pets, each larger and more troublesome than the last. Full color illustrations with white skeletal people and pets are vivid against a black background.

14 *Skeleton Crew*. Ill. by Andre Amstutz. Greenwillow, 1992. ISBN 0-688-11436-9. SERIES: Funnybones. SUBJECTS: Humorous stories; Vacations—Fiction. RL A.

Three skeletons on vacation are set adrift by pirates, floating in and out of danger. A choppy rhythm, some word play, and humor are accompanied by a vividly colored seascape and white skeletons against a black background.

Alexander, Ellen

15 *Llama and the Great Flood: A Folktale from Peru*. Ill. by author. HarperCollins, 1989. ISBN 0-690-04729-0. SUBJECTS: Folklore—Peru. RL C.

After a llama saves a Peruvian family from the Great Flood, llamas become very special. The appealing watercolor illustrations supply color and pattern to an account of everyday life high in the Andes.

Alexander, Liza

16 *Splish-Splashy Day: Featuring Jim Henson's Sesame Street Muppets*. Ill. by Joseph Ewers. Western, 1989, o.p. SERIES: Sesame Street. SUBJECTS: Humorous stories; Stories in rhyme; Weather—Rain—Fiction. RL A.

The Sesame Street characters enjoy playing and dancing in the mud and puddles of a rainy day—and the comfort of drying off at home. Cartoon illustrations accompany the text.

Alexander, Sue

17 *Marc the Magnificent*. Ill. by Tomie dePaola. Pantheon, 1978, o.p. SUBJECTS:

Imagination—Fiction; Magic—Fiction. RL C.
A boy's fantasy of fame as a magician contrasts with his first clumsy attempts at magic—but finally ends in success. Fantasy and reality are humorously contrasted through the use of language and simple pictures. Illustrations are primarily in plum, tan, and dull gold.

18 *More Witch, Goblin, and Ghost Stories*. Ill. by Jeanette Winter. Pantheon, 1978. ISBN 0-394-83933-1. SERIES: I Am Reading. SUBJECTS: Friendship—Fiction; Ghost stories; Witches—Fiction. RL C.
An indoor picnic, a faked illness, a tall tale, a day spent observing nature, all bring these three friends closer. Soft pencil drawings complement the theme well.

19 *Seymour the Prince*. Ill. by Lillian Hoban. Pantheon, 1979, o.p. SERIES: I Am Reading. SUBJECTS: Clubs—Fiction; Plays—Fiction. RL B.
Does Seymour want to be part of the Maple Street club badly enough to be laughed at as the prince in Sleeping Beauty? Soft pencil drawings are warm and appealing.

20 *Witch, Goblin, and Ghost Are Back*. Ill. by Jeanette Winter. Pantheon, 1985. ISBN 0-394-86296-1. SERIES: I Am Reading. SUBJECTS: Friendship—Fiction; Ghost stories; Witches—Fiction. RL C.
Lessons about friendship—and the consequences of eating nothing but fudge—are gently relayed in five chapters. Another book in a series about three friends. Illustrations are low-key and in soft pencil.

21 *Witch, Goblin, and Ghost in the Haunted Woods*. Ill. by Jeanette Winter. Pantheon, 1981. ISBN 0-394-84443-2. SERIES: I Am Reading. SUBJECTS: Friendship—Fiction; Ghost stories; Witches—Fiction. RL C.
Through a story, two friends help Goblin learn how to swim. Warm, supportive friends are very different from one another. Soft pencil drawings convey the feelings.

22 *Witch, Goblin, and Sometimes Ghost: Six Read-Alone Stories*. Ill. by Jeanette Winter. Pantheon, 1976. ISBN 0-394-93216-1. SERIES: I Am Reading. SUBJECTS: Friendship—Fiction; Ghost stories. RL B.

These six tales include friends telling stories so that fear of lightning is allayed, and friends collaborating in writing a book. Pencil drawings underscore the relationship of the three.

23 *World Famous Muriel*. Ill. by Chris Demarest. Little, Brown, 1984; Dell, pap., 1988. ISBN 0-440-40024-4. SUBJECTS: Humorous stories; Mystery and detective stories. RL B.
Muriel follows clues, including footprints, to discover who has stolen the decorations for the queen's party. Tongue-in-cheek humor is appropriately illustrated with comic watercolor drawings.

24 *World Famous Muriel and the Magic Mystery*. Ill. by Marla Frazee. HarperCollins, 1990. ISBN 0-690-04789-4. SUBJECTS: Libraries—Fiction; Magic—Fiction; Mystery and detective stories. RL B.
World Famous Muriel, fueled with peanutbutter cookies, tracks the missing magician, the Great Hokus Pokus, to the library, boning up on his less than perfect magic tricks. Vivid illustrations show a library full of people and activities, as well as a male children's librarian.

25 *World Famous Muriel and the Scary Dragon*. Ill. by Chris Demarest. Little, Brown, 1985; Dell, pap., 1988, o.p. SUBJECTS: Humorous stories; Mythical creatures—Fiction. RL B.
When the King of Pompandcircumstance sends for Muriel to rid the neighborhood of a dragon, she takes her tightrope and her favorite peanut butter cookies. Delightful humor is immeasurably heightened with cartoon drawings in watercolors.

Aliki

26 *At Mary Bloom's*. Ill. by author. Greenwillow, 1976. ISBN 0-688-02481-5. SUBJECTS: Cumulative tales; Pets—Fiction. RL A.
Mary Bloom helps a small girl celebrate her mouse's new babies. Marvelous animal ink drawings range from tiny mice to wall-to-wall pets and a story rebus.

27 *Communication*. Ill. by author. Greenwillow, 1993. ISBN 0-688-10529-7. SUBJECTS: Communication; Emotions. RL C.

Aliki (cont.)

Communicating shares knowledge, tells news, expresses feelings, and is being heard. With lively cartoon dialogue and drawings, the author talks about nonverbal communication including sign language, laughing and crying, and modern means of communication. Content and format are exceptional.

28 *Corn Is Maize: The Gift of the Indians*. Ill. by author. HarperCollins, 1976; HarperCollins, pap., 1976. ISBN 0-690-00975-5. SERIES: Let's-Read-and-Find-Out Science Books. SUBJECTS: Food; Native Americans. RL C.
The history of Native American corn cultivation going back 5,000 years is traced, as well as the ways it has been used and valued. Fascinating illustrations in gray, yellow, and green add immeasurably to the story. Illustrated instructions for making a corn husk wreath are appended.

29 *Digging Up Dinosaurs*. Ill. by author. HarperCollins, 1988. ISBN 0-690-04716-9. SERIES: Let's-Read-and-Find-Out Science Books. SUBJECTS: Dinosaurs; Science. RL B.
Of utmost interest in this story is the transporting of the dinosaur fossil finds to the museum and their preparation for exhibit. The dainty soft colored pencil drawings are augmented by cartoon comments from children, scientists, and museum buffs.

30 *Dinosaur Bones*. Ill. by author. HarperCollins, 1988. ISBN 0-690-04550-6. SERIES: Let's-Read-and-Find-Out Science Books. SUBJECTS: Dinosaurs; Fossils; Geology and geologists; Science and scientists. RL B.
With typically appealing colored pencil illustrations of dinosaurs and their discoverers, with lively dialogue accompanying the text, information about the several dozen dinosaurs is given.

31 *Dinosaurs Are Different*. Ill. by author. HarperCollins, 1985; HarperCollins, pap., 1986. ISBN 0-690-04456-9. SERIES: Let's-Read-and-Find-Out Science Books. SUBJECTS: Dinosaurs; Science. RL C.
Exceptionally well presented information on how one can distinguish the families of dinosaurs by their teeth and hips is illustrated with accurate sketches, color-coding, and cartoons of children. Length and weight, the name of each dinosaur, and the cartoons are hand-lettered.

32 *Fossils Tell of Long Ago*. Ill. by author. HarperCollins, pap., 1990. ISBN 0-06-445093-7. SERIES: Let's-Read-and-Find-Out Science Books. SUBJECTS: Fossils; Museums; Science and scientists. RL B.
Lively dialogue of children visiting a natural history museum adds flavor to the easy-reading information about fossils. Appealing ink and colored pencil drawings include children making their own imprints.

33 *How a Book Is Made*. Ill. by author. HarperCollins, 1985. ISBN 0-690-04498-4. SUBJECTS: Books and reading; Careers. RL C.
Aliki likes how a book feels, looks, and smells. She details the stages of a book's creation to publication. Cat characters in soft pastel cartoons even show details of color separation and printing.

34 *I'm Growing*. Ill. by author. HarperCollins, 1992. ISBN 0-06-020245-9. SERIES: Let's-Read-and-Find-Out Science Books. SUBJECTS: Human body—Growth. RL B.
A small Hispanic boy marks his growth by how his clothes fit, by how his measurements increase, and by looking at a photo album. Appealing presentation and illustrations.

35 *The King's Day: Louis XIV of France*. Ill. by author. HarperCollins, 1989. ISBN 0-690-04588-3. SUBJECTS: Biographies; France; Kings and queens. RL C.
The extravagant rituals of a day in the life of the Sun King are lavishly illustrated with detailed delicate watercolors and interesting text. A chronology and some French definitions are appended.

36 *Long-Lost Coelacanth and Other Living Fossils*. Ill. by author. HarperCollins, 1973, o.p. SERIES: Let's-Read-and-Find-Out Science Books. SUBJECTS: Animals—Fish, prehistoric; Fossils, living. RL C.
The drama of the 1938 discovery that the coelacanth was not extinct 70 million years ago is captured in simple language. Horses, starfish, algae, and horseshoe crabs are some of the other living fossils introduced. Children

are asked to guess what living fossil the author does *not* save!

37 *Milk: From Cow to Carton*. Ill. by author. HarperCollins, 1974, 1992. ISBN 0-06-020435-4. SERIES: Let's-Read-and-Find-Out Science Books. SUBJECTS: Animals—Cows; Food; Science. RL A.
From a pastoral landscape to a cow barn, from cow anatomy to a dairy schematic, the illustrations are tidy and appealing. The wonder of the process is not lost.

38 *My Feet*. Ill. by author. HarperCollins, 1990. ISBN 0-690-04815-7. SERIES: Let's-Read-and-Find-Out Science Books. SUBJECTS: Human body—Feet; Science. RL A.
Anatomy, size, differences, functioning, coverings, and comfort of feet are outlined, with the author/illustrator's characteristic simple colored pencil illustrations.

39 *My Hands*. Ill. by author. HarperCollins, 1990, 1992. ISBN 0-690-04880-7. SUBJECTS: Human body—Hands. RL A.
Appealing drawings of preschoolers working with clay, painting, sewing, buttoning, and petting a kitten illustrate the functions and usefulness of hands. Even sign language and gesturing are mentioned in this thorough and lively account for the younger set.

40 *My Visit to the Aquarium*. Ill. by author. HarperCollins, 1993. ISBN 0-06-021459-7. SUBJECTS: Animals—Fish; Oceans and ocean life; Science. RL A.
Drawings based on several aquariums narrow the field from the setting to individual animals in stages. Characteristics interesting to children are featured, from tidal pools to coastal streams to coral reefs.

41 *My Visit to the Dinosaurs*. 2nd ed. Ill. by author. HarperCollins, hb and pap., 1985. ISBN 0-690-04423-2. SERIES: Let's-Read-and-Find-Out Science Books. SUBJECTS: Dinosaurs; Science. RL C.
A small boy visits the natural history museum and learns about 15 common dinosaurs, as well as the work of paleontologists. Information is well presented and appealingly illustrated with ink sketches having green, turquoise, and gray washes.

42 *Story of Johnny Appleseed*. Ill. by author. Prentice-Hall, 1963, o.p. SUBJECTS: Biographies; Plants—Trees. RL C.
The outline of Johnny Appleseed's life and legend is given in sympathetic terms. Bold, decorative sketches underline his friendly relations with Native Americans and animals.

43 *A Weed Is a Flower: The Life of George Washington Carver*. Ill. by author. Simon & Schuster, hb and pap., 1988. ISBN 0-671-66118-3. SUBJECTS: Biographies; Science. RL C.
A laudatory outline of this talented man's life and accomplishments.

44 *Wild and Woolly Mammoths*. Ill. by author. HarperCollins, 1977; HarperCollins, pap., 1983. ISBN 0-690-01276-4. SERIES: Let's-Read-and-Find-Out Science Books. SUBJECTS: Animals, extinct. RL C.
In 1901 a frozen 10,000-year-old woolly mammoth was found with 30 pounds of flower, pine needles, moss, and pine cones in its stomach. Facts about Stone Age culture relating to mammoths is woven skillfully into this fascinating account. Ink and pencil sketches are in turquoise and brown.

Allard, Harry

45 *There's a Party at Mona's Tonight*. Ill. by James Marshall. Doubleday, 1979, o.p. SUBJECTS: Animals—Pigs—Fiction; Parties—Fiction. RL C.
Potter Pig repeatedly tries to inveigle an invitation to Mona's party; however, he's not invited because of his lack of tact. Arched-framed solid colors in sketches are in pig-pink, black, yellow, and turquoise.

Allen, Laura J.

46 *Ottie and the Star*. Ill. by author. HarperCollins, 1979, o.p. SERIES: Early I Can Read Books. SUBJECTS: Animals—Otters—Fiction. RL B.
A small otter encounters a shark, a dolphin, and a starfish trying to reach a star. Watercolor washes fit the watery setting well.

47 *Rollo and Tweedy and the Ghost at Dougal Castle*. Ill. by author. HarperCollins, 1992.

Allen, Laura J. (cont.)

ISBN 0-06-020107-X. SERIES: I Can Read Books. SUBJECTS: Animals—Mice—Fiction; Ghost stories; Mystery and detective stories. RL A.

Readers are challenged to decipher simple clues, false and true, to uncover the identity of the ghost impersonator at a Scottish castle. Full color illustrations are used against an inventive, interesting castle. backdrop.

48 *Where Is Freddy?* Ill. by author. HarperCollins, 1986, o.p. SERIES: I Can Read Books. SUBJECTS: Animals—Mice—Fiction; Imagination—Fiction; Mystery and detective stories. RL B.

When rich Mrs. Trumbly's grandson Freddy is missing, Rollo and Tweedy follow the clues of missing coat hangers, sheets, and laundry basket to track him down. This story of imagination and logic is illustrated with ink and wash drawings of expressive mice characters.

Allen, Marjorie N.

49 *One, Two, Three—Ah-Choo!* Ill. by Dick Gackenbach. Putnam, 1980, o.p. SERIES: Break-of-Day. SUBJECTS: Allergies—Fiction; Pets—Fiction. RL B.

Because of allergies, Wally cannot have the usual furry pets. Readers learn with him about hermit crabs. Gackenbach's warm, fuzzy drawings are in pumpkin and gray.

Allen, Marjorie N., and Allen, Carl

50 *Farley, Are You for Real?* Ill. by Joel Schick. Putnam, 1976, o.p. SUBJECTS: Humorous stories; Magic—Fiction. RL B.

The misadventures of an inept genie named Farley give Archie a taste of fear and wonder when he shrinks to two inches in height. Excellent pen and ink drawings give perspective, humor, and drama.

Alley, Robert

51 *Ghost in Dobbs Diner.* Ill. by author. Parents Magazine Pr., 1981. ISBN 0-8193-1055-7; Stevens, 1992. ISBN 0-8368-0884-3. SERIES: Read-Aloud Library. RL B.

Samuel Sheets, ghost and world traveler, makes himself useful at Mr. Dobbs's busy diner after appearing from a dusty pickle jar, but the busboy, cook, waitress, and customers are afraid. Soft pastel washes have milkshakes for the cover border and a very friendly ghost.

Allington, Richard L.

52 *Colors.* Ill. by Noel Spangler. Raintree, 1979. ISBN 0-8172-1280-9. SERIES: Beginning to Learn About. SUBJECTS: Concepts—Color. RL B.

In a very didactic manner, a girl introduces colors by drawing an item that is characteristically that color. Large drawings of an apple, bluebells, a mushroom, and so forth are shown on white with a border that matches the color of the item depicted.

53 *Hearing.* Ill. by Wayne Dober. Raintree, 1980, o.p. SERIES: Beginning to Learn About. SUBJECTS: Senses—Hearing; Sound. RL B.

The sounds of vehicles and animals are drawn with onomatopoeic words such as "caroo," "moo," and "crackle." Collages in soft colors draw attention to a myriad of familiar sounds.

Allington, Richard L., and Krull, Kathleen

54 *Reading.* Ill. by Joel Naprstek. Raintree, 1980. ISBN 0-8172-1322-8. SERIES: Beginning to Learn About. SUBJECTS: Books and reading. RL B.

A didactic text relates that one should learn to read for fun, to learn new things, to get around, and to avoid danger. Colored drawings are enclosed in large circles.

55 *Spring.* Ill. by Lynn Uhde. Raintree, 1981. ISBN 0-8172-1342-2. SERIES: Beginning to Learn About. SUBJECTS: Seasons—Spring. RL B.

The reader is asked about feelings, sounds, sports, and other signs of spring. Soft watercolors show the play, flora, and fauna of the season.

56 *Time.* Ill. by Yoshi Miyake. Raintree, 1983. ISBN 0-8172-1388-0. SERIES: Beginning to Learn About. SUBJECTS: Concepts—Time. RL B.

Minimal information about time is given; half of the text asks the reader didactic questions about when time goes slowly or what one would like to do in the future. Watercolor washes emphasize the patterns of clothing, walls, and a striped cat.

Alston, Edith

57 *Let's Visit a Space Camp*. Photos by Michael Plunkett. Troll, 1988. ISBN 0-8167-1743-5. SERIES: Let's Visit. SUBJECTS: Science; Space travel. RL C.
Youthful trainees fire model rockets, experience weightlessness in a 5DF chair and underwater, and suit up; the last day is for Lift Off, ending with debriefing. This is a fascinating look into a vocational experience that is becoming more accessible.

Anders, Rebecca

58 *Dolly the Donkey*. Orig. French by Anne-Marie Pajot, trans. by Dyan Hammarberg. Photos by Antoinette Barrere, drawings by L'Enc Matte. Carolrhoda, 1976, o.p. SERIES: Animal Friends. SUBJECTS: Animals—Donkeys; Pet care; Pets. RL C.
Four children acquire Dolly the donkey and her cart. They learn about the joys and aggravations of caring for a new pet. Color photos alternate with black and white. Occasional drawings give close-ups of hooves or carrying baskets.

59 *Lorito the Parrot*. Orig. French by Anne-Marie Pajot, trans. by Dyan Hammarberg. Ill. by Colyann, and L'Enc Matte. Carolrhoda, 1976, o.p. SERIES: Animal Friends. SUBJECTS: Animals—Parrots; Pet care; Pets. RL C.
Children visiting their neighbor who owns a parrot learn about its habits, beak, toes, diet, eyes, and native habitat. Black and white close-up photos alternate with color photos in this easy nonfiction book.

60 *Winslow the Hamster*. Orig. French by Anne-Marie Pajot, trans. by Dyan Hammarberg. Ill. by Rank, and L'Enc Matte. Carolrhoda, 1977, o.p. SERIES: Animal Friends. SUBJECTS: Animals—Hamsters; Pet care; Pets. RL C.
Well-presented facts about hamster habits, history, and charm. Excellent photos with some drawings.

Anderson, Peggy P.

61 *Time for Bed, the Babysitter Said*. Ill. by author. Houghton Mifflin, 1987. ISBN 0-395-41851-8. SUBJECTS: Animals—Frogs and toads—Fiction; Baby-sitting—Fiction; Bedtime—Fiction. RL A.
Joe is *very* elusive, and the baby-sitter unimaginative, when it is time for bed. A "please" finally turns the tables in this simplistic bedtime saga. Three-tone drawings have plenty of action and nice froglike touches.

Applebaum, Stan

62 *Going My Way: Nature's Hitchhikers*. Ill. by Leonard Shortall. Harcourt, 1976, o.p. SERIES: Let Me Read. SUBJECTS: Nature; Science. RL C.
Suckerfish, oxpeckers, burrs, fleas, and bee-eaters are some of the hitchhikers introduced. Illustrative sketches have a hint of color.

Archbold, Tim

63 *The Race*. Ill. by author. Holt, 1988, o.p. SUBJECTS: Concepts—Space—Fiction; Stories in rhyme. RL A.
A huge dog accompanies a gloved and helmeted boy on a headlong, crazy cart ride home for dinner. This outrageous adventure is underscored by ink washed sketches of a cart whose wheels rarely touch the ground. Very limited vocabulary is expanded by the illustrations.

Ardley, Neil

64 *The Science Book of Light*. Photos by Pete Gardner. Harcourt, 1991. ISBN 0-15-200577-3. SUBJECTS: Light; Science and scientists; Science experiments. RL C.
Experiments range from objects distorted in water to shadow puppets, periscopes, and kaleidoscopes. Color photos in primary colors against a white ground are very appealing. Ever-popular photographic paper is used to create silhouettes.

Armitage, Ronda, and Armitage, David

65 *Harry Hates Shopping!* Ill. by authors. Scholastic, 1993. pap. ISBN 0-590-45886-8. SERIES: Hello Reader! SUBJECTS: Animals—Koalas—Fiction; Behavior—Fiction; Humorous stories. RL A.

With a most imaginative twist, Mother Koala convinces her children that their teasing and bickering while shopping should stop. Acceptable illustrations show Mother's satisfaction with improved behavior clearly.

Arnosky, Jim

66 *Crinkleroot's Guide to Knowing the Birds*. Ill. by author. Macmillan, 1992. ISBN 0-02-705857-3. SUBJECTS: Animals—Birds; Nature. RL C.

Bearded Crinkleroot introduces some of the techniques and basics of bird-watching. Bird songs, coloring, habitat, anatomy, and life cycle are appealingly described and illustrated, as well as are ways to attract and feed familiar species.

67 *Crinkleroot's Guide to Knowing the Trees*. Ill. by author. Macmillan, 1991. ISBN 0-02-705855-7. SUBJECTS: Nature; Plants—Trees. RL C.

The droll, bearded naturalist, Crinkleroot, tells how a tree grows and introduces deciduous trees and conifers, the wildlife that inhabits various levels of the forest, and some of the idiosyncrasies of individual trees. Charming ink and wash sketches enhance the text.

Arnott, Kathleen

68 *Dragons, Ogres, and Scary Things: Two African Folktales*. Ill. by Cary. Garrard, 1974, o.p. SUBJECTS: Folklore—Africa; Mythical creatures. RL B.

In the first tale Gatsha saves the village girls from a dragon and wild animals with his magic drum. A gnome-woman's ingenuity saves Imtali from ogres in the second tale. The charcoal colored pen and wash drawings are highlighted in gold, which detracts from their quality.

69 *Spiders, Crabs, and Creepy Crawlers: Two African Folktales*. Ill. by Bette Davis. Garrard, 1978, o.p. SERIES: Imagination. SUBJECTS: Animals—Crabs—Fiction; Animals—Spiders—Fiction; Folklore—Africa. RL B.

Why Flamingo stands on one leg (to escape the notice of crabs angry that he ate the King of Crabs) and why Spider lives under a stone (because he stole the magic grinding stone) are well told in simple language. The colored drawings, however, are static and dull.

Asch, Frank

70 *Bread and Honey*. Ill. by author. Parents Magazine Pr., 1982; Crown, pap., 1988. ISBN 0-8193-1077-8. SERIES: Read Aloud and Easy Reading. SUBJECTS: Animals—Bears—Fiction. RL B.

Ben's picture of his mother is modified by all his animal friends until it has features taken from many animals, but his mother likes it anyway. A warm story is illustrated with large drawings in flat primary colors.

Aseltine, Lorraine

71 *First Grade Can Wait*. Ill. by Virginia Wright-Frierson. Whitman, 1988. ISBN 0-8075-2451-4. SUBJECTS: Behavior; Schools. RL B.

Luke likes singing, his teacher, and art in kindergarten, but has trouble paying attention, playing cooperatively, and sharing with the class. Pencil drawings and facing blue-type text are framed in light blue.

Aseltine, Lorraine; Mueller, Evelyn; and Tait, Nancy

72 *I'm Deaf and It's Okay*. Ill. by Helen Cogancherry. Whitman, 1986. ISBN 0-8075-3472-2. SERIES: Concept. SUBJECTS: Physically and mentally impaired; Senses—Hearing. RL B.

The way in which ordinary situations at home or school become scary or threatening to a deaf child is most sensitively told. Excellent pencil drawings help relay the emotional impact of deafness on the child.

Ashrose, Cara

73 *The Very First Americans*. Ill. by Bryna Waldman. Putnam, 1993. ISBN 0-448-

40168-1. series: All Aboard Books. subjects: Native Americans. rl B.
In three or four paragraphs, Native Americans from the Northwest, Southwest, Plains, and Woodlands are introduced. Nearly one-third still live on reservations, and the rest "walk in two worlds," keeping their traditions while living in cities and towns.

Averill, Esther

74 *Fire Cat*. Ill. by author. HarperCollins, 1960; pap., 1983. isbn 0-06-020196-7. series: I Can Read Books. subjects: Animals—Cats—Fiction. rl A.
Pickles makes up for some of his mischief when he becomes a fire cat. Stylized drawings are highlighted in red, black, and sunshine yellow.

Awdry, W.

75 *Thomas the Tank and the School Trip: Based on The Railway Series*. Ill. by Owain Bell. Random House, 1993. isbn 0-679-94365-X. series: Step into Reading. subjects: Trains—Fiction. rl A.
Thomas the Tank Engine tries to hurry through his route so he can take a group of children home from a school trip. Very limited vocabulary is illustrated with cartoons.

B

Baeten, Lieve

76 *Nicky at the Magic House*. Ill. by author. Annick, 1993. pap., isbn 1-55037-271-8. subjects: Witches—Fiction. rl B.
Nicky the witch and her cat Theodore, cruising on their broomstick late at night, find a house with all the lights on. They find a musical witch, a cooking witch, and a sleeping witch—but it is the fixing witch who sends them on their way. Wistful soft watercolor drawings set the tone.

Bailey, Donna

77 *Italy*. Photos. Raintree, 1990. isbn 0-8114-2553-3. series: Where We Live. subjects: Geography; Italy. rl C.

Although there are an aerial view and a kitchen and a market shot, most of the life of Venice centers on the water. Everyday and ceremonial activities are presented with large color photos and a few drawings.

Bailey, Donna, and Wong, Ansel

78 *Trinidad*. Photos. Raintree, 1990. isbn 0-8114-2550-9. series: Where We Live. subjects: Geography; Trinidad. rl B.
Trinidad is seen from the point of view of Keisha, a girl from capital city Port of Spain. The reader glimpses the city (when her dad goes to work), the fish market, the cricket field, and sugarcane and oil fields, and participates in Carnival. Large color photos and an index complement the text.

Baker, Barbara

79 *Digby and Kate*. Ill. by Marsha Winborn. Dutton, 1988. isbn 0-525-44370-3. series: Dutton Easy Reader. subjects: Animals—Dogs—Fiction; Friendship—Fiction. rl A.
Digby and Kate, a dog and cat respectively, are very different in temperament but still best friends. Pastel patterned drawings are somewhat stylized and romantic.

80 *Digby and Kate Again*. Ill. by Marsha Winborn. Dutton, 1989. isbn 0-525-44477-7. subjects: Animals—Cats—Fiction; Animals—Dogs—Fiction; Friendship—Fiction. rl A.
Four chapters show the relationship between the cat and dog friends—in the garden, with a new bicycle, raking leaves, and procrastinating about letter writing. Jewel-like colored drawings show the mishaps and antics of the pair.

81 *Staying with Grandmother*. Ill. by Judith B. Schachner. Dutton, 1994. isbn 0-525-44603-6. series: Dutton Easy Reader. subjects: Emotions—Homesickness; Grandparents—Fiction. rl A.
Clair feels more at home at her grandmother's after meeting a new friend, hearing her mother's favorite Alice in Wonderland story, and sleeping with her mother's old White Rabbit stuffed animal. Pencil and wash drawings supply a comfy, old-fashioned setting for grandmother's house.

Baker, Betty

82 *All-by-Herself*. Ill. by Catherine Stock.
    Greenwillow, 1980, o.p. SERIES: Read-
    alone. SUBJECTS: Giants—Fiction. RL B.
The villagers still do not welcome All-by-Herself after she kills the ice giant because she is
different. Three-tone washes on ink sketches
are striking.

83 *The Big Push*. Ill. by Bonnie Johnson.
    Putnam, 1972, o.p. SERIES: Break-of-Day.
    SUBJECTS: Native Americans—Hopi. RL B.
The Big Push was the final break between
those Hopi who accepted white influence,
however reluctantly, and those who did not.
Sympathetic historical treatment is illustrated
with shadowy pencil drawings.

84 *Little Runner of the Longhouse*. Ill. by
    Arnold Lobel. HarperCollins, 1962. ISBN 0-
    06-020341-2. SERIES: I Can Read Books.
    SUBJECTS: Cumulative tales; Native Ameri-
    cans—Fiction. RL B.
Little Runner tries to trade his baby brother
for some adventure in imitation of his elders
on New Year's Day. Lobel adds authentic
details of life in the longhouse.

85 *No Help at All*. Ill. by Emily Arnold
    McCully. Greenwillow, 1978, o.p. SERIES:
    Read-alone. SUBJECTS: Folklore—Mexico;
    Mexico—Fiction. RL B.
The West Wind puts a Mayan boy to work
after rescuing him from a man-eating "thing,"
but returns him home when all his own
efforts to escape end in disaster. Simple
expressive drawings are well suited to this
Mayan legend.

86 *Partners*. Ill. by Emily Arnold McCully.
    Greenwillow, 1978, o.p. SERIES: Read-
    alone. SUBJECTS: Animals—Fiction; Friend-
    ship—Fiction. RL B.
Badger and Coyote have an imperfect friendship as they hang stars, grow crops, and hunt
prairie dogs. Themes and humor have a folktale base. Pastel pencils color the excellent ink
drawings.

87 *Pig War*. Ill. by Robert Lopshire. Harper-
    Collins, 1969, o.p. SERIES: I Can Read
    History. SUBJECTS: Historical fiction; United
    States—1783–1865—Fiction. RL B.

A squabble about whether Britain or America
owns a Puget Sound island is settled when a
pig is paid for. Three-color comic illustrations
are simple, yet effective.

88 *Rat Is Dead and Ant Is Sad*. Ill. by Mamoru
    Funai. HarperCollins, 1981, o.p. SERIES: I
    Can Read Books. SUBJECTS: Cumulative
    tales; Native Americans—Legends; Native
    Americans—Pueblos. RL C.
An unusual cumulative tale includes a rat, an
ant, a jay, a cottonwood tree, a sheep, a Pueblo
family, and a horse. Illustrations pick up the
patterns and colors of the Southwest and
Pueblo culture.

89 *Three Fools and a Horse*. Ill. by Glen
    Rounds. Macmillan, 1975, o.p.; pap.,
    1987, o.p. SERIES: Ready-to-Read. SUBJECTS:
    Folklore—Native Americans; Humorous
    stories; Native Americans—Fiction. RL B.
The Apaches' Foolish People have trouble
locating a buffalo, cooking food, and staying
on a horse. Rounds' comic ink drawings
emphasize the People's potbellies and the
looks of disgust on the horses' faces. This nonsense tale is effectively told and illustrated.

90 *The Turkey Girl*. Ill. by Harold Berson.
    Macmillan, 1983, o.p. SERIES: Ready-to-
    Read. SUBJECTS: Animals—Turkeys—
    Fiction; Behavior—Brave—Fiction. RL B.
Elements of the Cinderella story are woven
into this tale of an orphan girl's devotion to
her turkeys. Her bravery, protecting them
from a wolf, earns her a family at last. Berson's
graceful line drawings have a folktale flavor.

91 *Worthington Botts and the Steam
    Machine*. Ill. by Sal Murdocca.
    Macmillan, 1981, o.p. SERIES: Ready-to-
    Read. SUBJECTS: Books and reading—
    Fiction; Robots—Fiction. RL C.
Worthington Botts reads *all* the time—until he
builds a labor-saving robot. His continuing
temptations to read are especially creative.
Murdocca's four-color cartoon drawings complement the text perfectly.

Baker, Eugene

92 *Outdoors*. Ill. by Tom Dunnington.
    Creative Ed., 1980, o.p. SERIES: Safety
    First. SUBJECTS: Safety. RL B.

Basil and Rover play in dangerous situations as the reader is asked what is wrong. Rules are then stated. They are restated in three black pages at the end. Animal characters are large and colorful.

Balestrino, Philip

93 *Fat and Skinny*. Ill. by Pam Makie. HarperCollins, 1975, o.p. SERIES: Let's-Read-and-Find-Out Science Books. SUBJECTS: Science. RL C.

Differences in body weight, activity, calories, and metabolism are discussed simply. Line drawings show children of all sizes eating, exercising, and playing.

94 *Hot as an Ice Cube*. Ill. by Tomie dePaola. HarperCollins, 1970, o.p. SERIES: Let's-Read-and-Find-Out Science Books. SUBJECTS: Science; Science experiments. RL C.

Household items provide a way to test many concepts relative to temperature. Well-presented facts are illustrated in turquoise and cocoa.

95 *The Skeleton Inside You*. Ill. by True Kelley. HarperCollins, 1989. ISBN 0-690-04733-9. SERIES: Let's-Read-and-Find-Out Science Books. SUBJECTS: Human body—Skeleton. RL C.

The function, parts, and connectors of human bones are outlined in a clear, understandable way. Large colorful framed drawings enliven the text.

Ball, Jacqueline A.

96 *What Can It Be? Riddles About the Senses*. Photos. Silver Burdett, 1989. ISBN 0-671-68580-5. SUBJECTS: Jokes and riddles. RL C.

Rhyming riddles are imaginative, tickling the senses: hearing, touch, taste, smell. Bright-colored close-up photos give the answers on the pages following the riddles, with additional facts about the subject or the riddle.

Bancroft, Catherine, and Gruenberg, Hannah Coale

97 *Felix's Hat*. Ill. by Hannah Coale Gruenberg. Macmillan, 1993. ISBN 0-02-708325-X. SUBJECTS: Animals—Frogs and toads—Fiction; Hats—Fiction; Imagination—Fiction. RL B.

Felix's family tries to cheer Felix up after he loses his favorite hat while floating in his inner tube. Only his imagination relieves his sadness. Lively ink and watercolor drawings show frog family life.

Bancroft, Henrietta

98 *Down Come the Leaves*. Ill. by Nonny Hogrogian. HarperCollins, 1961, o.p. SERIES: Let's-Read-and-Find-Out Science Books. SUBJECTS: Nature; Plants—Trees; Seasons—Fall. RL A.

Bancroft, from the point of view of two children playing in the leaves, focuses on the variety and wonder of trees, as she gives information about the life cycle of trees. The pencil silhouettes and leaf patterns are deceptively simple, drawn by a master illustrator.

Bang, Betsy

99 *Cucumber Stem*. Ill. by Tony Chen. Greenwillow, 1980, o.p. SERIES: Read-alone. SUBJECTS: India—Fiction. RL C.

A Bengali tale of a magic cucumber and a brave man who is two fingers tall. There are stylized Indian design details.

100 *Tuntuni the Tailor Bird*. Ill. by Molly G. Bang. Greenwillow, 1978, o.p. SERIES: Read-alone. SUBJECTS: Folklore—India; India—Fiction. RL C.

In the first cumulative tale, mosquitoes set off a chain of events in order to get the barber to remove a thorn from the bird Tuntuni's foot. In costume, design, characters, and vegetation, Molly Bang (daughter of the author) captures the flavor of Bengal and the humor of the tiny bird's escapades.

Bang, Molly G.

101 *Tye May and the Magic Brush*. Ill. by author. Greenwillow, 1981, o.p. SERIES: Read-alone. SUBJECTS: Folklore—China; Magic—Fiction. RL B.

Although the emperor tries to steal Tye May's magic brush, he gets his just reward. Satisfying tale of magic is illustrated by delicate pencil and ink drawings.

Bang, Molly G. (cont.)

102 *Wiley and the Hairy Man: Adapted from an American Folktale*. Ill. by author. Macmillan, 1976; pap., 1987. ISBN 0-02-708370-5. SERIES: Ready-to-Read. SUBJECTS: Folklore—African Americans; Folklore—United States; Magic—Fiction. RL B.

Following his mother's instructions, Wiley tricks the powerful Hairy Man who lives in the swamp near the Tombigbee River. Based on a well-known American folktale, this version is suitable for telling. Charcoal grays of pencil and paint are superbly apt for the Tennessee tale.

Bare, Colleen S.

103 *Never Grab a Deer by the Ear*. Ill. by author. Dutton, 1993. ISBN 0-525-65112-8. SUBJECTS: Animals—Deer; Nature. RL B.

Information about the deer's life cycle, enemies, food, and especially antlers is given in large, clear type with excellent color photos.

Barr, Catherine

104 *Bears In—Bears Out*. Ill. by author. Henry Z. Walck, 1967, o.p. SUBJECTS: Animals—Bears—Fiction. RL C.

At Yellowstone National Park two bear cubs get a car ride unbeknownst to the family. Credible story has child appeal. Crayon and ink drawings and hand-lettered text are very effective.

105 *Gingercat's Catch*. Ill. by author. Henry Z. Walck, 1970, o.p. SUBJECTS: Animals—Cats—Fiction; India—Fiction. RL C.

The competition is fierce when Gingercat tries out for a job as a watchcat at the state office in India. Hand-lettered text goes well with the yellow and gray pencil illustrations.

Barrett, Joyce D.

106 *Willie's Not the Hugging Kind*. Ill. by Pat Cummings. HarperCollins, 1989. ISBN 0-06-020416-8. SUBJECTS: African Americans—Fiction; Family Life—Fiction. RL C.

When Willie's friend Jo-Jo makes fun of hugging, Willie feels left out of the warm embraces in his family. His sister, Rose, lets

him know that it's "them that don't get hugging who think it's silly." An effective message is reinforced by the single-page color drawings and black and white headers.

Barrett, Judi

107 *I'm too small. YOU'RE TOO BIG*. Ill. by David Rose. Atheneum, 1981, o.p. SUBJECTS: Concepts—Size; Fathers. RL C.

Contrasts between father and small son are pleasantly exaggerated in framed ink and wash drawings.

Barrett, Norman

108 *Sharks*. Photos. Watts, 1989, o.p. SERIES: Picture Library. SUBJECTS: Animals—Sharks. RL C.

Varieties of sharks are described and shown in color photos or drawings. Different sizes of type are used for detailed captions, the general narrative, and supplementary information, including the glossary and index and "Facts and records."

Barrett, Ron

109 *Hi-Yo, Fido!* Ill. by author. Crown, 1984, o.p. SUBJECTS: Humorous stories. RL C.

This modern tall tale about how dogboys and doggirls become cowboys and cowgirls has many inventive touches. Rock formations include a huge fire hydrant and a bowl for dog biscuits; dog bones are carried on the "Bony Express." Busy four-color illustrations delight the eye.

Bartels, Alice L.

110 *The Grandmother Doll*. Ill. by Farida Zaman. Annick, 1993. ISBN 1-55037-337-4. SUBJECTS: Family life—Fiction; Imagination. RL B.

Grandmother Doll comes to the rescue when Katy and her mother are having a bad day and Katy is banished to her room. Katy ends up making a TV, a stove, and a bed for Grandmother. It seems that Mother also knows about Grandmother Doll. Framed watercolor wash drawings are lighthearted.

Bartlett, Margaret

111 *Where Does All the Rain Go?* Ill. by Patricia Collins. Putnam, 1973, o.p. SERIES: Science Is What and Why. SUBJECTS: Science; Water. RL C.
The rain cycle is simply and expertly described. Ink sketches have block printed highlights in gold and royal blue.

112 *Where the Brook Begins*. Ill. by Aldren A. Watson. HarperCollins, 1961, o.p. SERIES: Let's-Read-and-Find-Out Science Books. SUBJECTS: Nature; Science; Water. RL B.
In terms children can relate to, rhythmic language conveys good information about the origin of brooks. Graceful simple pencil drawings have turquoise and orange highlights.

Bason, Lillian

113 *Those Foolish Molboes!* Ill. by Margot Tomes. Putnam, 1977, o.p. SUBJECTS: Denmark—Fiction; Folklore—Denmark; Humorous stories. RL C.
In the first of three tales in this book, the foolish Molboes mark the watery hiding place of the village bell on the boat! Tomes's excellent illustrations have a homely folk flavor and interesting detail.

Baumgartner, Barbara, reteller

114 *Crocodile! Crocodile!: Stories Told Around the World*. Ill. by Judith Moffatt. Dorling Kindersley, 1994. ISBN 1-56458-463-1. SUBJECTS: Folklore; Puppets and puppetry; Storytelling. RL B.
Stories from India, Puerto Rico, China, Appalachia, and Native American peoples are retold by a Pennsylvania storyteller and illustrated with bold, unusual cut-paper graphics. Stories include two about money and crocodile, "The Squeaky Old Bed," "How the Chipmunk Got His Stripes," and "Sody Soleratus."

Baynton, Martin

115 *Fifty and the Fox*. Ill. by author. Crown, 1986, o.p. SERIES: It's Great to Read! SUBJECTS: Tractors—Fiction. RL B.
When soft-hearted Wally is assigned to rid the farm of a fox, Fifty the tractor finds a creative way to help. Comic drawings are bright with sunshine and help make a tractor protagonist plausible.

116 *Fifty and the Great Race*. Ill. by author. Crown, 1987, o.p. SERIES: It's Great to Read! SUBJECTS: Animals—Rats—Fiction; Fairs—Fiction; Tractors—Fiction. RL C.
Some farmers make fun of the old-fashioned tractor, Fifty, at the fair, so it is up to Fifty to win the big tractor race to redeem himself. In a surprise ending, Fifty's friend Norris the rat saves the day. Colored pencil drawings are in pale pastels.

117 *Fifty Gets the Picture*. Ill. by author. Crown, 1987, o.p. SERIES: It's Great to Read! SUBJECTS: Friendship—Fiction; Humorous stories; Tractors—Fiction. RL C.
It turns out that Fifty the tractor has more than one talent! He gets help from his animal friends with his artistic triumphs. Intriguing perspective is relayed as much by soft pastel drawings as by text.

118 *Fifty Saves His Friend*. Ill. by author. Crown, 1986, o.p. SERIES: It's Great to Read! SUBJECTS: Animals—Cats—Fiction; Animals—Rats—Fiction; Tractors—Fiction. RL C.
Fifty the tractor's ingenious trick scares the cat away from his friend Norris the rat permanently. Sunshine yellow predominates in soft pastel drawings.

Beckman, Beatrice

119 *I Can Be a Teacher*. Photos. Childrens Pr., hb and pap., 1985. ISBN 0-516-41843-2. SERIES: I Can Be. SUBJECTS: Careers. RL C.
A picture dictionary and an index accompany information about the variety of teaching positions, including the responsibilities both inside and outside the classroom. Color photos are plentiful, but occasionally they look static and posed.

Behrens, June

120 *How I Feel*. Photos by Vince Streano. Childrens Pr., 1973, o.p. SUBJECTS: Emotions. RL B.

Behrens, June (cont.)

Examples of situations demonstrating feelings of anger, loneliness, pride, and love are given simply. Some of the situational photos look posed, and the language is somewhat stilted.

121 *I Can Be a Truck Driver*. Ill. by author. Childrens Pr., hb and pap., 1985. ISBN 0-516-01848-5. SERIES: I Can Be. SUBJECTS: Careers; Trucks. RL C.

"If you've got it . . . a truck brought it." Training and techniques are illustrated with large sharp color photos that include women. Includes a picture dictionary, a glossary, and an index.

122 *I Can Be an Astronaut*. Photos. Childrens Pr., hb and pap., 1984. ISBN 0-516-01837-X. SERIES: I Can Be. SUBJECTS: Careers; Science; Space travel. RL C.

The need for teamwork and specialized training is emphasized in this basic career book. Excellent photos underline the opportunities in this exciting profession.

123 *Juliette Low: Founder of the Girl Scouts of America*. Photos. Childrens Pr., 1988. ISBN 0-516-04171-1. SUBJECTS: Biographies; Camps and camping. RL C.

One of the best biographies of Juliette Low, the energetic, eccentric founder of the Girl Scouts of the United States of America. Her childhood, jet-set marriage, and later dedication to providing unique opportunities for girls are detailed. Black and white photos illustrate the text.

124 *Look at the Sea Animals*. Photos by Vince Streano. Childrens Pr., 1975, o.p. SUBJECTS: Animals; Nature; Oceans and ocean life. RL C.

A sea turtle, an octopus, a hermit crab, a dolphin, and a stingray are some of the sea animals introduced. Full color photos are faced by basic information.

Benchley, Nathaniel

125 *George the Drummer Boy*. Ill. by Don Bolognese. HarperCollins, 1977; pap., 1987. ISBN 0-06-020500-8. SERIES: I Can Read Books. SUBJECTS: Historical fiction; United States—Revolution—Fiction. RL B.

A most unusual perspective on the beginning of the Revolutionary War told from the point of view of a British drummer boy. His feelings prior to and during the events at Concord are sketched. Red, blue, and gray drawings convey the flavor of the period.

126 *A Ghost Named Fred*. Ill. by Ben Shecter. HarperCollins, 1968; pap, 1979. ISBN 0-06-020474-5. SERIES: I Can Read Mystery. SUBJECTS: Ghost stories; Imagination—Fiction; Mystery and detective stories. RL B.

George's solitary, imaginative play directs him to a deserted house while he is still dressed as an astronaut. This leads to a treasure hunt with a gentle ghost named Fred. Four-color illustrations enhance this satisfying tale.

127 *Oscar Otter*. Ill. by Arnold Lobel. HarperCollins, 1966; pap., 1980. ISBN 0-06-020472-9. SERIES: I Can Read Books. SUBJECTS: Animals—Otters—Fiction. RL B.

Oscar's fancy slide takes him far from home—and his enemies spot him! He is chased by a procession of animals. Lively animal drawings are in earth tones against white.

128 *Red Fox and His Canoe*. Ill. by Arnold Lobel. HarperCollins, 1964; pap., 1985. ISBN 0-06-020476-1. SERIES: I Can Read Books. SUBJECTS: Animals—Fiction; Humorous stories; Native Americans—Fiction. RL B.

Red Fox is satisfied with a small canoe after three bears, two otters, a raccoon, and a moose wreck his larger one. Action illustrations concentrate on animal misadventures and add to the tongue-in-cheek humor.

129 *Running Owl the Hunter*. Ill. by Mamoru Funai. HarperCollins, 1979, o.p. SERIES: I Can Read Books. SUBJECTS: Growing-up—Fiction; Humorous stories; Native Americans—Fiction. RL C.

When all his independent hunting schemes go astray, Running Owl is assisted by an eagle who takes pity on him. Two-tone washes warm humorous ink sketches.

130 *Sam the Minuteman*. Ill. by Arnold Lobel. HarperCollins, 1969; pap., 1987. ISBN 0-06-020479-6. SERIES: I Can Read History.

SUBJECTS: Historical fiction; United States—Revolution—Fiction. RL B.

A bare and unromanticized account of the unintentional beginning of the Revolutionary War. It is told from the point of view of the young son of a Minuteman, who tells of the suspense, fear, excitement, and pain of the encounter. Pencil drawings are historically accurate in feeling and detail.

131 *Several Tricks of Edgar Dolphin*. Ill. by Mamoru Funai. HarperCollins, 1970. ISBN 0-06-020468-0. SERIES: I Can Read Books. SUBJECTS: Animals—Dolphins—Fiction. RL B.

Edgar the dolphin escapes his captors after adding water to his shallow tank aboard a ship. The conclusion is satisfying without creating villains. Pencil drawings have two-tone washes.

132 *Small Wolf*. Ill. by Joan Sandin. Harper-Collins, 1972, 1994. ISBN 0-06-020492-3. SERIES: I Can Read Books. SUBJECTS: Native Americans—Fiction; United States history—Colonial period—Fiction. RL A.

From the perspective of a Native American boy, the consequences of European encroachment are presented. This well-researched, unsentimental view of history is illustrated with rich, detailed drawings.

133 *Snorri and the Strangers*. Ill. by Don Bolognese. HarperCollins, 1976, o.p. SERIES: I Can Read History. SUBJECTS: Adventure stories; Canada; Historical fiction. RL B.

Snorri, the first white child born in North America, encounters some hostile natives before returning to Greenland with his family. Adventurous history is told in simple terms and illustrated with ink drawings having red and pale lemon washes.

134 *Strange Disappearance of Arthur Cluck*. Ill. by Arnold Lobel. HarperCollins, 1967; pap., 1979. ISBN 0-06-020478-8. SERIES: I Can Read Mystery. SUBJECTS: Mystery and detective stories. RL B.

Ralph the owl identifies the missing chick, Arthur, because he is the only chick who rides on someone's head. Wonderful animal expressions add zest to the pumpkin and green highlighted pencil drawings.

Bendick, Jeanne

135 *A Place to Live*. Ill. by author. Parents Magazine Pr., 1970, o.p. SERIES: Stepping-Stone. SUBJECTS: Communities. RL B.

The needs and interrelatedness of communities—of people, plants, and animals—are discussed. This concept of community is introduced in 13 short chapters with questions interspersed to involve the reader. Lively ink drawings have avocado highlights.

136 *The Planets: Neighbors in Space*. Ill. by Mike Roffe. Millbrook, 1991. ISBN 1-878841-03-3. SERIES: Early Bird. SUBJECTS: Astronomy; Science and scientists. RL C.

Placid drawings illustrate the simplest information about each planet; index appended.

137 *Shapes*. Ill. by author. Watts, 1968, o.p. SUBJECTS: Concepts—Shape. RL C.

Some shapes are flat, some three-dimensional; some names for shapes are specific and some general; shapes evoke a range of feelings. Fascinating ideas about shapes are interspersed with thought-provoking questions. Heavy ink and red drawings are somewhat dated, however.

Berenstain, Michael

138 *Michael Berenstain's Hop, Waddle, Swim!* Ill. by author. Western, 1992. ISBN 0-307-11578-X. SERIES: Fast Start. SUBJECTS: Animals—Fiction; Humorous stories; Stories in rhyme. RL A.

The movements of land and ocean creatures are suggested in rollicking. word play and rhyme with a very simple vocabulary. Cartoon illustrations unfortunately show a whale whose mouth is lined with shark-like teeth.

139 *Michael Berenstain's When I Grow Up Oh, the Things I Can Be!* Ill. by author. Western, 1992. ISBN 0-307-11579-8. SERIES: Fast Start. SUBJECTS: Careers; Stories in rhyme. RL A.

Parenting is included in a series of occupations sketched with broad strokes. They range from oil rig worker, teacher, farmer, cowboy or cowgirl, to a human cannonball for the circus. Characteristic Berenstain cartoon illustrations accompany the text.

Berenstain, Michael (cont.)

140 *The Panda Club's Tree House*. Ill. by author. Western, 1989. ISBN 0-307-11687-5. SERIES: Golden Easy Reader. SUBJECTS: Animals—Fiction. RL A.
Tiger Anne, Little Panda, Monkey Max, Rusty the Fox, and Polly, members of the Panda Club, look for the right tree in which to build a new clubhouse. Illustrations are cartoon ink in green, pink, orange, and yellow.

Berenstain, Stan, and Berenstain, Jan

141 *After the Dinosaurs*. Ill. by Michael Berenstain. Random House, 1988. ISBN 0-394-90518-0. SERIES: First Time Readers. SUBJECTS: Animals—prehistoric; Dinosaurs; Stories in rhyme. RL B.
A variety of familiar and unfamiliar prehistoric animals are illustrated with cartoon drawings whose accuracy becomes suspect when the drawings of cave and modern people are seen. Rhyming progression of animals.

142 *The Bear Detectives*. Ill. by authors. Beginner, 1975. ISBN 0-394-93127-0. SERIES: I Can Read It All by Myself. SUBJECTS: Animals—Bears—Fiction; Humorous stories; Mystery and detective stories. RL B.
Pa and Snuff the sniff hound lead the Bear detectives astray repeatedly. Cartoon illustrations exaggerate the miscues.

143 *Bear Scouts*. Ill. by authors. Random House, 1967. ISBN 0-394-90046-4. SUBJECTS: Animals—Bears—Fiction; Camps and camping—Fiction; Stories in rhyme. RL B.
The Scouts end up rescuing boastful Pa again and again, relying on their trusty guidebook. Cartoon illustrations help point out Pa's follies.

144 *Bears in the Night*. Ill. by authors. Random House, 1971. ISBN 0-394-92286-7. SERIES: Bright and Early. SUBJECTS: Animals—Bears—Fiction; Concepts—Space—Fiction; Emotions—Fear—Fiction. RL A.
The path through the woods to Spook Hill leads the Bear children over, under, and around obstacles in the landscape leading to nocturnal adventure. This traditionally for-matted tale is written with a simple vocabulary. Illustrations are in the blue-blacks and yellow of night.

145 *Bears on Wheels*. Ill. by authors. Random House, 1969. ISBN 0-394-90967-4. SERIES: Bright and Early Counting. SUBJECTS: Bicycles and bicycling—Fiction; Concepts—Numbers; Humorous stories. RL A.
Antics on a unicycle provide a humorous backdrop to this counting book with a primer vocabulary. Acrobatic bears perform against a very plain background.

146 *Bears' Vacation*. Ill. by authors. Beginner, 1968, o.p. SERIES: I Can Read It All By Myself. SUBJECTS: Animals—Bears—Fiction; Safety—Fiction; Stories in rhyme. RL A.
Papa demonstrates everything *not* to do for safety at the beach. Cartoon drawings exaggerate the action.

147 *The Berenstain Bears and the Big Road Race*. Ill. by authors. Random House, hb and pap., 1987. ISBN 0-394-99134-6. SERIES: First Time Readers. SUBJECTS: Animals—Bears—Fiction; Concepts—Color—Fiction; Fables. RL B.
The little red car putt-putts past the overconfident racers, including the green one with dirty tricks. Typical cartoon illustrations are in soft pastels.

148 *Berenstain Bears and the Ghost of the Forest*. Ill. by authors. Random House, 1988. ISBN 0-394-90565-2. SERIES: First Time Readers. SUBJECTS: Animals—Bears—Fiction; Ghost stories; Stories in rhyme. RL C.
Papa gets more than one scare himself after trying to scare the bear scouts on a campout by dressing as a ghost. Forced story is illustrated with typical Berenstain cartoons.

149 *The Berenstain Bears and the Missing Dinosaur Bone*. Ill. by authors. Beginner, 1980. ISBN 0-394-94447-X. SERIES: I Can Read It All By Myself. SUBJECTS: Animals—Bears—Fiction; Mystery and detective stories; Stories in rhyme. RL C.
With a crowd gathering to view the museum's dinosaur bones, the Bears and their hound

dog scour the museum looking for a missing thigh bone. The skillfully woven tale of suspense, humor, and mystery has the typical illustrations of the Berenstains.

150 *The Berenstain Bears and the Missing Honey*. Ill. by authors. Random House, hb and pap., 1987. ISBN 0-394-99133-8. SERIES: First Time Readers. SUBJECTS: Animals—Bears—Fiction; Mystery and detective stories; Stories in rhyme. RL C.
Following clues with Snuff their sniffer hound in the lead, the Bears have one disaster after another. Pastel colors catalog this humorous sleuthing.

151 *The Berenstain Bears and the Spooky Old Tree*. Ill. by authors. Random House, 1978. ISBN 0-394-93910-7. SERIES: Bright and Early. SUBJECTS: Animals—Bears—Fiction; Mystery and detective stories. RL B.
A well-crafted suspense story uses very basic vocabulary. The hazards are heightened in cartoon illustrations.

152 *Berenstain Bears Blaze a Trail*. Ill. by authors. Random House, 1987. ISBN 0-394-99132-X. SERIES: First Time Readers. SUBJECTS: Animals—Bears—Fiction; Hiking—Fiction; Stories in rhyme. RL C.
Scout Leader Jane awards Papa and the scouts merit badges despite Papa's failures to follow the guidebook. Pastel cartoons underline Papa's follies.

153 *The Berenstain Bears on the Moon*. Ill. by authors. Random House, 1985. ISBN 0-394-97180-9. SERIES: Bright and Early. SUBJECTS: Animals—Bears—Fiction; Space travel—Fiction; Stories in rhyme. RL B.
On the moon the Bears fly their flag, take moon notes, and collect moon rocks for their moon rock totes. This light introduction to space travel suggests that the stars are next. Cartoon illustrations are typical of the Berenstains.

154 *The Berenstain Kids: I Love Colors*. Ill. by authors. Random House, 1987, o.p. SERIES: First Time Readers. SUBJECTS: Concepts—Color; Stories in rhyme. RL B.
Uninspired verse reviews the colors of the rainbow and what primary colors produce each color. Pictures are typical.

155 *The Berenstains' B Book*. Ill. by authors. Random House, 1971. ISBN 0-394-92324-3. SERIES: Bright and Early. SUBJECTS: Alphabet—Fiction; Animals—Bears—Fiction; Nonsense. RL A.
Cumulative nonsense follows big brown bear and friends biking backward, who collectively break baby bird's balloon. Flat, colorful cartoon illustrations add lots of noise and action.

156 *Big Honey Hunt*. Ill. by authors. Beginner, 1962. ISBN 0-394-90028-6. SERIES: I Can Read It All By Myself. SUBJECTS: Animals—Bears—Fiction; Stories in rhyme. RL A.
Papa Bear encounters an owl, a porcupine, a skunk, and some angry bees while trying to find his own honey. Cartoon drawings are typical of the Berenstains.

157 *Bike Lesson*. Ill. by authors. Beginner, 1964, o.p. SERIES: I Can Read It All By Myself. SUBJECTS: Animals—Bears—Fiction; Bicycles and bicycling—Fiction. RL A.
Papa's "lessons" end disastrously until Small Bear finally gets his first turn on the new bicycle, and he rides Papa home on his handlebars. Humor is at the expense of sound bicycle safety. Drawings are typical of the Berenstains.

158 *C Is for Clown*. Ill. by authors. Random House, 1972. ISBN 0-394-92492-4. SERIES: Bright and Early. SUBJECTS: Alphabet—Fiction; Nonsense. RL B.
Clarence the clown carries a number of animals carrying things beginning with the letter "C" before the inevitable crash. Nonsense is illustrated with cartoon characters balancing higher and higher.

159 *He Bear, She Bear*. Ill. by authors. Random House, 1974. ISBN 0-394-92997-7. SERIES: Bright and Early. SUBJECTS: Animals—Bears—Fiction; Careers; Stories in rhyme. RL B.
Careers for both sexes are discussed and include cowboy, astronaut, and animal trainer. Far-reaching possibilities are presented in rhyme, illustrated with cartoons.

160 *Inside, Outside, Upside Down*. Ill. by authors. Random House, 1968. ISBN 0-394-91142-3. SERIES: Bright and Early.

**Berenstain, Stan, and
Berenstain, Jan (cont.)**

SUBJECTS: Animals—Bears—Fiction;
Concepts—Space—Fiction; Stories in
rhyme. RL A.
A small bear returns home to tell Mama about
his adventures in a box in which he traveled to
town inside, outside, upside down. Simple
rhythmic language and pictures focusing on
the yellow box give this story its appeal.

161 *Old Hat, New Hat*. Ill. by authors.
Random House, 1970. ISBN 0-394-90669-
1. SERIES: Bright and Early. SUBJECTS:
Animals—Bears—Fiction; Humorous
stories. RL A.
A bear shopping for a new hat finds himself
most satisfied with his old one. Cartoon drawings add humor.

162 *Ready, Get Set, Go!* Ill. by authors.
Random House, 1988. ISBN 0-394-90564-
4. SERIES: First Time Readers. SUBJECTS:
Animals—Bears—Fiction; Sports—
Fiction; Stories in rhyme. RL B.
In family Olympic events, Papa is best only at
sleeping. Stereotypes of Mama as timer and
starter and Papa as stupid are dull. Pastel cartoons are typical of the Berenstains.

Berg, Jean

163 *Nobody Scares a Porcupine*. Ill. by Robert
L. Jefferson. Westminster, 1969, o.p.
SUBJECTS: Animals—Porcupines—Fiction;
Behavior—Brave—Fiction. RL C.
The mouse, squirrel, muskrat, beaver, and
even the porcupine are all afraid of something,
but still go about their everyday tasks. Some
information about porcupines emerges. Pencil
drawings are warmed with turquoise and yellow colored pencil.

Berg, Julie

164 *The Berenstains: The Young at Heart*.
Photos. Abdo, 1993. ISBN 1-56239-224-7.
SUBJECTS: Biographies; Books and reading;
Writing and writers. RL C.
Jan and Stan met in art school, although they
didn't marry until Stan got out of the service.
They began as magazine illustrators and have

been successful with children's books featuring bears, while venturing into TV and other
related markets. Black and white photos add
little to the text.

165 *Maurice Sendak: The Young at Heart*.
Photos. Abdo, 1993. ISBN 1-56239-225-5.
SUBJECTS: Books and reading; Writing and
writers. RL C.
Berg includes a number of direct quotations as
she writes about the creative energy of a top
author and illustrator of children's books. The
son of Polish immigrants, Sendak apparently
had a loathing for school. Illustrations consist
of a few dull black and white photos.

Berger, Melvin

166 *Energy from the Sun*. Ill. by Giulio
Maestro. HarperCollins, 1976, o.p.
SERIES: Let's-Read-and-Find-Out Science
Books. SUBJECTS: Energy; Science experi-
ments. RL C.
Berger traces the broad outlines of how neces-
sary energy in its various forms is to our world.
Some simple solar experiments are included.
Graphically appealing drawings alternate gray
tones with four colors.

167 *Germs Make Me Sick!* Ill. by Marylin
Hafner. HarperCollins, 1985;
HarperCollins, pap., 1987. ISBN 0-690-
04429-1. SERIES: Let's-Read-and-Find-Out
Science Books. SUBJECTS: Diseases; Illness.
RL C.
The causes and treatment of common illnesses
are discussed in this book written by a former
teacher. Lively, bright illustrations include
some cartoon humor.

168 *Look Out for Turtles*. Ill. by Megan Lloyd.
HarperCollins, 1992. ISBN 0-06-022540-8.
SERIES: Let's-Read-and-Find-Out Science
Books. SUBJECTS: Animals—Turtles;
Nature; Science and scientists. RL A.
Characteristics of and differences between
turtles, from the smallest three-inch mud turtle to the 600-pound Galapagos turtle, are
described and illustrated with excellent soft
watercolors. Berger describes how turtles'
survival is being threatened by pollution and
loss of habitat in this sympathetic, interesting
account.

169 *Oil Spill!* Ill. by Paul Mirocha. HarperCollins, 1994. ISBN 0-06-022912-8. SERIES: Let's-Read-and-Find-Out Science Books. SUBJECTS: Oceans and ocean life; Pollution; Science. RL A.

The 1989 *Exxon Valdez*'s impact on 11,000 square miles of Alaska's coastline is described. Methods of containing and cleaning up the almost daily spills are discussed. Personal action—such as ways to use less fuel and how to write to congresspeople—is suggested in this well-written and illustrated book.

170 *Simple Science Says: Take One Mirror*. Ill. by G. Brian Karas. Scholastic, 1989, o.p. SUBJECTS: Science experiments. RL C.

Science experiments such as being able to look around corners, making a rainbow or a kaleidoscope, reading backward writing, or doing word magic are intriguingly presented. Pencil drawings with turquoise highlights add humor and expand the text.

171 *Stars*. Ill. by Marilyn Miller. Putnam, 1971, o.p. SERIES: Science Is What and Why. SUBJECTS: Astronomy; Science. RL B.

In simple terms, questions about the size and composition of stars, how far from earth they are, and why they shine and twinkle are answered. Red, white, and blue illustrations are effective.

172 *Switch On, Switch Off*. Ill. by Carolyn Croll. HarperCollins, 1989. ISBN 0-690-04786-X. SERIES: Let's-Read-and-Find-Out Science Books. SUBJECTS: Electricity; Energy; Science experiments. RL C.

Excellent well-presented information about how electricity is generated. Bright drawings feature familiar household scenes and pets. There are also diagrams of distribution systems.

173 *Why I Cough, Sneeze, Shiver, Hiccup, and Yawn*. Ill. by Holly Keller. HarperCollins, 1983. ISBN 0-690-04254-X. SERIES: Let's-Read-and-Find-Out Science Books. SUBJECTS: Human body—Reflexes; Science. RL C.

Comic sketches show how and why the reflexes work, using children and a cat as models. Well-presented information, with illustrations that lighten the tone.

Berger, Melvin, and Berger, Gilda

174 *Telephones, Televisions, and Toilets: How They Work—and What Can Go Wrong*. Ill. by Don Madden. Ideals, 1993. ISBN 0-8249-8645-8. SERIES: Discovery Readers. SUBJECTS: Telephones; Television. RL B.

In simple language, the authors describe how these appliances work, and how using a plunger sometimes helps. Simple color cartoons include a boy and his pets.

175 *Where Are the Stars During the Day? A Book About Stars*. Ill. by Blanche Sims. Ideals, 1993. ISBN 0-8249-8644-X. SERIES: Discovery Readers. SUBJECTS: Astronomy and astronomers; Science. RL A.

An exceptional introduction to the rotation of the earth, extending to the sun as a star, planets, the Big Dipper, the North Star, Orion, and the Milky Way. Simple illustrations make sky observation a family affair.

176 *Where Did Your Family Come From?* Ill. by Robert Quackenbush. Ideals, 1993. ISBN 0-8249-8647-4. SUBJECTS: Emigration and immigration. RL A.

Through the stories of children—Boris from Russia, Maria from Italy, Rosa from Mexico, and Chang from Korea—examples of the reasons immigrants settle in the United States are given. Typical vivid illustrations by Robert Quackenbush enhance the text.

177 *The Whole World in Your Hands*. Ill. by Robert Quackenbush. Ideals, 1993. ISBN 0-8249-8646-6. SERIES: Discovery Readers. SUBJECTS: Geography. RL A.

A masterful introduction to reading maps takes the reader from the map of a house to one of a neighborhood, a town, a state, a country, and the world, as well as a hint of what cultural habits can be inferred from a map. The text is appropriately and attractively illustrated.

Bernhard, Emery

178 *Spotted Eagle and Black Crow: A Lakota Legend*. Ill. by Durga Bernhard. Holiday House, 1993. ISBN 0-8234-1007-2. SUBJECTS: Native Americans—Lakota; Animals—Birds—Fiction; Folklore. RL C.

Bernhard, Emery (cont.)

A powerful tale of courage, love, and forgiveness in the wake of betrayal. The author and illustrator are "longtime students of traditional shamanism and tribal art." Stylized pastel illustrations are rich in Lakota imagery in close touch with the natural world.

Bernier-Grand, Carmen T.

179 *Juan Bobo: Four Folktales from Puerto Rico*. Ill. by Ernesto Ramos Nieves. HarperCollins, 1994. ISBN 0-06-023389-3. SERIES: I Can Read Books. SUBJECTS: Folklore; Nonsense; Spanish language. RL A.
Flaky Juan Bobo carries water in a basket, tries to dress a pig for church, tries to follow Mama's advice on table manners and goes home hungry, and "sells" syrup mistakenly to flies. Decorative illustrations are rich in texture and color.

Berry, Steve

180 *The Boy Who Wouldn't Speak*. Ill. by Deirdre Betteridge. Annick, 1992. ISBN 1-55037-231-9. SUBJECTS: Behavior—Shyness—Fiction; Giants—Fiction. RL B.
Owen, who at five has never spoken, befriends his new giant neighbors, Fred and Lola, and finally speaks up to defend them from nervous neighbors. Bright ink and watercolor cartoon drawings with lots of red and blue and orange enhance the text.

Bethell, Jean

181 *Three Cheers for Mother Jones*. Ill. by Kathleen Garry-McCord. Holt, 1980, o.p. SUBJECTS: United States—History. RL B.
Seventy-three-year-old Mary Harris Jones marched with mill children 125 miles, taking 22 days, to see President Theodore Roosevelt at his summer home to protest the conditions under which one million children under 14 worked. Federal legislation took another 35 years. Text is illustrated with pen and ink drawings.

Bianchi, John

182 *The Bungalo Boys III: Champions of Hockey*. Ill. by author. Bungalo, 1989.

ISBN 0-921285-18-3. SUBJECTS: Humorous stories; Sports—Hockey—Fiction. RL C.
In this tongue-in-cheek parody of more serious sports, Little Shorty, guided by Bungalo ghosts (from an ice floe after the ice shatters), scores the winning goal with time running out while the organ plays. Illustrations are colorful ink and watercolor cartoons.

Binnamin, Vivian

183 *The Case of the Planetarium Puzzle*. Ill. by Jeffrey S. Nelsen. Silver Burdett, 1989. ISBN 0-671-68819-7. SERIES: Field Trip Mysteries. SUBJECTS: Astronomy and astronomers—Fiction; Science. RL A.
Miss Whimsy's third-grade Fantastic Fifteen "peek, poke, and prove" on a class trip to the planetarium. Basic information about the size of the planets with a few other facts about meteors, comets, and stars is unearthed in this forced story with static illustrations.

184 *The Case of the Snoring Stegosaurus*. Ill. by Jeffrey S. Nelsen. Silver Burdett, 1989. ISBN 0-671-68818-9. SERIES: Field Trip Mysteries. SUBJECTS: Dinosaurs—Fiction; Science. RL A.
A few stray facts are given about the museum exhibits Miss Whimsy's third-grade class passes on the way to visit the stegosaurus at the museum. After the children climb over and under exhibits, they figure out why the stegosaurus snores, exhibiting some good detective work despite the inappropriate behavior.

Bishop, Ann

185 *Merry-Go-Riddle*. Ill. by Jerry Warshaw. Whitman, 1973, o.p. SUBJECTS: Jokes and riddles. RL C.
Interesting word play uses themes from the circus and circus performers so that the humor is cumulative. Illustrations are red and black ink cartoons.

Bishop, Bonnie

186 *No One Noticed Ralph*. Ill. by Jack Kent. Doubleday, 1978, o.p. SERIES: Reading On

My Own. SUBJECTS: Animals—Parrots—Fiction. RL C.
Ralph the parrot is noticed when he gives a fire alert. Lively drawings of Ralph and people are in browns and reds.

187 *Ralph Rides Away*. Ill. by Jack Kent. Doubleday, 1979, o.p. SERIES: Reading On My Own. SUBJECTS: Animals—Parrots—Fiction; Lost, being—Fiction. RL C.
Ralph gets lost in the zoo on his first adventurous picnic in the park with Mr. and Mrs. Muggs. The creative solution to his restitution to the family is matched by bright, comic four-color illustrations.

Bishop, Claire

188 *Georgette*. Ill. by Ursula Landshoff. Putnam, 1973, o.p. SERIES: Break-of-Day. SUBJECTS: Animals—Chickens—Fiction. RL B.
Georgette the chicken saves her neck with her dancing abilities in a tale of romance and suspense in a Paris apartment. Ink sketches add flavor to the setting.

189 *Truffle Pig*. Ill. by Kurt Wiese. Putnam, 1971, o.p. SERIES: Break-of-Day. SUBJECTS: Animals—Pigs—Fiction; France—Fiction. RL C.
The marvelous piglet Marcel saves his skin by his ability to dig for the elusive and costly truffles. The tale is told in simple language but not a controlled vocabulary. Distinctly French in character, illustrations are in ink with blue and yellow colored pencil.

Blakely, Cindy, and Drinkwater, Suzanne

190 *The Look Out! Book: A Child's Guide to Street Safety*. Ill. by Barbara Klunder. Scholastic, 1988, o.p. SUBJECTS: Safety. RL C.
Bright and action-filled sketches of animal children lighten the lists of rules for personal and traffic safety. There are a lot of "don'ts," and the illustrations are almost too busy.

Blassingame, Wyatt

191 *Bowleg Bill, Seagoing Cowboy*. Ill. by Herman Vestal. Garrard, 1976, o.p.

SUBJECTS: Humorous stories; Tall tales. RL C.
Sailing with 10,000 rabbits he had lassoed, Bowleg Bill has his hands full when they reproduce faster than the ship is moving. Bowleg Bill also discovers the thrill of whale riding. Runaway rabbits provide the most visual interest. The illustrations are in turquoise, orange, and gray.

192 *How Davy Crockett Got a Bearskin Coat*. Ill. by Mimi Korach. Garrard, 1972, o.p. SERIES: Tall Tales. SUBJECTS: Folklore—United States; Humorous stories; Tall tales. RL B.
While trying to replace his moth-eaten coat, Davy ends up being chased by his quarry, a bear. When he catches the bear and knots his tail through a hole in a tree, the bear runs on, skinless! Comic pencil drawings add to the fun of this tall tale.

193 *Pecos Bill and the Wonderful Clothesline Snake*. Ill. by Herman Vestal. Garrard, 1978, o.p. SERIES: American Folktales. SUBJECTS: Folklore—United States; Humorous stories; Tall tales. RL C.
Glass snakes that shatter and reassemble attached to other snakes, snakes with bells instead of rattles, snakes wild as broncos, and pancake snakes sunning under syrup and blueberries—these are some of the inventions of a tall tale enhanced by turquoise and gold drawings.

194 *Pecos Bill Catches a Hidebehind*. Ill. by Herman Vestal. Garrard, 1977, o.p. SERIES: American Folktales. SUBJECTS: Folklore—United States; Humorous stories; Tall tales. RL C.
After a roperite and a telescopo help Pecos Bill and Sluefoot Sue capture a hidebehind for a zoo, they feel sorry for the shy animal and send a roperite instead. Simple turquoise and orange illustrations add to the humor of this outrageous tall tale.

Blocksma, Mary

195 *Yoo Hoo, Moon!* Ill. by Patience Brewster. Bantam, 1992. ISBN 0-553-07094-0. SERIES: Bank Street Ready-to-Read. SUBJECTS: Animals—Fiction; Cumulative tales; Night—Fiction. RL A.

Blocksma, Mary (cont.)

As the animals wake up and shout for the moon to wake up, they mistake other lights for that of the moon. Language and story line are simple, and appealing clothed animals are painted in lavender, brown, and orange against the deep blues and greens of the night world.

Blocksma, Norma

196 *Best Dressed Bear*. Ill. by Sandra Kalthoff. Childrens Pr., 1984, o.p. SERIES: Just One More. SUBJECTS: Animals— Bears—Fiction; Animals—Fiction; Stories in rhyme. RL A.

Bear is dressed formally for a dance—but forgets his pants. Language is rhythmic and simple, but not predictable. Full color drawings of friendly animals add humor to a tale that uses an 80 word vocabulary.

Boegehold, Betty

197 *Chipper's Choices*. Ill. by Jim Arnosky. Putnam, 1981, o.p. SUBJECTS: Animals— Chipmunks—Fiction; Animals—Fiction. RL C.

Chipper the chipmunk tells stories about his friends Mole, Jay, Toad, and Squirrel in which the animals argue about who is boss, encounter a scary noise, and share riddles and some poems. Soft pencil drawings focus on nuts and individual animals.

198 *The Fight*. Ill. by Robin Oz. Bantam, 1991. ISBN 0-553-07086-X. SERIES: Bank Street Ready-to-Read. SUBJECTS: Cumulative stories; School stories. RL A.

A rhythmic modern cumulative tale detailing the sequence of insignificant events leading to a fight on the playground. Very effective illustrations are with ink and wash action.

199 *Here's Pippa Again*. Ill. by Cyndy Szekeres. Knopf, 1975, o.p. SERIES: Read-aloud/Read-alone. SUBJECTS: Animals—Fiction; Animals—Mice—Fiction; Growing-up—Fiction. RL B.

Pippa is often restless and ready for adventure. She wants to learn how to swim, play in the snow, find a pet, and have a party. Her animal friends' antics are shown in charming pencil drawings.

200 *Horse Called Starfire*. Ill. by Neil Waldman. Bantam, 1990. ISBN 0-553-05861-4. SERIES: Bank Street Ready-to-Read. SUBJECTS: Historical fiction; Horses—Fiction. RL A.

A magical telling of how Native Americans came to have horses, illustrated with flowing, stylized watercolors of the Southwest. Boegehold's story reads like a legend, despite its very simple vocabulary and story line.

201 *Hurray for Pippa!* Ill. by Cyndy Szekeres. Knopf, 1980, o.s.i. SERIES: Read-aloud/Read-alone. SUBJECTS: Animals— Fiction; Animals—Mice—Fiction. RL B.

Testing under the chin with a buttercup, cleaning out old toys, teaching a rabbit to play games, and playing dress-up occupy Pippa and her animal friends. Joyful pencil drawings suit the homely adventures.

202 *Pippa Pops Out!* Ill. by Cyndy Szekeres. Knopf, 1979, o.s.i.; pap., 1980. ISBN 0-440-46865-5. SERIES: Read-aloud/Read-alone. SUBJECTS: Animals—Mice—Fiction; Friendship—Fiction; Growing-up— Fiction. RL C.

The fears and feelings of inadequacy, as well as the warmth of friendship, are celebrated. Pencil drawings show expressive mice, squirrels, ducklings, and crickets.

203 *Small Deer's Magic Tricks*. Ill. by Jacqueline Chwast. Putnam, 1977, o.p. SERIES: Break-of-Day. SUBJECTS: Animals—Deer— Fiction; Folklore—Indonesia. RL B.

Four traditional Indonesian trickster tales about the tiny mouse deer, Kanchil. In one tale he outwits a tiger, some crocodiles, a wild pig, and an elephant. Comic-style ink drawings are mediocre.

204 *Three to Get Ready*. Ill. by Mary Chalmers. HarperCollins, 1965, o.p. SERIES: I Can Read Books. SUBJECTS: Animals—Cats—Fiction; Sibling rivalry—Fiction; Siblings—Fiction. RL A.

Mother Cat rescues and comforts her children Gigi, George, and Ginger as they explore the world at night outside their yard. Soft drawings in gray, green, and rose accompany this reassuring tale.

Boivin, Kelly

205 *What's in a Box?* Ill. by Janice Skivington. Childrens Pr., 1991. ISBN 0-516-02010-2. SERIES: Rookie Readers. SUBJECTS: Toys—Fiction. RL A.
Colored pencil and watercolor washes illustrate this story about different ways boxes can be used: for mail, tools, sand, hats, and jack-in-the boxes. A limited (55-word) vocabulary is used.

206 *Where Is Mittens?* Ill. by Clovis Martin. Childrens Pr., 1990. ISBN 0-516-02060-9. SERIES: Rookie Readers. SUBJECTS: Animals—Cats—Fiction; Stories in rhyme. RL A.
A young girl searches everywhere for her cat, finding her with new kittens in a closet. Large colorful watercolor closeups show a worried child.

Bonsall, Crosby

207 *The Amazing the Incredible Super Dog.* Ill. by author. HarperCollins, 1986. ISBN 0-06-020591-1. SUBJECTS: Animals—Cats—Fiction; Animals—Dogs—Fiction; Pets—Fiction. RL A.
A yawning puppy, Super Dog, chases a butterfly while his young mistress boasts to Willy, her cat, about all the tricks Super Dog can do. Exuberant, expressive ink and watercolor drawings of the three accompany the text.

208 *And I Mean It, Stanley.* Ill. by author. HarperCollins, 1974, o.p.; pap., 1984. ISBN 0-06-444046-X. SERIES: Early I Can Read Books. SUBJECTS: Animals—Dogs—Fiction; Imagination—Fiction. RL A.
A small boy's creations using things found in an alley are ruined when his pet, Shaggy Stanley, finally appears. Delightful ink drawings add warmth to an inventive tale.

209 *The Case of the Cat's Meow.* Ill. by author. HarperCollins, 1965, o.p.; pap., 1978. ISBN 0-06-444017-6. SERIES: I Can Read Books. SUBJECTS: Friendship—Fiction; Mystery and detective stories. RL A.

Four friends try to find the missing cat, Mildred, using cats, dogs, food, and alarms. Characters in this series are interesting individuals. Line drawings are colored with gray, red, salmon, and pumpkin.

210 *Case of the Dumb Bells.* Ill. by author. HarperCollins, 1966, o.p.; pap., 1982. ISBN 0-06-444030-3. SERIES: I Can Read Books. SUBJECTS: Friendship—Fiction; Mystery and detective stories. RL A.
Wizard, Skinny, Tubby, and Snitch have some difficulties with their phone system, cleverly conveyed by one-sided telephone conversations with irate parents. Excellent ink drawings convey relationships sympathetically.

211 *The Case of the Hungry Stranger.* Ill. by author. HarperCollins, 1992. ISBN 0-06-020571-7. SERIES: I Can Read Books. SUBJECTS: Friendship—Fiction; Mystery and detective stories. RL A.
Wizard, Tubby, Skinny, and Snitch check for blue teeth when on the trail of the blueberry pie thief. The mishaps of the friends provide gentle humor—Tubby gets tangled in a garden hose in a scary cellar; they follow false trails of their own making. Exceptional illustrations match text.

212 *Case of the Scaredy Cats.* Ill. by author. HarperCollins, 1971, o.p.; pap. 1984. ISBN 0-06-444047-8. SERIES: I Can Read Books. SUBJECTS: Friendship—Fiction; Mystery and detective stories. RL A.
During the fight between the boys in the gang and the girls who try to take the clubhouse over, little scaredy-cat Annie is lost and all join in to try to find her. Warm, reassuring, realistic ending is enhanced by ink drawings with marvelous cross-hatched patterns.

213 *The Day I Had to Play with My Sister.* Ill. by author. HarperCollins, 1972, o.p.; pap., 1988. ISBN 0-06-444117-2. SERIES: Early I Can Read. SUBJECTS: Siblings—Fiction. RL A.
A small sister's way of playing hide-and-seek does not satisfy her older brother. Appealing cross-hatched ink drawings with pale rose and gray show the antics of a devoted shaggy dog.

214 *Mine's the Best.* Ill. by author. HarperCollins, 1973; pap., 1984. ISBN 0-06-

Bonsall, Crosby (cont.)

020578-4. SERIES: Early I Can Read. SUBJECTS: Behavior—Argumentative—Fiction; Friendship—Fiction. RL A.
This classic argument between friends is resolved with the boys aligned together against a new antagonist—a girl. Visually fascinating inked patterned drawings of a parade of boardwalk people are in green and brown.

215 *Piggle*. Ill. by author. HarperCollins, 1973. ISBN 0-06-020580-6. SERIES: I Can Read Books. SUBJECTS: Dreams—Fiction; Imagination—Fiction; Nonsense. RL A.
Bear teaches Homer how to play "Piggle" (making nonsense rhymes), after his overtures are rejected by Duck, Rabbit, Pig, and his sisters. Charming, witty nonsense is illustrated with warm cross-hatched ink drawings during Homer's dream, and pale pink and brown while he is awake.

216 *Tell Me Some More*. Ill. by Fritz Siebel. HarperCollins, 1961. ISBN 0-06-020601-2. SERIES: I Can Read Books. SUBJECTS: Books and Reading—Fiction; Imagination—Fiction; Libraries—Fiction. RL A.
Andrew captures Tim's imagination with tales of elephants, camels, mountains and fountains, moons and spoons, rings and kings—which can be held in the hand or carried under his arm (in books)! The boys are drawn in ink, the imaginings are in color in this captivating tale.

217 *What Spot?* Ill. by author. HarperCollins, 1963, o.p.; pap., 1980. ISBN 0-06-020611-X. SERIES: I Can Read Books. SUBJECTS: Animals—Birds—Fiction; Animals—Walruses—Fiction. RL B.
Some polar animals puzzle over a mysterious black spot in the snow. This imaginative tale is illustrated with textured tones in pencil.

Boritzer, Etan

218 *What Is God?* Ill. by Robbie Marantz. Firefly, 1990. ISBN 0-920668-89-5. SUBJECTS: Religion. RL C.
Speculation about the nature of God begins with great teachers of a variety of faiths, and their holy books. The similarities between faiths and the meaning of prayer, the universal-ity of God, and connectedness through other people are outlined in fairly simple language.

Bourne, Miriam A.

219 *A Day in the Life of a Chef*. Photos. Troll, 1988. ISBN 0-8167-1115-1. SERIES: A Day in the Life of. SUBJECTS: Careers; Cookery. RL C.
For a day, Raymond Broat, head chef at a hotel restaurant, is followed around a clean, well-organized kitchen. From the glazes to the white chocolate roses, from the ice sculpture to the banquet manager, an array of coordinated jobs is introduced in fairly difficult language.

220 *A Day in the Life of a Cross-Country Trucker*. Photos by Gayle Jann. Troll, 1988. ISBN 0-8167-1117-8. SERIES: A Day in the Life of. SUBJECTS: Careers. RL C.
Trucker Mike Williams is shown on a two-week trip from New Jersey to California and back delivering textbooks with his partner. Information about the trucks, testing, planning, sleeping, fueling, and safety is given, accompanied by color photos.

221 *Four-Ring Three*. Ill. by Cyndy Szekeres. Putnam, 1973, o.p. SUBJECTS: Historical fiction; Plays—Fiction; Telephones—Fiction. RL C.
Frank and his sister Martha, with her friend Jean, convince their father to get a new-fangled telephone by producing a play. Characterizations, dialogue, and historical detail all ring true. The antics of cats and children enliven the period drawings.

222 *Let's Visit a Toy Factory*. Photos by Michael Plunkett. Troll, 1988. ISBN 0-8167-1159-3. SUBJECTS: Careers; Toys. RL B.
The coloring, molding, carving, painting, assembling, drilling, packaging, testing, and delivering of plastic toys is summarized with text and color photos.

223 *Second Car in Town*. Ill. by Ray Burns. Putnam, 1972, o.p. SERIES: Break-of-Day. SUBJECTS: Cars—Fiction; Historical fiction. RL B.
Garbed in a duster, Ellen felt like a princess on her first car ride. A feeling for the fear, wonder, and hazards of the new contraption is con-

veyed. Good ink sketches capture the action and humor.

Bowden, Joan C.

224 *Bean Boy*. Ill. by Sal Murdocca. Macmillan, 1978, o.p. SERIES: Ready-to-Read. SUBJECTS: Cumulative tales. RL A.
The adventures of a child carved from a bean by a childless couple are told in original cumulative fashion. Green and orange drawings have some folk flavor.

225 *Strong John*. Ill. by Sal Murdocca. Macmillan, 1979, o.p. SERIES: Ready-to-Read. SUBJECTS: Folklore. RL A.
John's hard work is repaid by worthless gifts; when he uses them to help a queen, he is richly rewarded. The characters are more flat and the rhythm of the tale less rich than in traditional tales. Turquoise and orange drawings are mediocre.

Boyd, Lizi

226 *Bailey, the Big Bully*. Ill. by author. Puffin, 1991. ISBN 0-14-054051-2. SUBJECTS: Behavior—Bullying. RL A.
Didactic story about a new boy who ignores the bully, Bailey, and then invites him to join the neighborhood children in building a treehouse. Ink and wash drawings are more appealing than the story.

Boynton, Alice Benjamin

227 *Priscilla Alden and the First Thanksgiving*. Ill. by Christa Kieffer. Silver Burdett, 1990. ISBN 0-671-69105-8. SERIES: Let's Celebrate. SUBJECTS: Holidays—Thanksgiving; United States—History. RL C.
In simple language, the story of the first colony at Plymouth, Massachusetts, is told. The hardships of life aboard ship as well as of the first winter are gently relayed, although the pastel illustrations help keep the tone light. The reader is hard pressed to find a picture of John Alden, often quoted.

Bozzo, Maxine Z.

228 *Toby in the Country, Toby in the City*. Ill. by Frank Modell. Greenwillow, 1982, o.p. SUBJECTS: City and town life—Fiction; Farm and country life—Fiction. RL A.
The similarities between the life-style of a country boy and a city boy are emphasized, from school and play to enjoyment of the seasons. Excellent comic watercolor illustrations add sparkle to the simple text.

Bram, Elizabeth

229 *Woodruff and the Clocks*. Ill. by author. Dial, hb and pap., 1980, o.p. SERIES: Dial Easy-to-Read. SUBJECTS: Animals—Cats—Fiction; Clocks—Fiction. RL B.
Woodruff finds out that his neglected cat, Muffin, is more important to him than his fascination with clocks, in the first of four stories in this book. Flat colors highlight simple ink drawings.

Brandenberg, Franz

230 *Aunt Nina and Her Nephews and Nieces*. Ill. by Aliki. Greenwillow, 1983. ISBN 0-688-01870-X. SUBJECTS: Animals—Cats—Fiction; Birthdays—Fiction; Family life—Fiction. RL B.
Aunt Nina's house provides more adventure than the zoo, the toy shop, the theater, the haunted house, and a treasure hunt combined when her nieces and nephews come to celebrate her cat's birthday. Lively watercolor and ink drawings add to the action.

231 *Everyone Ready?* Ill. by Aliki. Greenwillow, 1979, o.p. SERIES: Read-alone. SUBJECTS: Animals—Mice—Fiction; Family life—Fiction. RL B.
The Fieldmouse family is so busy they have trouble catching the train all at the same time. Delicate pen and ink drawings with washes of pink and green match the warmth and humor with human parallels.

232 *A Fun Weekend*. Ill. by Alexa Brandenberg. Greenwillow, 1991. ISBN 0-688-09721-9. SUBJECTS: Animals—Bears—Fiction; Family life—Fiction. RL B.
The bear family contentedly sleep in their van when they are too late for their reservations at a lodge after a long day of stops for stretching, swimming, eating ice cream, and shopping. Alexa Brandenberg illustrates her father's

Brandenberg, Franz (cont.)

story in colorful watercolor, crayon, and colored pencil drawings.

233 *Leo and Emily and the Dragon*. Ill. by Aliki. Greenwillow, 1984. ISBN 0-688-02532-3. SERIES: Read-alone. SUBJECTS: Baby-sitting—Fiction; Hiking—Fiction; Imagination—Fiction. RL A.
Leo and Emily have a long hike, complete with picnic, cave, sleeping bags, and sunbathing. When "boring" Harold baby-sits that night, they have another exhausting and imaginative hike indoors! Lively drawings in spring green and orange capture the delights, fears, and exhaustion well.

234 *Leo and Emily's Big Ideas*. Ill. by Aliki. Greenwillow, 1982. ISBN 0-688-00755-4. SERIES: Read-alone. SUBJECTS: Friendship—Fiction; Play—Fiction. RL B.
Leo and Emily's escapades include dressing up to scare people and making wet tracks and "back" marks all over the garage. The imaginative text and delicate, lively illustrations capture the spirit of adventure in everyday neighborhood play.

235 *Leo and Emily's Zoo*. Ill. by Yossi Abolafia. Greenwillow, 1988. ISBN 0-688-07457-X. SUBJECTS: Family life—Fiction. RL B.
Leo and Emily's backyard zoo is disappointing until some "zoo animals" appear next door. This is a very refreshing story enhanced by lively watercolors of children and animals.

236 *Nice New Neighbors*. Ill. by Aliki. Greenwillow, 1977; Scholastic, pap., 1980. ISBN 0-688-84105-8. SERIES: Read-alone. SUBJECTS: Animals—Mice—Fiction; Friendship—Fiction; Moving, household—Fiction. RL B.
Rejected by the other children on the street, the mice children decide to put on a play to attract their new neighbors' attention. Diminutive ink and wash drawings add to the charm of this book.

237 *A Robber! A Robber!* Ill. by Aliki. Greenwillow, 1976, o.p. SUBJECTS: Animals—Cats—Fiction; Emotions—Fear—Fiction. RL B.

The sound of snoring from their bottom bunk beds scares Edward and Elizabeth, who are in their respective rooms. In the morning they find out that visitors Uncle Peter and Aunt Ann were sharing their room. Darker penciled night scenes convey just enough feeling of fear.

238 *Six New Students*. Ill. by Aliki. Greenwillow, 1978, o.p. SERIES: Read-alone. SUBJECTS: Animals—Mice—Fiction; School stories. RL B.
Ferdinand the mouse's creative first-grade teacher introduces him to all the subjects he does not expect to enjoy in first grade. Gentle humor has marvelous small pastel watercolor mice illustrations.

239 *What Can You Make of It?* Ill. by Aliki. Greenwillow, 1977, o.p. SERIES: Read-alone. SUBJECTS: Animals—Mice—Fiction; Circuses—Fiction; Moving, household—Fiction. RL C.
The Fieldmouse family moves in seven vans because of all their "rubbish": magazines, toilet paper tubes, milk and egg cartons, and so on. However, they find creative uses for all their treasures. Whimsical ink sketches have yellow, orange, gray, and green colored pencil highlights.

Branley, Franklyn M.

240 *Beginning of the Earth*. Rev. ed. Ill. by Giulio Maestro. HarperCollins, hb and pap., 1972. ISBN 0-690-04676-6. SERIES: Let's-Read-and-Find-Out. SUBJECTS: Astronomy; Geology; Science. RL C.
Dark, abstract designs with ink and washes of black and gray with highlights of fuchsia and blue aptly illustrate Branley's speculation.

241 *The Big Dipper*. Ill. by Molly Coxe. HarperCollins, 1991. ISBN 0-06-445100-3. SERIES: Let's-Read-and-Find-Out. SUBJECTS: Astronomy and astronomers; Nature; Science. RL B.
A girl who loves to watch the night sky with her father and her dog gives information about the big (and little) dipper(s) and the North Star. She encourages the reader to take a friend outside on a still, dark night to starwatch. Simple pencil and watercolor illustrations add humor.

242 *North, South, East, and West*. Ill. by Robert Galster. HarperCollins, 1966, o.p. SERIES: Let's-Read-and-Find-Out. SUBJECTS: Concepts—Direction; Science. RL B.

After beginning with right and left, up and down, Branley invites children to learn compass directions by using their shadows. The printed graphics illustrate concepts extremely well and have excellent eye appeal.

243 *Oxygen Keeps You Alive*. Ill. by Don Madden. HarperCollins, 1971, o.p.; HarperCollins, pap., 1972, o.p. SERIES: Let's-Read-and-Find-Out Science Books. SUBJECTS: Air; Science; Science experiments—Air. RL C.

The text underlines the importance of oxygen to animals, birds, fish, and plants, but especially people—at high altitudes, in space, or under the sea—at every moment of life. Drawings complement the text to show how the lungs work.

244 *The Planets in Our Solar System*. Rev. ed. Ill. by Don Madden. HarperCollins, hb and pap., 1987. ISBN 0-690-04581-6. SERIES: Let's-Read-and-Find-Out. SUBJECTS: Astronomy; Science. RL C.

Basic size and distance between the planets in our solar system are introduced, with patterns and suggestions for making two models. Children and pets are included in the ink drawings to humanize the science facts.

245 *Rain and Hail*. Ill. by Harriett Barton. HarperCollins, 1983. ISBN 0-690-04353-8. SERIES: Let's-Read-and-Find-Out. SUBJECTS: Science; Weather. RL C.

Information about both rain and hail is logically presented. Illustrations and type are in royal blue.

246 *Shooting Stars*. Ill. by Holly Keller. HarperCollins, 1989. ISBN 0-06-020512-1. SERIES: Let's-Read-and-Find-Out. SUBJECTS: Astronomy and astronomers; Nature; Science. RL C.

One hundred tons of meteoroids fall on Planet Earth every day! When they make a light streak, they are called meteors, from a Greek word meaning "something in the sky." Informative text is illustrated with light-hearted ink and watercolor illustrations.

247 *The Sky Is Full of Stars*. Ill. by Felicia Bond. HarperCollins, 1981; HarperCollins, pap., 1983. ISBN 0-690-04123-3. SERIES: Let's-Read-and-Find-Out Science Books. SUBJECTS: Astronomy; Science. RL B.

Branley takes children out at night—with pet and blanket—to observe four common constellations, and gives directions for reproducing the configurations with a coffee can and a flashlight. Blue, light green, and various shades of gray show the children and the stars.

248 *Snow Is Falling*. Rev. ed. Ill. by Holly Keller. HarperCollins, hb and pap., 1986. ISBN 0-690-04548-4. SERIES: Let's-Read-and-Find-Out. SUBJECTS: Seasons—Winter; Weather—Snow. RL B.

The benefits as well as the hardships of snow to plants, animals, and people are presented. Details of wildlife winters and playing in the snow are drawn in ink against a sparkling blue sky.

249 *The Sun: Our Nearest Star*. Rev. ed. Ill. by Don Madden. HarperCollins, hb and pap., 1988. ISBN 0-690-04678-2. SERIES: Let's-Read-and-Find-Out. SUBJECTS: Astronomy; Science. RL C.

Besides information about the sun, a simple plant experiment and the idea that coal and oil are stored-up solar energy are introduced. Ink drawings in sky blue, apple green, and gray highlight and lighten the text.

250 *Sunshine Makes the Seasons*. Rev. ed. Ill. by Giulio Maestro. HarperCollins, 1985; HarperCollins, pap., 1986. ISBN 0-690-04482-8. SERIES: Let's-Read-and-Find-Out Science Books. SUBJECTS: Seasons; Science. RL B.

Good information about seasonal change is logically presented and related to a child's experience. Textured crayon against black is very effective.

251 *Tornado Alert*. Ill. by Giulio Maestro. HarperCollins, 1988. ISBN 0-690-04686-3. SERIES: Let's-Read-and-Find-Out. SUBJECTS: Weather—Storms. RL C.

Exceptionally well presented information about tornados is included along with simple safety precautions to follow during a tornado. Softly textured colored drawings are also factual but reassuring.

Branley, Franklyn M. (cont.)

252 *Volcanoes*. Ill. by Marc Simont. Harper-Collins, 1985; HarperCollins, pap., 1986. ISBN 0-690-04431-3. SERIES: Let's-Read-and-Find-Out Science Books. SUBJECTS: Geology; Science. RL C.
The examples of Pompeii, Krakatoa, and Mount St. Helen's provide good information about the movement of tectonic plates and associated earthquake/volcanic activity. Excellent watercolors show the above events, simple diagrams, and geologists at work.

253 *Weight and Weightlessness*. Ill. by Graham Booth. HarperCollins, 1971, o.p. SERIES: Let's-Read-and-Find-Out Science Books. SUBJECTS: Concepts—Weight; Science. RL B.
Well-described concepts of weight and weightlessness are illustrated with simple, decorative ink sketches.

254 *What Happened to the Dinosaurs?* Ill. by Marc Simont. HarperCollins, 1991. ISBN 0-690-04749-5. SERIES: Let's-Read-and-Find-Out. SUBJECTS: Dinosaurs; Science. RL C.
Theories of dinosaur extinction are examined: comet collisions caused by the twin to the sun, the Nemesis star, gathering clouds of dust into comets; or a cooler sun; or dinosaur egg predators; or some sickness. Marc Simont's exceptional watercolors illustrate current dinosaur research.

255 *What Makes Day and Night*. Rev. ed. Ill. by Helen Borten. HarperCollins, hb and pap., 1986. ISBN 0-690-04524-7. SERIES: Let's-Read-and-Find-Out Science Books. SUBJECTS: Astronomy; Science. RL B.
As a child turns in a circle before a lamp, so the earth turns in relation to the sun, creating light and dark periods we call day and night. Basic information is well illustrated with strong black prints on white or a solid color.

256 *What the Moon Is Like*. Rev. ed. Photos. Ill. by True Kelley. HarperCollins, 1986; HarperCollins, pap., 1986. ISBN 0-694-00205-4. SERIES: Let's-Read-and-Find-Out. SUBJECTS: Astronomy; Science. RL C.
Updated basic information about the moon is excellent. Illustrations are cutesy pastels, smudgy sketches, and mediocre photos.

Brenner, Barbara

257 *Baltimore Orioles*. Ill. by J. Winslow Higginbottom. HarperCollins, 1974, o.p. SERIES: I Can Read Books. SUBJECTS: Animals—Birds. RL A.
Besides mating and nesting habits, Brenner includes hazards in the lives of young orioles. Well-presented information is accompanied by appealing illustrations.

258 *Beavers Beware!* Ill. by Emily Arnold McCully. Bantam, 1992. ISBN 0-553-07498-9. SERIES: Bank Street Ready-to-Read. SUBJECTS: Animals—Beavers—Fiction. RL A.
A family with a house by the river find a beaver family taking over their dock. While they are discussing beaver, tree, and people rights, a storm takes the dock downstream. Vivid, full color illustrations are by a favorite, Emily McCully.

259 *Beef Stew*. Ill. by John E. Johnson. Knopf, 1965, o.p. SERIES: Read-alone. SUBJECTS: Grandparents—Fiction. RL B.
Nicky cannot seem to get any friends to come over for dinner for beef stew, but he gets a nice surprise. Four-color illustrations show Nicky's friends in school and in the neighborhood.

260 *Dinosaurium: The Museum That Explores the World of Living Dinosaurs*. Ill. by Donna Braginetz. Bantam, 1993. ISBN 0-553-07614-0. SERIES: A Bank Street Museum Book. SUBJECTS: Dinosaurs; Science and scientists. RL C.
Families move through the halls and labs of a museum to learn about time periods, bones, feeding, weight, and anatomy of dinosaurs. Insets show fossils, plate tectonics, skeletal details, eggs, and important paleontologists, which include several children.

261 *A Dog I Know*. Ill. by Fred Brenner. HarperCollins, 1983, o.p. SUBJECTS: Animals—Dogs—Fiction; Pets—Dogs—Fiction. RL B.
The special qualities of a boy's shaggy mutt are told in the first person. Brown pencil with washes focus on the brave-with-bear, scared-of-paper beloved pet.

262 *Moon Boy*. Ill. by J. Gaban. Bantam, 1990. ISBN 0-553-05858-4. SERIES: Bank

Street Ready-to-Read. SUBJECTS: Imagination—Fiction; Night—Fiction. RL A.
When a shiny dot on his windowsill turns out to be Moon Boy, shaped like a nightlight, a small boy shuts Moon Boy in his toy box to keep him. But when the gold balloon moon and the stars are dark with sadness, the boy releases Moon Boy. Illustrations are done in midnight blue and glowing white.

263 *Nicky's Sister*. Ill. by John E. Johnson. Knopf, 1966, o.p. SERIES: Read-alone. SUBJECTS: Behavior—Running away—Fiction; Sibling rivalry—Fiction. RL B.
Nicky prefers a hamster to a pesky baby sister until she is threatened by a bully. Details of home life are in ink with a three-color wash.

264 *Planetarium*. Ill. by Ron Miller. Byron Preiss, 1992. ISBN 0-553-35428-0. SERIES: A Bank Street Museum Book. SUBJECTS: Astronomy and astronomers; Science; Space. RL C.
Liberally illustrated, the bordered text is backed and surrounded with colored drawings, which include children exploring the planets without space suits. This browsing book has summary fact boxes, cartoon dialogue between the children, and a brief index.

265 *Rosa & Marco and the Three Wishes*. Ill. by Megan Halsey. Macmillan, 1992. ISBN 0-02-712315-4. SUBJECTS: Magic—Fiction; Siblings—Fiction; Sports—Fishing—Fiction. RL A.
A modern child's version of "The Fisherman and His Wife" has jealous older sister Rosa forced to use the third and last wish to get a taco unstuck from her brother's nose. Soft pencil and wash drawings of the pair undergird the storytelling.

266 *Wagon Wheels*. Ill. by Don Bolognese. HarperCollins, 1978; pap., 1984. ISBN 0-06-020669-1. SERIES: I Can Read History. SUBJECTS: Behavior—Brave; Frontier and pioneer life; Historical fiction. RL B.
This amazing adventure story of homesteading in the Kansas Territory was based on events in the lives of the Muldie boys and their father. Their resourcefulness and courage in facing starvation, grief, and a prairie fire are depicted. Effective pencil drawings have three-tone washes.

Brenner, Barbara, and Chardiet, Bernice

267 *Where's That Insect?* Ill. by Carol Schwartz. Scholastic, 1993. ISBN 0-590-45210-X. SERIES: Hide-and-Seek Science Book. SUBJECTS: Animals—Insects; Science. RL C.
Leafcutter ants, dragonflies, ladybugs, aphids, water bugs, sphinx moths, and walking sticks are some of the insects that can be identified after this introduction with full color drawings.

Brenner, Barbara, and Hooks, William H.

268 *Lion and Lamb Step Out*. Ill. by Bruce Degen. Bantam, 1990. ISBN 0-553-05860-6. SERIES: Bank Street Ready-to-Read. SUBJECTS: Animals—Fiction; Friendship—Fiction. RL A.
Lamb leads the way home after friend Lion's arrogance gets them lost; Lion decides his boring life is wonderful after visiting Uncle Leo at the circus; Lion learns that best friends don't give away secrets. Exuberant drawings are by Bruce Degen.

269 *Ups and Downs with Lion and Lamb*. Ill. by Bruce Degen. Bantam, 1991. ISBN 0-553-07088-6. SERIES: Bank Street Ready-to-Read. SUBJECTS: Animals—Lions—Fiction; Animals—Sheep—Fiction; Friendship—Fiction. RL A.
Lamb starts her own club when excluded from that of the other animals and finds a way to give Lion enough courage to save Lambkin from a wolf. Imagine their joy when Lion moves only across a small river, instead of across an ocean as they fear. Lively Degen animal drawings enhance the text.

Brinkloe, Julie

270 *Gordon Goes Camping*. Ill. by author. Doubleday, 1975, o.p. SUBJECTS: Animals—Bears—Fiction; Camps and camping—Fiction. RL B.
Gordon needs his friend Marvin's advice—and company—when he goes on his first camping trip. Patterned ink drawings have a green contrasting wash.

Broekel, Ray

271 *Experiments with Air.* Photos. Childrens Pr., hb and pap., 1988. ISBN 0-516-01213-4. SERIES: New True. SUBJECTS: Science experiments—Air. RL B.

A narrative describing the properties of air leads into simple experiments that clarify the text. The experiments are usually very simple, although two require adult supervision. Full color photos help readers follow the experiment instructions.

272 *Experiments with Straws and Paper.* Photos. Childrens Pr., 1990. ISBN 0-516-01104-9. SERIES: New True. SUBJECTS: Science and scientists; Science experiments. RL C.

Large-type narrative with smaller print experiments is illustrated with well-designed color photos. Straws and liquids and paper, the principles of flying and inertia, and various optical illusions are presented before the glossary and index.

273 *Experiments with Water.* Photos. Childrens Pr., 1988. ISBN 0-516-01215-0. SERIES: New True. SUBJECTS: Science and scientists; Science experiments—Water; Water. RL C.

The forms of water, the water cycle, water's reaction with heat and light, and buoyancy and pressure are discussed, and illustrated with photos of experiments, step-by-step. Brief index and glossary are included.

Bronin, Andrew

274 *Gus and Buster Work Things Out.* Ill. by Cyndy Szekeres. Putnam, 1975, o.p. SERIES: Break-of-Day. SUBJECTS: Animals—Raccoons—Fiction; Siblings—Fiction. RL B.

Squabbling over toys or the top bunk, or even how to eat properly, two brothers settle their differences by playing each other's favorite games—football and checkers. Soft pencil drawings with pale yellow warm this reassuring tale.

Brooks, Laura, adapter

275 *The Beast's Story.* Ill. by Ed Gutierrez and Serge Michaels. Western, 1992, o.p.

SERIES: Golden Easy Reader. SUBJECTS: Movies. RL A.

A drastically simplified adaptation of a Disney-stripped story uses the Disney illustrations so familiar to many movie viewers. The effect is sentimental. and cutesy.

Brown, Marc

276 *D.W. All Wet.* Ill. by author. Little, Brown, 1988. ISBN 0-316-11077-9. SERIES: Joy Street Books. SUBJECTS: Animals—Fiction; Sports—Swimming—Fiction. RL A.

When older brother Arthur dumps a reluctant D.W. into the water at the beach, she finds out she loves it! Soft pastel drawings add warmth to the family story.

277 *D.W. Flips!* Ill. by author. Little, Brown, 1987. ISBN 0-31611239-9. SERIES: Joy Street Books. SUBJECTS: Animals—Fiction; Sports—Gymnastics. RL A.

D.W., Arthur's younger sister, thinks she's in the baby class for gymnastics, but only learns how to somersault after much practice in this lighthearted, sympathetic view of childhood learning. Illustrations. of animal children are in soft pastels.

278 *D.W. Thinks Big.* Ill. by author. Little, Brown, 1993. ISBN 0-316-11305-0. SUBJECTS: Animals—Fiction; Siblings—Fiction; Weddings—Fiction. RL A.

When the ring bearer, D.W.'s older brother Arthur, drops Aunt Lucy's ring down the register, only smaller D.W. can rescue the ring. Humorous story is enhanced by the author's lively pastel drawings.

279 *The Silly Tail Book.* Ill. by author. Parents Magazine Pr., 1983; Stevens, 1994. ISBN 0-8368-0986-6. SUBJECTS: Mythical creatures—Fiction; Stories in rhyme. RL A.

New colored pencil illustrations of cartoon animals ranging from armadillos to camels, seals to turtles, show off the variety of tails—as well as some improbable ones. Lighthearted rhyme matches the fun.

280 *There's No Place Like Home.* Ill. by author. Parents Magazine Pr., 1984. ISBN 0-8193-1125-1. SUBJECTS: Houses; Stories in rhyme. RL A.

From a cave to a shell, from a spruce to a pocket, this inventive story about possible homes stretches the imagination. Friendly colored pencil drawings are by the author.

281 *Witches Four*. Ill. by author. Parents Magazine Pr., 1980, 1991. ISBN 0-448-41079-6. SERIES: Read Aloud Originals. SUBJECTS: Stories in rhyme; Witches—Fiction. RL A.

The witches four brush their teeth with spider paste and eat bat-wing sandwiches. When they lose their magic hats flying upside down on their broomsticks, they have to reclaim them from four homeless cats. Rhythmic rhyme is enhanced by the author's stylistic drawings, beginning with endpapers.

Brownell, M. Barbara

282 *Amazing Otters*. Photos. National Geographic, 1989, o.p. SERIES: Books for Young Explorers. SUBJECTS: Animals—Otters; Nature. RL C.

A most attractive book liberally illustrated with excellent land and underwater photos of sea otters at work and play. Additional information and reading suggestions, as well as a world map showing the range of river and sea otters, are appended.

283 *Busy Beavers*. Photos and drawings. National Geographic, 1988, o.p. SERIES: Books for Young Readers. SUBJECTS: Animals—Beavers; Nature. RL C.

This photoessay has good information about beavers. Especially well done are photos of a beaver swimming in clear water and of a beaver nursing her kit.

Bulla, Clyde R.

284 *Daniel's Duck*. Ill. by Joan Sandin. HarperCollins, 1977; pap., 1982. ISBN 0-06-020909-7. SERIES: I Can Read Books. SUBJECTS: Family life—Fiction; Wood carving—Fiction. RL A.

Everyone in Daniel's family spends long winter nights making crafts for the spring fair. When Daniel's carved duck evokes laughter, he thinks, at first, that people are laughing *at*

him. Watercolor illustrations primarily in grays and green give rich details of Tennessee Appalachian life.

285 *Poor Boy, Rich Boy*. Ill. by Marcia Sewell. HarperCollins, 1979, o.p. SERIES: I Can Read Books. SUBJECTS: Orphans—Fiction. RL A.

Orphaned by war, Coco is raised by a baker, Rosa, but later claimed by a rich and doting uncle. An unusual and touching story about worldly values is simply illustrated with light tones highlighting expressive ink drawings by a noted illustrator.

286 *Singing Sam*. Ill. by Susan Magurn. Random House, 1989. ISBN 0-394-91977-7. SERIES: Step into Reading. SUBJECTS: Animals—Dogs—Fiction; Pets—Fiction. RL A.

Rob only wants his former dog, Sam, when he sees him "singing" on television. Sam's new owner, Amy, doesn't care if Sam can sing or not. Rob takes Sam back, but Sam won't perform. Sam's expression when reunited with Amy is most fitting.

287 *A Tree Is a Plant*. Ill. by Lois Lignell. HarperCollins, 1960, o.p. SERIES: Let's-Read-and-Find-Out. SUBJECTS: Nature; Plants—Trees; Science. RL A.

Children follow an apple tree through the seasons. Boldly outlined sketches with apple green, gray, and red are in tune with the simply outlined information.

288 *What Makes a Shadow?* Ill. by June Otani. HarperCollins, 1962, 1994. ISBN 0-06-022915-2. SERIES: Let's-Read-and-Find-Out Science Books. SUBJECTS: Science; Shadows. RL A.

In the most simple terms, this experienced children's author introduces how shadows are formed. Warm pictures of children and their pets, homes, and cars illustrate the text.

Buller, Jon, and Schade, Susan

289 *Mike and the Magic Cookies*. Ill. by authors. Putnam, 1992, o.p.; pap., 1992. ISBN 0-448-40386-2. SERIES: All Aboard Reading. SUBJECTS: Fantasy—Fiction; Magic—Fiction. RL C.

Buller, Jon, and Schade, Susan (cont.)

A summer of boredom is broken when a wizard at the altered Shop and Spend sells animal cookies that transform Mike and his family into animals. Watercolor cartoon illustrations accompany the text.

290 *No Tooth, No Quarter!* Ill. by authors. Random House, 1989. ISBN 0-394-94956-0. SERIES: Step into Reading. SUBJECTS: Tooth fairy. RL A.

The tooth fairy gets bad grades for not collecting enough teeth. Walter expects a quarter even though he can't find the tooth that just fell out. He goes with the tooth fairy to Tooth Fairy Land with a chance to redeem the tooth fairy's record. This slim story has mediocre cartoon illustrations.

291 *The Video Kids*. Ill. by authors. Putnam, 1994. ISBN 0-448-40181-9. SERIES: All Aboard Reading. SUBJECTS: Imagination; Science fiction; Siblings—Fiction. RL B.

Jerome and Curtis get inside their video game via their fabulous invention and are saved only by Lavinia, Jerome's little sister, known as Lump until her heroics. Cartoon illustrations accompany the text.

292 *Yo! It's Captain Yo-Yo*. Ill. by authors. Putnam, 1993. ISBN 0-448-40191-6. SERIES: All Aboard Reading. SUBJECTS: Fantasy—Fiction; Magic—Fiction. RL B.

When a boy finds a magic yo-yo in his attic, he writes the magic password in code on his library card, which he deciphers in time to save his school—as Captain Yo-Yo—from the invading Blobs from outer space. Illustrations are typical cartoon drawings.

Bunting, Eve

293 *The Big Red Barn*. Ill. by Howard Knotts. Harcourt, 1979, o.p.; pap., 1979. ISBN 0-15-611938-2. SERIES: Let Me Read. SUBJECTS: Barns—Fiction; Farm and country life—Fiction; Stepparents—Fiction. RL C.

The hayloft is where a boy mourned his mother's death, so the barn fire represents a big loss to which he must adjust—with the help of an understanding grandpa. Knotts's

sympathetic pencil drawings add to the feelings of home.

294 *Goose Dinner*. Ill. by Howard Knotts. Harcourt, 1981, o.p. SERIES: Let Me Read. SUBJECTS: Animals—Geese—Fiction; Farm and country life—Fiction. RL C.

Because Goose rules the barnyard, the family does not appreciate her until she—and Dad—fend off a marauding raccoon. Warm pencil drawings glow.

295 *The Robot Birthday*. Ill. by Marie DeJohn. Dutton, 1980, o.p. SERIES: Smart Cat. SUBJECTS: Birthdays—Fiction; Moving, household—Fiction; Robots—Fiction. RL B.

A birthday with a new house and sitter turns out to be the most exciting one ever, thanks to a robot birthday present. Pencil drawings have a turquoise wash.

Burt, Denise

296 *Our Family Vacation*. Photos by Haworth Bartram. Stevens, 1985, o.p. SERIES: Growing Up. SUBJECTS: Seashore—Fiction; Vacations—Fiction. RL B.

Luis is shown packing for a trip; on the next page he is catching crabs on the beach, with no textual or visual transition. The full page color photos are somewhat posed looking, but give some feeling of sandcastles and shells.

Burton, Jane

297 *Caper the Kid*. Photos by author. Random House, 1989. ISBN 0-8368-0203-9. SERIES: How Your Pet Grows! SUBJECTS: Animals—Goats; Nature. RL C.

The growth of a pair of white-socked kids is detailed, from their food and play to exploration and climbing abilities. Excellent color photos capture the glint of sunlight, the sparkle of an eye, and the texture of a furry coat.

298 *Chester the Chick*. Photos by author. Random House, hb and pap., 1988, o.p. SERIES: How Your Pet Grows! SUBJECTS: Animals—Chickens; Pets. RL C.

The first year of a chick's life is described. Exceptional photos depict each stage in growth.

299 *Dabble the Duckling*. Photos by author. Random House, 1989. ISBN 0-8368-0205-5. SERIES: How Your Pet Grows! SUBJECTS: Animals—Ducks; Nature. RL C.
With excellent color photos the step-by-step development of a duck from egg to adulthood is illustrated.

300 *Fancy the Fox*. Photos by author. Random House, 1988, o.p. SERIES: How Animals Grow! SUBJECTS: Animals—Foxes; Nature. RL C.
The development of three orphan kits brought up in an animal shelter is traced with excellent color photos and interesting details of their learning to fend for themselves in the woods.

301 *Freckles the Rabbit*. Photos by author. Random House, hb and pap., 1988, o.p. SERIES: How Your Pet Grows! SUBJECTS: Animals—Rabbits; Pets. RL C.
The development of Freckles the rabbit is followed, from naked newborn to having her first litter. Exceptional photos of the lop-eared black and white rabbit are included, along with pictures of the cat, dog, and wild rabbit she encounters.

302 *Ginger the Kitten*. Photos by author. Stevens, 1989. ISBN 0-8368-0213-6. SERIES: Baby Animals Growing Up. SUBJECTS: Animals—Cats; Pets—Cats. RL C.
The weekly growth and exploration of a kitten are described in words and incredibly appealing color photos. Feast your eyes on the three backlit six-week-old ginger kittens among the ferns!

303 *Jack the Puppy*. Photos by author. Random House, hb and pap., 1989. ISBN 0-8368-0209-8. SERIES: How Your Pet Grows! SUBJECTS: Animals—Dogs; Pets—Dogs. RL C.
Jack's monthly growth from a groping newborn to a playmate for his mother's next litter is described in words and excellent color photos of puppies at play.

Busch, Phyllis

304 *Cactus in the Desert*. Ill. by Harriett Barton. HarperCollins, 1979, o.p. SERIES: Let's-Read-and-Find-Out. SUBJECTS: Nature; Science. RL C.
Although the text concentrates on how cacti conserve water, their uses by animals and people are touched on. Illustrations are apt.

Buss, Nancy

305 *The Lobster and Ivy Higgins*. Ill. by Kim Mulkey. Boyds Mills Pr., 1992. ISBN 1-56397-011-2. SUBJECTS: Animals—Lobsters—Fiction; Self-esteem—Fiction. RL C.
Ivy, the butt of her classmate's jokes because she smells like her father's fish market, comes out of her shell to try to save a 27-pound lobster her father plans to raffle. This is a satisfying story rich in dialogue, feelings, and detail.

Butterworth, Christine

306 *Ants*. Photos and drawings by Paula Chasty. Silver Burdett, 1988, o.p. SERIES: My World—Blue. SUBJECTS: Animals—Ants; Nature. RL C.
Pastel drawings of ant tunnels augment the information given by excellent photos in this photoessay. Several types of ants are depicted, which is a bit confusing.

307 *Beavers*. Photos and drawings by Paula Chasty. Silver Burdett, 1988, o.p. SERIES: My World—Blue. SUBJECTS: Animals—Beavers; Nature. RL B.
Marvelous photos of beavers cutting trees, building dams, defending and feeding themselves, and raising their babies are accompanied by simple text. Drawings show the interior of the lodge.

308 *Bees*. Photos by Paula Chasty. Silver Burdett, 1988, o.p. SERIES: My World—Blue. SUBJECTS: Animals—Bees. RL B.
Outstanding close-up photos provide the best information on bees. Language and drawings are somewhat stilted.

309 *Rabbits*. Photos and drawings by Paula Chasty. Silver Burdett, 1988, o.p. SERIES:

Butterworth, Christine (cont.)

My World—Blue. SUBJECTS: Animals—Rabbits. RL A.

With exceptional photos and some second-rate drawings, the first year of life of a young buck and doe is outlined. Habits, enemies, fast maturity, and habitat are covered.

310 *Squirrels*. Photos and drawings by Paula Chasty. Silver Burdett, 1988, o.p. SERIES: My World—Blue. SUBJECTS: Animals—Squirrels; Nature. RL B.

Some photos are exceptional, some less sharp, and some drawings are poor. There is confusion over types of squirrels being discussed, and neither the text nor the illustrations flow smoothly.

311 *Swallows*. Photos and drawings by Paula Chasty. Silver Burdett, 1988, o.p. SERIES: My World—Blue. SUBJECTS: Animals—Swallows; Nature. RL A.

The life cycle of migrating swallows is detailed. Text is illustrated with acceptable drawings and excellent color photos. One photo of a swallow drinking on the fly and another photo showing a swallow scooping up mud for a nest are exceptional.

Byars, Betsy

312 *The Golly Sisters Go West*. Ill. by Sue Truesdell. HarperCollins, 1985. ISBN 0-06-020884-8. SERIES: I Can Read Books. SUBJECTS: Frontier and pioneer life—Fiction; Humorous stories; Western stories. RL B.

May-May and Rose's naiveté and arguing lead to impromptu concerts, unnecessary night-time fears, and an unmanageable dancing horse. Six zany adventures are illustrated in full color, capturing the humor and action.

313 *The Golly Sisters Ride Again*. Ill. by Sue Truesdell. HarperCollins, 1994. ISBN 0-06-021563-1. SERIES: I Can Read Books. SUBJECTS: Frontier and pioneer life—Fiction; Siblings—Fiction. RL A.

In five brief chapters, the zany antics of the familiar Golly sisters, Rose and May-May, are resumed. A superstition about a goat in the audience being bad luck, an encounter with a talking rock, a singing and dancing "holiday,"

and finding comfort in a storm are grist for stories with cartoon drawings.

314 *Hooray for the Golly Sisters!* Ill. by Sue Truesdell. HarperCollins, 1990. ISBN 0-06-020898-8. SERIES: I Can Read Books. SUBJECTS: Emotions—Fear—Fiction; Frontier and pioneer life—Fiction; Humorous stories. RL A.

The bumbled navigation and magic of the entertaining Golly Sisters as they traverse the frontier west are enlivened by the zestful ink and wash drawings of Sue Truesdell. The chapter dealing with unnamed fears in the swamp is affecting.

315 *The Seven Treasure Hunts*. Ill. by Jennifer Barrett. HarperCollins, 1991. ISBN 0-06-020886-4. SUBJECTS: Friendship—Fiction; Sibling rivalry—Fiction. RL C.

Jackson and his friend Goat hide treasures from one another with many misfires, especially when Goat's older sister, the ogre, interferes. The treasures—M&Ms, breath mints from mother's purse, bird feathers, a Matchbox car with one wheel missing—give the story special appeal.

C

Calder, S. J.

316 *If You Were a Bird*. Ill. by Cornelius Van Wright. Silver Burdett, 1989. ISBN 0-671-68595-3. SERIES: First Facts. SUBJECTS: Animals—Birds. RL A.

Information about robins is given in simple language from the point of view of a young robin. Most interesting is his learning how to fly and taking a bath. Simple comparisons to other species of birds are made. Pastel illustrations complement the text.

317 *If You Were a Cat*. Ill. by Cornelius Van Wright. Silver Burdett, 1989. ISBN 0-382-24405-2. SERIES: First Facts. SUBJECTS: Animals—Cats; Pets—Cats. RL A.

The life cycle, diet, wild relatives, and habits of domestic cats are described in simple language with appealing watercolor drawings. Most interesting is the section showing how to tell whether a cat is playful or aggressive.

318 *If You Were a Fish*. Ill. by Cornelius Van Wright. Silver Burdett, 1989. ISBN 0-671-68596-1. SERIES: First Facts. SUBJECTS: Animals—Fish. RL A.

The food, anatomy, types, and enemies of goldfish are described and illustrated. Sketchy instructions for starting an aquarium are included.

319 *If You Were an Ant*. Ill. by Cornelius Van Wright. Silver Burdett, 1989. ISBN 0-671-68597-X. SERIES: First Facts. SUBJECTS: Animals—Ants; Animals—Insects; Science. RL A.

The home, work, life cycle, anatomy, food, and enemies of a wood ant are described. Pencil and wash drawings cover three-fourths of each double page spread to illustrate vocabulary that might otherwise be too difficult for young children. Directions for making an ant farm are included.

Calmenson, Stephanie

320 *The Little Witch Sisters*. Ill. by R. W. Alley. Parents Magazine Pr., 1989; Stevens, 1993. ISBN 0-8368-0970-X. SERIES: Read Aloud. SUBJECTS: Magic—Fiction; Siblings—Fiction; Witches—Fiction. RL A.

Notes to librarians, teachers, parents, and grownups precede and follow the story. Tinka, a small witch, agrees to help her sister Plinka only after she is rescued from being turned into an alligator, a bird, and an elephant. Ink and wash drawings soften the moral tale.

321 *Marigold and Grandma on the Town*. Ill. by Mary Chalmers. HarperCollins, 1994. ISBN 0-06-020813-9. SUBJECTS: Animals—Rabbits—Fiction; Grandparents—Fiction. RL A.

Marigold and her grandmother shop for a spring bonnet, make friends with the wind, and stop for a momentarily disastrous tea and for a photo. Delightfully imaginative and affirmative story illustrated by Chalmers's usual charming drawings.

322 *One Little Monkey*. Ill. by Ellen Appleby. Stevens, 1982. ISBN 0-8368-0988-2. SERIES: Read Aloud. SUBJECTS: Concepts—Numbers; Stories in rhyme. RL B.

Animal counting book with cross-eyed animals and forced rhyme is illustrated in watercolors. Notes to grown-ups are appended.

323 *Where's Rufus?* Ill. by Maxie Chambliss. Stevens, 1988. ISBN 0-8368-0990-4. SERIES: Read Aloud. SUBJECTS: Family life—Fiction; Picnics—Fiction. RL B.

A slim story about a family dog, Rufus, whom the reader is invited to trace as he hides all over the house to prevent the family from leaving on a picnic because rain is coming. Watercolor and ink drawings accompany the text.

Carley, Wayne

324 *Charley the Mouse Finds Christmas*. Ill. by Ruth Bagshaw. Garrard, 1972, o.p. SERIES: Venture. SUBJECTS: Animals—Mice—Fiction; Holidays—Christmas—Fiction. RL B.

By Christmas, a mouse living in a department store has lost all his toys, food, and companions. When a child spots the mouse in a window, the child tells Santa. Appealing mouse drawings are against a watercolor background.

325 *Here Comes Mirium, the Mixed-Up Witch*. Ill. by Ted Schroeder. Garrard, 1972, o.p. SUBJECTS: Magic—Fiction; Witches—Fiction. RL B.

Mirium's magic leads to adventures with an overfriendly dinosaur, a knight, a mummy, and a dog in the closed museum. Black and rose drawings are pedestrian.

326 *Mixed Up Magic*. Ill. by David Stone. Garrard, hb and pap., 1971, o.p. SERIES: Venture. SUBJECTS: Witches—Fiction. RL A.

Mirium's magic mistakes turn a dog show into pandemonium. Her cloak looks mysterious in black finger-painted design against the royal blue and orange of the policeman and dogs, respectively.

327 *Percy the Parrot Passes the Puck*. Ill. by Art Cumings. Garrard, 1972, o.p. SUBJECTS: Animals—Parrots—Fiction; Humorous stories; Sports—Ice hockey—Fiction. RL C.

Hockey fan Percy the Parrot appears on a television commercial for a food he dislikes in order to have a chance to see his home hockey

Carley, Wayne (cont.)

team in action. This lively and imaginative story is simply illustrated with apple green and orange highlights.

328 *Percy the Parrot Yelled Quiet!* Ill. by Art Cumings. Garrard, 1974, o.p. SERIES: Easy Venture. SUBJECTS: Animals—Parrots—Fiction; Pets—Fiction. RL B.

Percy turned out not to be the quiet pet Mrs. Gray originally wanted, but he sure was fun! Simple story is illustrated with comic watercolor drawings.

329 *Puppy Love*. Ill. by Erica Merkling. Garrard, hb and pap., 1971, o.p. SERIES: Venture. SUBJECTS: Pets—Dogs—Fiction; Sibling rivalry—Fiction. RL A.

Leslie discovered that looking after her new baby brother was like taking care of her puppy, Lickins. The analogy is satisfactory. Ink drawings show Leslie's pride in accomplishment.

330 *The Witch Who Forgot*. Ill. by Lou Cunette. Garrard, 1974, o.p. SUBJECTS: Witches—Fiction. RL A.

Mirium forgets where she put her shoe, hat, cat, and coat—even where she was going with a cake. Humor comes from unlikely places, as she looks for lost items. Cartoon drawings.

Carlson, Laurie

331 *EcoArt! Earth-Friendly Art and Craft Experiences for 3-to-9-Year-Olds*. Ill. by Loretta T. Braren. Williamson, pap., 1993. ISBN 0-913589-68-3. SERIES: Williamson Kids Can. SUBJECTS: Arts and crafts; Conservation. RL C.

Despite the large ink illustrations and appealing browsing format, some of the language and the amount of text will make this difficult for even third-graders. However, the intriguing ideas range from homemade supplies to things made with natural things or throwaways.

Carlson, Nancy

332 *Arnie and the New Kid*. Ill. by author. Viking, 1990. ISBN 0-670-82499-2. SUBJECTS: Animals—Dogs—Fiction; Physically and mentally impaired—Fiction. RL A.

After Arnie, a dog, falls and needs crutches, he finds a new friend, Phillip, who must use a wheelchair. As he experiences being handicapped, he learns to empathize rather than tease. Full color illustrations have eye-catching patterns on clothing.

333 *Arnie and the Stolen Markers*. Ill. by author. Viking, 1987. ISBN 0-670-81548-9. SUBJECTS: Behavior—Stealing—Fiction. RL B.

Arnie feels bad after stealing some markers until he confesses and has a chance to work off the cost. Full color drawings accompanying this straightforward moral seem to show the shopkeeper and mother angrier than the text indicates.

334 *Arnie Goes to Camp*. Ill. by author. Viking, 1988. ISBN 0-670-81549-7. SUBJECTS: Animals—Fiction; Camps and camping—Fiction. RL B.

Despite his misgivings and homesickness, Arnie enjoys the accomplishments and the camaraderie of summer camp. Bright colored drawings show action-filled days and nights.

335 *Harriet and the Garden*. Ill. by author. Carolrhoda, 1982; Penguin, pap., 1985. ISBN 0-87614-184-X. SUBJECTS: Animals—Dogs—Fiction; Behavior—Honest—Fiction. RL B.

After a sleepless night struggling with her conscience, Harriet, a dog, confesses to trampling Mrs. Hoozit's prize garden—and feels better. Colorful drawings focus on Harriet's long day.

336 *Harriet and the Roller Coaster*. Ill. by author. Carolrhoda, 1982; Penguin, pap., 1984. ISBN 0-87614-183-1. SUBJECTS: Amusement parks—Fiction; Animals—Dogs—Fiction; Emotions—Fear—Fiction. RL B.

Taunted by George, a rabbit, Harriet, a dog, reluctantly tries a roller coaster—and finds she likes it! Carlson's books challenge children to broaden their experiences and outlook. Bright colors convey feelings of fear and excitement.

337 *Harriet and Walt*. Ill. by author. Carolrhoda, 1982; Penguin, pap., 1984.

ISBN 0-87614-185-8. SUBJECTS: Animals—Dogs—Fiction; Siblings—Fiction. RL B. Harriet, originally burdened by her little brother when they go to play in the snow, ends up defending him against the impatience of her friend George. Quietly moral tale is illustrated with ink and colored pencil.

338 *Harriet's Halloween Candy*. Ill. by author. Carolrhoda, 1982; Penguin, pap., 1984. ISBN 0-87614-182-3. SUBJECTS: Animals—Dogs—Fiction; Behavior—Sharing—Fiction; Holidays—Halloween—Fiction. RL B.
Harriet shares her overabundance of Halloween candy only when she is sick from eating too much. Details of how she sorts her candy by color, size, and favorites add authenticity and humor. Pastel drawings have interesting patterns of clothes and candy.

339 *Harriet's Recital*. Ill. by author. Carolrhoda, 1982. ISBN 0-87614-181-5. SUBJECTS: Animals—Dogs—Fiction; Dancing—Fiction; Self-esteem—Fiction. RL A.
Harriet, a dog, is terrified of falling or having her costume rip during her ballet recital. After a shaky start, she blossoms, later denying being scared. The straightforward message is illustrated with typical Carlson framed drawings, in pinks and lavenders onstage.

340 *Loudmouth George and the Big Race*. Ill. by author. Carolrhoda, 1983; Penguin, pap., 1986. ISBN 0-87614-215-3. SUBJECTS: Animals—Rabbits—Fiction; Behavior—Excuses—Fiction. RL B.
George is too tired, too full, or too busy to train for the big race that Harriet ends up winning. His fatigue is graphically captured by corduroy legs and dragging limbs. Full color illustrations are on green or royal blue backgrounds.

341 *Loudmouth George and the Cornet*. Ill. by author. Carolrhoda, 1983; Penguin, pap., 1985. ISBN 0-87614-214-5. SUBJECTS: Animals—Rabbits—Fiction; Behavior—Excuses—Fiction; Musical instruments—Fiction. RL B.
George thinks he is too good at playing the cornet to take lessons, and when asked to leave the band, he has excuses and a better idea—he will take up the tuba, Colored pencil drawings show his family's consternation clearly.

342 *Loudmouth George and the Fishing Trip*. Ill. by author. Carolrhoda, 1983; Penguin, pap., 1985. ISBN 0-87614-213-7. SUBJECTS: Animals—Rabbits—Fiction; Behavior—Bragging—Fiction; Fishing—Fiction. RL B.
George's bragging is brought up short when Harriet's family takes him fishing. She is then on hand to keep his reports of success accurate. George in sky-blue pajamas with carrots on them is a nice touch.

343 *Loudmouth George and the Sixth-Grade Bully*. Ill. by author. Carolrhoda, 1983; Penguin, pap., 1985. ISBN 0-87614-217-X. SUBJECTS: Animals—Rabbits—Fiction; Behavior—Bullying—Fiction; School stories. RL B.
When a bully steals George's lunch every day, George's friend Harriet helps him prepare an unpleasant surprise in the next day's lunch! All who have suffered at the hands of a bully will be able to identify with George's creative revenge. Pencil drawings are in full color.

344 *Making the Team*. Ill. by author. Carolrhoda, 1985. ISBN 0-87614-281-1. SERIES: Louanne Pig. SUBJECTS: Animals—Pigs—Fiction; Sex roles—Fiction; Sports—Football—Fiction. RL B.
Louanne and Arnie, two pigs, practice together for cheerleading and football tryouts—but Louanne makes the football squad and Arnie the cheerleading. Pencil drawings are in red, blue, and green.

345 *The Mysterious Valentine*. Ill. by author. Carolrhoda, 1985, o.p. SERIES: Louanne Pig. SUBJECTS: Animals—Pigs—Fiction; Holidays—Valentine's Day—Fiction. RL C.
The reader finally figures out who Louanne the pig's secret admirer is, but Louanne never does. Familiar characters are drawn in full color with pencil.

346 *The Perfect Family*. Ill. by author. Carolrhoda, 1985. ISBN 0-87614-280-3. SERIES: Louanne Pig. SUBJECTS: Animals—Pigs—Fiction; Family life—Fiction; Siblings—Fiction. RL C.
Louanne the pig finds out that living in a family of ten siblings is not for her when she spends the weekend at her friend George's house. Colored pencil drawings add humor.

Carlson, Nancy (cont.)

347 *The Talent Show*. Ill. by author. Carolrhoda, 1985. ISBN 0-87614-284-6. SERIES: Louanne Pig. SUBJECTS: Animals—Pigs—Fiction; Self-esteem—Fiction. RL C.
Louanne the pig gets involved in the talent show even though she thinks she has nothing to contribute. Bright colored drawings add to the sympathetic treatment of feeling left out.

348 *Witch Lady*. Ill. by author. Carolrhoda, 1985. ISBN 0-87614-283-8. SERIES: Louanne Pig. SUBJECTS: Animals—Pigs—Fiction; Haunted houses—Fiction; Scary stories. RL C.
When Louanne the pig twists her ankle in the witch lady's yard, she finds out what *really* goes on in that scary house—but she may not tell her friends. Colored pencil drawings are in flat primary colors.

Carona, Philip

349 *Numbers*. Photos and drawings. Childrens Pr., hb and pap., 1982, o.p. SERIES: New True. SUBJECTS: Concepts—Numbers; Mathematics. RL B.
Watercolor illustrations and colored photos show a simple history and the uses of numbers.

Carrick, Carol

350 *Empty Squirrel*. Ill. by Donald Carrick. Greenwillow, 1981, o.p. SERIES: Read-alone. SUBJECTS: Pets—Fiction; Pets—Wild animals—Fiction. RL A.
Paul returns a fish he caught to the pond and a neglected toy squirrel that lost its stuffing outside over the winter to its owner, and keeps a turtle when he discovers it likes tuna. Soft pencil drawings are in brown and orange.

351 *The Longest Float in the Parade*. Ill. by Donald Carrick. Greenwillow, 1982, o.p. SERIES: Read-alone. SUBJECTS: Camps and camping—Fiction; Parades—Fiction. RL B.
At summer camp, Jimmy and Pinky's imaginative parade entry, a Chinese dragon, rivals all others. Warmly realistic from dialogue to atmosphere and characters, the text is complemented beautifully by the soft watercolor illustrations.

Carrick, Malcolm

352 *Happy Jack*. Ill. by author. HarperCollins, 1979, o.p. SERIES: I Can Read Books. SUBJECTS: Folklore. RL A.
The tale of foolish Jack who wins the princess is retold in simple language. Sepia drawings have avocado and peach washes.

353 *Mr. Tod's Trap*. Ill. by author. HarperCollins, 1980, o.p. SERIES: I Can Read Books. SUBJECTS: Animals—Foxes—Fiction. RL C.
Mr. Tod's ingenious rabbit traps work to Weasel's advantage, so Mrs. Tod takes over hunting and Mr. Tod takes over the housework. A houseful of appealing fox kits and lumpy clever rabbits enrich the tale.

354 *Today Is Shrew Day*. Ill. by author. HarperCollins, 1978, o.p. SERIES: I Can Read Books. SUBJECTS: Animals—Frogs and toads—Fiction; Animals—Shrews—Fiction; Friendship—Fiction. RL B.
Bullfrog gets all sorts of advice for babysitting—for a doll. Unusual perspectives add interest; illustrations are in gloomy, muddy colors.

Carter, Adam

355 *A Day in the Life of a Medical Detective*. Photos by Bob Duncan. Troll, 1985. ISBN 0-8167-0097-4. SERIES: A Day in the Life of. SUBJECTS: Careers. RL C.
Dr. Rick Richards is a medical detective for the Centers for Disease Control in Atlanta. The wide spectrum of work, from the lab to the computer, from all parts of the globe to community interviews and investigation into the life cycles of possible carriers, is shown.

Carter, Anne

356 *Bella's Secret Garden*. Ill. by John Butler. Crown, 1986, o.p. SERIES: It's Great to Read! SUBJECTS: Animals—Rabbits; Nature. RL C.
Human paws move Bella the rabbit from a suburban garden to a field away from the danger of cats, dogs, and machinery. Full page artwork is outstanding. From expressive eyes, fur that invites petting, down to the rabbit

endpapers, there is a consistent rabbit perspective.

357 *Molly in Danger*. Ill. by John Butler. Crown, 1986, o.p. SERIES: It's Great to Read! SUBJECTS: Animals—Moles—Fiction; Nature. RL C.
When Molly is forced out of her hole by floodwaters, she faces danger from a heron and an owl before finding new burrowing ground. Exceptional close-up full page drawings give a mole's view of the world.

358 *Ruff Leaves Home*. Ill. by John Butler. Crown, 1986, o.p. SERIES: It's Great to Read! SUBJECTS: Animals—Foxes; Nature. RL A.
A year of exploration and danger in the life of a young fox is exceptionally well portrayed in language and in effective full page drawings. Other wildlife is shown, as well as the dangers to which a fox on the fringe of a suburban area is exposed.

359 *Scurry's Treasure*. Ill. by John Butler. Crown, 1986, o.p. SERIES: It's Great to Read! SUBJECTS: Animals—Squirrels; Nature. RL B.
The content of finely drawn full color illustrations of the world from a young squirrel's perspective is well reflected in the text, as a squirrel mistakes a brooch for a nut.

Carter, Polly

360 *Harriet Tubman and Black History Month*. Ill. by Brian Pinkney. Silver Burdett, 1990. ISBN 0-671-69109-0. SERIES: Let's Celebrate. SUBJECTS: Biographies—African Americans; Holidays; United States—History—Civil War. RL A.
In simple language, some of the most colorful events in Harriet Tubman's adventures conducting some 300 slaves north to freedom are conveyed. Brian Pinkney's scratch drawings give a dark, shadowy background to the story of this heroine.

Cartwright, Sally

361 *Sunlight*. Ill. by Marylin Hafner. Putnam, 1974, o.p. SUBJECTS: Rainbows; Science experiments; Shadows. RL B.
Simple experiments with rainbows, reflections, and shadows are suggested. Visual interest is high with soft pencil drawings, varied in their use of space.

362 *The Tide*. Ill. by Marilyn Miller. Putnam, 1970, o.p. SERIES: Science Is What and Why. SUBJECTS: Oceans and ocean life; Science. RL C.
At the simplest level, Cartwright presents information about different kinds of tides and their causes. Interesting effects with printing and overlaid washes add visual appeal.

363 *Water Is Wet*. Ill. by Marylin Hafner. Putnam, 1973, o.p. SUBJECTS: Science experiments—Water; Water. RL A.
Ideas for simple science projects with water are appealingly presented. Illustrations are well suited to the text.

Caseley, Judith

364 *Harry and Willy and Carrothead*. Ill. by author. Greenwillow, 1991. ISBN 0-688-09493-7. SUBJECTS: Friendship—Fiction; Physically and mentally impaired—Fiction; School stories. RL B.
This story of a growing friendship among three boys focuses on what Harry, born without a left hand, *can* do. Full color illustrations show detail about school activities.

365 *Molly Pink*. Ill. by author. Greenwillow, 1985, o.p. SUBJECTS: Emotions—Fear—Fiction; Music—Fiction. RL C.
Despite Molly's singing practice, she freezes when she has a solo on stage—until members of her family turn their backs. Framed pictures in pink and yellow are well suited to the text.

366 *Three Happy Birthdays*. Ill. by author. Mulberry, 1993. pap., ISBN 0-688-11699-X. SUBJECTS: Birthdays—Fiction. RL A.
Benny, his dog, Charlie, and his sister, Marla, take turns celebrating their birthdays. Benny's favorite gift is an umbrella; Charlie's, a bone; and Marla's, stars. The family makes paper stars, star cookies and cake,. and snow stars. Whimsical pastel illustrations accompany the text.

Cassedy, Sylvia

367 *The Best Cat Suit of All*. Ill. by Rosekrans Hoffman. Dial, 1991. ISBN 0-8037-0517-4. SERIES: Dial Easy-to-Read. SUBJECTS: Animals—Cats—Fiction; Holidays—Halloween—Fiction; Moving, household—Fiction. RL A.

Matthew is sick and grumpy on Halloween in his new home where everything and everyone is different. A real black cat that matches his Halloween costume, and his parents, cheer him up. Pencil drawings have washes mainly with black, orange, and lavender.

368 *Zoomrimes: Poems About Things That Go*. Ill. by Michele Chessare. HarperCollins, 1993. ISBN 0-06-022632-3. SUBJECTS: Poetry; Transportation; Word play. RL B.

Poems range from the wondrous spring storm of maple tree "helicopters" to an escalator, from the efficient camel sedan to the zippered zeppelin. Imaginative word play and unusual perspectives make this anthology a delight. Lighthearted illustrations are in shades of gray.

Castiglia, Julie

369 *Jill the Pill*. Ill. by Steven Kellogg. Atheneum, 1979, o.p. SUBJECTS: Siblings—Fiction. RL B.

Jill's teenage behavior has nothing in common with her small brother's. Expressive, detailed ink drawings add authenticity to this story.

Catton, Chris, ed.

370 *Matchmaking*. Ill. by Oxford Scientific Films. Putnam, 1987, o.p. SUBJECTS: Nature. RL C.

A variety of mating activities is briefly described, from attracting mates with dramatic coloration or scent to presenting "gifts," to calling mates, or to fighting for them. Excellent color photos take the reader to woods, water, the Arctic, and garden.

Cauley, Lorinda B.

371 *Bake-Off*. Ill. by author. Putnam, 1978, o.p. SERIES: See and Read. SUBJECTS: Animals—Fiction; Bakers and baking—Fiction; Contests—Fiction. RL C.

Knowing sweets win votes, but committed to nutritious recipes, Mr. Hare wins the autumn bake-off with a surprise entry (recipe appended). Forest animals are given individual character through expressive ink drawings alternately colored in two-tone washes.

Cazet, Denys

372 *Saturday*. Ill. by author. Bradbury, 1985; Macmillan, pap., 1988, o.p. SUBJECTS: Animals—Dogs—Fiction; Grandparents—Fiction; Humorous stories. RL C.

Grandpa is always ready to leave work to play—or do a science project—with his grandson, Barney. Grandma's pancakes, cocoa, or a pillow help when Barney is unhappy. Humorous story illustrated with gray ink drawings captures the warmth of these relationships.

Cebulash, Mel

373 *Basketball Players Do Amazing Things*. Photos. Random House, 1976, o.p. SERIES: Step-Up. SUBJECTS: Sports—Basketball. RL C.

Outstanding basketball players discussed include the traveling female All American Red Heads, a trick shooter, and record foul shooters. The disputed 1972 Olympic game between the Soviet Union and the United States is covered. Brief, well-told stories are illustrated with black and white action photos.

374 *Willie's Wonderful Pet*. Ill. by George Ford. Scholastic, 1993. ISBN 0-590-45787-X. SERIES: Hello Reader! SUBJECTS: Animals; Pets; School stories. RL A.

Willie's wiggling worm stirs up all the classroom pets on Pet Day. A primer with simplest vocabulary is enhanced by uncluttered watercolor illustrations of children and pets.

Cerf, Bennett A.

375 *Bennett Cerf's Book of Animal Riddles*. Ill. by Roy McKie. Random House, 1964. ISBN 0-394-90034-0. SERIES: I Can Read It

All By Myself. SUBJECTS: Animals—Fiction; Jokes and riddles. RL A.

Dogs, turtles, hummingbirds, snails, and rabbits are some of the subjects of these clever, simple riddles. They are masterfully illustrated with McKie's bold line drawings.

376 *Bennett Cerf's Book of Laughs*. Ill. by Carl Rose. Beginner, 1959. ISBN 0-394-90011-1. SERIES: I Can Read It All By Myself. SUBJECTS: Jokes and riddles. RL A.

Standard jokes relying on wordplay are retold using a vocabulary of 232 words, well geared to second-grade humor. Dated drawings nevertheless illustrate the misconceptions of the words, thus adding humor.

377 *Bennett Cerf's Book of Riddles*. Ill. by Roy McKie. Random House, 1960. ISBN 0-394-90015-4. SERIES: I Can Read It All By Myself. SUBJECTS: Jokes and riddles. RL A.

Not too familiar standard riddles about dogs, cats, horses, pigs, and children are illustrated by a cartoon master of expressive line.

378 *More Riddles*. Ill. by Roy McKie. Random House, 1961. ISBN 0-394-90024-3. SERIES: I Can Read It All By Myself. SUBJECTS: Jokes and riddles. RL A.

Traditional riddles are retold simply. Comic illustrations extending the riddles are in primary colors.

Chalmers, Mary

379 *Merry Christmas, Harry*. Ill. by author. HarperCollins, 1992. ISBN 0-06-022739-7. SUBJECTS: Animals—Cats—Fiction; Holidays—Christmas—Fiction. RL A.

Harry's the cat's desire for a baby brother is realized on Christmas, when a kitten who drinks a little milk, takes a little nap, plays a little, and sleeps a little arrives. Chalmers's simple full color drawings hold center stage.

380 *Take a Nap, Harry*. Ill. by author. Harper-Collins, 1991. ISBN 0-06-021244-6. SUBJECTS: Animals—Cats—Fiction. RL A.

Harry the cat entertains a bee and himself when he should be napping. So he gets sleepy before "helping" his mother finish baking a cake, and finishes his nap while mother finishes the cake. Outstanding expressive watercolor animals match the gentle story admirably.

381 *Throw a Kiss, Harry*. Ill. by author. HarperCollins, 1990. O.P. SUBJECTS: Animals—Cats—Fiction. RL A.

Harry, a charming white kitten, goes exploring while Mother is talking to a friend, and has to be rescued from the roof of a house by a fireman. After refusing to blow the fireman a thank-you kiss, Harry sneaks back to do so. Simple pencil and wash drawings are very appealing.

Champion, Joyce

382 *Emily and Alice*. Ill. by Suçie Stevenson. Harcourt, 1993. ISBN 0-15-200588-9. SUBJECTS: Friendship—Fiction; Pets—Raccoons—Fiction. RL A.

Emily and Alice become fast friends when Alice moves in next door. They "baby-sit" Alice's pet raccoon, picnic, and play in rain puddles together despite occasional disagreements.

Chandler, Edna W.

383 *Cowboy Sam and Freddy*. Ill. by Jack Merryweather. Benefic, 1959. O.P. SUBJECTS: Cowboys—Fiction; Western stories. RL A.

Freddy is eager to become a cowboy, but he needs to be outfitted and learn a few things first. Blue, yellow, and red illustrations convey the action.

384 *Pony Rider*. Ill. by Jack Merryweather. Benefic, 1966, O.P. SERIES: Tom Logan. SUBJECTS: Cowboys—Fiction; Frontier and pioneer life—Fiction; Western stories. RL B.

Using a 60-word vocabulary, the author introduces a beginning reader to the West, including the Pony Express. Colored ink sketches are good.

Chardiet, Bernice, and Maccarone, Grace

385 *The Best Teacher in the World*. Ill. by G. Brian Karas. Scholastic, 1990. ISBN 0-590-43307-5. SERIES: School Friends. SUBJECTS:

**Chardiet, Bernice, and
Maccarone, Grace (cont.)**

Behavior—Lying—Fiction; School
stories. RL A.
When timid Bunny is chosen to deliver a
note to another teacher, she fails, but reports
otherwise. After a restless night, she confesses to a forgiving teacher. Pencil and wash
drawings suggest Bunny's feelings of bewilderment in a long, empty school hall particularly well.

386 *Martin and the Tooth Fairy*. Ill. by G.
Brian Karas. Scholastic, pap., 1991. ISBN
0-590-43305-9. SERIES: School Friends.
SUBJECTS: School stories; Tooth fairy—
Fiction. RL C.
Martin buys his friends' teeth when they fall
out, expecting to make a windfall from the
Tooth Fairy, in this story with pencil and
watercolor illustrations.

387 *We Scream for Ice Cream*. Ill. by G. Brian
Karas. Scholastic, 1992. ISBN 0-590-
44934-6. SERIES: School Friends. SUBJECTS:
Friendship—Fiction. RL A.
One disaster after another disrupts the neighborhood children's friendships when the ice
cream truck visits. Pencil and watercolor
stick figures accompany the straightforward
story.

Charles, Donald

388 *Calico Cat's Exercise Book*. Ill. by author.
Childrens Pr., hb and pap., 1982. ISBN 0-
516-33457-3. SERIES: Calico Cat. SUBJECTS:
Animals—Cats; Exercise. RL B.
Exuberant decorative cat drawings encourage
exercise, as does the very abbreviated text.

Chase, Catherine

389 *Pete, the Wet Pet*. Ill. by Gail Gibbons.
Elsevier-Dutton, 1981, o.p. SUBJECTS:
Animals—Dogs—Fiction; Pets—Dogs—
Fiction. RL A.
A simple story of the mess a big cuddly dog
makes in the house when he comes in to get
dry. Ink sketches with crayon and wash coloring add to the warmth of the tale.

Chenery, Janet

390 *Toad Hunt*. Ill. by Ben Shecter.
HarperCollins, 1967, o.p.; Dell, pap.,
1992. ISBN 0-440-40561-0. SERIES: Science I
Can Read. SUBJECTS: Animals—Reptiles
and amphibians; Nature; Science. RL B.
Teddy and Peter learn about turtles, salamanders, and frogs as they search for a toad. Soft
colored pencil and ink drawings show humor
and reverence for wild animals.

391 *Wolfie*. Ill. by Marc Simont.
HarperCollins, 1969, o.p.; Dell, pap.,
1991. ISBN 0-440-40496-7. SERIES: I Can
Read Books. SUBJECTS: Animals—Spiders;
Nature. RL B.
Good information about wolf spiders is spiced
with a younger sister's desire to feed "Wolfie";
she turns out to be a dead shot stunning flies
for Wolfie's meals with a rubber band. Two-
color illustrations are plain, yet expressive.

Chislett, Gail

392 *Whump*. Ill. by Vladyana Krykorka.
Annick, 1989. ISBN 1-55037-041-3.
SUBJECTS: Bedtime—Fiction. RL B.
Jeremy feels small and lonely in his new bed.
He "whumps" on his parents and brother,
keeping them awake, but finds them settled in
his bed instead. This slim story has illustrations in shades of blue and lavender, with a
most cozy black cat, teddies, and a shaggy
dog.

Chittenden, Margaret

393 *When the Wild Ducks Come*. Ill. by
Beatrice Darwin. Follett, 1972, o.p.
SERIES: Beginning to Read. SUBJECTS:
Animals—Ducks; Seasons. RL C.
A boy observes a pair of ducks through the
seasons. Colorful, impressionistic block prints
are exceptional.

Chlad, Dorothy

394 *In the Water . . . On the Water*. Ill. by
Lydia Halverson. Childrens Pr., 1988. ISBN
0-516-01974-0. SERIES: Safety Town.
SUBJECTS: Safety. RL B.

Some of the safety rules discussed include wearing a life jacket, not throwing sand, not jumping into a pool, using steps and railing, and not playing with faucets. Unimaginative text seems overcautious, for example, always wearing life jackets on the beach. Illustrations are done in watercolor.

395 *Matches, Lighters, and Firecrackers Are Not Toys*. Ill. by Lydia Halverson. Childrens Pr., hb and pap., 1982. ISBN 0-516-01982-1. SERIES: Safety Town. SUBJECTS: Safety. RL C.

The bare facts regarding the benefits and dangers of fire are flanked by a repetition of simple rules. Bright watercolors follow the text.

396 *Playing on the Playground*. Ill. by Lydia Halverson. Childrens Pr., 1987. ISBN 0-516-01989-9. SERIES: Safety Town. SUBJECTS: Playgrounds; Safety. RL B.

Six rules about playground safety begin with *"never* go alone." Following the explanations, the rules are repeated. Large drawings are of multiethnic children.

397 *Stop, Look, and Listen for Trains*. Ill. by Lydia Halverson. Childrens Pr., hb and pap., 1983. ISBN 0-516-01988-0. SERIES: Safety Town. SUBJECTS: Safety; Trains. RL C.

Chlad admonishes the reader to stop, look, and listen; never play near tracks; and wait until the train is gone before crossing tracks. A little information about trains is given as well. Large colorful paintings accompany the text.

398 *When I Ride in a Car*. Ill. by Lydia Halverson. Childrens Pr., hb and pap., 1983. ISBN 0-516-01987-2. SERIES: Safety Town. SUBJECTS: Safety. RL C.

Buckle-up, talk or play quietly, and never bother the driver are the safety rules introduced. Large watercolor drawings soften the presentation slightly.

Chorao, Kay

399 *Oink and Pearl*. Ill. by author. HarperCollins, 1981, o.p. SERIES: I Can Read Books. SUBJECTS: Animals—Pigs—Fiction; Siblings—Fiction. RL A.

The pigs Oink and PEARL feel frustrated, but find solace in each other's company. Elements

from four chapters are skillfully woven together. Pig-pink and soft apple green color sympathetic illustrations.

400 *Ups and Downs with Oink and Pearl*. Ill. by author. HarperCollins, 1986, o.p. SERIES: I Can Read Books. SUBJECTS: Animals—Pigs—Fiction; Sibling rivalry—Fiction. RL B.

Pearl's anger and jealousy of her little brother evaporate with laughter and sharing in this story about pig siblings. Soft pink, orange, and yellow washes warm this gentle tale.

Christensen, Nancy

401 *Good Night, Little Kitten*. Ill. by Dennis Hockerman. Childrens Pr., 1990. ISBN 0-516-05354-X. SERIES: My First Reader. SUBJECTS: Bedtime—Fiction; Family life—Fiction. RL A.

In simplest large-print language, Mama and Papa Kitten urge Little Kitten to go to sleep instead of playing. Story is simplistic for school age. Colored pencil and watercolor drawings show cute kittens and toys.

402 *Who Am I?* Ill. by Rowan Barnes-Murphy. Scholastic, 1993. ISBN 0-590-46192-3. SERIES: My First Hello Reader! SUBJECTS: Animals—Fiction; Stories in rhyme. RL A.

The rhyming riddle about someone who is not tall or small, has no spots or hat, or who doesn't swim or fly is a surprise, although a few visual clues have been given. Simple rhymes use very easy vocabulary. Flash cards and quizzes clutter the book.

Christian, Mary B.

403 *Devin and Goliath*. Ill. by Normand Chartier. Addison-Wesley, 1974, o.p. SUBJECTS: Animals—Turtles—Fiction; Pets—Wild animals—Fiction. RL B.

Devin finds that capturing a turtle named Goliath is not as satisfying as he expected. Pencil drawings with two-color highlights are especially sympathetic to animals.

404 *Doggone Mystery*. Ill. by Irene Trivas. Whitman, 1980. ISBN 0-8075-1656-2. SERIES: First Read-Alone Mystery. SUBJECTS:

Christian, Mary B. (cont.)

Animals—Dogs—Fiction; Mystery and detective stories. RL B.

The kids' dog, Ruffles, helps them uncover the thief. Ink and turquoise washed sketches add humor and help provide clues.

405 *Go West, Swamp Monsters*. Ill. by Marc Brown. Dial, 1985; pap., 1987. ISBN 0-8037-0144-6. SERIES: Dial Easy-to-Read. SUBJECTS: Behavior—Manners—Fiction; Humorous stories; Monsters—Fiction. RL B.

Four swamp monsters in cowboy attire join some child campers visiting their swamp. Humor comes from the monsters' literal interpretation of camping. Brown's illustrations of the monsters make them appear *very* friendly.

406 *Green Thumb Thief*. Ill. by Don Madden. Whitman, 1982, o.p. SERIES: First Read-alone. SUBJECTS: Animals—Dogs—Fiction; Mystery and detective stories. RL C.

The undercover kids and their shedding dog, Hercules, track down a plant thief. Far-fetched mystery has ink with gray and red wash drawings.

407 *J. J. Leggett, Secret Agent*. Ill. by Jacquie Hann. Lothrop, 1978, o.p. SUBJECTS: Mystery and detective stories. RL C.

A boy's walkie-talkie unexpectedly saves the day. Humorous pencil drawings have pumpkin highlights.

408 *Lucky Man*. Ill. by Glen Rounds. Macmillan, 1979, o.p. SERIES: Ready-to-Read. SUBJECTS: Folklore. RL A.

Felix got poorer and deeper and deeper in trouble for all his hard work until one unexpected day in court. Ink sketches have a folk flavor.

409 *Penrod Again*. Ill. by Jane Dyer. Macmillan, 1987. ISBN 0-02-718550-8. SERIES: Ready-to-Read. SUBJECTS: Animals—Bears—Fiction; Animals—Porcupines—Fiction; Friendship—Fiction. RL A.

Five chapters show the trials and satisfactions of friendship between a bear and a porcupine who have very different personalities. Jewel-like watercolors of the animal characters are outstanding.

410 *Penrod's Pants*. Ill. by Jane Dyer. Macmillan, 1986. ISBN 0-02-718520-6. SERIES: Ready-to-Read. SUBJECTS: Animals—Bears—Fiction; Animals—Porcupines—Fiction; Friendship—Fiction. RL B.

The friendship between a bear and a porcupine is strained when they shop for pants, pull a loose tooth, and decide who is to get the last cookie. Full color watercolors feature emerald greens, royal blues, and sunshine yellows.

411 *Penrod's Party*. Ill. by S. D. Schindler. Macmillan, 1990, o.p. SERIES: Ready-to-Read. SUBJECTS: Animals—Bears—Fiction; Animals—Porcupines—Fiction; Friendship—Fiction. RL B.

Since Penrod the Porcupine always seems to take advantage of their friendship, Griswold the Bear tries to sabotage Penrod's party when he's not invited. To his surprise, the party's really for him! The story is illustrated with appealing pastel drawings.

412 *Penrod's Picture*. Ill. by S. D. Schindler. Macmillan, 1991, o.p. SUBJECTS: Animals—Bears—Fiction; Animals—Porcupines—Fiction; Friendship—Fiction. RL B.

Penrod the Porcupine's best intentions mean disaster for Griswold the Bear's wall, and their camping trip. Penrod's misguided gardening and their garage sale end up more successfully, despite blunders. Friendly pencil and watercolor drawings add interesting details.

413 *Swamp Monsters*. Ill. by Marc Brown. Dial, hb and pap., 1983. ISBN 0-8037-7616-0. SERIES: Dial Easy-to-Read. SUBJECTS: Monsters—Fiction; School stories. RL B.

Swamp monsters Fenny and Crag decide they like snail stew and their own swamp after they go to school with a group of children. Children may gain some perspective on how others might view their everyday behavior. Literal-minded humor is illustrated with watercolors in rose, lemon, and brown.

414 *The Toady and Dr. Miracle*. Ill. by Ib Ohlsson. Macmillan, 1985; pap., 1987, o.p. SERIES: Ready-to-Read. SUBJECTS: Frontier and pioneer life—Fiction; Humorous stories. RL C.

In this frontier story, Luther proves he is not dumb when he outwits an itinerant medicine man. Vivid language and pen and ink drawings complement each other to set the mood, create interesting characters, and add humor to the story.

415 *Ventriloquist*. Ill. by Mamoru Roland Funai. Putnam, 1982, o.p. SERIES: Break-of-Day. SUBJECTS: Animals—Dogs—Fiction; Pets—Dogs—Fiction. RL B.

Arthur's dog Burford has marvelous gifts that go unrecognized, according to his master. Three-tone illustrations alternate with gray tones.

Chwast, Seymour

416 *The Twelve Circus Rings*. Ill. by author. Harcourt, 1993. ISBN 0-15-200627-3. SUBJECTS: Circuses—Fiction; Concepts—Numbers; Cumulative tales. RL A.

The flat pastel double spreads fill up with the animals and performers of the circus as the tale cumulates. Attention is drawn to the rather sophisticated counting and multiplying cunningly incorporated with a series of questions at the end.

Clark, Ann N.

417 *Little Indian Basket Maker*. Ill. by Harrison Begay. Melmont, 1957, o.p. SERIES: Look Read Learn. SUBJECTS: Art and artists; Native Americans—Papagos. RL C.

The basket making of Papago Native Americans involves hands and heart. Illustrations capture the color and texture of that culture with simply colored drawings featuring one little girl and her grandmother.

Claverie, Jean

418 *The Party*. Ill. by author. Crown, 1985, o.p. SERIES: It's Great to Read! SUBJECTS: Birthdays—Fiction; Costumes—Fiction; Parties—Fiction. RL B.

Some of the difficulties in choosing a costume and the squabbles during a birthday party are suggested in abbreviated text, using a child's perspective. Pale colored pencil drawings fill the pages. Binding is poor.

419 *The Picnic*. Ill. by author. Crown, 1985, o.p. SERIES: It's Great to Read! SUBJECTS: Family life—Fiction; Picnics—Fiction. RL B.

A family's relaxing day in the country ends up at a fast-food joint, ketchup-spattered, but with sun-yellow balloons with hearts. Muted pastel illustrations contrast adult and child response to events. Binding is poor.

420 *Shopping*. Ill. by author. Crown, 1985, o.p. SERIES: It's Great to Read! SUBJECTS: Humorous stories; Shopping—Fiction. RL B.

A small child's adventures at the grocery store and in the television department of a store have tongue-in-cheek adult humor. Misty yellows, reds, and blues draw the reader into a child's world. Binding is poor.

421 *Working*. Ill. by author. Crown, 1985, o.p. SERIES: It's Great to Read! SUBJECTS: Fathers—Fiction; Imagination—Fiction; Parents, working—Fiction. RL B.

A small boy's explorations at his father's work place provide varied adult reactions, judging by their expressions. This tale is warmed by the snowball play and hug on the way home. Light pastel drawings have a grainy texture.

Clifford, Eth

422 *Flatfoot Fox and the Case of the Missing Eye*. Ill. by Brian Lies. Houghton Mifflin, 1990. ISBN 0-395-51945-4. SUBJECTS: Animals—Fiction; Mystery and detective stories; Wordplay. RL B.

Flamboyant Fat Cat's beautiful sky-blue artificial eye is stolen when he serves no ice cream or cake at his birthday party because everyone is so mean to him. Ink drawings of Flatfoot Fox and his assistant, Secretary Bird, and his rabbit, pig, goat, and snake suspects add drama and humor.

Climo, Shirley

423 *King of the Birds*. Ill. by Ruth Heller. HarperCollins, 1988. ISBN 0-690-04623-5. SUBJECTS: Animals—Birds—Fiction; Folklore. RL C.

An appealing story of how Wren became King of the Birds by using his wits, though he never

Climo, Shirley (cont.)

affected a topknot or a robe of bright feathers. Illustrations in browns, blacks, and lavender show the rich variety of birds; the tale tells how they acquired their habits.

Clinton, Patrick

424 *I Can Be a Father*. Photos. Childrens Pr., 1988. ISBN 0-516-01904-X. SERIES: I Can Be. SUBJECTS: Fathers; Parent and child. RL B.

The varied ways in which fathers care for their children, teach them, and provide for them, are described in fluid, nonsexist language. A glossary and a picture glossary, many colored photos, and an index add to this warmly readable factual book.

Clithero, Sally

425 *Beginning-to-Read Poetry*. Ill. by Erik Blegvad. Follett, 1967, o.p. SUBJECTS: Imagination—Fiction; Poetry. RL C.

Poems such as "Holding Hands," "Mrs. Peck-Pigeon," and "The Make-Believe House" sparkle from this unusual collection. Watercolor washes show tiny animals, elves, snow people, and shoes.

Coatsworth, Elizabeth

426 *Bob Bodden and the Seagoing Farm*. Ill. by Frank Aloise. Garrard, 1970, o.p. SUBJECTS: Humorous stories; Tall tales. RL C.

This story explains how Maine sea-captain Bob Bodden's oceangoing farm caused the lakes and islands along Maine's shores. Ink sketches are a bit dated.

Cocca-Leffler, Maryann

427 *What a Pest!* Ill. by author. Putnam, 1994. ISBN 0-448-40399-4. SERIES: All Aboard Reading. SUBJECTS: Siblings—Fiction. RL A.

Little sister Jessie saves the day when one of the dance duo gets chicken pox. Appealing watercolor illustrations support this light-hearted story.

Coerr, Eleanor

428 *The Big Balloon Race*. Ill. by Carolyn Croll. HarperCollins, 1981, 1992. ISBN 0-06-021353-1. SERIES: I Can Read Books. SUBJECTS: Balloons; Biographies. RL A.

Ariel and her mother, Carlotta Myers, the most famous aeronaut of the 1880s, win a hot air balloon race by using their wits and courage. A stowaway, a thunderstorm, and an unscheduled touchdown in a pond, plus full color drawings, add to the drama.

429 *Chang's Paper Pony*. Ill. by Deborah Kogan Ray. HarperCollins, 1988. ISBN 0-06-021329-9. SERIES: I Can Read Books. SUBJECTS: Animals—Horses—Fiction; United States—1783–1865—Fiction. RL C.

A Chinese-American boy, Chang, growing up in a gold mining town, dreams of having a pony. Pencil drawings in turquoise and gold soften the harsh outlines of his life, and celebrate the realization of his dream.

430 *Jane Goodall*. Ill. by Kees de Kiefte. Putnam, 1976, o.p. SUBJECTS: Biographies; Science. RL C.

The outlines of Goodall's dreams, opportunities, and choices are given. Soft pencil sketches are appropriate.

431 *The Josefina Story Quilt*. Ill. by Bruce Degen. HarperCollins, 1986. ISBN 0-06-021349-3. SERIES: I Can Read Books. SUBJECTS: Frontier and pioneer life—Fiction; Quilting—Fiction; Western stories. RL B.

The hardships and satisfactions of wagon train travel are commemorated in a quilt by a young girl. Pencil outline drawings; each chapter is headed with a quilt patch significant to Josefina's experience.

432 *Mixed-Up Mystery Smell*. Ill. by Tomie dePaola. Putnam, 1976, o.p. SERIES: See and Read. SUBJECTS: Clubs—Fiction; Haunted houses—Fiction; Mystery and detective stories. RL B.

While hunting for a mysterious smell's source, the children nervously follow their noses to a "haunted" house, and discover the source of the delicious smell. Pale cocoa, avocado, and turquoise coloring alternates with pencil in dePaola's distinctive drawings.

433 *Waza Wins at Windy Gulch*. Ill. by Janet McCaffery. Putnam, 1977, o.p. SERIES: See and Read. SUBJECTS: Animals—Camels; Humorous stories; United States—1783–1865—Fiction. RL C.
A true story about the imported Camel Brigade of the 1850s that reads like a tall tale, as Dirtyshirt Dan tries to get the camels in trouble to save his mules. Excellent textured drawings are in shades of brown.

Cohen, Caron L.

434 *Three Yellow Dogs*. Ill. by Peter Sis. Greenwillow, 1986, o.p. SUBJECTS: Animals—Dogs—Fiction; Concepts—Numbers. RL A.
A five-word text is enlivened with dogs of all shapes and pastel colors. Some are shown close-up and others are seen from a distance.

Cole, Joanna

435 *Bony-Legs*. Ill. by Dirk Zimmer. Four Winds, 1983; Scholastic, pap., 1988. ISBN 0-02-722970-X. SUBJECTS: Folklore—Russia; Magic—Fiction; Russia—Fiction. RL A.
Sasha's kindness to Baba Yaga's creaking gate and a hungry cat and dog helps her escape from the Russian witch. Richly patterned illustrations embroider this simple version of a traditional tale of fear, magic, and kindness.

436 *Bully Trouble*. Ill. by Marylin Hafner. Random House, 1989. ISBN 0-394-94949-8. SERIES: Step into Reading. SUBJECTS: Behavior—Bullying—Fiction; Friendship—Fiction. RL A.
Best friends Arlo and Robby take revenge on bully Big Eddie with a hot soda concoction and a hot chili sandwich. Colored pencil and wash illustrations show the boys in action.

437 *Get Well, Clown-Arounds!* Ill. by Jerry Smath. Stevens, 1982, 1993. ISBN 0-8368-0895-9. SUBJECTS: Clowns—Fiction; Jokes and riddles; Wordplay. RL A.
Grandma Clown-Around's chicken soup and general clean-up "cures" her family of the green pox, caught when Baby paints green spots on the bathroom mirror. Games for learning are appended. Pastel drawings are busy and playful.

438 *Golly Gump Swallowed a Fly*. Ill. by Bari Weissman. Parents Magazine Pr., 1981. ISBN: 0-8193-1069-7. SUBJECTS: Humorous stories; Tall tales. RL B.
Golly Gump's adventures lead him to cover his mouth when he yawns in a tale paralleling "I Know an Old Lady Who Swallowed a Fly." Flat pastel colors and expressive animals add to the humor.

439 *How You Were Born*. Photos by Margaret Miller. Morrow, 1993. ISBN 0-688-12059-8. SUBJECTS: Human body—Birth; Nature. RL C
This is a slightly revised edition, leaving out diagrams of the male and female reproductive systems and the statement "During labor, your mother had to work hard."

440 *The Magic School Bus: At the Waterworks*. Ill. by Bruce Degen. Scholastic, 1986. ISBN 0-590-43739-9. SERIES: Magic School Bus. SUBJECTS: School stories; Science and scientists; Water. RL C.
This imaginative class trip takes the class in a raindrop from a cloud, downstream to a water filtration plant, into a water tower, and back through water pipes to the school. Irreverent dialogue, Ms. Frizzle's outrageous dresses, and the parting notes to "serious" students add humor.

441 *The Magic School Bus: Inside the Earth*. Ill. by Bruce Degen. Scholastic, 1987. ISBN 0-590-40759-7. SERIES: Magic School Bus. SUBJECTS: Geology and geologists; School stories; Science and scientists. RL C.
Ms. Frizzle, with her zany, unpredictable clothing, leads her third-grade class into the center of the earth in their air-conditioned magic school bus. A humorous conversation between a reader and the illustrator at the end sorts out the fiction from real science.

442 *The Magic School Bus: Inside the Human Body*. Ill. by Bruce Degen. Scholastic, 1989. ISBN 0-590-72633-1. SERIES: Magic School Bus. SUBJECTS: Human body; School stories; Science and scientists. RL C.
This magic school bus field trip takes the third-graders through Arnold's body, through the blood stream to the brain, exiting with a

Cole, Joanna (cont.)

sneeze. A humorous "test" at the end sorts out truth from fiction. Lively dialogue and fanciful illustrations add to the imaginative text.

443 *The Magic School Bus: Lost in the Solar System*. Ill. by Bruce Degen. Scholastic, 1989. ISBN 0-590-41428-3. SERIES: Magic School Bus. SUBJECTS: Astronomy; School stories; Science and scientists. RL C.
Ms. Frizzle, third-grade teacher extraordinaire, drives her class to the planets when they find the earthly planetarium closed. Through dialogue, school essays and adventures, narrative, a humorous appendix, and spirited ink and watercolor drawings, an introduction to outer space is given.

444 *The Magic School Bus: On the Ocean Floor*. Ill. by Bruce Degen. Scholastic, 1992. ISBN 0-590-41430-5. SERIES: Magic School Bus. SUBJECTS: Oceans and ocean life; School stories; Science and scientists. RL C.
This magic school bus drives right into the ocean where the class—and the lifeguard—don diving gear to explore various ocean layers, passing the tidal pools to visit the depths and a coral reef, visit with sharks and dolphins, and go bus surfing. Lively illustrations match imaginary trip.

445 *The Missing Tooth*. Ill. by Marylin Hafner. Random House, 1988. ISBN 0-394-99279-2. SERIES: Step into Reading. SUBJECTS: Friendship—Fiction; Human body—Teeth—Fiction. RL B.
Arlo and Robby had the same pets, liked the same games, and looked alike, down to the same missing teeth. After a bet about which one was going to lose the next tooth, the friendship becomes strained. Full colors warm this realistic story with a satisfying resolution.

446 *Mixed-Up Magic*. Ill. by True Kelley. Hastings House, 1987; Scholastic, pap., 1987. ISBN 0-8038-9298-5. SUBJECTS: Magic—Fiction; Nonsense; Stories in rhyme. RL A.
Rhyming nonsense is effectively paired with an elf's inept magic. Soft pastels warm the text.

447 *Plants in Winter*. Ill. by Kazue Mizumura. HarperCollins, 1973, o.p. SERIES: Let's-Read-and-Find-Out Science Books. SUBJECTS: Plants; Seasons—Winter. RL B.
A child finds out how various plants survive the winter from a botanist whose theories do not cover the hardy snowdrop blossom. Pale gray and green washes most appropriately illustrate each type of plant.

448 *Who Put the Pepper in the Pot?* Ill. by R. W. Alley. Parents Magazine Pr., 1989. ISBN 0-8193-1189-8. SERIES: Read Aloud Originals. SUBJECTS: Farm and country life—Fiction; Humorous stories. RL A.
Mama Sue and Papa Joe and their three kids live on hard work sweetened with love. They are nervous when their rich Aunt Tootie comes for dinner. Aunt Tootie surprises them by saving them from a disastrous stew. Illustrations suit the description of chaotic, cooperative farmlife.

449 *You Can't Smell a Flower with Your Ear! All About Your Five Senses*. Ill. by Mavis Smith. Putnam, 1994. ISBN 0-448-40470-2. SERIES: All Aboard Reading. SUBJECTS: Human body; Senses—Sight; Senses—Smell. RL A.
The senses are introduced in ten-page chapters that give anatomy, some background, and some experiments to try. Examples given are familiar to any child. Diverse ages and races are pictured in ink and watercolor drawings.

Cole, Joanna, and Calmenson, Stephanie

450 *Ready . . . Set . . . Read!* Ill. by Anne Burgess and Chris Demarest. Doubleday, 1990. ISBN 0-385-41416-1. SERIES: The Beginning Reader's Treasury. SUBJECTS: Books and reading; Poets and poetry. RL B.
Dr. Seuss, Arnold Lobel, Bernard Wiseman, and Joanna Cole are some of the authors whose stories are included in this anthology of poetry and stories with original art. Poets include Lilian Moore, Gwendolyn Brooks, David McCord, and other favorites.

Collins, David R.

451 *If I Could, I Would*. Ill. by Kelly Oechsli. Garrard, 1979, o.p. SERIES: Imagination.

SUBJECTS: Imagination—Fiction; Mothers—Fiction. RL B.

A small boy likes his mother so much he would give her lots of candy; take her for a wagon ride to the moon; give her a haunted house, lots of pets, and a castle—and even eat spinach! Gentle humor is reinforced by four-color cartoon drawings.

Conklin, Gladys

452 *I Caught a Lizard*. Ill. by Artur Marokvia. Holiday House, 1967, o.p. SUBJECTS: Animals—Lizards; Pet care; Pets—Wild animals. RL C.

Conklin conveys her fascination with many small wild animals and tells how to care for them, but she advocates letting them return to their natural environment after observing them for several days. Lightly colored pencil drawings reinforce this message.

Conway, Lisa

453 *I Like Ketchup Sandwiches*. Ill. by author. Random House, 1991. ISBN 0-679-81719-0. SERIES: Pictureback Reader. SUBJECTS: Family Life—Fiction. RL A.

The 48-word vocabulary appears at the end for cutting out as flash cards. A small child likes to burp, talk, dance, make her swing set bump, hang from trees, and visit her grandma. Soft colored-pencil drawings complement the story of a world familiar to a child.

Cooke, Ann

454 *Giraffes at Home*. Ill. by Robert Quackenbush. HarperCollins, 1972, o.p. SERIES: Let's-Read-and-Find-Out Science Books. SUBJECTS: Animals—Giraffes; Nature. RL C.

Information about giraffes' mating, birth, feeding, enemies, and herd behavior is presented in an interesting fashion. Excellent four-color illustrations alternate with gray ones.

Cooper, Jason

455 *Coral Reefs*. Photos. Rourke, 1992. ISBN 0-86593-229-8. SERIES: The Sea. SUBJECTS: Conservation; Oceans and ocean life. RL C.

Excellent close-up photos of coral reefs and their colorful fish are accompanied by brief information in large print. Short glossary and index are included.

456 *Fire Stations*. Photos. Rourke, 1992. ISBN 0-86593-210-7. SERIES: Great Places to Visit. SUBJECTS: Community helpers; Fire fighting. RL C.

Fire safety, fire equipment, and life in a fire station are described and illustrated with color photos. Women are shown as fire fighters and dispatchers when children visit the fire station. The text is in large print and a brief index is provided.

457 *Magnets*. Photos. Rourke, 1992. ISBN 0-86593-165-8. SERIES: Science Secrets. SUBJECTS: Magnets; Science. RL C.

Excellent full page color photos illustrate the text on half of each double spread. Magnetic rocks, electromagnets, and gravity are some of the topics introduced.

458 *Police Stations*. Photos by Lynn M. Stone. Rourke, 1992. ISBN 0-86593-213-1. SERIES: Great Places to Visit. SUBJECTS: Community helpers; Police. RL C.

The basics of police work are explained in unadorned language. Full page color photos accompany the text. D.A.R.E. is one of the police programs mentioned.

459 *Sea Shells*. Photos by Lynn M. Stone. Rourke, 1992. ISBN 0-86593-229-8. SERIES: Discovery Library of the Sea. SUBJECTS: Conservation; Oceans and ocean life; Shells. RL C.

The text highlights difficult words, which are defined in the glossary as well as in the text. Explanations are simple but informative, and are illustrated with outstanding close-up photos of different kinds of shells. Conservation as well as wonder is stressed.

460 *Wind*. Photos. Rourke, 1992. ISBN 0-86593-171-2. SERIES: Science Secrets. SUBJECTS: Science; Weather—Wind. RL C.

Basic concepts of the causes and effects of wind energy are introduced. Windmills, weather vanes, hurricanes, waterspouts, and tornadoes are illustrated with full page color photos. A brief glossary and an index are appended.

Corbett, Scott

461 *Boy Who Walked on Air*. Ill. by Ed Parker. Little, Brown, 1974, o.p. SUBJECTS: Humorous stories; Inventors and inventions—Fiction. RL B.
Max's willpower and Morry's inventiveness have disastrous results—most of the time—as they try to become airborne. Cartoon illustrations add humor.

Corey, Dorothy

462 *Everybody Takes Turns*. Ill. by Lois Axeman. Whitman, 1980, o.p. SERIES: Self-Starters. SUBJECTS: Behavior—Sharing. RL A.
At the most basic level, the text talks about people, including children, taking turns: in line, when only one toy is available, and crossing the street. Situations have child appeal, as do illustrations with varied patterns, cherry red washes, and pets.

Cossi, Olga

463 *Gus the Bus*. Ill. by Howie Schneider. Scholastic, 1989, o.p. SUBJECTS: Buses—Fiction. RL C.
After getting new tires, Gus, the school bus, has a day chasing a dog and horses, racing a fire truck, and attempting to take off at the airport. Pastel cartoons show the silly grin on his radiator and the wild flowers on his mirror.

Counsel, June

464 *But Martin!* Ill. by Carolyn Dinan. Faber & Faber, 1984, o.p. SUBJECTS: Cultural diversity—Fiction; School stories. RL B.
An intriguing, upbeat story celebrating diversity, play, and cooperative learning focuses on Martin, who is green and flies to school in a saucer. Ink drawings are brightened with washes and colored pencil.

Coville, Bruce, and Coville, Katherine

465 *The Foolish Giant*. Ill. by authors. HarperCollins, 1978. ISBN 0-397-31800-6. SERIES: I-Like-to-Read. SUBJECTS: Giants—Fiction. RL C.

A loving portrait of a brave, kind, and friendly giant named Harry is given, along with an explanation of his limitations and powers. All the tears are not Harry's in this evocative story illustrated with soft, detailed pencil drawings.

466 *Sarah's Unicorn*. Ill. by authors. Harper-Collins, 1979; HarperCollins, pap., 1985. ISBN 0-397-31873-1. SERIES: I-Like-to-Read. SUBJECTS: Mythical creatures—Fiction; Witches—Fiction. RL B.
Sarah's magical adventures with Oakhorn the unicorn nearly come to an end when Mag the evil witch discovers them together. Pencil drawings supply atmosphere and expressive details, especially of the forest animals.

Coxe, Molly

467 *The Great Snake Escape*. Ill. by author. HarperCollins, 1994. ISBN 0-06-022869-5. SERIES: I Can Read Books. SUBJECTS: Animals—Fiction; Friendship—Fiction. RL A.
Friends Mirabel the goose and Maxie the frog are helped by the feared king cobra who escaped from the zoo. Simple but absorbing story is illustrated in pencil and soft pastels.

Craig, Janet

468 *The Boo-Hoo Witch*. Ill. by Pat Schories. Troll, 1993. ISBN 0-8167-3186-1. SERIES: Giant First-Start. SUBJECTS: Holidays—Halloween—Fiction; Homelessness—Fiction; Witches—Fiction. RL A.
Little Witch is constantly crying because she has no home to go to. Her animal friends try to share their homes, but none work until a kitten shows her the perfect little house for the two of them. Very easy to read, the text is illustrated with colorful, though rather mediocre, pastel drawings.

469 A *Letter to Santa*. Ill. by Laura Rader. Troll, 1993. ISBN 0-8167-3252-3. SERIES: Giant First-Start. SUBJECTS: Holidays—Christmas—Fiction; Letters—Fiction. RL A.
Knowing that Christmas is coming, Mike, Jill, and Scott write letters to Santa. They tell him that they have been good and what they want for Christmas. After the holidays, the three

write a thank-you letter. Active, childlike watercolor and ink paintings illustrate the story.

470 *Max and Maggie in Summer*. Ill. by Paul Meisel. Troll, 1994. ISBN 0-8167-3348-1. SERIES: Nice Mice. SUBJECTS: Animals— Mice—Fiction; Friendship—Fiction; Seasons—Summer—Fiction. RL C.

Best friends Max and Maggie argue over what to do: fish or have a picnic. Friendship overcomes anger as they take turns. In the second story, Max's boredom is overcome as he watches clouds with Maggie. Humorous watercolor and ink paintings are delightful.

471 *Valentine's Day Mess*. Ill. by Deborah Morse. Troll, 1993. ISBN 0-8167-3254-X. SERIES: Giant First-Start. SUBJECTS: Animals—Mice—Fiction; Friendship—Fiction; Holidays—Valentine's Day—Fiction. RL A.

Friends Jan and Ken enjoy doing things together but when their special Valentine's Day surprises are accidentally destroyed, each blames the other. Friendship does win out though as they again do things together. Soft, carefully crafted pictures seem to be painted with an air brush.

472 *What's It Like to Be a Newspaper Reporter*. Ill. by Richard M. Kolding. Troll, 1989. ISBN 0-8167-1807-5. SERIES: What's It Like to Be a. . . . SUBJECTS: Careers. RL C.

The relationships of the reporter to the city editor, photographer, news writer, news service, and copy editors are seen through following the day of Scotty Hansen. Ink and wash drawings enliven his interviews for a string of stories.

Craig, M. Jean

473 *Spring Is Like the Morning*. Ill. by Don Almquist. Putnam, 1965, o.p. SUBJECTS: Seasons—Spring; Senses. RL B.

Outstanding textured prints in gray, brown, and avocado focus on the sights and feeling of spring.

Cresswell, Helen

474 *The Weather Cat*. Ill. by Barbara Walker. Forest House, 1990. ISBN 1-878363-06-9.

SERIES: Quality Time. SUBJECTS: Animals— Cats—Fiction; Family life—Fiction. RL B.

Mr. Briggs, the cat, adopts a family and spends nice mornings hunting birds, but colder ones hunting mice and spiders. Soon there are five weather cats! Soft colored pencil drawings accompany the text.

Cresswell, Helen, and Brown, Judy

475 *Almost Goodbye*. Dutton, 1990. ISBN 0-525-44858-6. SERIES: Speedsters. SUBJECTS: Magic—Fiction. RL A.

Gumball becomes invisible when he and his friend, Susie, wish on a white-elephant lamp. After a hobo picks up the lamp with one wish left, the panic and fun begin. A lighthearted twist on an old theme includes some cartoon dialogue with the ink and gray wash cartoon drawings.

Cristaldi, Kathryn

476 *Baseball Ballerina*. Ill. by Abby Carter. Random House, 1992. ISBN 0-679-91734-9. SERIES: Step into Reading. SUBJECTS: Dancing and dancers—Fiction; Sports—Baseball—Fiction. RL A.

A tomboy is afraid her Sharks baseball team will think she is a wimp in the ballet recital, but all ends well when she catches Princess Dandelion's flyaway crown. Text is illustrated with appealing watercolors in blue and lavender.

Croll, Carolyn

477 *Too Many Babas*. Ill. by author. HarperCollins, 1979, 1994. ISBN 0-06-021384-1. SERIES: I Can Read Books. SUBJECTS: Cookery—Fiction. RL A.

Each of Baba Eldis's visitors adds something to her soup until it is unpalatable. With the second batch, they work as a team. Inspired by the exhibition of Russian costumes at the Metropolitan Museum of Art, the story and illustrations do have a folk flavor.

Cromie, William J.

478 *Steven and the Green Turtle*. Ill. by Tom Eaton. HarperCollins, 1970, o.p. SERIES: I Can Read Science. SUBJECTS: Animals—

Cromie, William J. (cont.)

Turtles; Nature; Pets—Wild animals.
RL B.
Steven's rescue and later release of a tiny green turtle is sympathetically treated in this easy science book. Sketches have a predominantly turquoise wash.

Curran, Eileen

479 *Life in the Meadow*. Ill. by James Watling. Troll, hb and pap., 1985. ISBN 0-8167-0343-4. SUBJECTS: Animals; Animals—Insects. RL B.
A child frolics and observes the abundant life in a meadow. Textual illustrations are bright, with interesting perspectives; however, the cover is dull.

Curren, Polly

480 *I Know a Plumber*. Ill. by Frank Aloise. Putnam, 1976, o.p. SERIES: Community Helpers. SUBJECTS: Careers; Community helpers. RL C.
A picture glossary helps children clarify concepts regarding plumbing. A plumber's typical house call is shown. Ink sketches are good.

Cushman, Doug

481 *Aunt Eater Loves a Mystery*. Ill. by author. HarperCollins, 1987. ISBN 0-06-021327-2. SERIES: I Can Read Books. SUBJECTS: Animals—Anteaters—Fiction; Mystery and detective stories. RL C.
A missing suitcase, a mysterious shadow, a strange visitor next door, and a cat-sitting adventure are competently dealt with by Aunt Eater. Homey pictures are in turquoise, yellow, and forest green.

482 *Aunt Eater's Mystery Vacation*. Ill. by author. HarperCollins, 1992. ISBN 0-06-020514-8. SERIES: I Can Read Books. SUBJECTS: Animals—Anteaters—Fiction; Mystery and detective stories. RL A.
Aunt Eater alternates time reading mysteries and solving them on her vacation. She finds the missing ferry boat captain and recovers hotel guests' valuables, a valuable Swinesaurus bone, and a fellow mystery-lover. Sim-

ple stories illustrated in watercolor washes are dedicated to Prelutsky.

483 *Camp Big Paw*. Ill. by author. HarperCollins, 1990. ISBN 0-06-021368-X. SERIES: I Can Read Books. SUBJECTS: Animals—Fiction; Behavior—Bullying—Fiction; Camps and camping—Fiction. RL A.
Cyril, the bumbling tiger camper, is bullied by weasel Nigel Snootbutter. Cyril's bird house is messed up; he stands up in the canoe during a race, overturning it; he loses the baton in a swimming relay, and gets lost in the woods. Half-page pastel drawings focus on the animal campers.

484 *Uncle Foster's Hat Tree*. Ill. by author. Dutton, 1988. ISBN 0-525-44410-6. SERIES: Dutton Easy Reader. SUBJECTS: Aunts and uncles—Fiction; Tall tales. RL A.
Bored Merle becomes absorbed in the adventure stories attached to Uncle Foster's hats. Bright perky watercolors enliven the imaginative first person tall tales.

D

Daniel, Kira

485 *What's It Like to Be a Teacher*. Ill. by Diane Paterson. Troll, 1989. ISBN 0-8167-1430-4. SERIES: What's It Like to Be a . . . . SUBJECTS: Careers; School stories. RL C.
Mr. Benson gives the class a "smart start" with his morning puzzles, his problem-solving and comfort, his standards, creativity, and hard work. A joyful view of a satisfying career is illustrated with graphically pleasing watercolor and ink drawings.

Dauer, Rosamund

486 *Bullfrog and Gertrude Go Camping*. Ill. by Byron Barton. Greenwillow, 1980; Dell, pap., 1988. ISBN 0-440-40074-0. SERIES: Read-alone. SUBJECTS: Animals—Frogs and toads—Fiction; Animals—Snakes—Fiction; Camps and camping—Fiction. RL B.

Gertrude and Bullfrog come home a family after adopting Itsa Snake during a camping trip. Four-color framed drawings have shapeless friendly frogs and an expressive snake.

487 *Bullfrog Builds a House*. Ill. by Byron Barton. Greenwillow, 1976, o.p. SERIES: Read-alone. SUBJECTS: Animals—Frogs and toads—Fiction; Friendship—Fiction. RL B.

Bullfrog does not enjoy his new house with the front-porch diving board until he invites Gertrude to share it. Simple humor and a feeling of home regarding these two frogs are conveyed partly through avocado, rust, and cocoa drawings.

488 *Bullfrog Grows Up*. Ill. by Byron Barton. Greenwillow, 1976, o.p.; Dell, pap., 1988. ISBN 0-440-40007-4. SERIES: Read-alone. SUBJECTS: Animals—Frogs and toads—Fiction; Family life—Fiction; Growing-up—Fiction. RL B.

Bullfrog needs a lunch, a pack of cards, and a last bath before setting off on his own from his adopted mouse family (practicing his neglected frog talk). Interesting ideas for presentation to primary-school-age children are illustrated with humor, enhancing individual characters.

Daugherty, Charles M.

489 *Samuel Clemens*. Ill. by Kurt Werth. HarperCollins, 1970, o.p. SERIES: Harper-Collins Biography. SUBJECTS: Biographies; Writing. RL C.

The zestful life of this famous writer is well portrayed. Werth's expressive drawings give character and flavor to Clemens's adventures.

Davis, Gibbs

490 *Katy's First Haircut*. Ill. by Linda Shute. Houghton Mifflin, 1985, o.p. SUBJECTS: Haircutting—Fiction; School stories. RL C.

A simple topic, a first haircut, is dealt with sympathetically, especially by Katy's teacher (a male) and parents, who give her free choice about how her hair is to be cut. Full color illustrations are softened by pencil outlines and shading.

Davis, Maggie S.

491 *A Garden of Whales*. Ill. by Jennifer O'Connell. Camden House, 1993. ISBN 0-944475-36-1. SUBJECTS: Native Americans—Eskimos—Fiction; Animals—Whales—Fiction; Dreams—Fiction. RL C.

A boy dreams about danger to whales during his bath, and with other children (arriving in flying bathtubs) calls on the whales to give them tears to water their secret whale garden. Inspired by an Eskimo song, the story resonates with deep watercolors.

Day, Jenifer W.

492 *What Is a Flower?* Ill. by Dorothea Barlowe. Golden, 1975. ISBN 0-307-11800-2. SERIES: Child's Golden Science. SUBJECTS: Nature; Plants—Flowers. RL C.

A few sentences discuss various plants ranging from wild and garden flowers to vegetables, grasses, vines, and exotic flowers. Good information is illustrated with large, colorful watercolors.

493 *What Is a Fruit?* Ill. by Enid Kotschnig. Golden, 1976, o.p. SERIES: Child's Golden Science. SUBJECTS: Nature; Plants—Fruit. RL C.

Information is given about tomatoes and melons, grains, peas and berries, and the relationships between them. Word lists are appended. Large watercolor drawings add to the book's appeal.

Day, Marie

494 *Dragon in the Rocks*. Ill. by author. Firefly, 1991. ISBN 0-920775-76-4. SUBJECTS: Biographies; Geology; Science. RL C.

The remarkable story of young Mary Anning of Lyme Regis, England, who helped support her family after her father's death by selling the fossils she found in the sea cliffs. Cheerful watercolor washes illustrate this retelling of Mary's finds.

De Brunhoff, Laurent

495 *Babar's Little Circus Star*. Ill. by author. Random House, 1988. ISBN 0-394-98959-

De Brunhoff, Laurent (cont.)

> 7. SERIES: Step into Reading. SUBJECTS: Animals—Elephants—Fiction; Circuses—Fiction. RL A.

Isabelle cannot climb trees, ride a bike, or go to school, and she must go to bed early. However, small as she is, she has success in the circus. Flat decorative pastel drawings present the typical Babar family.

De Fossard, Esta

496 *Dinah the Dog with a Difference*. Photos by Haworth Bartram. Stevens, 1985, o.p. SERIES: Dial Easy-to-Read Animal Adventures. SUBJECTS: Animals—Dogs; Physically and mentally impaired. RL A.

Dinah's curiosity and fearlessness set her apart from her littermates, and fit her for work as a guide dog. Photo close-ups of puppy adventures are captivating.

Degen, Bruce

497 *The Little Witch and the Riddle*. Ill. by author. HarperCollins, 1980. ISBN 0-06-444125-3. SERIES: I Can Read Books. SUBJECTS: Friendship—Fiction; Jokes and riddles; Witches—Fiction. RL B.

The Little Witch needs the help of her friend Otto Ogre to solve the riddles that open the "Book of Magic." This witty, gentle story is enhanced by framed pencil drawings of the pair. The drawings are highlighted in rose and gold.

DeJong, David C.

498 *Happy Birthday Egg*. Ill. by Harvey Weiss. Little, Brown, 1962, o.p. SUBJECTS: Mystery and detective stories. RL C.

The nighttime mystery turns out to be an ostrich egg, not a dragon egg. Ink sketches have lavender colored pencil highlights.

DeLage, Ida

499 *ABC Pigs Go to Market*. Ill. by Kelly Oechsli. Garrard, 1977, o.p. SERIES: Once Upon an ABC. SUBJECTS: Alphabet—Fiction; Animals—Pigs—Fiction. RL B.

Pig children at the supermarket explore the *dairy*, look at *keys*, buy an *ounce* and a *pound* of nuts, and *wait* for change. Although the parts of speech are inconsistent and the vocabulary is not necessarily familiar, the mischief, curiosity, and setting of watercolor drawings definitely are.

500 *Beware! Beware! A Witch Won't Share*. Ill. by Ted Schroeder. Garrard, 1972, o.p.; Chelsea House, 1991. ISBN 0-7910-1473-8. SERIES: Old Witch. SUBJECTS: Gypsies—Fiction; Witches—Fiction. RL C.

Both the farmer and the witch have trouble with the gypsies. Pencil drawings are highlighted with chartreuse and yellow.

501 *A Bunny Ride*. Ill. by Tracy McVay. Garrard, 1975, o.p. SUBJECTS: Animals—Rabbits—Fiction. RL A.

Baby bunnies want to ride to town as their raccoon and opossum friends do. However, the baby bunnies find a pony ride too bumpy. Pastel drawings of the babies are most appealing.

502 *Farmer and the Witch*. Ill. by Gil Miret. Garrard, 1966, o.p.; Chelsea House, 1991. ISBN 0-7910-1474-6. SERIES: Old Witch. SUBJECTS: Witches—Fiction. RL C.

The witch's marvelous brew includes toadstools, feathers, worms, webs, and lizards. Her magic has the barnyard in chaos until the farmer's ingenuity and Hoppy Toad save the day. Pumpkin and black drawings add lively humor.

503 *Frannie's Flower*. Ill. by Ellen Sloan. Garrard, 1979, o.p. SUBJECTS: Imagination—Fiction. RL A.

A doll survives Frannie's milk-feeding, swinging, sleeping, and wagon-riding better than her flower. Soft pastel drawings focus on a small girl's play.

504 *Good Morning, Lady*. Ill. by Tracy McVay. Garrard, 1974, o.p. SUBJECTS: Animals—Fiction. RL A.

The possum tinker sells a pot to a mouse to use for an unusual purpose. Pastel colors show the smallest woodland creatures.

505 *Hello, Come In*. Ill. by John Mardon. Garrard, hb and pap., 1971. ISBN 0-8116-6708-1. SUBJECTS: Houses—Fiction. RL A.

Grandma, a witch, a pig, a ghost, a frog, a bird, a pony, a toymaker, and some children invite the reader into their abodes. Thin story line is supported by stylized, two-color drawings.

506 *Old Witch and the Crows*. Ill. by Marianne Smith. Garrard, 1983, o.p.; Chelsea House, 1991. ISBN 0-7910-1476-2. SERIES: Old Witch. SUBJECTS: Witches—Fiction. RL C.
When Old Witch helps the crows by chasing away the owl, they return the favor by bringing creepy crawlies for her brew. Bright purple and orange, with some gray and brown, keep the setting spooky.

507 *Old Witch Finds a New House*. Ill. by Pat Paris. Garrard, 1979, o.p.; Chelsea House, 1991. ISBN 0-7910-7481-9. SERIES: Old Witch. SUBJECTS: Witches—Fiction. RL C.
A woodcutter returns Old Witch's favor in full after she rescues him when he is trapped under a fallen tree. Comic drawings are in black, red, and green.

508 *Old Witch Goes to the Ball*. Ill. by Gustave E. Nebel. Garrard, 1969, o.p.; Chelsea House, 1991. ISBN 0-7910-1483-5. SERIES: Old Witch. SUBJECTS: Witches—Fiction. RL B.
The clever farmer's wife distracts Old Witch from getting even when the angry witch does not win the Halloween costume contest. Gray and gold washes highlight lively ink drawings.

509 *The Old Witch's Party*. Ill. by Mimi Korach. Garrard, 1976, o.p.; Chelsea House, 1991. ISBN 0-7910-1484-3. SERIES: Old Witch. SUBJECTS: Witches—Fiction. RL B.
Children mistake Old Witch for Grandma Petticoat twice. Turquoise and fuchsia highlight ink drawings.

510 *Pilgrim Children Come to Plymouth*. Ill. by Herman Vestal. Garrard, 1981, o.p. SUBJECTS: Holidays—Thanksgiving; Pilgrims. RL B.
Written from the point of view of Pilgrim children, the book focuses on the contributions and friendship of the Native Americans, without softening the fear and hardships. Warmth is added by watercolor drawings.

511 *Squirrel's Tree Party*. Ill. by Tracy McVay. Garrard, 1978, o.p. SUBJECTS: Animals—Squirrels—Fiction. RL A.
Cute animal children celebrate in the rain, sunshine, or wind. Appealing soft watercolors of animals complement the gentle story.

512 *Weeny Witch*. Ill. by Kelly Oechsli. Garrard, 1968, o.p.; Chelsea House, 1991. ISBN 0-7910-1485-1. SERIES: Old Witch. SUBJECTS: Fairies—Fiction; Witches—Fiction. RL C.
Weeny Witch does not fit in with those who try to darken the sky by capturing the night fairies. Some imaginative twists and rhymes give substance to the story. Drawings help set the atmosphere with lavender, blue, and pink.

513 *What Does a Witch Need?* Ill. by Ted Schroeder. Garrard, 1971, o.p.; Chelsea House, 1991. ISBN 0-7910-1486-X. SERIES: Old Witch. SUBJECTS: Witches—Fiction. RL B.
Old Witch discovers she needs a stray dog as much as a new kitten to make her brew and protect her toadstools from the gnomes. Nice touches of expression, both verbal and facial, enliven this tale.

Delton, Judy

514 *A Birthday Bike for Brimhall*. Ill. by June Leary. Carolrhoda, 1985. ISBN 0-87614-256-0. SERIES: On My Own. SUBJECTS: Animals—Bears—Fiction; Bicycles and bicycling—Fiction; Friendship—Fiction. RL B.
Did Bear trick Brimhall into learning how to ride his birthday bike? (Yes, and it worked!) Finely textured ink drawings add detail and drama to this story.

515 *Brimhall Turns Detective*. Ill. by Cherie R. Wyman. Carolrhoda, 1983. ISBN 0-87614-203-X. SERIES: On My Own. SUBJECTS: Animals—Bears—Fiction; Humorous stories; mystery and detective stories. RL A.
The antics of two friends that trace monster tracks have exaggerated humor. Ink drawings have sepia pencil accents.

516 *Brimhall Turns to Magic*. Ill. by Bruce Degen. Lothrop, 1979, o.p. SERIES: Fun-to-

Delton, Judy (cont.)

Read. SUBJECTS: Friendship—Fiction; Magic—Fiction. RL B.

When Roger the rabbit appears in Brimhall's hat by magic, it takes special friends to make him "disappear." Soon Bear regrets his grumpiness when Roger was around. Pencil drawings in gray and brown give detailed characterizations.

517 *The Goose Who Wrote a Book*. Ill. by Catherine Cleary. Carolrhoda, 1982. ISBN 0-87614-179-3. SERIES: On My Own. SUBJECTS: Writing—Fiction. RL B.

"Cheese Louise" says Goose when her friends want her absentminded fictional character to be a different animal. Pencil drawings are highlighted with turquoise and orange.

518 *Groundhog's Day at the Doctor*. Ill. by Giulio Maestro. Parents Magazine Pr., 1981, o.p. SUBJECTS: Animals—Fiction; Holidays—Groundhog Day—Fiction. RL C.

After Groundhog wakes up a day early feeling stiff and tired, he finds himself giving advice to animals he meets in the doctor's waiting room—and ends up going skiing with the doctor. Full color drawings have a textured background.

519 *I Never Win!* Ill. by Cathy Gilchrist. Carolrhoda, 1981. ISBN 0-87614-139-4. SERIES: On My Own. SUBJECTS: Self-esteem—Fiction. RL B.

Although a boy does not win birthday prizes or games, he takes his frustrations out on his piano practicing and eventually gets recognition for his talent. Ink drawings with black and red highlights are expressive of feelings.

520 *My Mom Made Me Go to Camp*. Ill. by Lisa McCue. Delacorte, 1990. ISBN 0-385-30113-8. SUBJECTS: Camps and camping—Fiction. RL B.

This is a reassuring book for child and parent about the fears and insecurities of going to summer camp—but the children in the illustrations look more like toddlers than children who would go to overnight camp.

521 *No Time for Christmas*. Ill. by Anastasia Mitchell. Carolrhoda, 1988. ISBN 0-87614-

327-3. SERIES: On My Own. SUBJECTS: Animals—Bears—Fiction; Holidays—Christmas—Fiction. RL B.

Bear and Brimhall are so busy working to buy each other Christmas presents that they don't see each other. Bright watercolors warm the friendship.

522 *Two Good Friends*. Ill. by Giulio Maestro. Crown, 1974, o.p.; pap., 1986, o.p. SUBJECTS: Animals—Bears—Fiction; Animals—Ducks—Fiction; Friendship—Fiction. RL B.

What good are a clean house and wonderful nut pies without an understanding friend? Differences that seem insurmountable are resolved with love. Soft colored pencil drawings complement the mood.

Demers, Jan

523 *What Do You Do with a . . . ?* Ill. by Don Robison. Willowisp, hb and pap., 1985, o.p. SERIES: Predictable Read Together. SUBJECTS: Stories in rhyme. RL A.

Rhythmic questions about familiar settings are answered in short rhyming phrases. Busy, brightly colored animals illustrate the questions.

Demuth, Patricia

524 *Inside Your Busy Body*. Ill. by Paige Billin-Frye. Putnam, 1993. ISBN 0-448-40189-4. SERIES: All Aboard Books. SUBJECTS: Human body; Science. RL C.

Muscles, lungs (air bags), digestion, brain (big boss on top), and senses are introduced in a few sentences, and illustrated with flat cutout collages, mostly of children.

525 *Snakes*. Ill. by Judith Moffatt. Photos by Paul Dyer. Putnam, 1993. ISBN 0-448-40514-8. SERIES: All Aboard Reading. SUBJECTS: Animals—Snakes; Science. RL A.

The characteristics of about a dozen snakes are introduced, and illustrated with exceptional colored and patterned heavy paper cutouts. The python, boa, cobra, rat, and rattlesnake, as well as the garter, green, thread, mud, cottonmouth, and sidewinder are included.

Dennis, Wesley

526 *Tumble: The Story of a Mustang*. Ill. by author. Hastings House, 1966, o.p. SUBJECTS: Animals—Horses—Fiction. RL C.
After a spell in a rodeo, Tumble succeeds his father as king of the mustangs. The sympathetic, elegant language has pencil illustrations.

Denzel, Justin

527 *Jumbo: Giant Circus Elephant*. Ill. by Richard Amundsen. Garrard, 1973, o.p. SERIES: Famous Animal Stories. SUBJECTS: Animals—Elephants; Circuses. RL B.
A true story tells about a small, gentle elephant who delighted fans for 20 years on both sides of the Atlantic. Full color illustrations show the drama of Jumbo's farewell to the circus.

dePaola, Tomie

528 *Cloud Book*. Ill. by author. Holiday House, 1975. ISBN 0-8234-0259-2. SUBJECTS: Weather—Clouds. RL C.
An index is included in this lively presentation of information and sayings about clouds. Children, animals, and imagination abound in the simple, decorative illustrations.

529 *The Kids' Cat Book*. Ill. by author. Holiday House, 1979. ISBN 0-8234-0365-3. SUBJECTS: Pet care; Pets—Cats. RL B.
Cat history and care is intriguingly presented when a boy visits Granny Twinkle. Add the author's outstanding creamy pastel illustrations to the text for a book that should be owned universally.

530 *Oliver Button Is a Sissy*. Ill. by author. Harcourt, hb and pap., 1979. ISBN 0-15-257852-8. SUBJECTS: Dancing—Fiction; Self-esteem—Fiction; Sex roles—Fiction. RL B.
Oliver likes to draw and read, play jump rope—and dance. Although the boys at school tease him, and his father thinks he is a sissy, Oliver revels in dance lessons and the teasing turns to admiration. Drawings are in turquoise and cocoa.

531 *The Quicksand Book*. Ill. by author. Holiday House, 1977; pap., 1984. ISBN 0-8234-0291-6. SUBJECTS: Nature; Science. RL C.
Jungle Boy corrects misconceptions people have about quicksand while Jungle GIRL sinks. When *he* falls in, she is in no hurry to help him out. Good information is presented in an arresting way and ably illustrated with hand-lettered cartoons and fact boxes.

de Saint Mars, Dominique

532 *Lily Fights with Her Brother*. Ill. by Serge Bloch and Cathy Mini. Child's World, 1993. ISBN 0-89565-980-8. SERIES: About Me. SUBJECTS: Behavior—Fiction; Siblings—Fiction. RL A.
Lily and Max turn the tables on their parents when they reflect their new lesson, "you are big enough and smart enough to solve your own problems, and I love both of you." Cartoon characters use very realistic dialogue and situations for significant learning.

533 *Max Is Shy*. Ill. by Serge Bloch and Cathy Mini. Child's World, 1992. ISBN 0-685-60114-5. SERIES: About Me. SUBJECTS: Behavior—Shyness; Self-esteem. RL B.
With exaggerated cartoons and pointed dialogue, Max's social terrors are illustrated, as well as the perceptions neighborhood children have of him. A few illustrated questions at the end point out some antidotes to shyness.

Dewey, Ariane

534 *Laffite, the Pirate*. Ill. by author. Greenwillow, 1985; ISBN 0-688-04578-2. SUBJECTS: Historical fiction; Pirates—Fiction; United States—1783–1865—Fiction. RL C.
Rousing stories of Laffite the pirate's bravado and occasional generosity and legends of treasure troves are retold by Dewey. Her colorful, decorative illustrations have clear lines and flat colors.

DeWitt, Lynda

535 *What Will the Weather Be?* Ill. by Carolyn Croll. HarperCollins, 1991. ISBN 0-06-021597-6. SERIES: Let's-Read-and-Find-Out Science Books. SUBJECTS: Science; Weather. RL C.

DeWitt, Lynda (cont.)

Descriptions of warm and cold fronts and air pressure and the way meteorologists measure them are simple and well illustrated. Information is related to predicting weather so farmers know when to plant, and people know what to wear, and when a storm is anticipated.

Dineen, Jacqueline

536 *Let's Look at Rain*. Ill. by Carolyn Scrace. Bookwright, 1989, o.p. SERIES: Let's Look At. SUBJECTS: Nature; Water. RL B.
The water cycle, collection and uses of water, weather, and storms related to the water cycle are introduced. Includes glossary and index. Acceptable pastel drawings.

Dines, Glen

537 *John Muir*. Ill. by author. Putnam, 1974, o.p. SERIES: See and Read Biography. SUBJECTS: Biographies; Nature. RL B.
Inventor and naturalist John Muir wrote lovingly about the wilderness. His work helped to save large tracts of land as parks for others to enjoy. This well-told, simple story has forest green, black, and gray colored drawings.

Dobkin, Bonnie

538 *Collecting*. Ill. by Rick Hackney. Childrens Pr., 1993. ISBN 0-516-02015-3. SERIES: Rookie Readers. SUBJECTS: Collecting and collectors; Stories in rhyme. RL A.
In a 96-word vocabulary, the fun of collecting—from stamps to shells, from comic books to insects, from posters to rockets—is shown. Colorful, lively illustrations accompany the text.

Dolch, Edward W., and Dolch, Marguerite P.

539 *Aesop's Stories*. Ill. by Marguerite P. Dolch. Garrard, 1951, o.p. SERIES: Pleasure Reading. SUBJECTS: Animals—Fiction; Fables. RL B.
Fifty-six familiar fables are retold in simple but smoothly flowing language, with morals

intact. Drawings with red coloring are dated, however.

540 *Circus Stories*. Ill. by Dee Wallace. Garrard, 1956, o.p. SERIES: Basic Vocabulary. SUBJECTS: Circuses—Fiction. RL B.
The quality of stories varies, from the sentimental one of a dog saving the audience from a lion on the loose, to the high drama of a fall by the famous Wallendas. Plain drawings add little.

541 *Folk Stories*. Ill. by Marguerite P. Dolch. Garrard, 1952, o.p. SERIES: Basic Vocabulary. SUBJECTS: Folklore—Europe. RL B.
Twenty folktales include nursery tales such as "The Pot That Would Not Walk," "Lazy Jack," and "The Three Wishes." Both the retelling and the drawings are plain, but they make traditional tales accessible to young readers.

542 *Lion and Tiger Stories*. Ill. by Charles Forsythe. Garrard, 1957, o.p. SERIES: Basic Vocabulary. SUBJECTS: Animals—Lions—Fiction; Animals—Tigers—Fiction; Folklore. RL B.
Traditional tales as well as circus adventures are retold well. Each story begins with an ink drawing with gold highlights.

543 *Lodge Stories*. Ill. by Billy M. Jackson. Garrard, 1957, o.p. SERIES: Basic Vocabulary. SUBJECTS: Folklore—Native Americans; Native Americans—Legends. RL A.
This book encompasses 18 authentic Native American tales coming from the Cherokee, Creek, Alabama, Yuchi, Choctaw, Natchez, and Seminole tribes. These well-told tales are headed by ink drawings of animals with orange background.

544 *Once There Was a Bear*. Ill. by Gerald McCann. Garrard, 1962, o.p. SERIES: First Reading. SUBJECTS: Animals—Bears; Folklore. RL B.
One hundred and ten sight words plus one new word per page are used to tell eight stories of bears, some true, some folktales. There is a good variety in style and outcome among the stories. The stories are illustrated with ink drawings highlighted in red and blue.

545 *Once There Was a Monkey*. Ill. by Kenyon Shannon. Garrard, 1962, o.p. SERIES: First

Reading. SUBJECTS: Animals—Monkeys—Fiction; Folklore. RL C.

The end of the book lists the eight stories about monkeys from India, Africa, Tibet, Brazil, and the Philippines. The language used in this book is very abbreviated. Rose and green highlight pedestrian drawings.

546 *Stories from Old Russia*. Ill. by James Lewicki. Garrard, 1964, o.p. SERIES: Folklore of the World. SUBJECTS: Folklore—Russia; Russia—Fiction. RL C.

Twenty-one traditional tales, of Vasilisa, Baba Yaga, and Ivan the Fool, are followed by a mini-pronunciation guide. Full color paintings are far superior to illustrations in most Dolch readers.

547 *Tepee Stories*. Ill. by Robert S. Kerr. Garrard, 1955, o.p. SERIES: Basic Vocabulary. SUBJECTS: Folklore—Native Americans; Native Americans—Fiction. RL C.

Blackfoot, Pawnee, Cheyenne, Kiowa, Wichita, Sioux, Crow, and Arikara tribal stories are retold in this book. Creation myths, tales of Coyote, and stories of giants, animals, and magic are exceptionally well told, but the drawings in red are very dated.

548 *"Why" Stories*. Ill. by Marguerite P. Dolch. Garrard, 1958, o.p. SERIES: Basic Vocabulary. SUBJECTS: Animals—Fiction; Folklore. RL A.

Stories, such as why Bear has a little tail, why Woodpecker looks for bugs, and why Jellyfish has no bones, are told in simple yet fluid, rhythmic language. Green colored drawings are dated.

Dolch, Marguerite P.

549 *Once There Was a Coyote*. Ill. by Carl Hauge and Mary Hauge. Garrard, 1975, o.p. SERIES: First Reading. SUBJECTS: Animals—Coyotes—Fiction; Folklore—Native Americans. RL B.

In simple, effective language, these stories tell why Coyote is smart, why he is a dirty color, why he does not crawl, why the volcano smokes, and how Coyote escaped from the Giants. Coyote looks appealingly doglike in simple drawings.

550 *Stories from Africa*. Ill. by Vincent Smith. Garrard, 1975, o.p. SERIES: Folklore of the World. SUBJECTS: Folklore—Africa. RL B.

Sixteen stories include the creation of man and woman, why we have rain, and a story about a "foolish" man who won a bet. Graphically pleasing illustrations are in flat primitive style with deep vivid colors.

Donnelly, Judy

551 *Tut's Mummy: Lost and Found*. Ill. by James Watling. Random House, hb and pap., 1988. ISBN 0-394-99189-3. SERIES: Step into Reading. SUBJECTS: Egypt, ancient. RL C.

The drama of finding of Tutankhamen's tomb is presented factually. Full color pastel drawings are taken from tomb paintings; the poor-quality black and white photos detract.

Donnelly, Liza

552 *Dinosaur Beach*. Ill. by author. Scholastic, 1989. SUBJECTS: Dinosaurs—Fiction; Fantasy. RL B.

A boy and his dog, Bones, are at a beach, where Bones' sand dinosaur creates a panic. The boy and Bones then travel to Dinosaur Beach, viewing a dozen dinosaurs who have created a sand sculpture of *them!* Simple, well-crafted story has soft pastel drawings and a brief description of each dinosaur.

Dorros, Arthur

553 *Ant Cities*. Ill. by author. HarperCollins, 1987. ISBN 0-690-04570-0. SERIES: Let's-Read-and-Find-Out Science Books. SUBJECTS: Animals—Ants; Nature. RL C.

An overview of the social organization, food, and types of ants is given, along with such details as how the antennae are used and how to build one's own ant city. Soft watercolors give cutaways and close-up views of ant cities.

554 *Elephant Families*. Ill. by author. HarperCollins, 1994. ISBN 0-06-022949-7. SERIES: Let's-Read-and-Find-Out Science Books. SUBJECTS: Animals—Elephants; Science. RL B.

Dorros, Arthur (cont.)

Elephants weigh as much as a large truck and may walk 40 miles a day looking for food and water. The watercolor illustrations are simple and appealing. Additional facts about elephants are added in small type.

555 *Feel the Wind*. Ill. by author. HarperCollins, 1989. ISBN 0-690-04741-X. SERIES: Let's-Read-and-Find-Out Science Books. SUBJECTS: Science. RL C.
Beginning by introducing familiar results that demonstrate the characteristics of wind, the text continues by describing the causes and uses of wind. Soft watercolors personalize and enhance this excellent text.

556 *Follow the Water from Brook to Ocean*. Ill. by author. HarperCollins, 1991. ISBN 0-06-021599-2. SERIES: Let's-Read-and-Find-Out Science Books. SUBJECTS: Nature; Science; Water. RL C.
The movement of water is traced downhill from the downspouts of houses to streams and rivers, over waterfalls and through canyons to the sea. Some of the plants, animals, and even smells en route are sketched. This is an excellent replacement for the Bartlett books, now out of print.

557 *Me and My Shadow*. Ill. by author. Scholastic, 1990. ISBN 0-590-42772-5. SUBJECTS: Science; Shadows. RL A.
Complex ideas such as sonar and x-ray shadows and eclipses are built on a simple base of chasing one's own shadow, trying shadow puppetry, or hand shadows. Simple drawings of children at play include their own dialogue.

558 *Pretzels*. Ill. by author. Greenwillow, 1981, o.p. SERIES: Read-alone. SUBJECTS: Humorous stories. RL C.
I Freyem Fine's biscuit dough, after being used as an anchor chain, is reconstituted as a pretzel. This tall tale is illustrated with ink and two-tone washes.

559 *Rain Forest Secrets*. Ill. by author. Scholastic, 1990. ISBN 0-590-43369-5. SUBJECTS: Rain Forests; Science. RL C.
The profusion of life in the rivers and in the rain forest, from the floor to the canopy, is suggested. There are 40 kinds of ants on one

tree! A backyard experiment and the author's early adventure as a four-year old sitting on the tail of the alligator add to rain forest lore.

Dorsky, Blanche

560 *Harry: A True Story*. Ill. by Muriel Batherman. Prentice-Hall, 1977, o.p. SUBJECTS: Animals—Rabbits—Fiction. School stories. RL C.
Harry, the nursery school's pet rabbit, is "not himself," and it takes a trip to the vet to find out why. Delicate ink sketches are in pastel colors except for the black rabbit.

Dreifus, Miriam

561 *Brave Betsy*. Ill. by Sheila Greenwald. Putnam, 1961, o.p. SERIES: See and Read. SUBJECTS: Lost, being—Fiction; Toys—Dolls and dollhouses—Fiction. RL A.
When Joan is trapped in the empty school, her doll Betsy leads her parents to her rescue. Green colored pencil alternating with red illustrates this simple tale.

Drescher, Henrik

562 *Whose Scaly Tail? African Animals You'd Like to Meet*. Ill. by author. Macmillan, 1987, o.p. SUBJECTS: Animals. RL A.
Despite limited vocabulary and liberal ink and watercolor clues, the animals—aardvark, elephant, giraffe, gorilla, pangolin, redtail monkey, and porcupine—are not all easy to identify. Appealing drawings accompany the question-and-answer format.

Dubowski, Cathy E., and Dubowski, Mark

563 *Pretty Good Magic*. Ill. by Mark Dubowski. Random House, hb and pap., 1987. ISBN 0-394-99068-4. SERIES: Step into Reading. SUBJECTS: Animals—Rabbits—Fiction; Humorous stories; Magic—Fiction. RL C.
The town of Forty Winks is so quiet that Presto decides to learn a new, impressive trick to wake everyone up—and finds himself stuck with dozens of rabbits. Comical pencil and wash drawings successfully complement the text.

E

Eastman, Patricia

564 *Sometimes Things Change*. Ill. by Seymour Fleischman. Childrens Pr., 1983. ISBN 0-516-02044-7. SERIES: Rookie Readers. SUBJECTS: Change. RL A.
Things change: caterpillars, tadpoles, eggs, grapes, seeds, buds, babies, strangers, clouds, and so forth. Some rather complex ideas for beginning readers using a 47 word vocabulary. Simple ink and wash drawings focus on children and animals.

Eastman, Philip D.

565 *Are You My Mother?* Ill. by author. Beginner, 1960. ISBN 0-394-90018-9. SERIES: I Can Read It All By Myself. SUBJECTS: Growing up—Fiction; Mothers—Fiction; Parent and child—Fiction. RL A.
Baby Bird hatches while Mother is out digging worms. He seeks her in the barnyard and is hoisted by a snorting machine—into his own nest just in time to meet his mother. Brown pencil drawings have yellow and red highlights, complementing this reassuring tale.

566 *Best Nest*. Ill. by author. Beginner, 1968. ISBN 0-394-90051-0. SUBJECTS: Animals—Birds—Fiction; Houses—Fiction. RL B.
Mr. Bird's search for a better nest demonstrates that a shoe, a mailbox, and a church steeple all have their drawbacks. Simple comic illustrations underline his relief when he finds his wife safe—back in the old nest.

567 *Flap Your Wings*. Ill. by author. Random House, 1969, o.p.; pap., 1984, o.p., 1991. ISBN 0-517-05445-0. SERIES: Early Bird. SUBJECTS: Animals—Birds—Fiction. RL A.
Mr. and Mrs. Bird hatch a foundling egg with surprising results. A well-constructed story that is illustrated simply. This reissue includes a cassette tape.

568 *Sam and the Firefly*. Ill. by author. Beginner, 1958, o.p. SERIES: I Can Read It All By Myself. SUBJECTS: Animals—Fireflies—Fiction; Animals—Owls—Fiction. RL A.
Gus the firefly's skill at spelling runs amok until he is saved from the consequences of his mischief by his friend Sam, an owl. Inventive humor has turquoise illustrations with yellow owl eyes and firefly writing.

Edwards, Anne

569 *Houdini*. Ill. by Joseph Ciardiello. Putnam, 1977, o.p. SERIES: See and Read. SUBJECTS: Biographies; Magic. RL C.
This true story of the best-known magician ever has great drama and human interest. Ink drawings add interesting details.

570 *P. T. Barnum*. Ill. by Marylin Hafner. Putnam, 1977, o.p. SERIES: See and Read Biography. SUBJECTS: Biographies; Circuses. RL C.
Barnum's colorful career is traced—from the small boy who always had a head for sums to the flamboyant showman. Gray tone drawings capture some of the excitement.

Edwards, Roberta

571 *Five Silly Fishermen*. Ill. by Sylvie Wickstrom. Random House, 1989. ISBN 0-679-80092-1. SERIES: Step into Reading. SUBJECTS: Folklore; Humorous stories; Storytelling. RL A.
A traditional tale about fishermen, each of whom forgets to count himself, is retold using very simple language. Pencil drawings with watercolor washes illustrate the large-type text.

Ehrlich, Amy

572 *Buck-Buck the Chicken*. Ill. by R. W. Alley. Random House, hb and pap., 1987. ISBN 0-394-98804-3. SERIES: Step into Reading. SUBJECTS: Animals—Chickens—Fiction; Humorous stories; Pets—Fiction. RL B.
Won by Nancy's father at the county fair, Buck-Buck is a pampered pet who does not seem to know how to act like a chicken. This delightfully silly story is illustrated with watercolors with ink detailing.

Ehrlich, Amy (cont.)

573 *Leo, Zack and Emmie*. Ill. by Steven Kellogg. Dial, hb and pap., 1981. ISBN 0-8037-4761-6. SERIES: Dial Easy-to-Read. SUBJECTS: Friendship—Fiction; School stories. RL B.

Emmie, as the newcomer, upsets the friendship between Leo and Zack. Four episodes of everyday experiences are warm and humorous, enhanced by delicious four-color action-filled illustrations.

574 *Leo, Zack and Emmie Together Again*. Ill. by Steven Kellogg. Dial, 1987. ISBN 0-8037-0382-1. SERIES: Dial Easy-to-Read. SUBJECTS: Friendship—Fiction. RL B.

Four stories tell how the friendship of these three is tested at school and in the neighborhood. The drawings add to the sense of mischief and express the emotions and warmth of childhood.

Ehrlich, Fred

575 *A Class Play with Ms. Vanilla*. Ill. by Martha Gradisher. Viking, 1992. ISBN 0-670-84651-1. SERIES: Hello Reading! SUBJECTS: Humorous stories; Plays—Fiction; Stories in rhyme. RL A.

The hunters grab the wolf's tail and pull his paws to save Little Red Riding Hood in this charming, reproducible play in rhyme for primary age children. Cartoon characters model the simple costumes and the action for a class production.

576 *Lunch Boxes*. Ill. by Martha Gradisher. Viking, 1991. ISBN 0-670-83860-8. SERIES: Hello Reading! SUBJECTS: School stories; Stories in rhyme. RL A.

Although a class at Oak Hill School walks peacefully to and from the lunchroom, they turn the lunchroom into a disaster area for a while. Cartoon drawings add action.

Elkin, Benjamin

577 *Big Jump and Other Stories*. Ill. by Katherine Evans. Beginner, 1958, o.p. SUBJECTS: Jokes and riddles—Fiction; Kings and queens—Fiction. RL A.

Ben solves the king's quandaries with creative thinking, but without high drama. Red and green colored pencil illustrations show the action but have minimal appeal except for those of Ben's puppy.

Elliott, Dan

578 *Ernie's Little Lie*. Ill. by Joe Mathieu. Random House, 1983. ISBN 0-394-85440-3. SERIES: Start-to-Read. SUBJECTS: Behavior—Lying—Fiction. RL B.

Ernie did not originally intend to claim someone else's artwork as his own, but he certainly feels better after confessing. Straightforward drawings show "Sesame Street" characters.

579 *Grover Learns to Read*. Ill. by Normand Chartier. Random House, 1985. ISBN 0-394-97498-0. SERIES: Start-to-Read. SUBJECTS: Books and reading—Fiction; Libraries—Fiction. RL B.

Grover is not sure he wants to learn to read if he misses out on his mother's bedtime story. Bright pastel drawings are of "Sesame Street" characters.

580 *My Doll Is Lost!* Ill. by Joe Mathieu. Random House, 1984. ISBN 0-679-83953-4; 0-394-96251-6. SERIES: Sesame Street Start-to-Read. SUBJECTS: Puppets and puppetry—Fiction; Toys—Fiction. RL A.

The characters of Sesame Street turn out to look for Herry's "beautiful" doll, but each is looking for a doll that resembles himself or herself. Sympathetic story with familiar characters.

581 *Oscar's Rotten Birthday*. Ill. by Normand Chartier. Random House, pap., 1992. ISBN 0-679-82400-6. SERIES: Sesame Street Start-to-Read. SUBJECTS: Birthdays—Fiction; Puppets and puppetry—Fiction. RL A.

Oscar the Grouch surprises everyone, including himself, by enjoying his birthday party, with presents of stinkweed, broken toys, peanut shells, and a jar of mud. Illustrations are typical cartoons of Sesame Street puppets.

Elting, Mary, and Folsom, Michael

582 *Q Is for Duck: An Alphabet Guessing Game*. Ill. by Jack Kent. Houghton

Mifflin, hb and pap., 1980. ISBN 0-395-29437-1. SUBJECTS: Alphabet—Fiction; Animals—Fiction. RL C.

This alphabet book is for older readers because the letters represent *verbs* not nouns. "L is for Frog Why? Because a Frog Leaps." However, the verbs used are not predictable or even logical. Drawings are charming.

Epstein, Sam, and Epstein, Beryl

583 *Hold Everything*. Ill. by Tomie dePaola. Holiday House, 1973, o.p. SUBJECTS: Science. RL C.

Sewing, adhesives, saliva, icing, staples, nails, and zippers are some of the ways things are held together. Creative possibilities such as holding hands and using "and" are suggested. Three-color illustrations give detail and humor.

584 *Pick It Up*. Ill. by Tomie dePaola. Holiday House, 1971, o.p. SUBJECTS: Human body—Hands; Science; Tools. RL C.

Using familiar objects or animals as examples, the many ways things are picked up are discussed. Alternating cocoa and turquoise and black and white drawings add humorous touches.

585 *Who Needs Holes?* Ill. by Tomie dePaola. Hawthorn, 1970, o.p. SUBJECTS: Concepts. RL A.

Armholes, buttonholes, colanders, shower heads, drills, lifesavers, and keyholes are some of the common holes explored in this creative text using a self-discovery experimental approach. DePaola's appealing people and animal drawings alternate ink with lavender and golden brown.

Esbensen, Barbara J.

586 *Baby Whales Drink Milk*. Ill. by Lambert Davis. HarperCollins, 1994. ISBN 0-06-021552-6. SERIES: Let's-Read-and-Find-Out Science Books. SUBJECTS: Animals—Whales; Science. RL A.

Information about mammals and the birth and habits of humpback whales is introduced in very simple vocabulary, accompanied by simple drawings of whales. A few facts about other types of whales and where whales can be observed is appended.

587 *Sponges Are Skeletons*. Ill. by Holly Keller. HarperCollins, 1993. ISBN 0-06-021034-6. SERIES: Let's-Read-and-Find-Out Science Books. SUBJECTS: Oceans and ocean life; Science. RL A.

Sponges have survived 700 million years. The parallels to the skeleton of a boy and his cat are shown, as well as the life of a sponge under the sea, and how the sponges get from there to the bathtub. Simple ink and watercolor illustrations accompany the text.

Eugenie, and Olson, Mary C., reteller

588 *Kittens for Keeps*. Ill. by Eugenie. Western, 1987. ISBN 0-307-03678-2. SERIES: Step Ahead Beginning Reader. SUBJECTS: Grandparents—Fiction; Pets—Cats—Fiction; Seashore—Fiction. RL A.

Visiting her grandmother at the seashore, Meg finds two kittens and keeps them until the end of the summer when one stays with her grandmother and the other goes home to the city with Meg. Illustrated with sweet watercolor paintings.

Evans, Katherine

589 *The Boy Who Cried Wolf*. Ill. by author. Whitman, 1960, o.p. SUBJECTS: Folklore. RL C.

This traditional tale of a shepherd boy who cries wolf once too often is retold well. Crayon drawings give a folktale flavor.

590 *Camel in the Tent*. Ill. by author. Whitman, 1961, o.p. SUBJECTS: Folklore—Turkey; Turkey—Fiction. RL C.

Traditional moral tale tells how a man lost a sultan's riches by letting a camel get his head in his tent. Textured crayon illustrates this foolish tale well.

591 *Maid and Her Pail of Milk*. Ill. by author. Whitman, 1959, o.p. SUBJECTS: Folklore—Netherlands; Netherlands—Fiction. RL B.

"Never count your chickens until they are hatched" is the moral a country maid longing for citified finery discovers. Crayon and pencil drawings are appropriate.

Evans, Katherine (cont.)

592 *The Man, the Boy, and the Donkey*. Ill. by author. Whitman, 1958, o.p. SUBJECTS: Folklore—Netherlands; Netherlands—Fiction. RL C.
This moral tale is well told with an authentic Dutch flavor. Black and white pencil drawings alternate with full color ones.

593 *One Good Deed Deserves Another*. Ill. by author. Whitman, 1964, o.p. SUBJECTS: Folklore—Mexico; Mexico—Fiction. RL C.
A traditional tale of Senor Coyote and Snake is retold with a boy's wise action saving a family from a ruffian. Ink drawings alternate with color, showing authentic folk details.

Eyles, Heather

594 *A Zoo in Our House*. Ill. by Andy Cooke. Warner, 1988, o.p. SERIES: Early Reader. SUBJECTS: Zoos—Fiction. RL C.
One by one some zoo animals visit a little boy's house, then *all* come for a party! Large, colorful zany animals and the messes they create are eye-catching.

F

Falken, Linda C.

595 *Kitty's First Airplane Trip*. Ill. by Lynn Adams. Scholastic, 1993. ISBN 0-590-45788-8. SERIES: Read with Me. SUBJECTS: Airplanes—Fiction; Pets—Fiction. RL A.
A toddler lets his kitty loose during their first airplane flight. Soft ink and wash drawings.

Farley, Walter

596 *Little Black, a Pony*. Ill. by James Schucker. Beginner, 1961. ISBN 0-394-90021-9. SUBJECTS: Animals—Horses—Fiction. RL A.
When his master begins riding a bigger horse, his former riding horse Little Black becomes sad and tries to keep up. Only when the boy is saved by Little Black after falling through the ice does he fully appreciate his faithful pony.

This is an absorbing horse story despite its dated illustrations.

Feder, Paula K.

597 *Where Does the Teacher Live?* Ill. by Lillian Hoban. Dutton, 1979, o.p. SUBJECTS: School stories. RL B.
The answer to a question many children ponder—"where does teacher live?"—is discovered by the reader, but not the children of this slight story. Hoban's soft watercolors are suitable.

Fehlner, Paul

598 *Dog and Cat*. Ill. by Maxie Chambliss. Childrens Pr., 1990. ISBN 0-516-05353-1. SERIES: My First Reader. SUBJECTS: Animals—Cats—Fiction; Animals—Dogs—Fiction. RL A.
In a text of just 20 words, the old dog chases, after a fashion, the fat cat, with disastrous results. The ink and watercolor illustrations carry most of the humor.

Feldman, Barbara

599 *Going, Going*. Ill. by author. Firefly, 1989. ISBN 1-55037-045-6. SERIES: Annick Toddler Series. SUBJECTS: Cars—Fiction; Dreams—Fiction. RL A.
With rich fabric appliqué, the author enriches the story of a boy whose world is enlarged when his mother learns to drive a car. Illustrations employ very detailed and inventive patterns and textures, and vivid colors.

600 *Stephen's Frog*. Ill. by author. Firefly, 1991. ISBN 1-55037-200-9. SUBJECTS: Animals—Frogs and toads—Fiction; Stories without words. RL A.
With colorful fabric collages, the author shows the story of a boy who takes his frog on an airplane to visit his grandparents, and ends up letting it go. The whole is very pleasing to eye and imagination.

Fernandes, Eugenie

601 *Just You and Me*. Ill. by author. Firefly, 1993. ISBN 1-55037-324-2. SUBJECTS: Babies—Fiction; Sleep—Fiction. RL A.

Neither the river nor the wind, nor the moon's story, nor the birds' lullaby, nor fishes' heads put the baby to sleep so Auntie Pearl will baby-sit so Mother and Heather can have some time together. Remarkable molded clay in crisp colors illustrates the whimsical story.

Fernandes, Kim

602 *Visiting Granny*. Ill. by author. Firefly, 1990. ISBN 1-55037-084-7. SUBJECTS: Concepts—Numbers—Fiction; Farm and country life—Fiction; Grandparents—Fiction. RL A.
While two children play, listen to a story, and help Granny in the kitchen, some lambs, goats, piglets, and kittens wander in and get shooed outside. Very appealing detailed molded clay scenes alternate with pages with large print.

603 *Zebo and the Dirty Planet*. Ill. by author. Firefly, 1991. ISBN 1-55037-183-5. SUBJECTS: Conservation—Fiction. RL B.
With very colorful dimensional clay figures and landscape, the author illustrates a slim story about Zebo, who brings pairs of animals from the dirty planet to earth. Illustrations are very appealing.

Fine, Jane

604 *Surprise!* Ill. by Mary Morgan. Viking, 1988. ISBN 0-670-82036-9. SERIES: Hello Reading! SUBJECTS: Birthdays—Fiction; Families—Fiction; Mothers—Fiction. RL B.
Three young children get up very early and quietly prepare a tray of juice and cookies for their mother's birthday. The text is very brief, relying on the pictures of the excited children and their rambunctious cat to help tell the story. Illustrations are in bright, vibrant watercolors.

Finsand, Mary J.

605 *The Town That Moved*. Ill. by Reg Sandland. Carolrhoda, 1983, o.p., 1991, pap. ISBN 0-440-40489-4. SERIES: On My Own. SUBJECTS: Historical fiction. RL C.
In the 1920s, when iron ore was discovered under the town of Hibbing, Minnesota, the buildings were rolled one by one on logs to a nearby location. Pencil drawings show the action.

Firmin, Peter

606 *Basil Brush and the Windmills*. Ill. by author. Prentice-Hall, 1979, o.p. SUBJECTS: Animals—Foxes—Fiction; Animals—Moles—Fiction; Inventors and inventions—Fiction. RL C.
Most of Basil the fox's inventions to save money turn out disastrously, save one. Humorous ink sketches are highlighted in red.

607 *Basil Brush Gets a Medal*. Ill. by author. Prentice-Hall, 1973, o.p. SUBJECTS: Animals—Foxes—Fiction; Animals—Moles—Fiction; Cumulative tales. RL C.
This original cumulative tale recounts Basil the fox and Harry the mole's adventures getting milk for the princess's porridge before deserved medals can be awarded. Red wash highlights ink animal drawings.

608 *Basil Brush Goes Boating*. Ill. by author. Prentice-Hall, 1969, o.p. SUBJECTS: Animals—Foxes—Fiction; Fishing—Fiction; Friendship—Fiction. RL B.
Basil the fox and his friend Harry the mole manage to leave all of their equipment behind when they go fishing. Gentle humor warms this tale of friendship; blue highlights ink drawings.

609 *Basil Brush Goes Flying*. Ill. by author. Prentice-Hall, 1977, o.p. SUBJECTS: Animals—Foxes—Fiction; Animals—Moles—Fiction. RL B.
Irrepressible optimism fuels Basil the fox and his friend Harry the mole's flying adventures. A blue wash brightens action-filled ink drawings.

610 *Basil Brush in the Jungle*. Ill. by author. Prentice-Hall, 1970, o.p. SUBJECTS: Animals—Foxes—Fiction; Humorous stories; India—Fiction. RL C.
Basil the fox takes the cage he makes to India, where the butterfly, crocodile, snake, and tiger are happier in the jungle than in his cage. Humor is used in this exotic adventure; ink and green wash sketches focus on animals, an

Firmin, Peter (cont.)

unforgettable Indian ferryman, and an umbrella man.

611 *Basil Brush on the Trail.* Ill. by author. Prentice-Hall, 1979, o.p. SUBJECTS: Animals—Foxes—Fiction; Animals—Moles—Fiction; Mystery and detective stories. RL B.

Basil the fox and Harry the mole's bungling attempts do not uncover the real thief of the silver tennis trophies until the owner returns home. Ink drawings have orange highlights.

612 *Boastful Mr. Bear.* Ill. by author. Delacorte, 1989. ISBN 0-440-50083-4. SERIES: The Old Tree Stories. SUBJECTS: Animals—Bears—Fiction; Animals—Foxes—Fiction; Behavior—Bragging—Fiction. RL A.

Mr. Bear rejects help from all his woodland friends—until he sits in a blackthorn bush. Typical cute pencil and watercolor illustrations depict a simplified traditional theme.

613 *Foolish Miss Crow.* Ill. by author. Delacorte, 1989. ISBN 0-440-50082-6. SERIES: The Old Tree Stories. SUBJECTS: Animals—Crows—Fiction; Animals—Foxes—Fiction. RL B.

Wily Mr. Fox lures vain Miss Crow with a scarf, a hat, jewelry, and his camera. Typical Firmin cartoon characters appear in illustrations.

614 *Happy Miss Rat.* Ill. by author. Delacorte, 1989. ISBN 0-440-50081-8. SERIES: The Old Tree Stories. SUBJECTS: Animals—Rats—Fiction; Music and musicians—Fiction. RL A.

Like Lionni's Frederick, Miss Rat plays her banjo and sings instead of preparing for winter, but shares in the harvest as she shares her songs. Typical Firmin cutesy watercolor forest animals are depicted in illustrations.

615 *Hungry Mr. Fox.* Ill. by author. Delacorte, 1989. ISBN 0-440-50034-6. SERIES: The Old Tree Stories. SUBJECTS: Animals—Fiction; Animals—Foxes—Fiction. RL A.

A watered-down version of "The Three Billy Goats Gruff" has the mouse, rat, and hare escaping Mr. Fox, who goes after the bigger one who follows—a warm fuzzy bear.

Fisher, Aileen

616 *Always Wondering: Some Favorite Poems of Aileen Fisher.* Ill. by Joan Sandin. HarperCollins, 1991. ISBN 0-06-022851-2. SUBJECTS: Poetry. RL C.

Appealing poems are loosely gathered into sections, and include such topics as animals, holidays, shooting stars, snails, and seasons. Pencil drawings begin each of four sections.

617 *The House of a Mouse.* Ill. by Joan Sandin. HarperCollins, 1988. ISBN 0-06-021849-5. SUBJECTS: Animals—Mice—Fiction; Poetry. RL C.

The world of different kinds of mice is explored—the dangers, tracks, nests, and habits—in lighthearted simple verse. Soft pencil drawings beautifully complement this rhythmic celebration of mice.

618 *My Cat Has Sapphire Eyes.* Ill. by Marie Angel. HarperCollins, 1973. o.p. SUBJECTS: Animals—Cats—Fiction; Pets—Cats—Fiction; Poetry. RL B.

Playful, sleepy-though-alert, acrobatic, protective cats and kittens live in this book of celebratory poetry. Expressive illustrations are in colored pencil.

619 *When It Comes to Bugs.* Ill. by Chris Degen and Bruce Degen. HarperCollins, 1986, o.p. SUBJECTS: Nature; Poetry. RL B.

Beetles and dragonflies, caterpillars, spiders, and centipedes are celebrated in inventive poetry with touches of whimsy. Text is becomingly illustrated with color overlays on black scratchboard by the Degens.

Fisher, Ronald M.

620 *Cottontails: Little Rabbits of Field and Forest.* Photos. National Geographic, 1989, o.p. SERIES: Books for Young Explorers. SUBJECTS: Animals—Rabbits; Nature. RL C.

Excellent color photos show some of the 14 kinds of cottontails at different stages of development in different habitats. A picture dictionary of appealing domestic rabbits, a bibliography, and additional facts are appended.

FitzGerald, Cathleen

621 *Let's Find Out about Words*. Ill. by
Georgia Froom. Watts, 1971, o.p.
SUBJECTS: English language. RL B.
FitzGerald celebrates the contributions of various cultures to the English language, as well
as the history and evolution of our language.
Information is well presented. Ink drawings
are against a gold or orange background.

Fitz-Gerald, Christine

622 *I Can Be a Mother*. Photos. Childrens Pr.,
1989. ISBN 0-516-41914-5. SERIES: I Can Be.
SUBJECTS: Mothers; Parent and child. RL B.
Good basic information regarding birth and
adoptive mothers and stepmothers is given. A
picture glossary precedes the text and a second glossary ends the book. Exceptional color
photos brighten the text.

Fleischman, Sid

623 *Kate's Secret Riddle Book*. Ill. by Barbara
Bottner. Watts, 1977, o.p. SERIES: Easy-
Read Story. SUBJECTS: Jokes and riddles.
RL B.
Riddles for young readers are woven into a
story about some girls trying to find out the
answer to their friend Wally's riddle. Yellow
and pumpkin colors predominate in illustrations with humor (but weird faces).

Florian, Douglas

624 *Monster Motel*. Ill. by author. Harcourt,
1993. ISBN 0-15-255320-7. SUBJECTS:
Monsters—Fiction; Poetry. RL C.
Shy Shegs who never come out of their eggs,
Gazzygoos who touch feet and grow a daisy
when they meet, the Crim who cries a river
(and luckily knows how to swim), share the
spotlight with the Brilly who takes its bath in
lemon Jell-O. Whimsical childlike watercolors
enhance imaginative poems.

625 *A Potter*. Ill. by author. Greenwillow, 1991.
ISBN 0-688-10101-1. SUBJECTS: Careers. RL A.
In simple rhythmic language and drawings
with black felt pen, crayon, and colored pencils and watercolor washes with immense

graphic appeal, the author describes the work
of a female potter.

Flower, Phyllis

626 *Barn Owl*. Ill. by Cherryl Pape.
HarperCollins, 1978, o.p. SERIES: I Can
Read Science. SUBJECTS: Animals—Owls;
Science. RL B.
The life cycle of a barn owlet is traced, simply
and eloquently. Pencil drawings with tan and
gray washes show the drama of learning to fly
and the first successful hunt.

Fowler, Allan

627 *How Do You Know It's Fall?* Photos.
Childrens Pr., 1992. ISBN 0-516-04922-4.
SERIES: Rookie Read-About Science.
SUBJECTS: Nature; Seasons—Fall. RL A.
The beginning of school and the picking of
apples, the jack-o-lanterns and the football
game, herald the season. Text is illustrated
with photos of landscapes, animals, and multiethnic children.

628 *How Do You Know It's Summer?* Photos.
Childrens Pr., 1992. ISBN 0-516-04923-2.
SERIES: Rookie Read-About Science.
SUBJECTS: Nature; Seasons—Summer. RL B.
The busy farmer and the fresh strawberries,
the beach and camp, the storm and the fireworks, illustrate the joys of summer. This book
has simple, large-print text with color photos
and a brief picture dictionary.

Fox, Charles P.

629 *When Autumn Comes*. Ill. by author.
Reilly & Lee, 1966, o.p. SERIES: Dial Easy-
to-Read-Photo-Story. SUBJECTS: Animals;
Nature; Seasons—Fall. RL A.
The changes before winter for birds, small
mammals, plants, and trees are described,
emphasizing observing and listening. Black
and white photos include many appealing
close-ups.

630 *When Summer Comes*. Ill. by author.
Reilly & Lee, 1966, o.p. SERIES: Dial Easy-
to-Read-Photo-Story. SUBJECTS: Animals;
Nature; Seasons—Summer. RL A.

Fox, Charles P. (cont.)

The reader is invited to observe frogs, ducks, snakes, skunks, dragonflies, woodchucks, raccoons, hawks, wasps, owls, and a mystery egg. Black and white photos include the young in their nests.

631 *When Winter Comes*. Ill. by author. Reilly & Lee, 1962, o.p. SERIES: Dial Easy-to-Read-Photo-Story. SUBJECTS: Animals; Nature; Seasons—Winter. RL A.
From raccoons and skunks to foxes and opossums, the animals' activities—and tracks—are described and illustrated with black and white photo close-ups.

Fradin, Dennis

632 *Cancer*. Photos. Childrens Pr., hb and pap., 1988. ISBN 0-516-01210-X. SERIES: New True. SUBJECTS: Diseases. RL C.
Facts about cancer and what is known about it; also focus on smoking as an avoidable carcinogen. Excellent photos show healthy people, hospital procedures, and some diseased organs.

633 *Declaration of Independence*. Photos and drawings. Childrens Pr., 1988. ISBN 0-516-01153-7. SERIES: New True. SUBJECTS: United States—Revolution. RL C.
An index and glossary accompany nine short chapters in large print giving background information about the Declaration of Independence as well as its effects on our government. Photos and many drawings are in color.

634 *The Flag of the United States*. Photos. Childrens Pr., 1988. ISBN 0-516-01158-8. SERIES: New True. SUBJECTS: Flags; United States—History. RL C.
Ten chapters give the history and care of the American flag, the writing of the Star Spangled Banner, and the pledge to the flag. A glossary and index are appended to basic, well-presented information, liberally illustrated with good photos.

635 *Mercury*. Photos. Childrens Pr., 1989. ISBN 0-516-01186-3. SERIES: New True. SUBJECTS: Astronomy and astronomers; Science and scientists. RL C.
The history of the discovery and exploration of Mercury through telescopes and Mariner X is outlined in nine short chapters. Photos, lithographs, and drawings stretch the text; short glossary and index are appended.

636 *Neptune*. Photos. Childrens Pr., 1990. ISBN 0-516-01187-1. SERIES: New True. SUBJECTS: Astronomy and astronomers; Science and scientists. RL C.
An overview of the discovery of planets and the Voyager II visit is extended by color photos and a few lithographs and paintings. The large-print text is supplemented by a brief index and a glossary.

637 *The Pawnee*. Photos. Childrens Pr., 1988. ISBN 0-516-01155-3. SERIES: New True. SUBJECTS: Native Americans—Pawnee. RL C.
The history and life-style of the Pawnee are described in ten short chapters, with a glossary and index appended. Excellent color photos give details of symbolism on clothing and sacred objects.

638 *Pluto*. Photos. Childrens Pr., 1989. ISBN 0-516-01175-8. SERIES: New True. SUBJECTS: Astronomy and astronomers; Science and scientists. RL C.
Clyde Tombaugh discovered Pluto in 1930 with his handmade home telescope. Drawings, black and white photos, and some poor quality color photos illustrate the text.

639 *The Shoshoni*. Photos. Childrens Pr., 1988. ISBN 0-516-01156-1. SERIES: New True. SUBJECTS: Native Americans—Shoshoni. RL C.
The importance of song, dance, and story in Shoshoni life is added to the history, which includes Sacajawea. Close-up color photos of traditional clothing are most captivating.

640 *Thirteen Colonies*. Photos and drawings. Childrens Pr., 1988. ISBN 0-516-01157-X. SERIES: New True. SUBJECTS: United States—Colonial period. RL C.
The reasons the Spanish, English, French, and Africans came to America, how they lived and broke away from England, and the fate of the Indians are introduced in six short chapters. A glossary and index add to its accessibility. A chart shows population of each colony by decade. Liberally illustrated with excellent color photos.

641 *Uranus*. Photos. Childrens Pr., 1989. ISBN 0-516-01177-4. SERIES: New True. SUBJECTS: Astronomy and astronomers; Science and scientists. RL C.

The exploration of Uranus led to the discovery of Neptune and Pluto. Color photos with some mediocre drawings expand the large-print narrative. There is a brief index and a glossary.

642 *Venus*. Photos. Childrens Pr., 1989. ISBN 0-516-01168-5. SERIES: New True. SUBJECTS: Astronomy and astronomers; Science and scientists. RL C.

A discussion of the possibility of Venus as Earth's twin is one of six chapters giving basic information in large print. Color and black and white illustrations and an index and a glossary complete the work.

643 *The Voyager Space Probes*. Photos. Childrens Pr., hb and pap., 1985, o.p. SERIES: New True. SUBJECTS: Astronomy; Science; Space travel. RL C.

Excellent color photos illustrate current information about Jupiter and Saturn garnered by the Voyager space probe, which is still headed for Neptune. A glossary and index are appended.

Frasier, Debra

644 *On the Day You Were Born*. Ill. by author. Harcourt, 1991. ISBN 0-15-257995-8. SUBJECTS: Ecology; Human body—Growth. RL C.

A grand celebration of the wonders of the natural world told in cumulative rhythmic language with stunning graphics. The text touches on migration, the spinning earth, gravity, the sun, stars, and moon, tides and rain, trees, air, and finally singing people.

Freedman, Russell

645 *Dinosaurs and Their Young*. Ill. by Leslie Morrill. Holiday House, 1983. ISBN 0-8234-0496-X. SUBJECTS: Dinosaurs; Science. RL C.

How the recent discovery of a duckbill dinosaur nursery by a Montana high school teacher has altered scientists' ideas about how dinosaurs lived is detailed by this 1984 Newbery award winner.

Freeman, Charlotte M.

646 *A Day in the Life of a Horse Trainer*. Photos by Gayle Jann. Troll, 1988. ISBN 0-8167-1111-9. SERIES: A Day in the Life of. SUBJECTS: Animals—Horses; Careers. RL C.

This book presents Leslie Lenehan, an equestrian World Cup champion and member of the Olympic team, as she trains a horse and teaches other equestrians. It is interesting, with some accommodation to primary vocabularies. Illustrations are color photos.

Freschet, Berniece

647 *Little Black Bear Goes for a Walk*. Ill. by Glen Rounds. Scribner, 1977, o.p. SUBJECTS: Animals—Bears—Fiction. RL B.

Little Bear's first exploration on his own introduces him to bugs, porcupines, water, bees—and *honey*. The expressive ink sketches add humor.

648 *Lizard Lying in the Sun*. Ill. by Glen Rounds. Scribner, 1975, o.p. SUBJECTS: Animals—Lizards; Nature; Science. RL B.

Good information about lizards is presented in an absorbing way by focusing on one lizard. Intriguing ink sketches enhance the text.

649 *Moose Baby*. Ill. by Jim Arnosky. Putnam, 1979, o.p. SERIES: See and Read Nature. SUBJECTS: Animals—Moose; Nature. RL C.

Encounters with a skunk, a coyote, and fighting bull moose mark a baby moose's first year. The ink and wash sketches are very appealing.

650 *Possum Baby*. Ill. by Jim Arnosky. Putnam, 1978, o.p. SERIES: See and Read Nature. SUBJECTS: Animals—Opossum; Growing-up; Nature. RL C.

The trials of growing up are told from the point of view of a young possum—from birth to independence. The tale is interrupted briefly to give information about other marsupials. Arnosky's black ink drawings are very appealing.

The Friendly Beasts

651 *The Friendly Beasts: A Traditional Christmas Carol*. Ill. by Sarah Chamberlain. Dutton, 1991. ISBN 0-525-44773-3. SUBJECTS: Cumulative tale; Holidays—Christmas; Music and musicians. RL B.

The Friendly Beasts (cont.)

Multicolored linoleum block prints are high-lighted by hand with pastels of wheat and blue to accentuate the pastoral wonder of Jesus' birth.

Friskey, Margaret

652 *Indian Two Feet and the Wolf Cubs*. Ill. by John Hawkinson. Childrens Pr., 1971, o.p. SUBJECTS: Animals—Wolves—Fiction; Native Americans—Fiction; Pets—Wild animals—Fiction. RL B.
Indian Two Feet spends so much time watching the wolf family that he is included in their family circle. When he tries to adopt a cub, he is advised that other wolves will take care of any orphans. Watercolor drawings are especially good of the animals.

653 *Mystery of the Farmer's Three Fives*. Ill. by Lucy Hawkinson and John Hawkinson. Childrens Pr., 1963, o.p. SERIES: Reading Lab. SUBJECTS: Concepts—Numbers—Fiction; Farm and country life—Fiction; Mathematics—Fiction. RL A.
A 145-word vocabulary is used to sketch arithmetic skills in an imaginative way, using barnyard animals. Delicate ink and wash drawings lighten the lesson.

654 *Three Sides and the Round One*. Ill. by Mary Gehr. Childrens Pr., 1973, o.p. SUBJECTS: Concepts—Shape; Mathematics; Stories in rhyme. RL B.
Creative, rhythmic language introduces shapes of ordinary objects. Striking, simple shapes stand out on bright solid backgrounds.

655 *The True Book of the Moonwalk Adventure*. Photos by NASA. Childrens Pr., 1970, o.p. SUBJECTS: Science; Space. RL C.
Information about the moon is gained, along with some of the drama of the first moon walk, and the appearance of Earth from space. Each NASA photo faces relevant text.

Frith, Michael K.

656 *I'll Teach My Dog One Hundred Words*. Ill. by P. D. Eastman. Beginner, 1973. ISBN 0-394-82692-2. SERIES: Bright and Early. SUBJECTS: Humorous stories; Stories in rhyme. RL B.
Rhythmic humor teaching the reader, as well as the dog, 100 new words; accented by excellent comic drawings.

Fritz, Jean

657 *Surprising Myself*. Photos by Andrea F. Pfleger. Richard Owen, 1992. ISBN 1-878450-37-9. SERIES: Meet the Author. SUBJECTS: Biographies—Women; Books and reading; Writing and writers. RL C.
In typically refreshing style, Jean Fritz outlines how she writes—and relaxes. Photos show her at play at Virgin Gorda, and with her grandsons, as well as at work. Lively and interesting text.

Froman, Robert

658 *Bigger and Smaller*. Ill. by Gioia Fiammenghi. HarperCollins, 1971, o.p. SUBJECTS: Concepts—Size. RL C.
The relative nature of size is emphasized and some entertaining relationships are explored. Ink and wash drawings are graphically interesting.

Funai, Mamoru

659 *Moke and Poki in the Rain Forest*. Ill. by author. HarperCollins, 1971, o.p. SERIES: I Can Read Books. SUBJECTS: Folklore—Hawaii; Hawaii—Fiction; Rainbows—Fiction. RL A.
Moke and Poki are six-inch menehunes. With the help of their friends they build a house, sing to the moon, sail a bean-pod canoe, and search for rainbows. Turquoise and rose-brown colors create a tropical setting for the wee friends.

G

Gackenbach, Dick

660 *Hattie Be Quiet, Hattie Be Good*. Ill. by author. HarperCollins, 1977. ISBN 0-06-

021952-1. SERIES: Early I Can Read. SUBJECTS: Animals—Rabbits—Fiction; Behavior—Obedient—Fiction. RL A.

Hattie's effort to please her mother by uncharacteristically spending time quietly is misinterpreted, as is her effort to help her friend Shirley feel perkier. Fat, cuddly rabbits with pumpkin coloring help portray Hattie's zest for life.

661 *Hattie Rabbit.* Ill. by author. HarperCollins, 1976. ISBN 0-06-021940-8. SERIES: Early I Can Read. SUBJECTS: Animals—Rabbits—Fiction; Friendship—Fiction. RL A.

Hattie makes two decisions: She likes her mother because she is warm, soft, and furry, and the money she won by tricking her friends is a poor substitute for their friendship. Brown and turquoise drawings are of appealing rabbits.

662 *Hattie, Tom and the Chicken Witch* (a play and a story). Ill. by author. HarperCollins, 1980. ISBN 0-06-021959-9. SERIES: I Can Read Books. SUBJECTS: Animals—Rabbits—Fiction; Holidays—Easter—Fiction; Plays—Fiction. RL A.

Hattie Rabbit is allowed a part in the Easter play only when Linda Chicken twists her ankle. Chickens and rabbits are important to Easter, they decide. Sympathetic animal characters are drawn in rose, beige, and gray.

663 *Hound and Bear.* Ill. by author. Houghton, 1976, o.p. SUBJECTS: Animals—Bears—Fiction; Animals—Dogs—Fiction; Friendship—Fiction. RL B.

Hound loses out on his own birthday when he tricks Bear into sleeping too long; he loses a present when he tries another trick. Bear gets the best present of all when Hound promises not to play any more tricks. Gentle moral is illustrated with gray and rust washes.

664 *Hurray for Hattie Rabbit!* Ill. by author. HarperCollins, 1986, o.p. SERIES: Early I Can Read. SUBJECTS: Animals—Rabbits—Fiction; Mothers—Fiction. RL B.

The mischievous, sad, smug, and repentant expressions of two cuddly friends, Hattie Rabbit and Rosie Pig, are captivating. Their mothers find creative solutions for sleeplessness and the girls have a bet for who will get her mother to say "yes" first.

665 *Mother Rabbit's Son Tom.* Ill. by author. HarperCollins, 1977, o.p. SERIES: Early I Can Read. SUBJECTS: Animals—Rabbits—Fiction. RL B.

Tom's steady diet of a hamburger with onion, ketchup, and pickles on a poppy-seed roll has results even his parents do not expect. It is also clear that Tom's mother should *never* have consented to a dinosaur for a pet! Gentle, simple illustrations are rust and beige with a dark outline.

Gage, Wilson

666 *The Crow and Mrs. Gaddy.* Ill. by Marylin Hafner. Greenwillow, 1984, o.p. SERIES: Read-alone. SUBJECTS: Humorous stories. RL C.

Mrs. Gaddy has a running feud with a mischievous crow. Broad humor is enhanced by detailed ink and wash drawings.

667 *Down in the Boondocks.* Ill. by Glen Rounds. Greenwillow, 1977, o.p. SERIES: Read-alone. SUBJECTS: Humorous stories; Stories in rhyme. RL C.

This sprightly comic story of a robber scared away by the racket in the boondocks that the deaf farmer cannot hear is told in wonderfully repetitive, rhythmic style. Scratchy ink drawings colored with textured brown and avocado are marvelously appropriate.

668 *Mrs. Gaddy and the Fast-Growing Vine.* Ill. by Marylin Hafner. Greenwillow, 1985, o.p. SERIES: Read-alone. SUBJECTS: Humorous stories. RL B.

The goat Mrs. Gaddy bought as a last resort to trim the vine that grew like lightning was almost as hard to get rid of as the vine. Comic sketches are in green and brown.

669 *Mrs. Gaddy and the Ghost.* Ill. by Marylin Hafner. Greenwillow, 1979. ISBN 0-688-84179-1. SERIES: Read-alone. SUBJECTS: Ghost stories. RL B.

Mrs. Gaddy's inventive devices for getting rid of a noisy ghost all fail, but she changes her mind about getting rid of the ghost when she

Gage, Wilson (cont.)

hears it crying. Excellent illustrations are in rose and brown.

670 *My Stars, It's Mrs. Gaddy!* Ill. by Marylin Hafner. Greenwillow, 1991. ISBN 0-688-10514-9. SUBJECTS: Farm and country life—Fiction; Ghost stories; Humorous stories. RL A.

This anthology of three previously published Mrs. Gaddy stories retains the original charming illustrations by Marylin Hafner. Mrs. Gaddy finds accommodation with her resident ghost, persists in her skirmishes of mean tricks with the crow, and deals with a goat and a vine devouring her house.

671 *Squash Pie*. Ill. by Glen Rounds. Greenwillow, 1976, o.p. SUBJECTS: Humorous stories; Wordplay. RL B.

The farmer's seeing-eye potatoes, corn ears, and dogwood tree's bark do not catch the thief stealing his squash. When the farmer's wife discovers she *likes* squash pie, no more are stolen. Droll pen and ink drawings have textured light blue and orange highlights.

Galbraith, Kathryn O.

672 *Roommates*. Ill. by Mark Graham. Macmillan, 1990. ISBN 0-689-50487-X. SUBJECTS: Babies, new—Fiction; Siblings—Fiction. RL A.

When a new baby is expected, Mimi and Beth become unwilling roommates. Their quarrels and their support of one another are presented sympathetically. Soft watercolor cover in blues with pencil drawings illustrates the text.

Gaskin, Carol

673 *A Day in the Life of a Circus Clown*. Photos. Troll, 1988. ISBN 0-8167-1107-0. SERIES: A Day in the Life of. SUBJECTS: Careers; Circuses. RL C.

Circus clown Mike Ridenour's day begins with practicing acrobatics, on his trumpet, or juggling. He applies his clown makeup an hour before the show to become Omar Gosh, the butt of most jokes in the clown act. Accessible language describes the circus in and out of the ring.

674 *A Day in the Life of a Racing Car Mechanic*. Photos by John F. Klein. Troll, 1985. ISBN 0-8167-0091-5. SERIES: A Day in the Life of. SUBJECTS: Careers; Cars. RL C.

Brian Dunkel is an auto mechanic at a school for racing car drivers, and sometimes gets to race. The photos are so dark that it is difficult to follow the steps he and the chief mechanic, Frank, take to remove an engine and do repairs. Of course Brian wins the test race!

Gauch, Patricia L.

675 *Aaron and the Green Mountain Boys*. Ill. by Margot Tomes. McDonald, 1987, o.p. SUBJECTS: Historical fiction; United States—Revolution—Fiction. RL C.

Although an eager boy wants to help in the fight against the British, his part of chopping wood and washing mugs at first seems very unglamorous. A well-told history from a child's view has exceptional, authentic pen and ink drawings.

Gave, Marc

676 *Monkey See, Monkey Do*. Ill. by Jacqueline Rogers. Scholastic, 1993. ISBN 0-590-45801-9. SERIES: Hello Reader! SUBJECTS: Animals—Monkeys—Fiction; Stories in rhyme. RL A.

Playful watercolor illustrations make the best of a limited, repetitive text, adding humor, visual interest, and an appealing punch line.

Gelman, Rita G.

677 *Hey, Kid!* Ill. by Carol Nicklaus. Watts, 1977, o.p. SERIES: Easy-Read Story. SUBJECTS: Gifts and gift-giving—Fiction; Stories in rhyme. RL B.

A girl's surprise box holds a friendly critter who talks and sings until she gives it to another curious child. Ink drawings have colored pencil and three-color painted background. The ghostlike visitor is defined with pencil.

678 *More Spaghetti, I Say!* Ill. by Mort Gerberg. Scholastic, 1992. ISBN 0-590-45783-7. SERIES: Hello Reader! SUBJECTS: Animals—Monkeys—Fiction; Humorous stories; Stories in rhyme. RL A.

Gelman, Rita G. (cont.)

Minnie is so busy eating spaghetti she hasn't time to play with Freddy. Lively watercolor illustrations match the light tone of the rhyme.

Gemme, Leila B.

679 *T-Ball Is Our Game*. Photos by Richard Marshall. Childrens Pr., 1978, o.p. SUBJECTS: Sports—T-Ball. RL B.
Abbreviated text accompanies large action color photos underlining the learning and fun aspects of T-ball. The rules are appended.

Gibbons, Gail

680 *Dinosaurs, Dragonflies & Diamonds. All About Natural History Museums*. Ill. by author. Macmillan, 1988. ISBN 0-02-737240-5. SUBJECTS: Dinosaurs; Museums. RL B.
The variety and development of exhibits, the many people who work behind the scenes in a museum, as well as the research being done are skillfully outlined and illustrated with fascinating glimpses of museum life that includes child visitors.

681 *Happy Birthday!* Ill. by author. Holiday House, 1986. ISBN 0-8234-0614-8. SUBJECTS: Birthdays. RL C.
Basic information about birthdays is illustrated in full color decorative style with bright blue predominating.

682 *The Magnificent Morris Mouse Clubhouse*. Ill. by author. Watts, 1981. o.p. SERIES: Easy-Read Story. SUBJECTS: Animals—Fiction. RL A.
Morris the mouse's long, unwieldy tail knocks over the bucket of nails and one of paint and then a ladder when he tries to help his friends build a clubhouse. With care, he finds his tail useful for measuring, lifting, and balancing when he builds his own clubhouse. Blue and yellow washes illustrate the text.

683 *The Planets*. Ill. by author. Holiday House, 1993. ISBN 0-8234-1040-4. SUBJECTS: Astronomy and astronomers. Science and scientists. RL B.
Sketchy information about the planets, the "wanderers" in Greek, is given on double spreads with the author's colorful drawings.

684 *Puff . . . Flash . . . Bang! A Book about Signals*. Morrow, 1993. ISBN 0-688-07378-6. SUBJECTS: Signs and symbols. RL C.
Familiar sight and sound signals are described, from an alarm clock to a buoy, from sign language to a lighthouse. Vivid blues and greens predominate in the author's appealing drawings.

685 *Sharks*. Ill. by author. Holiday House, 1992. ISBN 0-8234-0960-0. SUBJECTS: Animals—Sharks; Oceans and ocean life. RL B.
There are about 350 different kinds of sharks, some of which are introduced with a gray drawing highlighted with chalk against the stylized bright blue and green of the sea. Details show the egg cases or live young, teeth, gills, and fins of a variety of sharks.

686 *Spiders*. Ill. by author. Holiday House, 1993. ISBN 0-8234-1006-4. SUBJECTS: Animals—Spiders. RL B.
The author describes and illustrates the differences between spiders and insects, molting and balooning of spiderlings, spinning, and enemies of spiders. Basic information is presented with vivid blue, green, and brown illustrations.

687 *Stargazers*. Ill. by author. Holiday House, 1992. ISBN 0-8234-0983-X. SUBJECTS: Astronomy. Science and scientists. RL C.
A little history, the difference between a refracting and a reflecting telescope, and a few of the most prominent features to be seen with the naked eye or binoculars are included in this simple book featuring a family of stargazers.

688 *Sun up, Sun Down*. Ill. by author. Harcourt, 1983. ISBN 0-15-282781-1. SUBJECTS: Astronomy and astronomers. RL B.
The effect of the sun on the everyday life of a small girl is outlined, from the patterns of sun and shadow to the grains that she eats. Rain, storms, and rainbows are discussed briefly in a text accompanied by the author's appealing illustrations.

Gibbons, Gail (cont.)

689 *Trains*. Ill. by author. Holiday House, 1987; pap., 1988. ISBN 0-8234-0640-7. SUBJECTS: Trains. RL C.
Information regarding trains, such as types of engines and cars, loading and unloading, and signals for engineers and drivers of cars near tracks, is given. Strong primary-color graphics add appeal.

Gibson, Gertrude

690 *CAT-CAT*. Ill. by Darrell Wiskur. Childrens Pr., 1970. o.p. SUBJECTS: Animals—Cats—Fiction; Pets—Fiction. RL A.
Cat-Cat ruled the roost even after a dog, Butch, came into the household. Chalk sketches give Cat-Cat distinction.

Giff, Patricia R.

691 *The Almost Awful Play*. Ill. by Susanna Natti. Viking, 1984; Puffin, pap., 1985. ISBN 0-14-050530-X. SUBJECTS: Plays— Fiction; School stories. RL B.
Thespian disaster turns into triumph with Ronald Morgan's quick thinking. Colored drawings help capture the spirit of school rivalries and friendship.

692 *Happy Birthday, Ronald Morgan!* Ill. by Susanna Natti. Viking, 1986; Penguin, pap., 1988. ISBN 0-670-80741-9. SUBJECTS: Birthdays—Fiction; Friendship—Fiction; School stories. RL A.
Ronald Morgan has bad news—his birthday comes after school is out, and he lost the friendship of his best friend. His teacher encourages him to make up; he does not notice the surreptitious preparations under-way for a party. Full color drawings illustrate very real situations.

693 *Ronald Morgan Goes to Bat*. Ill. by Susanna Natti. Viking, 1988. ISBN 0-670-81457-1. SUBJECTS: Self-esteem—Fiction; Sports—Baseball—Fiction. RL A.
Ronald's enthusiasm for baseball is originally outstripped by his skill, but some tips and practice improve his confidence. Bright, lively watercolors warm the sympathetic tale.

694 *Today Was a Terrible Day*. Ill. by Susanna Natti. Viking, 1980; Puffin, pap., 1984; ISBN 0-670-71830-0. SUBJECTS: Books and reading—Fiction; School stories; Self-esteem—Fiction. RL B.
One upbeat note from his teacher turns a day full of misery into one of joy for second grader Ronald Morgan. Comic drawings underline the mishaps and teasing of a boy anxious to please.

695 *Watch Out, Ronald Morgan!* Ill. by Susanna Natti. Viking, 1985; Puffin, pap., 1986. ISBN 0-670-80433-9. SUBJECTS: Eyeglasses—Fiction; School stories. RL B.
Ronald's teacher encourages him to have his eyes checked when he seems to be tripping and squinting, and has trouble making visual distinctions. This upbeat book has emerald greens and royal blues in lively child-centered drawings.

Giganti, Paul, Jr.

696 *Each Orange Had Eight Slices: A Counting Book*. Ill. by Donald Crews. Greenwillow, 1992. ISBN 0-688-10429-0. SUBJECTS: Concepts—Numbers. RL B.
Using familiar objects such as fruit with seeds, flowers with bugs, ducks with ducklings, and clowns with balloons, multiplication concepts are simply. introduced. Graphically striking illustrations in primary colors are by Donald Crews.

Gilchrist, Theo E.

697 *Halfway Up the Mountain*. Ill. by Glen Rounds. HarperCollins, 1978, o.p. SUBJECTS: Folklore—United States; Humorous stories. RL C.
Vivid, colorful language spices this traditional tale of a nearly blind old woman scaring off the bandit, Bloodcoe, as she tries to salt and pep-per the beef and push the garlic bits inside. Wry pen and ink drawings are masterful.

Gillham, Bill

698 *What's the Difference?* Photos by Fiona Horne. Putnam, 1986, o.p. SERIES: Look and Talk. SUBJECTS: Concepts; Visual perception. RL B.

The reader is asked to describe the differences between such things as a girl with long hair and one with braids and a big wheel and a bicycle. Basic differentiation is easy with excellent color photos featuring primary colors.

Ginsburg, Mirra

699 *The Night It Rained Pancakes*. Ill. by Douglas Florian. Greenwillow, 1975, o.p. SERIES: Read-alone. SUBJECTS: Folklore—Russia; Russia—Fiction. RL B.
Clever Ivan's trickery enables his simple brother's tale of finding gold to be discredited. A traditional tale is told and illustrated with appropriately plain ink and wash drawings.

Gise, Joanne

700 *Dogs*. Ill. by Roseanna Pistolesi. Troll, 1990. ISBN 0-8167-1902-0. SERIES: A Picture Book of. SUBJECTS: Animals—Dogs. RL B.
Each page is shared by background and a drawing of a breed of dog, from the nonbarking Basenji to more familiar household breeds. A line or two about why breeds developed special characteristics is included. This is a good introduction to dogs.

Glaser, Linda

701 *Keep Your Socks On, Albert!* Ill. by Sally G. Ward. Dutton, 1992. ISBN 0-525-44838-1. SERIES: Dutton Easy Reader. SUBJECTS: Animals—Opossums—Fiction; Siblings—Fiction. RL A.
Albert's older sister, Shirley, tells him moral tales that are a little too scary—but Albert reciprocates when the blame shifts. Imaginative dialogue fits situations familiar to all siblings. Appealing drawings are primarily in royal blue, red, and palest green washes.

Gleiter, Jan, and Thompson, Kathleen

702 *Sequoya*. Ill. by Tom Redman. Raintree, 1988. ISBN 0-8172-2678-8. SUBJECTS: Native Americans—Cherokees; Biographies; Language. RL C.
Sequoya had the ingenuity to turn the Cherokee language into a written language—twice, as his first efforts burned up in a fire. Then he had to convince the elders that his work was not witchcraft in this simple story with watercolor illustrations.

Glendinning, Sally

703 *Jimmy and Joe Find a Ghost*. Ill. by Paul Frame. Garrard, 1969, o.p. SERIES: Jimmy and Joe. SUBJECTS: Ghost stories. RL A.
The only twist in this pedestrian story is that the "flippety-flops" and objects thrown by the "ghost" are traced to a seal. The realistic drawings place multiracial boys in the city.

Goennel, Heidi

704 *My Day*. Ill. by author. Little, Brown, 1988, o.p. SUBJECTS: Growing up; Play. RL B.
This tale of a girl's ordinary school day takes on special qualities because of the simple graphics of the artwork.

Goldin, Augusta

705 *Ducks Don't Get Wet*. Ill. by Leonard Kessler. HarperCollins, 1989. ISBN 0-690-04782-7. SERIES: Let's-Read-and-Find-Out Science Books. SUBJECTS: Animals—Ducks; Nature. RL C.
An introduction to various kinds of ducks and their characteristics. Facts that are included are: some ducks can dive 100 feet deep and some can fly 70 miles per hour! Charming ducks and neighboring pond animals are in watercolors.

706 *Spider Silk*. Ill. by Joseph Low. HarperCollins, 1964, o.p. SERIES: Let's-Read-and-Find-Out Science Books. SUBJECTS: Animals—Spiders; Nature. RL C.
Silk is used for navigation and for cocoons. Webs are for catching food. Simple information concentrates on the common grass spider. Ink drawings have two-tone washes on alternate pages.

707 *Straight Hair, Curly Hair*. Ill. by Ed Emberley. HarperCollins, 1966; pap., 1972. ISBN 0-690-77921-6. SERIES: Let's-Read-and-Find-Out Science Books.

Goldin, Augusta (cont.)

SUBJECTS: Human body—Hair; Science experiments. RL C.

Information about hair is interspersed with simple experiments and suggested observations. Accompanying sketches have touches of humor to lighten the text.

Goldman, Susan

708 *Grandma Is Somebody Special.* Ill. by author. Whitman, 1976. ISBN 0-8075-3034-4. SERIES: Self Starters. SUBJECTS: Grandparents—Fiction. RL C.

The joy and comfort in simple activities with Grandma, such as looking at a fire engine, photos, and her jewelry box; cooking; playing games; telling and reading stories; and singing old songs are clearly conveyed. Full color watercolors also have a homey everyday appeal.

Gordon, Jeffie R.

709 *Muriel and Ruth: A Book about Friendship.* Ill. by Lane Yerkes. Bell Books, 1992. ISBN 1-878093-18-5. SUBJECTS: Animals—Pigs—Fiction; Friendship—Fiction; School stories. RL B.

Muriel meets Ruth the first day of school, and they become best friends. Despite a squabble when Ruth doesn't want to share her new birthday present, they remain pals. Fat, rosy-cheeked pig characters predominantly in green and orange people the story.

Gordon, Sharon

710 *What a Dog!* Ill. by Deborah Sims. Troll, 1980. ISBN 0-89375-393-9. SERIES: First-Start Easy Reader. SUBJECTS: Animals—Dogs—Fiction; Pets—Dogs—Fiction. RL A.

Only 9 of the 56 words in the book have more than 1 syllable. Bernie walks the eager dog—or is it the other way around? Line drawings focus on a roly-poly pet.

Gordon, Shirley

711 *Crystal's Christmas Carol.* Ill. by Edward Frascino. HarperCollins, 1989. ISBN 0-06-

022239-5. SUBJECTS: Friendship—Fiction; Holidays—Christmas—Fiction. RL C.

Susan and Sherri are embarrassed when their friend Crystal sings Christmas carols everywhere—but then they notice the happy faces of people on the street and in the mall, and join her more enthusiastically. Pen and wash drawings are expressive, featuring holiday colors.

Graham, Bob

712 *Crusher Is Coming.* Ill. by author. Viking, 1988, o.p. SUBJECTS: Friendship—Fiction; Self-esteem—Fiction. RL B.

Peter introduces many activities to impress an older friend, Crusher, but Crusher enjoys most playing with Peter's baby sister. Excellent watercolor and ink sketches underline the contrast between how Crusher looks and how he acts.

Gramatky, Hardie

713 *Bolivar.* Ill. by author. Putnam, 1961, o.p. SUBJECTS: Animals—Donkeys—Fiction; Ecuador—Fiction. RL C.

Despite his spirited mistakes, Bolivar the burro grows into his famous name as he courageously saves the revelers from a raging bull. Pictures are as exuberant as the little donkey.

Granowsky, Alvin; Tweedt, Joy A.; and Tweedt, Craig L.

714 *Chicken Salad Soup.* Ill. by Michael L. Denman. Modern Curriculum, 1985, o.p. SERIES: Beginning to Read. SUBJECTS: Computers—Fiction; Cookery—Fiction. RL B.

When Eric follows a computer recipe for lunch, he ends up with chicken salad instead of soup. Only 77 words are used in this story. Cartoon drawings show the kitchen mess.

715 *Computer Park.* Ill. by Michael L. Denman. Modern Curriculum, 1985, o.p. SUBJECTS: Computers—Fiction. RL B.

The chaos in a computer entertainment park when the computers go down is suggested in this 77-word text. Busy cartoons add to the fun.

716 *Robert's Robot*. Ill. by Michael L. Denman. Modern Curriculum, 1985, o.p. SUBJECTS: Robots—Fiction. RL B.
Robert dreams of his very own robot cleaning his room and doing his yard work and his homework! Ninety-two word text is illustrated with busy cartoons.

717 *Who Said That?* Ill. by Michael L. Denman. Modern Curriculum, 1985, o.p. SERIES: Beginning to Read. SUBJECTS: Birthdays—Fiction; Computers—Fiction; School stories. RL A.
With a 77-word vocabulary, some children surprise their teacher with a birthday message from the new talking computer. Large pastel cartoons are action-filled and busy.

Graves, Charles P.

718 *Fourth of July*. Ill. by Ken Wagner. Garrard, 1963, o.p. SERIES: Holiday. SUBJECTS: Holidays—Fourth of July. RL C.
In ten short chapters the history, music, symbols, and celebrations of the Fourth of July are presented. Illustrated in red, white, and blue.

719 *Wright Brothers*. Ill. by Fermin Rocker. Putnam, 1973, o.p. SERIES: See and Read Beginning to Read Biography. SUBJECTS: Airplanes; Biographies. RL C.
The author traces the history of the Wright brothers' determined efforts to fly. Good ink sketches give a flavor of the times.

Greene, Carla

720 *Truck Drivers: What Do They Do?* Ill. by Leonard Kessler. HarperCollins, 1967. ISBN 0-06-022099-6. SERIES: I Can Read Books. SUBJECTS: Careers; Trucks. RL B.
A picture glossary precedes a lively look at the multitude of jobs truck drivers and their trucks perform. A view of the cab and engine is also provided. Simple pen and ink drawings have red and yellow highlights.

721 *What Do They Do? Policemen and Firemen*. Ill. by Leonard Kessler. Harper-Collins, 1962, o.p. SERIES: I Can Read Books. SUBJECTS: Community helpers; Fire fighting; Police. RL B.
Basic facts include equipment, safety, and training in these helpers' most familiar roles. A picture glossary introduces the text. Bold sketches are effective.

Greene, Carol

722 *Benjamin Franklin: A Man with Many Jobs*. Photos by Steve Dobson. Childrens Pr., 1988. ISBN 0-516-04202-5. SERIES: Rookie Biography. SUBJECTS: Biographies; United States—History. RL B.
Aided by a simple, well-illustrated format, the creative accomplishments of Benjamin Franklin are outlined. Five short chapters are augmented by a time line and index.

723 *Black Elk: A Man with a Vision*. Drawings and photos. Childrens Pr., 1990. ISBN 0-516-04213-0. SERIES: Rookie Biography. SUBJECTS: Native Americans; Biographies. RL C.
Black Elk, an Oglala Sioux, was born in 1863 and died in 1950. Despite his recurring visions of peace, he endured the routing of the Indians from their ancestral homes, traveled in Europe with the Buffalo Bill Cody's Wild West show, and survived the Wounded Knee massacre.

724 *Christopher Columbus: A Great Explorer*. Photos and drawings. Childrens Pr., 1989. ISBN 0-516-04204-1. SERIES: Rookie Biography. SUBJECTS: Biographies; Explorers and exploration; United States—History. RL C.
This is a very simple version of the successes and frustrations of Columbus's explorations, illustrated with lithographs, paintings, photos, and drawings.

725 *Daniel Boone: Man of the Forests*. Drawings and photos. Childrens Pr., 1990. ISBN 0-516-04210-6. SERIES: Rookie Biography. SUBJECTS: Biographies; Explorers and exploration; Frontier and pioneer life. RL C.
One of 11 children born to a blacksmith and his wife, Daniel Boone fathered 10. He opened Kentucky and Missouri to settlers against the active opposition of Indians, whom he befriended, fought, and escaped from after being captured more than once. In his eighties, he walked to Yellowstone and back.

Greene, Carol (cont.)

726 *Elie Wiesel: Messenger from the
Holocaust.* Photos. Childrens Pr., 1987,
o.p. SUBJECTS: Biographies; History;
Religion. RL C.

Elie Wiesel's acceptance speech for the 1986
Nobel Peace Prize concludes the outline of
his concentration camp ordeals and later witness. A time line is appended to this moving
tribute.

727 *George Washington: First President of the
United States.* Photos. Childrens Pr.,
1991. ISBN 0-516-04218-1. SERIES: Rookie
Biography. SUBJECTS: Biographies;
Presidents—United States; United
States—History. RL C.

A pedestrian account of George Washington's
career, beginning when he was a surveyor at
age 16. Black and white photos predominate;
time line and index are appended.

728 *Hi, Clouds.* Ill. by Gene Sharp. Childrens
Pr., hb and pap., 1983. ISBN 0-516-02036-
6. SERIES: Rookie Readers. SUBJECTS:
Weather—Clouds—Fiction. RL A.

Many shapes are seen in the clouds by two city
children. A 27-word vocabulary and simple
bright illustrations make this an appealing
beginning reader.

729 *I Can Be a Football Player.* Color photos
and drawings. Childrens Pr., 1984. ISBN 0-
516-01839-6. SERIES: I Can Be. SUBJECTS:
Sports—Football. RL B.

Well-organized information about being a
football player at different levels and about
related careers is introduced. A glossary is
appended. Small cartoon drawings assist with
vocabulary and ideas.

730 *Ice Is . . . Whee!* Ill. by Paul Sharp.
Childrens Pr., 1983. ISBN 0-516-02037-4.
SERIES: Rookie Readers. SUBJECTS:
Seasons—Winter—Fiction. RL A.

The beauty of ice and the fun of sliding on it or
playing with icicles are celebrated with a 21
word vocabulary. Cartoon drawings are colorful, yet simple.

731 *Indira Nehru Gandhi: Ruler of India.*
Photos. Childrens Pr., 1985, o.p. SUBJECTS:
Biographies—Women; India. RL C.

Born to an Indian ruling family, Indira followed her father in becoming prime minister
of India. Political issues are touched on lightly.
Photos trace the maturing political leader
until her assassination.

732 *Jackie Robinson: Baseball's First Black
Major-Leaguer.* Photos. Childrens Pr.,
1990. ISBN 0-516-04211-4. SERIES: Rookie
Biography. SUBJECTS: African Americans;
Biographies; Sports—Baseball. RL C.

Raised by his mother in a poor Pasadena
neighborhood, Jackie went on to earn letters
in four sports at UCLA. Branch Rickey of the
Brooklyn Dodgers gave him an opportunity to
play professionally. He was Rookie of the Year
despite discrimination, and went on to fight
racial prejudice on and off the field.

733 *Jacques Cousteau: Man of the Oceans.*
Photos. Childrens Pr., 1990. ISBN 0-516-
04215-7. SERIES: Rookie Biography.
SUBJECTS: Biographies; Oceans and ocean
life; Science and scientists. RL C.

Cousteau discovered three wonderful things
as a boy: water, machines, and film, all of
which shaped his life. While in the navy, he
explored the sea and sea life, all of which he
shared through film, books, TV, and live
appearances.

734 *John Chapman: The Man Who Was
Johnny Appleseed.* Photos and drawings.
Childrens Pr., 1991. ISBN 0-516-04223-8.
SERIES: Rookie Biography. SUBJECTS:
Biographies; Plants—Trees. RL C.

The legend and the skimpy facts known about
Johnny Appleseed are given in this interesting
tale of an eccentric, Bible-toting vegetarian.
who "lived for others" and planted apple trees
throughout Pennsylvania, Ohio, and Indiana.
Lithographs, drawings, and photos illustrate
this text.

735 *John Philip Sousa: The March King.*
Black and white photos. Childrens Pr.,
1992. ISBN 0-516-04226-2. SERIES: Rookie
Biography. SUBJECTS: Biographies; Music
and musicians. RL C.

The outline of John Philip Sousa's life, with
his successful career composing music, especially marches, and directing the Marine
Corps Band. A time. line and an index are

appended to this work liberally illustrated with black and white photos.

736 *Louis Pasteur: Enemy of Disease*. Photos. Childrens Pr., 1990. ISBN 0-516-04216-5. SERIES: Rookie Biography. SUBJECTS: Biographies; Medicine; Science and scientists. RL C.
Pasteur's life is outlined in five chapters, with a time line and an index appended. Through painstaking work he discovered microbes and developed vaccines; the Pasteur Institute was founded as more and more people came for help. Three of his five children died in childhood. Illustrations are black and white photos.

737 *Margaret Wise Brown: Author of Goodnight Moon*. Photos and illustrations. Childrens Pr., 1993. ISBN 0-516-04254-8. SERIES: Rookie Biography. SUBJECTS: Biographies—Women; Books and reading; Writers and writing. RL C.
Margaret Wise Brown's love of cats and rabbits, woods and fields, is described, as well as her dissatisfaction with her life and the many changes in it. She died at age 42, engaged to be married. Black and white photos of Brown, color photos of the woods, and some famous book illustrations appear throughout.

738 *Martin Luther King, Jr.: A Man Who Changed Things*. Photos. Childrens Pr., 1989. ISBN 0-516-04205-X. SERIES: Rookie Biography. SUBJECTS: African Americans; Biographies; Holidays—Martin Luther King, Jr., Day. RL C.
With many black and white photos and some in color, and stirring language augmenting the narrative outline of King's life, the author brings King's message and roots to the young reader.

739 *Mother Teresa: Friend of the Friendless*. Photos. Childrens Pr., 1983, o.p. SUBJECTS: Biographies. RL C.
The inspiring story of the way in which one determined, dedicated person can change the world. Mother Teresa, born in Yugoslavia, began work as a missionary in India while a young woman, and has inspired people all over the globe.

740 *Please Wind?* Ill. by Gene Sharp. Childrens Pr., 1982. ISBN 0-516-02033-1.
SERIES: Rookie Readers. SUBJECTS: Seasons—Spring—Fiction; Stories in rhyme. RL A.
A child's wish for a brisk wind is granted, blowing clothes on the clothesline, a balloon, a hat, and even her kite. Creative story uses only 22 words and has simple watercolor drawings.

741 *Pocahontas: Daughter of a Chief*. Ill. by Steven Dobson. Childrens Pr., 1988. ISBN 0-516-04203-3. SERIES: Rookie Biography. SUBJECTS: Native Americans; Biographies; United States—Colonial period. RL C.
A bare-bones account of Pocahontas's lasting friendship with the settlers at Jamestown, first John Smith, then John Rolfe, whom she married. While with her husband and son in England, she died and was buried at Gravesend. Paintings, lithographs, photos, and drawings are used liberally.

742 *Rain! Rain!* Ill. by Larry Frederick. Childrens Pr., 1982. ISBN 0-516-42034-8. SERIES: Rookie Readers. SUBJECTS: Stories in rhyme; Weather—Rain. RL A.
Twenty-nine words celebrate rain (especially puddles to play in). Cheerful, action-filled illustrations feature emerald green and royal blue watercolors.

743 *Shine, Sun!* Ill. by Gene Sharp. Childrens Pr., 1983. ISBN 0-516-02038-2. SERIES: Rookie Readers. SUBJECTS: Play—Fiction; Seasons—Summer—Fiction. RL A.
Twenty-seven words and bright watercolors focus on a little girl dancing and wading on a sunny day, as well as her admiring the flowers, butterflies, and birds singing.

744 *Snow Joe*. Ill. by Paul Sharp. Childrens Pr., hb and pap., 1982. ISBN 0-516-02035-8. SERIES: Rookie Readers. SUBJECTS: Seasons—Winter—Fiction; Stories in rhyme. RL A.
Remarkable interest is generated in snow play using just 15 words. Large comic illustrations are in pastels.

745 *Wolfgang Amadeus Mozart: Musical Genius*. Childrens Pr., 1993. ISBN 0-516-04256-4. SERIES: Rookie Biography. SUBJECTS: Biographies; Music and musicians. RL C.

Greene, Carol (cont.)

The difficulties and triumphs of Mozart's music-making are celebrated in this short biography with five chapters, a time line, and an index. Photos, lithographs, paintings, and playbills illumine the text.

Greene, Laura

746 *I Am an Orthodox Jew*. Ill. by Lisa C. Wesson. Holt, Rinehart, 1978, o.p. SUBJECTS: Religion. RL B.

The weekly rituals and restrictions of Orthodox Jews are shown from the point of view of a boy, his sister, and his gentile friend. Ink drawings underline the warmth of family tradition.

Greenwood, Pamela D.

747 *I Found Mouse*. Ill. by Jennifer Plecas. Clarion, 1994. ISBN 0-395-65478-5. SUBJECTS: Emotions—Loneliness—Fiction; Parent and child—Fiction; Pets—Cats—Fiction. RL C.

Tessie's big brother is camping with their grandmother, her best friend has gone to visit her father, and her mother is at school in Colorado. What starts out as a very long three weeks turns into a growing experience for Tessie when she finds a stray kitten and gives it a home. Illustrated with childlike watercolors with ink definition, the story is divided into chapters and uses humor well to balance Tessie's concerns.

748 *What About My Goldfish?* Ill. by Jennifer Plecas. Houghton Mifflin, 1993. ISBN 0-395-64337-6. SUBJECTS: Moving, household—Fiction; Pets—Dogs—Fiction; Pets—Fiction. RL A.

When a boy moves, he makes new friends only after he brings his goldfish, Merlin and Skunk, for show-and-tell, and has a Pond Party (since his birthday is too far away). Simple ink and watercolor drawings complement the text.

Greve, Andreas

749 *The Good Night Story*. Ill. by Kitty Macaulay. Annick, 1993. ISBN 1-55037-288-2. SUBJECTS: Animals—Fiction; Bedtime—Fiction; Storytelling. RL B.

A small boy finishes the bedtime story his grandfather began—with startlingly realistic results.

Grey, Judith

750 *What Time Is It?* Ill. by Susan Hall. Troll, 1981. ISBN 0-89375-509-5. SUBJECTS: Animals—Fiction; Books and reading—Fiction; Concepts—Time. RL A.

A boy squirrel asks whether it is time to eat or play. Rhythmic language is used with a basic vocabulary of 25 words. Pastel washes feature cute animals, butterflies, and birds.

751 *Yummy, Yummy*. Ill. by Joan E. Goodman. Troll, 1981. ISBN 0-89375-543-5. SUBJECTS: Animals—Hippos—Fiction; Bakers and baking—Fiction. RL A.

A hippo makes an apple-carrot-honey-chocolate cake for a yummy treat. Slight story has a 37 word vocabulary and soft pastel illustrations.

Greydanus, Rose

752 *Double Trouble*. Ill. by Roland Rodegast. Troll, 1981. ISBN 0-89375-529-X. SUBJECTS: Animals—Raccoons—Fiction; Siblings—Twins—Fiction. RL B.

Jim and Tim, raccoon twins, blame each other for messes, but end up doing the cleaning together. Limited story line uses a 34-word vocabulary. Large textured drawings are in bright colors.

753 *Let's Pretend*. Ill. by Marsha Winborn. Troll, hb and pap., 1981. ISBN 0-89375-545-1. SERIES: Giant First-Start. SUBJECTS: Imagination—Fiction. RL B.

Children "spy" on their dog and cat. A slim story line and text are expanded by attractive marbelized watercolors on white.

Gridley, Marion

754 *Osceola*. Ill. by Lloyd E. Oxendine. Putnam, 1972, o.p. SERIES: See and Read Beginning to Read Biography. SUBJECTS: Biographies; Native Americans—Seminoles. RL B.

The bravery and determination of one man to preserve his native culture culminates in his early death. Crude ink sketches have orange highlights.

Grindley, Sally, ed.

755 *A Day with Alice and Sam. Ten Stories and a Picture Dictionary*. Ill. by Maureen Galvani. Kingfisher, 1993. ISBN 1-85697-912-1. SERIES: Kingfisher Ready-to-Read. SUBJECTS: Family life—Fiction. RL B.

The activities of a family with three children from sunup to bedtime include teasing, pretending, planting a tree, baking cupcakes, going to a street fair, hunting for the family dog, and a bedtime story. Ink and wash drawings include a picture dictionary.

Gross, Ruth B.

756 *A Book about Pandas*. Photos. Dial, 1972; Scholastic, pap., 1991. ISBN 0-590-43492-6. SUBJECTS: Animals—Pandas; Nature. RL C.

Habits and characteristics of pandas learned from studying their behavior in a zoo are related in this photoessay. Black and white pictures are numerous, catching pandas in a variety of poses.

Gruber, Suzanne

757 *The Monster under My Bed*. Ill. by Stephanie Britt. Troll, hb and pap., 1985. ISBN 0-8167-0456-2. SERIES: Giant First-Start. SUBJECTS: Animals—Bears—Fiction; Bedtime—Fiction. RL C.

A small bear, certain that he hears noises under his bed, calls his mother repeatedly for reassurance. He settles down only when the source of the disturbance is found—his cat, Fluffy. The reassuring tale has excellent watercolor drawings with royal blue predominating.

Gunther, Louise

758 *A Tooth for the Tooth Fairy*. Ill. by Jim Cummins. Garrard, 1978, o.p. SUBJECTS: Tooth fairy—Fiction. RL B.

When Rose loses her tooth in the grass at the playground and tries to substitute a fake, she finds that her trouble was not necessary. Straightforward story has full color illustrations.

H

Haddad, Helen R.

759 *Truck and Loader*. Ill. by Donald Carrick. Greenwillow, 1982, o.p. SERIES: Read-alone. SUBJECTS: Trucks. RL B.

The complementary work of loader and dump truck doing road building, tree removal, and pond building is well described. Carrick's exceptional drawings are in muted orange, beige, and green.

Hall, Katy, and Eisenberg, Lisa

760 *Buggy Riddles*. Ill. by Simms Taback. Dial, 1986. ISBN 0-8037-0140-3. SERIES: Dial Easy-to-Read. SUBJECTS: Jokes and riddles. RL B.

Each of the 41 riddles (with answers) featuring insects is given in a full page. The illustrations are bold, brightly colored, and humorous.

761 *Fishy Riddles*. Ill. by Simms Taback. Dial, hb and pap., 1983. ISBN 0-8037-2431-4. SERIES: Dial Easy-to-Read. SUBJECTS: Jokes and riddles. RL B.

The riddles all have pleasing, but not always predictable, plays on words. Fittingly illustrated in cartoon style with turquoise and orange.

762 *Grizzly Riddles*. Ill. by Nicole Rubel. Dial, 1989. ISBN 0-8037-0376-7. SERIES: Dial Easy-to-Read. SUBJECTS: Jokes and riddles; Word play. RL B.

Inventive twists on old riddles revolve around grizzly bears in school, on picnics, on airplanes, or fishing. Cartoon drawings feature grisly grizzlies and eye-catching patterns.

763 *Snakey Riddles*. Ill. by Simms Taback. Dial, 1990. ISBN 0-8037-0669-3. SERIES: Dial Easy-to-Read. SUBJECTS: Animals—Snakes; Jokes and riddles; Word play. RL B.

Delightful play with language with dozens of riddles about snakes. Watercolor drawings show richly textured snakes.

Hall, Kirsten

764 *Bunny, Bunny*. Ill. by Kathy Wilburn. Childrens Pr., 1990. ISBN 0-516-05352-3.

Hall, Kirsten (cont.)

SERIES: My First Reader. SUBJECTS: Animals—Rabbits—Fiction; Stories in rhyme. RL A.

Blue-jacketed Bunny romps in the meadow with his friends all day, before returning to his hollow in tree roots to be tucked into bed by his parents. Light, playful illustrations accompany the simple rhymed text, limited to 24 words.

Hall, Lynn

765 *Captain: Canada's Flying Pony*. Ill. by Tran Mawicke. Garrard, 1976, o.p. SERIES: Famous Animal Stories. SUBJECTS: Animals—Horses. RL C.

A true story of a mud-colored pony and a girl who outjumped larger horses all over the world is told with drama and humor. Watercolor drawings focus on the pony and girl.

Hall, Malcolm

766 *CariCATures*. Ill. by Bruce Degen. Putnam, 1978, o.p. SERIES: Break-of-Day. SUBJECTS: Animals—Fiction; Jokes and riddles—Fiction; Newspapers—Fiction. RL B.

The Claws and Paws newspaper begins to thrive only when some cat cartoons and riddles are added. Excellent ink and wash drawings of the animal characters enhance the good characterizations.

767 *Derek Koogar Was a Star*. Ill. by Joel Schick. Putnam, 1975, o.p. SUBJECTS: Animals—Cougars—Fiction; Animals—Fiction; Humorous Stories. RL B.

With tongue-in-cheek humor, a tricky potbellied washed-up movie star cougar has the tables turned by Maxine Bear. Expressive ink drawings and good dialogue exaggerate the humor.

768 *Edward, Benjamin and Butter*. Ill. by Tomie dePaola. Putnam, 1981, o.p. SUBJECTS: Animals—Horses—Fiction; Animals—Tapirs—Fiction; Friendship—Fiction. RL B.

The tables are turned when Edward tries to cheer up his gloomy friend Benjamin with a trick. Pencil and yellows illustrate this story with gentle humor and unexpected twists.

769 *Headlines*. Ill. by Wallace Tripp. Putnam, 1973, o.p. SERIES: Break-of-Day. SUBJECTS: Animals—Fiction; Books and reading—Fiction; Newspapers—Fiction. RL C.

Editor Theodore Cat's newspaper headlines come out wrong because a pack rat family steals type. Good characterization comes from text and Tripp's outstanding ink drawings.

Hamilton, Virginia M.

770 *Jahdu*. Ill. by Jerry Pinkney. Greenwillow, 1980, o.p. SERIES: Read-alone. SUBJECTS: Fantasy; Shadows—Fiction. RL B.

Accompanied by his independent shadow, Jahdu rolls up the sky to crawl behind, and sticks his finger in the cup of night to taste it. Rich language patterns and pencil drawings on palest lavender stimulate the imagination.

Hamsa, Bobbie

771 *Dirty Larry*. Ill. by Paul Sharp. Childrens Pr., 1983. ISBN 0-516-02040-4. SERIES: Rookie Readers. SUBJECTS: Play—Fiction. RL C.

Larry's dirty anatomy from ears and knees to nose and neck are detailed in 32 familiar words. Cartoons show how much fun he has getting so dirty. (Beginning readers will be able to enjoy this book despite the Spache reading level assignment.)

772 *Fast Draw Freddie*. Ill. by Stephen Hayes. Childrens Pr., hb and pap., 1984. ISBN 0-516-02046-3. SERIES: Rookie Readers. SUBJECTS: Art and artists; Stories in rhyme. RL B.

The 31-word rhymed text celebrates the possibilities for drawing on paper. Ink sketches of multiethnic children are set in a city environment.

773 *Polly Wants a Cracker*. Ill. by Jerry Warshaw. Childrens Pr., hb and pap., 1986. ISBN 0-516-02071-4. SERIES: Rookie Readers. SUBJECTS: Animals—Parrots—Fiction; Concepts—Numbers; Stories in rhyme. RL B.

A simple 32-word vocabulary is used for a story counting the crackers Polly wants. Lively full color drawings of three children and a dog pampering Polly keep the story moving.

Hancock, Sibyl

774 *Bill Pickett: First Black Rodeo Star*. Ill. by Lorinda B. Cauley. Harcourt, 1977, o.p. SERIES: Let Me Read. SUBJECTS: African Americans; Biographies; Western stories. RL B.

The rodeo adventures of the first black international rodeo star. The close relationship he had with his horse, Spradley, is also emphasized. Sepia drawings add to the story.

775 *Old Blue*. Ill. by Erick Ingraham. Putnam, 1980, o.p. SERIES: See and Read. SUBJECTS: Cowboys; Western stories. RL C.

The remarkable true story of a tame lead longhorn steer named Old Blue is told from the point of view of a novice on one particular drive in 1878. This tale is exceptional in its telling, as well as in its soft pencil drawings.

Hare, Norma Q.

776 *Wish Upon a Birthday*. Ill. by Diane Dawson. Garrard, 1979, o.p. SUBJECTS: Bakers and baking—Fiction; Birthdays—Fiction; Kings and queens—Fiction. RL B.

The cook's helper, Gabe, makes the very first birthday cake as his gift for Princess Melinda. Busy, bright cartoon-style drawings show the bustle in the castle kitchen.

Harrison, David

777 *Case of the Missing Frog*. Ill. by Jerry Warshaw. Rand McNally, 1972, o.p. SERIES: Fledgling. SUBJECTS: Animals—Frogs and toads—Fiction; City and town life—Fiction; Stories in rhyme. RL A.

A search for their missing pet, Og the frog, leads two boys all over their city neighborhood. Sketches shows expressive animal faces and the flavor of the neighborhood.

778 *Little Turtle's Big Adventure*. Ill. by J. P. Miller. Random House, 1969, o.p. SERIES: Early Bird. SUBJECTS: Animals—Turtles; Nature. RL B.

When road construction forces Little Turtle to relocate, a boy helps him find a new home. The cover is dated, but the other illustrations are excellent, with good graphics, textures, and an interesting variety of techniques.

779 *Wake Up, Sun*. Ill. by Hans Wilhelm. Random House, hb and pap., 1986. ISBN 0-394-98256-8. SERIES: Step into Reading. SUBJECTS: Cumulative tales; Farm and country life—Fiction. RL A.

The animals were very nice to the farmer's baby after her cries coincided with the sunrise. Appealing simple watercolors focus on friendly farm animals.

Harrison, Virginia

780 *The World of a Falcon*. Photos by Oxford Scientific Films. Stevens, 1988. ISBN 1-55532-308-1. SERIES: Where Animals Live. SUBJECTS: Animals—Falcons; Nature. RL C.

The habitat, life cycle, and special characteristics of kestrels (a kind of falcon), and their adjustment to people are covered. Index and glossary are helpful. Close-up color photos are exceptional, especially of kestrels "hovering" with feathers extended. Adapted from Mike Birkhead's *The Falcon Over the Town* (Stevens, 1988).

781 *The World of Dragonflies*. Photos by Oxford Scientific Films. Stevens, 1988. ISBN 1-55532-310-3. SERIES: Where Animals Live. SUBJECTS: Animals—Dragonflies; Nature. RL C.

The habitat, anatomy, and life cycle of dragonflies are introduced, along with their enemies and relationships with people. Spectacular close-up photos of dragonflies at every stage of their life cycle accompany the informative text. Adapted from Christopher O'Toole's *The Dragonfly Over the Water* (Stevens, 1988).

782 *The World of Lizards*. Photos by Oxford Scientific Films. Stevens, 1988. ISBN 1-55532-307-3. SERIES: Where Animals Live. SUBJECTS: Animals—Lizards; Nature. RL C.

Information about the variety, habitats, anatomy, and life cycle of lizards, particularly their protective coloration and habits, is giv-

Harrison, Virginia (cont.)

en. Exceptional close-up color photos are up to Oxford Scientific Films' standards. Adapted from Mike Linley's *The Lizard in the Jungle* (Stevens, 1988).

783 *The World of Mice.* Photos by Oxford Scientific Films. Stevens, 1988. ISBN 1-55532-309-X. SERIES: Where Animals Live. SUBJECTS: Animals—Mice. RL C.

The habitat, life cycle, senses, and food, as well as the enemies of mice are described. Mice as pests and pets for people are also discussed. Exceptional close-up color photos add immeasurably to the book. Adapted from Robert Burton's *The Mouse in the Barn* (Stevens, 1988).

Harshman, Terry Webb

784 *Porcupine's Pajama Party.* Ill. by Doug Cushman. HarperCollins, 1988; pap., 1990. ISBN 0-06-444140-7. SERIES: I Can Read Books. SUBJECTS: Animals—Fiction; Friendship—Fiction; Scary stories. RL A.

Porcupine invites friends Owl and Otter to a pajama party, where they watch a scary movie and bake chocolate chip cookies. The movie turns out to be a little too scary for a good night's sleep. This is a reassuring story with very appealing ink and watercolor drawings of the friends.

Hasler, Eveline

785 *Winter Magic.* Trans. of *In Winterland.* Ill. by Michele Lemieux. Morrow, 1985. ISBN 0-688-05258-4. SUBJECTS: Animals—Cats—Fiction; Fantasy; Seasons—Winter—Fiction. RL B.

Peter takes a winter ride on his cat, Sebastian, through the caves, forest, and underground. Somewhat impressionistic paintings reinforce the dreamy qualities of his adventure.

Hatch, Shirley C.

786 *Wind Is to Feel.* Ill. by Marilyn Miller. Putnam, 1973, o.p. SUBJECTS: Senses—Touch; Weather. RL B.

The wind is described through a variety of familiar sensory experiences and experiments.

Effective pencil sketches have pale blue, yellow, and gray washes.

Hautzig, Deborah

787 *Handsomest Father.* Ill. by Muriel Batherman. Greenwillow, 1979, o.p. SERIES: Read-alone. SUBJECTS: Fathers—Fiction; School stories; Self-esteem—Fiction. RL B.

A child's agonies regarding his father's personal appearance are sympathetically portrayed when the father attends open house at school. Ink and wash sketches blend superbly.

788 *Happy Birthday, Little Witch.* Ill. by Marc Brown. Random House, hb and pap., 1985. ISBN 0-394-97365-8. SERIES: Step into Reading. SUBJECTS: Birthdays—Fiction; Witches—Fiction. RL B.

When Little Witch's Halloween friends surprise her with a birthday party, she plays pin the tail on the devil, it rains black and blue jellybeans, and there are firecrackers. Expectations are gently overturned in this story illustrated with Brown's humorous drawings.

789 *It's a Secret!* Ill. by Tom Leigh. Random House, 1988. ISBN 0-394-99672-0. SERIES: Start-to-Read. SUBJECTS: Concepts—Numbers. RL A.

Bert's feelings are hurt when Ernie tells others that Bert can't count past 100. The Sesame Street group then learns to count together. Characters are in bright colors.

790 *It's Easy!* Ill. by Joe Mathieu. Random House, 1988. ISBN 0-394-91376-0. SUBJECTS: Friendship—Fiction; Gardening—Fiction; Puppets—Fiction. RL A.

Big Bird finds he needs help with his sunflower garden after all to keep the birds away. Large colored drawings are of Sesame Street characters.

791 *It's Not Fair! Featuring Jim Henson's Sesame Street Muppets.* Ill. by Tom Leigh. Random House, 1986; pap., 1993. ISBN 0-679-83951-8. SERIES: Start-to-Read. SUBJECTS: Friendship—Fiction. RL B.

After Bert does all the work and Ernie gets the credit, Ernie gives Bert an unusual gift—a dustpan and brush. Realistic differences are dealt with sympathetically. Colorful cartoons of familiar television characters illustrate the text.

792 *Little Witch's Big Night*. Ill. by Marc Brown. Random House, hb and pap., 1984. ISBN 0-394-96587-6. SERIES: Step into Reading. SUBJECTS: Witches—Fiction. RL C.
Little Witch, left behind on Halloween because she had been too good, gives some trick-or-treaters a night to remember. Friendly watercolor drawings take away all fear.

793 *The Nutcracker Ballet*. Ill. by Carolyn Ewing. Random House, 1992. ISBN 0-679-92385-3. SERIES: Step into Reading. SUBJECTS: Dancing; Fairy tales; Music and musicians. RL B.
When Marie helps break the spell on the curious nutcracker given her by her eccentric godfather, the nutcracker turns into a prince in this simple retelling with watercolor drawings.

794 *Why Are You So Mean to Me?* Ill. by Tom Cooke. Random House, 1986. ISBN 0-394-88060-9. SERIES: Start-to-Read. SUBJECTS: Friendship—Fiction; Self-esteem—Fiction. RL B.
Grover's mother tells him he will always be good at being himself, regardless of how he plays baseball. Feelings are expressed and friends forgiven in another Henson Muppet series book, illustrated in bright pastels.

Hawes, Judy

795 *Fireflies in the Night*. Ill. by Ellen Alexander. HarperCollins, 1990. ISBN 0-06-022485-1. SERIES: Let's-Read-and-Find-Out. SUBJECTS: Animals—Fireflies; Nature; Science. RL B.
The ways in which firefly light is generated, changes with the temperature, and is used by people are simply outlined, with suitable illustration of nighttime scenes. The fireflies are always released by bedtime.

796 *Why Frogs Are Wet*. Ill. by Don Madden. HarperCollins, 1968, o.p. SERIES: Let's-Read-and-Find-Out Science Books. SUBJECTS: Animals—Frogs and toads; Science. RL B.

Frogs preceded dinosaurs by 50 million years, have 2,000 varieties, were the first animals to have a voice. Fascinating frog facts are illustrated by bright, decorative drawings with bold strokes.

Hawkins, Colin, and Hawkins, Jacqui

797 *I'm Not Sleepy!* Ill. by authors. Crown, 1985, o.p.; Orchard, 1992. ISBN 0-531-05898-0. SERIES: It's Great to Read! SUBJECTS: Animals—Bears—Fiction; Bedtime—Fiction. RL A.
Not until Mommy comes to tuck him in does Baby Bear settle down for the night. Abbreviated dialogue between mother and child is illustrated showing only rotund baby's delaying antics.

798 *Jen the Hen*. Ill. by authors. Putnam, 1985, o.p. SERIES: Flip-the-Page Rhyming. SUBJECTS: Birthdays—Fiction; Stories in rhyme. RL A.
Ken, Ben, Wren, and a hen called Jen meet in the glen at ten—for a birthday party. Wordplay using basic vocabulary is illustrated with rotund cartoon characters in pastels, and two tiny bookish worms.

799 *Mig the Pig*. Ill. by Colin Hawkins. Putnam, 1986, o.p. SERIES: Flip-the-Page Rhyming. SUBJECTS: Animals—Pigs—Fiction; Stories in rhyme; Wordplay. RL A.
The beginning consonant of "pig" changes to make "big," "wig," "twig," and five other rhyming words. Zany cartoons include "talking" scallop-edged worms.

800 *Pat the Cat*. Ill. by authors. Putnam, 1983, o.p.; pap., 1986. ISBN 0-399-20957-3. SUBJECTS: Animals—Cats—Fiction; Stories in rhyme. RL A.
Pat the fat cat has a rat named Nat and a bat named Tat in his hat on the mat. Story is as lively as vocabulary allows, brightened by scallop-edged animals and worms.

801 *Tog the Dog*. Ill. by Colin Hawkins. Putnam, 1986, o.p. SERIES: Flip-the-Page Rhyming. SUBJECTS: Animals—Dogs—Fiction; Stories in rhyme; Wordplay. RL A.
Jog, fog, cog, frog, bog, hog, log, and a dog named Tog are rhyming words produced by

**Hawkins, Colin, and
Hawkins, Jacqui (cont.)**

changing initial consonants and accenting them with humorous wordplay. Visual humor is added with lumpy cartoon animals.

802 *Zug the Bug.* Ill. by Colin Hawkins. Putnam, 1988, o.p. SERIES: Flip-the-Page Rhyming. SUBJECTS: Animals—Insects—Fiction; Stories in rhyme; Wordplay. RL A.
Seven words rhyming with bug are made by changing the initial consonant. Cartoons are enlivened by the humorous commentary of two worms.

Hayes, Geoffrey

803 *The Mystery of the Pirate Ghost: An Otto and Uncle Tooth Adventure.* Ill. by author. Random House, hb and pap., 1985. ISBN 0-394-97220-1. SERIES: Step into Reading. SUBJECTS: Dinosaurs—Fiction; Mystery and detective stories; Pirates—Fiction. RL B.
Dinosaurs Otto and Uncle Tooth uncover a pirate "ghost" with a trumpet. The mystery is well constructed with some humor and a satisfying conclusion. Koalas, puffins, and octopi complete the cast of characters. Illustrations are in watercolor.

804 *The Secret of Foghorn Island.* Ill. by author. Random House, hb and pap., 1988. ISBN 0-394-99614-3. SERIES: Step into Reading. SUBJECTS: Dinosaurs—Fiction; Mystery and detective stories. RL B.
Dinosaurs Otto and Uncle Tooth save Auntie Hicks from Sid Rat, Weasel, and the magical Doctor Ocular in an adventure with sea witches and shipwrecks. Pastel comic drawings keep the tone light.

Hayward, Linda

805 *Biggest Cookie in the World.* Ill. by Joe Ewers. Random House, 1989. ISBN 0-394-84049-6. SERIES: Pictureback Reader. SUBJECTS: Bakers and baking—Fiction; Monsters—Fiction; Puppets and puppetry—Fiction. RL A.
While Sesame Street's Cookie Monster waits for a batch of chocolate chip cookies to bake, he dreams about the largest cookie in the world, losing track of baking time—with disastrous results. Ideas for using the 32 vocabulary words on flash cards are included on the back cover.

806 *Hello, House!* Ill. by Lynn Munsinger. Random House, hb and pap., 1988. ISBN 0-394-98864-7. SERIES: Step into Reading. SUBJECTS: Folklore—African Americans; Folklore—United States. RL A.
Brer Rabbit outsmarts Brer Wolf again in a classic trickster tale. Pastel drawings with expressive main characters enhance this simple, effective retelling.

Hearn, Emily

807 *Ring around Duffy.* Ill. by Paul Frame. Garrard, 1974, o.p. SERIES: Venture. SUBJECTS: Animals—Ducks—Fiction; Pollution—Fiction. RL B.
An injured duckling, rescued by a family dog, is returned to the wild, but needs to be rescued again when he gets a soda can ring stuck around his bill. Pencil and turquoise wash drawings present animals best.

808 *TV Kangaroo.* Ill. by Tom Eaton. Garrard, 1975, o.p. SUBJECTS: Animals—Fiction; Weather—Fiction. RL B.
No matter what weather the television kangaroo announces, some animals like it and others "avoid" it. Simple text and idea illustrated with light-hearted animal cartoons.

Heide, Florence

809 *Lost and Found.* Photos and drawings. Macmillan, 1975, o.p. SUBJECTS: Animals—Fiction; City and country life—Fiction; Water—Fiction. RL A.
Although the language is pedestrian, the illustrations are varied and interesting, ranging from block printing to black and white or color photos to cartoons.

Heide, Florence P., and Heide, Roxanne

810 *A Monster Is Coming! A Monster Is Coming!* Ill. by Rachi Farrow. Watts, 1980, o.p. SUBJECTS: Monsters—Fiction; Television—Fiction. RL B.

Neither her younger brother, Eddie, nor a monster can distract Alice from television. Pale lemon and lavender on a strong black and white checked floor contrast with the fuchsia, red, and gold monster.

**Heide, Florence, and
Van Clief, Sylvia Worth**

811 *Hats and Bears*. Drawings. Macmillan, 1975, o.p. SUBJECTS: Animals—Bears—Fiction; Hats—Fiction. RL A.
Short stories and verse touch on familiar things to children. Chapters have colorful humorous watercolor drawings by different illustrators. Writing is unimaginative.

Heilbroner, Joan

812 *The Happy Birthday Present*. Ill. by Mary Chalmers. HarperCollins, 1962, o.p. SERIES: I Can Read Books. SUBJECTS: Birthdays—Fiction; Siblings—Fiction. RL A.
Peter takes his little brother, Davy, shopping for Mother's birthday. With limited resources they end up with an imaginative birthday tree. Very realistic dialogue, childlike misconceptions, and soft pencil drawings add to the appeal.

813 *Robert the Rose Horse*. Ill. by P. D. Eastman. Random House, 1962. ISBN 0-394-90025-1. SERIES: I Can Read It All By Myself. SUBJECTS: Allergies—Fiction; Animals—Horses—Fiction; Humorous stories. RL A.
Robert's allergies cause him to end several careers prematurely, but when his big sneeze captures some bank robbers, he finally finds his calling. Cartoon sketches fit the humor.

814 *This Is the House Where Jack Lives*. Ill. by Aliki. HarperCollins, 1962. ISBN 0-06-022286-7. SERIES: I Can Read Books. SUBJECTS: Cumulative tales. RL A.
The very best of modern cumulative tales includes an assortment of apartment dwellers, from the maid and window-washer to a boy walking a dog and Jack taking an exuberant bath on an upper floor. Drawings are fun in gray and fuchsia.

815 *Tom the TV Cat: A Step Two Book*. Ill. by Sal Murdocca. Random House, hb and pap., 1984. ISBN 0-394-96708-9. SERIES: Step into Reading. SUBJECTS: Animals—Cats—Fiction; Self-esteem—Fiction; Television—Fiction. RL A.
Tom the cat tests some television roles by imitating the song man, the strong man, superman, and a ball man—with disastrous results. Murdocca's cartoons underline the humor of Tom's antics.

Heller, Ruth

816 *A Cache of Jewels and Other Collective Nouns*. Ill. by author. Putnam, 1987. ISBN 0-448-19211-X. SUBJECTS: English language; Word play. RL C.
In imaginative rhythmic, rhyming language, an array of collective nouns is presented—a gam of whales and a muster of peacocks, a parcel of penguins and a drift of swans. Double-spread, dramatic, realistic drawings show animals, fruit, flowers, and trees.

817 *Kites Sail High: A Book About Verbs*. Ill. by author. Putnam, 1988. ISBN 0-448-10480-6. SUBJECTS: English language; Word play. RL C.
Verbs are highlighted in bold, large type in the playful rhyming text. Tenses, moods, and contractions and voices are introduced, and illustrated with bold, double-page drawings from under the sea and from fairy tales, of animals and a single peacock feather quill, to a close-up box of candy.

818 *Many Luscious Lollipops: A Book About Adjectives.*. Ill. by author. Putnam, 1989. ISBN 0-448-03151-5. SUBJECTS: English language; Word play. RL C.
Demonstratives and possessives, comparative and irregular and superlative adjectives are introduced painlessly in this introduction to grammar and language. The playful rhyming text has sweeping illustrations of animals, ice cream, mazes, tree ornaments, and space.

819 *Merry-Go-Round: A Book About Nouns*. Ill. by author. Putnam, 1990. ISBN 0-448-40085-5. SUBJECTS: English language; Word play. RL C.
Stunning full-page thematic illustrations extend the unpatronizing vocabulary and grammar of nouns, ranging from medieval to

Heller, Ruth (cont.)

space-age themes. The language and the format are imaginative and instructive, covering plurals and possessives, compound and collective nouns, and determiners.

820 *Up, Up and Away: A Book About Adverbs.* Ill. by author. Putnam, 1991. ISBN 0-448-40249-1. SUBJECTS: English language; Word play. RL C.

Three large owls in a spruce illustrate the introduction of the questions adverbs ask: when, how, where, and why. Illustrations range from a monochromatic long-haired cat, to black-and-white pandas among the bright green bamboo, to the eerie purple and orange of the genies.

Henderson, Kathy

821 *Dairy Cows. Photos.* Childrens Pr., 1988. ISBN 0-516-01152-9. SERIES: New True. SUBJECTS: Animals—Cows; Farm and country life. RL B.

Seven brief chapters give information on the anatomy and digestive system of cows and on dairy farming. Glossary and index are appended. Excellent color photos accent the information.

Henriod, Lorraine

822 *Marie Curie.* Ill. by Fermin Rocker. Putnam, 1970, o.p. SERIES: See and Read. SUBJECTS: Biographies; Careers; Science. RL B.

In simple terms, without neglecting the hardships or hazards, the story of Marie Curie's amazing accomplishments in science is told. Ink drawings have a pale blue wash.

Henwood, Chris

823 *Frogs.* Photos by Barrie Watts. Watts, 1988, o.p. SERIES: Keeping Minibeasts. SUBJECTS: Animals—Frogs and toads; Pets. RL C.

Background information about frogs is geared for the catching, caring, and feeding of frogs as pets. Exceptional color photos give additional information about their habitat and handling.

824 *Spiders.* Photos by Barrie Watts. Watts, 1988. ISBN 0-531-10642-X. SERIES: Keeping Minibeasts. SUBJECTS: Animals—Spiders; Pets. RL C.

The handling and feeding of spiders of different sizes are described and illustrated with excellent color photos. Information on webs and the exaggerated danger to man from spiders is given.

Herman, Gail

825 *Double Header.* Ill. by Jerry Smath. Putnam, 1993. ISBN 0-448-40157-6. SERIES: All Aboard Reading. SUBJECTS: Monsters—Fiction; Sports—Baseball—Fiction. RL A.

Although the two heads of a double-headed boy monster almost always agree, their disagreement on the baseball diamond costs their team the game. Seeing a good scary double feature—*Human Beings* and *Human Beings 2*—at Fright Night unites the two again. Friendly colored pencil drawings complement the text.

826 *What a Hungry Puppy!* Ill. by Norman Gorbaty. Putnam, 1993. ISBN 0-448-40537-7. SERIES: All Aboard Reading. SUBJECTS: Animals—Dogs—Fiction; Pets—Fiction. RL A.

Despite the admonition that dinner is almost ready, Lucky the puppy strays, sniffing, digging, and chewing, until chased home by a big white sheepdog, who turns out not to be threatening after all. Raggedy puppy drawings are appealing.

Hewett, Joan

827 *Tiger, Tiger, Growing Up.* Photos by Richard Hewett. Houghton Mifflin, 1993. ISBN 0-395-61583-6. SUBJECTS: Animals—Tigers; Conservation; Zoos. RL C.

The development of a newborn tiger cub, Tara, into a cat ambassador for Marine World Africa USA is traced through playful, affectionate color photos and narrative.

Hilker, Cathryn H.

828 *A Cheetah Named Angel.* Photos. Watts, 1992. ISBN 0-531-15252-9. SUBJECTS:

Animals—Cheetahs; Conservation; Zoos. RL C.

Cathryn raises a cheetah cub from the Columbus, Ohio, zoo at her farm near Cincinnati, along with her Great Dane and, later, a mountain lion cub, Carrie. Both the cubs become TV stars and international ambassadors to lobby for preservation of habitat for wild cats. Excellent photos accompany the text.

Hillert, Margaret

829 *Circus Fun*. Ill. by Elaine Raphael. Modern Curriculum, 1969, o.p. SUBJECTS: Circuses—Fiction. RL A.

Fifty words are used to tell about the circus. Watercolors focus on clowns, lions, and elephants.

830 *Come Play with Me*. Ill. by Kinuko Craft. Follett, 1975, o.p. SERIES: Just Beginning-To-Read. SUBJECTS: Poetry. RL A.

Simple poems about familiar things, composed of 75 pre-primer words, are illustrated with imaginative watercolors in a fairy tale atmosphere.

831 *Come to School, Dear Dragon*. Ill. by David Helton. Modern Curriculum, 1985. ISBN 0-8136-5133-6. SERIES: Beginning to Read. SUBJECTS: Mythical creatures—Fiction; Pets—Dragons—Fiction; School stories. RL A.

A dragon makes himself useful when his boy takes him to school. This primer employs a 75-word vocabulary and typically cutesy Helton drawings.

832 *A Friend for Dear Dragon*. Ill. by David Helton. Modern Curriculum, 1985. ISBN 0-8136-5136-0. SERIES: Beginning to Read. SUBJECTS: Friendship—Fiction; Mythical creatures—Fiction; Pets—Fiction. RL A.

Using a 67-word vocabulary, a former first grade teacher relays the moral play of a boy and his pet dragon, and the new neighbor girl and her unicorn. Cutesy drawings and unimaginative text limit the appeal of this book.

833 *Go to Sleep, Dear Dragon*. Ill. by David Helton. Modern Curriculum, 1985. ISBN 0-8136-5023-2. SERIES: Beginning to Read.

SUBJECTS: Dreams—Fiction; Mythical creatures—Fiction; Pets—Fiction. RL A.

Using a 74-word vocabulary, the author spins a tale of how the dreaming boy finds his dear dragon's egg in medieval times. This is more interesting than many Hillert books with such limited vocabularies, but has typical drawings.

834 *Happy Birthday, Dear Dragon*. Ill. by Carl Kock. Modern Curriculum, hb and pap., 1977. ISBN 0-8136-5021-6. SERIES: Just Beginning-To-Read. SUBJECTS: Concepts—Color—Fiction; Holidays—Valentine's Day—Fiction; Mythical creatures—Fiction. RL A.

A child and a baby dragon celebrate Valentine's Day by focusing on red things familiar to children: a cardinal, a fire truck, a stop light, school, apples, and a valentine. Drawings are simple.

835 *It's Circus Time, Dear Dragon*. Ill. by David Helton. Modern Curriculum, 1984. ISBN 0-8136-5132-8. SUBJECTS: Circuses—Fiction; Dragons—Fiction. RL A.

In text with a 65-word vocabulary, a boy and his pet dragon visit the circus. The book is dry and unimaginative in text and illustration, except for the dragon's mild mischief in trying the tuba or joining the parade of elephants.

836 *Little Puff*. Ill. by Sid Jordan. Modern Curriculum, hb and pap., 1973. ISBN 0-8136-5014-3. SUBJECTS: Trains—Fiction. RL A.

Sixty words are used to tell the slight story of a train that is not wanted in town or at the zoo, only on the tracks with children as passengers. Drawings have color and pattern reminiscent of a mosaic.

837 *Play Ball*. Ill. by Dick Martin. Follett, hb and pap., 1978. ISBN 0-8136-5034-8. SERIES: Just Beginning-To-Read. SUBJECTS: Play—Fiction; Toys—Fiction. RL A.

Interest and humor are generated with 58 words as two boys look for balls and equipment to play various games. There are unexpected and magical qualities to their play. Pale tans and yellows predominate in clever illustrations.

838 *Run to the Rainbow*. Ill. by Barbara Corey. Modern Curriculum, hb and pap.,

Hillert, Margaret (cont.)

1981. ISBN 0-8136-5065-8. SERIES: Beginning-To-Read. SUBJECTS: Rainbows; Science. RL A.

The text, even though a bit choppy, introduces some interesting, commonplace ways to produce rainbows. Watercolor illustrations are a bit busy to locate the "rainbows."

839 *Snow Baby.* Ill. by Liz Dauber. Follett, hb and pap., 1969. ISBN 0-8136-5065-8. SERIES: Just Beginning-To-Read. SUBJECTS: Seasons—Winter—Fiction; Weather—Snow—Fiction. RL A.

Children's play in the snow leads to a surprise find in this pre-primer with a 50-word vocabulary. Full color drawings fill the pages.

840 *What Is It?* Ill. by Kinuko Craft. Modern Curriculum, hb and pap., 1978. ISBN 0-8136-5056-9. SERIES: Just Beginning-To-Read My Stories in Verse. SUBJECTS: Imagination—Fiction; Stories in rhyme. RL A.

Two elflike children follow a string through an imaginary land. The rhymed text uses 55 simple words. Illustrations are stilted pastels.

841 *Who Goes to School?* Ill. by Nan Brooks. Modern Curriculum, hb and pap., 1981. ISBN 0-8136-5075-5. SERIES: Just Beginning-To-Read. SUBJECTS: Animals—Cats; Animals—Dogs; School stories. RL A.

Circus, television commercial, and police dogs go to school, as do children. A vocabulary of 65 words is used to give very basic information about school. Folk-style illustrations add appeal.

842 *The Witch Who Went for a Walk.* Ill. by Krystyna Stasiak. Follett, hb and pap., 1982, o.p. SERIES: Just Beginning-To-Read. SUBJECTS: Holidays—Halloween—Fiction; Witches—Fiction. RL A.

Sixty-seven words are used to show the witch's fear of children dressed for Halloween. Some scary elements such as owls, caves, bats, and trees are shown with wide eyes in dark colors.

Himmelman, John

843 *The Day-Off Machine.* Ill. by author. Silver Burdett, 1990. ISBN 0-671-69635-1.
SERIES: Fix-It Family. SUBJECTS: Animals—Beavers—Fiction; Family life—Fiction; Inventors and inventions—Fiction. RL A.

Graham, a boy from a very inventive beaver family, finds an ingenious way to get the whole family to take a day off—and then another. Delightful warm family relations are pictured with ink and wash drawings.

844 *Great Leaf Blast-Off.* Ill. by author. Silver Burdett, 1990. ISBN 0-671-69634-3. SERIES: Fix-It Family. SUBJECTS: Animals—Beavers—Fiction; Humorous stories; Inventors and inventions—Fiction. RL A.

Pen and wash drawings add humor to this chapter story of inventive beavers named Wright. The brothers make unsuccessful machines to avoid raking, their parents invent new contraptions to replace appliances the boys "borrowed," but "space girl" Belle steals the day.

845 *Ibis: A True Whale Story.* Ill. by author. Scholastic, 1990. ISBN 0-590-42848-9. SUBJECTS: Animals—Whales; Nature. RL A.

A true story about a small whale saved by scientists from net entanglement off Provincetown, Massachusetts, in 1984. Simple friendly whale illustrations accompany the text.

846 *Simpson Snail Sings.* Ill. by author. Dutton, 1992. ISBN 0-525-44978-7. SERIES: Dutton Easy Reader. SUBJECTS: Animals—Fiction; Animals—Snails—Fiction; Friendship—Fiction. RL A.

Imaginative gentle tales of friends Simpson the Snail and Gypsy Moth are accompanied by delicate, expressive ink and wash drawings. The two share a trophy for best costume; Simpson learns to sing his own song; Simpson loses—and regains—a friend; and he and Tucker Turtle have a sleep-over.

847 *The Ups and Downs of Simpson Snail.* Ill. by author. Dutton, 1989. ISBN 0-525-44542-0. SERIES: Dutton Easy Reader. SUBJECTS: Animals—Snails—Fiction; Animals—Turtles—Fiction; Friendship—Fiction. RL A.

Tucker Turtle rescues Simpson Snail, whose pride doesn't allow him to ask for help; friends Gypsy Moth and Tucker rescue him after he tries flying against their advice. The characters appear in whimsical ink and watercolor.

Hindley, Judy

848 *Zoom on a Broom! Six Fun-Filled Stories.* Ill. by Tony Goffe. Kingfisher, 1991. ISBN 1-85697-826-5. SERIES: Kingfisher Read-Alone. SUBJECTS: Cumulative tales; Folklore. RL A.
Elements of familiar folktales and themes are rewoven, some with more success than others. "The Magical Apple Tree" and "Tricky Tom" (royal suitor outwits giant) work well, but "The Wonderful Turnip" and "What Do Witches Like?" are flat. Excellent light-hearted ink and wash drawings illustrate the tales.

Hirschi, Ron

849 *Fall.* Photos by Thomas D. Mangelsen. Cobblehill, 1981. ISBN 0-525-65053-9. SUBJECTS: Animals—Birds; Seasons—Fall. RL B.
Excellent photos of a web, a flower, a squirrel eating a mushroom, salmon, an eagle, and deer are shown against the rich tapestry of fall colors. Large print is used for vividly described seasonal changes.

850 *Spring.* Photos by Thomas D. Mangelsen. Cobblehill, 1990. ISBN 0-525-65037-7. SERIES: A Wildlife Seasons Book. SUBJECTS: Nature; Seasons—Spring. RL B.
From the golden weasel to the nest of baby owls, from the marmot atop his rocky hill to a vivid mountain bluebird perched on the top of a pine tree, this photo essay celebrates the wonder and diversity at the beginning of spring.

851 *What is a Bird?* Photos by Galen Burrell. Walker, 1987. ISBN 0-8027-6721-4. SUBJECTS: Animals—Birds. RL B.
Short, expressive descriptions of a variety of birds are stunningly illustrated with close-up framed photo of birds against their native settings. This book is full of wonder and poetry.

Hiscock, Bruce

852 *The Big Rock.* Ill. by author. Atheneum, 1988. ISBN 0-689-31402-7. SUBJECTS: Geology; Science. RL C.
The geological history of the Adirondacks is presented in an interesting and understandable way by following the movement of one rock. The watercolor illustrations complement the text well.

Hoban, Brom

853 *Jason and the Bees.* Ill. by author. HarperCollins, 1980, o.p. SERIES: Nature I Can Read. SUBJECTS: Animals—Bees; Nature. RL A.
It takes 20,000 bees to collect a pound of nectar, which makes a pound of honey. Jason, who originally throws rocks at hives, learns from a neighbor how to care for the bees safely. Pen and wash drawings are a bit stilted.

Hoban, Julia

854 *Buzby.* Ill. by John Himmelman. HarperCollins, 1990. ISBN 0-06-022399-5. SERIES: I Can Read Books. SUBJECTS: Animals—Fiction; Humorous stories. RL A.
When polite, clean Buzby, who is also a good mouser, finds a job as a hotel busboy, he spills icewater on an opera singer and slips in the butter on the king's table. Gentle humor is enhanced by ink and wash illustrations.

855 *Buzby to the Rescue.* Ill. by John Himmelman. HarperCollins, 1993. ISBN 0-06-021024-9. SERIES: I Can Read Books. SUBJECTS: Animals—Cats—Fiction. RL A.
Buzby, the proud hotel cat, saves a hotel guest, star Serena Lovejoy, from herself, and some suspected robbers. Fine, simple drawings show the innocent hotel cat and the other characters.

856 *Quick Chick.* Ill. by Lillian Hoban. Dutton, 1989. ISBN 0-525-44490-4. SUBJECTS: Animals—Chickens—Fiction. RL B.
The littlest slow-learning chick is renamed after escaping from a cat. Friendly barnyard animals are in soft pastels.

Hoban, Lillian

857 *Arthur's Camp-out.* Ill. by author. HarperCollins, 1993. ISBN 0-06-020526-1. SERIES: I Can Read Books. SUBJECTS: Animals—Chimpanzees—Fiction; Camps and camping—Fiction; Siblings—Fiction. RL B.

Hoban, Lillian (cont.)

Arthur's fears and problems when he follows his younger sister's friends on a campout are eased when the girls feed him and keep him company. The baby-sitter welcomes campers home with a banner and breakfast pancakes. Reassuring pencil and wash drawings accompany the text.

858 *Arthur's Christmas Cookies*. Ill. by author. HarperCollins, 1972, pap., 1984. ISBN 0-06-022368-5. SERIES: I Can Read Books. SUBJECTS: Animals—Chimpanzees—Fiction; Bakers and baking—Fiction; Holidays—Christmas—Fiction. RL B.
Arthur again turns defeat into triumph when his Bake E-Z Christmas cookies are rock-hard. Pencil and wash drawings complement this story of childhood mishaps featuring a loving chimp family.

859 *Arthur's Funny Money*. Ill. by author. HarperCollins, 1980; pap., 1984. ISBN 0-06-022344-8. SERIES: I Can Read Books. SUBJECTS: Animals—Chimpanzees—Fiction; Mathematics—Fiction; Siblings—Fiction. RL B.
Violet finds out Arthur does not know numbers as well as he says when they go into the bike-washing business. Realistic characterization is underlined by soft pencil drawings with a four-color wash.

860 *Arthur's Great Big Valentine*. Ill. by author. HarperCollins, 1988. ISBN 0-06-022407-X. SERIES: I Can Read Books. SUBJECTS: Animals—Chimpanzees—Fiction; Friendship—Fiction; Holidays—Valentine's Day—Fiction. RL B.
Arthur makes up with his friends by sending an unusual valentine. The pain and humor of childhood are shown throughout the book. Illustrations are of chimpanzee children.

861 *Arthur's Honey Bear*. Ill. by author. HarperCollins, 1974; pap., 1982. ISBN 0-06-022370-7. SERIES: I Can Read Books. SUBJECTS: Animals—Chimpanzees—Fiction; Growing-up—Fiction; Siblings—Fiction. RL B.
Arthur becomes his Honey Bear's *uncle* when he reluctantly trades his beloved toy to Violet and regrets it. The sadness and joy of growing up are celebrated here.

862 *Arthur's Loose Tooth*. Ill. by author. HarperCollins, 1985; pap., 1987. ISBN 0-06-022354-5. SERIES: I Can Read Books. SUBJECTS: Animals—Chimpanzees—Fiction; Baby-sitting—Fiction; Human body—Teeth—Fiction. RL B.
A cozy book has excellent dialogue, good relationships, and gentle humor. Arthur the chimp's loose tooth does not keep him from enjoying s'mores and taffy apples. Expressive chimps have child fears and childlike misbehaviors.

863 *Arthur's Pen Pal*. Ill. by author. HarperCollins, 1976; pap., 1982. ISBN 0-06-022372-3. SERIES: I Can Read Books. SUBJECTS: Animals—Chimpanzees—Fiction; Baby-sitting—Fiction; Siblings—Fiction. RL B.
Arthur decides he does not want to trade families with his pen pal after all, despite the irritations of baby-sitting for a younger sister. Good characterization and dialogue. Softly colored pencil drawings capture the feeling of everyday family life.

864 *Arthur's Prize Reader*. Ill. by author. HarperCollins, 1978; pap., 1984. ISBN 0-06-022380-4. SERIES: I Can Read Books. SUBJECTS: Animals—Chimpanzees—Fiction; Books and reading—Fiction; Siblings—Fiction. RL B.
While trying to help her older brother, Arthur, with a Super Chimp Comic contest, Violet learns to read hard words. Dialogue and pencil and wash drawings capture the flavor of childhood.

865 *The Case of the Two Masked Robbers*. Ill. by author. HarperCollins, 1986. ISBN 0-06-022299-9. SERIES: I Can Read Books. SUBJECTS: Animals—Raccoons—Fiction; Animals—Turtles—Fiction; mystery and detective stories. RL B.
Raccoons Arabella and Albert, seeking the turtle-egg robber, have some nocturnal adventures and find a way to safeguard the eggs. The nighttime fears are most effectively portrayed in pencil with dusky violet, tan, and green.

866 *Mr. Pig and Sonny Too*. Ill. by author. HarperCollins, 1977. ISBN 0-06-022341-3. SERIES: I Can Read Books. SUBJECTS: Animals—Pigs—Fiction; Friendship—Fiction. RL B.

Mr. Pig's mishaps while skating, picnicking, and going to a wedding (his own) have amusing and loving resolutions. The pigs are drawn with lumpy detail in pastel greens and pale oranges dominating.

867 *Silly Tilly and the Easter Bunny*. Ill. by author. HarperCollins, 1986. ISBN 0-06-022393-6. SERIES: Early I Can Read. SUBJECTS: Animals—Moles—Fiction; Animals—Rabbits—Fiction; Holidays—Easter—Fiction. RL B.
Silly Tilly nearly misses the Easter Bunny's visit by her forgetful behavior. Slight story has friendly pastel, lumpy animal watercolors.

868 *Silly Tilly's Thanksgiving Dinner*. Ill. by author. HarperCollins, 1990. ISBN 0-06-022423-1. SERIES: I Can Read Books. SUBJECTS: Friendship—Fiction; Holidays—Thanksgiving. RL A.
Silly Tilly's vision problems lead to a series of mistakes, which are solved when her Thanksgiving guests provide all the food. Gentle humor is amplified by the author's appealing animal drawings.

869 *Stick-in-the-Mud Turtle*. Ill. by author. Greenwillow, 1977, o.p. SERIES: Read-alone. SUBJECTS: Animals—Turtles—Fiction. RL C.
Fred, his wife, and their ten turtle children live simply and well until another turtle family moves into their pond. Pastel sketches with dominant green underline their contentment—shattered and then regained.

870 *Turtle Spring*. Ill. by author. Greenwillow, 1978, o.p. SERIES: Read-alone. SUBJECTS: Animals—Turtles—Fiction; Seasons—Spring—Fiction. RL B.
Turtle gossip and spring newborns flavor a gentle seasonal tale with interesting character sketches. Spring green, yellow, and brown show the animals on the pond with their new babies.

Hoban, Lillian, and Hoban, Phoebe

871 *Laziest Robot in Zone One*. Ill. by Lillian Hoban. HarperCollins, 1983; pap., 1985. ISBN 0-06-022352-9. SERIES: I Can Read Books. SUBJECTS: Robots—Fiction; Science Fiction. RL C.

Robots Sola and Sol's search for Big Rover leads them to rescue Power Puss and get a lot of help with their household chores. Interesting differences from and similarities to life familiar to modern children are illustrated in lavender, orange, gray, and fuchsia watercolor sketches in this science fiction story.

872 *Ready-Set-Robot*. Ill. by Lillian Hoban. HarperCollins, 1982; pap., 1985. ISBN 0-06-022346-4. SERIES: I Can Read Books. SUBJECTS: Humorous stories; Robots—Fiction; Science fiction. RL C.
Space and robot humor evolves from a messy robot's involvement in a space race, which he wins only with his robot dog's help. Interesting ideas about life for robots are illustrated in pastels.

Hoban, Russell

873 *Ace Dragon Ltd*. Ill. by Quentin Blake. Jonathan Cape, 1980, o.p. SUBJECTS: Mythical creatures—Fiction. RL B.
John's astute observation earns him a day of high adventure with a dragon named Ace in Wellingtons. This playful and imaginative tale has some amusing twists of plot. Lively pen sketches have light orange and gray washes.

874 *Bargain for Frances*. Ill. by Lillian Hoban. HarperCollins, 1970; pap., 1978. ISBN 0-06-444001-X. SERIES: I Can Read Books. SUBJECTS: Animals—Badgers—Fiction; Friendship—Fiction. RL B.
Frances finds that carefully avoiding her friend's tricks is not as much fun as being friends. Fairly sophisticated ideas are presented in a reassuring, simple manner. Soft pencil drawings maintain that tone.

875 *Tom and the Two Handles*. Ill. by Lillian Hoban. HarperCollins, 1965; pap., 1984. ISBN 0-06-022431-2. SERIES: I Can Read Books. SUBJECTS: Fathers—Fiction; Friendship—Fiction. RL A.
After Tom has a fight with his best friend, his father tells him about a jug having two handles. In other words, Tom can choose to pick up his friendship by the same handle next time, or choose the other. In ink and wash drawings Lillian Hoban's illustrations of the children capture the essence of the spat.

Hodgman, Ann

876 *Day in the Life of a Fashion Designer.* Photos. Troll, 1988. ISBN 0-8167-1119-4. SERIES: A Day in the Life of. SUBJECTS: Careers. RL C.

From the sketch to the muslin pattern to the actual sample, from selecting fabrics to computerizing a fabric design for the loom, the text suggests the talent, hard work, and advance preparation needed to have fashionable clothes ready for sale. An interesting view of a glamorous career.

877 *Day in the Life of a Theater Set Designer.* Photos by Gayle Jann. Troll, 1988. ISBN 0-8167-1127-5. SERIES: A Day in the Life of. SUBJECTS: Careers. RL C.

Linda at work at her home and in New York studios is described in rather difficult language accompanied by color photos. This book would be hard for readers in primary grades to use without guidance.

Hoff, Syd

878 *Albert the Albatross.* Ill. by author. HarperCollins, 1961. ISBN 0-06-022446-0. SERIES: Early I Can Read. SUBJECTS: Animals—Albatrosses—Fiction. RL B.

While lost from his ship, Albert encounters a parrot, a cuckoo, a woodpecker, and a weathervane bird. When he roosts on a hat belonging to a lady off on a cruise, he finds his ship again. Plain cartoons follow Albert's adventures.

879 *Barney's Horse.* Ill. by author. HarperCollins, 1987. ISBN 0-06-022450-9. SERIES: Early I Can Read. SUBJECTS: Animals—Horses—Fiction; City and town life—Fiction. RL B.

Barney the peddler's horse runs away—once. Warm view of city life is illustrated with cartoon drawings.

880 *Bernard on His Own.* Ill. by author. Houghton Mifflin, 1993. ISBN 0-395-65226-X. SUBJECTS: Animals—Bears—Fiction. RL A.

Bernard has to be rescued by his parents repeatedly because he is too young to stand on his hind legs or growl. Very simple colored pencil drawings are nevertheless comforting to a young reader.

881 *Captain Cat.* Ill. by author. HarperCollins, 1993. ISBN 0-06-020527-X. SERIES: I Can Read Books. SUBJECTS: Animals—Cats—Fiction. RL A.

Soldiers, particularly one named Pete, befriend a tiger cat—soon named Captain Cat, since he has more stripes than anyone else. Captain Cat enjoys mess duty, and marching—although not in the rain. Typical Hoff drawings show a very contented cat.

882 *Chester.* Ill. by author. HarperCollins, 1961; pap., 1986. ISBN 0-06-022456-8. SERIES: I Can Read Books. SUBJECTS: Animals—Horses—Fiction. RL A.

The horse Chester's search for loving leads him to a farm, a market, a park, a carousel, and a firehouse. Simple cartoon drawings and predicaments evoke gentle humor.

883 *Danny and the Dinosaur.* Ill. by author. HarperCollins, 1958; pap., 1978. ISBN 0-06-022466-5. SERIES: I Can Read Books. SUBJECTS: Dinosaurs—Fiction. RL B.

A dinosaur takes a day off from the museum to frolic with Danny. This imaginative tale is very appealing to children. Flat drawings have humor in the episodes, from the dinosaur's large size to its delighted expression.

884 *Happy Birthday, Henrietta!* Ill. by author. Garrard, 1983, o.p. SERIES: Imagination. SUBJECTS: Animals—Chickens—Fiction; Birthdays—Fiction. RL A.

Besides being treated to flowers, a movie, and popcorn in town, Henrietta has yet another birthday surprise in store. Watercolors make the cartoon animals appear warm.

885 *Henrietta, the Early Bird.* Ill. by author. Garrard, 1978, o.p. SERIES: Imagination. SUBJECTS: Animals—Chickens—Fiction; Farm and country life—Fiction. RL A.

Henrietta mistakenly tries to arouse the barnyard and town in the middle of the night. Comic watercolors are simple and expressive.

886 *Henrietta Goes to the Fair.* Ill. by author. Garrard, 1979, o.p. SERIES: Imagination.

SUBJECTS: Animals—Chickens—Fiction; Fairs—Fiction; Farm and country life—Fiction. RL A.
Henrietta accidentally wins a blue ribbon at the fair, but her real concern is for Winthrop the pig's feelings. Simple watercolors focus on the animals.

887 *Henrietta's Fourth of July*. Ill. by author. Garrard, 1981, o.p. SERIES: Imagination. SUBJECTS: Animals—Chickens—Fiction; Farm and country life—Fiction; Holidays—Fourth of July—Fiction. RL A.
Henrietta carries the flag when the farm animals participate in the Fourth of July festivities. Cartoon drawings add humor.

888 *The Horse in Harry's Room*. Ill. by author. HarperCollins, 1970; pap., 1985. ISBN 0-06-022483-5. SERIES: Early I Can Read. SUBJECTS: Animals—Horses—Fiction; Imagination—Fiction. RL B.
Even after a trip to the country to see real horses, Harry knows that his imaginary horse will stay in his room as long as Harry wants. Typical Hoff cartoons have either turquoise or brown wash.

889 *Ida the Bareback Rider*. Ill. by author. Putnam, 1972, o.p. SERIES: See and Read. SUBJECTS: Circuses—Fiction. RL C.
Ida the circus bareback rider wants all the applause until a fire teaches her that teamwork is more important. A sampling of circus acts with a fairly didactic story is illustrated with typical Hoff cartoons in yellow, pink, and orange washes.

890 *Jeffrey at Camp*. Ill. by author. Putnam, 1968, o.p. SUBJECTS: Camps and Camping—Fiction. RL C.
Jeffrey's moaning from overeating scares a bear away from camp, and changes Jeffrey's eating habits permanently. Cartoon drawings have yellow highlights.

891 *Julius*. Ill. by author. HarperCollins, 1959; pap., 1988. ISBN 0-06-022491-6. SERIES: I Can Read Books. SUBJECTS: Animals—Gorillas—Fiction; Circuses—Fiction. RL B.
A circus gorilla gets lost when he tries to find the people he has just scared away. Simple sketches are typical of Hoff.

892 *The Lighthouse Children*. Ill. by author. HarperCollins, 1994. ISBN 0-06-022959-4. SUBJECTS: Lighthouses—Fiction. RL A.
Sam and Rose fed the gulls and kept the lighthouse until a storm ruined the lighthouse, forcing the couple to move away. Lonely for their gulls, they found a way to entice the gulls to follow them. Typical Hoff cartoons illustrate the story.

893 *Mrs. Brice's Mice*. Ill. by author. HarperCollins, 1988. ISBN 0-06-022452-5. SERIES: Early I Can Read. SUBJECTS: Animals—Mice—Fiction. RL A.
Mrs. Brice fed her 25 mice the finest cheese, and washed and dried behind their ears so they were always clean. However, one mouse is always the nonconformist in Mrs. Brice and the mice's collective activities. Cartoon illustrations underline the humor.

894 *Sammy the Seal*. Ill. by author. HarperCollins, 1959; pap., 1980. ISBN 0-06-022526-2. SERIES: I Can Read Books. SUBJECTS: Animals—Seals—Fiction. RL A.
Despite success in learning how to read at school, Sammy the seal discovers that at the zoo he can swim and have a tasty diet more easily than in his city explorations. Cartoon illustrations are appropriate for the slight tale.

895 *Soft Skull Sam*. Ill. by author. Harcourt, 1981, o.p. SERIES: Let Me Read. SUBJECTS: Sports—Soccer—Fiction. RL B.
Sam's afraid of hitting the ball with his head in soccer, but he discovers it doesn't hurt. Didactic story is illustrated with Hoff's cartoons that have gray and green washes.

896 *Stanley*. Ill. by author. HarperCollins, 1992. ISBN 0-06-022535-1. SERIES: I Can Read Books. SUBJECTS: Man, prehistoric—Fiction; Self-esteem—Fiction. RL A.
A new, full color edition of Syd Hoff's tale of a prehistoric man whose seed-planting, picture-painting, and kindness distances him from other cave-dwellers. This is a rhythmic, imaginative, simple tale.

897 *Thunderhoof*. Ill. by author. HarperCollins, 1971. ISBN 0-06-022560-2. SERIES: Early I Can Read. SUBJECTS: Animals—Horses—Fiction; Cowboys—

Hoff, Syd (cont.)

Fiction; Pets—Wild animals—Fiction. RL C.
Wild Thunderhoof throws every comer from his saddle, but after escaping to the range, he misses the brushing and currying, so he returns to the ranch more docile. Illustrations are very simple.

898 *A Walk Past Ellen's House*. Ill. by author. McGraw-Hill, 1972, o.p. SUBJECTS: Behavior—Shyness—Fiction; Friendship—Fiction. RL B.
Harvey overcomes his shyness only when he forgets himself to help someone else. Comic drawings have brown and blue wash.

899 *Walpole*. Ill. by author. HarperCollins, 1977, o.p. SERIES: Early I Can Read. SUBJECTS: Animals—Walruses—Fiction. RL B.
Big, strong Walpole does not want to be leader of the walrus pack; he is busy caring for orphan walruses. Although the language is simple, there are some nice touches and real warmth. Illustrations in brown and blue match the quality of the text.

900 *Who Will Be My Friends?* Ill. by author. HarperCollins, 1960; pap., 1985. ISBN 0-06-022556-4. SERIES: Early I Can Read. SUBJECTS: Friendship—Fiction; Moving, household—Fiction. RL A.
Freddy's ability to play baseball gives him an entry into a new neighborhood. This simple story is illustrated with typically simple Hoff pencil drawings, alternating sepia with four colors.

901 *Wilfred the Lion*. Ill. by author. Putnam, 1970, o.p. SUBJECTS: Animals—Lions—Fiction; Behavior—Bravery—Fiction; Friendship—Fiction. RL B.
Wilfred's attempts to act as brave as his favorite animal, the lion, help him to be less fearful in the playground, but he ends up lonely—until his mother helps him become a boy again. Typical Hoff cartoons have pale blue and tan washes.

Hogan, Paula Z.

902 *The Honeybee*. Ill. by Geri K. Strigenz. Raintree, 1979. ISBN 0-8172-1256-6.

SERIES: Life Cycles. SUBJECTS: Animals—Bees; Nature. RL C.
A glossary is appended to an outline of the life of a honeybee hive. Full page paintings show bee behavior.

Hogrogian, Nonny

903 *Billy Goat and His Well-Fed Friends*. Ill. by author. HarperCollins, 1972, o.p. SERIES: I Can Read Books. SUBJECTS: Animals—Goats—Fiction. RL B.
Together Billy Goat and four friends escape being some farmers' dinner, and they scare wolves away from their new house in the woods. In cadence and result, the tale is reminiscent of the "Musicians of Bremen." Pale pastel pencil drawings are very appealing.

Holding, James

904 *The Robber of Featherbed Lane*. Ill. by author. Putnam, 1970, o.p. SERIES: See and Read. SUBJECTS: Mystery and detective stories. RL B.
An imaginative cumulation of lost items includes a diamond ring, a banana cake, a monkey, a small child, and a kitten. Ink sketches are in yellow and avocado.

Holl, Adelaide

905 *Bedtime for Bears*. Ill. by Cyndy Szekeres. Garrard, hb and pap., 1973, o.p. SERIES: Venture. SUBJECTS: Animals—Bears—Fiction; Seasons—Fall—Fiction. RL B.
Full of curiosity, Small Bear succumbs to sleep only after finding the other animals too busy preparing for winter to have time to play. Pencil drawings with a pale blue wash give the animals a very appealing mien.

906 *George the Gentle Giant*. Ill. by Frank Daniel. Golden, 1962, o.p. SERIES: Read It Yourself. SUBJECTS: Friendship—Fiction; Giants—Fiction. RL B.
George the Giant tries unsuccessfully with a picnic and singing to make friends with the village children. When his tears make a pool, friendly contact is made. Plain colored drawings have little imaginative detail.

907 *If We Could Make Wishes*. Ill. by Judy Pelikan. Garrard, 1977, o.p. SERIES: Imagination. SUBJECTS: Imagination—Fiction. RL C.
Two children play with dragons, ghosts, mermaids, and giants—in their imaginations! They are content with being themselves in real life. Message and pastel watercolors are a bit stilted.

908 *The Long Birthday*. Ill. by Ethel Gold. Garrard, 1974, o.p. SERIES: Venture. SUBJECTS: Birthdays—Fiction. RL B.
Jody finds a butterfly chrysalis, earns money to buy some seeds, and makes a card for her mother's birthday after giving away or losing her precious three dimes. Drawings in kelly green and pencil are static.

909 *Small Bear and the Secret Surprise*. Ill. by Tien. Garrard, 1978, o.p. SERIES: Small Bear Adventures. SUBJECTS: Friendship—Fiction; Siblings—Fiction. RL A.
Small Bear's "secret surprise" is a new baby sister, who wanders off while under his care, climbs a tree and will not come down. This quiet, gentle adventure is suitably illustrated with soft ink drawings with a turquoise wash.

910 *Small Bear Builds a Playhouse*. Ill. by Cyndy Szekeres. Garrard, 1978, o.p. SERIES: Small Bear Adventures. SUBJECTS: Animals—Bears—Fiction; Behavior—Sharing—Fiction; Friendship—Fiction. RL B.
Small Bear does not enjoy his new playhouse much until he invites his friends to share it. Pencil drawings of animals have a green wash.

911 *Small Bear's Birthday Party*. Ill. by Leigh Grant. Garrard, 1977, o.p. SERIES: Small Bear Adventures. SUBJECTS: Animals—Bears—Fiction; Birthdays—Fiction. RL B.
When Small Bear's friends are too busy to play, his feelings are hurt, but the party they are planning for him changes his feelings. Patterned ink drawings with a pale turquoise wash suit the gentleness of the story.

912 *Small Bear's Name Hunt*. Ill. by Pat Bargielski. Garrard, 1977, o.p. SERIES: Small Bear Adventures. SUBJECTS: Animals—Bears—Fiction. RL A.

Small Bear's gentle encounters with other animals convince him that his own name is most appropriate. Bargielski's use of cool green detracts from the warmth of her drawings.

913 *Sylvester: The Mouse with the Musical Ear*. Ill. by N. M. Bodecker. Golden, 1973, o.p. SERIES: Read It Yourself. SUBJECTS: Animals—Mice—Fiction; City and town life—Fiction; Farm and country life—Fiction. RL B.
When development encroaches on the pastoral music of his fields, Sylvester finds a home that suits his musical ear—a guitar! In delightful progression, a town-city mouse story becomes a tall tale, well underscored by delicate line drawings.

914 *Too Fat to Fly*. Ill. by Bill Morrison. Garrard, hb and pap., 1973, o.p. SERIES: Venture. SUBJECTS: Animals—Elephants—Fiction; Self-esteem—Fiction. RL B.
Marco's attempts to imitate Lark, Butterfly, and Fish are disastrous, but he is just right for being an elephant. Illustrations are adequate.

915 *Wake Up, Small Bear*. Ill. by Pat Bargielski. Garrard, 1977, o.p. SERIES: Small Bear Adventures. SUBJECTS: Animals—Bears—Fiction; Seasons—Spring—Fiction. RL A.
Joyfully Small Bear greets the spring after his winter nap, as he searches for his friend, Binky. Fuzzy ink animals have an apple green backdrop.

Holland, Marion

916 *Big Ball of String*. Ill. by author. Beginner, 1958. ISBN 0-394-90005-7. SUBJECTS: Imagination—Fiction; Stories in rhyme. RL B.
A boy's adventures while adding to his ball of string and using it when he is confined to bed are highly creative. Red and blue colored pencil highlights the drawings.

Hong, Lily T.

917 *Two of Everything*. Ill. by author. Whitman, 1993. ISBN 0-8075-8157-7. SUBJECTS: Folklore—China; Humorous stories. RL B.

Hong, Lily T. (cont.)

A wonderful retelling of a Chinese folktale about a magic pot that makes two of everything. It even clones its owners! Striking design, color, and details are shown with appealing, roly-poly Mr. and Mrs. Haktak.

Hood, Flora

918 *One Luminaria for Antonio*. Ill. by Ann Kirn. Putnam, 1966, o.p. SERIES: See and Read. SUBJECTS: Holidays—Christmas—Fiction; Mexico—Fiction. RL C.
Antonio gets a candle for a luminaria and an accompanying blessing despite his poverty and a temptation he has trouble resisting. Earth-tone textured sand paintings have an authentic flavor.

Hooks, William H.

919 *The Gruff Brothers*. Ill. by Pierre Cornuel. Bantam, 1990. ISBN 0-553-05855-X. SERIES: Bank Street Ready-to-Read. SUBJECTS: Animals—Fiction; Rebuses. RL A.
This retelling is lively and original, despite the simple language and the rebuses giving colors and animals (fox, snake, sheep, duck, and bird). The troll is not too scary, with his "pickles and popcorn" retorts when he lets the first two goats cross the bridge. Ink and washes complement the text.

920 *How Do You Make a Bubble?* Ill. by Doug Cushman. Bantam, 1992. ISBN 0-553-35487-6. SERIES: Bank Street Ready-to-Read. SUBJECTS: Animals—Fiction; Humorous stories; Stories in rhyme. RL A.
Humorous ink and wash cartoon animal characters help a beginning reader answer a question on each page. "How do you make a pie? You bake it. . . . make a malted? You shake it."

921 *Little Poss and Horrible Hound*. Ill. by Carol Newsom. Bantam, 1992. ISBN 0-553-07881-X. SERIES: Bank Street Ready-to-Read. SUBJECTS: Animals—Dogs—Fiction; Animals—Opossums—Fiction. RL B.
Little Poss escapes from Horrible Hound three times with his ingenious reworking of his father's cautions. "One a day keeps the doctor away" becomes the apple jammed into Hound's mouth giving time for Little Poss to escape. Illustrations are shallow except for Hound's expressions.

922 *Lo-Jack and the Pirates*. Ill. by Tricia Tusa. Bantam, 1991. ISBN 0-553-07092-4. SERIES: Bank Street Ready-to-Read. SUBJECTS: Humorous stories; Pirates—Fiction. RL B.
A boy enamored of the glamorous life of pirates is hijacked by real pirates. When he takes all orders literally, he ends up saving a ship full of men, women, and children from being blown to bits for treasure. Lively illustrations add much to the humor of the misunderstandings.

923 *Mr. Baseball*. Ill. by Paul Meisel. Bantam, 1991. ISBN 0-553-07315-X. SERIES: Bank Street Ready-to-Read. SUBJECTS: Siblings—Fiction; Sports—Baseball—Fiction. RL A.
Little brother Eli becomes the water boy, then the mascot of his brother's Little League team. Slight story is illustrated with cartoon ink and wash drawings of multicultural characters.

924 *Mr. Monster*. Ill. by Paul Meisel. Bantam, 1990. ISBN 0-553-05897-5. SERIES: Bank Street Ready-to-Read. SUBJECTS: Siblings—Fiction; Toys—Fiction. RL A.
Eli, otherwise known as Mr. Monster, has so many monster toys that his brother invents a gobble monster to scare the monsters into their closet. When the plot backfires, Eli begins collecting scare nooks. Watercolor and ink cartoon illustrations.

925 *Where's Lulu?* Ill. by R. W. Alley. Bantam, 1991. ISBN 0-553-07093-2. SERIES: Bank Street Ready-to-Read. SUBJECTS: African Americans—Fiction; Family life—Fiction. RL A.
A small girl searches the house and yard for Lulu to play ball with—the reader is surprised to find that Lulu is a very playful black dog. Dad joins in the fun. Dialogue is realistic. Illustrations in pencil and wash reflect warm family life.

Hopkins, Lee Bennett

926 *Good Books, Good Times!* Ill. by Harvey Stevenson. HarperCollins, 1990. ISBN 0-06-022528-9. SUBJECTS: Books and reading; Poetry. RL C.

Whimsical bold watercolors use unusual perspective to stimulate the imagination in this celebration of the joys of reading. Arnold Lobel, Jack Prelutsky, David McCord, and X. J. Kennedy are some of the poets lending their talent to this delightful collection.

927 *Happy Birthday*. Ill. by Hilary Knight. Simon & Schuster, 1991. ISBN 0-671-70973-9. SUBJECTS: Birthdays—Fiction; Poetry. RL B.

Charming ink and wash drawings capture the excitement of birthdays for a young child. Familiar favorite poets such as Dr. Seuss, Aileen Fisher, Myra Cohn Livingston, Margaret Hillert, and Shakespeare create the party atmosphere.

928 *It's About Time!* Ill. by Matt Novak. Simon & Schuster, 1993. ISBN 0-671-78512-5. SUBJECTS: Concepts—Time; Poetry. RL B.

Poems by favorites such as Charlotte Zolotow, Karla Kuskin, Gwendolyn Brooks, Harry Behn, Aileen Fisher, and Dorothy Aldis—about spaghetti, bedtime, and a new puppy—are illustrated with graphically pleasing colored pencil drawings.

929 *More Surprises*. Ill. by Megan Lloyd. HarperCollins, 1987. ISBN 0-06-022605-6. SERIES: I Can Read Books. SUBJECTS: Poetry. RL C.

Poems by poets such as Aileen Fisher and Charlotte Zolotow deal with seasons, books, and nonsense. Faintly textured soft pastels give variety and humor.

930 *Questions*. Ill. by Carolyn Croll. HarperCollins, 1992. ISBN 0-06-022413-4. SERIES: I Can Read Books. SUBJECTS: Poetry. RL A.

Felice Holman, Margaret Wise Brown, Eve Merriam, Christina Rossetti, and Karla Kuskin are some of the many quality poets represented in this excellent collection of poems. All ask questions, dealing with friendship, pretending, feelings, and humor.

931 *Ragged Shadows: Poems of Halloween Night*. Ill. by Giles Laroche. Little, Brown, 1993. ISBN 0-316-37276-5. SUBJECTS: Holidays—Halloween; Poetry. RL C.

Laroche uses cut-paper illustrations to create the mystery of Halloween through bare tree branches, from the inside of a jack-o'-lantern, with costumed skeletons passing the cemetery. Poems are by a variety of poets, including Valerie Worth, Nancy Willard, and Aileen Fisher.

932 *Weather*. Ill. by Melanie Hall. HarperCollins, 1994. ISBN 0-06-021462-7. SUBJECTS: Poetry; Weather—Fiction. RL A.

Poems about the sun, wind, rain, and snow are imaginative and lively. X. J. Kennedy has a spider making a snowflake soufflé, Isabel Glaser's lion-maned sun scorches the earth. Valerie Worth has a cat purring on a warm flat quilt made by the sun through the window panes. Pastel illustrations enhance the poems.

Hornblow, Leonora, and Hornblow, Arthur

933 *Insects Do the Strangest Things*. Ill. by Michael K. Frith. Random House, 1968. ISBN 0-394-94306-6. SERIES: Step-Up. SUBJECTS: Animals—Insects; Nature; Science. RL C.

The 17 insects shown are illustrated in four color. They range from caddis fly to flea and walking stick to termite.

934 *Reptiles Do the Strangest Things*. Ill. by Michael K. Frith. Random House, 1970. ISBN 0-394-90074-X. SERIES: Step-Up. SUBJECTS: Animals—Reptiles and amphibians; Nature; Science. RL C.

Among the 25 reptiles introduced is the brontosaurus; however, the information is out of date. The wonder and variety of reptiles is stressed. Good watercolors dominate each double page spread.

Howe, James

935 *Pinky and Rex and the Mean Old Witch*. Ill. by Melissa Sweet. Macmillan, 1991. ISBN 0-689-31617-8. SUBJECTS: Emotions—

Howe, James (cont.)

Loneliness—Fiction; Friendship—Fiction. RL A.
A well-crafted story of the "mean old witch" next door who chases friends Pinky and Rex and Pinky's little sister, Amanda, when they set foot in her yard. The story is suspenseful, with a satisfying ending, not overdone. Melissa Sweet's watercolor illustrations are charming.

936 *Pinky and Rex and the New Baby.* Ill. by Melissa Sweet. Macmillan, 1993. ISBN 0-689-31717-4. SUBJECTS: Babies, new—Fiction. Family life—Fiction; Friendship—Fiction. RL B.
The dialogue and relationships between friends and family members is engaging and realistic. The arrival of Rex's new baby engenders a discussion of adoption as well. Seven short chapters are tightly woven and illustrated with the author's appealing watercolor paintings.

937 *Pinky and Rex and the Spelling Bee.* Ill. by Melissa Sweet. Macmillan, 1991. ISBN 0-689-31618-6. SUBJECTS: Friendship—Fiction; Schools—Fiction. RL C.
When Pinky wins the class spelling bee—but wets his pants—his friend Rex restores his humor with a friendship stone. Story has realistic dialogue, humor, and suspense, besides having emotional impact. Watercolor drawings are excellent.

938 *Pinky and Rex Go to Camp.* Ill. by Melissa Sweet. Macmillan, 1992. ISBN 0-689-31718-2. SUBJECTS: Camps and camping—Fiction; Friendship—Fiction. RL B.
Pinky's letter to the advice column gets him to talk with his mom, who says he doesn't have to go to camp, but he decides to go when friend Rex confesses his fear. Appealing watercolors accompany this warm tale.

939 *Rabbit-Cadabra!* Ill. by Alan Daniel. Morrow, 1993. ISBN 0-688-10403-7. SUBJECTS: Animals—Cats—Fiction; Magic—Fiction; Pets—Fiction. RL C.
Harold the dog and Chester the cat manage to turn the Amazing Karlovsky's magic show at the local elementary school into chaos. Vivid, engaging watercolor illustrations enhance the text; instructions for pulling a rabbit from a hat are appended.

Huber, M. B.

940 *It Happened One Day.* HarperCollins, 1976, o.p. SERIES: Wonder-Story. SUBJECTS: Fables; Folklore. RL B.
The 11 folktales come from England, Finland, France, Germany, East Africa, and India, plus two of Aesop's fables. Tales retold, ranging from "Drakestail" to "Jack and the Beanstalk," are somewhat stilted. Pastel washes with textured gray sketches are varied and appealing.

Hudlow, Jean

941 *Eric Plants a Garden.* Ill. by author. Whitman, 1979, o.p. SUBJECTS: Gardening. RL B.
In a photoessay a young boy is shown preparing the soil and planting, tending, and harvesting his vegetable garden. Serial photos, close-ups, some in color, show the progress from planning the garden to carving a jack-o'-lantern.

Hulbert, Jay

942 *Pete Pig Cleans Up.* Ill. by John Killgrew. Raintree, 1989. ISBN 0-8172-3504-3. SERIES: Real Readers. SUBJECTS: Animals—Pigs—Fiction; Toys—Fiction. RL A.
Pete Pig cleans his room, only to mess it up immediately. Text is accompanied by cartoon illustrations.

Hurd, Edith T.

943 *Come and Have Fun.* Ill. by Clement Hurd. HarperCollins, 1962. ISBN 0-06-022681-1. SERIES: Early I Can Read. SUBJECTS: Animals—Cats—Fiction; Animals—Mice—Fiction. RL A.
A simple story deals with a cat chasing a mouse, incorporating some nice twists of language and cozy sketches that focus on the two animals.

944 *Johnny Lion's Bad Day.* Ill. by Clement Hurd. HarperCollins, 1970. ISBN 0-06-022708-7. SERIES: I Can Read Books. SUBJECTS: Animals—Lions—Fiction; Illness—Fiction; Parent and child—Fiction. RL A.

Johnny Lion's cold miseries are accentuated by bad dreams and comforted by loving parents. Ink sketches with textured soft coloring convey a small child's feelings.

945 *Johnny Lion's Book.* Ill. by Clement Hurd. HarperCollins, 1965; pap., 1985. ISBN 0-06-022706-0. SERIES: I Can Read Books. SUBJECTS: Animals—Lions—Fiction; Behavior—Obedient—Fiction; Books and reading—Fiction. RL A.
Johnny Lion is reading his first book. The story teaches him about some of the consequences of not minding his parents. Text and pencil illustrations are gently reassuring.

946 *Johnny Lion's Rubber Boots.* Ill. by Clement Hurd. HarperCollins, 1972. ISBN 0-06-022710-9. SERIES: I Can Read Books. SUBJECTS: Animals—Lions—Fiction; Imagination—Fiction. RL A.
After a rainy day's play inside, Johnny gets to play outside in his new rubber boots. Delightful friendly lion sketches warm the small adventures of Johnny's imaginative day.

947 *Last One Home Is a Green Pig.* Ill. by Clement Hurd. HarperCollins, 1959. ISBN 0-06-022716-8. SERIES: I Can Read Books. SUBJECTS: Animals—Ducks—Fiction; Animals—Monkeys—Fiction. RL A.
Duck and Monkey have a great race, hitching rides on everything from a bicycle and a horse to a submarine and a fire engine. They even vow to race again the next day. The language is simple, but with the rhythm of a cumulative tale. Sketchy action drawings have a green wash.

948 *Look for a Bird.* Ill. by Clement Hurd. HarperCollins, 1977, o.p. SERIES: Science I Can Read. SUBJECTS: Animals—Birds; Nature; Science. RL B.
Robins, blue jays, hummingbirds, pigeons, cardinals, and crows are some of the birds that appear on double spreads, half text and half watercolor illustrations. Tips for identifying each are included.

949 *Mother Kangaroo.* Ill. by Clement Hurd. Little, Brown, 1976, o.p. SERIES: Mother Animal. SUBJECTS: Animals—Kangaroos; Growing-up; Nature. RL C.

The growth of one "joey" is described in an intriguing fashion. Exceptional shaded block prints rivet one's attention.

950 *No Funny Business.* Ill. by Clement Hurd. HarperCollins, 1962, o.p. SERIES: I Can Read Books. SUBJECTS: Animals—Cats—Fiction; Dreams—Fiction; Picnics—Fiction. RL A.
When the family goes on a picnic, their cat, Carl, is left at home. However, he has imaginary picnic adventures in his dreams. Carl's expressive, mischievous eyes are the focal point of ink and two-tone wash drawings.

951 *Sandpipers.* Ill. by Lucienne Bloch. HarperCollins, 1961, o.p. SERIES: Let's-Read-and-Find-Out Science Books. SUBJECTS: Animals—Sandpipers; Nature. RL B.
In rhythmic language, the life cycle of sandpipers is lovingly recounted. Exceptional block prints in a variety of perspectives are in khaki, gray, and blue.

952 *Stop Stop.* Ill. by Clement Hurd. HarperCollins, 1961. ISBN 0-06-022746-X. SERIES: I Can Read Books. SUBJECTS: Babysitting—Fiction; Humorous stories. RL A.
Suzie's favorite baby-sitter Miss Mugs has an exaggerated passion for cleanliness, until the elephant at the zoo gives her a shower. Comic ink sketches add to the fun.

953 *White Horse.* Ill. by Tony Chen. HarperCollins, 1970, o.p. SUBJECTS: Emotions—Loneliness—Fiction; Imagination—Fiction. RL A.
A lonely boy, Jimmie Lee, on a class trip to the zoo, takes a magical trip on a white horse in his imagination. Evocative story has four-color drawings that focus on the boy and an unusually textured white horse.

Hutchins, Hazel

954 *And You Can Be the Cat.* Ill. by Ruth Ohi. Annick, 1992. ISBN 1-55037-219-X. SUBJECTS: Imagination; Siblings—Fiction. RL B.
Leanna's little brother, Norman, is an increasingly disruptive cat when Neil comes to play with Leanna. But after being banished, Nor-

Hutchins, Hazel (cont.)

man creates such a wonderful castle that he gets a better offer. Full color illustrations show the action.

Hutchins, Pat

955 *The Best Train Set Ever*. Ill. by author. Greenwillow, 1978, o.p. SERIES: Read-alone. SUBJECTS: Birthdays—Fiction; Family life—Fiction; Holidays—Halloween—Fiction. RL B.
Very satisfying stories are told of Peter's birthday wish coming true, little Maria creating a prize-winning Halloween costume, and a family laid low by measles saving their Christmas celebration for July. The family is drawn in avocado, pumpkin, cocoa, and lemon.

956 *The Tale of Thomas Mead*. Ill. by author. Greenwillow, 1980. ISBN 0-688-84282-8. SERIES: Read-alone. SUBJECTS: Books and reading—Fiction; Stories in rhyme. RL C.
Thomas discovers that not knowing how to read gets him in lots of awkward situations. The rhyming of this exaggerated story is reminiscent of Maurice Sendak's *Pierre* (HarperCollins, 1962). Pastel paintings complement text well.

I

I Can Add

957 *I Can Add*. Ill. by Simone Abel. Bantam, 1994. ISBN 0-553-09564-1. SERIES: Math Fun Flip Books. SUBJECTS: Animals—Fiction; Concepts—Numbers. RL B.
By matching up color-coded sections on the spiral binder, the reader learns to add. Appealing animals and boats, chicks and bees can be counted on the sturdy glossy pages.

Impey, Rose, and Knox, Jolyne

958 *Desperate for a Dog*. Dutton, 1988; Puffin, pap., 1991. ISBN 0-14-034798-4. SERIES: Speedsters. SUBJECTS: Animals—Dogs—Fiction; Family life—Fiction; Pets—Fiction. RL B.

After two sisters lobby unsuccessfully for a dog, their parents agree to shelter their elderly neighbor's dog, Toby. When he is reunited with his owner, the house seems dull and empty. Ink drawings are a little too busy, and the format a bit cluttered for a beginning reader.

J

Jacobs, Francine

959 *Supersaurus*. Ill. by D. D. Tyler. Putnam, 1982, o.p. SERIES: See and Read. SUBJECTS: Dinosaurs; Science. RL C.
The true story of "Dinosaur Jim" Jensen's discovery of Supersaurus is heralded. Unusual dot-shaped pencil drawings are especially effective in showing fossils in the matrix as they are uncovered.

Jacobs, Leland B.

960 *April Fool!* Ill. by Lou Cunette. Garrard, 1973, o.p. SERIES: Venture. SUBJECTS: Holidays—April Fool's Day. RL B.
A series of standard April Fool's jokes played on Nancy gives her an idea on how to enjoy this holiday. Well written and illustrated with pencil and pale blue wash.

961 *Hello, Pleasant Places!* Ill. by Kelly Oechsli. Garrard, 1972, o.p. SUBJECTS: Animals—Fiction; Poetry; Zoos—Fiction. RL A.
Inventive poetic wordplay is grouped by settings: city, park, zoo, shore, woods, and country. Includes average ink drawings with an apple green or orange wash.

962 *Hello, Year!* Ill. by Frank Aloise. Garrard, 1972, o.p. SERIES: Venture. SUBJECTS: Holidays—Fiction; Poetry; Seasons—Fiction. RL B.
Poets such as Maurice Sendak and Aileen Fisher celebrate sensory experiences around various holidays. Bright orange and fuchsia highlight small ink sketches.

963 *I Don't, I Do*. Ill. by Frank Carlings. Garrard, hb and pap., 1971, o.p. SERIES:

Venture. SUBJECTS: Animals—Fiction; Poetry. RL B.

In this poem, children *don't* want to be fish, penguins, or camels, but they *do* want to play, row, or eat ice cream. Mediocre ink drawings have flat apple green highlights.

964 *Just Around the Corner: Poems About the Seasons*. Ill. by Jeff Kaufman. Henry Holt, 1993. ISBN 0-8050-2676-2. SUBJECTS: Holidays; Poetry; Seasons. RL C.

The flowers, birds, and leaves of fall; snowprints, sneezes, and New Year's bells; the rain and flowers of spring; the shadows, shore, and sun of summer—all are celebrated in poetry. Intriguing rhyming patterns and word play are illustrated with bold graphic colors.

965 *Playtime in the City*. Ill. by Kelly Oechsli. Garrard, hb and pap., 1971, o.p. SERIES: Venture. SUBJECTS: City and town life; Poetry. RL A.

Poems about swinging, playing games, blowing soap bubbles, and pretending are written by children's poets such as Aileen Fisher. Line drawings have turquoise highlights.

966 *Poems about Fur and Feather Friends*. Ill. by Frank Aloise. Garrard, hb and pap., 1971, o.p. SERIES: Venture. SUBJECTS: Animals; Pets; Poetry. RL A.

Simple verse about pets, birds, and farm animals is written by such poets as John Ciardi and Lois Lenski. Line drawings have chartreuse highlights.

967 *Poetry for Autumn*. Ill. by Stina Nagel. Garrard, 1968, o.p. SUBJECTS: Holidays—Fiction; Poetry; Seasons—Fall—Fiction. RL C.

Robert Frost and David McCord are some of the poets who write about animals, voters, fall holidays, and books in simple poems. Ink sketches show tiny children and animals.

968 *Poetry for Chuckles and Grins*. Ill. by Tomie dePaola. Garrard, 1968, o.p. SERIES: Poetry. SUBJECTS: Humorous stories; Poetry. RL B.

Mary O'Neill opens this good anthology of humorous verse by such poets as Ogden Nash and Aileen Fisher. Broadly outlined humorous sketches have gold and pink coloring.

969 *Poetry for Space Enthusiasts*. Ill. by Frank Aloise. Garrard, 1971, o.p. SUBJECTS: Imagination—Fiction; Poetry; Space travel—Fiction. RL C.

Planes, zeppelins, bubbles, planets, clouds, stars, and witches are the stuff dreams are made of. This collection of poems is illustrated with ink sketches highlighted in sky blue.

970 *Teeny-Tiny*. Ill. by Marilyn Lucey. Garrard, 1976, o.p. SERIES: Easy Venture. SUBJECTS: Imagination—Fiction; Stories in rhyme. RL B.

An enchanting adventure of teeny-tiny children in a teeny-tiny toy store is told in rhythmic rhyme. Bright watercolor pictures focus on the children's play.

Jameson, Cynthia

971 *The House of Five Bears*. Ill. by Lorinda Bryan Cauley. Putnam, 1978, o.p. SUBJECTS: Animals—Bears—Fiction; Folklore—Russia. RL A.

An old man and an old woman seeking shelter from a blizzard stumble into the cave of five bears, who abandon the cave, thinking a dragon is there. Detailed ink drawings have royal highlights of palest gold and purple.

972 *Winter Hut*. Ill. by Ray Cruz. Putnam, 1973, o.p. SUBJECTS: Folklore—Russia; Russia—Fiction. RL C.

In this retelling of a Russian folktale, only by working together can the animals scare off Wolf and Bear from the shelter Bull has had to build alone. Ink drawings with beige focus on close-ups of the animals.

Janice

973 *Little Bear Learns to Read the Cookbook*. Ill. by Mariana. Lothrop, 1969, o.p. SUBJECTS: Animals—Bears—Fiction; Books and reading—Fiction; Cookery—Fiction. RL B.

Little Bear learns to read so she can bake a chocolate cake. Of course she relates the alphabet to food, as do her animal friends. Pencil drawings and washes showcase the animals.

Jann, Gayle

974 *A Day in the Life of a Construction Foreman*. Photos by author. Troll, 1988. ISBN 0-8167-1121-6. SERIES: A Day in the Life of. SUBJECTS: Careers. RL C.
Without a glossary, readers will have to rely on good color photos for assistance with the fairly technical language, as the work of a construction foreman supervising electricians building a skyscraper is outlined.

975 *A Day in the Life of a Photographer*. Photos by author. Troll, 1988. ISBN 0-8167-1123-2. SERIES: A Day in the Life of. SUBJECTS: Careers. RL C.
Technical language for professional commercial photography abounds with little background given. Equipment, exposure, layout, marketing, accounting, and the personal qualities necessary for running one's own photography business are outlined.

Jaspersohn, William

976 *How the Forest Grew*. Ill. by Chuck Eckart. Greenwillow, 1980, o.p. SERIES: Read-alone. SUBJECTS: Nature; Plants—Trees; Science. RL C.
The life cycle of a forest and its dependent wildlife is related in rich detail. The framed ink drawings have the same wealth of detail.

Jennings, Terry

977 *Time*. Ill. by David Anstey. Gloucester, 1988, o.p. SERIES: Junior Science. SUBJECTS: Concepts—Time; Science; Science experiments. RL B.
Activities and experiments with water and candle clocks and a sundial are simply illustrated in bright watercolors.

Jensen, Patricia

978 *A Funny Man*. Ill. by Wayne Becker. Scholastic, 1993. ISBN 0-590-46193-1. SERIES: My First Hello Reader! SUBJECTS: Humorous stories; Stories in rhyme. RL A.
In crisp, rhythmic language, the idiosyncrasies of a man who drives a teapot and has a banjo-playing crocodile and a bed with work boots and a propeller, are outlined. Flash cards and quizzes detract from the fun.

979 *The Mess*. Ill. by Molly Delaney. Childrens Pr., 1990. ISBN 0-516-05357-4. SERIES: My First Reader. SUBJECTS: Family life—Fiction. RL A.
A small boy with a most sympathetic dog thinks of all the fun his friends are having outside before he decides to clean up his room. Soft pencil and watercolors are used in illustrations. The story uses just 20 words.

Jensen, Patsy

980 *Monster Party*. Ill. by Patrick Girouard. Troll, hb and pap., 1994. ISBN 0-8167-3184-5. SERIES: Giant First-Start Readers. SUBJECTS: Birthdays—Fiction; Monsters—Fiction; Sibling rivalry—Fiction. RL A.
Though he tries to get his sister to leave his birthday party, Little Monster has no success. All is forgiven when she gives him the best present ever. A very easy to read book, this is illustrated with far from scary and rather silly monsters.

Jeunesse, Gallimard

981 *Castles*. Ill. by C. Millet and D. Millet. Scholastic, 1990. ISBN 0-590-46377-2. SERIES: First Discovery Book. SUBJECTS: Castles. RL C.
Clear overlays show inside and outside the turret, the whole family sharing a bed, and both sides of the wall during an assault. The design adds dimension and visual interest. Spiral binding is inside a traditional one. Information is provided on everyday life in a castle as well as during wartime.

Jeunesse, Gallimard, and Bour, Laura

982 *The River*. Ill. by Laura Bour. Scholastic, 1992. ISBN 0-590-47128-7. SERIES: First Discovery Book. SUBJECTS: Animals; Nature; Plants. RL C.
Clear overlays shows the river level during flood and drought, birds swimming and diving or nesting, dragonflies molting, and riverbanks clean or polluted. Drawings of birds,

fish, amphibians, people, and insects along the river are detailed and fascinating.

Jeunesse, Gallimard; Delafosse, Claude; and Valat, Pierre-Marie

983 *The Camera: Snapshots, Movies, Videos, and Cartoons*. Ill. by Pierre-Marie Valat. Scholastic, 1993. ISBN 0-590-47129-5. SERIES: First Discovery Book. SUBJECTS: Photography and photographers. RL C.

A fascinating first look at point-and-shoot, Polaroid, and video cameras and animated cartoons using images painted on clear pages to show the front and back of the image. Pages move easily on spiral binding.

Jewell, Nancy

984 *Two Silly Trolls*. Ill. by Lisa Thiesing. HarperCollins, 1992. ISBN 0-06-022830-X. SERIES: I Can Read Books. SUBJECTS: Humorous stories; Siblings—Fiction. RL A.

When a bear sits on their mushroom house, troll brothers build another—alas, a roofless one. They end up having their picnic in their own back yard, and share a traveling itch. Gentle, unassuming humor is complemented by watercolor trolls in a woodland habitat.

Johnson, Crockett

985 *Picture for Harold's Room*. Ill. by author. HarperCollins, 1960; pap., 1985. ISBN 0-06-023006-1. SERIES: I Can Read Books. SUBJECTS: Imagination—Fiction. RL A.

With a magic crayon, Harold travels the world, changing size and perspective with a stroke of the crayon. Very spare drawings of a boy show his artistic creations with a purple line.

Johnson, Jean

986 *Librarians A to Z*. Photos. Walker, 1988. ISBN 0-8027-6842-3. SERIES: Community Helpers. SUBJECTS: Alphabet; Books and reading; Community helpers. RL C.

An alphabet presents various aspects of librarianship, from cataloging, programming, videos, weeding, and zigzag books. Excellent close-up black and white photos show librarianship as an active, current, and vital profession.

Johnson, Mildred

987 *Wait, Skates!* Ill. by Tom Dunnington. Childrens Pr., hb and pap., 1983. ISBN 0-516-02039-0. SERIES: Rookie Readers. SUBJECTS: Sports—Roller skating—Fiction. RL A.

With a 30-word vocabulary, a boy is shown learning how to roller skate. Action and humor are captured well in the bright colored drawings.

Johnson, Sylvia A.

988 *Elephants around the World*. Orig. French by Anne-Marie Pajot, trans. by Dyan Hammarberg. Photos by Guy Dhuit, Jean-Louis Nou, and Rapho; drawings by L'Enc Matte. Carolrhoda, 1977, o.p. SERIES: Animal Friends. SUBJECTS: Animals—Elephants; Nature. RL C.

Although Frank's introduction to elephants is in the zoo, most of the information in this book is from their natural habitat. Appendix suggests elephants are now successfully protected from human hunters, which is *not* now true. Colored and black and white photos are combined with some drawings.

989 *Lions of Africa*. Orig. French by Anne-Marie Pajot, trans. by Dyan Hammarberg. Photos by Guy Dhuit, Klaus Paysan, and Rapho; drawings by L'Enc Matte. Carolrhoda, 1977, o.p. SERIES: Animal Friends. SUBJECTS: Animals—Lions; Nature. RL C.

Uncle David shows Luke and Ted his movies of African lions, while they and the reader learn of the lions' habits. Excellent black and white photos alternate with color photos.

990 *Penney and Pete the Lambs*. Orig. French by Anne-Marie Pajot, trans. by Dyan Hammarberg. Photos by Antoinette Barrere, drawings by L'Enc Matte. Carolrhoda, 1976, o.p. SERIES: Animal Friends. SUBJECTS: Animals—Sheep; Nature; Pets. RL C.

Information about sheep is imparted from the point of view of two children. Additional details are included in an appendix. Some drawings appear among the black and white photos.

Johnston, Tony

991 *The Adventures of Mole and Troll*. Ill. by Wallace Tripp. Putnam, 1972, o.p. SUBJECTS: Animals—Moles—Fiction; Friendship—Fiction; Trolls—Fiction. RL B.
The friendship of neighbors Mole and Troll survives a day at the beach, shoelaces that constantly come untied, and attempts to live like the other. Outstanding ink and wash drawings by Tripp add to the humor and appeal.

992 *Farmer Mack Measures His Pig*. Ill. by Megan Lloyd. HarperCollins, 1986, o.p. SUBJECTS: Animals—Pigs—Fiction; Farm and country life—Fiction; Humorous stories. RL B.
Farmer Mack and Farmer Tubb compete to determine whose pig is fatter and the better jumper. Slapstick humor is delightful. Colorful comic drawings add to the spirited humor.

993 *I'm Gonna Tell Mama I Want An Iguana*. Ill. by Lillian Hoban. Putnam, 1990, o.p. SUBJECTS: Humorous stories; Poetry. RL B.
Strong rhythm and delightful humor characterize short, memorable poems with unusual twists. Illustrated by Lillian Hoban's soft colored pencil children comforting a dog on the way to the vet, or watching Grandma let down her hair.

994 *Night Noises and Other Mole and Troll Stories*. Ill. by Cyndy Szekeres. Putnam, 1977, o.p. SUBJECTS: Animals—Moles—Fiction; Friendship—Fiction; Trolls—Fiction. RL B.
Troll is Mole's rain-or-shine friend. He sneezes a tooth out after Mole's helpful schemes, such as slamming a door, fail. Chapters about this special friendship are illustrated with pencil-drawn friendly looking critters.

995 *Odd Jobs*. Ill. by Tomie dePaola. Putnam, 1977, o.p. SERIES: See and Read. SUBJECTS: Humorous stories. RL C.
Washing an uncooperative dog, Bouncer (not once but four times!), subbing in dance class, and balloon-sitting are some of the jobs undertaken by a sometimes successful Odd Jobs. Pencil drawings are gloriously appropriate.

996 *Odd Jobs and Friends*. Ill. by Tomie dePaola. Putnam, 1982, o.p. SERIES: See and Read. SUBJECTS: Friendship—Fiction; Humorous stories. RL C.
Odd Jobs takes on some odd tasks—protecting an arm cast from a romantic scribbler, teaching Annie how to blow bubble-gum bubbles, and keeping a new kid company until he finds a friend. Warm, expressive pencil drawings are of multiethnic friends.

Jordan, Helene J.

997 *How a Seed Grows*. Ill. by Loretta Krupinski. HarperCollins, 1992. ISBN 0-06-020185-1. SERIES: Let's-Read-and-Find-Out. SUBJECTS: Nature; Plants—Seeds, roots, and bulbs; Science experiments. RL B.
The author suggests planting ten bean seeds and digging up one each day to understand the way in which a seed begins to develop. Sketches are accurate and visually interesting.

Judson, Clara I.

998 *Christopher Columbus*. Ill. by Polly Jackson. Follett, 1960, o.p. SERIES: Beginning to Read. SUBJECTS: Biographies. RL A.
In 368 basic vocabulary words, the outline of Columbus's dream and the suspense of whether he would achieve it before his crew mutinied are well portrayed. Full color drawings are a bit dated.

Justus, May

999 *Surprise for Perky Pup*. Ill. by Mimi Korach. Garrard, hb and pap., 1971, o.p. SERIES: Venture. SUBJECTS: Animals—Dogs—Fiction. RL A.
When Perky Pup is hit over the head, his howling alarms all the dogs until they find the source of the blow. Delightful simple drawings are in emerald green, royal blue, and cocoa.

K

Kalish, Muriel, and Kalish, Lionel

1000 *Bears on the Stairs. A Beginner's Book of Rhymes*. Ill. by authors. Scholastic, 1993. ISBN 0-590-44918-4. SERIES:

Cartwheel. SUBJECTS: Stories in rhyme; Toy and movable books. RL A.

Six rhymes about animals are completed only when the 3/4-page flap is opened. Pencil and wash drawings are large and simple.

1001 *Who Says Moo? A Beginner's Book of Animal Sounds.* Ill. by authors. Scholastic, 1993. ISBN 0-590-44917-6. SERIES: Cartwheel. SUBJECTS: Animals— Fiction; Stories in rhyme; Toy and movable books. RL A.

The sounds made by six familiar animals are uncovered as the 3/4-page flap is opened. The friendly animals are shown in simple pencil and wash drawings.

Kantrowitz, Mildred

1002 *Willy Bear.* Ill. by Nancy W. Parker. Parents Magazine Pr., 1976, o.p.; Macmillan, pap., 1989. ISBN 0-689-71345-2. SUBJECTS: School stories; Toys— Teddy bears—Fiction. RL B.

A small boy eases his anxiety about his first day at school by talking to his faithful teddy bear. Neat pastel drawings have an appropriate simplicity and comfort.

Kaye, Marilyn

1003 *Will You Cross Me?* Ill. by Ned Delaney. HarperCollins, 1985, o.p. SERIES: Early I Can Read. SUBJECTS: City and town life— Fiction; Friendship—Fiction. RL A.

Two friends need frequent help to cross a city street to play together. Comic details of animals and newspapers add to the picture of the busy neighborhood.

Keller, Beverly

1004 *Beetle Bush.* Ill. by Marc Simont. Putnam, 1975, o.p. SUBJECTS: Self-esteem—Fiction. RL C.

Arabella becomes an ex-failure when her garden produces snails, moles, beetles, and one overlooked melon. This story is sensitively told and illustrated sympathetically in colored pencil.

1005 *Don't Throw Another One, Dover.* Ill. by Jacqueline Chwast. Putnam, 1975, o.p.

SERIES: Break-of-Day. SUBJECTS: Emotions—Anger—Fiction; Grandparents—Fiction; Sibling rivalry—Fiction. RL B.

To his surprise, Dover is drawn into the daily activities of his grandmother's simple lifestyle. He is visiting her while his mother is having a baby; Grandma gets his attention by throwing her own "tantrum," since Dover has thrown some of his own while with his mother. Pencil drawings have a burnt orange wash.

1006 *When Mother Got the Flu.* Ill. by Maxie Chambliss. Putnam, 1984, o.p. SERIES: Break-of-Day. SUBJECTS: Humorous stories; Illness—Fiction. RL C.

Despite his best intentions not to bother his mother, who has the flu, a small boy breaks the knob on the television set, gets bubble gum all over the cat, melts crayons on the television, and falls into a well while chasing the cat. Black and white illustrations alternate with two colors, thus exaggerating the mess.

Keller, Holly

1007 *Geraldine's Big Snow.* Ill. by author. Greenwillow, 1988. ISBN 0-688-07514-2. SUBJECTS: Animals—Pigs—Fiction; Weather—Snow—Fiction. RL B.

During Geraldine's impatient wait for the first snow she meets neighbors preparing for a blizzard. The story is simply told and joyfully illustrated in bright watercolors.

Kelley, Emily

1008 *Happy New Year.* Ill. by Priscilla Kiedrowski. Carolrhoda, 1984. ISBN 0-87614-269-2. SERIES: On My Own. SUBJECTS: Holidays—New Year's Day. RL C.

New Year's customs in seven countries, some jokes, food, songs, and games are described. Colored pencil drawings give some of the details of the various cultures.

Kennedy, Richard

1009 *Contests at Cowlick.* Ill. by Marc Simont. Little, Brown, 1975, o.p. SUBJECTS: Humorous stories; Tall tales; Western stories. RL C.

Kennedy, Richard (cont.)

A small boy single-handedly rounds up an entire outlaw gang of 15 by trickery in this most satisfying book. Colored pencil drawings add humor and action.

Kent, Jack

1010 *The Biggest Shadow in the Zoo*. Ill. by author. Parents Magazine Pr., 1980. ISBN 0-8193-1048-4. SUBJECTS: Animals—Elephants—Fiction; Shadows—Fiction; Zoos—Fiction. RL A.

Goober the elephant refuses to give rides to zoo visitors while mourning the loss of his shadow, which fell in the moat. This charming, lighthearted story is illustrated with ink and crayon cartoon characters.

1011 *Hoddy Doddy*. Ill. by author. Greenwillow, 1979, o.p. SERIES: Read-alone. SUBJECTS: Folklore—Denmark; Humorous stories; Nonsense. RL C.

Three Danish tales of fools are retold, one about the Norse lobster sailors, another about marking the watery hiding place of the village clock, and the final one about the human winner of a cuckoo contest. Illustrations are well-suited to the simple retellings.

1012 *Socks for Supper*. Ill. by author. Parents Magazine Pr., 1978; Crown, pap., 1988. ISBN 0-8193-0965-6. SUBJECTS: Farm and country life—Fiction; Humorous stories. RL C.

A poor farmer and his wife unravel his sweater to knit socks to trade for milk in order to make butter and cheese. The ending has a nice twist, with Kent's excellent full color drawings spicing the simple tale.

1013 *Wizard of Wallaby Wallow*. Ill. by author. Parents Magazine Pr., 1971, o.p. SUBJECTS: Animals—Mice—Fiction; Magic—Fiction; Self-esteem—Fiction. RL C.

When discontented Mouse acquired one of the Wizard's unlabeled bottles containing a magic spell, he decides he likes being a mouse best. Comic illustrations underline the gentle humor.

Kessel, Joyce K.

1014 *St. Patrick's Day*. Ill. by Cathy Gilchrist. Carolrhoda, 1982. ISBN 0-87614-193-9. SERIES: On My Own. SUBJECTS: Holidays—St. Patrick's Day; Ireland. RL B.

The holiday celebrating Patrick's unifying and bringing Christianity to the tribes of Ireland 1,600 years ago is outlined. Ink drawings with green accents and borders underline the seriousness of this religious holiday.

Kessler, Ethel, and Kessler, Leonard

1015 *The Big Fight*. Ill. by Pat Paris. Garrard, 1981, o.p. SERIES: Begin to Read with Duck and Pig. SUBJECTS: Animals—Ducks—Fiction; Animals—Pigs—Fiction; Friendship—Fiction. RL A.

Pig and Duck both make an effort to make up after they have a name-calling fight. Comic drawings add good characterization.

1016 *Grandpa, Witch, and the Magic Doobelator*. Ill. by authors. Macmillan, 1981, o.p. SERIES: Ready-to-Read. SUBJECTS: Humorous stories; Magic—Fiction; Witches—Fiction. RL B.

When Wanda and Willy learn magic tricks for Halloween, they find that Grandpa Witch's magic sometimes has unexpected results. Ink and wash drawings feature pet cats and a fabulous fantasy machine—the Doobelator.

1017 *Our Tooth Story: A Tale of Twenty Teeth*. Ill. by authors. Dodd, Mead, 1972, o.p. SUBJECTS: Doctors and nurses; Human body—Teeth. RL B.

A story for kindergartners about teeth gives simple facts from a child's perspective, as well as tips for good dental hygiene. Bold childlike line drawings extend the text.

1018 *Pig's Orange House*. Ill. by Pat Paris. Garrard, 1981, o.p. SERIES: Begin to Read with Duck and Pig. SUBJECTS: Animals—Fiction; Concepts—Color—Fiction; Humorous stories. RL A.

When Pig's friends help him paint his house, it ends up with a most unusual effect. Full color comic drawings are appropriate for the fun.

1019 *Stan the Hot Dog Man*. Ill. by authors. HarperCollins, 1990. ISBN 0-06-023280-3. SERIES: I Can Read Books. SUBJECTS: Family life—Fiction; Retirement—Fiction. RL A.

Stan retires from a bakery to become a compassionate hot dog man who feeds those who are short of money, or caught in a blizzard. After work, he and his wife, Emma, go fishing. Ink and watercolor wash drawings enhance the warm, neighborly story.

1020 *The Sweeneys from 9D*. Ill. by Leonard Kessler. Macmillan, 1985, o.p. SERIES: Ready-to-Read. SUBJECTS: Friendship—Fiction; Latchkey children—Fiction; Moving, household—Fiction. RL B.

Tommy's nervous stomach disappears after his first full day in a new school and a new apartment. Ink sketches have orange, gray, and beige washes.

1021 *What's Inside the Box?* Ill. by Leonard Kessler. Dodd, Mead, 1976, o.p. SUBJECTS: Animals—Fiction; Concepts—Fiction; Mystery and detective stories. RL B.

Seven animals find a box in the woods and scatter fearfully at each new noise or clue to its contents. Simple suspense and humor are effective, especially when matched with Kessler's three-color comic drawings.

Kessler, Leonard

1022 *Are We Lost, Daddy?* Ill. by author. Putnam, 1967, o.p. SUBJECTS: Family life—Fiction; Humorous stories. RL A.

After taking a circuitous back route, a family succeeds in finding Big Valley. However, they find it after they get a map. The humor and aggravations are in a childlike view.

1023 *The Big Mile Race*. Ill. by author. Greenwillow, 1983. ISBN 0-688-01421-6. SERIES: Read-alone. SUBJECTS: Animals—Fiction; Sports—Running—Fiction. RL B.

Animals with individual characteristics learn about running, and practice for the big race. The dialogue is lively, but the strength of the story is in the support and encouragement the animals provide for each other. Kessler's sketches add humor and action.

1024 *Do You Have Any Carrots?* Ill. by Lori Pierson. Garrard, 1979, o.p. SUBJECTS: Animals—Fiction; Animals—Rabbits—Fiction; Farm and country life—Fiction. RL A.

Cuddly bunnies find out that none of the barnyard or woodland animals likes carrots as much as they do. Sunny yellow and apple greens set off a variety of animals in this slight story.

1025 *The Forgetful Pirate*. Ill. by author. Garrard, 1974, o.p. SERIES: Venture. SUBJECTS: Animals—Parrots—Fiction; Pirates—Fiction. RL C.

The cider-drinking pirate is so forgetful that only his parrot can lead the crew to gold. Simple watercolors illustrate this thin tale.

1026 *Here Comes the Strikeout*. Ill. by author. HarperCollins, 1965, 1992. ISBN 0-06-023156-4. SERIES: I Can Read Books. SUBJECTS: Sports—Baseball—Fiction. RL A.

Thanks to help from his friend, Willie, Bobby finds out that neither lucky bats nor helmets, only hard work, will help him learn how to improve his batting record (all strikeouts). Pen and wash illustrations have typical Kessler appeal.

1027 *Hey Diddle Diddle*. Ill. by author. Garrard, 1980, o.p. SERIES: Young Mother Goose. SUBJECTS: Mother Goose—Fiction; Nonsense; Stories in rhyme. RL C.

Inventive rhyming wordplay nonsense is illustrated with cartoon drawings of animals.

1028 *Hickory Dickory Dock*. Ill. by Doug Cushman. Garrard, 1980, o.p. SERIES: Young Mother Goose. SUBJECTS: Concepts—Time—Fiction; Mother Goose—Fiction; Stories in rhyme. RL A.

The hours of the day are celebrated with nonsense rhymes as the clock strikes each hour. Colored ink drawings focus on a cat and a mouse.

1029 *Kick, Pass and Run*. Ill. by author. HarperCollins, 1966; pap., 1978. ISBN 0-06-023160-2. SERIES: Sports I Can Read. SUBJECTS: Animals—Fiction; Sports—Football—Fiction. RL B.

Kessler, Leonard (cont.)

Exceptionally well presented facts about football from the point of view of animals who find a football, watch the game being played, and then try to play themselves. Very simple drawings with rust and green capture the humor and action.

1030 *Mixed-Up Mother Goose*. Ill. by Diane Dawson. Garrard, 1980, o.p. SERIES: Young Mother Goose. SUBJECTS: Mother Goose—Fiction; Stories in rhyme. RL C.
After a collision in which she hurts her head, Mother Goose thinks Little Bo Peep herds goats, and Little Miss Muffet is eating pink ice cream. Humor is illustrated with pastel drawings in this rhyming story.

1031 *The Mother Goose Game*. Ill. by Pat Paris. Garrard, 1980, o.p. SERIES: Young Mother Goose. SUBJECTS: Mother Goose—Fiction; Stories in rhyme. RL A.
Mother Goose makes friends with Mole, Hen, Pig, Cat, Goat, Cow, Frog, Dog, Fox, Bird, Ant, Duck, and Mouse, who introduce themselves in rhyme. Comic animal drawings suit this simple text.

1032 *Old Turtle's 90 Knock-Knocks, Jokes, and Riddles*. Ill. by author. Greenwillow, 1991. ISBN 0-688-09586-0. SUBJECTS: Animals—Fiction; Jokes and riddles; Wordplay. RL B.
Dog, Rabbit, Mouse, Duck, Chicken, Cat, Bird, and Owl have sections on Jokes and Riddles followed by Knock-Knocks. All were apparently tested on the children at Indian Rock and East York Elementary schools, to whom the book is dedicated. Watercolors are as entertaining as the humorous text.

1033 *Old Turtle's Riddle and Joke Book*. Ill. by author. Greenwillow, 1986. ISBN 0-688-05954-6. SERIES: Read-alone. SUBJECTS: Jokes and riddles. RL B.
Standard riddles familiar to many adults, but new to children, are illustrated with apple green and pumpkin cartoons that exaggerate the humor.

1034 *Old Turtle's Soccer Team*. Ill. by author. Greenwillow, 1988. ISBN 0-688-07158-9.

SERIES: Read-alone. SUBJECTS: Animals—Fiction; Sports—Soccer—Fiction. RL B.
The no-name animals have *much* to learn about soccer, and about cooperation, before they become a team. Colorful comic animal drawings add to the excellent simple dialogue, interesting characterization, and humorous wordplay.

1035 *Old Turtle's Winter Games*. Ill. by author. Greenwillow, 1983, o.p; Dell, pap., 1990. ISBN 0-440-40261-1. SERIES: Read-alone. SUBJECTS: Animals—Fiction; Sports—Winter—Fiction. RL A.
The animals help each other—out of the snowbank after a ski jump, and down the hill when there are not enough sleds. With imaginative humor beginning readers are introduced to Olympic events. Four-color comic illustrations are simple, yet expressive.

1036 *On Your Mark, Get Set, Go!* Ill. by author. HarperCollins, 1972, o.p. SERIES: Sports I Can Read. SUBJECTS: Animals—Fiction; Sports—Olympics—Fiction. RL B.
In the animal Olympics, everyone can do something and everybody learns something. Exceptionally imaginative presentation of information and values is illustrated with comic ink drawings colored in three tones.

1037 *The Pirate's Adventure on Spooky Island*. Ill. by author. Garrard, 1979, o.p. SERIES: Imagination. SUBJECTS: Animals—Parrots—Fiction; Pirates—Fiction. RL A.
An inept pirate, Captain Ben, needs his parrot's help to capture Bad Bart. Lively drawings by Kessler add to the fun.

1038 *The Worst Team Ever*. Ill. by author. Greenwillow, 1985. ISBN 0-688-04235-X. SERIES: Read-alone. SUBJECTS: Animals Fiction; Sports—Baseball—Fiction. RL B.
Melvin Moose, Bobo Bullfrog, and Pickles Frog improve at swampball with Old Turtle's encouragement and discipline. Clever humor lightens the lesson, as do the two-tone comic drawings.

Kim, Joy

1039 *Come On Up!* Ill. by Paul Harvey. Troll, hb and pap., 1981. ISBN 0-89375-511-7. SERIES: Giant First-Start. SUBJECTS:

Animals—Cats—Fiction; Animals—Dogs—Fiction. RL A.

A small cat is afraid to climb a tree—until a dog comes along. Unfortunately the author puts the dog in the tree as well as the cat at the end. Bright comic illustrations show a rotund, timid yellow kitten and her raggedy playmate.

1040 *Rainbows and Frogs: A Story about Colors*. Ill. by Paul Harvey. Troll, hb and pap., 1981. ISBN 0-89375-505-2. SUBJECTS: Concepts—Color. RL A.

Using a 35-word vocabulary, Kim asks the reader what color he or she likes and what feelings each color generates. Rich, rainbow-colored close-ups are humorous.

King, P. E.

1041 *Down on the Funny Farm: A Step Two Book*. Ill. by Alastair Graham. Random House, hb and pap., 1986. ISBN 0-394-97460-3. SERIES: Step into Reading. SUBJECTS: Farm and country life—Fiction; Humorous stories. RL B.

As soon as the farmer trains his animals properly, the old owner shows up to confuse them all again. This well-paced story has an open ending. Full color comic illustrations suit the text.

King-Smith, Dick

1042 *All Pigs Are Beautiful*. Ill. by Anita Jeram. Candlewick, 1993. ISBN 1-56402-148-3. SERIES: Read and Wonder. SUBJECTS: Animals—Pigs; Farm and country life. RL B.

The author loves pigs, and, if pressed, will say that a black and white spotted medium-snouted, flop-eared Gloucestershire pig is his favorite. He imagines what his pig, Monty, is thinking when he gets his head scratched after he eats. Delightful pen and wash sketches illustrate the text.

Kirk, Ruth

1043 *Desert Life*. Ill. by author and Louis Kirk. Natural History, 1970, o.p. SUBJECTS: Deserts; Nature; Science. RL C.

Kirk describes the birds, mammals, reptiles, insects, weather, and plants of the desert. Colored close-up photos are compelling.

Kirkpatrick, Rena K.

1044 *Look at Magnets*. Ill. by Ann Knight. Raintree, 1985. ISBN 0-8172-2354-1. SERIES: Look at Science. SUBJECTS: Magnets; Science; Science experiments. RL C.

Simple tests to see the power of magnets, and how to make electromagnets and a compass are shown in an elementary fashion. Children doing the experiments are in brightly colored clothing on a white background.

1045 *Look at Rainbow Colors*. Ill. by Anna Barnard. Raintree, 1985. ISBN 0-8172-2356-8. SERIES: Look at Science. SUBJECTS: Concepts—Color; Rainbows; Science. RL C.

Ordinary sources of rainbows and some exploration of how colors change are introduced. Bright drawings show flowers and animals.

Kiser, SuAnn

1046 *Hazel Saves the Day*. Ill. by Betsy Day. Dial, 1994. pap., ISBN 0-8037-1488-2; 0-8037-1489-0. SERIES: Dial Easy-to-Read. SUBJECTS: Animals—Chickens—Fiction; Friendship—Fiction. RL A.

In four short chapters, Hazel Hen moves in, foils a thief, and makes a party-full of new animal friends. Cheery colored pencil and watercolor drawings augment the text.

Kite, Patricia

1047 *Down in the Sea: Jellyfish*. Photos. Whitman, 1993. ISBN 0-8075-1712-7. SUBJECTS: Animals—Jellyfish; Nature; Oceans and ocean life. RL B.

Exceptional close-up photos of a wondrous variety of jellyfish are accompanied by a rhythmic, poetic text. Jellyfish come smaller than a grape and bigger than a bed, with tentacles less than an inch to longer than a basketball court.

1048 *Down in the Sea: The Crab*. Photos. Whitman, 1994. ISBN 0-8075-1709-7. SUBJECTS: Animals—Crabs. RL B.

Using colorful photographs and short, easily understood sentences, the author introduces a great variety of true crabs (those with ten legs visible) to young readers. The format is attrac-

Kite, Patricia (cont.)

tive, some of the photographs are beautiful, and the text is interesting. A final page of facts about crabs brings the information together.

1049 *Down in the Sea: The Octopus*. Photos. Whitman, 1993. ISBN 0-8075-1715-1. SUBJECTS: Animals—Octopi; Nature; Oceans and ocean life—Octopi. RL B.
Exceptionally interesting information about octopi is illustrated with appropriate close-up photos of octopi in hiding, guarding eggs, escaping in a cloud of ink, and eating a crab.

1050 *Down in the Sea: The Sea Slug*. Photos. Whitman, 1994. ISBN 0-8075-1717-8. SUBJECTS: Animals—Sea slugs. RL B.
Through photographs of these brightly colored shell-less creatures (captioned with their scientific names) and a brief interesting text, children are offered an opportunity to learn about sea slugs, their habits, enemies, and life cycle. A final lengthier page of text brings the information together and adds to it.

Klasky, Charles

1051 *Rugs Have Naps (But Never Take Them)*. Ill. by Mike Venezia. Childrens Pr., hb and pap., 1984, o.p. SERIES: Easy Reading. SUBJECTS: English language—Homonyms. RL C.
Twenty-four homonyms include ones about knots and fillings in their double meanings. Illustrations are in watercolor cartoon format.

Klein, Howard

1052 *My Best Friends Are Dinosaurs*. Ill. by Windrow. McKay, 1965, o.p. SUBJECTS: Dinosaurs—Fiction; Stories in rhyme. RL C.
A boy's affinity for dinosaurs is conveyed in simple verse. Ink drawings of dinosaurs are paralleled by the boy's imaginative play.

Klein, John F., and Gaskin, Carol

1053 *A Day in the Life of a Commercial Fisherman*. Photos by John F. Klein. Troll, 1988. ISBN 0-8167-1109-7. SERIES: A Day in the Life of. SUBJECTS: Careers. RL C.

Commercial fisherman Mark Brown is shown preparing the specialized gear on board his boat for an eight-day fishing trip with his partner, Curt. The camera follows them from port to fish house. Text is detailed for a third-grader.

Klein, Monica

1054 *Backyard Basketball Superstar*. Ill. by Nola Langner. Pantheon, 1981, o.p. SERIES: I Am Reading. SUBJECTS: Sex roles—Fiction; Sports—Basketball—Fiction. RL B.
After some mental adjustments, the Flyers, the neighborhood basketball team, vote unanimously to have Melanie join the all-male team. Excellent pencil drawings lighten the message.

Klingel, Cindy

1055 *Harriet Tubman: Black Liberator (1820–1913)*. Ill. by John Keely and Dick Brude. Creative Ed., 1987. ISBN 0-88682-166-5. SERIES: We the People. SUBJECTS: African Americans; Biographies; United States—Civil War. RL C.
An easy-reading recap of Tubman's courage in helping over 300 slaves escape to the North, many as far as Canada. Pencil and gray wash sketches alternate with colored ones; large print.

1056 *Susan Anthony: Crusader for Women's Rights (1820–1906)*. Ill. by John Keely and Dick Brude. Creative Ed., 1987. ISBN 0-88682-164-9. SERIES: We the People. SUBJECTS: Biographies. RL C.
Daughter of a mill owner, Anthony escaped to teaching, and then crusading for the abolitionist cause, then rights for women. She was inspired by Frederick Douglass, and worked hand-in-hand with Elizabeth Cady Stanton. Indifferent watercolor drawings accompany the large-type text.

Knight, David

1057 *Let's Find Out about Earth*. Ill. by Linda Chen. Watts, 1975, o.p. SUBJECTS: Astronomy; Science; Seasons. RL C.

The topics of the seasons, gravity, the world, the oceans, and planetary travel are introduced by a good science author. Illustrations are brightly colored.

1058 *Let's Find Out about Sound.* Ill. by Ulrick Schramm. Watts, 1974, o.p. SUBJECTS: Science; Sound. RL C.
The variety of sources, kinds, and transmitters of sound to the human ear are introduced. Line drawings help convey the well-organized and carefully presented information.

Knowlton, Jack

1059 *Geography from A to Z: A Picture Glossary.* Ill. by Harriett Barton. HarperCollins, 1988. ISBN 0-690-04618-9. SUBJECTS: Geography. RL C.
Zones, palisade, key, and crevasse are some of the geographic terms defined and illustrated here. Large paintings are in flat primary colors. Very appealing, informative, and readable.

Koch, Michelle

1060 *Just One More.* Ill. by author. Greenwillow, 1989. ISBN 0-688-08127-4. SUBJECTS: Concepts—Numbers; Language. RL A.
Each double spread has singular and plural nouns illustrated with small, graphically pleasing soft watercolors in a box. Numbers range from 3 geese to 13 sharks or 15 sheep.

Kohlenberg, Sherry

1061 *Sammy's Mommy Has Cancer.* Ill. by Lauri Crow. Stevens, 1994. ISBN 0-8368-1071-6. SUBJECTS: Diseases; Illness. RL B.
The author is a young mother with cancer who wrote the book first for her toddler, and has added notes for parents with cancer to use with their children before, during, and after treatment. With bright affirming drawings, the text gives a child's view of changes in his mother.

Kohn, Berniece

1062 *Echoes.* Ill. by Albert Pucci. Putnam, 1965, o.p. SUBJECTS: Science; Sound. RL C.

The scientific applications for sonar properties are touched on by a scientist and science writer. The text is still useful despite dated prints and an old copyright.

Komaiko, Leah

1063 *Earl's Too Cool for Me.* Ill. by Laura Cornell. HarperCollins, 1988, o.p.; pap., 1990. ISBN 0-06-443245-9. SUBJECTS: Fantasy; Friendship—Fiction. RL C.
A boy imagines that Earl has accomplished exotic feats. After making Earl's acquaintance, the boy discovers that Earl is more ordinary than he had imagined. So begins a real cool friendship. Rhythmic text has appropriately exaggerated watercolor comic illustrations.

Koontz, Robin M.

1064 *Chicago and the Cat.* Ill. by author. Cobblehill, 1993. ISBN 0-525-65097-0. SERIES: A Little Chapter Book. SUBJECTS: Animals—Cats—Fiction. RL A.
A cat moves in on Chicago, the rabbit, and turns out to be a really good cook—even though he ruins Chicago's garden. And their trip to the animal shelter for a protector puppy has unexpected success. Charming watercolor illustrations enhance the story.

Kotzwinkle, William

1065 *Up the Alley with Jack and Joe.* Ill. by Joe Servello. Macmillan, 1974, o.p. SERIES: Ready-to-Read. SUBJECTS: City and town life—Fiction; Imagination—Fiction. RL C.
Three boys and an old dog spend a Saturday full of adventure just "up the alley." The story captures the spirit of childhood. Servello's two-tone ink drawings add flavor to the characters and suspense to the adventures.

Kowalczyk, Carolyn

1066 *Purple Is Part of a Rainbow.* Ill. by Gene Sharp. Childrens Pr., hb and pap., 1985. ISBN 0-516-02068-4. SERIES: Rookie Readers. SUBJECTS: Stories in rhyme. RL B.

Kowalczyk, Carolyn (cont.)

A simple vocabulary is used to present interesting ideas about the parts that make up a whole of familiar things, such as a rainbow. Rhyming couplets are accompanied by vivid, sprightly drawings.

Krasilovsky, Phyllis

1067 *The Man Who Cooked for Himself*. Ill. by Mamoru Funai. Parents Magazine Pr., 1981, o.p.; Stevens, 1994. ISBN 0-8368-0984-X. SERIES: Read Aloud and Easy Reading. SUBJECTS: Food—Fiction; Sex roles—Fiction. RL C.

A lazy man living on the edge of a wood discovers he can be self-sufficient in feeding himself and his cat. The colorful pictures have a fuzzy appearance from poor reproduction.

1068 *The Man Who Entered a Contest*. Ill. by Yuri Salzman. Doubleday, 1980, o.p. SERIES: Reading On My Own. SUBJECTS: Bakers and baking—Fiction; Contests—Fiction; Humorous stories. RL B.

A man who had one last cake left from his old stove gets help from his cat to win a new stove in a contest for the most unusual cake. Two-color line drawings are original and effective in design and humor.

1069 *The Man Who Tried to Save Time*. Ill. by Marcia Sewell. Doubleday, 1979, o.p. SERIES: Reading On My Own. SUBJECTS: Behavior—Efficient—Fiction; Concepts—Time—Fiction. RL B.

A man's orderly life with his cat is disrupted by his efforts to save time by doing everything ahead of time. For example, he sleeps in his clothes, on top of the covers, and eats peculiarly. Three-color washes on ink have a folksy flavor.

Kraske, Robert

1070 *Daredevils Do Amazing Things*. Ill. by Ivan Powell. Random House, 1978, o.p. SERIES: Step-Up. SUBJECTS: Adventure stories; Biographies. RL B.

True stories about Blondin (a Niagara Falls tightrope walker), Houdini, Annie Oakley, a deep-sea fight with a 24-foot octopus, and Evel Knievel's skycycle jump over Snake River Canyon are extremely well told. Ink sketches are appropriate.

Kraus, Robert

1071 *Dance, Spider, Dance!* Ill. by author. Western, 1992. ISBN 0-307-11566-6. SERIES: Golden Easy Reader. SUBJECTS: Animals—Spiders—Fiction; Friendship—Fiction. RL A.

Spider is the hit of the dance contest when he jumps to rescue his friend—and her balloons—and lands on a banana peel. With friends Fly and Ladybug, he celebrates with a banana split. Typical wry cartoon characters are by the author.

1072 *Trouble with Spider*. Ill. by author. HarperCollins, 1962, o.p. SUBJECTS: Animals—Flies—Fiction; Animals—Spiders—Fiction; Friendship—Fiction. RL B.

Fly overcomes his suspicion of Spider when Spider needs help. Good dialogue and excellent ink and wash drawings have a marvelous sense of scale and provide selective detail.

Krensky, Stephen

1073 *Lionel and Louise*. Ill. by Susanna Natti. Dial, 1992. ISBN 0-8037-1056-9. SERIES: Dial Easy-to-Read. SUBJECTS: Imagination; Siblings—Fiction. RL A.

Lionel saves older sister Louise from a dragon (a fly buzzing inside her window), lets his sister build a fancy sand castle when the waves are threatening, "helps" Louise clean up muddy footprints and handprints, and worries Louise when they leave the water. Illustrations are appealing watercolors.

1074 *Lionel-at-Large*. Ill. by Susanna Natti. Dial, 1986. ISBN 0-8037-0241-8. SERIES: Dial Easy-to-Read. SUBJECTS: Family life—Fiction; Growing-up—Fiction. RL B.

Lionel finds his "vegetable shelf" (when deprived of dessert), and survives his first sleepover and a shot at the doctor's office. Familiar fears are overcome in the five humorous chapters on family life. Full color illustrations keep the tone light.

1075 *Lionel in the Spring*. Ill. by Susanna
Natti. Dial, 1990. ISBN 0-8037-0631-6.
SERIES: Dial Easy-to-Read. SUBJECTS:
Family life—Fiction. RL A.
Lionel's ambitious gardening plan gets pared
down, he and his sister fix breakfast for their
parents, he and his friend make a super-
strength potion that neither can drink, and
Lionel has trouble throwing away any toys
during spring cleaning. Captivating pencil and
wash drawings enhance the story.

1076 *Lionel in the Winter*. Ill. by Susanna
Natti. Dial, 1994. ISBN 0-8037-1334-7.
SERIES: Dial Easy-to-Read. SUBJECTS:
Seasons—Winter—Fiction. RL A.
Lord Lionel, explorer, escapes the grizzly
bears, an avalanche, and an earthquake, and
builds some friends so his snowman won't be
lonely in this inventive and humorous look at
a small boy's winter world. Illustrations augment text.

1077 *Snow and Ice*. Ill. by John Hayes.
Scholastic, 1989. ISBN 0-590-41449-6.
SERIES: Science Is Fun. SUBJECTS: Science;
Science experiments; Seasons—Winter.
RL C.
Besides basic information and simple experi-
ments about snow and ice, including icicles,
simple directions for making a snow fort are
included. Humorous line drawings have a roy-
al blue wash.

Krinsley, Jeanette

1078 *The Cow Went over the Mountain*. Ill. by
Feodor Rojankovsky. Golden, 1963, o.p.
SUBJECTS: Animals—Fiction; Wordplay.
RL A.
Five animals conclude after exploring the next
mountain that conditions are best right at
home. The language is playful and the full col-
or drawings show friendly animals.

Kroll, Steven

1079 *The Goat Parade*. Ill. by Tim Kirk.
Parents Magazine Pr., 1983. ISBN 0-8193-
1100-6. SUBJECTS: Humorous stories;
Parades—Fiction; Stories in rhyme. RL B.
Sam leads the goat parade into school—with
memorable results. Lively, rhythmic, zany

humor is illustrated with full color cartoon
drawings.

1080 *Pigs in the House*. Ill. by Tim Kirk.
Stevens, 1983, 1992. ISBN 0-8368-0879-7.
SUBJECTS: Animals—Pigs—Fiction; Farm
and country life—Fiction; Stories in
rhyme. RL A.
Three errant pigs turn the farmhouse into a
disaster area. Cartoon illustrations accompany
the simple rhyming text.

Krulik, Nancy E.

1081 *Animals on the Job*. Photos. Scholastic,
1990, o.p. SUBJECTS: Animals. RL B.
The usefulness of animals, from dogs and
camels to elephants and chimpanzees, is
described and illustrated with a photo per
double page spread. Language, photos, and
format are unexceptional.

1082 *My Picture Book of the Planets*. Photos
by NASA. Scholastic, 1991. ISBN 0-590-
43907-3. SUBJECTS: Astronomy and
astronomers; Science. RL A.
In large type, each of the planets is described
in a few sentences. Attractive format shows
the position of each planet, along with a photo
of each planet's surface.

Kuller, Alison M.

1083 *An Outward Bound School*. Photos by
Thomas R. Stewart. Troll, 1990. ISBN 0-
8167-1731-1. SUBJECTS: Schools. RL C.
A class of ten students experience an 18-day
course in sailing. Each day begins with a run
and a dip in the cool Atlantic Ocean, a group
meeting, possibly some rock climbing instruc-
tion, or experiencing the ropes course. Navigation, nature study, and "going solo" are all part
of the project.

Kumin, Maxine W.

1084 *Paul Bunyan*. Ill. by Dirk Gringhuis.
Putnam, 1966, o.p. SERIES: See and Read
Beginning to Read. SUBJECTS: Folklore—
United States; Tall tales. RL B.
Paul's antics account for the sun in the morn-
ing, the tides in the Bay of Fundy, a pancake

Kumin, Maxine W. (cont.)

griddle large enough to skate on, and the formation of the Rocky Mountains. Tall-tale humor shown in pencil with a blue wash.

Kumin, Maxine W., and Sexton, Anne

1085 *Eggs of Things*. Ill. by Leonard Shortall. Putnam, 1963, o.p. SERIES: See and Read Beginning to Read. SUBJECTS: Animals—Frogs and toads; Nature; Seasons—Spring. RL B.
Skippy and Buzz raise tadpoles secretly in a third-floor bathtub. Cowboy, a dog, and Skippy's sister, Pest, add to their difficulties in parenting. This creative presentation about spring eggs is well-illustrated by Shortall's ink with two-tone wash drawings.

Kunhardt, Edith

1086 *Danny's Birthday*. Ill. by author. Greenwillow, 1986, o.p. SUBJECTS: Animals—Alligators—Fiction; Birthdays—Fiction. RL B.
A slight story of the repeated viewing of a fifth birthday party videotape has short choppy sentences and dull language. Colorful animals attend the party—and save the text.

1087 *Honest Abe*. Ill. by Malcah Zeldis. Greenwillow, 1993. ISBN 0-688-11189-0. SUBJECTS: Biographies; United States—Presidents. RL B.
Some interesting facts are included in the rather choppy outline of Lincoln's life. Illustrations in primary colors are in folk style.

Kunnas, Mauri

1088 *Ricky, Rocky, and Ringo Count on Pizza*. Ill. by author. Crown, o.p. SERIES: It's Great to Read! SUBJECTS: Animals—Rhinoceroses—Fiction; Concepts—Numbers—Fiction; Cookery—Fiction. RL A.
Wheelbarrows and buckets of ingredients are assembled for a present for hungry rhino cousins on National Pizza Day. Simple counting book with riotous cartoon illustrations.

Kuskin, Karla

1089 *Soap Soup*. Ill. by author. Harper-Collins, 1991. ISBN 0-06-023571-3. SERIES: I Can Read Books. SUBJECTS: Family life; Poetry; Wordplay. RL A.
Small children's exploration of the world around them includes their own bodies, the seasons, friends, and their families. Simple, playful language describes how to eat an egg, how a stew turns into you, and a stroll through clover with Granny. Very simple illustrations match.

1090 *Something Sleeping in the Hall*. Ill. by author. HarperCollins, 1985. ISBN 0-06-023634-5. SERIES: I Can Read Books. SUBJECTS: Animals—Fiction; Poetry. RL B.
Gently humorous rhymed wordplay involves familiar animals and events. Tiny, fuzzy colored pencil drawings are equally warm and imaginative.

Kwitz, Mary D.

1091 *Gumshoe Goose, Private Eye*. Ill. by Lisa Campbell Ernst. Dial, 1988. ISBN 0-8037-0424-0. SERIES: Dial Easy-to-Read. SUBJECTS: Animals—Geese—Fiction; Mystery and detective stories. RL A.
In four short chapters, Gumshoe Goose solves the kidnapping of baby chick. Appealing drawings and simple style make this accessible to beginning readers.

1092 *Little Chick's Breakfast*. Ill. by Bruce Degen. HarperCollins, 1983, o.p. SERIES: Early I Can Read. SUBJECTS: Animals—Chickens—Fiction; Farm and country life—Fiction. RL B.
Little Chick sees the whole barnyard awaken and get breakfast before she gets hers. Colored pencil illustrations are rich in design and detail.

1093 *Little Chick's Friend Duckling*. Ill. by Bruce Degen. HarperCollins, 1992. ISBN 0-06-023639-6. SERIES: I Can Read Books. SUBJECTS: Animals—Chickens—Fiction; Animals—Ducks—Fiction; Friendship—Fiction. RL A.
While waiting for Broody Hen's other chicks to hatch, Little Chick and his friend Duckling

encounter some big, scary things—a horse and a dog—then find that the hatchlings think *they* are big and scary. Gentle, reassuring tale is matched by Degen's soft illustrations.

1094 *Little Chick's Story*. Ill. by Cyndy Szekeres. HarperCollins, 1978, o.p. SERIES: Early I Can Read. SUBJECTS: Animals—Chickens—Fiction; Growing-up—Fiction. RL B.

Broody Hen's bedtime story about Little Chick's future is comforting to both. Blue and cocoa highlight complementary pencil drawings.

L

LaFarge, Phyllis

1095 *Joanna Runs Away*. Ill. by Trina Schart Hyman. Holt, Rinehart, 1973, o.p. SUBJECTS: Behavior—Running away—Fiction; City and town life—Fiction; Emotions—Loneliness—Fiction. RL B.

A lonely girl who loves animals, especially an old vegetable cart horse, stows aboard the cart, and finds on her triumphant return that she does have friends. Hyman's pencil drawings are rich in detail and feeling.

Landshoff, Ursula

1096 *Cats Are Good Company*. Ill. by author. HarperCollins, 1983, o.p. SERIES: I Can Read Books. SUBJECTS: Animals—Cats; Pet care; Pets—Cats. RL B.

Care of cats, cat characteristics, and the benefits of owning a cat are given in a fascinating and humorous text. Childlike sketches match the tone perfectly.

1097 *Okay, Good Dog*. Ill. by author. Harper-Collins, 1978, o.p. SERIES: I Can Read Books. SUBJECTS: Animals—Dogs; Pet Care; Pets—Dogs. RL B.

Loving training directions include house-breaking and teaching the dog to sit, come, heel, stay, and lie down. Whimsical pencil drawings keep the tone light.

Langerman, Jean

1098 *No Carrots for Harry!* Ill. by Frank Remkiewicz. Stevens, 1992. ISBN 0-8368-0876-2. SERIES: Read Aloud. SUBJECTS: Animals—Rabbits—Fiction. RL A.

Harry's dislike for carrots keeps growing as he avoids eating them, despite wanting his favorite sweetgrass tart for dessert. Of course he discovers he likes carrots. Expressive rabbit cartoons.

Langner, Nola

1099 *Dusty*. Ill. by author. Putnam, 1976, o.p. SERIES: Break-of-Day. SUBJECTS: Animals—Cats—Fiction. RL B.

A girl's patience in gaining a stray cat's trust leads to a friendship that warms her even after Dusty no longer appears. This affecting story is illustrated with unsentimental soft pencil drawings.

Lapp, Eleanor J.

1100 *The Mice Came in Early This Year*. Ill. by David Cunningham. Whitman, 1976, o.p. SUBJECTS: Grandparents—Fiction; Seasons—Fall—Fiction. RL B.

A boy helps his grandfather prepare for winter by digging up potatoes, chopping wood, picking apples and hazelnuts, and watching a neighbor pull in his boat. Wonderful watercolors capture the atmosphere of homely seasonal preparations.

Larrick, Nancy, ed.

1101 *More Poetry for Holidays*. Ill. by Harold Berson. Garrard, 1973, o.p. SERIES: Poetry. SUBJECTS: Poetry. RL C.

Poetry about holidays, including Jewish ones, is presented chronologically with brief notes appended. One holiday included is Children's Book Week. Fanciful ink sketches enliven the space and enrich the mental images.

1102 *Poetry for Holidays*. Ill. by Kelly Oechsli. Garrard, 1966, o.p. SERIES: Poetry. SUBJECTS: Poetry. RL C.

John Ciardi, Aileen Fisher, and Henry Longfellow are among the noted poets celebrating ten

Larrick, Nancy, ed. (cont.)

holidays. This good selection has somewhat stilted tiny drawings.

Latham, Jean L.

1103 *What Tabbit the Rabbit Found*. Ill. by Bill Dugan. Garrard, 1974, o.p. SERIES: Easy Venture. SUBJECTS: Animals—Rabbits—Fiction. RL A.

Using primer vocabulary, a small rabbit finds everything except the blue ball he was looking for. Childlike drawings are appropriate.

Lattimore, Deborah N.

1104 *The Flame of Peace: A Tale of the Aztecs*. Ill. by author. HarperCollins, 1991. ISBN 0-06-023709-0. SUBJECTS: Cumulative tales; Folklore—Mexico; Peace—Fiction. RL C.

An Aztec boy braves the road past the nine demons of darkness to seek the flame of peace to reconcile his people with their enemy in this dramatic tale with a familiar cumulative rhythm. Illustrations are decorative Aztec symbols with primary colors against earth-tones.

Lauber, Patricia

1105 *Be a Friend to Trees*. Ill. by Holly Keller. HarperCollins, 1994. ISBN 0-06-021529-1. SERIES: Let's-Read-and-Find-Out Science Books. SUBJECTS: Plants—Trees; Science. RL B.

Holly Keller's strong graphic design and rich colors enhance the. well-written basic information about trees. The fruits and nuts, the tree eaters, the uses of trees, and how to be a friend to trees are introduced.

1106 *Clarence and the Burglar*. Adapted by F. N. Monjo. Ill. by Paul Galdone. Putnam, 1973, o.p. SERIES: Break-of-Day. SUBJECTS: Animals—Dogs—Fiction; Humorous stories; Pets—Fiction. RL B.

Adapted from a chapter in *Clarence the TV Dog* (Putnam, 1955). Clarence, the friendliest of dogs, overwhelms a burglar by untying the burglar's shoes when he refuses to play. Fun to read, with lively ink and wash pictures.

1107 *Clarence and the Cat*. Ill. by Paul Galdone. Putnam, 1977, o.p. SERIES: Break-of-Day. SUBJECTS: Animals—Cats—Fiction; Animals—Dogs—Fiction; Humorous stories. RL B.

Clarence the dog is an incredibly generous host to a visiting cat, even sharing his food and toys, his favorite chair—and his canine friends. Cat is not so bossy after their visit! Galdone captures Clarence's irrepressible friendliness and Cat's hauteur perfectly.

1108 *How We Learned the Earth Is Round*. Ill. by Megan Lloyd. HarperCollins, 1990. ISBN 0-690-04860-2. SERIES: Let's-Read-and-Find-Out Science Books. SUBJECTS: Explorers and exploration; Geography; Science. RL B.

Using simple language and suggested experiments, a noted science author shows how early geographers and explorers proved the Earth is round. The illustrations augment the text with simple maps, diagrams, sketches, and—finally—a photo of the Earth from space.

1109 *An Octopus Is Amazing*. Ill. by Holly Keller. HarperCollins, 1990. ISBN 0-690-04803-3. SERIES: Let's-Read-and-Find-Out Science Books. SUBJECTS: Animals—Octopi; Science. RL B.

A female octopus takes a week to lay her 200,000 eggs, which she glues onto stems hanging in her den. She then spends all her time guarding them and. cleaning them; when they hatch, she dies. Very light pastel line drawings. give a friendly sense of the octopus world.

1110 *Snakes Are Hunters*. Ill. by Holly Keller. HarperCollins, 1988. ISBN 0-690-04630-8. SERIES: Let's-Read-and-Find-Out Science Books. SUBJECTS: Animals—Snakes; Nature. RL C.

This clear, factual presentation about snakes of all sizes and kinds offers information on the life cycles and physical characteristics of snakes, and methods of hunting and feeding them. The spare cartoons present a nonmenacing animal that is sure to engage the interest of children.

Lawrence, James

1111 *Binky Brothers and the Fearless Four*. Ill. by Leonard Kessler. HarperCollins,

1970, o.p. SERIES: I Can Read Books. SUBJECTS: Clubs—Fiction; Mystery and detective stories. RL A.

For a price, younger brother Dinky helps find out who wrecked the Fearless Four's snow fort. Dialogue is good in text illustrated simply with flat orange, turquoise, and black.

1112 *Binky Brothers, Detectives*. Ill. by Leonard Kessler. HarperCollins, 1968; pap., 1978. ISBN 0-694-00018-3. SERIES: I Can Read Books. SUBJECTS: Clubs—Fiction; Mystery and detective stories; Siblings—Fiction. RL B.

Dinky thinks he has the solution to the mystery—but has to be rescued by his younger brother, Binky, who demands full partnership in the detective business. Very simple ink drawings have orange and cocoa washes.

Lawrence, Judith

1113 *Goat for Carlo*. Ill. by Liz Dauber. Garrard, hb and pap., 1971. ISBN 0-8116-6709-X. SERIES: Venture. SUBJECTS: Animals—Goats—Fiction; Mexico—Fiction. RL A.

Carlo's new goat produces a surprise bonus. Red serapes, sashes, and skirts highlight the setting of this simple tale.

Lazarus, Keo F.

1114 *Billy Goat in the Chili Patch*. Ill. by Carol Rogers. University of Chicago Pr., 1975, o.p. SUBJECTS: Folklore—Mexico; Mexico—Fiction. RL C.

A burro, a dog, a cock, and an ant try to help Pepito get a billy goat out of his chili patch. They discover that sometimes little and wise is better than big and strong. Simple earth-tone paintings enhance the Mexican flavor.

Lear, Edward

1115 *Edward Lear's Nonsense*. Ill. by P. Mark Jackson. William Collins, 1990, o.p. SUBJECTS: Nonsense; Poets and poetry. RL C.

The limericks of the master, Edward Lear, are printed in large type, accompanied by full page interesting, eccentric illustrations with a British look. Lear was the first children's author to delight in nonsense.

Leech, Jay, and Spencer, Zane

1116 *Bright Fawn and Me*. Ill. by Glo Coalson. HarperCollins, 1979, o.p. SUBJECTS: Native Americans—Cheyennes—Fiction; Sibling rivalry—Fiction. RL B.

A young girl caring for her toddler sister explores a trading fair. As the toddler draws a lot of attention, the older sister experiences a wide range of emotions. Earth-tone drawings give a feeling of the Native American culture and of relationships.

Leedy, Loreen

1117 *Postcards from Pluto: A Tour of the Solar System*. Ill. by author. Holiday House, 1993. ISBN 0-8234-1000-5. SUBJECTS: Astronomy; Science and scientists; Space. RL C.

Tour guide Dr. Quasar conducts a group of multicultural children on an abbreviated tour of the solar system. Dialogue and postcards convey facts about the tour. Vivid purple, blue, and green acrylics are set against the black background of space.

Lerner, Sharon

1118 *Big Bird Says . . . : A Game to Read and Play*. Ill. by Joe Mathieu. Random House, 1985. pap. ISBN 0-394-87499-4. SERIES: Step into Reading. SUBJECTS: Humorous stories; Puppets—Fiction; Stories in rhyme. RL A.

Jim Henson's puppets play a rhyming Sesame Street version of "Simon Says." Language and actions are playful and varied. Cartoon characters in ink with watercolor are unexceptional.

1119 *Big Bird's Copycat Day*. Ill. by Joe Mathieu. Random House, 1984. ISBN 0-394-96912-X. SERIES: Step into Reading. SUBJECTS: Puppets and puppetry—Fiction; Stories in rhyme. RL A.

Big Bird copies the Sesame Street characters, as well as a baby, a dog, an owl, and a bee. Simple language and ideas in rhyme make

Lerner, Sharon (cont.)

easy reading. Typical Sesame Street characters appear in illustrations.

1120 *Follow the Monsters*. Ill. by Tom Cooke. Random House, hb and pap., 1985. ISBN 0-394-97126-4. SERIES: Step into Reading. SUBJECTS: Concepts—Space—Fiction; Puppets—Fiction; Stories in rhyme. RL B.
The monsters' destination is of course Sesame Street; they demonstrate a dozen spatial terms en route there. Drawings of Henson muppets in this rhyming story are in pastel colors.

LeSieg, Theo

1121 *Come Over to My House*. Ill. by Richard Erdoes. Random House, 1966. ISBN 0-394-90044-8. SERIES: I Can Read It All By Myself. SUBJECTS: Cultural diversity; Houses; Stories in rhyme. RL B.
After skimming the world celebrating its diversity of housing, the tour concludes that despite the differences, houses are alike when friends are invited in. Indifferent comic illustrations keep the tone light in this rhyming story.

1122 *Eye Book*. Ill. by Roy McKie. Random House, 1968. ISBN 0-394-91094-X. SERIES: Bright and Early. SUBJECTS: Human body—Eyes—Fiction; Stories in rhyme. RL A.
Eyes that see blue, red, a bird and a bed, trees and clocks, bees and socks, are celebrated. Lively, simply outlined cartoons are in primary color watercolors.

1123 *In a People House*. Ill. by Roy McKie. Random House, 1972. ISBN 0-394-92395-2. SERIES: Bright and Early. SUBJECTS: Houses; Stories in rhyme. RL C.
A lively, rhyming catalog of household objects is illustrated with full color line drawings.

1124 *Maybe You Should Fly a Jet! Maybe You Should Be a Vet!* Ill. by Michael J. Smollin. Random House, hb and pap., 1980. ISBN 0-394-94448-8. SERIES: I Can Read It All By Myself. SUBJECTS: Careers; Stories in rhyme. RL C.
Lively suggestions of career options range from teaching and preaching to being a turkey farmer. Cartoon sketches show mostly males.

1125 *Please Try to Remember the First of Octember*. Ill. by Art Cumings. Random House, 1977. ISBN 0-394-93563-2. SERIES: I Can Read It All By Myself. SUBJECTS: Nonsense; Stories in rhyme. RL B.
In this rhyming story, wonderful, magical things come true by wishing on the first of Octember. Pastel drawings are more static than those in LeSieg's other books.

1126 *Ten Apples Up on Top*. Ill. by Roy McKie. Random House, 1961. ISBN 0-394-80019-2. SERIES: I Can Read It All by Myself. SUBJECTS: Humorous stories; Stories in rhyme. RL A.
Toe-tapping rhythm, outrageous bragging, and a marvelous chase draw the reader into this story. Simple, expressive line drawings are accented with red and yellow.

1127 *The Tooth Book*. Ill. by Roy McKie. Random House, 1981. ISBN 0-394-94825-4. SERIES: Bright and Early. SUBJECTS: Human body—Teeth—Fiction; Humorous stories; Stories in rhyme. RL C.
Creative, humorous uses of teeth are detailed using rhyming text; the closing admonishes the readers to remember, no matter what, that the dentist is their teeth's best friend. Comic illustrations are lively and appropriate.

1128 *Wacky Wednesday*. Ill. by George Booth. Random House, 1974. ISBN 0-394-92912-8. SERIES: I Can Read It All By Myself. SUBJECTS: Concepts—Numbers; Puzzles; Stories in rhyme. RL A.
Comic visual and rhyming puzzles intrigue the reader as well as delight the eye, as the reader is invited to identify all the errors in the pictures.

1129 *Would You Rather Be a Bullfrog?* Ill. by Roy McKie. Random House, 1975, o.p. SERIES: Bright and Early. SUBJECTS: Humorous stories; Nonsense; Stories in rhyme. RL C.
Rhymed couplets ask readers what outrageous animals or things they would like to be, from hammers or nails to minnows or whales. Humor is accentuated with McKie's usual comic drawings, with strong simple lines and bold colors.

Leverich, Kathleen

1130 *The Hungry Fox and the Foxy Duck*. Ill. by Paul Galdone. Parents Magazine Pr., 1978. ISBN 0-8193-0988-5. SUBJECTS: Animals—Ducks—Fiction; Animals—Foxes—Fiction; Folklore. RL A.

Foxy Duck requires hungry Fox to bring a table, dishes, and a tablecloth before she leaves the pond to join him for breakfast. Fox finds out the pond has a fence around it for a reason in this original and clever retelling of an old tale with flowing, simple Galdone watercolors.

Levinson, Nancy S.

1131 *Clara and the Bookwagon*. Ill. by Carolyn Croll. HarperCollins, 1988. ISBN 0-06-023838-0. SERIES: I Can Read Books. SUBJECTS: Books and reading—Fiction; Farm and country life—Fiction; Libraries—Fiction. RL B.

Though Clara works hard on the family farm, her father, who feels that books are only for rich people, will not help her learn to read—until the bookwagon librarian changes his attitude. Simple colored pencil drawings add to this moving story of a child's determination to read.

1132 *Snowshoe Thompson*. Ill. by Joan Sandin. HarperCollins, 1992. ISBN 0-06-023802-X. SERIES: I Can Read Books. SUBJECTS: Biographies; Explorers and exploration; Frontier and pioneer life. RL A.

John Thompson earned his nickname from his many trips over the Sierra Nevadas delivering mail on homemade skis. The simple retelling focuses on a boy's desire to send a letter to his father, who is off seeking gold, and is enhanced by appealing pastel pictures by Joan Sandin.

Levitt, Sidney

1133 *Mighty Movers*. Ill. by author. Hyperion, 1994. ISBN 1-56282-422-8. SUBJECTS: Animals—Fiction; Ghost stories; Moving, household—Fiction. RL A.

Movers Fred and Ted moved a family of polar bears, a statue of a giant foot, and a 500-pound gorilla, but have trouble moving a ghost. Very plain pastel drawings show the bear movers and their clients.

Lewis, Thomas P.

1134 *The Blue Rocket Fun Show: Or Friends Forever*. Ill. by Ib Ohlsson. Macmillan, 1986, o.p. SERIES: Ready-to-Read. SUBJECTS: Amusement parks—Fiction; Friendship—Fiction; Science fiction. RL B.

Leslie and Niki's summer friendship is not interrupted by surprise revelations about Niki's origin at summer's end. Well-constructed story has imaginative details and two-tone pencil highlights.

1135 *Clipper Ship*. Ill. by Joan Sandin. HarperCollins, 1978. ISBN 0-06-023809-7. SERIES: I Can Read History. SUBJECTS: Historical fiction; Sex roles—Fiction; Ships—Fiction. RL C.

Based on true-life stories of captains' wives who took over responsibility for ships, this book details one such passage to the California gold fields via the treacherous Cape Horn. Absorbing adventure shown in gray and beige with a touch of turquoise.

1136 *Hill of Fire*. Ill. by Joan Sandin. Harper-Collins, 1971; pap., 1983. ISBN 0-06-023804-6. SERIES: I Can Read History. SUBJECTS: Geology; Historical fiction; Mexico. RL A.

The true story of the 1943 eruption of Paricutin in a Mexican farmer's field is told from the point of view of his son, Pablo. Authentic ink drawings feature earth tones.

1137 *Mr. Sniff and the Motel Mystery*. Ill. by Beth L. Weiner. HarperCollins, 1984, o.p. SERIES: I Can Read Books. SUBJECTS: Animals—Dogs—Fiction; Mystery and detective stories. RL B.

Mr. Sniff identifies the perpetuator of motel mischief as someone without hay fever, who knows where to find lipstick, chews bubble gum, and is not afraid of crabs or jellyfish. Challenging puzzle has a compassionate conclusion and illustrations in turquoise, pumpkin, and avocado.

Lexau, Joan M.

1138 *The Dog Food Caper*. Ill. by Marylin Hafner. Dial, 1985; pap., 1987. ISBN 0-8037-0108-X. SERIES: Dial Easy-to-Read. SUBJECTS: Mystery and detective stories; Witches—Fiction. RL B.
Willy gets help from a neighborhood witch, Miss Happ, when dog food is found all over Mr. Spring's house, for whom Willy is dog-sitting. Colored pencil drawings enhance the characterization.

1139 *Don't Be My Valentine*. Ill. by Syd Hoff. HarperCollins, 1985; pap., 1988. ISBN 0-06-023873-9. SERIES: I Can Read Books. SUBJECTS: Friendship—Fiction; Holidays—Valentine's Day—Fiction; School stories. RL C.
Even after Albert helps them make up, Sam and Amy Lou are bugging each other on Valentine's Day at school. Realistic relationships with typical Hoff comic drawings in strong colors.

1140 *Finders Keepers, Losers Weepers*. Ill. by Tomie dePaola. HarperCollins, 1976, o.p. SUBJECTS: Siblings—Fiction. RL B.
Max tries to cover for his sister Amanda, but he has some hardships along the way. Stylized drawings have gold, blue, and avocado coloring.

1141 *I Hate Red Rover*. Ill. by Gail Owens. Dutton, 1979, o.p. SERIES: Fat Cat. SUBJECTS: Emotions—Fear—Fiction; Grandparents—Fiction; Self-esteem—Fiction. RL A.
Jill's skill at playing Red Rover at school is strengthened by her desire to help Grandpa adjust to his new dentures—neither like being laughed at. Expressive pencil drawings have a pale red wash.

1142 *Miss Happ in the Poison Ivy Case*. Ill. by Marylin Hafner. Dial, 1983, o.p. SERIES: Dial Easy-to-Read. SUBJECTS: Mystery and detective stories; Witches—Fiction. RL A.
When the magical peanut butter and grape seed concoction of Miss Happ, a neighbor, does not cure his sister's poison ivy, Willy Nilly discovers the cure himself. Expressive, action-filled drawings are brightened with shades of orange and turquoise.

1143 *The Rooftop Mystery*. Ill. by Syd Hoff. HarperCollins, 1968. ISBN 0-06-023865-8. SERIES: I Can Read Books. SUBJECTS: Moving, household—Fiction; Siblings—Fiction; Toys—Dolls and dollhouses—Fiction. RL B.
When Sam loses his sister's doll, for which he was responsible during a move, his detective work saves his skin. Flat comic drawings are a bit dull.

1144 *T for Tommy*. Ill. by Janet Compere. Garrard, hb and pap., 1971, o.p. SERIES: Venture. SUBJECTS: Storytelling. RL A.
Another version of a familiar tell-and-draw story with primary school-level vocabulary. Very basic ink illustrations.

1145 *That's Just Fine and Who-O-O Did It?* Ill. by Dora Leder. Garrard, hb and pap., 1971, o.p. SERIES: Venture. SUBJECTS: Fairies—Fiction; Magic—Fiction. RL A.
A story of a magic pot and a boy's adventures with a fairy girl are retold by Lexau. No background for the tales is given. Ink drawings show intriguing ash colored folk creations.

Lillegard, Dee

1146 *I Can Be a Baker*. Photos and drawings. Childrens Pr., hb and pap., 1986. ISBN 0-516-01892-2. SERIES: I Can Be. SUBJECTS: Careers; Food. RL C.
A picture glossary and an index accompany information about machine- and hand-baking, emphasizing the necessary speed and teamwork. Excellent color photos and a few drawings amplify the text.

1147 *Where Is It?* Ill. by Gene Sharp. Childrens Pr., hb and pap., 1984. ISBN 0-516-42065-8. SERIES: Rookie Readers. SUBJECTS: Lost and found possessions—Fiction. RL A.
A small boy messes up his room looking for his red cap. He finds it in an unexpected way. Cheery full color illustrations.

Ling, Mary

1148 *Calf*. Photos by Gordon Clayton. Ill. by Dan Wright. Dorling Kindersley, 1993. ISBN 1-56458-205-1. SERIES: See How

They Grow. SUBJECTS: Animals—Cows; Nature. RL A.

Excellent color photos trace the growth of a calf from birth to two years old. Calf borders and endpapers further decorate the simple text.

1149 *Foal*. Photos by Gordon Clayton. Ill. by Jane Cradock-Watson. Dorling Kindersley, 1992. ISBN 1-56458-113-6. SERIES: See How They Grow. SUBJECTS: Animals—Horses; Nature. RL A.

Exceptional photos of a foal from birth to five months are further enhanced by watercolor horse borders and endpapers. Text is simple.

1150 *Fox*. Photos by Jane Burton. Ill. by Rowan Clifford and Dan Wright. Dorling Kindersley, 1992. ISBN 1-56458-114-4. SERIES: See How They Grow. SUBJECTS: Animals—Foxes; Nature. RL A.

Playful kits, from birth to 12 weeks old, are illustrated with excellent close-up color photos, and a watercolor border and endpapers. Text is simple.

1151 *Giraffe*. Photos by Peter Anderson. Ill. by Sandra Pond and Will Giles. Dorling Kindersley, 1993. ISBN 1-56458-311-2. SERIES: See How They Grow. SUBJECTS: Animals—Giraffes; Nature. RL A.

A close-up look at giraffes, from birth to one year old. Simple text is dominated by excellent photos as well as giraffe borders and endpapers.

1152 *Owl*. Photos by Kim Taylor. Ill. by Jane Cradock-Watson. Dorling Kindersley, 1992. ISBN 1-56458-115-2. SERIES: See How They Grow. SUBJECTS: Animals—Owls; Nature. RL B.

Color photos show an owl from the incredibly ugly and helpless newly hatched baby to the fully grown beauty at 12 weeks. Simple text has decorative borders and endpapers.

1153 *Penguins*. Photos by Neil Fletcher. Ill. by Sandra Pond and Will Giles. Dorling Kindersley, 1993. IBSN 1-56458-312-0. SERIES: See How They Grow. SUBJECTS: Animals—Penguins; Nature. RL B.

Seven stages in the growth of a penguin, from birth to two and a half years, are shown in exceptional close-up photos, limited text, and decorative borders.

1154 *Pig*. Photos by Bill Ling. Ill. by Jane Cradock-Watson. Dorling Kindersley, 1993. ISBN 1-56458-204-3. SERIES: See How They Grow. SUBJECTS: Animals—Pigs; Nature. RL A.

Exceptional photos of pigs against a white ground are accented by watercolor borders and endpapers of pigs, and a simple text.

Little, Emily

1155 *David and the Giant*. Ill. by Hans Wilhelm. Random House, hb and pap., 1987. ISBN 0-394-98867-1. SERIES: Step into Reading. SUBJECTS: Bible stories. RL A.

This very simplified version of the story of David and Goliath stays close to the Old Testament but omits any encounter with King Saul. The pencil and watercolor pictures are cartoon style and upbeat.

Littledale, Freya

1156 *The Snow Child*. Ill. by Barbara Lavallee. Scholastic, pap., 1989. ISBN 0-590-42141-7. SUBJECTS: Folklore—Russia; Russia—Fiction. RL C.

A childless couple make a snow child who teaches the villagers how to make snow sculptures, but the snow child disappears with the spring thaw. This tale of renewal has the lavenders, blues, and whites of fantasy.

Lobel, Anita

1157 *The Straw Maid*. Ill. by author. Greenwillow, 1983, o.p. SUBJECTS: Folklore. RL B.

A girl escapes from three robbers by dressing a straw figure in her clothes, and dressing herself in feathers stuck on with honey. This original folktale has a satisfying ending. Delicate ink drawings and patterns emphasize the folk flavor.

Lobel, Arnold

1158 *Days with Frog and Toad*. Ill. by author. HarperCollins, 1978; pap., 1984. ISBN 0-06-023964-6. SERIES: I Can Read Books. SUBJECTS: Animals—Frogs and toads; Friendship—Fiction. RL B.

Lobel, Arnold (cont.)

Procrastination, kite-flying frustration, scary-story shivers, a too-big birthday hat, and two close friends, Frog and Toad, sitting alone together are the themes of the five chapters. Green and brown soft pencil drawings are reassuring and warm, like the friendship.

1159 *Frog and Toad All Year*. Ill. by author. HarperCollins, 1976; pap., 1984. ISBN 0-06-023951-4. SERIES: I Can Read Books. SUBJECTS: Animals—Frogs and toads—Fiction; Friendship—Fiction. RL B.
Toad needs Frog's encouragement to go sledding; they search together for spring and share chocolate ice cream cones and a late Christmas. Story and earth-tone drawings have humor and compassion.

1160 *Frog and Toad Are Friends*. Ill. by author. HarperCollins, 1970; pap., 1979. ISBN 0-06-023958-1. SERIES: I Can Read Books. SUBJECTS: Animals—Frogs and toads—Fiction; Friendship—Fiction. RL B.
Frog and Toad, as usual, support and encourage each other, in searching for spring and a lost button, and in waiting for a letter. Drawings focus closely on the two friends.

1161 *Frog and Toad Together*. Ill. by author. HarperCollins, 1972; pap., 1979. ISBN 0-06-023960-3. SERIES: I Can Read Books. SUBJECTS: Animals—Frogs and toads—Fiction; Friendship—Fiction. RL B.
Toad can do nothing without his list and he finds that helping frightened seeds is very hard work. With Frog's assistance everything becomes easier. The author's splendid illustrations help show the ways in which friends overcome irritations and frustrations.

1162 *Grasshopper on the Road*. Ill. by author. HarperCollins, 1978; pap., 1986. ISBN 0-06-023962-X. SERIES: I Can Read Books. SUBJECTS: Animals—Grasshoppers—Fiction. RL B.
Lobel writes powerfully about the joys of embracing new experiences in six small tales about Grasshopper. Grasshopper meets some small critters so involved in one narrow activity that they will not risk traveling with him. Rhythmic, imaginative language is accompanied by sympathetic drawings typical of Lobel.

1163 *Lucille*. Ill. by author. HarperCollins, 1964; pap., 1986. ISBN 0-06-023966-2. SERIES: I Can Read Books. SUBJECTS: Animals—Horses—Fiction; Self-esteem—Fiction. RL B.
Lucille considers herself dull and dirty as a workhorse, but chooses that role after she dresses up and tries to act like a lady. The lively drawings add humor and keep the tone light.

1164 *Mouse Soup*. Ill. by author. HarperCollins, 1977; pap., 1983. ISBN 0-06-023968-9. SERIES: I Can Read Books. SUBJECTS: Animals—Mice—Fiction; Humorous stories. RL B.
A mouse's tales of bees, thorns, stones, and mud help him escape from being the weasel's soup. Imaginative and varied ideas have excellent illustrations, highlighted by the picture of bee stings on the weasel's head.

1165 *Mouse Tales*. Ill. by author. HarperCollins, 1972; pap., 1978. ISBN 0-06-023942-5. SERIES: I Can Read Books. SUBJECTS: Animals—Mice—Fiction; Friendship—Fiction. RL B.
Seven simple tales of friendship and kindness deal with a child mouse afraid of a cloud that looks like a cat, and a wishing well that grants every wish after being given a pillow to cushion the impact of pennies being dropped in. Some drawings are small, some open and flowing.

1166 *Owl at Home*. Ill. by author. HarperCollins, 1975; pap., 1982. ISBN 0-06-023949-2. SERIES: I Can Read Books. SUBJECTS: Animals—Owls—Fiction; Emotions—Fear—Fiction. RL B.
Owl has Winter for an unwelcome guest, strange bumps under his blanket, and some comforting tear-water tea. Humor warms Owl's apprehensions, as do the soft pencil drawings.

1167 *Small Pig*. Ill. by author. HarperCollins, 1969; pap., 1988. ISBN 0-06-023932-8. SERIES: I Can Read Books. SUBJECTS: Animals—Pigs—Fiction; Farm and country life—Fiction; Humorous stories. RL B.
When the farmer's wife cleans up Small Pig's beloved mud puddle, he goes in search of a new place to wallow—and chooses unwisely.

Very effective story has expressive four-color drawings.

1168 *Uncle Elephant*. Ill. by author. HarperCollins, 1981; pap., 1986. ISBN 0-06-023980-8. SERIES: I Can Read Books. SUBJECTS: Animals—Elephants—Fiction; Emotions—Loneliness—Fiction; Illness—Fiction. RL B.

An old elephant helps a small, sick, lonely elephant while away the time. They share peanuts, have supper by moonlight, and trumpet in the dawn. Rose and pale green washes embellish the wrinkly pair's adventures.

Lohf, Sabine

1169 *Things I Can Make with Buttons*. Ill. by author. Chronicle, 1990. ISBN 0-87701-687-9. SERIES: Things I Can Make with. SUBJECTS: Arts and crafts. RL C.

Creative ideas for button craft are introduced by a child gnome cartoon figure in large colorful photos on a white ground. One can count or paint buttons, make jewelry or animals, stitchery or collages, games, gardens, or puppets.

1170 *Things I Can Make with Leaves*. Ill. by author. Chronicle, 1990. ISBN 0-87701-763-8. SERIES: Things I Can Make with. SUBJECTS: Arts and crafts. RL C.

Imaginative leaf animals and people, cards, dolls, crowns, collages, jewelry, puppets, prints, and tea are illustrated with large color photos against a white ground, with a Swedish child gnome making suggestions.

1171 *Things I Can Make with Paper*. Ill. by author. Chronicle, 1989. ISBN 0-87701-671-2. SERIES: Things I Can Make with. SUBJECTS: Arts and crafts. RL C.

Torn paper collage, crumbled paper pictures, greeting cards, woven paper, stars and snowflakes, play money, pinwheels, masks, and accordion animals are some of the creative ideas for paper crafts. A Swedish elf helps amplify each double spread illustrated with a color photo.

Long, Ruthanna

1172 *Tiny Bear Goes to the Fair*. Ill. by Joan Allen. Golden, 1969, o.p. SERIES: Beginning Readers. SUBJECTS: Animals—Bears—Fiction; Kites and kite flying—Fiction; Stories in rhyme. RL B.

Precise, neat watercolors complement this rhyming story of Tiny Bear's adventure with a kite at the fair.

Lopshire, Robert

1173 *How to Make Snop Snappers and Other Fine Things*. Ill. by author. Greenwillow, 1977, o.p. SERIES: Read-alone. SUBJECTS: Imagination; Toys. RL B.

A tantalizing table of contents shows toys to be created, from an airboat and a sock puppet to a Ballimp (balloon-turned-blimp). Exceptionally imaginative ideas, directions, and wordplay. The comic illustrations are humorous, yet precise.

1174 *I Am Better Than You!* Ill. by author. HarperCollins, 1968, o.p. SERIES: I Can Read Books. SUBJECTS: Animals—Lizards—Fiction; Behavior—Bragging—Fiction. RL A.

In this story about two lizards, Sam tries to outdo Pete in *everything*, but oversells his abilities; perhaps he will make a new friend. Lovely lizard activities like zapping flies and changing colors are illustrated in avocado green.

1175 *I Want to Be Somebody New!* Ill. by author. Beginner, 1986. ISBN 0-394-97616-9. SERIES: I Can Read It All By Myself. SUBJECTS: Animals—Fiction; Self-esteem—Fiction; Stories in rhyme. RL A.

The disadvantages of being an elephant, a giraffe, or a mouse become apparent when a zoo animal uses its magic to try different shapes. Light tone is conveyed by rhyme and comic drawings.

Lorian, Nicole

1176 *A Birthday Present for Mama: A Step Two Book*. Ill. by J. P. Miller. Random House, hb and pap., 1984. ISBN 0-394-96755-0. SERIES: Step into Reading. SUBJECTS: Animals—Rabbits—Fiction; Birthdays—Fiction; Mothers—Fiction. RL B.

Little Rabbit seeks help in finding a birthday present for his mother from a sheep, a frog, a

Lorian, Nicole (cont.)

cat, a fox, and a squirrel—but a hug is enough! Spring colors brighten friendly cartoon drawings.

Low, Alice

1177 *Zena and the Witch Circus*. Ill. by Laura Cornell. Dial, 1990. ISBN 0-8037-0404-6. SERIES: Dial Easy-to-Read. SUBJECTS: Magic—Fiction; Witches—Fiction. RL A.

A small witch, Zena, has trouble with her magic, but succeeds in taming the witches' dragon, a dog, by shrinking him into a puppy with softly spoken magic. Whimsical, lively pen and wash sketches add dashes of color and humor.

Low, Joseph

1178 *Benny Rabbit and the Owl*. Ill. by author. Greenwillow, 1978, o.p. SERIES: Read-alone. SUBJECTS: Animals—Rabbits—Fiction; Emotions—Fear—Fiction. RL B.

Father Rabbit has an ingenious way to allay Benny's fear of an owl in his closet. Imaginative, reassuring story has expressive ink and wash drawings.

1179 *Mad Wet Hen and Other Riddles*. Ill. by author. Greenwillow, 1977, o.p.; Morrow, pap., 1992. ISBN 0-688-11511-X. SERIES: Read-alone. SUBJECTS: Jokes and riddles; Wordplay. RL B.

People, pigs, elephants, peacocks, and umbrellas are the focus of these refreshingly original riddles. Pen and wash drawings spark the imagination.

Lowery, Barbara

1180 *Mammals*. Ill. by Michael Charlton. Watts, 1976, o.p. SERIES: Easy-Read Fact. SUBJECTS: Animals; Nature; Science. RL C.

Good descriptions of mammal characteristics and behavior are accompanied by two-tone pencil illustrations and an index.

Lowery, Janette S.

1181 *Six Silver Spoons*. Ill. by Robert Quackenbush. HarperCollins, 1971, o.p. SERIES:

I Can Read History. SUBJECTS: Historical Fiction; United States—Revolution—Fiction. RL A.

Some of the fear of the Redcoats' presence in Boston and the battle at Lexington are conveyed from a young girl's perspective. Pencil drawings with two-tone washes portray the spirit of the times.

Lowery, Linda

1182 *Martin Luther King Day*. Ill. by Hetty Mitchell. Carolrhoda, 1987. ISBN 0-87614-299-4. SERIES: On My Own. SUBJECTS: African Americans; Biographies; Holidays—Martin Luther King, Jr., Day. RL B.

Lowery focuses on the injustices children can understand in talking about Martin Luther King, Jr.,'s concerns. Black pencil drawings alternate with colored ones to show scenes and people important to the civil rights movement.

Lowery, Linda, and Lorbiecki, Marybeth

1183 *Earthwise at School: A Guide to the Care and Feeding of your Planet*. Ill. by David Mataya. Carolrhoda, 1993. ISBN 0-87614-731-7. SUBJECTS: Conservation. RL C.

Headings for this environmental action book include Cloudy Skies, Tree Treasures, Sea Sickness, Land's End (waste management), People Power, and Where Do We Go from Here? Following outlines of environmental problems, specific examples of positive action from around the world are given.

Lunn, Carolyn

1184 *Bobby's Zoo*. Ill. by Tom Dunnington. Childrens Pr., 1989. ISBN 0-516-02089-7. SERIES: Rookie Readers. SUBJECTS: Animals—Fiction; Humorous stories; Stories in rhyme. RL A.

This humorous story uses a 53-word vocabulary and bright watercolors to tell of all the wild animals who've taken over Bobby's house.

1185 *Spiders and Webs*. Ill. by Tom Dunnington. Childrens Pr., 1989. ISBN 0-516-02093-5. SERIES: Rookie Readers. SUBJECTS: Stories in rhyme. RL A.

Rhythmic imaginative associations of things familiar to children, from baths and bubbles and lightning and thunder to why and wonder. Watercolor illustrations are lively, of multicultural children. Text employs a 61-word vocabulary.

Luttrell, Ida

1186 *The Bear Next Door*. Ill. by Sarah Stapler. HarperCollins, 1991. ISBN 0-06-024024-5. SERIES: I Can Read Books. SUBJECTS: Animals—Bears—Fiction; Friendship—Fiction; Animals—Gophers—Fiction. RL A.
Arlo Gopher's sprinkler soaks the belongings of his new neighbor, Vic, in the first of three chapter stories about their budding friendship. A gentle humor infuses all three. Colorful, wry ink and watercolor illustrations match the text.

1187 *Lonesome Lester*. Ill. by Megan Lloyd. HarperCollins, 1984, o.p. SUBJECTS: Animals—Prairie dogs—Fiction; Solitude—Fiction. RL C.
Prairie dog Lester finds that ants, his super-clean Aunt Martha, and a crying lost baby rabbit do not make good company—you cannot be just plain peaceful with company around. Soft colored drawings, particularly of frowning Aunt Martha, are especially effective.

1188 *Milo's Toothache*. Ill. by Enzo Giannini. Dial, 1992. ISBN 0-8037-1035-6. SERIES: Dial Easy-to-Read. SUBJECTS: Animals—Fiction; Dentists—Fiction; Friendship—Fiction. RL A.
Dan the Dog recruits other friends to help him accompany his friend Milo to the dentist. Only Milo is cool when his female dentist calls him in. Soft watercolor washes show friendly animals.

1189 *One Day at School*. Ill. by Jared D. Lee. Harcourt, 1984, o.p. SERIES: Let Me Read. SUBJECTS: Humorous stories; School stories. RL C.
Arnold B. Lipton finds he is in charge of the third grade—composed of his teachers—one topsy-turvy day. Some ideas intriguing to children are broached, but the theme falls apart in

places. Wavy comic cartoons with red accents add to the humor.

1190 *Tillie and Mert*. Ill. by Doug Cushman. HarperCollins, 1985, o.p.; pap., 1992. ISBN 0-06-444159-8. SERIES: I Can Read Books. SUBJECTS: Animals—Skunks—Fiction; Friendship—Fiction. RL B.
The strong friendship of two skunks, Tillie and Mert, survives bad judgment in their small business and Tillie's success in fortune telling. Good characterization and cozy watercolors complement the theme well.

Lynn, Sara, and James, Diane

1191 *Growing Up: A First Look at Development*. Ill. by Joe Wright. Thomson Learning, 1994. ISBN 1-56847-144-0. SERIES: Play & Discover. SUBJECTS: Growing up. RL B.
In spectacular full page color photos in primary colors of animals and people from birth to elderly, and appealing drawings, the stages of development are introduced. Some projects, such as watching a bean seed grow, are suggested; a quiz reviews information given.

1192 *What We Wear: A First Look at Clothes*. Ill. by Joe Wright. Thomson Learning, 1994. ISBN 1-56847-143-2. SERIES: Play & Discover. SUBJECTS: Clothing; Costumes; Crafts. RL B.
A wonderfully creative book combining information about colorful clothing in different cultures with crafts for weaving, dress-up, making beads, printing, and so on. Illustrations are oversize full-color photo close-ups and Joe Wright's drawings.

M

Maass, Robert

1193 *Fire Fighters*. Photos by author. Scholastic, 1989. ISBN 0-590-41459-3. SUBJECTS: Fire fighting. RL C.
This photoessay looks at a fire station on a quiet day and follows fire fighters doing main-

Maass, Robert (cont.)

tenance work and relaxing while on call. When an alarm sounds, readers follow the fire fighters to the scene of a fire. Clear color photos and text explain what fire fighting is all about.

McArthur, Nancy

1194 *Megan Gets a Dollhouse*. Ill. by Megan Lloyd. Scholastic, 1988, o.p. SERIES: Hello Reader! SUBJECTS: Self-esteem—Fiction; Toys—Dolls and dollhouses—Fiction. RL C.
Her cousin Sharon has a beautiful but fragile dollhouse and Megan would like one of her own. When Mom and Dad say such a dollhouse is too expensive, Megan uses a lot of ingenuity to create her own from a cardboard box and odds and ends. Lively, humorous illustrations are in vibrant colors.

1195 *Pickled Peppers*. Ill. by Denise Brunkus. Scholastic, 1988, o.p. SERIES: Hello Reader! SUBJECTS: Behavior—Responsible—Fiction; Pet care—Fiction; Pets—Birds—Fiction. RL B.
Suzie wants to keep her aunt's dog, Pud, but she did not take good care of the dog when he visited and now her Mom and Dad say no. To prove that she is responsible, Suzie pet-sits for her neighbors' tongue-twister-reciting parakeet. The humorous story is illustrated with comic drawings with green accents.

Maccarone, Grace

1196 *Pizza Party!* Ill. by Emily A. McCully. Scholastic, 1994. ISBN 0-590-47563-0. SERIES: Hello Reader! SUBJECTS: Cookery—Fiction; Stories in rhyme. RL A.
Four children, with some adult assistance, work together to create a pizza. Very short rhyming sentences convey the enthusiasm with which the children approach their project. The watercolors capture perfectly and extend the theme of the text.

McCauley, Jane

1197 *Animals in Summer*. Photos. National Geographic, 1988. ISBN 0-87044-738-6. SERIES: Books for Young Readers.

SUBJECTS: Animals; Seasons—Summer. RL C.
A potpourri of impressive color photos has "animals" and "summer" as loose themes with the text serving mostly as captions. The book excites readers and interests them in nature rather than providing information or answering questions on nature. A brief bibliography is included.

1198 *Let's Explore a River*. Ill. by Joseph H. Bailey. National Geographic, 1988. ISBN 0-87044-741-6. SERIES: Books for Young Explorers. SUBJECTS: Nature. RL C.
A Florida park manager and his three children take a canoe trip on a river. Readers see the great diversity of nature through large color photos and a clear simple text. A two-page addendum suggests ways for parents to make such a trip with their children. A bibliography is included.

McClintock, Mike

1199 *A Fly Went By*. Ill. by Fritz Siebel. Beginner, 1958. ISBN 0-394-90003-0. SERIES: I Can Read It All By Myself. SUBJECTS: Cumulative tales; Stories in rhyme. RL A.
As he relaxes next to a lake, a little boy watches one animal after another race by. Each animal thinks it is being chased by the animal behind it. The charcoal and wash illustrations reflect the fast pace and the humor of the rhyming text.

1200 *What Have I Got?* Ill. by Leonard Kessler. HarperCollins, 1961, o.p. SERIES: Early I Can Read. SUBJECTS: Imagination—Fiction; Stories in rhyme. RL A.
A little boy tells in rhyme about all the things he could do with what he has in his pockets. At times forced or awkward, the text is brief, easy to read, and helped by the simple line drawings with color accents.

McClung, Robert M.

1201 *Horseshoe Crab*. Ill. by author. Morrow, 1967, o.p. SUBJECTS: Animals—Horseshoe crabs. RL C.
Not really a crab but an ancient form of sea life, the horseshoe crab goes through many

years of molting its shells before it becomes an adult. Watercolor pictures aid a carefully prepared text in describing this curious animal and its life cycle.

1202 *Ladybug*. Ill. by author. Morrow, 1966, o.p. SUBJECTS: Animals—Ladybugs. RL C.
The ladybug is one of the farmer's most valued insects. This book about its life cycle and habits makes fascinating reading. The illustrations are done in watercolors, and although the portraits of insects are good, larvae and eggs do not always seem to be drawn to the same scale.

McCrady, Lady

1203 *The Perfect Ride*. Ill. by Dennis Kendrick. Parents Magazine Pr., 1981, o.p. SUBJECTS: Amusement parks—Fiction; Animals—Dogs—Fiction. RL B.
The Dog family spends Saturday at Play Land amusement park. With only four tickets left, they decide to take a boat ride to the "Bermuda Triangle." Scary and full of surprises, the ride is the perfect end to their day. The marker drawings show stodgy dogs finally enjoying themselves.

McCully, Emily Arnold

1204 *The Grandma Mix-Up*. Ill. by author. HarperCollins, hb and pap., 1988. ISBN 0-06-024201-9. SERIES: I Can Read Books. SUBJECTS: Babysitting—Fiction; Grandparents—Fiction. RL B.
Pip's parents have asked their respective mothers to baby-sit Pip and so the child is stuck with both. Grandma Nan is too strict and Grandma Sal is too easygoing until Pip asks them to do things Pip's way. A delightful portrait of a child of indeterminate sex is illustrated in ink and wash.

1205 *Grandmas at the Lake*. Ill. by author. HarperCollins, 1990. ISBN 0-06-024126-8. SERIES: I Can Read Books. SUBJECTS: Grandparents—Fiction; Vacations—Fiction. RL B.
Pip and her friend Ski join her constantly arguing grandmas for and lakeside vacation. Tired of the adults' arguments, the two young children attempt to teach them a lesson by refusing to bring their boat back to shore. Attractive watercolors make light of a potentially dangerous situation.

McDaniel, Becky B.

1206 *Katie Can*. Ill. by Lois Axeman. Childrens Pr., hb and pap., 1987. ISBN 0-516-02082-X. SERIES: Rookie Readers. SUBJECTS: Asian Americans—Fiction; Sibling rivalry—Fiction. RL A.
Katie's older brother and sister seem to watch her only when she *cannot* do something. Finally they do see her do just what she said she could—teach the dog to catch the ball. Brightly colored ink and paint pictures capture the frustrations of a young child in this very short book.

1207 *Katie Couldn't*. Ill. by Lois Axeman. Childrens Pr., hb and pap., 1985. ISBN 0-516-02069-2. SERIES: Rookie Readers. SUBJECTS: Asian Americans—Fiction; Growing-up—Fiction; Siblings—Fiction. RL A.
Katie watches her older brother and sister do many things she is not big enough to do. Then Daddy comes home and picks up Katie but not the others because they are too big. The very brief text and colorful paintings capture the frustration of being youngest in a warm Asian-American family.

1208 *Katie Did It*. Ill. by Lois Axeman. Childrens Pr., hb and pap., 1983. ISBN 0-516-02043-9. SERIES: Rookie Readers. SUBJECTS: Asian Americans—Fiction; Behavior—Fiction; Siblings—Fiction. RL A.
The youngest child in a close-knit Asian-American family, Katie is always being blamed for things. Tired of hearing her sister and brother say Katie did it, she responds that she did it when mother asks who gave her flowers. Attractive, colorful pictures accompany a brief text.

1209 *Larry and the Cookie*. Ill. by Clovis Martin. Childrens Pr., 1993. ISBN 0-516-02014-5. SERIES: Rookie Readers. SUBJECTS: Food—Fiction; Play—Fiction. RL A.
Larry puts one of his favorite cookies into the front of his overalls and goes to play football.

McDaniel, Becky B. (cont.)

When the game is over, Larry cannot find the cookie until he discovers crumbs. The simple colored paintings and minimal text work well together.

MacDonald, Maryann

1210 *The Pink Party*. Ill. by Abby Carter. Hyperion, 1994. ISBN 1-56282-620-4. SUBJECTS: Emotions—Jealousy—Fiction; Friendship—Fiction. RL B.
Best friends Lisa and Amy live next door to each other and both love pink. When the two try to keep up with each other's purchases, Lisa finds herself jealous of Amy, who seems to get anything she wants. Pencil drawings with pastel washes gently support the text.

1211 *Rabbit's Birthday Kite*. Ill. by Lynn Munsinger. Bantam, 1991. ISBN 0-553-05876-2. SERIES: Bank Street Ready-to-Read. SUBJECTS: Animals—Hedgehogs—Fiction; Animals—Rabbits—Fiction; Kites and kite flying—Fiction. RL B.
Hedgehog decides to make a kite for his friend rabbit's birthday. The excitable rabbit cannot restrain himself, and though he knows nothing about kite flying, decides he needs no help. Happily resolved, the story is complemented by gentle watercolors of the two good friends.

McDonnell, Janet

1212 *Animal Camouflage: Hide-and-Seek Animals*. Ill. by Diana Magnuson. Child's World, 1990. ISBN 0-89565-562-4. SERIES: Discovery World: First Steps to Science. SUBJECTS: Animals—Camouflage. RL B.
Professor Facto takes readers to different areas of the world to discover how camouflage helps animals survive. Watercolor illustrations effectively draw children in as the text asks them to find hidden animals. Camouflage activities are also included.

1213 *Animal Talk: Barks, Growls, Hisses, Howls*. Ill. by Ching. Child's World, 1990. ISBN 0-89565-558-6. SERIES: Discovery World: First Steps to Science.

SUBJECTS: Animals—Communication. RL B.
Text and illustrations combine to explain how animals use body language, sound, and smell to get their messages across. Brief but very interesting text and pen and wash pictures show a dog begging, a cat with raised back, a peacock displaying feathers, and so on.

1214 *Baby Animals: Safe and Sound*. Ill. by Linda Hohag and Lori Jacobson. Child's World, 1990. ISBN 0-89565-554-3. SERIES: Discovery World: First Steps to Science. SUBJECTS: Animals—Baby. RL B.
Professor Facto takes a little boy to see the new babies at the zoo and on an imaginary trip to Antarctica to see emperor penguins. The brief information is accompanied by a pictorial listing of baby animals with their names (e.g., kid for goat). Illustrations are rather flat, lifeless.

1215 *Celebrating Earth Day*. Ill. by Diana Magnuson. Childrens Pr., 1994. ISBN 0-516-00689-4. SERIES: Circle the Year with Holidays. SUBJECTS: Conservation; Holidays—Earth Day; Recycling. RL C.
With Earth Day approaching, the children in Ms. Webster's class begin to learn about taking care of the earth by not polluting and by being recyclers. Useful and attractive illustrations complement the text. A section of experiments is at the end.

1216 *Space Travel: Blast-Off Day*. Ill. by Rondi Collette. Child's World, 1990. ISBN 0-89565-556-X. SERIES: Discovery World: First Steps to Science. SUBJECTS: Space travel. RL B.
From strapping in to blast-off to their return, a space shuttle crew is followed in words and pictures as they work inside and outside the spacecraft. Following the main text is a section of activities and a brief index. Illustrated with realistic color pictures.

1217 *Wind: What Can It Do?* Ill. by Gwen Connelly. Child's World, 1990. ISBN 0-89565-555-1. SERIES: Discovery World: First Steps to Science. SUBJECTS: Weather; Weather—Wind. RL B.
This is not an explanation of how winds are formed, but an exploration of the things winds do and become: tornadoes, drying the clothes,

moving clouds, bringing warm or cold air, and so on. Includes an activity section, an index, and bright but hurried-looking watercolors with pencil detailing.

McGoldrick, Jane R.

1218 *Animal Clowns*. Photos. National Geographic, 1989, o.p. SERIES: Books for Young Explorers. SUBJECTS: Animals. RL C.

Animals are photographed in amusing postures or performing rituals that appear comical. A very brief and superficial text merely calls attention to and identifies the animals. A section for adults is included.

McGovern, Ann

1219 *Little Wolf*. Ill. by Nola Langner. Abelard-Schuman, 1965, o.p. SUBJECTS: Native Americans—Fiction; Self-esteem—Fiction. RL A.

Little Wolf is often ridiculed by his tribe because he cannot kill an animal. He is wise in the lore of the forest, a knowledge that he uses to save the chief's son from poisoning and gain the tribe's respect. Sepia-colored drawings are lovely and restrained, complementing the fine story.

McInnes, John

1220 *The Chocolate Chip Mystery*. Ill. by Paul Frame. Garrard, 1972, o.p. SERIES: Venture. SUBJECTS: Business enterprises—Fiction; City and town life—Fiction; Mystery and detective stories. RL A.

Forced to move, Max opens his ice cream store in a building that everyone thinks is haunted. His customers do not come and his chocolate chip ice cream starts disappearing. Max's young helper Peppino solves the mystery of the missing ice cream and finds a way to bring customers in. Realistic sketches.

1221 *Have You Ever Seen a Monster?* Ill. by Tom Eaton. Garrard, 1974, o.p. SERIES: Easy Venture. SUBJECTS: Monsters—Fiction. RL B.

On every other page there are questions about things that a monster might do that are then answered with fantastic things that the narrator claims to have seen them do. Predictable refrains build the confidence of children struggling with reading. Illustrated with energetic cartoonlike artwork.

1222 *How Pedro Got His Name*. Ill. by Edward Malsberg. Garrard, 1974, o.p. SERIES: Venture. SUBJECTS: City and town life—Fiction; Pets—Dogs—Fiction. RL A.

To earn enough money to buy a puppy, Tony works for a shoemaker. Once he has the money saved he gets sick and his physician, Dr. Pedro, promises he will buy the dog for Tony. The story has a Hispanic setting and is illustrated with full color realistic paintings.

1223 *Leo Lion Paints It Red*. Ill. by Tom Eaton. Garrard, 1974, o.p. SERIES: Easy Venture. SUBJECTS: Animals, zoo—Fiction; Humorous stories; Zoos—Fiction. RL A.

When a little girl gives him red paint, clever Leo the Lion starts making signs for himself and the other zoo animals. Children respond to the signs by giving the animals what they want. Simple, colorful pictures illustrate this silly but engaging story.

1224 *On with the Circus!* Ill. by William Hutchinson. Garrard, hb and pap., 1973, o.p. SERIES: Venture. SUBJECTS: Circuses—Fiction. RL B.

Judy gets a chance to be a part of the circus when the littlest clown gets sick. No one knows who she is when she is dressed in Bingo's clothes and she has a wonderful time. The realistic color illustrations recreate the old Big Top ambience.

McIntyre, Ida M.

1225 *Unicorn Magic*. Ill. by Don Hedin. Garrard, 1972, o.p. SERIES: Venture. SUBJECTS: Magic—Fiction; Mythical creatures—Fiction. RL B.

A unicorn tells a tale of sorcery, a beautiful princess made from straw, and a prince seeking a bride. It is the unicorn's magic that saves the princess from being returned to straw by the sorcerer. The lack of unicorn stories has made this book popular despite the undistinguished illustrations.

McKie, Roy, and Eastman, Philip D.

1226 *Snow*. Ill. by Roy McKie. Beginner, 1962. ISBN 0-394-90027-8. SERIES: I Can Read It All By Myself. SUBJECTS: Stories in rhyme; Weather—Snow—Fiction. RL A.

Two children and their dog explore all the things that are fun to do with snow. Bold, lively pictures in blue, red, and yellow with heavy outlining and a rhyming text have the children sledding, making snow angels, and doing snow-related activities.

McKissack, Patricia

1227 *The Apache*. Photos. Childrens Pr., hb and pap., 1984. ISBN 0-516-01925-2. SERIES: New True. SUBJECTS: Native Americans—Apaches. RL C.

The text begins with the Apaches' Canadian origins, and then discusses their descendants (for example, Navajo, Chiricahua, and Jicarilla), ways of life, religious beliefs, great leaders, and wars. Well written, the text is illustrated with color photographs.

1228 *The Maya*. Photos. Childrens Pr., hb and pap., 1985. ISBN 0-516-01270-3. SERIES: New True. SUBJECTS: Native Americans—Mayas. RL C.

A great deal of information on Mayan history and culture is presented in an interesting text that might provoke youngsters to want to read more. As in other books in the New True series, this is illustrated with good full color photographs and has a glossary and an index.

1229 *Monkey-Monkey's Trick*. Ill. by Paul Meisel. Random House, 1988. ISBN 0-394-99173-7. SERIES: Step into Reading. SUBJECTS: Animals—Hyenas—Fiction; Animals—Monkeys—Fiction; Folklore—Africa. RL B.

Monkey-Monkey is pleased when a strange creature offers to help him build his house in exchange for food. Then, tricked out of the food, Monkey-Monkey finds a clever way to get what he needs. A funny retelling of an African tale. Illustrated with colorful, child-like, and humorous paintings.

1230 *Our Martin Luther King Book*. Ill. by Helen Endres. Child's World, 1986. ISBN 0-89565-342-7. SERIES: A Special Day. SUBJECTS: African Americans; Biographies; Holidays—Martin Luther King, Jr., Day. RL C.

A class of young children learns from their teacher about Martin Luther King, Jr., and his commitment to equal rights for African Americans. The children role-play segregation, sing "We Shall Overcome," and have a party in King's honor. Illustrated with full color paintings and photos.

1231 *Who Is Coming?* Ill. by Clovis Martin. Childrens Pr., hb and pap., 1986. ISBN 0-516-02073-0. SERIES: Rookie Readers. SUBJECTS: Africa—Fiction; Animals—Fiction; Animals—Monkeys—Fiction. RL A.

Little monkey runs up, down, in, out, and always *away* from the large African animals until an illustration shows a tiger. Little monkey does not run away then because, as everyone knows, there are no tigers in Africa. The simple, repetitive text has sketchy but colorful pictures.

1232 *Who Is Who?* Ill. by Elizabeth Allen. Childrens Pr., hb and pap., 1983. ISBN 0-516-02042-0. SERIES: Rookie Readers. SUBJECTS: English language—Synonyms and antonyms; Siblings—Twins—Fiction. RL A.

The clues to help tell twins Bobby and Johnny apart are in their preferences for opposites. One likes up, the other down; one front, the other back, and so on. The very brief text and colorful illustrations feature two lively African American boys in a variety of situations cleverly introducing opposites.

McKissack, Patricia, and McKissack, Fredrick

1233 *Booker T. Washington: Leader and Educator*. Ill. by Michael Bryant. Enslow, 1992. ISBN 0-89490-314-4. SERIES: Great African Americans. SUBJECTS: African Americans; Biographies; Teachers and teaching. RL C.

Born into slavery, Booker T. Washington is shown as an individual with determination and a commitment to his people. He works his way through Hampton Institute, founds Tuskegee Institute, and begins teaching African Americans the trades necessary for independence. Black-and-white illustrations accompany the text.

1234 *Bugs!* Ill. by Clovis Martin. Childrens Pr., 1988. ISBN 0-516-02088-9. SERIES: Rookie Readers. SUBJECTS: Animals—Insects—Fiction; Concepts—Numbers—Fiction. RL A.

Two exuberant children explore the countryside and happily discover all kinds of fanciful bugs and show the numbers 1 to 5. The McKissacks and Martin successfully combine forces in their use of a very brief text and attractive watercolor pictures to tell their story.

1235 *Carter G. Woodson: The Father of Black History*. Ill. by Edward Ostendorf. Enslow, 1991. ISBN 0-89490-309-8. SERIES: Great African Americans. SUBJECTS: African Americans; Biographies; Teachers and teaching. RL B.

The founder of Black History Month is shown as a determined man who came to education at age 18 and stuck with it. He became a teacher, a principal, and an innovative educator. Well and clearly written, the text is illustrated with black-and-white pictures.

1236 *Constance Stumbles*. Ill. by Tom Dunnington. Childrens Pr., hb and pap., 1988. ISBN 0-516-02086-2. SERIES: Rookie Readers. SUBJECTS: Bicycles and bicycling—Fiction. RL A.

Prone to accidents, Constance nevertheless determines to learn to ride her bicycle. A very brief text relies on full color pictures of an ebullient African American child and a watchful owl to capture children's interest.

1237 *Frederick Douglass; Leader Against Slavery*. Ill. by Edward Ostendorf. Enslow, 1991. ISBN 0-89490-306-3. SERIES: Great African Americans. SUBJECTS: African Americans; Biographies; Civil rights. RL B.

A stirring look at the life of the one-time slave, abolitionist, writer, and tireless worker for civil rights, the story of Douglass gives young readers a taste of his life and the evils of slavery. Illustrated in black and white, the book also contains an index and glossary.

1238 *George Washington Carver: The Peanut Scientist*. Ill. by Edward Ostendorf. Enslow, 1991. ISBN 0-89490-308-X. SERIES: Great African Americans. SUBJECTS: African Americans; Biographies; Science and scientists. RL C.

Born into slavery, Carver worked and studied hard and became a professor at Tuskegee Institute. There he taught science and introduced many uses for the peanut and the sweet potato. Illustrated in black and white with drawings and photos. Glossary and index are included.

1239 *Ida B. Wells-Barnett*. Ill. by Edward Ostendorf. Enslow, 1991. ISBN 0-89490-301-2. SERIES: Great African Americans. SUBJECTS: African Americans; Biographies; Civil rights. RL C.

Determined to stop the violence against African Americans from the Ku Klux Klan and others filled with hate, Wells-Barnett spoke out and wrote to make people, including the president, aware of lynchings and other acts of violence. Text is illustrated with black-and-white photos and prints.

1240 *Jesse Owens: Olympic Star*. Ill. by Michael David Biegel. Enslow, 1992. ISBN 0-89490-312-8. SERIES: Great African Americans. SUBJECTS: African Americans; Biographies; Sports—Running. RL B.

Owens was born into a poor southern family. His father moved the family north, where Jesse became a runner and a track star, ultimately becoming a member of the U.S. track and field team at the Olympics in 1936. There he won four gold medals and became an inspiration to children everywhere. Well written, the book is illustrated with photographs and occasionally awkward pen-and-ink drawings. Index and glossary are included.

1241 *Langston Hughes: Great American Poet*. Ill. by Michael David Biegel. Enslow, 1992. ISBN 0-89490-315-2. SERIES: Great African Americans. SUBJECTS: African Americans; Biographies; Poets and poetry. RL C.

Inspired by African American people throughout the country, Langston Hughes wrote poetry, fiction, and plays. He traveled but spent most of his time in Harlem. An inspiring look

**McKissack, Patricia, and
McKissack, Fredrick (cont.)**

at not just the poet but his family, the book is illustrated with pen-and-ink drawings and photographs.

1242 *Louis Armstrong: Jazz Musician*. Ill. by Edward Ostendorf. Enslow, 1991. ISBN 0-89490-307-1. SERIES: Great African Americans. SUBJECTS: African Americans; Biographies; Music and musicians. RL B.
From his early years in a poor section of New Orleans, to reform school and the discovery of his musical talent, an overview is given of Armstrong's life and especially his career. A substantial biography for this level, it is well organized, interesting, and illustrated with photos and ink drawings.

1243 *Marian Anderson: A Great Singer*. Ill. by Edward Ostendorf. Enslow, 1991. ISBN 0-89490-303-9. SERIES: Great African Americans. SUBJECTS: African Americans; Biographies; Music and musicians. RL C.
A gifted singer, Miss Anderson sang throughout the United States and the world, breaking racial barriers in Washington and in the American opera world. The story of Anderson's rise from poverty and her commitment to music is illustrated with black-and-white pictures and photographs.

1244 *Mary Church Terrell: Leader for Equality*. Ill. by Edward Ostendorf. Enslow, 1991. ISBN 0-89490-305-5. SERIES: Great African Americans. SUBJECTS: African Americans; Biographies; Civil rights. RL C.
Born into a wealthy Memphis family, Mary Church Terrell was a well-educated woman who dedicated her life to fighting for the civil rights of African Americans and women. Well written, her story is illustrated with black-and-white pictures and photographs. Glossary and index are appended.

1245 *Mary McLeod Bethune: A Great Teacher*. Ill. by Edward Ostendorf. Enslow, 1991. ISBN 0-89490-304-7. SERIES: Great African Americans. SUBJECTS: African Americans; Biographies; Teaching and teachers. RL B.
As a small child, Bethune was determined to learn to read. She went on to graduate from college and start a school for African Americans, which earned her respect, fame, and a place in the Roosevelt administration. This well-written book has black-and-white drawings and photographs.

1246 *Messy Bessey*. Ill. by Richard Hackney. Childrens Pr., 1987. ISBN 0-516-02083-8. SERIES: Rookie Readers. SUBJECTS: Behavior—Fiction; Cleanliness—Fiction; Stories in rhyme. RL A.
Bessey's room and her clothes are a terrible mess. Finally she cleans herself and her room, stuffing most things into her closet. Attractive and colorful pictures help the very brief rhyming text tell the story.

1247 *Messy Bessey's Closet*. Ill. by Rick Hackney. Childrens Pr., 1989. ISBN 0-516-02091-9. SERIES: Rookie Readers. SUBJECTS: Behavior—Sharing; Cleanliness; Stories in rhyme. RL A.
After cleaning her room, Bessey opens the closet and all kinds of things tumble out. Then she discovers things she no longer wants and decides to give them away. A very brief rhyming text is lively enough to encourage reading. Colorful illustrations are simple and realistic.

1248 *Messy Bessey's Garden*. Ill. by Richard Hackney. Childrens Pr., 1991. ISBN 0-516-02008-0. SERIES: Rookie Readers. SUBJECTS: Gardening—Fiction; Stories in rhyme. RL A.
Messy Bessey plants a garden but forgets about it until it is filled with weeds. Then she works hard to earn her pumpkin harvest. A very limited text and full-color illustrations invite children into this story.

1249 *Paul Robeson: A Voice to Remember*. Ill. by Michael David Biegel. Enslow, 1992. ISBN 0-89490-310-1. SERIES: Great African Americans. SUBJECTS: African Americans; Biographies; Civil rights. RL B.
Taught to never give up, Paul Robeson fought for his education and his place in the world of music and theater. An outspoken advocate of equal rights for African Americans and all people, Robeson is an example of courage for all children. Illustrations are pen-and-ink and photographs.

1250 *Ralph J. Bunche: Peacemaker*. Ill. by Edward Ostendorf. Enslow, 1991. ISBN

0-89490-300-4. SERIES: Great African Americans. SUBJECTS: African Americans; Biographies; United Nations. RL B.

Born into a family that gave him love and determination, Ralph Bunche was the first African American to earn a Ph.D. in political science from Harvard. After his work to end fighting in Israel, Dr. Bunche became the first African American to win the Nobel Peace Prize. Black-and-white illustrations.

1251 *Satchel Paige: The Best Arm in Baseball.* Ill. by Michael David Biegel. Enslow, 1992. ISBN 0-89490-317-9. SERIES: Great African Americans. SUBJECTS: African Americans; Biographies; Sports—Baseball. RL C.

A star of the Negro Baseball League before baseball was integrated, Satchel Paige was a great pitcher who, in his forties, was one of the first to integrate baseball. Accented with black-and-white photos and pen-and-ink drawings, the story of Paige's life is well written and interesting.

1252 *Sojourner Truth: A Voice for Freedom.* Ill. by Michael Bryant. Enslow, 1992. ISBN 0-89490-313-6. SERIES: Great African Americans. SUBJECTS: African Americans; Biographies; Civil rights. RL C.

Born into slavery in New York, Sojourner Truth fought long and hard for the rights of slaves and former slaves and the rights of women. Through charcoal drawings, photos, reproductions of art, and a good text, the life of an unusual and brave woman is made real. Index and glossary are included.

1253 *Zora Neale Hurston: Writer and Storyteller.* Ill. by Michael Bryant. Enslow, 1992. ISBN 0-89490-316-0. SERIES: Great African Americans. SUBJECTS: African Americans; Biographies; Writing and writers. RL C.

Coming from a small Florida town, Zora Neale Hurston worked hard to earn an education, graduating from college when she was 37. The story of her life, her determination to write, and her pride in her heritage makes inspirational reading. Glossary and index are included.

McLenighan, Valjean

1254 *One Whole Doughnut, One Doughnut Hole.* Ill. by Steven Roger Cole. Childrens Pr., hb and pap., 1982. ISBN 0-516-02031-5. SERIES: Rookie Readers. SUBJECTS: English language—Homonyms. RL C.

Pairs of humorous captioned pictures show the different meanings of words that sound the same. The series and format would indicate that this is meant for a child just beginning to read, but the subject might be more fun for older children. The illustrations are colorful and comical.

1255 *Stop-Go, Fast-Slow.* Ill. by Margrit Fiddle. Childrens Pr., hb and pap., 1982. ISBN 0-516-03617-3. SERIES: Rookie Readers. SUBJECTS: English language—Synonyms and antonyms. RL B.

A very brief, rhyming text and comical full color pictures successfully explain opposites such as left/right, day/night, and in/out.

McMorrow, Catherine

1256 *The Jellybean Principal.* Ill. by Amy Wummer. Random House, hb and pap., 1994. ISBN 0-679-94743-4. SERIES: Step into Reading. SUBJECTS: Friendship—Fiction; School stories—Fiction. RL C.

After ending up in the principal's office several times, three friends resolve to stay out of trouble. Yet when they hear someone calling for help from inside the closed school, they cannot resist helping. Exaggerated situations and humor are illustrated with cartoonlike color drawings.

McMullan, Kate

1257 *Dinosaur Hunters.* Ill. by John R. Jones. Random House, 1989. ISBN 0-394-91150-4. SERIES: Step into Reading. SUBJECTS: Dinosaurs. RL C.

Separated into lengthy chapters, this history of paleontology gives young enthusiasts good information about searching for fossils and what is done with them after they are found. One error: Brontosaurus is now called apatosaurus. Illustrated with utilitarian paintings.

**McNamara, Louise G., and
Litchfield, Ada B.**

1258 *Your Busy Brain.* Ill. by Ruth Hartshorn.
Little, Brown, 1973, o.p. SERIES: All
about you. SUBJECTS: Human body—
Brain; Science. RL C.
Using simple language and good, clear diagrams and pictures, the authors explain the
many bodily functions that the human brain
and nervous system control.

1259 *Your Living Bones.* Ill. by Patricia Grant
Porter. Little, Brown, 1973, o.p. SERIES:
All about you. SUBJECTS: Human body—
Skeleton; Science. RL C.
A lively text discusses the function and growth
of bones and encourages children to feel their
own bones and pay attention to how they
move. The pictures of children and bones are
realistic.

McNulty, Faith

1260 *Dancing with Manatees.* Ill. by Lena
Shiffman. Scholastic, pap., 1994. ISBN 0-
590-46401-9. SERIES: Hello Reader!
SUBJECTS: Animals—Endangered;
Animals—Manatees. RL C.
A child and her adult friend snorkle amidst
manatees in a river in Florida. As she swims
she learns about the gentle sea mammal from
her friend and from her own experience. A
good, informative text and realistic watercolor
paintings should make readers sensitive to the
manatee's plight.

1261 *The Elephant Who Couldn't Forget.* Ill.
by Marc Simont. HarperCollins, 1980.
ISBN 0-06-024146-2. SERIES: I Can Read
Books. SUBJECTS: Animals—Elephants—
Fiction; Memory and memorization—
Fiction; Sibling rivalry—Fiction. RL B.
Congo, the youngest elephant in his family,
prides himself on his extraordinary memory
and tries hard not to forget anything. Unfortunately he remembers things better left forgotten. Filled with good information, this story
has lovely pencil and wash illustrations.

1262 *How to Dig a Hole to the Other Side of
the World.* Ill. by Marc Simont. Harper-
Collins, hb and pap., 1979. ISBN 0-06-

024148-9. SUBJECTS: Earth; Geology and
geologists. RL C.
A child takes an imaginary journey through
the earth and out again on the other side. A
geological adventure, the book uses humor
and lots of good information to explain the
construction of the earth. Attractive watercol-
or and pencil pictures help to make the story
fun.

1263 *Woodchuck.* Ill. by Joan Sandin.
HarperCollins, 1974, o.p. SERIES: Science
I Can Read. SUBJECTS: Animals—Ground-
hogs; Animals—Woodchucks. RL A.
Readers first meet the woodchuck when she is
hibernating, then observe her meeting a male,
giving birth to and raising young, and finally
being alone again. There is no romanticizing
here, just an honest view of animal life. Realistic and detailed pencil and wash drawings.

McPhail, David M.

1264 *Lorenzo.* Ill. by author. Doubleday, 1984,
o.p. SUBJECTS: Animals—Fiction; Art and
artists—Fiction; Houses—Fiction. RL B.
Tired of his life as an itinerant painter, Lorenzo moves into a deserted house in a hollow
tree and paints while making friends with the
woodland animals. Illustrated with appealing
ink sketches that have red and brown washes.

1265 *Snow Lion.* Ill. by author. Parents
Magazine Pr., 1982; Crown, pap., 1987.
ISBN 0-8193-1098-0. SERIES: Read Aloud
and Easy Reading. SUBJECTS: Animals—
Lions—Fiction; Weather—Fiction;
Weather—Snow—Fiction. RL B.
Tired of the torrid jungle weather, Lion climbs
into the mountains and discovers snow. When
no one believes his story of the fluffy cold
stuff, lion takes the disbelievers into the mountains, where they have a wonderful time.
Expressive, semirealistic pictures are lively
and fun.

MacQuitty, Miranda, ed.

1266 *Side by Side.* Photos. Putnam, 1988, o.p.
SUBJECTS: Animals; Plants; Symbiosis.
RL C.
Symbiosis and parasitism, examples of how
animals or plants live "side by side," are

explained with excellent color photographs captioned with explanatory text showing animals and plants from around the world. An addendum offers more in-depth information on the animals and plants mentioned in the text.

McRae, Rodney

1267 *The Trouble with Heathrow*. Ill. by author. Childrens Pr., 1987, o.p. SERIES: Sunshine Books. SUBJECTS: Humorous stories; Pets—Dogs—Fiction. RL B.
Heathrow, a big, lovable Afghan hound, is always into mischief and never seems to learn a lesson. The brief text is dominated by vibrant and expressive paintings of the playful dog.

Madsen, Ross M.

1268 *Perrywinkle and the Book of Magic Spells*. Ill. by Dirk Zimmer. Dial, 1986; pap., 1988. ISBN 0-8037-0243-4. SERIES: Dial Easy-to-Read. SUBJECTS: Humorous stories; Magic—Fiction. RL B.
Perrywinkle practices spells from the wizard's books and creates havoc for everyone. His pet bird and his new friend Andromeda try to help him control his "spelling." The budding wizard's frustrations at mastering magic are apparent in the lively pencil and wash pictures.

1269 *Stewart Stork*. Ill. by Megan Halsey. Dial, 1993. ISBN 0-8037-1325-8. SERIES: Dial Easy-to-Read. SUBJECTS: Animals—Storks—Fiction; Self-esteem—Fiction. RL B.
Stewart Stork wants to be bigger, taller, and faster than he is and goes to unusual lengths to achieve this. By book's end, he accepts who he is and decides that his talent is humor. Amusing text and colored pencil and ink drawings work well together.

Maestro, Betsy

1270 *All Aboard Overnight: A Book of Compound Words*. Ill. by Giulio Maestro. Houghton Mifflin, 1992. ISBN 0-395-51120-8. SUBJECTS: English

language—Compound words—Fiction; Trains—Fiction. RL B.
While preparing for and actually taking a train trip, a little girl describes the things she does and sees, introducing many compound words. The attractive book, illustrated throughout with realistic watercolor and pencil pictures, also presents a fine look at railroad travel.

1271 *Ferryboat*. Ill. by Giulio Maestro. HarperCollins, 1986. ISBN 0-690-04520-4. SUBJECTS: Boats and boating. RL B.
Attractive watercolor paintings and a simple text tell the story of a river crossing on the modern ferryboat *Selden III* in Connecticut. Readers learn how cars are loaded and how captain and crew manage the boat. The brief text gives a good sense of what it is like to take a ferryboat trip.

1272 *How Do Apples Grow?* Ill. by Giulio Maestro. HarperCollins, 1992. ISBN 0-06-020055-3. SERIES: Let's-Read-and-Find-Out Science Books. SUBJECTS: Plants—Fruit; Plants—Trees. RL B.
The development of apples—from the winter bud on a branch to the final ripened fruit in the fall—is followed through text and carefully crafted pencil and watercolor pictures. The care with which this was created makes it an especially fine nonfiction book.

1273 *A More Perfect Union: The Story of Our Constitution*. Ill. by Giulio Maestro. Lothrop, 1987. ISBN 0-688-06839-1. SUBJECTS: History—United States. RL C.
The difficulties in writing a plan for governing the new United States are shown in the very interesting and carefully worded text and in the art. Pencil and watercolor pictures carefully recreate a post-revolutionary America in this story of the writing of the Constitution of the United States. Appended are a summary of the Constitution, a list of the signers, and pertinent dates and facts.

1274 *Why Do Leaves Change Color?* Ill. by Loretta Krupinksi. HarperCollins, hb and pap., 1994. ISBN 0-06-022873-3. SERIES: Let's-Read-and-Find-Out Science Books. SUBJECTS: Seasons—Fall; Plants—Trees. RL B.
Gouache and colored pencil pictures fill the pages and vibrantly accent and extend the text,

Maestro, Betsy (cont.)

which explores how and why leaves change color. This reads well and children will enjoy the appended activities that include appropriate safety precautions.

Maestro, Betsy, and DelVecchio, Ellen

1275 *Big City Port*. Ill. by Giulio Maestro. Scholastic, pap., 1984. ISBN 0-590-41577-8. SUBJECTS: Ports and harbors; Ships and shipping. RL B.
A picture of the activity in the harbor or port of a large city is carefully drawn in ink and watercolor pictures and in the text. Use of gray tones gives the pictures a dark look.

Maestro, Giulio

1276 *Leopard and the Noisy Monkeys*. Ill. by author. Greenwillow, 1979, o.p. SERIES: Read-alone. SUBJECTS: Animals—Fiction; Humorous stories; Sleep—Fiction. RL B.
Escaping from the noise of the 20 monkeys he has allowed to use his treehouse, Leopard goes to Crocodile's house, and Crocodile goes to Aardvark's to escape Leopard, Aardvark to Hippo's, Hippo to Leopard's. Amusing illustrations and story are silly enough to please young readers.

1277 *Leopard Is Sick*. Ill. by author. Greenwillow, 1978, o.p. SERIES: Read-alone. SUBJECTS: Animals—Fiction; Humorous stories; Illness—Fiction. RL B.
Bored with being sick but ordered by his doctor to rest, Leopard feels better only when his three friends disguise themselves as doctors to cheer him up. Simple yet interesting paintings with gray outlining and details fit well with the funny story.

Mallett, Anne

1278 *Here Comes Tagalong*. Ill. by Steven Kellogg. Parents Magazine Pr., 1971, o.p. SUBJECTS: Emotions—Loneliness—Fiction; Humorous stories; Siblings—Fiction. RL B.
Steve does not know any children his own age so he tags along after his older brother and his friends. Finally old enough to go around the block, he makes his own friends and his younger brother becomes Tagalong. Spirited pictures catch the humor as well as Steve's initial loneliness.

Malone, Mary

1279 *Annie Sullivan*. Ill. by Lydia Rosier. Putnam, 1971, o.p. SERIES: See and Read Beginning to Read Biography. SUBJECTS: Biographies; Physically and mentally impaired. RL B.
Annie Sullivan's life story is told in a concise and straightforward way beginning with her childhood poverty and going through her years as "Teacher" to Helen Keller. No dates are provided, although World War I is mentioned. Illustrated with realistic ink drawings.

Mantinband, Gerda B.

1280 *Bing Bong Bang and Fiddle Dee Dee*. Ill. by Anne Rockwell. Doubleday, 1979, o.p. SERIES: Reading On My Own. SUBJECTS: Farm and country life—Fiction; Marriage—Fiction; Music—Fiction. RL B.
To his wife's dismay, an old man buys a fiddle and tries to play it. She starts banging on pots to stop his squeaking and their music drives the animals from their farm. An affectionate reconciliation ends this story of marital discord. Simple, childlike drawings accompany the humorous story.

Manushkin, Fran

1281 *Buster Loves Buttons!* Ill. by Dirk Zimmer. HarperCollins, 1985. ISBN 0-06-024108-X. SERIES: I Can Read Books. SUBJECTS: Behavior—Greedy—Fiction; Collecting and collectors—Fiction; Pets—Dogs—Fiction. RL B.
Buster is a compulsive collector of buttons, even cutting them off people's clothing, until he is given his comeuppance by Kippy and her dog. Full color humorous drawings effectively extend and make more exciting this occasionally plodding story.

1282 *Hocus and Pocus at the Circus*. Ill. by Geoffrey Hayes. HarperCollins, 1983, o.p. SERIES: I Can Read Books. SUBJECTS: Circuses—Fiction; Holidays—Halloween—Fiction; Witches—Fiction. RL C.

Intent on creating chaos, Hocus takes her little witch sister Pocus to the circus on Halloween night. Pocus uses her talent to thwart Hocus's spells in this slight but enjoyable story. The comic-style drawings are in full color with characters round and toylike rather than realistic.

1283 *The Perfect Christmas Picture*. Ill. by Karen A. Weinhaus. HarperCollins, 1980; pap., 1987. ISBN 0-06-444112-1. SERIES: I Can Read Books. SUBJECTS: Family life—Fiction; Photography—Fiction. RL C.

All year Mr. Green has tried with no success to take a perfect Christmas picture of his six children. His frustrations and the children's antics will have readers laughing. The spare, humorous ink and wash drawings work very well with the story.

Margolis, Richard J.

1284 *Big Bear, Spare That Tree*. Ill. by Jack Kent. Greenwillow, 1980, o.p. SERIES: Read-alone. SUBJECTS: Animals—Bears—Fiction; Animals—Blue Jays—Fiction. RL B.

Trying to save her soon-to-hatch eggs, a blue jay screams for Bear to stop chopping down her tree. He ignores her until he sees that the eggs are hatching and then he must really come to the rescue. The conflict is handled well and Kent's humorous drawings keep the story light.

1285 *Homer the Hunter*. Ill. by Leonard Kessler. Macmillan, 1972, o.p. SERIES: Ready-to-Read. SUBJECTS: Animals—Fiction; Humorous stories; Hunting—Fiction. RL B.

Rabbit, Squirrel, and Crow initially fool Homer, a terrible hunter, into believing they are ghosts haunting him. Finally Homer decides to share in the fun and pretends that he is a ghost too. Comical sketches in gray, brown, and red complement the story.

1286 *Wish Again, Big Bear*. Ill. by Robert Lopshire. Macmillan, 1972, o.p. SERIES:

Ready-to-Read. SUBJECTS: Animals—Bears—Fiction; Animals—Fish—Fiction; Wishes—Fiction. RL B.

To save himself from being eaten, Fish tells Big Bear he is magic and will grant him three wishes. Fish saves himself and Bear gets what he wished for—a friend. The humor in Fish's trickery and Bear's gullibility acts as a perfect complement to Lopshire's comic ink drawings.

Markert, Jenny

1287 *Hippos*. Photos. Child's World, 1993. ISBN 1-56766-003-7. SUBJECTS: Animals—Hippopotami. RL C.

Sharp color photographs and a focused text show how the third largest land animal lives, protects its territory, and cares for its young. Slightly more difficult than the others in the Naturebooks series. Includes an index.

1288 *Reptiles*. Photos. Child's World, 1993. ISBN 0-89565-850-X. SERIES: Wildlife Library. SUBJECTS: Animals—Reptiles and amphibians. RL C.

Alternating pages of large, well-spaced text and striking color photographs should lure young readers into this introductory look at reptiles such as the basilisk lizard, the gila monster, and the gavial.

Markham, Marion M.

1289 *The Halloween Candy Mystery*. Ill. by Emily A. McCully. Houghton Mifflin, 1982, o.p.; Avon, pap., 1990. ISBN 0-380-70965-1. SUBJECTS: Holidays—Halloween—Fiction; Mystery and detective stories; Siblings—Twins—Fiction. RL B.

Dressed in their panda costumes and ready to go trick-or-treating, twin sisters Mickey and Kate get involved in reporting a robbery and in helping to find the missing robber. Longer than most first readers, this is entertaining and has good black and white drawings.

Marshall, Edward

1290 *Four on the Shore*. Ill. by James Marshall. Dial, 1985; pap., 1987. ISBN 0-8037-0142-X. SERIES: Dial Easy-to-Read.

Marshall, Edward (cont.)

SUBJECTS: Humorous stories; Siblings—Fiction; Storytelling—Fiction. RL B.
Three children, Lolly, Spider, and Sam, share stories around a fire hoping to frighten Spider's little brother Willie into going home. Drawn in ink with colorful washes, the pictures are simple yet comical, adding to the already delightful humor of the stories.

1291 *Fox All Week*. Ill. by James Marshall. Dial, 1984; pap., 1987. ISBN 0-8037-0066-0. SERIES: Dial Easy-to-Read. SUBJECTS: Animals—Foxes—Fiction; Friendship—Fiction; Humorous stories. RL B.
From Monday morning to Sunday evening, Fox, his friends, and his family face situations that are sure to stir memories in adults and be very funny to children. The book is illustrated with humorous full color ink and watercolor paintings.

1292 *Fox and His Friends*. Ill. by James Marshall. Dial, hb and pap., 1982. ISBN 0-8037-2669-4. SERIES: Dial Easy-to-Read. SUBJECTS: Animals—Foxes—Fiction; Baby-sitting—Fiction; Humorous stories. RL B.
In each of three stories, Fox cannot seem to get away with anything. In two stories he is stuck taking care of his spunky little sister Louise and in the third his conscience gets the better of him. Each story is very funny, the third hilarious, especially with the deadpan, comic illustrations.

1293 *Fox at School*. Ill. by James Marshall. Dial, hb and pap., 1983. ISBN 0-8037-2675-9. SERIES: Dial Easy-to-Read. SUBJECTS: Animals—Foxes—Fiction; Humorous stories; School stories. RL B.
Always wanting the easy way out, egocentric Fox is surprised that it takes hard work to act in the class play or control the class. Children are sure to identify with the imperfect but lovable Fox. Illustrated with comic ink drawings with coral and green tints.

1294 *Fox in Love*. Ill. by James Marshall. Dial, hb and pap., 1982. ISBN 0-8037-2433-0. SERIES: Dial Easy-to-Read. SUBJECTS: Animals—Foxes—Fiction; Humorous stories; Romance—Fiction. RL B.
Forced to take his little sister Louise to the park, Fox is surprised to meet Raisin, a lovely white fox, and is soon swooning over her as well as Millie, Rose, and Lola. Fun to read, this book has whimsical ink cartoon drawings with orange and green washes.

1295 *Fox on Wheels*. Ill. by James Marshall. Dial, hb and pap., 1983. ISBN 0-8037-0002-4. SERIES: Dial Easy-to-Read. SUBJECTS: Animals—Foxes—Fiction; Baby-sitting—Fiction; Bicycles and bicycling—Fiction. RL B.
In three stories with surprise endings, Fox gets into more trouble than he bargained for—especially when he baby-sits for his little sister Louise or goes biking through the park. Illustrations are ink line drawings with color overlays in a whimsical style.

1296 *Three by the Sea*. Ill. by James Marshall. Dial, hb and pap., 1981. ISBN 0-8037-8687-5. SERIES: Dial Easy-to-Read. SUBJECTS: Friendship—Fiction; Storytelling—Fiction. RL B.
After a filling picnic lunch at the beach, Lolly decides to share a story from her reader with Spider and Sam. Bored, they try to create their own stories. Sure to appeal to children and adults, this book is illustrated with humorous ink and pencil drawings.

1297 *Troll Country*. Ill. by James Marshall. Dial, 1980, o.s.i.; pap., 1980. ISBN 0-8037-6210-0. SERIES: Dial Easy-to-Read. SUBJECTS: Fantasy; Humorous stories; Trolls—Fiction. RL B.
After hearing her mother's story of her encounter with a troll, Elsie Fay is sure she will know exactly how to handle one. Droll ink drawings with colored pencil accents in gray, green, and rust are perfect for this entertaining story.

Marshall, James

1298 *Fox on Stage*. Ill. by author. Dial, 1993. ISBN 0-8037-1356-8. SERIES: Dial Easy-to-Read. SUBJECTS: Animals—Foxes—Fiction; Magic—Fiction; Plays—Fiction. RL B.
In three stories, Fox continues to cause laughter as he very seriously tries to entertain his

bedridden Grannie, refuses to believe in magic, and attempts to put on a scary play. The watercolor paintings are a perfect match for the stories' humor.

1299 *Fox on the Job*. Ill. by author. Dial, 1988. ISBN 0-8037-0351-1. SERIES: Dial Easy-to-Read. SUBJECTS: Animals—Foxes—Fiction; Humorous stories. RL B.

To impress the girls, Fox shows off on his bike and ends up demolishing it. When Mom refuses to buy him a new one, Fox goes through several jobs before he finds one just right for his special talents. Story and artwork continue to be as witty and satisfying as in the earlier Fox stories.

1300 *Fox Outfoxed*. Ill. by author. Dial, 1992. ISBN 0-8037-1036-4. SERIES: Dial Easy-to-Read. SUBJECTS: Animals—Foxes—Fiction; Holidays—Halloween—Fiction; Humorous stories. RL B.

Three hilarious stories feature Fox, his little sister Louise, and his friends as they stage a race; Fox gets tricked out of his comics; they go trick-or-treating and end up tricked. Marshall's text and delightfully humorous watercolor pictures are sure winners with young readers.

1301 *Three up a Tree*. Ill. by author. Dial, 1986. ISBN 0-8037-0329-5. SERIES: Dial Easy-to-Read. SUBJECTS: Friendship—Fiction; Storytelling—Fiction; Treehouses—Fiction. RL B.

To get into Spider and Sam's treehouse, Lolly promises to tell a story. Soon the other two are trying to outdo Lolly with their storytelling. The colorful, often silly illustrations and stories are sure to evoke appreciative smiles.

Martin, Claire

1302 *I Can Be a Weather Forecaster*. Photos. Childrens Pr., hb and pap., 1987. ISBN 0-516-01908-2. SERIES: I Can Be. SUBJECTS: Careers; Weather. RL C.

Weather forecasting is presented as an interesting and demanding profession with much more involved than what is seen on a television weather report. Illustrated with color photographs and simple drawings, the text

mentions weather satellites, stations, computers, and other forecasting tools.

Martin, C. L. G.

1303 *Day of Darkness, Night of Light*. Ill. by Victoria M. Williams. Dillon, 1988, o.p. SERIES: It Really Happened! SUBJECTS: Fire fighting—Fiction; Historical fiction. RL C.

Fire breaks out threatening to destroy Menominee, Michigan, in October 1871. After getting his mother and sisters to safety, Daniel and his grandfather help battle the blaze and save their town. Based on an actual event, this suspenseful story is effectively illustrated in pencil.

Martin, Louise

1304 *Alligators*. Photos. Rourke, 1989. ISBN 0-86592-579-8. SERIES: Reptile Discovery Library. SUBJECTS: Animals—Alligators and crocodiles; Animals—Reptiles and amphibians. RL C.

Good photographs add appeal to a very brief text divided into nine paragraph-size sections. The various aspects of alligators' lives are mentioned. A limited glossary and an index are included.

1305 *Chameleons*. Photos. Rourke, 1989. ISBN 0-86592-576-3. SERIES: Reptile Discovery Library. SUBJECTS: Animals—Chameleons; Animals—Reptiles and amphibians. RL C.

Nine sections of text with paragraph-size bits of information are augmented by photographs. Together they offer an introduction to the life of a number of chameleons. A confusing section says the tongue is half the size of its body and shows a tongue twice the size. There is a minimal glossary and an index.

1306 *Panda*. Photos. Rourke, 1988. ISBN 0-86592-996-3. SERIES: Wildlife in Danger. SUBJECTS: Animals—Endangered; Animals—Pandas. RL B.

Martin provides interesting information to support her plea for the preservation of the panda, stressing threats to its existence such as poaching and loss of habitat. Some photographs are not matched correctly to the text

Martin, Louise (cont.)

but the information is good enough to compensate for that.

1307 *Rhinoceros*. Photos. Rourke, 1988. ISBN 0-86592-997-1. SERIES: Wildlife in Danger. SUBJECTS: Animals—Endangered; Animals—Rhinoceroses. RL B.
The threat of extinction is mentioned on nearly every page of this simply written and useful book. There is a good deal of information about rhinos: types, habitat, diet, poaching, protection, and horns. Color photos are not always matched to the text and captions could be more informative.

1308 *Seals*. Photos. Rourke, 1988. ISBN 0-86592-999-8. SERIES: Wildlife in Danger. SUBJECTS: Animals—Endangered; Animals—Seals. RL B.
Using only 18 pages of alternating text and photographs, Martin presents well-documented threats to the existence of seals without presenting much information on the various species of seals. The brief information could be useful for reports on endangered animals.

1309 *Tigers*. Photos. Rourke, 1988. ISBN 0-86592-995-5. SERIES: Wildlife in Danger. SUBJECTS: Animals—Endangered; Animals—Tigers. RL B.
The emphasis here is on the threat to Asian tigers through poaching and habitat destruction rather than on the general characteristics of the largest member of the cat family. Good information and attractive color photographs are provided.

1310 *Trapdoor Spiders*. Photos. Rourke, 1988. ISBN 0-86592-963-7. SERIES: Spiders Discovery Library. SUBJECTS: Animals—Spiders. RL B.
An excellent text describes the unusual burrow and some of the habits of the trapdoor spiders that are found all over the world. The scope of information is limited and a discussion of the spider's life cycle could have been included. The photos include two that have mismatched captions.

Martin, Patricia M.

1311 *The Pumpkin Patch*. Ill. by Tom Hamil. Putnam, 1966, o.p. SUBJECTS: Holidays—

Halloween—Fiction; School stories. RL B.
Kate loves kindergarten and cannot wait for her class to go to the pumpkin patch so she can pick out her very own pumpkin. Once there she discovers that the perfect pumpkin already has an owner—a field mouse. Very sketchy drawings are busy and childlike and work well with this story.

1312 *Thomas Alva Edison*. Ill. by Fermin Rocker. Putnam, 1971, o.p. SERIES: See and Read Beginning to Read Biography. SUBJECTS: Biographies; Inventors and inventions. RL C.
Focusing on Edison's curiosity about all kinds of scientific ventures, this interesting text highlights his youthful adventures in school and at work and his adult scientific study. Pen and ink cross-hatchings are used to create the pictures of Edison and his work.

Martini, Teri

1313 *Cowboys*. Photos. Childrens Pr., 1981. ISBN 0-516-01611-3. SERIES: New True. SUBJECTS: Cowboys. RL C.
Rounding up and branding cattle, taking care of the ranch, being in a rodeo, and feeding cattle in winter are some of the parts of a cowboy's work that are presented in this short book with colorful photographs, a glossary, and an index.

Marzollo, Jean

1314 *Amy Goes Fishing*. Ill. by Ann Schweninger. Dial, 1980, o.p. SERIES: Dial Easy-to-Read. SUBJECTS: Fishing—Fiction; Parent and child—Fiction. RL B.
On her first fishing trip with father, Amy remembers how boring her brother and sister thought fishing was. She is pleasantly surprised at how much she enjoys their day together. An understated text and quiet, soft-hued pictures blend to create an enjoyable, low-key story.

1315 *Cannonball Chris*. Ill. by Blanche Sims. Random House, hb and pap., 1987. ISBN 0-394-98512-5. SERIES: Step into Reading. SUBJECTS: Emotions—Fear—Fiction; Parent and child—Fiction; Sports—Swimming—Fiction. RL B.

Realizing that something is wrong, Chris's father convinces Chris to say what is bothering him—a fear of diving into deep water. His father helps Chris to face his fear, name it, and finally overcome it with his support. This very well done story has lively multiracial children drawn in pencil and wash.

1316 *Happy Birthday, Martin Luther King*. Ill. by J. Brian Pinkney. Scholastic, 1993. ISBN 0-590-44065-9. SUBJECTS: African Americans; Biography; Holidays—Martin Luther King, Jr., Day. RL B.
In simple words and beautiful scratchboard illustrations, the story of King's life and his commitment to understanding between races is told. Though this is in a picture-book format, the care taken in writing the text has made it very accessible to young readers.

1317 *Musical Instruments*. Translated from the French and rewritten. Ill. by Donald Grant. Scholastic, 1992. ISBN 0-590-47729-3. SERIES: First Discovery Book. SUBJECTS: Musical instruments. RL C.
On heavy paper with occasional transparent overlays that attract the interest of young readers, explanations are provided for how classical, popular, and folk instruments are made. Illustrations are colorful paintings set against a white background.

1318 *The Rain Forest*. Translated from the French and rewritten. Ill. by Rene Mettler. Scholastic, 1992. ISBN 0-590-47728-5. SERIES: First Discovery Book. SUBJECTS: Animals; Conservation; Rain forest. RL C.
Heavy-weight glossy paper with occasional transparent overlays displays the rain forest and its plants and animals. Colors are vibrant and the overlays add surprises and fun to an interesting subject. On darker pages, however, the text is often difficult to read.

1319 *Red Sun Girl*. Ill. by Susan Meddaugh. Dial, 1983. ISBN 0-8037-7494-X. SERIES: Dial Easy-to-Read. SUBJECTS: Animals—Fiction; Magic—Fiction; Science fiction. RL B.
Everyone on the planet is a human during Red Sun and an animal during Blue Sun except Kiri. Tired of being laughed at, she finds a way to get her own animal shape. This is an appealing, well-paced book that is divided into chapters. Simple, cartoon style pictures are drawn with colored pencil.

1320 *Soccer Sam*. Ill. by Blanche Sims. Random House, hb and pap., 1987. ISBN 0-394-98406-4. SERIES: Step into Reading. SUBJECTS: Cultural diversity—Fiction; Sports—Soccer—Fiction. RL C.
Although Sam's Mexican cousin Marco does not understand English, his prowess at soccer earns him friends. This well-done book about overcoming cultural differences has pencil and watercolor pictures.

1321 *Whales*. Ill. by Ute Fuhr and Raoul Sautai. Scholastic, 1991. ISBN 0-590-47130-9. SERIES: First Discovery Book. SUBJECTS: Animals—Whales. RL B.
Clever plastic overlays extend an interesting text and add child appeal to an already intriguing animal. The plastic overlays give readers an opportunity to see different views and even a skeleton of a whale. One difficulty may be reading text that is set against blue.

Marzollo, Jean, and Marzollo, Claudio

1322 *Blue Sun Ben*. Ill. by Susan Meddaugh. Dial, hb and pap., 1984. ISBN 0-8037-0063-6. SERIES: Dial Easy-to-Read. SUBJECTS: Animals—Fiction; Magic—Fiction; Science fiction. RL B.
On Ben's planet everyone is an animal during Blue Sun and a human during Red Sun. Caught by the evil Animal Singer while in his chipmunk shape, Ben manages to escape with the help of his cousin Kiri and the Fox Woman. Colored pencil drawings effectively delineate the exciting story.

1323 *Jed and the Space Bandits*. Ill. by Peter Sis. Dial, 1987. ISBN 0-8037-0136-5. SERIES: Science Fiction Dial Easy-to-Read. SUBJECTS: Science fiction. RL C.
Since she is able to become invisible, Molly is not seen by the space bandits who kidnap her scientist parents. Jed, his cogs (telepathic half-dog, half-cat animals), and his robot Teddy Bear join Molly in an exciting rescue of her parents. The story is illustrated with good full color pictures.

**Marzollo, Jean, and
Marzollo, Claudio (cont.)**

1324 *Jed's Junior Space Patrol.* Ill. by David S. Rose. Dial, 1982. ISBN 0-8037-4287-8. SERIES: Dial Easy-to-Read. SUBJECTS: Science fiction. RL B.

Left alone while his space pilot parents work, Jed hears a call for help and rescues two cogs—telepathic half-dog, half-cat animals. Taken from Jed, the little animals use telepathy to get him to rescue them again. This time they stay with him. The futuristic pictures are done in ink and washes.

1325 *Robin of Bray.* Ill. by Diane Stanley. Dial, hb and pap., 1982. ISBN 0-8037-7332-3. SERIES: Dial Easy-to-Read. SUBJECTS: Fairy tales; Magic—Fiction; Trolls—Fiction. RL B.

In this creative and appealing fairy tale, Robin is stuck being a shepherd when he has talent enough to be a magician. After rescuing a princess from trolls, he discovers his true identity. Contains suitably fanciful pointillist ink drawings with washes.

1326 *Ruthie's Rude Friends.* Ill. by Susan Meddaugh. Dial, 1984; pap., 1987. ISBN 0-8037-0116-0. SERIES: Dial Easy-to-Read. SUBJECTS: Behavior—Manners—Fiction; Friendship—Fiction; Science fiction. RL B.

Ruthie, newly arrived from Earth, is just as rude to the strange beings she meets as she believes they are to her until they rescue her from a terrible three-headed monster. Ink line drawings with vibrant colored pencil details carry and expand the successful science-fiction theme.

Mason, Margo

1327 *Go Away, Crows!* Ill. by David Prebenna. Bantam, hb and pap., 1989. ISBN 0-553-05817-7. SERIES: Little Rooster Read-A-Story. SUBJECTS: Animals—Birds—Fiction; Animals—Pigs—Fiction. RL A.

When a bunch of crows descend on the two pigs' home, nothing Big Pig does seems to work. Finally Little Pig finds the solution—a scarecrow. Soft pencil and watercolor pictures comically illustrate this very brief story.

1328 *Good Dog, Rover.* Ill. by Sandy Hoffman Bantam, hb and pap., 1989. ISBN 0-553-05814-2. SERIES: Little Rooster Read-A-Story. SUBJECTS: Pets—Dogs—Fiction. RL A.

Amy and Andy and their parents know they do not want a black or white, a large or small dog. They find Rover, a medium-size spotted dog, at the pound and he is perfect. The children begin training him and he quickly learns. Cartoonish ink and watercolor pictures augment the very brief text.

1329 *Ready, Alice?* Ill. by Catherine Siracusa. Bantam, hb and pap., 1990. ISBN 0-553-05816-9. SERIES: Little Rooster Read-A-Story. SUBJECTS: Behavior—Fiction. RL A.

Despite her parents' impatience and constant reminders, Alice dawdles getting up, getting dressed, eating, and, finally, getting ready for the beach. Pencil and watercolor drawings ably illustrate this very short story.

1330 *Winter Coats.* Ill. by Laura Rader. Bantam, hb and pap., 1989. ISBN 0-553-05818-5. SERIES: Little Rooster Read-A-Story. SUBJECTS: Animals; Clothing; Seasons—Winter. RL A.

Using large type and very short sentences as captions to pictures of animals and humans in winter, the book shows how animals and people use "coats" to stay warm. Illustrations are not skillfully done and appear similar to those used in old school primers.

Massie, Diane R.

1331 *The Komodo Dragon's Jewels.* Ill. by author. Macmillan, 1975, o.p. SERIES: Ready-to-Read. SUBJECTS: Animals—Lizards—Fiction; Humorous stories. RL C.

The Komodo Dragon, a giant lizard, gets his chance to see the jewels shining from the mainland when he is mistaken for a passenger and is allowed aboard a tour boat. The fun found in the text is augmented by the outlandish ink and wash illustrations.

Mathis, Sharon Bell

1332 *Red Dog Blue Fly: Football Poems.* Ill. by Jan Spivey Gilchrist. Viking, 1991. ISBN

0-670-83623-0. SUBJECTS: African Americans; Poetry; Sports—Football. RL C.
The fears and glories, the coaches and parents, the cheerleaders and playoff pizza, are all a part of the pulsing, rhythmic poems about America's favorite sport. Strong illustrations are done primarily in blues and greens, with yellow and purple accents.

Matthews, Morgan

1333 *What's It Like to Be a Farmer*. Ill. by Anne Kennedy. Troll, hb and pap., 1990. ISBN 0-8167-1803-2. SERIES: What's It Like to Be a . . . . SUBJECTS: Careers; Farm and country life. RL C.
The Smith family has a large farm with a variety of crops and animals. Readers follow the Smiths through a year as they plant, tend crops and animals, and harvest. Ink drawings with color washes effectively illustrate the text.

1334 *What's It Like to Be a Postal Worker*. Ill. by Mark A. Hicks Troll, hb and pap., 1990. ISBN 0-8167-1813-X. SERIES: What's It Like to Be a . . . . SUBJECTS: Careers; Mail. RL C.
Readers follow letters through the postal system and learn about the various jobs and machines involved in getting mail from place to place. Illustrations, done with pen and ink drawings with color washes, help to explain the system.

1335 *What's It Like to Be a Railroad Worker*. Ill. by Lynn Sweat. Troll, 1990. ISBN 0-8167-1815-6. SERIES: What's It Like to Be a . . . . SUBJECTS: Careers; Trains. RL C.
As Jimmy and his parents travel on the passenger train, the conductor tells the boy about trains and how they operate. Ink drawings with color washes supplement the text.

Matthias, Catherine

1336 *I Can Be a Police Officer*. Photos. Childrens Pr., hb and pap., 1984. ISBN 0-516-01840-X. SERIES: I Can Be. SUBJECTS: Careers; Police. RL B.
Supported by full color photographs and drawings, this book gives an overview of police work in the United States and abroad.

It also discusses the type of work done by American police officers and the educational requirements for entry into the force.

1337 *I Love Cats*. Ill. by Tom Dunnington. Childrens Pr., hb and pap., 1983. ISBN 0-516-02041-2. SERIES: Rookie Readers. SUBJECTS: Pets—Cats—Fiction; Stories in rhyme. RL B.
A plump little boy admits that he likes all kinds of animals but he *loves* cats. Like other books in the Rookie Reader series, the text here is very brief. It relies on its rhyme and humorous pictures to interest readers.

1338 *Out the Door*. Ill. by Eileen M. Neill. Childrens Pr., hb and pap., 1982. ISBN 0-516-03560-6. SERIES: Rookie Readers. SUBJECTS: School stories. RL A.
A forgetful little girl has to go back home for her lunchbox and then her umbrella as she tries to get to the school bus and a full day at school. The very brief text relies on the flat ink and wash pictures to carry the story.

1339 *Over-Under*. Ill. by Gene Sharp. Childrens Pr., hb and pap., 1984. ISBN 0-516-02048-X. SERIES: Rookie Readers. SUBJECTS: Concepts—Fiction; Playgrounds—Fiction. RL A.
A young African American child demonstrates on/off, in/out, over/under, around/between, inside/outside, above/below, and up/down using playground equipment. Cheerful ink and watercolor paintings illustrate the concepts mentioned in the very brief text.

1340 *Too Many Balloons*. Ill. by Gene Sharp. Childrens Pr., hb and pap., 1982. ISBN 0-516-03633-5. SERIES: Rookie Readers. SUBJECTS: Balloons—Fiction; Concepts—Numbers—Fiction; Zoos—Fiction. RL A.
Buying one balloon to correspond to the first animal she sees at the zoo, the little girl keeps buying balloons as she visits animals until she has 55 balloons and starts to float away. The brief and simple text has full color paintings with ink details.

May, D. J.

1341 *Mr. Marble's Moose*. Ill. by Sabra Smith. Word, 1991. ISBN 0-8499-0969-4. SERIES:

May, D. J. (cont.)

Word Kids! SUBJECTS: Animals—Moose—Fiction; Christian life—Fiction. RL B.
Though Mr. Marble's moose Sam loves to express his happiness with life and his joy in God by singing, the noise bothers others. Sam learns how to "make a joyful noise" while being kind to others. Bold cartoonlike pictures fill the picture book–size reader.

May, Julian

1342 *The Life Cycle of an Opossum*. Photos by Allan Roberts. Creative Ed., 1973, o.p. SERIES: Life Cycle. SUBJECTS: Animals—Opossum. RL C.
Facts about the opossum's rearing of its young, its eating habits, its enemies, and its relationship to humankind are accompanied by color photographs and a map showing the animal's territorial range. Also mentioned is the fact that the opossum has existed since the time of the dinosaurs and is a living fossil.

1343 *These Islands Are Alive*. Ill. by Rod Ruth. Hawthorne, 1971, o.p. SUBJECTS: Islands; Oceans and ocean life. RL C.
Coral islands, such as the Florida Keys, grow continuously as offshore reefs, since reefs are formed as coral live and die. This book describes and explains some of the sea creatures found among the reefs. Illustrated with black and white realistic pencil and wash drawings with maps and diagrams.

Mayer, Gina, and Mayer, Mercer

1344 *Rosie's Mouse*. Ill. by Mercer Mayer. Western, 1992. ISBN 0-307-11468-6. SERIES: Golden Star Reader. SUBJECTS: Animals—Hippopotami—Fiction; Animals—Mice—Fiction; Cleanliness—Fiction. RL C.
Rosie, a hippo, has the neatest of houses until a little uninvited mouse moves in. Then things become very messy and the big but gentle-hearted hippo tries to find ways to get rid of the mouse. Humorous, cartoonlike paintings are done in Mayer's typical high-child-appeal style.

Mayer, Mercer

1345 *Herbert the Timid Dragon*. Ill. by author. Western, 1991. ISBN 0-307-11463-5. SERIES: Golden Star Reader. SUBJECTS: Dragons—Fiction; Emotions—Fear—Fiction; Knights and knighthood—Fiction. RL C.
Herbert, a fearful dragon, thinks he is rescuing a princess and ends up with a spunky young woman who terrorizes him. When she really is in danger the dragon comes to her rescue. The busy watercolor and ink-lined comic pictures have more child appeal than the rather forced text.

1346 *Little Critter's Read-It-Yourself Storybook: Six Funny Easy-to-Read Stories*. Ill. by author. Western, 1993. ISBN 0-307-16840-9. SUBJECTS: Family life—Fiction; Friendship—Fiction; Sibling rivalry—Fiction. RL A.
Little Critter shares his family, pets, and friends in six brief but humorous stories. The text is intentionally straightforward while the comic watercolor animal characters inject humor and fun into the stories.

1347 *This Is My Friend*. Ill. by author. Western, 1989. ISBN 0-307-11685-9. SERIES: Easy Readers. SUBJECTS: Friendship—Fiction. RL A.
The ins and outs of friendship are seen in the humorous illustrations and brief text of this story. The pictures are done in watercolors with ink definition.

Maynard, Christopher

1348 *Incredible Dinosaurs*. Photos. Covent Garden Books, pap., 1994. ISBN 1-56458-551-4. SERIES: Snap Shot. SUBJECTS: Dinosaurs. RL C.
A chatty tone and colorful photographic layout let children know that this is not only about their favorite topic but it is also fun. Most dinosaurs are given a double page spread with much of the information in captions. Table of contents and index provide access.

1349 *Incredible Flying Machines*. Photos. Covent Garden Books, pap., 1994. ISBN

1-56458-552-2. SERIES: Snap Shot. SUBJECTS: Aeronautics; Airplanes. RL C.
A light tone, creative layout of photographs, and unusual placement of some text should make this highly attractive to young readers. The brief text is helped by the captioning of pictures, which as a whole present a limited history of flight.

1350 *Incredible Little Monsters*. Photos. Covent Garden, pap., 1994. ISBN 1-56458-553-0. SERIES: Snap Shot. SUBJECTS: Animals; Animals—Bats; Animals—Reptiles and amphibians. RL C.
Lizards, bats, fish, turtles, and other unusual animals are given double page spreads with many photographic silhouettes to highlight their special features. The text is chatty and fun, and the entire book has much child appeal. Tight binding causes some of the text or pictures to be lost.

1351 *Incredible Mini-Beasts*. Photos. Covent Garden Books, pap., 1994. ISBN 1-56458-554-9. SERIES: Snap Shot. SUBJECTS: Animals; Animals—Insects; Animals—Spiders. RL C.
Words and phrases like "Deadly jaws . . ." and "Beware the poison fang!" are in bold type near colorful photographs and are sure to attract the interest of readers. The insects and spiders focused on include the tarantula, praying mantis, and cockroach. Format and information are guaranteed to be fun.

Mayo, Gretchen

1352 *Big Trouble for Tricky Rabbit*. Ill. by author. Walker, 1994. ISBN 0-8027-8275-2. SERIES: Native American Trickster Tales. SUBJECTS: Animals—Rabbits; Folklore—Native Americans. RL B.
Gathered from a variety of sources, the six stories in this collection are all very well done. The rhythm of the language and the subtle paintings expertly capture the spirit of these stories. After each story, sources are given and the final section of the book gives additional source information.

1353 *Here Comes Tricky Rabbit!* Ill. by author. Walker, 1994. ISBN 0-8027-8273-6. SERIES: Native American Trickster Tales.

SUBJECTS: Animals—Rabbits—Fiction; Folklore—Native Americans. RL B.
Cherokee, Kickapoo, and Apache stories are the roots for three of the six tales in this volume. Carefully retold, including the sources at the end of each story, and illustrated with subtle yet effective paintings, these folktales will be entertaining for young readers and useful for storytelling.

Meddaugh, Susan

1354 *Too Short Fred*. Ill. by author. Houghton Mifflin, 1978, 1985, o.p. SUBJECTS: Animals—Cats—Fiction; Self-esteem—Fiction. RL A.
Though he constantly complains of being short, Fred's size is usually no hindrance to having fun. Pencil and chalk drawings show an assortment of humanized cats illustrating the action in the text. Children will enjoy Fred and his friends in this well-written, well-illustrated piece.

Meeks, Esther

1355 *The Dog That Took the Train*. Ill. by Ted Schroeder. Follett, 1972, o.p. SERIES: Beginning-to-Read. SUBJECTS: Animals—Dogs—Fiction; Lost, being—Fiction; Trains—Fiction. RL B.
The conductor of a train tries to find the owner of a dog that has strayed onto the passenger line. The lively full color pictures add excitement to this book.

Mercer, Charles

1356 *Roberto Clemente*. Ill. by George Loh. Putnam, 1974, o.p. SERIES: See and Read Beginning to Read Biography. SUBJECTS: African Americans; Biographies. RL C.
Hard work, determination, and a strong sense of honor help Roberto Clemente to become a great baseball player for the Pittsburgh Pirates and a great humanitarian. Coming from Puerto Rico he faces bigotry in the United States but overcomes it. Illustrated with realistic black, white, and yellow drawings.

Merriam, Eve

1357 *The Birthday Cow*. Ill. by Guy Michel. Knopf, 1978, o.p. SUBJECTS: Nonsense; Poetry. RL B.
This book contains fifteen nonsensical poems about silly things that children will be familiar with and enjoy, such as birthdays, Halloween, clowns, and cows. Illustrated with suitably whimsical multicolored drawings.

Meyers, Susan

1358 *The Truth about Gorillas*. Ill. by John Hamberger. Dutton, 1980, o.p. SERIES: Smart Cat. SUBJECTS: Animals—Gorillas. RL C.
Children reading this introduction to gorillas will find that it presents the gorilla's life in an interesting way. The book is well researched and well written, and encourages its readers to care about wildlife. The realistic illustrations are done with pencil and washes.

Michel, Anna

1359 *Little Wild Chimpanzee*. Ill. by Peter Parnall and Virginia Parnall. Pantheon, 1978, o.p. SERIES: I Am Reading. SUBJECTS: Animals—Chimpanzees. RL B.
The first five years of a chimpanzee's life are observed as he grows and interacts with his family and other animals. This carefully written story includes much factual information as well as lovely realistic drawings of chimpanzees and their environment.

1360 *Little Wild Elephant*. Ill. by Peter Parnall and Virginia Parnall. Pantheon, 1979, o.p. SERIES: I Am Reading. SUBJECTS: Animals—Elephants. RL B.
The first four years of Little Elephant's life, his relationships with family members, and his ability to care for himself are carefully examined. Soft, realistic pencil drawings complement and extend the text.

1361 *Little Wild Lion Cub*. Ill. by Tony Chen. Pantheon, 1980, o.p. SERIES: I Am Reading. SUBJECTS: Animals—Growth and development; Animals—Lions. RL B.
Readers follow Little Lion from birth until he is two years old—not yet grown up but no longer a cub. The place of a cub in a pride and a cub's relationship to its parents are seen in this informative and interesting story. Detailed, realistic watercolor paintings add to the appeal.

Miklowitz, Gloria

1362 *Sad Song, Happy Song*. Ill. by Earl Thollander. Putnam, 1973, o.p. SERIES: See and Read. SUBJECTS: Animals—Alligators; Conservation. RL C.
A baby alligator is captured and taken to a pet store, where he is sold. His life is frightening, and becomes hopeful only when he is returned to his natural environment. A well-done look at the plight of wild animals kept as pets; it is illustrated with bold black paintings with some color washes.

Milburn, Constance

1363 *The Seasons*. Ill. by Ann Baum. Bookwright, 1988. ISBN 0-531-18179-0. SERIES: Let's Look At. SUBJECTS: Seasons. RL C.
Originally published in England, this book offers a clear explanation of why we have seasons and how they differ in various parts of the world. Illustrated with full color pictures, including one that shows the Earth's rotation around the sun and how this causes the seasons.

Miles, Miska

1364 *Noisy Gander*. Ill. by Leslie Morrill. Dutton, 1978, o.p. SERIES: Unicorn Book. SUBJECTS: Animals—Geese—Fiction; Farm and country life—Fiction. RL C.
The other animals mock the little gosling's father for his constant honking at animals until his vigilance—and honking—rids the barnyard of a coyote. The story, told simply and well, has realistic pencil drawings.

1365 *Tree House Town*. Ill. by Emily A. McCully. Little, Brown, 1974, o.p. SUBJECTS: Conservation—Fiction. RL C.
As children come into the forest to build tree houses, they drive out the animals. Night after night, as the tree houses multiply during the

day, the animals leave for the other side of the forest. With its expressive ink and colored pencil drawings, this story could lead to discussion of conservation.

Milgrim, David

1366 *Why Benny Barks*. Ill. by author. Random House, hb and pap., 1994. ISBN 0-679-96157-7. SERIES: Step into Reading. SUBJECTS: Animals—Dogs—Fiction. Stories in rhyme. RL A.
A little boy tries to understand what makes his dog, Benny, bark so much. Finally, he decides that, even though he has no answer, Benny is still his friend. Cartoonish and childlike watercolors are very effective with this humorous text.

Milgrom, Harry

1367 *Adventures with a Ball*. Ill. by the Strimbans. Dutton, 1965, o.p. SERIES: First Science Experiments. SUBJECTS: Science experiments. RL B.
A variety of simple experiments entices children into discovering the properties of spheres. No elaborate equipment is necessary for these learning experiences. Illustrations have a flat geometric look to them and are in dark blue, orange, and black.

1368 *Adventures with a Cardboard Tube*. Ill. by Tom Funk. Dutton, 1972, o.p. SERIES: First Science Experiments. SUBJECTS: Mathematics; Science experiments. RL C.
The properties of cylinders are discussed and explored in a variety of experiments that are relatively easy and fun for younger children to perform. The simple pencil and wash drawings add to a child's understanding of how to do the experiments.

1369 *Adventures with a Party Plate*. Ill. by George Wilde. Dutton, 1968, o.p. SERIES: First Science Experiments. SUBJECTS: Mathematics; Science experiments. RL C.
Using a paper plate, children learn about circles; their radii, diameters, and circumferences; some aerodynamic principles; how a turbine works; and much, much more. Simple ink line drawings help to explain the experiments.

1370 *Adventures with a Straw*. Ill. by Leonard Kessler. Dutton, 1967, o.p. SERIES: First Science Experiments. SUBJECTS: Science experiments. RL C.
Nearly every page of this book has an activity that will help children discover the properties of cylinders. The many science experiments use straws and household materials. Though the simple ink line drawings with washes are somewhat dated, they are still effective with the text.

1371 *Adventures with a String*. Ill. by Tom Funk. Dutton, 1965, o.p. SERIES: First Science Experiments. SUBJECTS: Science experiments. RL C.
By using a piece of string and different household objects, children learn how string can make sounds and be used for a pulley or a pendulum, along with other interesting science facts. The book encourages children's experimentation and observation. The rather dated drawings are done in ink and wash.

Milios, Rita

1372 *Bears, Bears, Everywhere*. Ill. by Tom Dunnington. Childrens Pr., hb and pap., 1988. ISBN 0-516-02085-4. SERIES: Rookie Readers. SUBJECTS: Concepts—Numbers—Fiction; Stories in rhyme; Toys—Teddy bears—Fiction. RL B.
A very brief rhyming text and soft watercolor pictures present bears in combinations from one to ten and in a variety of humorous situations. The vocabulary is very limited and the pictures play an important part in telling the story.

1373 *The Hungry Billy Goat*. Ill. by Mary C. Walters. Childrens Pr., 1989. ISBN 0-516-02090-0. SERIES: Rookie Readers. SUBJECTS: Animals—Goats—Fiction; Humorous stories. RL A.
A little boy describes the things a very hungry goat eats, including the child's shoe, shirt, hat, and scarf. The limited vocabulary is supported by pen and ink drawings with color washes.

1374 *I Am*. Ill. by Clovis Martin. Childrens Pr., hb and pap., 1987. ISBN 0-516-42081-X. SERIES: Rookie Readers. SUBJECTS: English language—Synonyms and

Milios, Rita (cont.)

antonyms—Fiction; Stories in rhyme.
RL A.
Attractive full color pictures of children with different cultural backgrounds, some with physical impairments, accompany a brief rhyming text. Together they explain opposites like *up* and *down*, and compare and contrast words like *say* and *do*, and *one* and *many*.

1375 *Sneaky Pete*. Ill. by Clovis Martin. Childrens Pr., 1989. ISBN 0-516-02092-7. SERIES: Rookie Readers. SUBJECTS: Games—Fiction; Hiding—Fiction. RL A.
No one can find Pete at home or with his friends. Pete is clever enough to be the best at hide-and-seek and at finding himself a good place to hide and read. Colorful ink and watercolor pictures give clues to Pete's whereabouts while adding fun to the story.

Miller, Jay

1376 *The Delaware*. Photos and archival pictures. Childrens Pr., 1994. ISBN 0-516-01053-0. SERIES: New True. SUBJECTS: Native Americans—Delawares. RL C.
Divided into chapters, this book offers basic information on the history, culture, and current life of the Delaware nation. Along with photographs, archival pictures, and sketches, a glossary and an index are included.

Milton, Joyce

1377 *Bats: Creatures of the Night*. Ill. by Judith Moffatt. Putnam, hb and pap., 1993. ISBN 0-448-40193-2. SERIES: All Aboard Reading. SUBJECTS: Animals—Bats. RL B.
How bats live and raise their young, what they eat, and their relationship to humans and the environment are touched on in this carefully and interestingly written look at the only flying mammal. Excellent art is created from pictures using paper-cut figures and designs.

1378 *Dinosaur Days*. Ill. by Richard Roe. Random House, hb and pap., 1985. ISBN 0-394-97023-3. SERIES: Step into Reading. SUBJECTS: Dinosaurs. RL B.

Fans of dinosaurs will enjoy the brief but informative text. When a dinosaur is introduced, the pronunciation of its name is given along with a few important facts about it. The detailed drawings are in colored pencil.

1379 *Secrets of the Mummies*. Ill. by Dolores Santoliquido. Random House, 1984, o.p. SERIES: Step-Up. SUBJECTS: Egypt, ancient; Mummies. RL C.
An interesting and instructive narrative tells about mummies in general and those of ancient Egypt in particular. The description of the making of mummies is fascinating as are the sections on tombs and animal mummies. The lengthy text dominates well-chosen black and white photos.

1380 *Wild, Wild Wolves*. Ill. by Larry Schwinger. Random House, hb and pap., 1992. ISBN 0-679-91052-2. SERIES: Step into Reading. SUBJECTS: Animals—Wolves. RL B.
Their dwindling population worldwide and their misunderstood nature are mentioned along with discussion of the life cycle and behavior of wolves and their place in nature, plus some American Indian folklore. Fine watercolor and pencil pictures beautifully capture the animal.

Minarik, Else H.

1381 *Cat and Dog*. Ill. by Fritz Siebel. HarperCollins, 1960. ISBN 0-06-024221-3. SERIES: Early I Can Read. SUBJECTS: Animals—Cats—Fiction; Animals—Dogs—Fiction; Pets—Fiction. RL A.
The rivalry between a little girl's cat and dog creates havoc as they chase each other through the house and garden. Pencil drawings with some wash accents add to the fun of the story.

1382 *Father Bear Comes Home*. Ill. by Maurice Sendak. HarperCollins, 1959; pap., 1978. ISBN 0-06-024231-0. SERIES: I Can Read Books. SUBJECTS: Animals—Bears—Fiction; Family life—Fiction; Mythical creatures—Fiction. RL A.
Father Bear is finally home from ocean fishing and Little Bear and his family now share problems with hiccups, a picnic by the river, and

fantasizing about a mermaid. This delightful story is a good portrayal of a nuclear family. Detailed drawings are of dignified turn-of-the-century bears.

1383 *A Kiss for Little Bear.* Ill. by Maurice Sendak. HarperCollins, 1968; pap., 1984. ISBN 0-06-024299-X. SERIES: I Can Read Books. SUBJECTS: Animals—Bears—Fiction; Grandparents—Fiction. RL A.
When Little Bear sends a picture to his grandmother via Hen, his grandmother sends back a kiss that is passed from animal to animal until it reaches Little Bear. The realistic drawings of animals, some in turn-of-the-century garb, are set in beautiful and detailed woodland areas.

1384 *Little Bear.* Ill. by Maurice Sendak. HarperCollins, 1957; pap., 1978. ISBN 0-06-024241-8. SERIES: I Can Read Books. SUBJECTS: Animals—Bears—Fiction; Birthdays—Fiction; Family life—Fiction. RL A.
This perennial favorite has childlike Little Bear in a variety of adventures, including a birthday party, that always lead him to a warm and loving family and friends. The detailed, realistic ink drawings show a happy bear cub, his friends, and his mother dressed in turn-of-the-century clothing.

1385 *Little Bear's Friend.* Ill. by Maurice Sendak. HarperCollins, 1960; pap., 1984. ISBN 0-06-024256-6. SERIES: I Can Read Books. SUBJECTS: Animals—Bears—Fiction; Fantasy; Friendship—Fiction. RL A.
Little Bear meets a little lost girl and in taking her home becomes her friend. During the summer he introduces her to Duck, Hen, Cat, and Owl and knows he will miss her when she goes home to attend school. Little Bear's story is illustrated with lovely, detailed drawings.

1386 *Little Bear's Visit.* Ill. by Maurice Sendak. HarperCollins, 1961; pap., 1979. ISBN 0-06-024266-3. SERIES: I Can Read Books. SUBJECTS: Animals—Bears—Fiction; Grandparents—Fiction. RL A.
Little Bear spends a lovely day with his grandparents. They eat, play, and tell stories—all to Little Bear's delight. The detailed realistic illustrations of bears dressed in turn-of-the-

century clothing are part of what makes this book memorable.

1387 *No Fighting, No Biting!* Ill. by Maurice Sendak. HarperCollins, 1958; pap., 1978. ISBN 0-06-024291-4. SERIES: I Can Read Books. SUBJECTS: Animals—Alligators—Fiction; Sibling rivalry—Fiction. RL B.
Rosa and Willie pester Cousin Joan until she finally tells them stories about two little alligators who are so busy bickering that they are nearly eaten. The text is simple yet fascinating, especially with Sendak's detailed drawings setting the story at the turn of the century.

1388 *Percy and the Five Houses.* Ill. by James Stevenson. Greenwillow, 1989. ISBN 0-688-08104-5. SUBJECTS: Animals—Beavers—Fiction; Houses—Fiction; Humorous stories. RL A.
After Percy, a beaver, finds gold in the stream, he is invited by Ferd Fox to become a member of the House of the Month Club. Percy has fun playing with each fragile dwelling he receives, but finally decides home is the best house of all. Illustrated with zany, comic watercolors.

Mitchell, Barbara

1389 *Cornstalks and Cannonballs.* Ill. by Karen Ritz. Carolrhoda, 1980, o.p. SERIES: On My Own. SUBJECTS: United States—War of 1812. RL B.
Besieged by English warships, the people of Lewes, Delaware, wait until the middle of the night and then, dressed like American soldiers, with cornstalks for guns, scare the English ships away. Based on an actual event, this story is illustrated with realistic blue ink drawings.

1390 *Hush, Puppies.* Ill. by Cherie R. Wyman. Carolrhoda, 1983. ISBN 0-87614-201-3. SERIES: On My Own. SUBJECTS: Cookery—Fiction; United States—1783–1865—Fiction. RL C.
Southern folk legends say that hush puppies were created by a clever slave cook to quiet the hounds at her master's fish fry. An entertaining and almost upbeat look at an unfortunate time, this book offers a good story as well as a

Mitchell, Barbara (cont.)

recipe for hush puppies. Illustrated with ink drawings.

1391 *Tomahawks and Trombones*. Ill. by George Overlie. Carolrhoda, 1982, o.p. SERIES: On My Own. SUBJECTS: Native Americans—Delaware; Religion; United States—French and Indian War. RL B.

Waiting for the Delaware Indians to attack on Christmas day, the Moravians of Bethlehem, Pennsylvania, hide in their homes. Four men take their trombones and play them from a housetop—scaring away the Delaware. This interesting bit of U.S. history is illustrated with realistic paintings.

Mitgutsch, Ali

1392 *From Gold to Money*. Ill. by author. Carolrhoda, 1985. ISBN 0-87614-230-7. SERIES: Start To Finish. SUBJECTS: Money. RL C.

Starting with prehistoric times, Mitgutsch looks at the development of bartering, the use of gold, and then the minting of money. The text is clearly written with good examples and colorful, humorous illustrations that further a child's understanding of trade and money.

1393 *From Idea to Toy*. Ill. by author. Carolrhoda, 1988. ISBN 0-87614-352-4. SERIES: Start to Finish. SUBJECTS: Toys—Teddy bears. RL B.

From reading about the artist sketching live bears at the zoo to learning about the final "blowing in" of foam filling, children are presented with the rudiments of teddy bear creation. The simple, colorful paintings help to describe the process.

1394 *From Picture to Picture Book*. Ill. by author. Carolrhoda, 1988. ISBN 0-87614-353-2. SERIES: Start to Finish. SUBJECTS: Books and reading; Publishing. RL C.

One picture book is followed from an artist's idea and his interpretation of it in words and pictures through the steps leading to the book's sale in a bookstore. Simple yet colorful paintings help to explain the publishing process.

Mizumura, Kazue

1395 *Opossum*. Ill. by author. HarperCollins, 1974, o.p. SERIES: Let's-Read-and-Find-Out. SUBJECTS: Animals—Opossum. RL C.

After seeing an opossum playing dead in the woods, a little boy goes home to find out everything he can about the animal. The interesting information is supported by well-done watercolor pictures in soft hues.

Moncure, Jane B.

1396 *The Biggest Snowball of All*. Ill. by Joy Friedman. Child's World, 1988. ISBN 0-89565-391-5. SERIES: Magic Castle Readers. SUBJECTS: Animals—Bears—Fiction; Concepts—Size—Fiction; Weather—Snow—Fiction. RL A.

In the library a little girl reads about Little Bear and her adventure with a snowball that grows from being tiny to very big. She and her friends build a snowbear and snowhouse and then watch them melt down to a tiny size. The pencil and wash paintings seem geared toward preschoolers.

1397 *Butterfly Express*. Ill. by Linda Hohag. Child's World, 1988. ISBN 0-89565-392-3. SERIES: Magic Castle Readers. SUBJECTS: Animals—Butterflies and moths—Fiction. RL A.

A little girl reads about another little girl's adventure—finding a caterpillar, watching it metamorphose, and finally seeing it become a butterfly. With snow on the ground, the little girl in the story's father finds a pilot to take the butterfly with him to California where it is warm. Watercolor illustrations seem geared toward preschoolers.

1398 *Caring for My Baby Sister*. Ill. by Clovis Martin. Child's World, 1991. ISBN 0-89565-669-8. SERIES: Growing Responsible. SUBJECTS: Behavior—Responsible—Fiction; Family life—Fiction; Siblings—Fiction. RL B.

Becoming a big brother means learning how to hold and feed and watch out for a baby sister. The child in this story positively takes on his new responsibilities and enjoys most of them. The text is illustrated with color paintings with ink definition.

1399 *Caring for My Body*. Ill. by Jodie McCallum. Child's World, 1991. ISBN 0-89565-668-X. SERIES: Growing Responsible. SUBJECTS: Health; Human body. RL B.

A little boy enthusiastically recounts how he and his classmates learned about the importance of healthy behavior: getting exercise, eating properly, and so on. Brief, useful text is illustrated with "cute" colored pictures.

1400 *Caring for My Home*. Ill. by Gwen Connelly. Child's World, 1991. ISBN 0-89565-667-1. SERIES: Growing Responsible. SUBJECTS: Behavior—Helpful; Behavior—Responsible; Cleanliness. RL B.

A child describes how she and everyone in her family pitches in to get things done. She also talks about being responsible for her own things and her room. A very brief and upbeat text, this is illustrated with textbookish color paintings.

1401 *Caring for My Kitty*. Ill. by Christina Rigo. Child's World, 1990. ISBN 0-89565-666-3. SERIES: Growing Responsible. SUBJECTS: Pet care; Pets—Cats. RL B.

A little girl explains the pleasures and the work involved in having her own kitten. The brief text is accompanied by "cute" watercolor paintings. Information on pet care is provided to children in a positive way.

1402 *Caring for My Things*. Ill. by Rondi Collette. Child's World, 1991. ISBN 0-89565-670-1. SERIES: Growing Responsible. SUBJECTS: Behavior—Responsible—Fiction; Lost and found possessions—Fiction. RL B.

A little boy learns what it means to be responsible for his belongings as he listens to stories told by his mother and grandparents. Although definitely didactic, this is still thoughtfully written and has child appeal. Illustrations are adequate watercolors with ink definition.

1403 *A Color Clown Comes to Town*. Ill. by Linda Hohag. Child's World, hb and pap., 1988. ISBN 0-89565-369-9. SERIES: Magic Castle Readers. SUBJECTS: Concepts—Color. RL A.

An imaginative child encounters a clown who introduces her to colors. The little girl insists on their proper use for painting but also learns about mixing primary colors to get secondary colors. Very limited text is accompanied by unimaginative art.

1404 *Courage: What Is It?* Ill. by Helen Endres. Child's World, 1981. ISBN 0-89565-202-1. SERIES: What Is It? SUBJECTS: Behavior—Brave. RL B.

A rather timid girl is shown doing things that for a shy child would require courage: getting back on a bicycle, petting a friendly but large dog, meeting new people, and so on. Rather dated in its look and concentration on a female character, the book is illustrated in color.

1405 *Dinosaurs: Back in Time*. Ill. by Linda Hohag and Lori Jacobson. Child's World, 1990. ISBN 0-89565-550-0. SERIES: Discovery World. SUBJECTS: Dinosaurs. RL B.

A trip to the museum to see the dinosaur models is made even better by an imaginary trip back in time to see them as they lived then. An index and two pages of activities end the book. Illustrations are childlike and done in watercolors.

1406 *Here We Go 'Round the Year*. Ill. by Linda Hohag. Child's World, hb and pap., 1988. ISBN 0-89565-402-4. SERIES: Magic Castle Readers. SUBJECTS: Concepts—Time; Stories in rhyme. RL A.

Twelve teddy bears introduce a little girl to the months of the year and the enjoyable things to do during each. Illustrated in childlike watercolors, the story reinforces the progression of the months.

1407 *Hop-Skip-Jump-a-Roo Zoo*. Ill. by Linda Hohag. Child's World, hb and pap., 1988. ISBN 0-89565-371-0. SERIES: Magic Castle Readers. SUBJECTS: Concepts—Numbers—Fiction; Stories in rhyme; Zoos—Fiction. RL A.

Andy visits the zoo, seeing animals numbering one to ten and learning ten action verbs. The rhyming and repetitive text is helped by the watercolor pictures, though they seem geared to younger than school-age children.

1408 *How Seeds Travel: Popguns and Parachutes*. Ill. by Helen Endres. Child's

Moncure, Jane B. (cont.)

World, 1990. ISBN 0-516-08116-0. SERIES: Discovery World. SUBJECTS: Plants—Seeds, roots, and bulbs. RL B.
The many ways plant seeds travel to new areas are shown by the examples of a cherry tree's fruit being eaten by birds, a squirrel burying an oak's acorn, a dandelion's seeds being carried by the wind, and so on. Brief but clear explanations are helped by full color paintings.

1409 *Ice-Cream Cows and Mitten Sheep.* Ill. by Joy Freidman. Child's World, hb and pap., 1988. ISBN 0-89565-403-2. SERIES: Magic Castle Readers. SUBJECTS: Animals; Farm and country life. RL A.
David visits a farm and learns about cows, sheep, and chickens and the things they produce. Illustrated with soft watercolors, the book gives a very basic introduction to farming.

1410 *Kinds of Animals: Flyers, Leapers, Crawlers, Creepers.* Ill. by Linda Hohag and Lori Jacobson. Child's World, 1990. ISBN 0-89565-567-5. SERIES: Discovery World. SUBJECTS: Animals—Classification. RL B.
The classification of animals by insect, reptile, amphibian, and other groups is reinforced as a child sees animal after animal. Distinctive physical characteristics are mentioned for each. A section of reinforcing activities and an index follow. Undistinguished color illustrations accompany the text.

1411 *Little Too-Tall.* Ill. by Linda Hohag and Dan Spoden. Child's World, hb and pap., 1988. ISBN 0-89565-374-5. SERIES: Magic Castle Readers. SUBJECTS: Animals—Fiction; Animals—Ostriches—Fiction; Friendship—Fiction. RL A.
An ostrich, Little Too-Tall, is looking for friends. The first animals she meets find her odd. Then she warns an antelope and a zebra of a lion's approach and they gratefully accept her. A repetitive refrain and a limited text are augmented by childlike watercolor pictures.

1412 *The Magic Moon Machine.* Ill. by Linda Hohag. Child's World, hb and pap.,

1988. ISBN 0-89565-410-5. SERIES: Magic Castle Readers. SUBJECTS: Concepts—Numbers—Fiction; Fantasy; Space travel—Fiction. RL B.
After he decides to join an astronaut on his way to the moon, a boy keeps delaying to gather things he wants to take with him: pets, food, and so on. He has so many things the spacecraft cannot go. A silly story with some chances for counting objects, it is illustrated with "cute" watercolors.

1413 *Mr. Doodle Had a Poodle.* Ill. by Linda Hohag. Child's World, hb and pap., 1988. ISBN 0-89565-409-1. SERIES: Magic Castle Readers. SUBJECTS: Pets—Dogs—Fiction; Stories in rhyme. RL A.
Mr. Doodle's poodle can do just about anything, including reading and mowing the lawn, but she refuses to bark until she meets a cat. A very short rhyming text has childlike watercolor pictures.

1414 *Night Animals: Wake Up, Little Owl!* Ill. by Lydia Halverson. Child's World, 1990. ISBN 0-89565-568-3. SERIES: Discovery World. SUBJECTS: Animals—Nocturnal. RL C.
With Grandpa as her guide, a child goes into a rural area looking for night animals, including the bat, raccoon, beaver, and owl. Good information is included in the brief but rather difficult text, illustrated with suitably dark watercolors. Index and activity section included.

1415 *Our Christmas Book.* Ill. by Krystyna Stasiak and Gwen Connelly. Child's World, 1986. ISBN 0-89565-341-9. SERIES: Special-Day. SUBJECTS: Arts and crafts; Holidays—Christmas. RL C.
To get into the Christmas spirit, the children in Miss Berry's room create books, put on a puppet show, make piñatas, and much more. Instructions for the crafts are included. Watercolor paintings and ink drawings tend to have a textbookish look.

1416 *Our Columbus Day Book.* Ill. by Jean Shackelford. Child's World, 1986. ISBN 0-89565-347-8. SERIES: Special-Day. SUBJECTS: Biographies; Explorers and exploration; Holidays—Columbus Day. RL C.

Good ideas for introducing the explorations of Columbus and the difficulties he faced are presented in this introduction to the holiday.

1417 *Our Easter Book*. Ill. by Lois Axeman. Child's World, 1987. ISBN 0-89565-345-1. SERIES: Special-Day. SUBJECTS: Arts and crafts; Holidays—Easter. RL C.

In the classroom children learn to make and do a variety of things to celebrate spring rather than to emphasize the religious aspect of the holiday. They make bird nests, bunny hats, flower baskets, and much more. The textbookish illustrations provide explanations/instructions for many of the crafts.

1418 *Our Halloween Book*. Ill. by Pam Peltier. Child's World, 1986. ISBN 0-89565-348-6. SERIES: Special-Day. SUBJECTS: Arts and crafts; Holidays—Halloween. RL C.

Cutesy paintings of a classroom of primary-age children illustrate the crafts and activities that go on there. The children gather fall leaves, make a jack-o'-lantern, write stories, and much more as they celebrate the popular holiday.

1419 *Our Mother's Day Book*. Ill. by Susan Lexa. Child's World, 1987. ISBN 0-89565-346-X. SERIES: Special-day. SUBJECTS: Holidays—Mother's Day; School stories. RL C.

The week before Mother's Day a class studies how mothers are celebrated in different parts of the world, makes gifts, listens to a classmate's great-grandmother tell about life when she was a child, and much more. Useful for classrooms, this is illustrated with prosaic watercolors.

1420 *Rain: A Great Day for Ducks*. Ill. by Joy Friedman. Child's World, hb and pap., 1990. ISBN 0-89565-553-5. SERIES: Discovery World. SUBJECTS: Science experiments—Weather; Weather. RL B.

While a little boy walks in the rain looking at ducks and frogs and plants, the text explains how rain helps things grow, keeps animals alive, and so forth. Following the text is a section of activities and experiments. An index is included. Pictures are attractive watercolor with pencil definition.

1421 *Step into Spring: A New Season*. Ill. by Jenny Williams. Child's World, 1990.

ISBN 0-89565-571-3. SERIES: Discovery World. SUBJECTS: Seasons—Spring. RL B.

A boy and his dog use their senses to discover that spring has finally returned. They taste strawberries, smell lilacs, touch a pussy willow, and listen to birds. Then they explore the farm for signs of the new season. Illustrations are in colored pencil. Activity section and index are included.

1422 *What's So Special about Today? It's My Birthday*. Ill. by Jenny Williams. Child's World, 1988. ISBN 0-89565-414-8. SERIES: What's So Special. SUBJECTS: Birthdays—Fiction; Pets—Dogs—Fiction. RL B.

For his fifth birthday Ben gets all kinds of surprises but the best one of all is the treasure hunt that leads to his puppy. Illustrated with expressive watercolors, the story is one many children will enjoy.

1423 *What Was It Before It Was Bread?* Ill. by Elizabeth Nygaard. Child's World, 1985. ISBN 0-89565-323-0. SERIES: Sequence Books. SUBJECTS: Farm and country life; Food. RL B.

As John eats wheat bread he asks about its origins. The book explains how wheat is grown, made into bread at a factory, and shipped to stores. A recipe for whole-wheat muffins is included along with a list of other wheat products. The text is illustrated with awkward watercolor pictures.

1424 *A Wish-For Dinosaur*. Ill. by Vera K. Gohman. Child's World, 1988. ISBN 0-89565-393-1. SERIES: Magic Castle Readers. SUBJECTS: Dinosaurs—Fiction; Fantasy; Wishes—Fiction. RL A.

Darrin wishes for a dinosaur for a day and that is what he gets. The huge animal causes problems at Darrin's house but in the park he quickly wins the prize for best pet and gives the little boy a wonderful day. The text is illustrated with watercolor pictures.

1425 *Word Bird's Dinosaur Days*. Ill. by Linda Hohag and Lori Jacobson. Child's World, 1991. ISBN 0-89565-617-5. SERIES: Word Bird Readers. SUBJECTS: Dinosaurs—Fiction; School stories. RL B.

Word Bird and his school friends take a trip to the museum to see dinosaurs. Back at school they sing dinosaur songs, draw dinosaur pic-

Moncure, Jane B. (cont.)

tures, and play dinosaur games—even the timid Bee, who slowly loses her fear. Text is illustrated with cutesy watercolors geared to the very young.

1426 *Word Bird's Magic Wand.* Ill. by Linda Hohag and Lori Jacobson. Child's World, hb and pap., 1990. ISBN 0-89565-580-2. SERIES: Word Bird Readers. SUBJECTS: Animals—Fiction; School stories; Writing—Fiction. RL B.

In school Word Bird and his animal friends use their pencils, Magic Wands, to write special words and create word pictures. By the end of the school year, they are all creating their own books. Illustrated with "cute" watercolor pictures geared to very young children.

Monjo, F. N.

1427 *The Drinking Gourd.* Ill. by Fred Brenner. HarperCollins, 1970; pap., 1983. ISBN 0-06-024330-9. SERIES: I Can Read History. SUBJECTS: Historical fiction; Slavery—Fiction; Underground railroad—Fiction. RL B.

Sent home from church for misbehaving, Tommy discovers a family of fugitive slaves. He becomes involved with helping his father get them to the next station on the family's journey to Canada and freedom. Realistic drawings add to the drama of the story.

1428 *Indian Summer.* Ill. by Anita Lobel. HarperCollins, 1968, o.p. SERIES: I Can Read Books. SUBJECTS: Frontier and pioneer life—Fiction; Historical fiction; United States—Revolution—Fiction. RL C.

With their father away fighting the British, four children and their mother have to fight off an attack by Indians. Detailed ink and wash pictures show an ingenious and brave woman and her family.

1429 *The One Bad Thing about Father.* Ill. by Rocco Negri. HarperCollins, 1970; pap., 1987. ISBN 0-06-444110-5. SERIES: I Can Read Books. SUBJECTS: Family life—Fiction; Historical fiction; Presidents—United States—Fiction. RL C.

Quentin's father, Theodore Roosevelt, could have been just about anything, but Quentin thinks that his father's being president makes life very difficult for the family. The entertaining yet informative text has pictures with detailed ink cross-hatchings with color overlays.

Montgomery, Elizabeth R.

1430 *The Mystery of the Boy Next Door.* Ill. by Ethel Gold. Garrard, 1978, o.p. SERIES: For Real. SUBJECTS: Friendship—Fiction; Physically and mentally impaired—Fiction. RL A.

To the children the new boy on their street seems unfriendly and intent on ignoring them. They understand his behavior and renew their offers of friendship when they discover he is deaf. An attempt to further the acceptance of the impaired, this book has realistic ink and wash drawings.

Moon, Cliff

1431 *Dairy Cows on the Farm.* Ill. by Anna Jupp. Bookwright, 1983, o.p. SERIES: Down on the Farm. SUBJECTS: Animals—Cows; Farm and country life. RL B.

At a typical modern British dairy farm, calves are taken from cows so that milk can be used for humans. The text and full color pictures then take the reader to the milking area, where modern machinery is discussed and pictured, and finally to a local dairy where milk is bottled.

1432 *Pigs on the Farm.* Ill. by Anna Jupp. Bookwright, 1983, o.p. SERIES: Down on the Farm. SUBJECTS: Animals—Pigs; Farm and country life. RL B.

Children are introduced to pig farming in this British book. They are told in text and in full color realistic pictures how pigs are raised and butchered, and how their meat is sold in markets. Throughout the book questions are occasionally asked so that children get involved in what they are reading.

1433 *Poultry on the Farm.* Ill. by Bill Donohoe. Bookwright, 1983, o.p. SERIES: Down on the Farm. SUBJECTS: Animals—Poultry; Farm and country life. RL B.

Both traditional and modern methods of raising poultry are discussed and shown in full color realistic pictures in this British book. Chickens, ducks, and turkeys are shown on farms and information is provided on hatcheries and the preparation of poultry for markets.

1434 *Sheep on the Farm*. Ill. by Anna Jupp. Bookwright, 1983, o.p. SERIES: Down on the Farm. SUBJECTS: Animals—Sheep; Farm and country life. RL C.

In this British book, sheep are shown wandering fields and hills under the protection of a shepherd and his dog. The way in which sheep are shorn and dipped as well as the products that come from their wool and meat are discussed and shown in full color realistic paintings.

Moore, Lilian

1435 *Junk Day on Juniper Street and Other Easy-to-Read Stories*. Ill. by Arnold Lobel. Parents Magazine Pr., 1969, o.p. SUBJECTS: Family life—Fiction; Farm and country life—Fiction. RL B.

This is a collection of short stories with perfectly plausible happy endings. They are about families, neighbors, old married couples, a silly dog guarding a duckling, and a donkey who helps a boy find a silver mine. The gentle, whimsical stories have detailed and humorous ink drawings.

1436 *Little Raccoon and the Outside World*. Ill. by Gioia Fiammenghi. McGraw-Hill, 1965, o.p. SUBJECTS: Animals—Fiction; Animals—Raccoons—Fiction; Behavior—Curiosity—Fiction. RL A.

Little Raccoon is anxious to learn what really is in the outside world. With two little skunks following him, he wanders away, discovers a house, and then decides that his own woodland home is preferable. This funny story has ink drawings with chartreuse accents.

1437 *A Pickle for a Nickel*. Ill. by Susan Perl. Golden, 1961, o.p. SERIES: Read It Yourself. SUBJECTS: Animals—Parrots—Fiction; Humorous stories; Noise—Fiction. RL B.

Mr. Bumble likes everything quiet—his house, his car, and even his parrot. While he is work-ing, a neighbor boy talks to the parrot who, to Bumble's consternation, begins to squawk continuously. Detailed, comic illustrations in full color ink and wash add to the humor.

Mooser, Stephen

1438 *Funnyman and the Penny Dodo*. Ill. by Tomie dePaola. Watts, 1984, o.p. SERIES: Easy-Read Story. SUBJECTS: Humorous stories; Jokes and riddles—Fiction; mystery and detective stories. RL C.

Detective Funnyman uses his jokes to find Putty Face Pete and reclaim valuable stolen stamps. Both the story and the jokes are enjoyable. Text is illustrated with humorous pencil drawings with beige and blue washes.

1439 *Funnyman's First Case*. Ill. by Tomie dePaola. Watts, 1981, o.p. SERIES: Easy-Read Story. SUBJECTS: Humorous stories; Jokes and riddles—Fiction; Mystery and detective stories. RL C.

Forever cracking jokes to his customers, Archie finds his job as a waiter is in jeopardy until he uses his talent to capture Big Red, a local thief. Though the jokes are old, children will enjoy them, the silly plot line, and the comical pencil drawings with pink and beige tones.

1440 *The Ghost with the Halloween Hiccups*. Ill. by Tomie dePaola. Watts, 1977; Avon, pap., 1981. ISBN 0-380-40287-4. SERIES: Easy-Read Story. SUBJECTS: Hiccups—Fiction; Holidays—Halloween—Fiction; Humorous stories. RL C.

Mr. Penny's appearance in the Halloween play is a tradition that may be stopped by a bad case of hiccups. Almost scary full color pictures of Halloween creatures trying to cure him of the hiccups add to the fun.

Mooser, Stephen, and Oliver, Lin

1441 *The Fat Cat*. Ill. by Susan Day. Warner, 1988, o.p. SERIES: Catch the Reading Bug. SUBJECTS: Animals—Cats—Fiction; Animals—Rats—Fiction; Humorous stories. RL A.

Two stories, one with a fat cat and a hat and the other with a cat and a rat, rely on humorous ink and wash paintings to tell the stories.

Mooser, Stephen, and Oliver, Lin (cont.)

Meant as an introduction to reading alone, the texts use four sight words and ten words with "at" as their base.

1442 *Tad and Dad*. Ill. by Susan Day. Warner, 1988. ISBN 1-55782-023-6. SERIES: Catch the Reading Bug. SUBJECTS: Animals—Bears—Fiction; Behavior—Fiction; Parent and child—Fiction. RL A.

In two nearly wordless stories, a small bear and his father share adventures that need the ink and wash pictures to create their rather thin plots. Meant to facilitate reading for the very beginner, this book uses four sight words and eight words with "ad" as their base.

Morgan, Michaela

1443 *Helpful Betty Solves a Mystery*. Ill. by Moira Kemp. Carolrhoda, 1994. ISBN 0-87614-832-1. SERIES: Helpful Betty. SUBJECTS: Animals—Hippopotami—Fiction; Humorous stories. RL B.

Bumbling Betty the hippo finds a magnifying glass and decides that she should be solving mysteries. In her zeal she mixes up two eggs—one a bird's, the other a crocodile's. Humorous illustrations and text complement each other.

1444 *Helpful Betty to the Rescue*. Ill. by Moira Kemp. Carolrhoda, 1994. ISBN 0-87614-831-3. SERIES: Helpful Betty. SUBJECTS: Animals—Hippopotami; Humorous stories. RL B.

Wanting to show how brave and helpful she is, a little hippo runs to the rescue when she hears a monkey cry—not realizing the monkey is fine. Along the way she accidentally saves a frog from a variety of animals. Delightfully funny pictures should appeal to children.

Morley, Diana

1445 *Marms in the Marmalade*. Ill. by Kathy Rogers. Carolrhoda, 1984, o.p. SERIES: On My Own. SUBJECTS: English language; Nonsense; Stories in rhyme. RL C.

Poking fun at the illogical way that many English words are constructed, this rhyming book takes familiar words like *caterpillar* and gives logical though silly definitions for them. Chil-

dren and adults will enjoy the nonsense and the attractive full color drawings.

Morris, Ann

1446 *How Teddy Bears Are Made: A Visit to the Vermont Teddy Bear Factory*. Ill. by Ken Heyman. Scholastic, 1994. ISBN 0-590-47152-X. SUBJECTS: Toys—Teddy bears. RL B.

Three children take a tour of a factory that makes all kinds of teddy bears. Through appealing color photographs and a brief text, readers are taken through most of the steps in the manufacturing of the toys.

Morris, Johnny

1447 *Animal-Go-Round: Turn the Wheel and See the Animals Grow*. Photos. Dorling Kindersley, 1993. ISBN: 1-56458-329-5. SUBJECTS: Animals—Growth; Toy and movable books. RL B.

Appealing, excellent color photos on a white ground show the growth of cuddly animals familiar to children, from chicks and puppies to butterflies and frogs. Lambs are shown from birth to 12 weeks, frogs from egg to full grown on a full-page rotating wheel revealing one stage at a time.

Morris, Robert

1448 *Dolphin*. Ill. by Mamoru Funai. Harper-Collins, 1975; pap., 1983. ISBN 0-06-024342-2. SERIES: Science I Can Read Books. SUBJECTS: Animals—Dolphins; Conservation; Nature. RL C.

Much can be learned about the bottle-nosed dolphin in this story of the birth and growth of a baby dolphin. Illustrated with realistic watercolor paintings, the book helps to promote a concern for nature and conservation.

1449 *Seahorse*. Ill. by Arnold Lobel. Harper-Collins, 1972, o.p. SERIES: Science I Can Read. SUBJECTS: Animals—Seahorses. RL A.

A carefully worded and fascinating text with lovely, detailed pencil, ink, and wash drawings explains how seahorses live, travel, bear young, and hide from predators.

Moses, Amy

1450 *I Am an Explorer*. Ill. by Rick Hackney. Childrens Pr., 1990. ISBN 0-516-02059-5. SERIES: Rookie Readers. SUBJECTS: Concepts—Opposites—Fiction; Explorers and exploration—Fiction; Imaginative play—Fiction. RL B.

A lively little boy imagines himself a world explorer going in and out of caves, over and under water, up and down a mountain, and so on. Along the way, through the very brief text and clear watercolor pictures, children are introduced to concepts.

Moskin, Marietta

1451 *Lysbet and the Fire Kittens*. Ill. by Margot Tomes. Putnam, 1973, o.p. SERIES: Break-of-Day. SUBJECTS: Fire fighting—Fiction; Pets—Cats—Fiction; United States—Colonial period—Fiction. RL C.

Left for a short time to care for the house and her cat Stuyver, who is about to have kittens, Lysbet builds a fire that accidentally sets the house ablaze while she is ice skating. After alerting her New Amsterdam neighbors, Lysbet rescues the cat and her new kittens. Ink drawings ably capture the 1662 setting.

Mozelle, Shirley

1452 *Zack's Alligator*. Ill. by James Watts. HarperCollins, 1989. ISBN 0-06-024309-0. SERIES: I Can Read Books. SUBJECTS: Animals—Alligators and crocodiles—Fiction; Fantasy; Imaginative play—Fiction. RL B.

When water is added to Zack's keychain, it grows into a real live alligator named Bridget who is full of energy and mischief and fun. The colorful pencil drawings, the magical change, and the great dose of humor have much child appeal.

1453 *Zack's Alligator Goes to School*. Ill. by James Watts. HarperCollins, 1994. ISBN 0-06-022887-3. SERIES: I Can Read Books. SUBJECTS: Animals—Alligators and crocodiles—Fiction; Imaginative play; School stories. RL B.

When the class bully sees Zack with his keychain alligator, he is sure his robot will be the star of show and tell. But Bridget gets dropped in the fish tank and is soon a full size 'gator with plenty of mischief. Enjoyable reading is accented by lively colored pencil drawings.

Mueller, Virginia

1454 *A Halloween Mask for Monster*. Ill. by Lynn Munsinger. Whitman, 1986. ISBN 0-8075-3134-0. SERIES: Just-for-Fun. SUBJECTS: Holidays—Halloween—Fiction; Monsters—Fiction. RL A.

The little green monster tries on human and animal masks but finds them too scary. Finally he decides to go trick-or-treating as himself. The predictable repetition of phrases in the very brief story and the delightful color pictures make this just right for the beginning reader.

Munsil, Janet

1455 *Where There's Smoke*. Ill. by Michael Martchenko. Annick, 1993. ISBN 1-55037-291-2. SUBJECTS: Behavior—Fiction. RL B.

Daisy and Dad help each other stop nail-biting and smoking, respectively. They share an inventive list of new hobbies together. The punch line is a bit forced, however. Lively watercolor drawings accompany the text.

Muntean, Michaela

1456 *Bicycle Bear*. Ill. by Doug Cushman. Stevens, 1994. ISBN 0-8368-0963-7. SERIES: Read Aloud Originals. SUBJECTS: Animals—Bears—Fiction; Humorous stories; Stories in rhyme. RL B.

Bicycle Bear delivers a moose for Ima Goose in this humorous rhyming story illustrated with funny watercolor pictures. Following the story is a section featuring advice for adults using books with young readers.

1457 *A Garden for Miss Mouse*. Ill. by Christopher Santora. Parents Magazine Pr., 1993. ISBN 0-8368-0891-6. SERIES: Read Aloud Library. SUBJECTS: Animals—Mice—Fiction; Gardening—Fiction; Stories in rhyme. RL B.

Miss Mouse impulsively digs up her whole yard for a huge garden. At first, it is lovely.

Muntean, Michaela (cont.)

Then it really starts to grow and Miss Mouse is a captive of her lush vegetable garden until friends join in for the harvest. Lively rhyming text is illustrated with exuberant watercolors.

1458 *The Old Man and the Afternoon Cat*. Ill. by Bari Weissman. Parents Magazine Pr., 1982. ISBN 0-8193-1072-7. SERIES: Read Aloud and Easy Reading. SUBJECTS: Animals—Cats—Fiction; Old age—Fiction; Pets—Cats—Fiction. RL B.

The lonely and grumpy old man looks forward to his afternoons at the park with a friendly cat. When the cat disappears, the old man begins a search that earns him friends, the cat, and a new outlook on life. This satisfying story has attractive full color illustrations.

Murata, Michinori

1459 *Water and Light: Looking Through Lenses*. Photos by Isamu Sekido. Lerner, 1993. ISBN 0-8225-2904-1. SERIES: Science All Around You. SUBJECTS: Light; Science experiments; Water. RL C.

Clear color photographs and straightforward explanations of how light is magnified or changed through lenses and water are supported by easy-to-follow experiments.

Murdocca, Sal

1460 *Take Me to the Moon!* Ill. by author. Lothrop, 1976, o.p. SERIES: Fun-to-Read. SUBJECTS: Fantasy; Kings and queens—Fiction. RL B.

When the queen orders that she be taken to the moon, an astrologer, a carpenter, and a knight scramble to find a way to get her there, finally deciding on a dragon-propelled spaceship. Illustrated with humorous cartoon-type pictures in shades of blue and yellow.

1461 *Tuttle's Shell*. Ill. by author. Lothrop, 1976, o.p. SERIES: Fun-to-Read. SUBJECTS: Animals—Turtles—Fiction. RL B.

Louis the Rat steals Tuttle Turtle's shell while he is bathing. It takes the combined cunning of Tuttle and his friends to win it back. Comic pen and ink drawings with detailed cross-hatchings illustrate the silly but fun-to-read story.

Murphy, Jim

1462 *Harold Thinks Big*. Ill. by Susanna Natti. Crown, 1980, o.p. SUBJECTS: Animals—Pigs—Fiction; Romance—Fiction; Sports—Football—Fiction. RL A.

Smitten with Esther, a porcine cheerleader, Harold goes to lawyer Owl for advice. "Think big" is his suggestion and Harold does, with disastrous results. Comic line and wash illustrations complement this story of unrequited love that is sure to bring empathetic smiles to its readers.

Murray, Peter

1463 *Beavers*. Photos. Child's World, 1992. ISBN 0-89565-844-5. SERIES: Nature Books. SUBJECTS: Animals—Beavers. RL C.

Alternating pages of well-spaced, boldfaced type and color photographs introduce children to the many facets of the world of the beaver.

1464 *Chameleons*. Photos. Child's World, 1993. ISBN 1-56766-016-9. SERIES: Nature Books. SUBJECTS: Animals—Chameleons; Animals—Reptiles and amphibians. RL C.

Many misconceptions about chameleons and their habits are clarified by Murray through his brief text and the very well done color photographs. Among other things, readers learn that chameleons do not change color to match their environment. A great many different chameleons are pictured but not identified.

1465 *Frogs*. Photos. Child's World, 1993. ISBN 1-56766-010-X. SERIES: Nature Books. SUBJECTS: Animals—Frogs and toads; Animals—Reptiles and amphibians. RL C.

The many kinds and sizes of frogs, their life cycle, and their predators are discussed in a text complemented by attractive color photographs. The pictures would have been more effective if they had specific captioning to identify a type of frog. Index is included.

1466 *Gorillas*. Photos. Child's World, 1993. ISBN 1-56766-020-7. SERIES: Nature Books. SUBJECTS: Animals—Endangered; Animals—Gorillas. RL C.

Color photographs and a carefully worded text afford young readers a good look at some of the kinds of gorillas found in Africa. The book explains some of their habits, the foods they eat, and the danger man and the loss of the rainforest are to them.

1467 *Hummingbirds*. Photos. Child's World, 1993. ISBN 1-56766-011-8. SERIES: Nature Books. SUBJECTS: Animals—Birds; Animals—Hummingbirds. RL C.
An attractive format featuring colored pages, full color photographs, and widely spaced lines of text will draw readers into this well-written look at hummingbirds of the Americas. Though most pictures are identified in the text, some birds are frustratingly without identification.

1468 *Parrots*. Photos. Child's World, 1993. ISBN 1-56766-015-0. SERIES: Nature Books. SUBJECTS: Animals—Birds; Animals—Endangered; Animals—Parrots. RL C.
Native to rainforest areas and attractive to man because of their plumage and ability to mimic, parrots are endangered. Murray discusses their habits, calls, and life cycle. Full color photographs are beautiful but could use captioning. Index is included.

1469 *Porcupines*. Photos. Child's World, 1994. 1-56766-019-3. SERIES: Nature Books. SUBJECTS: Animals—Porcupines. RL C.
Good full page color photographs complement an interesting text that presents the life of the porcupine, its young, its food, and other porcupines found throughout the world. One quibble: On page 29, the author mentions two different porcupines without identifying the one pictured.

1470 *Tarantulas*. Photos. Child's World, 1993. ISBN 1-56766-060-6. SERIES: Nature Books. SUBJECTS: Animals—Spiders. RL C.
A gentle but sometimes frightening-looking spider, the tarantula lives in the Southwest in burrows or trees. Through clear color photographs and well-spaced lines of text, children learn a great deal about the habits and life-style of a spider that can also be a pet.

Muschg, Hanna

1471 *Two Little Bears*. Trans. by Anthea Bell. Ill. by Kaethe Bhend-Zaugg. Bradbury, 1986, o.p. SUBJECTS: Animals—Bears—Fiction; Animals—Growth and development—Fiction. RL B.
During the first year of their lives, two roly-poly bear cubs wrestle and play as they learn to fish, hunt for food, and hide from danger. This accurate fictionalized account of the growth of cubs is charming and has very detailed pen and ink pictures.

Myers, Bernice

1472 *Not at Home?* Ill. by author. Lothrop, 1981, o.p. SUBJECTS: Friendship—Fiction. RL A.
When she arrives at Lorraine's to spend the night, the new baby-sitter tells Sally that Lorraine is not at home. Hurt, Sally rushes home vowing not to speak to Lorraine again. Later both girls discover that there was a mix-up. Illustrated with sketchy comic ink drawings.

Myrick, Mildred

1473 *Ants Are Fun*. Ill. by Arnold Lobel. HarperCollins, 1968, o.p. SERIES: I Can Read Books. SUBJECTS: Animals—Ants—Fiction; Friendship—Fiction; Moving, household—Fiction. RL B.
From their treehouse observatories, two boys see a new neighbor who is their age carrying a mysterious box. Later they learn it is an ant nest. Through the boys' curiosity, a great deal is discovered about ants. Charming pencil drawings with color washes add much to the story.

1474 *Secret Three*. Ill. by Arnold Lobel. HarperCollins, 1963; pap., 1982. ISBN 0-06-024356-2. SERIES: I Can Read Books. SUBJECTS: Clubs—Fiction; Codes and secret messages—Fiction; Friendship—Fiction. RL B.
Finding a bottle on the beach with a secret message in it starts an exchange of coded messages and inspires the creation of the Secret Three Club. The codes, included in the detailed and attractive ink drawings with color washes, will be easily deciphered by readers.

N

Naden, Corinne

1475 *Let's Find Out about Frogs*. Ill. by Jerry Lang. Watts, 1972, o.p. SERIES: Let's Find Out About. SUBJECTS: Animals—Frogs and toads. RL C.
The life cycle, physical characteristics, and general behavior of frogs are discussed in this brief, factual, and interesting book. The illustrations are carefully drawn in ink with some green accents.

Namm, Diane

1476 *Little Bear*. Ill. by Lisa McCue. Childrens Pr., 1990. ISBN 0-516-05356-6. SERIES: My First Reader. SUBJECTS: Animals—Bears—Fiction; Food—Fiction; Stories in rhyme. RL A.
A 16-word rhyming vocabulary and sweet watercolor pictures tell the story of a baby bear who refuses to be tempted by good food. Instead the little animal wants only honey. The limited vocabulary will make this accessible to the very beginning reader.

1477 *Monsters*. Ill. by Maxie Chambliss. Childrens Pr., 1990. ISBN 0-516-05358-2. SERIES: My First Reader. SUBJECTS: Concepts—Numbers; Monsters—Fiction; Stories in rhyme. RL A.
Cute and colorful monsters—just out of the child's sight—gather as the child looks for them. The very brief text is sure to be fun for the child just beginning to read as it reinforces counting skills.

Neasi, Barbara

1478 *Listen to Me*. Ill. by Gene Sharp. Childrens Pr., hb and pap., 1986. ISBN 0-516-02072-2. SERIES: Rookie Readers. SUBJECTS: Grandparents—Fiction; Listening—Fiction. RL C.
When the little boy feels neglected and not listened to, his grandma comes to the rescue. She spends time with him and carefully listens to everything the little boy says. Sketchy line drawings with full color washes help to tell this very short story.

1479 *Sweet Dreams*. Ill. by Clovis Martin. Childrens Pr., hb and pap., 1987. ISBN 0-516-02084-6. SERIES: Rookie Readers. SUBJECTS: Dreams—Fiction; Stories in rhyme. RL A.
A little girl looks forward to all the different kinds of dream stories she may encounter while sleeping. The dreams she imagines she might have and the entire text are illustrated with bright comic-style watercolor and ink pictures.

Newman, Alyse

1480 *It's Me, Claudia!* Ill. by author. Watts, 1981, o.p. SERIES: Easy-Read Story. SUBJECTS: Human body—Ears—Fiction; Self-esteem—Fiction. RL B.
Thinking her large ears make her look like a mouse, Claudia tries different ways to hide them, finally settling on wearing a large hat. The hat acts as a barrier to friends and fun and Claudia finally gives it up. Ink and wash drawings show a little girl coming to terms with how she looks.

Newman, Nanette

1481 *That Dog!* Ill. by Marylin Hafner. HarperCollins, 1983, o.p., pap., 1992. ISBN 0-06-440363-7. SUBJECTS: Death—Fiction; Pets—Dogs—Fiction. RL B.
Ben and his dog Barnum are inseparable and when Barnum dies, Ben is sure he can never love another dog. With the support of loving family and friends, Ben finally does make room for a stray puppy. The gently humorous illustrations capture Ben and Barnum's very special relationship.

Newton, James R.

1482 *The March of the Lemmings*. Ill. by Charles Robinson. HarperCollins, 1976, o.p. SERIES: Let's-Read-and-Find-Out. SUBJECTS: Animals—Lemmings. RL C.
When food and room are plentiful, the lemming population of northern Norway grows continuously until both food and room are scarce. Then many of the little animals leave their homes and head westward, toward the ocean. Good information and realistic pencil drawings make this a very useful book.

Nicklaus, Carol

1483 *Come Dance with Me*. Ill. by author.
Silver Burdett, 1991. ISBN 0-671-73503-9.
SERIES: Silver Sower Easy Reader.
SUBJECTS: Animals—Fiction; Dancing
and dancers—Fiction. RL A.
A group of animals expressively dance in all
kinds of ways: fast, slow, together, apart, looking mean or pretty, like a snake, and so on.
The few words per page combine with the cartoonlike color paintings to give children an
idea of dance as a personal statement.

1484 *The GO Club*. Ill. by author. Silver
Burdett, 1991. ISBN 0-671-73500-4.
SERIES: Silver Sower Easy Reader.
SUBJECTS: Bicycles and bicycling—
Fiction; Safety—Fiction. RL A.
Animal characters ride bikes with one, two,
three, and four wheels. All are heading to the
park and along the way share safety tips. Few
words per page are helped by cartoon-like
color illustrations set against much white.

1485 *Harry the Hider*. Ill. by author. Watts,
1979, o.p.; Avon, pap., 1980, o.p. SERIES:
Easy-Read Story. SUBJECTS: Humorous
stories; Pets—Cats—Fiction. RL A.
Miranda thinks it is fruitless to try to enter
her cat Harry in the circus—all he can do is
hide. However, it is his camouflaging ability
that not only wins him first prize but also
intrigues the reader, who must look carefully
at the ink line drawings to try to find the
missing Harry.

1486 *Head Over Heels*. Ill. by author. Silver
Burdett, 1991. ISBN 0-671-73506-3.
SERIES: Silver Sower Easy Reader.
SUBJECTS: Animals—Fiction; Sports—
Gymnastics—Fiction. RL A.
With the help of an instructor, a reluctant puppy begins to learn the fun of basic gymnastic
movements. By book's end the puppy is introducing others to things he has learned. Illustrated with colorful cartoonlike paintings that
work with the brief text to show the power of
determination.

1487 *Sidekicks*. Ill. by author. Silver Burdett,
1991. ISBN 0-671-73504-7. SERIES: Silver
Sower Easy Reader. SUBJECTS: Animals—
Fiction; Sports—Soccer—Fiction. RL A.

Two young animals of opposite temperament
join a soccer team, learn to play by the rules,
and try hard to be members of the team. The
importance of teamwork is reinforced by the
colorful cartoonlike artwork.

Nixon, Hershell H., and Nixon, Joan L.

1488 *Oil and Gas: From Fossils to Fuels*. Ill.
by Jean Day Zallinger. Harcourt, 1977,
o.p. SERIES: Let Me Read. SUBJECTS:
Energy; Geology. RL C.
The origins and nature of gas and oil deposits,
oil exploration and recovery, uses of oil and
gas, and the need for alternative energy
sources are topics in this introduction to
petroleum geology. The two-color illustrations
are well done and sometimes more symbolic
than literally accurate.

Nixon, Joan L.

1489 *Bigfoot Makes a Movie*. Ill. by Syd Hoff.
Putnam, 1979, o.p.; Scholastic, pap.,
1983, o.p. SUBJECTS: Fantasy; Humorous
stories; Mythical creatures—Fiction.
RL B.
Young Bigfoot naively believes the film crew
want to be his friends when they mistake him
for an actor dressed as Bigfoot. The exaggerated cartoonlike illustrations are childlike and
guarantee that the story is not taken seriously.

1490 *Danger in Dinosaur Valley*. Ill. by Marc
Simont. Putnam, 1978, o.p. SERIES: See
and Read. SUBJECTS: Dinosaurs—Fiction;
Science fiction; Sports—Baseball—
Fiction. RL B.
The climate is growing colder and the
Diplodocus family must go south. Little
Diplodocus, watching a baseball game on a
Back Into Time tourist's television, learns to
pitch rocks to help the family escape Tyran-
nosaurus Rex. Subject matter and humorous
illustrations are sure to appeal to children.

1491 *Muffie Mouse and the Busy Birthday*. Ill.
by Geoffrey Hayes. Seabury, 1978, o.p.
SUBJECTS: Animals—Mice—Fiction;
Birthdays—Fiction; Family life—
Fiction. RL B.
It is mother mouse's birthday and little Muffie
decides to make it extra special. She concocts

Nixon, Joan L. (cont.)

a very unusual birthday breakfast, teaches Tommy Mouse to share, and stops horrible cousin Harry from scaring her. The detailed drawings show a secure, well-loved, turn-of-the-century mouse.

1492 *The Mysterious Prowler*. Ill. by Berthe Amoss. Harcourt, 1976, o.p. SERIES: Let Me Read. SUBJECTS: Behavior—Shyness—Fiction; Moving, household—Fiction; mystery and detective stories. RL B.

Spotting someone peeking in the window and later ringing his doorbell and vanishing, Jonathan decides to track down the mysterious prowler. He discovers it is his new neighbor, a boy too shy to stay and talk. The ink drawings add to the suspense created by Nixon's careful pacing.

1493 *The Thanksgiving Mystery*. Ill. by Jim Cummins. Whitman, 1980. ISBN 0-8075-7820-7. SERIES: First Read-Alone Mystery. SUBJECTS: Holidays—Thanksgiving—Fiction; Mystery and detective stories. RL B.

Positive that she has seen a ghost, Susan, with Mark and Mrs. Pickett, devises a plan to trap it during their Thanksgiving holiday. This is a lengthier book than most readers are used to and may be just right for youngsters wanting a "long" book. Illustrated with prosaic ink and wash pictures.

1494 *The Valentine Mystery*. Ill. by Jim Cummins. Whitman, 1979. ISBN 0-8075-8450-9. SERIES: First Read-Alone Mystery. SUBJECTS: Holidays—Valentine's Day—Fiction; Mystery and detective stories. RL C.

Susan's two-year-old brother's clue to the identity of the giver of her Valentine card creates a mystery. Children reading the book will be trying to guess how to decipher the clue as well as the mystery. Illustrated with realistic ink and wash sketches.

Nobens, C. A.

1495 *The Happy Baker*. Ill. by author. Carolrhoda, 1979, o.p. SERIES: On My Own. SUBJECTS: Bakers and baking—Fiction; Food—Fiction. RL B.

Having left his bakery and friends, Joseph travels the world sampling and refusing other countries' breads while relishing their soups. When he returns home, he reopens his bakery, adding soup to his menu. Illustrated with flat, humorous watercolor pictures in green and rust tones.

Norman, Gertrude

1496 *Johnny Appleseed*. Ill. by James Caraway. Putnam, 1960, o.p. SERIES: See and Read. SUBJECTS: Biographies; Legends. RL A.

Although dated in format, this simple telling of the life of John Chapman, or Johnny Appleseed, is still good reading. It presents the man as nonviolent and as a friend to both settlers and Native Americans. The illustrations are realistic paintings in brown and green.

1497 *A Man Named Columbus*. Ill. by James Caraway. Putnam, 1960, o.p. SERIES: See and Read. SUBJECTS: Biographies; Explorers and exploration. RL A.

A generally factual and interesting account of the life of Columbus, children will find this useful for school reports or to satisfy their curiosity about the great explorer. The illustrations are in blue and taupe and somewhat dated.

1498 *A Man Named Lincoln*. Ill. by Joseph Cellini. Putnam, 1960, o.p. SERIES: See and Read. SUBJECTS: Biographies; Presidents—United States. RL A.

This is a well-written and useful book offering a simple, uncomplicated look at Lincoln's life. It includes some folklore, such as Lincoln's walking miles to return six cents, but generally remains factual. Brown-toned illustrations appear somewhat dated.

Nottridge, Rhoda

1499 *Big Cats*. Ill. by David Nockels. Watts, 1990. ISBN 0-531-18285-1. SERIES: Let's Look At. SUBJECTS: Animals—Cats; Animals—Endangered. RL B.

This overview of the lives of lions, cougars, tigers, and other big cats, offers general information on their size, environment, and prey. It also encourages the conservation of animal life. Illustrations are realistic color paintings. Index and habitat map are included.

Numeroff, Laura J.

1500 *Amy for Short*. Ill. by author. Macmillan, 1976, o.p. SERIES: Ready to Read. SUBJECTS: Friendship—Fiction; Self-esteem—Fiction. RL C.
Amy has no problem with being the tallest in her class but she worries that her friend Mark may not like her as much now that she is taller than he is. A good depiction of a child whose family and friends help her to accept and like herself. Illustrations are in coral and black.

1501 *Beatrice Doesn't Want To*. Ill. by author. Watts, 1981, o.p. SERIES: Easy-Read Story. SUBJECTS: Books and reading—Fiction; Libraries—Fiction. RL B.
Not liking books or reading, Beatrice resents her trips to the library until she hears the children's librarian read aloud. This upbeat look at nonreading children captures Beatrice's resistance to books and her reluctant capitulation. Illustrations are ink drawings and color washes.

1502 *Does Grandma Have an Elmo Elephant Jungle Kit?* Ill. by author. Greenwillow, 1980, o.p. SERIES: Read-Alone. SUBJECTS: Grandparents—Fiction. RL C.
Though Donald is afraid there will be nothing to do at Grandma and Grandpa's house, the weekend is full of fun and Donald is anxious to visit again. This positive look at active, loving grandparents is well done and has appropriate, simple ink and wash drawings.

1503 *The Ugliest Sweater*. Ill. by author. Watts, 1980, o.p. SERIES: Easy-Read Story. SUBJECTS: Gifts and gift giving—Fiction. RL B.
Grandmother's intricately designed multicolored sweater seems ugly to Peter until his teacher says the student wearing red, white, and blue may bring in the class's special guest from France. Outlined in heavy ink with blue and red washes, the illustrations boldly complement the story.

Nussbaum, Hedda

1504 *Animals Build Amazing Homes*. Ill. by Christopher Santoro. Random House, 1979. ISBN 0-394-83850-5. SERIES: Step-Up. SUBJECTS: Animals—Homes. RL B.
Whether it is mound-building termites, pond-digging alligators, or tunnel-digging prairie dogs, the animals and the homes in this book make fascinating reading. The clear text is illustrated with realistic drawings with some washes.

1505 *Plants Do Amazing Things*. Ill. by Joe Mathieu. Random House, 1977. ISBN 0-394-93232-3. SERIES: Step-Up. SUBJECTS: Plants. RL B.
In brief, entertaining, and informative chapters, many unusual plants and plant characteristics are described, including lichens, flytraps, cacti, and examples of symbiosis. The two-color illustrations are cartoonlike but appear to depict natural objects accurately.

O

O'Connor, Jane

1506 *EEK! Stories to Make You Shriek*. Ill. by Brian Karas. Putnam, hb and pap., 1992. ISBN 0-448-40383-8. SERIES: All Aboard Reading. SUBJECTS: Behavior—Greedy—Fiction; Holidays—Halloween—Fiction; Scary stories. RL B.
Three spooky stories (one about a mysterious Halloween visitor, one about a doll that comes to life, and the last about a ghostly dog) are accented by cartoonlike illustrations that lessen the scariness of the tales.

1507 *Lulu and the Witch Baby*. Ill. by Emily A. McCully. HarperCollins, 1986. ISBN 0-06-024627-8. SERIES: I Can Read Books. SUBJECTS: Sibling rivalry—Fiction; Witches—Fiction. RL C.
Witch Baby seems to get all the attention and Lulu Witch would like nothing better than for Baby to disappear. When Mama Witch flies off to the market, Lulu concocts a spell to do just that. Pencil and wash pictures show pointy-eared and disheveled but not menacing witches.

1508 *Lulu Goes to Witch School*. Ill. by Emily A. McCully. HarperCollins, 1987, o.p., pap., 1990. ISBN 0-06-444138-5. SERIES: I Can Read Books. SUBJECTS: School stories; Witches—Fiction. RL C.

O'Connor, Jane (cont.)

Though Lulu Witch tries to be good-natured and friendly, Sandy Witch's meanness and constant besting of everyone annoy her. Lulu finally gets the best of Sandy. Fans of witch stories will enjoy Lulu's story and the full color humorous drawings accompanying it.

1509 *Molly the Brave and Me*. Ill. by Sheila Hamanaka. Random House, hb and pap., 1990. ISBN 0-394-94175-6. SERIES: Step into Reading. SUBJECTS: Behavior—Courageous—Fiction; Country life—Fiction; Friendship—Fiction. RL B.
In Beth's eyes Molly is afraid of nothing. When Molly invites Beth to spend the night at her country home, Beth is afraid Molly will learn she is a coward. In a surprise twist, Beth ends up comforting Molly when they are lost. Lively colored pencil drawings.

1510 *Sir Small and the Dragonfly*. Ill. by John O'Brien. Random House, 1988. ISBN 0-394-89625-4. SERIES: Step into Reading. SUBJECTS: Concepts—Size—Fiction; Fantasy; Knights and knighthood—Fiction. RL B.
Smaller even than the very small people of Pee Wee, Sir Small is the only one brave enough to try to rescue Lady Teena from the dragonfly's cave. The fanciful color pictures have sketchy ink detailing and a need for more differentiation among the characters' faces.

1511 *Super Cluck*. Ill. by Megan Lloyd. HarperCollins, 1991. ISBN 0-06-024594-8. SERIES: I Can Read Books. SUBJECTS: Animals—Chickens—Fiction; Fantasy; Humorous stories. RL B.
Left behind when the others returned to planet Nestron, Cluck hatches and is raised as a regular but very strong—and flying—chicken. When a rat steals eggs from the hen house, Super Cluck comes to the rescue. Colorful comic illustrations capture the story's fun.

1512 *The Teeny Tiny Woman*. Ill. by R. W. Alley. Random House, hb and pap., 1986. ISBN 0-394-98320-3. SERIES: Step into Reading. SUBJECTS: Folklore—England; Ghost stories. RL B.

A well-known folktale frequently told to children, this version does not maintain the suspense as well as others. Its pacing is often awkward and the full color pictures are a little too "cute." Still, many young readers, having heard the story, will want to read this on their own.

Oda, Hidetomo

1513 *Insect Hibernation*. Trans. by Jun Amano. Ill. by Hidekazu Kubo. Raintree, hb and pap., 1986. ISBN 0-8172-2551-X. SERIES: Nature Close-Ups. SUBJECTS: Animals—Hibernation. RL C.
A clear text and excellent color photos follow a variety of insects from fall to winter, when they hibernate hidden away in trees and earth, to spring when they emerge again. Detailed captions significantly supplement the text, which was originally published in Japan.

Oechsli, Kelly

1514 *Mice at Bat*. Ill. by author. HarperCollins, 1986. ISBN 0-06-024624-3. SERIES: I Can Read Books. SUBJECTS: Animals—Mice—Fiction; Sports—Baseball—Fiction. RL C.
After the human crowd leaves the stadium, two teams of mice, the Mighty Mites and the Boomers, have an action-packed game of their own. Multiethnic names and a knowledge of the sport provide broad appeal. Illustrations are ink drawings with orange- and blue-toned washes.

Older, Jules

1515 *Don't Panic: A Book about Handling Emergencies*. Ill. by J. Ellen Dolce. Golden, 1986. SERIES: Learn about Living. SUBJECTS: Emergencies; Safety. RL B.
A bee sting, a broken jar, burned fingers, a nosebleed, and trying the high slide for the first time all present problems for which "Don't Panic!" is the first step to finding a solution. The rather "preachy" text has full color drawings of cute children at home, school, and play.

Olsen, Glenda P.

1516 *Birds of Prey*. Photos. Child's World, 1994. ISBN 1-56766-059-2. SUBJECTS: Animals—Birds of prey; Animals—Endangered. RL C.
Each of a dozen birds of prey or raptors is given a page of text and a full color photograph. Text at times attempts to be funny and occasionally needs more explanation than is provided. Photos could use captioning to distinguish particular birds. Table of contents is provided.

Olson, Mary C., ed.

1517 *Elephant on Skates*. Ill. by Jerry Scott. Golden, pap., 1987. ISBN 0-307-03676-6. SERIES: Step Ahead Beginning Reader. SUBJECTS: Animals—Elephants—Fiction; Self-esteem—Fiction; Sports—Roller Skating—Fiction. RL A.
Everyone in her family tries to convince Edna that elephants do not belong on roller skates. Undaunted, she finally manages to get her family to try roller skating too. The story is fun as are the full color comic drawings of the elephant family.

1518 *Fly, Max, Fly!* Ill. by Donald Leake. Golden, 1976, o.p.; pap., 1987. ISBN 0-307-03677-4. SERIES: Step Ahead Beginning Reader. SUBJECTS: Circuses—Fiction; Pets—Dogs—Fiction. RL A.
All the human members of the family are trapeze artists and Max, their dog, longs to be up flying with them. With the help of a clown, the children of the family train Max to be a part of their troupe. Children will enjoy the story and the boldly colored pictures, each with borders and stars.

1519 *The Magic Friend Maker*. Ill. by Renee Graef. Golden, 1976; pap., 1987. ISBN 0-307-03682-0. SERIES: Step Ahead Beginning Reader. SUBJECTS: Friendship—Fiction. RL A.
Kate meets Jill and becomes her friend after admiring her beautiful rock. Jill and Kate both think it is the magic of the rock that made them friends. Somewhat superficial, the story is illustrated with full color pictures.

Difficult nouns are printed along with rebus silhouettes of them.

1520 *Race Down the Mountain*. Ill. by Giannini. Golden, 1976; pap., 1987. ISBN 0-307-03675-8. SERIES: Step Ahead Beginning Reader. SUBJECTS: Trains—Fiction. RL A.
As the little train travels down the mountain, animals try to warn it that it has lost its caboose. The train misunderstands them, thinking they are urging it to race faster. Soft full color watercolor paintings give a clear view of the train and animals in this very slight story.

1521 *This Room Is Mine!* Ill. by Gwen Connelly. Golden, 1976, o.p.; pap., 1987. ISBN 0-307-03681-2. SERIES: Step Ahead Beginning Reader. SUBJECTS: Sibling rivalry—Fiction. RL A.
Mad at his older brother Bob, Dan decides to divide their room in half, not realizing that the door is on Bob's side. Bob ends the dispute by including his little brother in a ball game. The familiar family situation is illustrated with realistic full color pencil and wash drawings.

Oneal, Zibby

1522 *Maude and Walter*. Ill. by Maxie Chambliss. HarperCollins, 1985, o.p. SUBJECTS: Siblings—Fiction. RL A.
Walter is often too ready to tell his little sister Maude to go away. Maude is clever enough to get him to realize her importance as she helps him out in some situations and makes him jealous in others. Watercolor illustrations present Maude and Walter as rather ordinary children.

Oppenheim, Joanne

1523 *The Christmas Witch*. Ill. by Annie Mitra. Bantam, hb and pap., 1993. ISBN 0-553-09392-4. SERIES: Bank Street Ready-to-Read. SUBJECTS: Folklore—Italy; Holidays—Christmas. RL C.
Too late, Befana, an old Italian woman, decides to follow the three kings in search of the Christ child. Not able to find him, she searches every year at Christmas, leaving gifts, according to

Oppenheim, Joanne (cont.)

the old Italian legend. Illustrations are simply designed, childlike watercolors.

1524 *Could It Be?* Ill. by S. D. Schindler. Bantam, hb and pap., 1990. ISBN 0-553-05893-2. SERIES: Bank Street Ready-to-Read. SUBJECTS: Animals—Bears—Fiction; Seasons—Spring—Fiction. RL B.

None of the usual signs or sounds of spring can awaken the hibernating bear. It takes a buzzing bumblebee and its connection to honey to get the bear up. The gentle text is illustrated with watercolors with ink definition.

1525 *Do You Like Cats?* Ill. by Carol Newsom. Bantam, hb and pap., 1993. ISBN 0-553-09116-6. SERIES: Bank Street Ready-to-Read. SUBJECTS: Animals—Cats—Fiction; Stories in rhyme. RL B.

Detailed, realistic paintings and a rhyming text introduce the many kinds of domestic cats that people see and with whom they choose to live. Readers will meet a great many purebred as well as mixed-breed cats.

1526 *The Donkey's Tale.* Ill. by Chris Demarest. Bantam, hb and pap., 1991. ISBN 0-553-07090-8. SERIES: Bank Street Ready-to-Read. SUBJECTS: Folklore; Stories in rhyme. RL B.

An old man and his son decide to take their donkey to market to sell. Along the way they get all kinds of advice and, trying to please everyone, take it and end up with nothing. Based on a traditional tale, the story is illustrated with humorous watercolor and ink pictures.

1527 *Eency Weency Spider.* Ill. by S. D. Schindler. Bantam, hb and pap., 1991. ISBN 0-553-07316-8. SERIES: Bank Street Ready-to-Read. SUBJECTS: Nursery rhymes; Stories in rhyme. RL B.

The eency weency spider rhyme is introduced and verses added to ease the introduction of little Miss Muffet, Humpty Dumpty, Little Jackie Horner, and Jack be nimble, Jack be quick. Only the eency weency spider rhyme is given. Illustrated with detailed, comical watercolors.

1528 *Follow That Fish.* Ill. by Devis Grebu. Bantam, hb and pap., 1990. ISBN 0-553-05857-6. SERIES: Bank Street Ready-to-Read. SUBJECTS: Animals—Fish—Fiction; Fantasy; Stories in rhyme. RL B.

Imaginative ink and watercolor pictures illustrate a fantasy rhyme about a little girl pulled under water by a big fish. Along the way she has fanciful encounters with an eel, a flatfish, a seaturtle, a shark, and octopi.

1529 *"Not Now!" Said the Cow.* Ill. by Chris Demarest. Bantam, hb and pap., 1989. ISBN 0-553-05826-6. SERIES: Bank Street Ready-to-Read. SUBJECTS: Animals—Fiction; Folklore. RL B.

A variant of "The Little Red Hen," this has Crow finding corn seed and having no luck getting other animals to help him plant it and care for it. Sketchy comic paintings show Crow struggling and finally getting his reward: popcorn to eat by himself.

1530 *Row, Row, Row Your Boat.* Ill. by Kevin O'Malley. Bantam, hb and pap., 1993. ISBN 0-553-09498-X. SERIES: Bank Street Ready-to-Read. SUBJECTS: Boats and boating—Fiction; Music—Fiction. RL B.

From a toy-filled bathtub a little boy imaginatively sails away and onto all kinds of boats. The text follows the rhythm of the well-known children's song. Illustrations combine watercolors and colored pencils to effectively capture the mood of the book.

1531 *The Show-and-Tell Frog.* Ill. by Kate Duke. Bantam, hb and pap., 1992. ISBN 0-553-08134-9. SERIES: Bank Street Ready-to-Read. SUBJECTS: Animals—Frogs and toads—Fiction; Humorous stories; School stories. RL B.

Allie thinks she has lost her show-and-tell frog but the mischievous animal is always lurking just out of sight, hopping from hiding place to hiding place until show-and-tell time. Illustrations really make the story fun while the text never gives away where the frog is at any moment.

1532 *"Uh-Oh!" Said the Crow.* Ill. by Chris Demarest. Bantam, 1993. ISBN 0-553-09387-8. SERIES: Bank Street Ready-to-Read. SUBJECTS: Animals—Farmyard—

Fiction; Farm and country life—Fiction; Noise—Fiction. RL B.

Huddled in the barn, the animals begin to hear a loud and almost spooky noise followed by thuds. One by one the animals refuse to find out what it is. Then Crow goes and they discover the wind knocking apples down. Zany watercolor paintings show comical animals in a familiar situation.

Orgel, Doris

1533 *Cindy's Snowdrops*. Ill. by Ati Forberg. Knopf, 1966, o.p. SUBJECTS: Gardening—Fiction; Plants—Flowers—Fiction; Plants—Seeds, roots and bulbs—Fiction. RL B.

Cindy decides to plant snowdrop bulbs and carefully plans where to put them, hoping they will bloom in time for her March birthday. Impressionistic watercolor and ink pictures with blotted blackgrounds carry out the dreamy, expectant feeling of the story.

1534 *The Mouse Who Wanted to Marry*. Ill. by Holly Hannon. Bantam, hb and pap., 1993. ISBN 0-553-09235-9. SERIES: Bank Street Ready-to-Read. SUBJECTS: Animals—Mice—Fiction; Folklore. RL B.

A variant of a folktale told in Asian countries, this features a lovely mouse trying to find the most steadfast husband. She tries the sun, the clouds, the wind, a wall, and finally discovers that a mouse is the strongest of them all. The story is illustrated with attractive, colorful paintings.

1535 *Next Time I Will*. Ill. by Betsy Day. Bantam, hb and pap., 1993. ISBN 0-553-09031-3. SERIES: Bank Street Ready-to-Read. SUBJECTS: Folklore—England; Humorous stories. RL B.

Bill, a boy who does exactly as he is told, tries to earn extra money for food. Instead he does one thing after another wrong. Finally even his mistakes are redeemed because his actions make a rich man's daughter laugh. Illustrations are colorful paintings that look stiff.

Orgel, Doris, and Schecter, Ellen

1536 *The Flower of Sheba*. Ill. by Laura Kelly. Bantam, 1994. ISBN 0-553-09041-0.

SERIES: Bank Street Ready-to-Read. SUBJECTS: Bible stories. RL C.

Hoping to learn from the wisest man in the world, the Queen of Sheba travels to Israel to meet King Solomon. To prove his wisdom, she gives him a great test: finding a real flower amid thousands of false ones. The text is illustrated with dramatic full color paintings.

Orlowsky, Wallace, and Perera, Thomas B.

1537 *Who Will Wash the River?* Ill. by Richard Cuffari. Putnam, 1970, o.p. SERIES: Science Is What and Why. SUBJECTS: Conservation; Pollution—Water. RL C.

Since the last time Tommy and Sue visited the river, it has become terribly polluted with sewage and rubbish. The two then learn about the importance of water treatment plants in halting pollution. Though published a while ago this book is still valid. It is well written and has good realistic ink and wash drawings.

Osborne, Mary P.

1538 *Mo and His Friends*. Ill. by DyAnne DiSalvo-Ryan. Dial, 1989. ISBN 0-8037-0504-2. SERIES: Dial Easy-to-Read. SUBJECTS: Animals—Fiction; Friendship—Fiction. RL B.

In four quiet stories set in the different seasons, the value and fun of friendship are seen through Sheriff Mo (a beaver), Peewee and Pearl (mice), Chicken Lucille, and the other Smith Pond characters. The pictures are in watercolor and pencil and reflect the gentle nature of the stories.

1539 *Mo to the Rescue*. Ill. by DyAnne DiSalvo-Ryan. Dial, 1985; pap., 1987. ISBN 0-8037-0182-9. SERIES: Dial Easy-to-Read. SUBJECTS: Animals—Fiction; Friendship—Fiction; Sheriffs—Fiction. RL A.

Kind-hearted sheriff Mo Beaver welcomes newcomers, cleverly breaks up fighting blue jays, sees monsters in the shadows, and finally gets away to just sit and read a book. The gentle, "folksy" story is illustrated with full color pencil sketches with watercolor washes.

Osinski, Alice

1540 *The Chippewa*. Photos. Childrens Pr., hb and pap., 1987. ISBN 0-516-01230-4. SERIES: New True. SUBJECTS: Native Americans—Chippewas. RL C.
Information about the Chippewa—history, hunting, farming, religious traditions, life today, and the effects of treaties on them—is provided in this brief book. There are good full color photographs as well as reproductions of historical prints accompanying the interesting text.

Osinski, Christine

1541 *I Can Be a Photographer*. Photos. Childrens Pr., 1986, o.p. SERIES: I Can Be. SUBJECTS: Careers; Photography and photographers. RL C.
In a brief overview, the author offers a glimpse of some of the many kinds of photographic work. She also offers some explanations of how photographs are produced and the pleasure picture taking can be. Illustrated with color photographs, the book also has an index and a glossary.

Otto, Carolyn

1542 *I Can Tell by Touching*. Ill. by Nadine B. Westcott. HarperCollins, hb and pap., 1994. ISBN 0-06-023324-9. SERIES: Let's-Read-and-Find-Out Science Books. SUBJECTS: Senses—Touch. RL B.
A child notices the difference in the way things around the house feel—a pet rabbit and a drawing of a rabbit, gravel, a hillside he rolls down, and more. Westcott's simple and attractive pencil drawings with watercolors add to the text. A list of supplementary activities is appended.

Overbeck, Cynthia

1543 *The Vegetable Book*. Ill. by Sharon Lerner. Lerner, 1975, o.p. SERIES: Early Nature Picture Book. SUBJECTS: Gardening; Vegetables. RL C.
In a tour of a vegetable garden, this book comments on a dozen common edibles: how they are grown and used as food. The brightly colored illustrations are semirealistic.

P

Packard, David

1544 *The Ball Game*. Ill. by Robert W. Alley. Scholastic, pap., 1993. ISBN 0-590-46190-7. SERIES: My First Hello Reader! SUBJECTS: Sports—Baseball—Fiction; Stories in rhyme. RL A.
A very young ball player describes being up at bat and hitting the winning run. Short sentences and lots of action in the watercolor illustrations give the story a "you are there" feeling. The book also includes tear-out flashcards and a section of activities to reinforce language skills.

Packard, Mary

1545 *The Kite*. Ill. by Benrei Huang. Childrens Pr., 1990. ISBN 0-516-05355-8. SERIES: My First Reader. SUBJECTS: Kites and kite flying—Fiction. RL A.
A small child gets his kite to fly and watches as it soars and then imagines riding on it. A few words per page are expanded by the expressive yet childlike watercolor pictures.

1546 *My Messy Room*. Ill. by Stephanie Britt. Scholastic, pap., 1993. ISBN 0-590-46191-5. SERIES: My First Hello Reader! SUBJECTS: Cleanliness—Fiction; Stories in rhyme. RL A.
An exuberant little girl celebrates the messiness of her room, finally admitting that no matter how much she likes it, her mother does not. Bold pictures with strong colors and black outlining have great appeal. The book also includes language-reinforcement activities and flash cards.

1547 *Surprise!* Ill. by Benrei Huang. Childrens Pr., 1990. ISBN 0-516-05360-4. SERIES: My First Reader. SUBJECTS: Birthdays—Fiction. RL A.
A very young child, opening birthday gifts, is happily surprised by the last, which holds a puppy. The 16-word vocabulary briefly describes the event, which is illustrated with pastel colored watercolors featuring chubby, round-faced little children.

1548 *Where Is Jake?* Ill. by Carolyn Ewing. Childrens Pr., 1990. ISBN 0-516-05361-2. SERIES: My First Reader. SUBJECTS: Animals—Pets—Dogs—Fiction; Concepts. RL A.

As two children search for their dog, they also demonstrate spatial concepts such as up/down, in/out, and so on. Each double page spread is illustrated with attractive pencil and watercolor pictures and captioned with just three words, usually in the form of a question.

Palacios, Argentina

1549 *A Christmas Surprise for Chabelita.* Ill. by Lori Lohsteter. BridgeWater, 1993. ISBN 0-8167-3131-4. SUBJECTS: Grandparents—Fiction; Panama—Fiction; Parent and child—Fiction. RL B.

Living with her grandparents while her mother teaches far away, Chabelita memorizes a special poem and gets to recite it at the school holiday program. Spanish phrases, explained in context, and a beautifully illustrated Panamanian setting reinforce the uniqueness of this fine book. ·

1550 *Viva Mexico! A Story of Benito Juarez and Cinco de Mayo.* Ill. by Howard Berelson. Raintree, hb and pap., 1993. ISBN 0-8114-7214-0. SERIES: Stories of America. SUBJECTS: Biographies; Holidays—Cinco de Mayo; Mexico. RL C.

A Zapotec Indian, Benito Juarez worked hard for an education and then worked equally hard to help others—finally becoming president of Mexico. When the country was invaded he helped to fight off the French and make May 5 a time to remember. The text is illustrated with expressive ink and watercolor drawings.

Palmer, Helen M.

1551 *A Fish Out of Water.* Ill. by P. D. Eastman. Beginner, 1961. ISBN 0-394-90023-5. SERIES: I Can Read It All By Myself. SUBJECTS: Animals—Fish—Fiction; Humorous stories; Pets—Fish—Fiction. RL A.

A little boy is warned that he must feed his new goldfish, Otto, no more than a spot of food, but he still feeds him the entire box. Otto grows and grows until the pet store own-er, Mr. Carp, must use his magic to return him to goldfish size. Never having waned in popularity, this book remains a delight with its humorous yet simple drawings.

Papajani, Janet

1552 *Museums.* Photos. Childrens Pr., 1983. ISBN 0-516-01682-2. SERIES: New True. SUBJECTS: Museums. RL C.

From a discussion of the things Alexander the Great collected to a look at the Baseball Hall of Fame, museums of all kinds are mentioned. Young people are encouraged to visit and explore a variety of museums and the good color photographs of exhibits are an extra enticement to reading and visiting.

Pape, Donna L.

1553 *The Big White Thing.* Ill. by Bill Morrison. Garrard, 1975, o.p. SERIES: Easy Venture. SUBJECTS: Animals—Raccoons—Fiction; Humorous stories. RL A.

Not until a rainstorm fills it with water do the raccoons realize what the big white bathtub might be. Then they jump right in, swimming and bathing. The pictures are a bit sweet but their comic portrayal of the woodland animals is appealingly done in colored pencil and wash.

1554 *The Book of Foolish Machinery.* Ill. by Fred Winkowski. Scholastic, 1988. ISBN 0-590-40907-7. SUBJECTS: Nonsense; Poetry. RL C.

Nearly tongue twisters with their contortions of familiar words and with their silly rhymes, these poems about nonsensical machines and how they work are ideal for reading aloud by a confident young reader. The humorous, colorful illustrations are of complex machines.

1555 *Count on Leo Lion.* Ill. by Tom Eaton. Garrard, 1973, o.p. SERIES: Venture. SUBJECTS: Animals, zoo—Fiction; Concepts—Numbers—Fiction; Humorous stories. RL A.

Asleep in his zoo cage, Leo Lion is awakened by two monkeys squabbling over how they should divide the peanuts they have. Deciding that they need to learn to count, Leo tries all

Pape, Donna L. (cont.)

kinds of ways to teach the monkeys their numbers. Illustrated with colorful and amusing drawings.

1556 *A Gerbil for a Friend*. Ill. by Diane Martin. Prentice-Hall, 1973, o.p. SUBJECTS: Pets—Gerbils. RL B.

Mark already has a cage waiting for the little gerbil when she is finally old enough for him to take home. By following Mark's example, children will be able to provide a good home for a pet gerbil. Illustrated with expressive ink drawings.

1557 *Leo Lion Looks for Books*. Ill. by Tom Eaton. Garrard, 1972, o.p. SERIES: Venture. SUBJECTS: Animals—Lions—Fiction; Books and reading—Fiction; Humorous stories. RL A.

Leo likes reading but there is not much to read in the zoo. He leaves his cage and wanders through town, discovers a bookstore, and ends up in the library. When the zookeeper comes for him, Leo does not want to leave the books. Full color cartoon pictures show a dramatic lion who loves books.

1558 *The Mouse at the Show*. Ill. by Gail Gibbons. Elsevier-Dutton, 1981. o.p. SUBJECTS: Animals—Fiction; Animals—Mice—Fiction; Circuses—Fiction. RL A.

One animal after another trades places with a little mouse. By the time she gets to just the right seat, the circuslike show is over. Simple sentences are repeated or paraphrased to make reading this story very easy. Good layout and attractive ink and wash drawings will appeal to children.

1559 *Mr. Mogg in the Log*. Ill. by Mimi Korach. Garrard, 1972, o.p. SERIES: Venture. SUBJECTS: Humorous stories. RL B.

Trying to retrieve a quarter he has dropped, Mr. Mogg gets stuck in a log. Mrs. Mogg and their friend Mr. Jones try pulling him loose, having a helicopter shake him free, and more until they finally find a simple but sloppy solution. Illustrated with colorful, sketchy marker drawings.

1560 *Mrs. Twitter the Animal Sitter*. Ill. by Dora Leder. Garrard, 1972, o.p. SERIES: Venture. SUBJECTS: Animals—Fiction; Business enterprises—Fiction; Pet care—Fiction. RL A.

Mrs. Twitter answers an ad for a sitter and ends up taking care of a horse. She does everything wrong until a child helps her. Next she takes care of a seal and teaches it to balance a ball on its nose. The very silly story has realistic yet comical illustrations.

1561 *Snowman for Sale*. Ill. by Raymond Burns. Garrard, 1977, o.p. SERIES: For Real. SUBJECTS: Birthdays—Fiction; Siblings—Fiction; Weather—Snow—Fiction. RL A.

To get enough money to buy mother a birthday present, Terry and Jerry build a huge snowman to sell. Not allowed to help them, their younger brother Todd makes little snowmen, which sell while the big one does not. The watercolor illustrations for this story are rather bland.

1562 *Where Is My Little Joey?* Ill. by Tom Eaton. Garrard, 1978, o.p. SERIES: Imagination. SUBJECTS: Animals—Kangaroos—Fiction; Humorous stories. RL A.

After napping in a park, poor Kara Kangaroo notices her little joey is gone. She searches everywhere for him but is hampered by having her pouch used for all kinds of things whenever she stops. The humorous story has colorful, cartoonlike pictures.

Parish, Peggy

1563 *Amelia Bedelia*. Ill. by Fritz Siebel. HarperCollins, 1992. ISBN 0-06-020186-X. SERIES: I Can Read Books. SUBJECTS: Humorous stories. RL B.

Amelia Bedelia is hired by the Rogerses and left with a list of chores. Following their instructions exactly, she "dusts" the furniture with dusting powder, "dresses" the chicken in clothes—and more. This perennial favorite has been newly illustrated in full color.

1564 *Amelia Bedelia and the Baby*. Ill. by Lynn Sweat. Greenwillow, 1981; Avon, pap., 1982. ISBN 0-688-00316-8. SERIES: Read-alone. SUBJECTS: Baby-sitting—Fiction; Humorous stories. RL A.

Mrs. Rogers insists that Amelia Bedelia take care of the neighbor's baby. The child's mother leaves detailed instructions for Amelia Bedelia to follow and to the baby's delight, she follows them exactly. The ink and wash pictures add to the fun.

1565 *Amelia Bedelia and the Surprise Shower*. Ill. by Fritz Siebel. HarperCollins, 1966; pap., 1979. ISBN 0-06-024643-X. SERIES: I Can Read Books. SUBJECTS: Humorous stories. RL B.
Not familiar with "showers," Amelia Bedelia assumes she is to spray the bride-to-be with water. In a story filled with her literal and very funny interpretations of instructions, Amelia Bedelia's antics will keep children laughing. The book has humorous ink and wash sketches.

1566 *Amelia Bedelia Goes Camping*. Ill. by Lynn Sweat. Greenwillow, 1985; Avon, pap., 1986. ISBN 0-688-04058-6. SERIES: Read-alone. SUBJECTS: Camps and camping—Fiction; Humorous stories. RL A.
When Mr. Rogers says to hit the road, of course Amelia Bedelia takes a stick and hits the road. After creating her usual havoc on their camping trip, Amelia Bedelia again redeems herself with her cooking. This book is illustrated with spare ink drawings and washes.

1567 *Amelia Bedelia Helps Out*. Ill. by Lynn Sweat. Greenwillow, 1979; Avon, pap., 1982. ISBN 0-688-84231-3. SERIES: Read-alone. SUBJECTS: Humorous stories. RL B.
When Miss Emma's gardener is ill, Amelia Bedelia and her niece offer to help. They create the usual problems because of Amelia Bedelia's literal interpretation of orders. Adding to the hilarity are the ink and wash pictures.

1568 *Amelia Bedelia's Family Album*. Ill. by Lynn Sweat. Greenwillow, 1988. ISBN 0-688-07677-7. SUBJECTS: Families—Fiction; Humorous stories. RL B.
Mr. and Mrs. Rogers decide to have a party for their silly maid Amelia Bedelia and want to invite her family. When she shows them her family album, the Rogerses realize that her family is as unusual as Amelia Bedelia. A new format and full color pictures are used for this twenty-fifth anniversary book.

1569 *Be Ready at Eight*. Ill. by Leonard Kessler. Macmillan, 1979, o.p.; pap., 1987, o.p. SERIES: Ready-to-Read. SUBJECTS: Birthdays—Fiction; Memory and memorization—Fiction. RL B.
Miss Molly cannot remember why she has a string tied around her finger although everybody in town is reminding her that they will see her at eight. Her forgetfulness turns her birthday party into a surprise. Simple line drawings with orange and green accents add to the fun.

1570 *The Cats' Burglar*. Ill. by Lynn Sweat. Greenwillow, 1983; Dell, pap., 1988. ISBN 0-688-01826-2. SERIES: Read-alone. SUBJECTS: Pets—Cats—Fiction; Robbers and outlaws—Fiction. RL A.
Aunt Emma refuses to give up any of her nine cats. When a burglar breaks in, the cats gang up on the very allergic man. The independent Aunt Emma and the police know how lucky she is not to be hurt while the humorous drawings and antics of the cats keep the tone light.

1571 *Come Back, Amelia Bedelia*. Ill. by Wallace Tripp. HarperCollins, 1971; pap., 1978. ISBN 0-06-024668-5. SERIES: I Can Read Books. SUBJECTS: Humorous stories. RL B.
After being fired by Mrs. Rogers for her latest literal interpretation of instructions, Amelia Bedelia starts looking for work with predictable and often hilarious results. The ink and wash drawings give Amelia Bedelia an innocence that adds to the story's humor and success.

1572 *Dinosaur Time*. Ill. by Arnold Lobel. HarperCollins, 1974; pap., 1983. ISBN 0-06-024654-5. SERIES: Early I Can Read. SUBJECTS: Dinosaurs. RL B.
Eleven dinosaurs are introduced, giving the pronunciation of their names and facts about their size and life-style. The never waning popularity of dinosaurs and the attractive detailed drawings and brief text have made this a continual favorite.

1573 *Good Hunting, Blue Sky*. Rev. ed. Ill. by James Watts. HarperCollins, 1988. ISBN 0-06-024661-8. SERIES: I Can Read Books. SUBJECTS: Hunting—Fiction; Native Americans—Fiction. RL B.

Parish, Peggy (cont.)

In a good revision of *Good Hunting, Little Indian* (HarperCollins, 1962), Blue Sky goes out hunting with bow and arrow and misses everything he aims for. Walking home he is chased by a boar and ends up riding it into his village where his father kills it. This book is illustrated with attractive full color drawings.

1574 *Good Work, Amelia Bedelia*. Ill. by Lynn Sweat. Greenwillow, 1976; Avon, pap., 1982. ISBN 0-688-84022-1. SERIES: Read-alone. SUBJECTS: Humorous stories. RL B.
Amelia Bedelia's well-known literal approach to following instructions gets her in more trouble as she patches a screen with cloth, serves cracked corn as a chicken dinner, and puts pieces of sponge in batter for a sponge cake. Ink and colored pencil drawings add to the humor.

1575 *Granny and the Desperadoes*. Ill. by Steven Kellogg. Macmillan, 1970, o.p. SUBJECTS: Humorous stories; Robbers and outlaws—Fiction; Western stories. RL B.
The threat of Granny's shotgun, which does not work, is the reason the robbers are helping Granny repair her house and capture ducks. Kellogg's hilarious pencil sketches guarantee fun.

1576 *Merry Christmas, Amelia Bedelia*. Ill. by Lynn Sweat. Greenwillow, 1986; Avon, pap., 1987. ISBN 0-688-06102-8. SERIES: Read-alone. SUBJECTS: Holidays—Christmas—Fiction; Humorous stories. RL B.
When Mrs. Rogers leaves to pick up Aunt Myra, who is spending Christmas with the Rogers family, Amelia Bedelia is left with a list of instructions for trimming the tree, stuffing stockings, and more, all of which she interprets literally and humorously. Ink and wash sketches support the zaniness of the story.

1577 *Mind Your Manners*. Ill. by Marylin Hafner. Greenwillow, 1978. pap., ISBN 0-688-84157-0. SERIES: Read-alone. SUBJECTS: Behavior—Manners. RL B.
A humorous, light-handed approach to manners gives children the appropriate behavior for 18 situations—from meeting new people to chewing gum. The ink and wash illustrations reinforce the importance of good manners.

1578 *Mr. Adams's Mistake*. Ill. by Gail Owens. Macmillan, 1982. ISBN 0-02-769800-9. SERIES: Ready-to-Read. SUBJECTS: Animals—Chimpanzees—Fiction; Humorous stories; School stories. RL B.
Mr. Adams, a nearsighted truant officer, mistakes a chimpanzee for a child and hurries it off to school with riotous results. Realistic full-color drawings add to the humor in the story.

1579 *No More Monsters for Me!* Ill. by Marc Simont. HarperCollins, 1981; pap., 1987. ISBN 0-06-024658-8. SERIES: I Can Read Books. SUBJECTS: Monsters—Fiction; Parent and child—Fiction; Pets—Fiction. RL B.
After arguing with her mother about having a pet, Minn finds a gentle baby monster and hides it in the basement. While there, it starts to grow at an alarming rate. In the end, it is taken back to its home and replaced by a more ordinary pet. Humorous ink and wash pictures show a huge but still lovable monster.

1580 *Ootah's Lucky Day*. Ill. by Mamoru Funai. HarperCollins, 1970, o.p. SERIES: I Can Read Books. SUBJECTS: Hunting—Fiction; Native Americans—Eskimos—Fiction. RL A.
With nothing to eat and no oil for a fire, little Ootah, an Eskimo boy, takes his dogs and goes hunting alone. Using all his training and courage, Ootah surprises everyone by killing a walrus, thus providing meat for all the people in his village. Simple, realistic drawings illustrate the book.

1581 *Play Ball, Amelia Bedelia*. Ill. by Wallace Tripp. HarperCollins, 1972; pap., 1978. ISBN 0-06-024656-1. SERIES: I Can Read Books. SUBJECTS: Humorous stories; Sports—Baseball—Fiction. RL B.
When the Grizzlies are short one player in their game with the Tornadoes, Amelia Bedelia volunteers to help out. Putting paper tags on players, stealing bases, and carrying boys "out" are typical of the good-natured misunderstandings depicted in the ink and wash line drawings.

1582 *Scruffy*. Ill. by Kelly Oechsli. Harper-Collins, 1988. ISBN 0-06-024660-X.

SERIES: I Can Read Books. SUBJECTS: Animal shelters—Fiction; Birthdays—Fiction; Pets—Cats—Fiction. RL B.

For his birthday Todd gets a trip to the animal shelter to pick out a kitten. While there Todd chooses an older cat—Scruffy. Information on shelters and responsible pet ownership is provided. The sketchy ink and wash pictures capture the concern and fun in looking for a pet.

1583 *Teach Us, Amelia Bedelia*. Ill. by Lynn Sweat. Greenwillow, 1977; Scholastic, pap., 1987. ISBN 0-688-84069-8. SERIES: Read-alone. SUBJECTS: Humorous stories; School stories. RL B.

Taking a message to the principal, Amelia Bedelia is mistaken for the new teacher and hurried into a classroom. She diligently follows a list of instructions, concocting her own hilarious way of teaching. Illustrated with funny ink, colored pencil, and wash pictures.

1584 *Thank You, Amelia Bedelia*. Newly Illustrated Edition. Ill. by Barbara Siebel Thomas. HarperCollins, 1964, 1992. ISBN 0-06-022979-9. SERIES: I Can Read Books. SUBJECTS: Humorous stories. RL B.

In her usual way, Amelia Bedelia follows instructions exactly as she gets ready for Mrs. Rogers's Great-Aunt Myra's visit. She does nothing right but manages to win everyone to her side by cooking a wonderful apple pie. New pictures, based on the 1964 edition, are in full color.

1585 *Too Many Rabbits*. Ill. by Leonard Kessler. Macmillan, 1974, o.p. SERIES: Ready-to-Read. SUBJECTS: Animals—Rabbits—Fiction; Pets—Rabbits—Fiction. RL A.

When the rabbit she takes in has a litter, Miss Molly decides to keep them all until they start multiplying. Humorous line drawings and a simple text tell the story of a kindhearted woman who just cannot say no to stray animals.

1586 *Zed and the Monsters*. Ill. by Paul Galdone. Doubleday, 1979, o.p. SERIES: Reading On My Own. SUBJECTS: Monsters—Fiction; Tall tales. RL B.

An offer of gold entices lazy Zed to match wits with and overcome four monsters. Humorous and good for storytelling, the story is illus-trated with outlandishly funny ink and wash pictures.

Park, Margaret

1587 *Harvey and Rosie . . . and Ralph*. Ill. by Ann Iosa. Dutton, 1992. ISBN 0-525-44836-5. SERIES: Speedsters. SUBJECTS: Animals—Dogs—Fiction; Magic—Fiction; Sports—Soccer—Fiction. RL C.

Harvey is such a poor soccer player that even his dog Rosie is better. On the day of their big game, Rosie is magically transformed into a soccer-playing child who helps them win. Black and white pictures are scattered throughout this engaging sports story.

Park, W. B.

1588 *The Costume Party*. Ill. by author. Little, Brown, 1983, o.p. SUBJECTS: Costumes—Fiction; Humorous stories; Parties—Fiction. RL B.

All of her friends are annoyed at the antics of the rude stranger in the bear costume, so Shirley Cat takes charge, getting him to behave so that everyone can have fun. A good lesson in party behavior and a funny story, this has pencil sketches with fuchsia accents.

Parker, Philip

1589 *The Life Cycle of a Stickleback*. Ill. by Jackie Harland. Bookwright, 1988, o.p. SERIES: Life Cycles. SUBJECTS: Animals—Fish. RL B.

Sticklebacks are notable in that they lay eggs in a nest and then the male guards the nest and looks after the hatchlings. The tiny three spined freshwater stickleback is seen in its habitat as readers learn about its breeding and diet. Full color paintings accurately depict the excellent text.

1590 *The Life Cycle of a Sunflower*. Ill. by Jackie Harland. Bookwright, 1988, o.p. SERIES: Life Cycles. SUBJECTS: Plants—Flowers. RL B.

Using clear, carefully executed paintings that work very well with an excellent text, this book presents a good description of the growth of a sunflower from seed to maturity.

Parker, Philip (cont.)

Attention is also paid to clear instructions for growing a sunflower. A glossary, bibliography, and index are included.

Parramon, J. M.

1591 *My First Visit to a Farm*. Ill. by G. Sales. Barron's, 1990. ISBN 0-8120-4305-7. SERIES: My First Visit. SUBJECTS: Farm and country life; School stories. RL B.

A class visits an old-fashioned family farm where cows are milked by hand and horses are used to pull wagons of hay. Following the story is a two-page section geared to adults about domestic animals and farming. The illustrations are sweet watercolors.

1592 *My First Visit to the Aviary*. Ill. by G. Sales. Barron's, 1990. ISBN 0-8120-4303-0. SERIES: My First Visit. SUBJECTS: Animals—Birds; School stories. RL B.

A teacher takes her students to an aviary where they learn a little about the habits of some common and some exotic birds. Paintings are colorful and somewhat realistic. A section intended for parents and teachers offers additional information.

1593 *My First Visit to the Zoo*. Ill. by author. Barron's, 1990. ISBN 0-8120-4302-2. SERIES: My First Visit. SUBJECTS: School stories; Zoos. RL B.

A class visits the zoo and identifies the animals and comments on their zoo habitats. Illustrations of the animals are realistic watercolors while those of the people gazing at them are more cartoonlike. One mistake: Baboons are identified as monkeys.

Patent, Dorothy H.

1594 *All about Whales*. Photos. Holiday House, 1987. ISBN 0-8234-0644-X. SUBJECTS: Animals—Whales; Conservation. RL C.

This book characterizes whales as mammals belonging to two groups (baleen and toothed) and discusses their growth, feeding, senses, and communication, and the efforts of humans to save them from extinction. An index is included. Black and white photos accompany an extensive text.

Paterson, Diane

1595 *Someday*. Ill. by author. Macmillan, 1993. ISBN 0-02-770565-X. SUBJECTS: Animals—Fiction; Boats and boating—Fiction; Humorous stories. RL B.

For three clams, a shell, and a pebble, a sea gull purchases a sailboat, names it *Someday*, and invites his animal friends to go sailing with him. One misadventure after another fills their day with fun. Text is illustrated with watercolor paintings with much child appeal.

Paterson, Katherine

1596 *The Smallest Cow in the World*. Ill. by Jane C. Brown. HarperCollins, 1991. ISBN 0-06-024690-1. SERIES: I Can Read Books. SUBJECTS: Animals—Cows—Fiction; Farm and country life—Fiction; Imagination—Fiction. RL B.

Forced not only to move but to see Rosie, his favorite cow, sold, Marvin gets so angry that he imagines a miniature Rosie—a Rosie who does mean things until Marvin gives her a good home. The problems of moving and of having little control over anything are well handled in text and pictures.

Patrick, Gloria

1597 *This Is*. Ill. by Joan Hanson. Carolrhoda, 1970, o.p. SUBJECTS: Stories in rhyme. RL B.

Not so much a story as a collection of very brief rhyming phrases that accumulate into several short unrelated rhyming verses, the book is popular with many children just starting to read. The simple block print illustrations show a mouse, a house, and a boy.

Patterson, Lillie

1598 *Haunted Houses on Halloween*. Ill. by Doug Cushman. Garrard, 1979, o.p. SERIES: First Holiday. SUBJECTS: Folklore; Ghost stories; Holidays—Halloween—Fiction. RL B.

The first of two stories of ghostly hauntings has a penniless youth bravely facing a skeletal apparition and earning a treasure. The second story has a hunter outwitting a dangerous witch. The ink and watercolor pictures reflect the plot, which is sure to attract young readers.

Payne, Elizabeth

1599 *Meet the Pilgrim Fathers*. Ill. by H. B. Vestal. Random House, 1966, o.p. SERIES: Step-Up. SUBJECTS: Holidays—Thanksgiving; Pilgrims; United States—Colonial period. RL B.
The story of the Pilgrims begins when they flee to Holland for religious freedom. The detailed and interesting narrative follows the Pilgrims to America and through their first very difficult years in Plymouth and, of course, the thanksgiving celebration. This book is illustrated with textbook-like drawings.

Pearce, Q. L., and Pearce, W. J.

1600 *In the African Grasslands*. Ill. by Delana Bettoli. Silver Burdett, 1990. ISBN 0-671-68831-6. SERIES: Nature's Footprints. SUBJECTS: Animals—Baby; Animals—Habits and behavior; Grasslands—Africa. RL A.
Mother and young of cheetah and antelope, jackal and leopard, baboon and ostrich, and two other pairs are shown and minimal information is provided about each. Realistic watercolor pictures are framed with the tracks of the animals.

1601 *In the Barnyard*. Ill. by Delana Bettoli. Silver Burdett, 1990. ISBN 0-671-68828-6. SERIES: Nature's Footprints. SUBJECTS: Animals—Farm; Animals—Habits and Behavior; Animals—Tracks. RL A.
Ten farm animals in five sets (duck and cat, dog and sheep, and so on) are shown in a farm setting. The minimal text starts with the animal's sound then briefly states the animal's use. Rather sweet watercolor pictures use animal tracks to lead readers forward and introduce an animal.

1602 *In the Desert*. Ill. by Delana Bettoli. Silver Burdett, 1990. ISBN 0-671-68829-4.
SERIES: Nature's Footprints. SUBJECTS: Animals—Desert; Animals—Habits and behavior; Animals—Tracks. RL A.
With emphasis on their tracks, five sets of animals (tortoise and vulture, roadrunner and prairie dog, and so on) are shown with tracks leading to them and tracks framing the pictures. Text merely captions the full color realistic pictures and provides little information.

1603 *In the Forest*. Ill. by Delana Bettoli. Silver Burdett, 1990. ISBN 0-671-68830-8. SERIES: Nature's Footprints. SUBJECTS: Animals—Habits and behavior; Animals—Tracks; Forestry and forest rangers. RL A.
Five sets of woodland and pond animals (beaver and frog, owl and skunk, and so on) are pictured in their natural environment with minimal information. Readers are urged to use the tracks that frame the colorful, rather sweet, paintings to find the appropriate animal.

Pearson, Susan

1604 *Molly Moves Out*. Ill. by Steven Kellogg. Dial, 1979, o.p. SERIES: Dial Easy-to-Read. SUBJECTS: Animals—Rabbits—Fiction; Friendship—Fiction; Siblings—Fiction. RL B.
Tired of her little siblings taking her things and of their constant noise, Molly moves to her own house. There she makes a new friend and appreciates her family as visitors. The story and ebullient line drawings capture the chaos and love of this large and noisy rabbit family.

1605 *Monday I Was an Alligator*. Ill. by Sal Murdocca. HarperCollins, 1979, o.p. SERIES: I-Like-To-Read. SUBJECTS: Humorous stories; Imagination—Fiction. RL C.
Each day of the week a little girl imagines that she is a different animal terrorizing someone in her family. When she finally decides to be herself, everyone is relieved. Humorous ink sketches with some color capture the fun.

Pellowski, Michael J.

1606 *What's It Like to Be a Fire Fighter*. Ill. by John Lawn. Troll, 1989. ISBN 0-8167-1428-2. SERIES: What's It Like to Be a . . . .

Pellowski, Michael J. (cont.)

SUBJECTS: Careers; Community helpers; Fire fighters and fire fighting. RL C.
Members of a fire-fighting crew are shown battling a large fire. Then other types of fire fighting are shown: fire boats, airborne fighters, and smoke jumpers. The colorful watercolor illustrations have captioning to identify important tools.

1607 *What's It Like to Be a Forest Ranger*. Ill. by George Ulrich. Troll, hb and pap., 1989. ISBN 0-8167-1422-3. SERIES: What's It Like to Be a . . . . SUBJECTS: Careers; Forestry and forest rangers. RL C.
A boy learns that being a forest ranger involves much more than just fighting fires. He sees how rangers are caretakers of the trees and animals and water. A good introduction to this career, the book is illustrated with realistic watercolors defined with ink.

1608 *What's It Like to Be a Police Officer*. Ill. by Mena Dolobowsky. Troll, 1990. ISBN 0-8167-1811-3. SERIES: What's It Like to Be a . . . . SUBJECTS: Careers; Community helpers; Police. RL C.
After losing her bike, a little girl and her father go to the police station to report it missing. There she asks questions about police work that lead into a discussion of the career. The text is illustrated with flat, stylized watercolor pictures.

Penner, Lucille Recht

1609 *Dinosaur Babies*. Ill. by Peter Barrett. Random House, 1991. ISBN 0-679-91207-X. SERIES: Step into Reading. SUBJECTS: Dinosaurs. RL A.
Scientific in its approach to what is known about dinosaurs and their young, this book lets children know what has been verified and what is supposition with few words and realistic, well-designed pictures of the dinosaurs.

1610 *Snakes!* Ill. by Peter Barrett. Random House, hb and pap., 1994. ISBN 0-679-94777-9. SERIES: Step into Reading. SUBJECTS: Animals—Reptiles and amphibians; Animals—Snakes. RL B.
Engaging, realistic paintings of snakes and their environments will attract children to this

book and the well-done text will maintain their interest. The author includes information on physical aspects of snakes, their food, social behavior, and the important part they play in the balance of nature.

1611 *The True Story of Pocahontas*. Ill. by Pamela Johnson. Random House, hb and pap., 1994. ISBN 0-679-96166-6. SERIES: Step into Reading. SUBJECTS: Biographies; Native Americans; United States—History. RL B.
In a brief look at the life of the young American Indian woman alleged to have saved the life of John Smith, readers get a glimpse of the life of her people and her own character. The ending unfortunately says only that she spent the remainder of her life in England, not that disease killed her as she was returning to Virginia. Watercolor and pencil pictures attractively depict her life.

Penney, Richard L.

1612 *Penguins Are Coming!* Ill. by Tom Eaton. HarperCollins, 1969, o.p. SERIES: Science I Can Read. SUBJECTS: Animals—Penguins. RL B.
A fascinating eyewitness account of life among the Adelie penguins in Antarctica is given. The book should be useful and interesting to children of all ages—not just beginning readers. It is illustrated with bold and lively ink drawings.

Penny, Malcolm

1613 *Let's Look at Sharks*. Ill. by Wendy Meadway. Watts, 1990. ISBN 0-531-18308-4. SERIES: Let's Look At. SUBJECTS: Animals—Fish; Animals—Sharks. RL B.
Detailed and realistic watercolors show many different kinds of sharks—including the ray and the hammerhead—while the text explains where they live and how. There is also information on sharks dangerous to humans. A brief glossary is included.

Perkins, Al

1614 *The Ear Book*. Ill. by William O'Brien. Random House, 1968. ISBN 0-394-91199-7. SERIES: Bright and Early. SUBJECTS:

Human body—Ears—Fiction; Stories in rhyme. RL B.

A short, rhythmic text leads children not only to consider the many ways and things that ears hear but also offers children a chance for a successful beginning reading experience. Full color comic paintings of people and things are arranged on a white background.

1615 *Hand, Hand, Fingers, Thumb*. Ill. by Eric Gurney. Random House, 1969. ISBN 0-394-91076-1. SERIES: Bright and Early. SUBJECTS: Animals—Monkeys—Fiction; Stories in rhyme. RL C.

A rhyming text introduces the reader to one monkey drumming, then more and more monkeys using their hands in a variety of ways. Finally millions of monkeys are drumming in this catchy nonstory that both readers and listeners enjoy. Illustrated with detailed line drawings and washes.

1616 *Hugh Lofting's Travels of Doctor Dolittle*. Ill. by Philip Wende. Random House, 1967. ISBN 0-394-80048-6. SERIES: Beginner Books. SUBJECTS: Adventure stories; Animals—Fiction; Fantasy. RL C.

This very abbreviated version of the classic story is abridged well, and children will enjoy this taste of Doctor Dolittle's adventures. Here he travels to Africa by ship to cure the monkeys of a terrible disease. Illustrations, similar in style to Lofting's, are done in color.

1617 *The Nose Book*. Ill. by Roy McKie. Random House, 1970. ISBN 0-394-90623-3. SERIES: Bright and Early. SUBJECTS: Human body—Nose—Fiction; Stories in rhyme. RL A.

A brown dog explores the great variety of noses among animals and humans and notes the things noses are used for, such as holding up glasses and smelling food. The lively, rhyming text is matched to bright, bold paintings with black outlinings.

1618 *Tubby and the Lantern*. Ill. by Rowland Wilson. Beginner, 1971, o.p. SERIES: I Can Read It All By Myself. SUBJECTS: Adventure stories; Animals—Elephants—Fiction. RL B.

Ah Mee, the son of a lantern maker, has Tubby, a small elephant, as his very special pet and friend. The two are lifted away by a huge lantern and carried out to sea and they have a great adventure. Illustrated with lively full-color pictures.

Peters, Sharon

1619 *Animals at Night*. Ill. by Paul Harvey. Troll, 1983. ISBN 0-89375-903-1. SERIES: Now I Know. SUBJECTS: Animals—Nocturnal—Fiction. RL A.

After being put to bed, the little bear looks out his window and wonders who is there. Very brief sentences and very simple, stylized paintings show a variety of nighttime animals hunting for food, calling to each other, or building new homes.

1620 *The Goofy Ghost*. Ill. by Tom Garcia. Troll, 1981. ISBN 0-89375-533-8. SERIES: Giant First-Start. SUBJECTS: Ghost stories; Haunted houses—Fiction. RL B.

A family of rather innocuous ghosts haunts a large old house. All the family members are competent ghosts except for the youngest, who is a klutz. When a mean old ghost tries to move in on the family, the bumbling little ghost scares him away. Illustrated with non-threatening pastel paintings.

1621 *Here Comes Jack Frost*. Ill. by Eulala Connor. Troll, hb and pap., 1981. ISBN 0-89375-513-3. SERIES: Giant First-Start. SUBJECTS: Fantasy; Seasons—Winter—Fiction. RL A.

A short text with a very limited vocabulary works with rather sweet, colorful paintings to describe and illustrate an elflike Jack Frost painting winter windows. The text and illustrations are adequate to the subject.

1622 *Puppet Show*. Ill. by Alana Lee. Troll, hb and pap., 1980. ISBN 0-89375-385-8. SERIES: First-Start Easy Reader. SUBJECTS: Puppets—Fiction. RL A.

Four children work together to make puppets and a stage and to put on a puppet show. The very brief story is good for children just beginning to read. The red and black illustrations are simple yet lively.

Petersen, David L.

1623 *Airplanes*. Photos. Childrens Pr., hb and pap., 1981. ISBN 0-516-01606-7.

Petersen, David L. (cont.)

> SERIES: New True. SUBJECTS: Airplanes.
> RL C.

Full color photographs of a variety of airplanes add interest to this brief look at aircraft from the time of the Wright brothers to that of the space shuttle. Also looked at are the way planes are used and the people who fly them.

1624 *Airports.* Photos. Childrens Pr., 1981,
> o.p. SERIES: New True. SUBJECTS: Airports.
> RL B.

The different parts and services of a modern airport are explored with full color photographs. There is also a glossary and an index. This book provides useful introductory information that may lead a child to read other books about aeronautics.

1625 *Apatosaurus.* Photos. Childrens Pr.,
> 1989. ISBN 0-516-01159-6. SERIES: New
> True. SUBJECTS: Dinosaurs. RL C.

After clarifying the confusing "renaming" of brontosaurus to apatosaurus, the book goes on to discuss the discovery of the dinosaur's bones, theories concerning its habits and behavior, and much more. Well done, the book is illustrated with color photographs and includes a glossary and index.

1626 *Carlsbad Caverns National Park.*
> Photos. Childrens Pr., 1994. ISBN 0-516-
> 01051-4. SERIES: New True. SUBJECTS:
> Geology and geologists; National parks;
> Nature. RL C.

After receiving an explanation of how stalactites, stalagmites, and other geologic formations are created, young readers will be introduced to the wonders of Carlsbad Cavern and given a photographic tour of it and the park. Good photos, an upbeat tone, a glossary, and an index round out the work.

1627 *Helicopters.* Photos. Childrens Pr., hb
> and pap., 1983. ISBN 0-516-01680-6.
> SERIES: New True. SUBJECTS: Helicopters.
> RL C.

A brief history of the development of helicopters is followed by chapters that discuss the kinds of helicopters and their operation, mechanical parts, and safety requirements. There is a glossary and an index. The book is illustrated with full color photographs.

1628 *Yosemite National Park.* Photos.
> Childrens Pr., 1993. ISBN 0-516-01335-1.
> SERIES: New True. SUBJECTS: National
> parks—Yosemite; Nature. RL C.

The history of the famous park, including the role of John Muir in preserving it, the places to see, and the animals that inhabit it are exhibited in both text and clear color photographs. The book includes a glossary, an index, and a table of contents.

1629 *Zion National Park.* Photos. Childrens
> Pr., 1993. ISBN 0-516-01336-X. SERIES:
> New True. SUBJECTS: National parks;
> Native Americans; Nature. RL C.

Zion Canyon in Utah—its landscape, animals, and plant life—is observed in good color photographs and a well-written text. Facts about the settling of the land by Native American peoples and then by the Mormons in the 1800s broaden the scope. Index, glossary, and table of contents are included.

Petersen, P. J.

1630 *The Fireplug Is First Base.* Ill. by Betsy
> James. Dutton, 1990. ISBN 0-525-44587-
> 0. SERIES: Speedsters. SUBJECTS: Siblings—
> Fiction; Sports—Baseball—Fiction.
> RL B.

Joe's little brother "Flea" finally gets a chance to bat in the Big Boys' street game of baseball. Through a series of mishaps, Flea gets a triple home run. Black and white pencil and wash pictures are lively and have balloons filled with dialogue. The format makes it appear to be aimed at older readers.

Petrie, Catherine

1631 *Hot Rod Harry.* Ill. by Paul Sharp.
> Childrens Pr., hb and pap., 1982. ISBN 0-
> 516-03493-6. SERIES: Rookie Readers.
> SUBJECTS: Bicycles and bicycling—
> Fiction. RL A.

Hot Rod Harry is a terror on his bicycle because he cares about nothing but speed. The full color expressive pictures do more to tell the story than does the very brief text.

1632 *Joshua James Likes Trucks.* Ill. by Jerry
> Warshaw. Childrens Pr., hb and pap.,

1982. ISBN 0-516-03525-8. SERIES: Rookie Readers. SUBJECTS: Trucks—Fiction. RL A.
At home and in town, Joshua James spots all types and sizes of trucks. A very limited vocabulary, brief text, and bright pictures with black outlining make this book attractive to children.

1633 *Sandbox Betty*. Ill. by Sharon Elzaurdia. Childrens Pr., hb and pap., 1982. ISBN 0-516-03578-9. SERIES: Rookie Readers. SUBJECTS: Sandcastles—Fiction; Stories in rhyme. RL B.
A very limited and repetitious text tells of Betty and her meticulously crafted and elaborate sandcastles. Simple, childlike colored drawings with black outlining are necessary to the telling of the story, since the text is so brief.

Petty, Kate

1634 *Dinosaurs*. Ill. by Richard Orr and Stephen Bennett. Watts, 1988, o.p. SERIES: Small World. SUBJECTS: Dinosaurs. RL C.
Dinosaurs are colorfully painted in their surroundings as the illustrators perceive them to be in order to show a straightforward presentation of rather superficial information on dinosaurs. Several dinosaurs, early reptiles, and birds are described and their Latin names given.

1635 *Guinea Pigs*. Photos. Gloucester, 1989. ISBN 0-531-17131-0. SERIES: First Pets. SUBJECTS: Pets—Guinea pigs. RL B.
More of an introduction to guinea pigs than a pet care book, this book offers good color photos and paintings, brief and rather casual information on care, and some background facts on guinea pigs. Children should find this an enticement to guinea pig ownership as well as interesting reading.

1636 *Whales*. Ill. by Norman Weaver. Watts, 1988, o.p. SERIES: Small World. SUBJECTS: Animals—Whales. RL C.
A descriptive account of different kinds of whales, this book offers little in-depth information. Instead it introduces a variety of whales and gives brief facts on them and their behavior and habitat. Paintings are realistic and attractive.

Pfeffer, Wendy

1637 *From Tadpole to Frog*. Ill. by Holly Keller. HarperCollins, hb and pap., 1994. ISBN 0-06-023044-4. SERIES: Let's-Read-and-Find-Out Science Books. SUBJECTS: Animals—Frogs and toads; Animals—Reptiles and amphibians. RL B.
Using the bullfrog as an example, the author and illustrator take a fascinating step-by-step approach to the frog's development. Watercolor illustrations are detailed and attractive. A final section, geared to older readers, provides more information on frogs. A map concludes the book.

Phillips, Joan

1638 *Lucky Bear*. Ill. by J. P. Miller. Random House, hb and pap., 1986. ISBN 0-394-97987-7. SERIES: Step into Reading. SUBJECTS: Toys—Teddy bears—Fiction. RL A.
Named Lucky by the toymaker, a teddy bear falls out of a window and into a series of adventures that earn him a friend. A very brief text with large print is complemented by soft watercolor pictures.

1639 *My New Boy*. Ill. by Lynn Munsinger. Random House, hb and pap., 1986. ISBN 0-394-98277-0. SERIES: Step into Reading. SUBJECTS: Animals—Dogs—Fiction; Humorous stories; Pets—Dogs—Fiction. RL A.
In this brief whimsical story a puppy teaches his boy tricks and takes care of him. Simple paintings with ink details effectively convey the humor and warmth of the story.

1640 *Tiger Is a Scaredy Cat*. Ill. by Norman Gorbaty. Random House, hb and pap., 1986. ISBN 0-394-98056-5. SERIES: Step into Reading. SUBJECTS: Animals—Cats—Fiction; Animals—Mice—Fiction; Emotions—Fear—Fiction. RL A.
Tiger, a young cat, is afraid of dogs, trucks, the vacuum cleaner, the dark, and even mice. When a baby mouse is lost and needs help, Tiger gathers his courage and returns the mouse to its home. Pictures are simple yet bold and colorful and work with the text to create an appealing book.

Phleger, Frederick B.

1641 *Red Tag Comes Back*. Ill. by Arnold Lobel. HarperCollins, 1961. ISBN 0-06-024706-1. SERIES: Science I Can Read. SUBJECTS: Animals—Fish. RL A.

After explaining the purpose of tagging to a young boy, a naturalist tags a salmon just for him. The well-done book follows Red Tag the salmon's journey to the sea, her growth, and finally her return to the same area to spawn. Detailed ink and wash drawings realistically portray the life of the salmon.

Pickering, Robert

1642 *I Can Be an Archaeologist*. Photos. Childrens Pr., hb and pap., 1987. ISBN 0-516-01909-0. SERIES: I Can Be. SUBJECTS: Careers. RL C.

Study, persistence, painstaking care, and curiosity are the traits most important to becoming an archaeologist according to this brief look at the profession. The text and photographs have people doing all aspects of the work in the field and in museums.

Pickett, Anola

1643 *Old Enough for Magic*. Ill. by Ned Delaney. HarperCollins, 1989. hb and pap. ISBN 0-06-024732-0. SERIES: I Can Read Books. SUBJECTS: Magic—Fiction; Sibling rivalry—Fiction. RL B.

For his birthday Peter gets a very special magic set. His older sister insists he is too young for magic. Yet she is the one who does not read the directions and gets turned into a frog and Peter comes to her rescue. Text is illustrated with cartoonlike color paintings.

Pilkey, Dav

1644 *Dragon Gets By: Dragon's Second Tale*. Ill. by author Orchard, 1991. ISBN 0-531-05935-9. SERIES: Dragon Tales. SUBJECTS: Dragons—Fiction; Humorous stories. RL B.

Waking up groggy, the little blue dragon proceeds to do just about everything not only wrong but usually backward. He sweeps his dirt floor until he has a huge hole, eats so much he cannot fit into the car, and so on. Vibrant watercolors capture the humor and are sure to attract readers.

1645 *Dragon's Fat Cat: Dragon's Fourth Tale*. Ill. by author. Orchard, 1992. ISBN 0-531-05982-0. SERIES: Dragon Tales. SUBJECTS: Dragons—Fiction; Pet care—Fiction; Pets—Cats—Fiction. RL B.

On a snowy winter day, Dragon notices a fat cat sitting near his door. After adopting the cat, Dragon finds he knows nothing about caring for it. In five brief chapters, illustrated with vividly colored paintings, the kindly but bumbling blue dragon humorously entertains readers.

1646 *Dragon's Halloween: Dragon's Fifth Tale*. Ill. by author. Orchard, 1993. ISBN 0-531-08590-2. SERIES: Dragon Tales. SUBJECTS: Dragons—Fiction; Holidays—Halloween—Fiction. RL B.

The gentle blue giant gets into the spirit of Halloween by creating a pumpkin monster that scares even him, has a great costume until he is rained on, and scares himself with his own hungry stomach rumblings. Vibrant colors and active shapes invite children into the stories.

1647 *Dragon's Merry Christmas: Dragon's Third Tale*. Ill. by author. Orchard, 1991. ISBN 0-531-05957-X. SERIES: Dragon Tales. SUBJECTS: Dragons—Fiction; Holidays—Christmas—Fiction. RL B.

Four stories featuring the gentle blue dragon capture perfectly the fun and joy of the Christmas holidays. Pilkey's colors are vibrant, his comic character endearing, and the van Gogh–like starry night in the final chapter is just right.

1648 *A Friend for Dragon: Dragon's First Tale*. Ill. by author. Orchard, 1991. ISBN 0-531-05934-0. SERIES: Dragon Tales. SUBJECTS: Dragons—Fiction; Friendship—Fiction. RL B.

The lonely little blue dragon is tricked into believing an apple can talk and want to be his friend. Humorous and brightly colored watercolors help to carry the brief story and work to attract a readers attention.

Pillar, Marjorie

1649 *Pizza Man*. Photos. HarperCollins, 1990. ISBN 0-690-04836-X. SUBJECTS: Business enterprises; Food—Pizza. RL C.

Through black-and-white photographs and a very brief text in large type, readers can follow the "pizza man" as he prepares to make pizzas. Readers should be impressed by the amount of work that goes into making this favorite food.

Pitt, Valerie

1650 *Let's Find Out about Names*. Ill. by Patricia Grant Porter. Watts, 1971, o.p. SERIES: Let's Find Out About. SUBJECTS: Names. RL B.

Surnames, Christian names, and meanings and origins of some names are clearly and entertainingly explained. This book might inspire children to start investigating the origins of their given names. Illustrated with representative black, fuchsia, and ocher sketches.

1651 *Let's Find Out about the Community*. Ill. by June Goldsborough. Watts, 1972, o.p. SERIES: Let's Find Out About. SUBJECTS: Communities; Community helpers. RL C.

A clear and simple text and watercolor pictures together define what a community is made up of: libraries, schools, community helpers, citizens, and government. The community is then examined to see how the many parts work together to run smoothly.

Platt, Kin

1652 *Big Max*. Ill. by Robert Lopshire. HarperCollins, 1965, 1992. ISBN 0-06-024750-9. SERIES: I Can Read Books. SUBJECTS: Animals—Elephants—Fiction; Humorous stories; Mystery and detective stories. RL B.

Big Max, a diminutive detective, hurries via a hot-air umbrella to Pooka Pooka. Using his look-and-find method, Big Max finds a missing elephant. A clever text and newly colored comic-style illustrations combine to keep this a perennial favorite.

1653 *Big Max in the Mystery of the Missing Moose*. Ill. by Robert Lopshire. HarperCollins, 1977; pap., 1983, o.p. SERIES: I Can Read Mystery. SUBJECTS: Humorous stories; Mystery and detective stories. RL B.

Traveling by hot-air umbrella, Big Max heads for the zoo and begins his search for Marvin the missing moose. By trial and error and with plenty of humor, Max finds Marvin in Moose Land with his family. Comical pencil and wash drawings suit the text well.

Pluckrose, Henry

1654 *Changing Seasons*. Photos. Childrens Pr., 1994. ISBN 0-516-08116-0. SERIES: Walkabout. SUBJECTS: Seasons. RL B.

The signs of seasonal change are noted in a brief text and full page color photographs. The changes are seen in animals, plants, and weather. Many unfamiliar animals are not named, the illustrations are grainy, and the pages seem crowded.

1655 *Flowers*. Photos. Childrens Pr., 1994. ISBN 0-516-08117-9. SERIES: Walkabout. SUBJECTS: Plants—Flowers. RL B.

An appreciation of flowering plants without much detailed information about them individually, this does encourage observation and an interest in the ways in which plants grow and reproduce. Color photographs are rather grainy and layout is not always appealing.

1656 *In the Air*. Photos. Childrens Pr., 1994. ISBN 0-516-08118-7. SERIES: Walkabout. SUBJECTS: Air. RL B.

A brief text set against full color, often grainy and unappealing photographs helps children to gain an understanding of how air is a vital part of the world of animals and plants.

1657 *Look at Tongues and Tasters*. Photos. Watts, 1990, o.p. SERIES: Look At. SUBJECTS: Animals—Senses; Human body—Tongue; Senses—Taste. RL B.

Text and color photographs work together to demonstrate how tongues in humans and other animals not only provide a sense of taste but also help with speech, food gathering, grooming, and so on. Experiments and an index are also provided.

Pluckrose, Henry (cont.)

1658 *Minibeasts*. Photos. Childrens Pr., 1994. ISBN 0-516-08119-5. SERIES: Walkabout. SUBJECTS: Animals—Insects; Animals—Invertebrates. RL C.

The brief text and full-page color photographs (which are often grainy and with a crowded effect) attempt to encourage children to look at the world around them and especially at insects, slugs, snails, and other invertebrates.

1659 *Seashore*. Photos. Childrens Pr., 1994. ISBN 0-516-08120-9. SERIES: Walkabout. SUBJECTS: Seashore. RL C.

Tides, shells, animal life, and human use are discussed in this look at what constitutes a seashore. The text is brief but introduces many proper names for creatures found in this environment—making it somewhat more difficult. Photos are grainy and not always attractive.

1660 *Trees*. Photos. Childrens Pr., 1994. ISBN 0-516-08121-7. SERIES: Walkabout. SUBJECTS: Plants—Trees. RL B.

A brief and superficial look at trees and what they contribute, this book could encourage observation of trees and nature by young readers. The photographs are often grainy and the book design is rather crowded. A glossary would have helped for pronunciation of some words.

1661 *Under the Ground*. Photos. Childrens Pr., 1994. ISBN 0-516-08122-5. SERIES: Walkabout. SUBJECTS: Animals, burrowing; Tunnels. RL C.

A look at not only some of the kinds of animals that live underground but also the ways in which the underground areas are used by man, this brief book encourages observation. Photographs are often grainy and poorly placed or chosen.

1662 *Ways to Clean It!* Photos by Chris Fairclough. Watts, 1990, o.p. SERIES: Ways to . . . . SUBJECTS: Cleanliness. RL B.

Pluckrose explains how important it is to keep things clean and free from bacteria—a child's face and hands or the dishes used for dinner. Color photographs help clarify the text. Simple experiments are also included.

1663 *Weather*. Photos. Childrens Pr., 1994. ISBN 0-516-08123-3. SERIES: Walkabout. SUBJECTS: Weather. RL C.

The kinds of weather—hot, cold, windy, dry, rainy, and so on—are discussed briefly along with some information about those who forecast the weather. A glossary would have been helpful for pronunciation of some unfamiliar words. Photographs are grainy and sometimes poorly chosen.

Podendorf, Illa

1664 *Energy*. Photos. Childrens Pr., 1982. ISBN 0-516-01625-3. SERIES: New True. SUBJECTS: Energy. RL C.

Very simple language is used to provide basic information on a variety of energy sources from food for humans to wind for electricity. The emphasis is on the forms and uses of energy most noticeable in a child's environment with little on technology. Illustrated with color photographs.

1665 *Spiders*. Photos. Childrens Pr., hb and pap., 1982. ISBN 0-516-01653-9. SERIES: New True. SUBJECTS: Animals—Spiders. RL C.

Children will learn to distinguish spiders from insects and to appreciate the way the spiders weave their webs and help humans by eating harmful insects. The text is clear and easy to understand. The color photographs attest to the great many sizes, shapes, and kinds of spiders that exist.

1666 *Trees*. Photos. Childrens Pr., hb and pap., 1982. ISBN 0-516-01657-1. SERIES: New True. SUBJECTS: Plants—Trees. RL B.

The parts of trees, the way they grow, the different varieties, their uses, and the need to protect them from damage are clearly and concisely described. The text is accompanied by suitable full color photographs, a glossary, and an index.

Pollock, Penny

1667 *Ants Don't Get Sunday Off*. Ill. by Lorinda B. Cauley. Putnam, 1978, o.p. SERIES: See and Read. SUBJECTS: Animals—Ants—Fiction. RL C.

Anya, an old ant, is tired of constantly taking care of the nursery yet she is the first to try to rescue the eggs from flooding. Caught in the water, she is carried away on a great adventure. Facts about ants are interspersed in the text, which is complemented by clever ink and chalk pictures.

1668 *The Slug Who Thought He Was a Snail.* Ill. by Lorinda B. Cauley. Putnam, 1980, o.p. SERIES: See and Read. SUBJECTS: Animals—Slugs—Fiction; Animals—Snails—Fiction; Self-esteem—Fiction. RL C.

A forceful snail convinces Sam Slug that he is a snail who has lost his house and must find a new one. Sam does exactly as the snail tells him until he meets another slug who assures him he is fine as he is. Detailed pictures are slightly comical while the text provides accurate information on slugs.

1669 *The Spit Bug Who Couldn't Spit.* Ill. by Lorinda B. Cauley. Putnam, 1982, o.p. SERIES: See and Read. SUBJECTS: Animals—Insects—Fiction. RL C.

Ezra, a newly hatched spittlebug, has little success making spit until he grows and matures, but each step in the process is difficult for the timid little bug. Factual information about spittlebugs is included at the end of this story, which has humorous colored pencil drawings.

Pomerantz, Charlotte

1670 *Buffy and Albert.* Ill. by Yossi Abolafia. Greenwillow, 1982, o.p. SERIES: Read-alone. SUBJECTS: Animals—Cats—Fiction; Grandparents—Fiction; Old age—Fiction. RL B.

The two children's grandfather complains about having to take care of his two old cats. When their grandfather has an accident and is bedridden, the younger child lovingly shows him that the cats cannot help being old anymore than he can. The ink drawings with pastel accents are perfect for the story.

1671 *The Outside Dog.* Ill. by Jennifer Plecas. HarperCollins, 1993. ISBN 0-06-024782-7. SERIES: I Can Read Books. SUBJECTS: Grandparents—Fiction; Pets—Dogs—Fiction; Spanish language. RL B.

Marisol lives with her grandfather in a small Puerto Rican village. He says they can never have a dog, but a stray and the little girl slowly change his mind. Spanish words are nicely mixed into the text and explained in a glossary. Childlike ink drawings with color washes illustrate the story.

Porte, Barbara Ann

1672 *Harry Gets an Uncle.* Ill. by Yossi Abolafia. Greenwillow, 1991. ISBN 0-688-09389-2. SUBJECTS: Families—Fiction; Marriage and wedding customs—Fiction. RL B.

Though Harry's friend Dorcas scares him with tales of terrible wedding mishaps, Aunt Rose and Uncle Leo's wedding turns out just right—even though Harry's dog gets loose. Delightful watercolor pictures are perfect. Flip through the pages and look at the bottom right for a special treat!

1673 *Harry in Trouble.* Ill. by Yossi Abolafia. Greenwillow, 1989. ISBN 0-688-07633-5. SUBJECTS: Behavior—Responsible—Fiction; Humorous stories; Lost and found possessions—Fiction. RL A.

Harry is on his third library card: the first his dog ate, the second his father put in the wash, and the third he can't find. Now he has to face the librarian and tell her what he's done. Harry's humorous first person account is accompanied by warm and lively watercolor paintings.

1674 *Harry's Birthday.* Ill. by Yossi Abolafia. Greenwillow, 1994. ISBN 0-688-12142-X. SUBJECTS: Birthdays—Fiction; Parties—Fiction; Single parent families—Fiction. RL B.

Harry keeps telling his friends and father that he hopes to get a cowboy hat for his birthday. On the big day, he has a wonderful party and gets not one but seven hats. Gentle humor, a grasp of the concerns of young children, and delightful watercolor art fill this book.

1675 *Harry's Dog.* Ill. by Yossi Abolafia. Greenwillow, 1984; Scholastic, pap., 1986. ISBN 0-688-02556-0. SERIES: Read-alone. SUBJECTS: Allergies—Fiction; Families, single parent—Fiction; Pets—Dogs—Fiction. RL B.

Porte, Barbara Ann (cont.)

Knowing his father is allergic to dogs, Harry nonetheless accepts one. He tells outlandish stories to explain her presence and to convince his father to allow him to keep her. Aunt Rose finds the perfect solution to Harry's dilemma. Illustrated in soft colors with gentle humor.

1676 *Harry's Mom*. Ill. by Yossi Abolafia. Greenwillow, 1985. ISBN 0-688-04818-8. SERIES: Read-alone. SUBJECTS: Families, single parent—Fiction; Parent and child—Fiction. RL B.

When the dictionary says an orphan is someone with one parent, Harry rushes home to his father for comfort. His dad assures him that, even though his mother is dead, he is not an orphan. Harry also gets to hear more about his sports reporter mom. Ink and pencil drawings and text are excellent.

1677 *Harry's Visit*. Ill. by Yossi Abolafia. Greenwillow, 1983, o.p., Dell, pap., 1990. ISBN 0-440-40331-6. SERIES: Read-alone. SUBJECTS: Behavior—Shyness—Fiction. RL B.

When his father's friends invite him to spend the day, Harry inaccurately predicts that he will have a terrible time. The reluctance of this shy and very polite only child to venture beyond his territory is capably portrayed. Simple pastel colored pictures help tell the story.

Porter, Wesley

1678 *About Monkeys in Trees*. Ill. by Dominique Churchill. Watts, 1979, o.p. SUBJECTS: Animals—Monkeys—Fiction; Folklore—Africa. RL B.

This reworking of an African folktale tells how sly tortoise borrows money from monkey and, when the time comes to repay it, convinces monkey that she has thrown it away. This folktale explains why monkeys stay in trees (to search for the lost money). Illustrations are simple, uninspiring, but colorful paintings.

1679 *The Magic Kettle*. Ill. by Lynn Sweat. Watts, 1979, o.p. SUBJECTS: Folklore—Japan. RL C.

An old man finds a kettle, polishes it, and sees it transformed into a wild little animal. Once it is back in its kettle form, the old man sells it to a merchant who gets wealthy by holding shows where the kettle changes into its animal form. Expressively illustrated in bright colors and ink.

Posell, Elsa

1680 *Cats*. Photos. Childrens Pr., hb and pap., 1983. ISBN 0-516-01671-7. SERIES: New True. SUBJECTS: Animals—Cats; Pets—Cats. RL B.

Good basic information on well-known wild and domestic cats is given in a clear text. The book is divided into chapters with full color photographs of the animals and includes a glossary and an index. Some general information on pet care is also provided.

1681 *Dogs*. Photos. Childrens Pr., hb and pap., 1981. ISBN 0-516-01614-8. SERIES: New True. SUBJECTS: Animals—Dogs; Pets—Dogs. RL B.

Types of dogs, such as sport and working, specific breeds, and pointers for their care and training are accompanied by full color photographs. The text is carefully and clearly written and an index and glossary are included.

1682 *Elephants*. Photos. Childrens Pr., 1982. ISBN 0-516-01621-0. SERIES: New True. SUBJECTS: Animals—Elephants; Animals—Endangered. RL B.

A simple text describes types of elephants, their diet, and their lives in the wild and as captives of man. It is supplemented by color photos of elephants in the wild, at zoos, and at work. Although nothing here is in depth, the information is adequate for most young children.

1683 *Whales and Other Sea Mammals*. Photos. Childrens Pr., hb and pap., 1982. ISBN 0-516-01663-6. SERIES: New True. SUBJECTS: Animals—Endangered; Animals—Whales. RL C.

This informative look at whales includes material on their origins and physiology, their many kinds, and the possibility of their extinction from whale hunting. Short chapters are accompanied by excellent color photos and a few drawings; also included is an index and a glossary.

Poskanzer, Susan C.

1684 *What's It Like to Be a Chef.* Ill. by Karen E. Pellaton. Troll, hb and pap., 1990. ISBN 0-8167-1797-4. SERIES: What's It Like to Be a . . . . SUBJECTS: Careers; Cookery. RL C.

While visiting her Uncle Peppi at the restaurant where he is chef, Casey gets to watch and help with the preparation of lunch. Some of the many duties of a professional chef are lightly touched on. Illustrated with watercolors outlined in ink, the book offers a good look at a career.

1685 *What's It Like to Be a Dairy Farmer.* Ill. by George Ulrich. Troll, hb and pap., 1989. ISBN 0-8167-1426-6. SERIES: What's It Like to Be a . . . . SUBJECTS: Careers; Farm and country life. RL B.

At Sunrise Dairy Farm Kira and her parents all begin work early in the morning. Her parents milk the cows as Kira fixes breakfast, then Kira has her other chores to do. This is a nonglamorized look at dairy farming as a career. The illustrations are ink and watercolor washes.

1686 *What's It Like to Be a Puppeteer.* Ill. by Diane Paterson. Troll, hb and pap. 1989. ISBN 0-8167-1432-0. SERIES: What's It Like to Be a . . . . SUBJECTS: Careers; Puppets and puppetry. RL C.

Two puppeteers get ready for their regular weekend performance in the park. They check their puppets and stage and allow a young boy and his grandmother to watch them practice. Lots of good information on using puppets is provided. The illustrations are well-done watercolors with ink.

1687 *What's It Like to Be a Sanitation Worker.* Ill. by Allan Eitzen. Troll, hb and pap., 1989. ISBN 0-8167-1436-3. SERIES: What's It Like to Be a . . . . SUBJECTS: Careers; Community helpers; Garbage and garbage disposal. RL C.

Tom, Mary, and Frank are followed through a complete day of gathering garbage from their town, taking it to the landfill, and finally returning to the garage and cleaning the truck. A positive look at this career, the book is illustrated in realistic watercolor pictures.

1688 *What's It Like to Be an Astronaut.* Ill. by Allan Eitzen. Troll, hb and pap., 1990. ISBN 0-8167-1793-1. SERIES: What's It Like to Be a . . . . SUBJECTS: Astronauts; Careers; Space travel. RL C.

Andrew excitedly greets his mission specialist mom as she returns from a space shuttle flight. She explains to him many of the things that happen on a shuttle as well as telling him about the special training she has had in preparation for it.

Potter, Tessa, and Bailey, Donna

1689 *Ducks and Geese.* Ill. by Gill Tomblin. Raintree, 1990. ISBN 0-8114-2628-9. SERIES: Animal World. SUBJECTS: Animals—Ducks; Animals—Geese. RL B.

Good color photographs and paintings illustrate the habits of ducks and geese while a short but clear text provides basic information on these waterfowl. Index is included.

1690 *Goats.* Ill. by Gill Tomblin. Raintree, 1990. ISBN 0-8114-2629-7. SERIES: Animal World. SUBJECTS: Animals—Goats; Farm and country life. RL B.

Using full color realistic paintings and photographs and very short sentences providing the simplest of information, the authors introduce domestic and wild goats from different areas of the world to children. The focus is on the domestic animal and its uses.

1691 *Hens.* Ill. by Gill Tomblin. Raintree, 1990. ISBN 0-8114-2627-0. SERIES: Animal World. SUBJECTS: Animals—Chickens; Animals—Poultry; Farm and country life. RL B.

Free-range and factory-raised chickens are introduced through color photographs, drawings, and a brief text. The difference in quality of life for the animals is apparent in the illustrations and just might spark discussion. In both instances the hens are used for egg production.

1692 *Sheep.* Ill. by Gill Tomblin. Raintree, 1990. ISBN 0-8114-2630-0. SERIES: Animal World. SUBJECTS: Animals—Sheep; Farm and country life; Wool. RL B.

After initially showing sheep grazing on a British farm and then being sheared, the book changes its focus to the use of wool in fabric

Potter, Tessa, and Bailey, Donna (cont.)

production. Illustrated with full color photographs and paintings. Index is included.

Poulin, Stephane

1693 *Can You Catch Josephine?* Ill. by author. Tundra, 1987. ISBN 0-88776-198-4. SUBJECTS: Humorous stories; Pets—Cats—Fiction; School stories. RL A.
When Daniel's cat Josephine sneaks into his backpack and into his school, she creates havoc as Daniel and others try to catch her. Set in Montreal, the detailed and colorful paintings show an old-fashioned school staffed by modern multiracial teachers and students.

1694 *Could You Stop Josephine?* Ill. by author. Tundra, 1988. ISBN 0-88776-216-6. SUBJECTS: Farm and country life—Fiction; Humorous stories; Pets—Cats—Fiction. RL A.
Thinking they have left Daniel's cat Josephine safely home in Montreal, Daniel and his father drive out to the country to visit cousins. When they arrive, the spunky Siamese who has been hiding in the car gets loose and leads them on a merry chase. Illustrated with vibrant pictures of the Quebec countryside in summer.

1695 *Have You Seen Josephine?* Ill. by author. Tundra, 1988. ISBN 0-88776-180-1. SUBJECTS: City and town life—Fiction; Pets—Cats—Fiction. RL A.
Daniel decides to follow his cat Josephine to see where she goes every Saturday. He chases her through his Montreal neighborhood and finally to a neighbor's for a special Saturday cat party. The colorful paintings and black and white sketches offer readers a chance to view French Canadian culture.

Powell, E. Sandy

1696 *Rats*. Photos by Jerry Boucher. Lerner, 1994. ISBN 0-8225-3003-1. SERIES: Early Bird Nature Books. SUBJECTS: Animals—Rats. RL C.
Attractive photographs of pet rats at all stages of development support a text full of facts about the animal. Also appealing to young readers is the chatty tone and the positive atti-

tude toward rats as pets—though not toward wild rats. A glossary and index are included.

Powell, Jillian

1697 *Climbers*. Photos. Carolrhoda, 1991. ISBN 0-87614-700-7. SERIES: Things That Move. SUBJECTS: Animals; Animals—Climbing. RL B.
From cats, snakes, and snails to firefighters and children on playground equipment, this book explores the many ways that animals climb. A few sentences on each page caption full color photographs depicting the animal in action.

1698 *Flyers*. Photos. Carolrhoda, 1992. ISBN 0-87614-701-5. SERIES: Things That Move. SUBJECTS: Animals—Flying; Flight. RL B.
Birds, kites, balloons, arrows, and helicopters are some of the things mentioned here that fly. Each page has color photographs and very brief information that acts almost like captioning. Very basic, this is identification rather than explanation of principles.

1699 *Jumpers*. Photos. Carolrhoda, 1992. ISBN 0-87614-702-3. SERIES: Things That Move. SUBJECTS: Animals—Jumping; Sports—Jumping. RL B.
Animals and insects as well as sports-minded humans are pictured jumping. The brief text acts as captioning for the color photographs. Some of those pictured are frogs, squirrels, kangaroos, parachutists, and skiers.

1700 *Swimmers*. Photos. Carolrhoda, 1992. ISBN 0-87614-703-1. SERIES: Things That Move. SUBJECTS: Animals—Aquatic. RL B.
Color photographs of aquatic animals dominate this book about animals and the means by which they move or swim in water. Though many different animals are looked at (beavers, otters, fish, frogs, and so on), the text concentrates on just the movement of each animal.

Power, Barbara

1701 *I Wish Laura's Mommy Was My Mommy*. Ill. by Marylin Hafner. HarperCollins, 1979. ISBN 0-397-31859-6. SERIES: I-Like-To-Read. SUBJECTS: Family life—

Fiction; Humorous stories; Mothers, working—Fiction. RL C.

It is not until Laura's mommy agrees to baby-sit for Jennifer and her two little brothers that Laura has to wash dishes and make her own bed. A good job is done showing how much work is involved in caring for children. Pencil drawings, often humorous, are a good match for the text.

Prager, Annabelle

1702 *The Spooky Halloween Party*. Ill. by Tomie dePaola. Pantheon, 1981. ISBN 0-394-94370-8. SERIES: I Am Reading. SUBJECTS: Holidays—Halloween—Fiction; Humorous stories; Parties—Fiction. RL B.

Albert is sure he will not be frightened at Nicky's spooky Halloween party. Once there, he is surprised that he cannot identify any of the children until he realizes he is at the wrong party. Suitably scary black and white illustrations and the delightful story will be enjoyed by youngsters.

1703 *The Surprise Party*. Ill. by Tomie dePaola. Random House, hb and pap., 1988. ISBN 0-394-99596-1. SERIES: Step into Reading. SUBJECTS: Birthdays—Fiction; Friendship—Fiction; Parties—Fiction. RL B.

A little boy convinces his best friend to plan a "surprise" party for his birthday. Fortunately the best friend is wise enough to really make it a surprise. The full color pictures of multiracial children add to the warmth and humor of the story.

Prall, Jo

1704 *My Sister's Special*. Photos by Linda Gray. Childrens Pr., 1985, o.p. SERIES: Real-life Photo Stories. SUBJECTS: Physically and mentally impaired. RL B.

Angie cannot walk, talk, or use her arms and hands very well because she is brain damaged. However, she goes to school in a wheelchair and communicates with symbols. Black and white photos of a smiling child and loving family are accompanied by a proud brother's description of his special sister.

Prather, Ray

1705 *Double Dog Dare*. Ill. by author. Macmillan, 1975, o.p. SERIES: Ready-to-Read. SUBJECTS: Dares—Fiction; Friendship—Fiction. RL B.

Finding a quarter leads Eddie and Rudy, two young black friends, on a series of "daring" adventures through town. Illustrated with pencil drawings with green and brown washes.

Preller, James

1706 *Wake Me in Spring*. Ill. by Jeffrey Scherer. Scholastic, pap., 1994. ISBN 0-590-47500-2. SERIES: Hello Reader! SUBJECTS: Animals—Bears—Fiction; Animals—Hibernation—Fiction; Animals—Mice—Fiction. RL B.

As Bear gets ready to hibernate for the winter, his friend Mouse tries to get him to stay awake to enjoy sleigh rides, snowmen, and so on. Bear will not miss winter, but he will miss his friend. Simply designed, colored, cartoonlike pictures extend the text.

Prelutsky, Jack

1707 *It's Christmas*. Ill. by Marylin Hafner. Greenwillow, 1981; Scholastic, pap., 1986. ISBN 0-688-00440-7. SERIES: Read-alone. SUBJECTS: Holidays—Christmas—Fiction; Poetry. RL C.

A dozen whimsical poems reflect a child's view of the celebration of Christmas at home and in school. The illustrations of vivacious families of various races capture the humor and warmth of these holiday poems.

1708 *It's Halloween*. Ill. by Marylin Hafner. Greenwillow, 1977; Scholastic, pap., 1986. ISBN 0-688-84102-3. SERIES: Read-alone. SUBJECTS: Holidays—Halloween—Fiction; Poetry. RL C.

Excitement, fun, and a little bit of fear—necessary ingredients for a memorable Halloween night—are in these 13 poems and in the ink and wash pictures that accompany them. The poems are great fun for reading aloud and alone.

1709 *It's Thanksgiving*. Ill. by Marylin Hafner. Greenwillow, 1982; Scholastic, pap.,

Prelutsky, Jack (cont.)

1987. ISBN 0-688-00442-3. SERIES: Read-alone. SUBJECTS: Holidays—Thanksgiving; Poetry. RL C.

Twelve warm and witty poems about all aspects of Thanksgiving—from football to leftover turkey—are fun for children to read aloud or alone. The ink line drawings with orange and brown washes add to the reader's enjoyment.

1710 *Rainy Rainy Saturday*. Ill. by Marylin Hafner. Greenwillow, 1980. ISBN 0-688-84252-6. SERIES: Read-alone. SUBJECTS: Poetry; Weather—Rain. RL B.

In 14 delightful poems, children's views of the fun, boredom, or disappointment caused by rainy Saturdays are presented in rhythmic and thoughtful verses. The pencil and wash comic drawings complement the poetry.

1711 *What I Did Last Summer*. Ill. by Yossi Abolafia. Greenwillow, 1984. ISBN 0-688-01755-X. SERIES: Read-alone. SUBJECTS: Poetry; Seasons—Summer—Fiction. RL B.

In 13 poems a little boy remembers his summer: going on a picnic, having a nasty cousin visit, being sick, being hot, and so on. His memories are humorous now that he is back at school even though some of the actual events were not so funny when they were taking place. The softly colored drawings capture the emotions—especially the humor—of the delightful poetry.

Pringle, Laurence

1712 *Twist, Wiggle, and Squirm: A Book about Earthworms*. Ill. by Peter Parnall. HarperCollins, 1973, o.p. SERIES: Let's Read and Find Out. SUBJECTS: Animals—Earthworms. RL C.

From why earthworms are found on sidewalks after a heavy rainfall to details of how and where they live and what they eat, this presents an interesting look at an important form of animal life. The illustrations are detailed, realistic pen and ink drawings.

1713 *Water Plants*. Ill. by Kazue Mizumura. HarperCollins, 1975, o.p. SERIES: Let's-Read-and-Find-Out Science Books. SUBJECTS: Plants; Pond life. RL C.

One animal after another feeds and is fed upon in this story of the food chain of a freshwater pond. Readers learn a great deal about the plants of the pond as they follow the animals. Well written and very interesting, it is illustrated with realistic watercolor paintings.

Putnam, Polly

1714 *Mystery of Sara Beth*. Ill. by Judith Friedman. Follett, hb and pap., 1981. ISBN 0-8136-5116-6. SUBJECTS: Mystery and detective stories; School stories; Siblings—Twins—Fiction. RL B.

Sara Beth, the new girl, is decidedly unfriendly in spite of her classmates' attempts to welcome her. Only Becky guesses that Sara Beth is really a twin coming on different days because she and her sister share a winter coat. The multiracial class is realistically portrayed in ink and colored washes.

Q

Quackenbush, Robert

1715 *Animal Cracks*. Ill. by author. Lothrop, 1975, o.p. SERIES: Fun-to-Read. SUBJECTS: Fables; Humorous stories. RL C.

Seven short, humorous stories about animals present situations explaining well-known sayings such as "his bark is worse than his bite." All are illustrated with boldly outlined gold and black pencil sketches and are fun to read.

1716 *Calling Doctor Quack*. Ill. by author. Lothrop, 1978, o.p. SERIES: Fun-to-Read. SUBJECTS: Animals—Fiction; Doctors and nurses—Fiction; Pollution—Water—Fiction. RL C.

Dr. Quack, a duck, is besieged by patients blaming their sudden illnesses on the bad-tempered Mr. Snapping Turtle. The poor animal is sick and disagreeable because the pond has become polluted and trash has lodged in his shell. Good pictures illustrate an amusing, pointed tale.

1717 *Detective Mole*. Ill. by author. Lothrop, 1976, o.p. SERIES: Fun-to-Read. SUBJECTS:

Animals—Moles—Fiction; mystery and detective stories. RL C.

Almost as soon as he finishes detective school, Mole begins solving mysteries. The five entertaining stories here involve the animals in Mole's community and are accompanied by bold pencil drawings.

1718 *Detective Mole and the Circus Mystery.* Ill. by author. Lothrop, 1980, o.p. SERIES: Fun-to-Read. SUBJECTS: Animals—Moles—Fiction; Circuses—Fiction; Mystery and detective stories. RL C.

Melba the tatooed cow disappears from the circus the day of her marriage to Boris the bull. Mole masterfully pieces together the clues and finds Melba in time for her wedding. The illustrations, in full color with blue outlining, are as imaginative as the story.

1719 *Detective Mole and the Seashore Mystery.* Ill. by author. Lothrop, 1976, o.p. SERIES: Fun-to-Read. SUBJECTS: Animals—Moles—Fiction; Mystery and detective stories. RL C.

Called to Land's End Island to find Captain Bill's stolen pearl, Mole carefully listens for clues and discovers the culprit—a giant clam. Humorous heavy line drawings add to the seaside flavor and to the fun of the story.

1720 *Detective Mole and the Secret Clues.* Ill. by author. Lothrop, 1977, o.p. SERIES: Fun-to-Read. SUBJECTS: Animals—Moles—Fiction; Mystery and detective stories. RL C.

A mysterious stranger hands Mole a small green pea as he sets off to help the Chicken family claim their Uncle Ebenezer's mansion. Clues are easy enough for children to work out in order to solve the mystery. Animal characters are drawn in heavy blue and black pencil.

1721 *Detective Mole and the Tip-Top Mystery.* Ill. by author. Lothrop, 1978, o.p. SERIES: Fun-to-Read. SUBJECTS: Animals—Moles—Fiction; Mystery and detective stories. RL C.

Down to their last guests, Mr. and Mrs. Goat call in Mole to stop the strange occurrences that are driving guests away from their mountain lodge. Humorous pencil drawings and a bit of suspense make this an exciting mystery.

1722 *Henry Goes West.* Ill. by author. Parents Magazine Pr., 1982; Crown, pap., 1988. ISBN 0-8193-1090-5. SERIES: Read Aloud and Easy Reading. SUBJECTS: Animals—Ducks—Fiction; Humorous stories; Western stories. RL B.

Henry, a duck, misses Clara and decides to join her on her guest ranch vacation out west. When he arrives everyone is gone. As he waits for their return, Henry accidentally creates one catastrophe after another. A very funny story with a nice ending, it is illustrated in full color.

1723 *Henry's Awful Mistake.* Ill. by author. Parents Magazine Pr., 1980. ISBN 0-8368-0882-7. SERIES: Read Aloud Library. SUBJECTS: Animals—Ants—Fiction; Animals—Ducks—Fiction; Humorous stories. RL B.

Henry is cooking supper for Clara when he notices an ant. Determined to get rid of it, Henry creates havoc. He ends up bursting pipes, flooding the house, and canceling supper. Text is illustrated with energetic watercolor pictures heavily outlined in ink.

1724 *Henry's Important Date.* Ill. by author. Parents Magazine Pr., 1981. ISBN 0-8193-1068-9. SERIES: Read Aloud and Easy Reading. SUBJECTS: Animals—Ducks—Fiction; Birthdays—Fiction; Concepts—Time—Fiction. RL B.

Henry, a duck, tries his best to get to Clara's birthday party on time—but he gets stuck in traffic, locks his keys in his car, and then gets on a bus that breaks down. Poor Henry's awful day is funny but one that everyone can empathize with. Illustrated in full color with bold comic drawings.

1725 *Moose's Store.* Ill. by author. Lothrop, 1979, o.p. SERIES: Fun-to-Read. SUBJECTS: Animals—Fiction; Farm and country life—Fiction; Friendship—Fiction. RL C.

When Beaver and the other animals decide to help Moose by transforming his friendly, old-fashioned store into a deli, Moose feels uncomfortable and out of place. Bold pencil drawings are a good complement to this tale of tradition versus modernization.

1726 *Mr. Snow Bunting's Secret.* Ill. by author. Lothrop, 1978, o.p. SERIES: Fun-

Quackenbush, Robert (cont.)

to-Read. SUBJECTS: Animals—Fiction; Holidays—Christmas—Fiction. RL C.
Only able to stay until November, Mr. Snow Bunting, a bird, opens a gift-wrapping business for the Christmas season that makes Mr. Dog jealous and suspicious. When Dog accuses Snow Bunting of being a sorcerer, Dog learns Snow Bunting's secret and is embarrassed. Illustrated with humorous heavy line drawings in red and black.

1727 *No Mouse for Me*. Ill. by author. Watts, 1981, o.p. SERIES: Easy-Read Story. SUBJECTS: Animals-Mice-Fiction; Cumulative tales; Humorous stories. RL B.
A little boy returns a mouse to the pet shop demanding his money back. He claims that a mouse would attract a cat that would attract a dog and on and on until a catastrophe would occur and, anyway, he would rather have a snake. Outrageously silly, this is illustrated with bold drawings.

1728 *Pete Pack Rat*. Ill. by author. Lothrop, 1976, o.p. SERIES: Fun-to-Read. SUBJECTS: Animals—Fiction; Robbers and outlaws—Fiction; Western stories. RL C.
Pete Pack Rat repeatedly outwits the notorious outlaw Gizzard Coyote in this old west style story with desert animals as characters. Illustrated with heavy line drawings, the book has humor and suspense that should appeal to young readers.

1729 *Pete Pack Rat and the Gila Monster Gang*. Ill. by author. Lothrop, 1978, o.p. SERIES: Fun-to-Read. SUBJECTS: Animals—Fiction; Robbers and outlaws—Fiction; Western stories. RL C.
The Gila Monster Gang not only robs the Pebble Junction Bank but also kidnaps Sheriff Sally Gopher. Only Pete Pack Rat is clever enough to rescue Sally and capture the gang. The delightful old west story has bold black and purple drawings.

1730 *Sheriff Sally Gopher and the Haunted Dance Hall*. Ill. by author. Lothrop, 1977, o.p. SERIES: Fun-to-Read. SUBJECTS: Animals—Fiction; Ghost stories; Western stories. RL C.

In spite of warnings that the old dance hall is haunted, Sheriff Sally Gopher tries to get it ready for a grand performance by dancer Lola Field Mouse. Suspense and humor combine in this story of an almost haunted hall. Illustrations are black and maroon pencil drawings.

1731 *Sherlock Chick and the Giant Egg Mystery*. Ill. by author. Parents Magazine Pr., 1989. ISBN 0-8368-0897-5. SERIES: Read Aloud Originals. SUBJECTS: Animals—Chickens—Fiction; Farm and country life—Fiction; Mystery and detective stories. RL B.
When little Sherlock Chick discovers a giant egg, he quickly gets his mother hen to identify it. The egg is much too big for her to do anything but try to warm it, but mother hen sits while Sherlock figures out what is hatching from it. Humorous text and quirky colored paintings have child appeal.

1732 *Sherlock Chick and the Peekaboo Mystery*. Ill. by author. Parents Magazine Pr., 1987. ISBN 0-8193-1149-9. SERIES: Read Aloud Originals. SUBJECTS: Animals—Chickens—Fiction; Animals—Fiction; Mystery and detective stories. RL B.
Mother Mouse hires Sherlock Chick to find her lost son. As the little chick searches, he notices lots of eyes in dark places and says again and again "Peekaboo! I see you . . ." before finding the mouse. Colorful paintings have much ink detailing.

1733 *Sherlock Chick's First Case*. Ill. by author. Parents Magazine Pr., 1986. ISBN 0-8368-0892-4. SERIES: Read Aloud Originals. SUBJECTS: Animals—Chickens—Fiction; Mystery and detective stories. RL B.
Hatched wearing a detective hat, Sherlock Chick starts right in to solve the mystery of the missing corn. He follows a trail of corn and finds the culprits. Illustrated with heavily outlined watercolor pictures, the silly story is appealing.

Quin-Harkin, Janet

1734 *Helpful Hattie*. Ill. by Susanna Natti. Harcourt, 1983, o.p. SERIES: Let Me

Read. SUBJECTS: Birthdays—Fiction; Haircutting—Fiction; Human Body—Teeth—Fiction. RL A.

Hattie has lots of ideas and little patience, which sometimes leads to trouble. She frosts her birthday cake with catsup, cuts her own hair, and disrupts her class picture-taking with her lost tooth. A funny story illustrated with droll ink line drawings.

1735 *Magic Growing Powder*. Ill. by Art Cumings. Parents Magazine Pr., 1980. ISBN 0-8193-1038-7. SUBJECTS: Fairy tales; Magic—Fiction; Self-esteem—Fiction. RL B.

King Max hates being short and will do just about anything to be taller. He is ready to give away half his kingdom and his daughter to two tricksters for their growing powder. Princess Penny cleverly outwits the two tricksters and saves the kingdom. Illustrated with humorous full color pictures.

Quinlan, Patricia

1736 *Anna's Red Sled*. Ill. by Lindsay Grater. Firefly, hb and pap., 1989. ISBN 1-55037-073-1. SUBJECTS: Parent and child—Fiction; Seasons—Winter—Fiction; Sports—Sledding—Fiction. RL B.

Mom wants to sell Anna's old red sled at the bazaar but Anna refuses to let her. Instead Anna takes it to the park and starts remembering all the times she and mother shared when she was only three. Soft watercolors and a quiet text work well in this story.

R

Rabinowitz, Sandy

1737 *How I Trained My Colt*. Ill. by author. Doubleday, 1980, o.p.; Bantam, pap., 1991. ISBN 0-553-15848-1. SERIES: Reading On My Own. SUBJECTS: Animals—Horses—Training; Pets—Horses. RL B.

On the day of Sunny's birth, the colt's training begins. Told in the first person, the story shows how much patience and care go into the training of a horse during its first year. As a story or a horse-training book, this is very well done. Good watercolor illustrations.

Radford, Ruby

1738 *Robert Fulton*. Ill. by Salem Tamer. Putnam, 1970, o.p. SERIES: See and Read Beginning to Read Biography. SUBJECTS: Art and artists; Biographies; Inventors and inventions. RL B.

Trained as an artist and a craftsman, Robert Fulton invented many things, including a submarine called the *Nautilus*, before he gained fame with the steamboat. Although fictionalized conversations are added, a good portrait of a brilliant man is still provided. Realistic ink drawings.

The Random House Book of Easy-to-Read Stories

1739 *The Random House Book of Easy-to-Read Stories*. Dr. Seuss, Richard Scarry, et al. Random House, 1993. ISBN 0-679-83438-9. SUBJECTS: Stories. RL B.

Sixteen popular books for beginning readers by such authors as Dr. Seuss, the Berenstains, and P. D. Eastman, illustrated by artists such as Tomie de Paola and Marc Brown, are presented here either in their entirety or excerpted. Format and selections are sure to be winners.

Rappaport, Doreen

1740 *The Boston Coffee Party*. Ill. by Emily A. McCully. HarperCollins, 1988. ISBN 0-06-024825-4. SERIES: I Can Read Books. SUBJECTS: Historical fiction; United States—Revolution—Fiction. RL C.

When Thomas, a greedy merchant, locks away all his coffee until the price rises, the women of Boston decide to hold a coffee "party" and break into his warehouse. Based on an actual occurrence, this story could lead children to a discussion of ethics. Illustrated with ink and wash sketches.

Reidel, Marlene

1741 *From Egg to Bird*. Ill. by author. Carolrhoda, 1981. ISBN 0-87614-159-9. SERIES:

Reidel, Marlene (cont.)

Start to Finish. SUBJECTS: Animals—
Birds; Animals—Reproduction. RL B.
The process of rearing young birds, from nest-
building to the time of the young birds' depar-
ture, is told very simply and nicely. Text is
perfectly coordinated with the artwork, full-
color paintings of birds raising their young.
Paintings are somewhat stylized but clearly
depict their subject.

Reit, Seymour

1742 *The Rebus Bears.* Ill. by Kenneth Smith.
Bantam, 1989. ISBN 0-553-05822-3.
SERIES: Bank Street Ready-to-Read.
SUBJECTS: Folklore; Rebuses. RL A.
Picture clues behind or next to words will help
beginning readers handle this very familiar
Goldilocks folktale. Although this is longer
than most of the very easy books for young
readers, the combination of a familiar story
and rather large full color rebus illustrations
makes it accessible.

1743 *Things That Go: A Traveling Alphabet.*
Ill. by Fulvio Testa. Bantam, hb and
pap., 1990. ISBN 0-553-05856-8. SERIES:
Bank Street Ready-to-Read. SUBJECTS:
Alphabet; Vehicles. RL B.
Surprisingly full of descriptive information, this
alphabet book covers all kinds of land, sea, and
air vehicles including an ambulance, a garbage
truck, and a spaceship. The illustrations are
detailed and fun, and augment the text.

Renard, Judith E.

1744 *Animals of the High Mountains.* Photos.
National Geographic, 1989, o.p. SERIES:
Books for Young Explorers. SUBJECTS:
Animals—Alpine; Mountains. RL B.
Divided according to continents of the world,
this look at mountain animals highlights a
variety of them including marmots, ibex, gua-
nacos, chamois, and snow leopards. Lush color
photographs will entice young readers while
the notes to adults give needed additional
information.

Retan, Walter

1745 *Armies of Ants.* Ill. by Jean Cassels.
Scholastic, pap., 1994. ISBN 0-590-

47616-5. SERIES: Hello Reader! SUBJECTS:
Animals—Ants; Animals—Insects. RL C.
This fascinating look at a number of ant varieties and their lives touches on food gathering
and production, rearing of young, and interaction with other ant species. Watercolor art is
detailed and important to the lengthy text.

Ricciuti, Edward R.

1746 *An Animal for Alan.* Ill. by Tom Eaton.
HarperCollins, 1970, o.p. SERIES: Science
I Can Read. SUBJECTS: Pets; Pets—Wild
animals. RL B.
In trying to select the perfect pet, Alan slowly
learns that most wild animals are not meant to
be pets. Alan's father suggests that he might
like a dog or a cat. The animals are realistically portrayed in ink and colored pencil drawings and the story has a good message for
children.

1747 *Catch a Whale by the Tail.* Ill. by
Geoffrey Moss. HarperCollins, 1969,
o.p. SERIES: Science I Can Read. SUBJECTS:
Animals—Whales. RL C.
Hoping to find a way to get Robert, a Beluga
whale, to sing or whistle, his curator heads
to the far north to find a mate for him. Readers are taken on a whaling expedition and
given good information on the Beluga whale.
Illustrated with exuberant blue and brown
sketches.

1748 *Donald and the Fish That Walked.* Ill. by
Syd Hoff. HarperCollins, 1974, o.p.
SERIES: Science I Can Read. SUBJECTS:
Animals—Fish; Conservation. RL B.
Donald thinks the walking catfish that begin to
appear in his neighborhood are fun. Then Mr.
Walter explains that they were brought from
Asia and are driving out other fish. A thought-
provoking look at a conservation problem, this
story is illustrated in a cartoon style.

Rice, Eve

1749 *Mr. Brimble's Hobby and Other Stories.*
Ill. by author. Greenwillow, 1975, o.p.
SERIES: Read-alone. SUBJECTS: Family
life—Fiction. RL C.
What first seems to be a very traditional fami-
ly is far more. All of its members are strong

individuals who value themselves and each other and together create enjoyable stories of a loving family. The simple warmth of the ink and wash drawings are a perfect complement to the text.

1750 *Once in a Wood: Ten Fables from Aesop.* Ill. by author. Greenwillow, 1979, o.p. SERIES: Read-alone. SUBJECTS: Fables. RL B.
The essence of Aesop is captured in Rice's adaptations of ten familiar fables. Each is carefully constructed with a final few lines devoted to a rhyming moral. The illustrations are very detailed, whimsical black and white drawings.

1751 *Papa's Lemonade and Other Stories.* Ill. by author. Greenwillow, 1976, o.p. SERIES: Read-alone. SUBJECTS: Animals—Dogs— Fiction; Family life—Fiction. RL B.
Papa and Mama dog and their five pups share gentle yet whimsical adventures that include trying to find a substitute for a broken bank, going for a walk in the country, and making lemonade with oranges. Ink drawings of very humanized animals are given soft color washes.

Richardson, Joy

1752 *Air.* Photos. Watts, 1992. ISBN 0-531-14201-9. SERIES: Picture Science. SUBJECTS: Air; Science. RL C.
What air means to human beings, animals, plants, airplanes, and so on is discussed in brief chapters with one page of text and one color photograph. Occasional painted diagrams extend and help explain the text. An index is included.

1753 *Day and Night.* Photos. Watts, 1991. ISBN 0-531-14139-X. SERIES: Picture Science. SUBJECTS: Day; Night. RL C.
First observing how day and night are experienced, the author then explains how the earth's turning creates daytime and nighttime. Clear explanations are presented in a rather dull format with color photographs. Index is included.

1754 *Rocks and Soil.* Photos. Watts, 1992. ISBN 0-531-14206-X. SERIES: Picture Science. SUBJECTS: Geology and geologists. RL C.

How soil, mountains, oil, coal, crystals, and other materials are formed is given brief but clear coverage. A textbookish format with grainy color photographs makes this less appealing than other books. Index is included.

1755 *The Seasons.* Photos. Watts, 1991. ISBN 0-531-14158-6. SERIES: Picture Science. SUBJECTS: Seasons. RL C.
Through textbookish color photographs and some explanatory diagrams, a look at how the world changes from season to season is presented along with some brief explanatory paragraphs on how the movement of the earth around the sun causes the changes. Index is included.

1756 *The Water Cycle.* Photos. Watts, 1992. ISBN 0-531-14205-1. SERIES: Picture Science. SUBJECTS: Science; Water. RL C.
The water cycle, water purification, and principles of water are covered without great depth, at a level suitable for most beginning readers. Format and bland color photographs have a textbookish look. Index is included.

1757 *The Weather.* Photos. Watts, 1992. ISBN 0-531-14164-0. SERIES: Picture Science. SUBJECTS: Weather. RL C.
The formation of rain, snow, frost, and fog; weather forecasting; and the climate are all covered in this brief look at the various aspects of weather. Rather dull format and mediocre color photographs lessen the appeal of the book.

1758 *What Happens When You Breathe?* Ill. by Colin Maclean and Moira Maclean. Stevens, 1986, o.p. SERIES: What Happens When . . . ? SUBJECTS: Human body—Respiration. RL C.
A clear, easily understood text helps children learn how breathing works. Simple experiments simulate or measure the lung's activities and further clarify the respiration process. An index and a bibliography are included. Illustrated with colored diagrams and drawings.

1759 *What Happens When You Eat?* Ill. by Colin Maclean and Moira Maclean. Stevens, 1986, o.p. SERIES: What Happens When . . . ? SUBJECTS: Human body—Digestion. RL C.
This explanation of digestion is clear and easily understood. Colored diagrams and draw-

Richardson, Joy (cont.)

ings help show how food reaches the stomach and goes through the intestines. A bibliography and an index are included.

1760 *What Happens When You Listen?* Ill. by Colin Maclean and Moira Maclean. Stevens, 1986, o.p. SERIES: What Happens When . . . ? SUBJECTS: Human body—Ears; Senses—Hearing. RL C.
A clear, straightforward text helps children understand how ears work. A number of simple experiments are also suggested. There is an index, a bibliography, and a list of nonbook sources for additional information. Colored diagrams and drawings aid in conveying the message.

1761 *What Happens When You Sleep?* Ill. by Colin Maclean and Moira Maclean. Stevens, 1986, o.p. SERIES: What Happens When . . . ? SUBJECTS: Human body—Sleep; Sleep. RL B.
Basic information about how and why people sleep, dream, and wake up is conveyed in a simple writing style. A few experiments are suggested along with some questions to prod young readers. Included is a bibliography, a subject index, and an experiment and question index. Attractive full color pictures.

Richter, Alice, and Numeroff, Laura J.

1762 *You Can't Put Braces on Spaces.* Ill. by Laura J. Numeroff. Greenwillow, 1979, o.p. SERIES: Read-alone. SUBJECTS: Human body—Teeth—Fiction; Orthodontics—Fiction. RL B.
A little boy can hardly wait for his teeth to grow in so that he can have braces like his brother and other older children. Good information on orthodontia is given as the older brother goes to have his braces put on. Boldly outlined pictures are flat and childlike but lively.

Rickard, Graham

1763 *Tractors.* Ill. by Clifford Meadway. Bookwright, 1988, o.p. SERIES: Let's Look At. SUBJECTS: Farm and Country Life; Tractors. RL C.

After presenting a brief history of the tractor, the machine's many uses and types are then looked at. Rickard also includes a thoughtful section on some of the disadvantages of modern farming methods. Illustrated with realistic watercolor paintings. Includes a brief glossary.

Ridlon, Marci

1764 *A Frog Sandwich: Riddles and Jokes.* Ill. by Pat Dypold. Follett, 1973, o.p. SERIES: Beginning to Read. SUBJECTS: Jokes and riddles. RL B.
The 33 riddles and jokes that are presented in this book are well known to older children and adults. However, these riddles and jokes will still be fun for the reader encountering them for the first time. They are illustrated with appropriately silly ink and wash pictures.

1765 *Kittens and More Kittens.* Ill. by Liz Dauber. Follett, 1967, o.p. SERIES: Beginning to Read. SUBJECTS: Animals—Cats—Fiction; Pets—Cats—Fiction. RL A.
Finally old enough to own a pet, Jennifer Joan posts flyers in her neighborhood asking for a kitten and even gets into the newspaper. The inevitable donations of kittens occur and the little girl is fortunate to find someone to take them. Illustrated with colorful, attractive paintings.

Riehecky, Janet

1766 *Anatosaurus.* Ill. by Diana Magnuson. Child's World, hb and pap., 1989. ISBN 0-89565-545-4. SERIES: Dinosaur Books. SUBJECTS: Dinosaurs. RL C.
A dinosaur about which much is known because two mummified bodies have been found, the plant-eating anatosaurus is thought to have been able to swim. Carefully written, this book is illustrated with watercolor pictures of the duck-billed dinosaur.

1767 *Brachiosaurus.* Ill. by Jim Conaway. Child's World, hb and pap., 1989. ISBN 0-89565-542-X. SERIES: Dinosaur Books. SUBJECTS: Dinosaurs. RL C.
About 43 feet tall and weighing over 85 tons, the brachiosaurus was one of the biggest dinosaurs. Speculation about the animal's habits and herd life is presented as such. Infor-

mation on current discoveries of dinosaurs that may have been larger is also given. Watercolor pictures accompany the text.

1768 *Cooperation*. Ill. by Kathryn Hutton. Child's World, hb and pap., 1990. ISBN 0-89565-565-9. SERIES: Values to Live By. SUBJECTS: Behavior—Cooperative. RL B.
Twin boys and their Asian American family and multicultural friends demonstrate the many ways in which people can cooperate. Meant to reinforce and encourage positive values, the book is illustrated with sweet watercolor paintings with pencil definition.

1769 *Good Sportsmanship*. Ill. by Christina Rigo. Child's World, hb and pap., 1990. ISBN 0-89565-563-2. SERIES: Values to Live By. SUBJECTS: Behavior—Sportsmanship; Values. RL B.
A little girl demonstrates the many ways to be a good sport: with friends, playing a game; at school. The rather saccharine watercolor illustrations help the very brief text reinforce the book's message.

1770 *Iguanodon*. Ill. by Diana Magnuson. Child's World, hb and pap., 1989. ISBN 0-89565-544-6. SERIES: Dinosaur Books. SUBJECTS: Dinosaurs. RL C.
The first dinosaur discovered (1822), the iguanodon was first thought to resemble a rhinoceros. The story of its finding and attempts to identify it make fascinating and lively reading. The tone of the book is light but scientific. Text is illustrated with watercolors.

1771 *Maiasaura*. Ill. by Diana Magnuson. Child's World, hb and pap., 1989. ISBN 0-89565-543-8. SERIES: Dinosaur Books. SUBJECTS: Dinosaurs. RL C.
A duck-billed dinosaur, the maiasaura, built nests for its young and watched over them until they could be independent. In 1978 remains of over 10,000 maiasaura were found in Montana. An interesting mix of information, the text is accompanied by watercolor pictures.

1772 *Saving the Forests: A Rabbit's Story*. Ill. by Linda Hohag and Lori Jacobson. Child's World, 1990. ISBN 0-89565-561-6. SERIES: Discovery World: First Steps to Science. SUBJECTS: Animals—Fiction; Conservation—Fiction; Pollution—Fiction. RL B.
Through a very anthropomorphized rabbit, the story of the destruction of a forest and its animals is told. Far from polished, the art is "cute" with its watercolor animals and childlike paintings of nature. Yet children will understand the message and enjoy the reinforcing experiments.

1773 *Snow: When Will It Fall?* Ill. by Joy Friedman. Child's World, 1990. ISBN 0-89565-560-8. SERIES: Discovery World: First Steps to Science. SUBJECTS: Weather—Snow. RL B.
The importance of snow to plants and animals, the problems it can create, the structure of snowflakes, and experiments are all included in this look at one aspect of weather. Illustrated with pencil and watercolors. Index is included.

1774 *What Plants Give Us: The Gift of Life*. Ill. by Rondi Collette. Child's World, 1990. ISBN 0-89565-570-5. SERIES: Discovery World: First Steps to Science. SUBJECTS: Plants. RL B.
Beautifully illustrated with detailed watercolors set into artfully designed frames, this book has a slightly more difficult and lengthier text than others in the series. It explores the ways in which plants help people and the text is followed by a section of experiments.

Rinkoff, Barbara

1775 *Guess What Rocks Do*. Ill. by Leslie Morrill. Lothrop, 1975, o.p. SERIES: Guess What . . . SUBJECTS: Geology. RL B.
An appreciation rather than a scientific look at rocks is presented. The book shows the many ways humans have used rocks—as weapons, for building, and for grinding. The illustrations give the reader a sense of time passing with realistic figures drawn against swaths of rust or olive.

1776 *Guess What Trees Do*. Ill. by Beatrice Darwin. Lothrop, 1974, o.p. SERIES: Guess What . . . SUBJECTS: Plants—Trees. RL C.
An appreciation of the many things that trees do for people rather than a botanical study of trees, the text reminds readers that trees provide oxygen, sap for maple syrup, wood for

Rinkoff, Barbara (cont.)

furniture, and much more. The illustrations, which add little to the text, are in turquoise, black, and olive.

1777 *No Pushing, No Ducking: Safety in the Water*. Ill. by Roy Doty. Lothrop, 1974, o.p. SUBJECTS: Boats and boating; Safety; Sports—Swimming. RL B.
A girl surprises her show-offish friend Tom with her knowledge of water safety and her swimming skill. The book offers a humorous but very effective approach to water safety—swimming or boating—and includes a list of water safety rules. It is nicely illustrated with cartoonlike pictures.

1778 *Rutherford T. Finds 21B*. Ill. by Tomie dePaola. Putnam, 1970, o.p. SERIES: See and Read. SUBJECTS: Moving, household—Fiction; School stories. RL B.
Rutherford bravely heads for school alone but cannot find his room. New to the area, he asks a succession of children for directions and all of them end up helping him not only to find the room but to feel less like a newcomer. Illustrated with simple taupe and blue pictures.

Robbins, Ken

1779 *Make Me a Peanut Butter Sandwich and a Glass of Milk*. Ill. by author. Scholastic, 1992. ISBN 0-590-43550-7. SUBJECTS: Food; Farm and country life. RL B.
The production of peanut butter, bread, and milk—from farm to the store to the table—is shown in hand-tinted photographs and explained in an understandable text. The attractive format will invite readers to learn just how much work is involved in the production of favorite foods.

Robert, Adrian

1780 *The "Awful Mess" Mystery*. Ill. by Paul Harvey. Troll, hb and pap., 1985. ISBN 0-8167-0402-3. SUBJECTS: Clubs—Fiction; Mystery and detective stories. RL B.
After Katie tries on her mother's new bracelet, she loses it, creating an awful mess. Katie's fellow club members help her retrace her steps, and they finally find the bracelet. The detect-

ing in this story is complex enough to interest young readers. Illustrated with very simple, childlike pictures.

Robins, Joan

1781 *Addie Meets Max*. Ill. by Sue Truesdell. HarperCollins, 1985; pap., 1988. ISBN 0-06-025064-X. SERIES: Early I Can Read. SUBJECTS: Friendship—Fiction; Moving, household—Fiction; Pets—Dogs—Fiction. RL A.
Addie's new neighbor Max seems unfriendly and so does his dog Ginger until Addie gets a chance to know them. Lively watercolor paintings expressively illustrate this light but realistic story of a blossoming friendship.

1782 *Addie Runs Away*. Ill. by Sue Truesdell. HarperCollins, 1989. ISBN 0-06-025080-1. SERIES: Early I Can Read. SUBJECTS: Behavior—Running away—Fiction; Friendship—Fiction. RL A.
Awakened by his dog Ginger, Max discovers that his neighbor—and friend—Addie is running away from home rather than going to camp. Max finally convinces her and himself that camp is not so bad. Expressive watercolor pictures add a light touch to a story about misunderstanding.

1783 *Addie's Bad Day*. Ill. by Sue Truesdell. HarperCollins, 1993. ISBN 0-06-021298-5. SERIES: I Can Read Books. SUBJECTS: Birthdays—Fiction; Friendship—Fiction; Haircutting—Fiction. RL B.
Addy is mortified! Her new haircut is awful, she refuses to take off her hat and will not go to Max's birthday party. But good friend Max finds just the right way to get Addie to have fun again. Lively and realistic, this story is illustrated with sketchy, humorous ink-and-wash pictures.

Robinson, Fay

1784 *A Frog Inside My Hat: A First Book of Poems*. Ill. by Cyd Moore. BridgeWater, hb and pap., 1993. ISBN 0-8167-3129-2. SUBJECTS: Poets and poetry. RL B.
Lively, attractive, full of humorous poems and sprightly illustrations, this collection is perfect for introducing beginning readers to the best

of poetry and poets. Included are selections by Ciardi, McCord, Lear, Nikki Giovanni, Prelutsky, Milne, and other well-known poets.

1785 *A Ghost in the Toy Box*. Ill. by Ann Iosa. Childrens Pr., 1992. ISBN 0-516-02371-3. SERIES: Bear & Alligator Tales. SUBJECTS: Animals—Hamsters; Toys. RL A.
When Ape hears a strange noise in the toy box, Bear and Alligator decide to investigate. Though Alligator runs away when he hears it, Bear bravely opens the lid to let Hamster out. The story is illustrated in cartoonlike watercolors with pencil definition.

1786 *Old MacDonald Had a Farm*. Ill. by Ann Iosa. Childrens Pr., 1993. ISBN 0-516-02372-1. SERIES: Bear & Alligator Tales. SUBJECTS: Music—Fiction; Toys—Fiction; Toys—Teddy Bears—Fiction. RL A.
After spending the day at school with his little girl, a teddy bear teaches the other toy animals how to sing their own special version of "Old MacDonald." The short, repetitive text has pencil-and-watercolor illustrations.

1787 *Pizza Soup*. Ill. by Ann Iosa. Childrens Pr., 1993. ISBN 0-516-02373-X. SERIES: Bear & Alligator Tales. SUBJECTS: Cookery—Fiction; Stories in rhyme. RL B.
Father and daughter go shopping for ingredients for their favorite pizza soup and then make it and serve it. A lively, repetitive rhyming text and active pencil-and-watercolor pictures will draw children in, as will the inclusion of the recipe.

1788 *Real Bears and Alligators*. Photos. Ill. by Ann Iosa. Childrens Pr., 1992. ISBN 0-516-02374-8. SERIES: Bear & Alligator Tales. SUBJECTS: Animals—Alligators and crocodiles; Animals—Bears; Toys—Fiction. RL A.
Series characters, illustrated with comic watercolor paintings, decide to find out which is better: alligators or bears. The body of the book is made up of alternating, often grainy, photographs of the two animals and comparisons of their behavior, life cycle, and food.

1789 *Sound All Around*. Photos. Childrens Pr., 1994. ISBN 0-516-06024-4. SERIES: Rookie Read-About Science. SUBJECTS: Sound. RL B.

Using a minimal number of words and full color photographs, the concept of sound is explained in terms that a beginning reader can understand. Index is included.

1790 *When Nicki Went Away*. Ill. by Ann Iosa. Childrens Pr., 1992. ISBN 0-516-02376-4. SERIES: Bear & Alligator Tales. SUBJECTS: Toys—Fiction. RL A.
With their little girl gone for a week, her toy animals have a great time playing and messing up the house. Just before she returns they all pitch in and clean the house. Text is illustrated with humorous watercolor pictures.

Robinson, Marileta

1791 *Mr. Goat's Bad Good Idea: Three Stories*. Ill. by Arthur Getz. HarperCollins, 1977. ISBN 0-690-03864-X. SUBJECTS: Animals—Fiction; Native Americans—Navajos—Fiction. RL B.
In the first of three entertaining stories set in Navajo country, lazy Mr. Goat tries to get dirt for his hogan from other animals. Instead of less work, this cumulative tale shows he has far more. The other two stories are quiet yet fun. Illustrated with engaging ink and wash pictures.

Robison, Nancy

1792 *Izoo*. Ill. by Edward Frascino. Lothrop, 1980, o.p. SERIES: Fun-to-Read. SUBJECTS: Science fiction; Zoos—Fiction. RL B.
On their way to a space show, Max and Charlie are picked up by aliens and transported to their ice zoo; they escape just before they are to be cloned. Comical yet suitably sinister drawings add to the fun of this science fiction adventure.

1793 *The Mystery at Hilltop Camp*. Ill. by Ethel Gold. Garrard, 1979, o.p. SERIES: Garrard Mystery. SUBJECTS: Camps and camping—Fiction; Mystery and detective stories. RL B.
Equipped with her detective's magnifying glass, Patty is sure she can solve the mystery of the camp's missing milk. Although lacking real suspense, this is still a story that children will be comfortable reading. Illustrated with realistic pencil drawings in turquoise and chartreuse.

Robison, Nancy (cont.)

1794 *Space Hijack!* Ill. by Edward Frascino. Lothrop, 1979, o.p. SERIES: Fun-to-Read. SUBJECTS: Science fiction. RL B.

While Mark and Ted are on their way to the moon with their prize-winning experiment, their ship is hijacked by an invisible alien who wants their atomic batteries. The two boys outwit the invisible man and finally return to Earth. Illustrated with comical ink and wash sketches.

1795 *UFO Kidnap!* Ill. by Edward Frascino. Lothrop, 1978, o.p. SERIES: Fun-to-Read. SUBJECTS: Science fiction; UFOs—Fiction. RL A.

Roy and Barney are mistaken for interplanetary jewel thieves and are taken to another planet. When the stolen gem appears, Roy is designated the new ruler of the planet. In the end the boys use the gem's power to escape and get home. Illustrated with humorously weird comic line drawings.

Roche, P. K.

1796 *Webster and Arnold and the Giant Box*. Ill. by author. Dial, 1980. ISBN 0-8037-9436-3. SERIES: Dial Easy-to-Read. SUBJECTS: Animals—Mice—Fiction; Imagination—Fiction; Sibling rivalry—Fiction. RL B.

Two little mouse brothers find a large box and let their imaginations run wild as they play at being cave dwellers, engineers on an African train, restaurant owners, and more. The story is nicely illustrated with soft pastel drawings outlined in ink.

Rocklin, Joanne

1797 *Three Smart Pals*. Ill. by Denise Brunkus. Scholastic, pap., 1994. ISBN 0-590-47431-6. SERIES: Hello Reader! SUBJECTS: Friendship—Fiction; Humorous stories. RL B.

Three smart pals are actually three very silly friends as they use their brains to conclude that Mr. Bing does not need to mention the word *fish* on his store sign, that green is the perfect color for lunch, and so on. Text is illustrated with cartoonish paintings.

Rockwell, Anne

1798 *A Bear, a Bobcat, and Three Ghosts*. Ill. by author. Macmillan, 1977, o.p. SERIES: Ready-to-Read. SUBJECTS: Ghost stories; Holidays—Halloween—Fiction. RL B.

Three strange ghosts lead Timothy Todd, the miller and his wife, and Widow Wilson on a chase through the woods in search of three missing children. Flat, childlike ink drawings with washes of orange create a suitably "spooky" effect.

1799 *Big Bad Goat*. Ill. by author. Dutton, 1982, o.p. SERIES: Smart Cat. SUBJECTS: Animals—Fiction; Humorous stories. RL B.

In this very brief story, Tommy goes from larger to larger animal trying to get one of them to help him get Big Bad Goat out of the flower garden. When all have refused, a bee stings Goat and Goat finally leaves. The simple ink and watercolor pictures are childlike and appealing.

1800 *Big Boss*. Ill. by author. Macmillan, 1975, o.p.; pap., 1985, o.p. SERIES: Ready-to-Read. SUBJECTS: Animals—Frogs and toads—Fiction; Animals—Tigers—Fiction; Folklore—China. RL B.

A clever little frog outwits a huge tiger by claiming he is the Big Boss who eats tigers for dinner. Whimsical ink and watercolor pictures have a primitive look that fits this folk story well.

1801 *The Bump in the Night*. Ill. by author. Greenwillow, 1979, o.p. SERIES: Read-alone. SUBJECTS: Folklore—Spain; Ghost stories. RL B.

Based on a Spanish folktale, the story has Toby, a boy who likes to fix things, agree to spend the night in a castle and face its ghost. His courage never wanes as the ghost, appearing in pieces, tests him. Flat, childlike ink drawings with yellow and brown are well suited to the story.

1802 *The Gollywhopper Egg*. Ill. by author. Macmillan, 1974, o.p.; pap., 1986, o.p. SERIES: Ready-to-Read. SUBJECTS: Tall tales. RL C.

Timothy Todd sells a farmer a coconut telling him it is the egg of the Gollywhopper, a bird as big as a cow and as strong as a mule, which has unlimited talent. The simple, flat ink drawings have a primitive charm and humor that is perfect for the story.

1803 *Honk Honk!* Ill. by author. Dutton, 1980, o.p. SERIES: Smart Cat. SUBJECTS: Animals—Geese—Fiction; Farm and country life—Fiction. RL B.

Gray Goose nips Billy Boy and the barnyard animals. After a chase the ornery goose flees to the pond, safe from everyone's anger. The brief text has flat, childlike pictures that are attractive and full of the story's vigor and humor.

1804 *No More Work*. Ill. by author. Greenwillow, 1976, o.p. SERIES: Read-alone. SUBJECTS: Animals—Monkeys—Fiction; Boats and boating—Fiction; Mythical creatures—Fiction. RL B.

Trying to escape from hard work and boring food, the three little monkeys run away from their ship and land on an island with a dragon ready to eat them. Shipboard life has new appeal for the three as they head back. The very simple and childlike watercolor pictures are just right.

1805 *The Story Snail*. Ill. by author. Macmillan, 1974, o.p.; pap., 1987, o.p. SERIES: Ready-to-Read. SUBJECTS: Fantasy; Self-esteem—Fiction; Storytelling—Fiction. RL B.

Though kind and good, John seems to have no special talent until he meets a very unusual silver snail who gives him 100 stories to tell. Tired of repeatedly telling them, John gains confidence as he searches for other tales. The book has simple, childlike drawings with pastel washes.

1806 *Thump Thump Thump!* Ill. by author. Dutton, 1981, o.p. SERIES: Smart Cat. SUBJECTS: Folklore—United States; Monsters—Fiction. RL B.

Using the simplest language, the familiar story of the "hairy toe"—a monster coming to reclaim his missing toe—is nicely paced and retold. Illustrations are childlike and not too scary.

1807 *Timothy Todd's Good Things Are Gone*. Ill. by author. Macmillan, 1978, o.p. SERIES: Ready-to-Read. SUBJECTS: Mystery and detective stories. RL B.

Running from a thunderstorm, Timothy Todd takes refuge in an apparently deserted house and falls asleep. When he awakens, his pack full of goods is gone and he sets off to find it. The story is ably illustrated with Rockwell's easily recognizable, uncluttered ink and wash drawings.

1808 *Up a Tall Tree*. Ill. by Jim Arnosky. Doubleday, 1981, o.p. SERIES: Reading On My Own. SUBJECTS: Fantasy; Monsters—Fiction. RL B.

Nick, the son of poor woodcutters, discovers a bottle with a little monster inside. After setting it free, Nick is rewarded with three berries that can turn any metal into gold. This gift makes his family rich. Ink and pencil drawings show an incongruously modern family of woodcutters.

1809 *Walking Shoes*. Ill. by author. Doubleday, 1980, o.p. SERIES: Reading On My Own. SUBJECTS: Fairy tales; Houses—Fiction. RL A.

Lonely, neglected, and unwanted, the little house is granted magic walking shoes and uses them to go in search of people who will really love her. The simple story has childlike line drawings with red and green washes.

Rockwell, Anne, and Brion, David

1810 *Space Vehicles*. Ill. by author. Dutton, 1994. ISBN 0-525-45270-2. SUBJECTS: Astronomy and astronomers; Space travel. RL B.

After a kitten watches a spaceship blast off, she explains some of the things done in the space program and identifies things that astronauts do and use. She ends by saying she wants to be an astronaut one day. Good childlike illustrations and simple text clearly explain the subject.

Rockwell, Anne, and Rockwell, Harlow

1811 *Blackout*. Ill. by authors. Macmillan, 1979, o.p. SERIES: Ready-to-Read. SUBJECTS: Blackouts, electric power failures—Fiction; Emergencies—Fiction; Family life—Fiction. RL B.

An ice storm and broken power lines mean Dan and his family must find ways to stay

**Rockwell, Anne, and
Rockwell, Harlow (cont.)**

warm for three days with no heat and electricity. The story realistically presents a family
doing its best during very difficult times. Illustrated with simple pictures that underscore
the story's seriousness.

1812 *The Night We Slept Outside.* Ill. by Anne
Rockwell. Macmillan, 1983; pap., 1986,
o.p. SERIES: Ready-to-Read. SUBJECTS:
Camps and camping—Fiction;
Emotions—Fear—Fiction; Night—
Fiction. RL B.
Anxious to try out their new sleeping bags,
two brothers spend the night on their deck
and are frightened by the night noises and
animals. Ink drawings with dark blue and
gray watercolors capture the feeling of night
outdoors while the story effectively shows
children trying to combat fears.

1813 *Out to Sea.* Ill. by authors. Macmillan,
1980, o.p. SERIES: Ready-to-Read.
SUBJECTS: Boats and boating—Fiction;
Emergencies—Fiction. RL B.
Two children playing in a boat are washed out
to sea. Their desperate parents get the Coast
Guard to try to rescue them in this suspenseful and realistic story. The simple yet effective
ink drawings have aqua and gray washes.

Rockwell, Harlow

1814 *I Did It.* Ill. by author. Macmillan, 1974,
o.p.; pap., 1987. ISBN 0-689-71126-3.
SERIES: Ready-to-Read. SUBJECTS: Arts and
crafts. RL B.
Children explain how to create something they
have enjoyed making: a paperbag mask, a bean
mosaic, a papier-mache fish, a paper airplane,
invisible messages, and bread. Although no
special safety precautions are given, the simple
ink pictures show children working with adult
supervision.

1815 *Look at This.* Ill. by author. Macmillan,
1978, o.p.; pap., 1987. ISBN 0-689-71165-
4. SERIES: Ready-to-Read. SUBJECTS: Arts
and crafts. RL B.
Three children from different families explain
how to make a dancing frog, applesauce, and
a noisemaker. The instructions and the pic-

tures accompanying them are clear and are
easy for young children to follow.

Ronai, Lili

1816 *Corals.* Ill. by Arabelle Wheatley.
HarperCollins, 1976, o.p. SERIES: Let's-
Read-and-Find-Out. SUBJECTS: Oceans
and ocean life. RL C.
By means of an imaginary underwater journey through coral reefs and atolls and along
the ocean floor, readers learn about corals and
the ocean life around them. Simple ink and
watercolor pictures are attractive and extend
the information in the text.

Roop, Peter, and Roop, Connie

1817 *Keep the Lights Burning, Abbie.* Ill. by
Peter E. Hanson. Carolrhoda, 1985. ISBN
0-87614-275-7. SERIES: On My Own.
SUBJECTS: Behavior—Brave—Fiction;
Historical fiction; Lighthouses—
Fiction. RL B.
For four weeks in 1856 a ferocious storm
delays Abbie's father's return to their island
lighthouse home. Young Abbie keeps the lights
burning and tends to her ill mother until her
father finally gets through to them. Excellent
watercolors illustrate this understated tale of
bravery.

1818 *Snips the Tinker.* Ill. by Craig M. Brown.
Milliken, hb and pap., 1990. ISBN 0-
88335-785-2. SERIES: Reading Well.
SUBJECTS: Fairy tales. RL B.
Snips notices that the people in the kingdom
he visits have no money and poor supplies
because taxes are so high. To show the king
how hard the taxes are on his people, Snips
gives him a gift that teaches him a lesson.
Watercolors with pointillistic definition accompany the text.

Rosen, Ellsworth

1819 *Spiders Are Spinners.* Ill. by Teco
Slagboom. Houghton Mifflin, 1968, o.p.
SUBJECTS: Animals—Spiders. RL C.
Using a rhyming text, Rosen discusses a vari-
ety of spiders and webs without much atten-
tion to detail or specifics. The verse and

carefully created pencil drawings act as an invitation to further reading about arachnids and should work well with children.

Rosen, Sidney

1820 *How Far Is a Star?* Ill. by Dean Lindberg Carolrhoda, 1992. ISBN 0-87614-684-1. SERIES: Question of Science. SUBJECTS: Astronomy and astronomers; Space. RL C.
A conversational tone using questions and answers posed by a child and answered by an adult is used to explain about stars, distance in space, supernovas, and so forth. Cartoon illustrations are combined with photographs to create a jumbled look with much child appeal. Glossary is included.

1821 *Where Does the Moon Go?* Ill. by Dean Lindberg. Carolrhoda, 1992. ISBN 0-87614-685-X. SERIES: Question of Science. SUBJECTS: Astronomy and astronomers; Space; Space travel. RL C.
Through a combination of good photographs, cartoon overlays, and questions and answers, a child's concerns about the moon, what and where it is, are explained. For more difficult concepts, simple experiments are used to clarify facts. A glossary is included.

Rosenberg, Amye

1822 *Rabbit's Rainy Day*. Ill. by author. Western, 1989. ISBN 0-307-11689-1. SERIES: Golden Easy Reader. SUBJECTS: Animals—Rabbits—Fiction; Behavior—Bored—Fiction; Weather—Fiction. RL A.
Forced to stay indoors on a rainy day, a restless bunny tries to find something to do. His efforts lead him into mischief and wear out the rest of the family. Full color cartoonlike pictures capture the bunny's energy but otherwise exhibit little skill.

Rosenbloom, Joseph

1823 *Deputy Dan and the Bank Robbers*. Ill. by Tim Raglin. Random House, hb and pap., 1985. ISBN 0-394-97045-4. SERIES: Step into Reading. SUBJECTS: Humorous stories; Robbers and outlaws—Fiction; Western stories. RL C.
A literal-minded, persevering deputy, Dan accidentally uncovers clues to the identity of the notorious Scrambled Eggs Gang and captures them. Pen and wash pictures help to show the absurdity of this very funny story.

1824 *Deputy Dan Gets His Man*. Ill. by Tim Raglin. Random House, hb and pap., 1985. ISBN 0-394-97250-3. SERIES: Step into Reading. SUBJECTS: Humorous stories; Robbers and outlaws—Fiction; Western stories. RL C.
Dan, an old west version of Amelia Bedelia who does everything exactly as instructed, catches the pearl thief Shootin' Sam and foils a train robbery. The story is accompanied by humorous full color ink and wash pictures.

1825 *The Funniest Dinosaur Book Ever!* Ill. by Hans Wilhelm. Sterling, 1987, o.p. SUBJECTS: Dinosaurs—Fiction; Jokes and riddles. RL B.
This collection of old jokes is bound to get laughs from young readers and groans from older siblings and adults who will be forced to hear them again. The jokes are arranged around and among funny and colorful pictures of dinosaurs that are in a variety of situations.

Rosenthal, Bert

1826 *Basketball*. Photos. Childrens Pr., hb and pap., 1983. ISBN 0-516-01674-1. SERIES: New True. SUBJECTS: Sports—Basketball. RL C.
This book explains the game, its rules and equipment, and the team composition. The differences among professional, college, and high school rules are also noted. Full color photographs of players of all ages, male and female, accompany the text.

Rosenthal, Mark

1827 *Bears*. Photos. Childrens Pr., hb and pap., 1983. ISBN 0-516-01675-X. SERIES: New True. SUBJECTS: Animals—Bears. RL B.
In brief chapters with short sentences, this volume presents a variety of bears, their habitats,

Rosenthal, Mark (cont.)

and their habits. A glossary and an index are included. Illustrated with full color photographs.

Ross, Dave, and Wilson, Jeanne

1828 *Mr. Terwilliger's Secret*. Ill. by authors. Watts, 1981, o.p. SERIES: Easy-Read Story. SUBJECTS: Dinosaurs—Fiction; Fantasy. RL B.

Mr. Terwilliger lets Margaret and Joel in on his secret: He has a real triceratops, Sara, in his basement. On the day the two children agree to feed Sara, she gets loose and does damage to the neighbors' yards. Sketchy childlike drawings fit this fantasy well.

Ross, Jan

1829 *Dogs Have Paws*. Ill. by Robert Masheris. Follett, 1982, o.p. SERIES: Beginning to Read. SUBJECTS: Families, single parent—Fiction; Pets—Dogs—Fiction. RL B.

When his father reminds him to wash his hands or put on boots, a little boy enviously thinks of his dog's paws, which are not washed and do not wear boots. Then he realizes that having hands means he can do many things a dog cannot do. Good realistic pictures show a close-knit single-parent family.

Ross, Katherine

1830 *Grover, Grover, Come on Over*. Ill. by Tom Cooke. Random House, hb and pap., 1991. ISBN 0-679-91117-0. SERIES: Step into Reading. SUBJECTS: Friendship—Fiction; Kites and kite flying—Fiction. RL A.

Though Grover refuses to come over when his friends ask, he does borrow one thing after another and surprises them with a kite. Muppet characters fill the story and are illustrated with pencil and watercolor pictures.

Ross, Pat

1831 *M and M and the Bad News Babies*. Ill. by Marylin Hafner. Pantheon, hb and

pap., 1983, o.p.; Puffin, pap., 1985. ISBN 0-14-31851-8. SERIES: I Am Reading. SUBJECTS: Baby-sitting—Fiction; Friendship—Fiction; Siblings—Twins—Fiction. RL B.

Trying to earn money for a new fish tank, two friends, Mimi and Mandy, agree to baby-sit for the twins, Richie and Benjie. The girls' spunk and ingenuity in the face of two very lively babies make this story a lot of fun. Pencil and wash pictures of the four further the humor.

1832 *M and M and the Big Bag*. Ill. by Marylin Hafner. Pantheon, 1981, o.p.; Penguin, pap., 1985. ISBN 0-14-031852-6. SERIES: I Am Reading. SUBJECTS: Friendship—Fiction; Shopping—Fiction. RL C.

On their first solo trip to the grocery store, two friends, Mandy and Mimi, lose their shopping list and almost buy all the wrong things. Fortunately they find the list just in time. This delightful story has humorous pencil and wash pictures.

1833 *M and M and the Halloween Monster*. Ill. by Marylin Hafner. Viking, 1991. ISBN 0-670-83003-8. SUBJECTS: Emotions—Fear—Fiction; Friendship—Fiction; Holidays—Halloween—Fiction. RL C.

Best friends Mandy and Mimi decide to win the Halloween costume prize in their building. As they search in their lockers in the basement, the two are sure they have seen a monster or a ghost. Longer and more difficult than the other M & M books, this is also illustrated in black and white.

1834 *M and M and the Haunted House Game*. Ill. by Marylin Hafner. Pantheon, 1980, o.p.; Dell, pap., 1981. ISBN 0-440-45544-8. SERIES: I Am Reading. SUBJECTS: Emotions—Fear—Fiction; Friendship—Fiction; Games—Fiction. RL C.

The haunted house game seems a perfect choice for a boring afternoon until two friends, Mimi and Mandy, accidentally scare themselves. A sense of fun—and near fear—in the characters' imaginative play is successfully created. The lively pictures add to the humor.

1835 *M and M and the Mummy Mess*. Ill. by Marylin Hafner. Viking, 1985, o.p.; Puffin, pap., 1986. ISBN 0-14-032084-9.

SUBJECTS: Friendship—Fiction; Mummies—Fiction; Museums—Fiction. RL C. Too early for the Egyptian mummy show, two friends, Mandy and Mimi, sneak into the exhibit area and become fascinated by the mummies and the museum before being caught by the director. The light, humorous illustrations are in gray-toned pencil and wash.

1836 *M and M and the Santa Secrets*. Ill. by Marylin Hafner. Viking, 1985, o.p.; Puffin, pap., 1987. ISBN 0-14-032222-1. SUBJECTS: Friendship—Fiction; Holidays—Christmas—Fiction. RL C.

Two best friends, Mimi and Mandy, do not know what to get each other for Christmas until each hears the other tell Santa what she wants most. The story realistically captures the joys and frustrations of best friends while the illustrations depict the girls in lighthearted pencil sketches.

1837 *M and M and the Superchild Afternoon*. Ill. by Marylin Hafner. Viking, 1987, o.p.; Puffin, pap., 1989. ISBN 0-14-032145-4. SUBJECTS: Dancing—Fiction; Friendship—Fiction; Sports—Gymnastics—Fiction. RL C.

Unable to decide which Superchild activity to join, two friends, Mimi and Mandy, try each other's choices—ballet and gymnastics—and discover hidden talents. Pencil and wash pictures effectively complement the text.

1838 *Meet M and M*. Ill. by Marylin Hafner. Pantheon, 1980, o.p.; Puffin, pap., 1988. ISBN 0-14-032651-0. SERIES: I Am Reading. SUBJECTS: Behavior—Argumentative—Fiction; Friendship—Fiction. RL C.

Two best friends, Mandy and Mimi, seem inseparable until one day they are crabby and fight. Slowly they overcome their anger and hurt and decide to renew their friendship. The pencil and wash drawings in gray and white capture the emotions of these two little girls.

1839 *Molly and the Slow Teeth*. Ill. by Jerry Milord. Lothrop, 1980, o.p. SUBJECTS: Human body—Teeth—Fiction; Tooth fairy—Fiction. RL C.

Everyone in second grade but Molly has lost a tooth so she tries ways to fool her friends and the tooth fairy into believing that she is missing a tooth. Sketchy ink drawings with some color accents create pictures of less than pristine but very appealing children.

Rothaus, James R.

1840 *Squanto: The Indian Who Saved the Pilgrims (1500[?]–1622)*. Ill. by John Nelson and Harold Henriksen. Creative Ed., 1988, o.p. SERIES: We the People. SUBJECTS: Native Americans—Wampanoag; United States—Colonial period. RL C.

Young Tisquantum lived in England for four years after being captured, only to be betrayed, and captured again. Having been befriended by John Smith, he supported the colony that sprang up on the site of his village, which had been decimated by disease in his absence. Large print and watercolors are used in this story.

Rotter, Charles

1841 *Walruses*. Photos. Child's World, 1993. ISBN 0-89565-841-0. SERIES: Nature Books. SUBJECTS: Animals—Walruses. RL C.

The life cycle, enemies, and environment of the walrus are carefully covered in alternating pages of text and color photographs. The information is interesting and the format, using a variety of colored pages for text, is also appealing.

Rowan, James P.

1842 *Ants*. Photos. Rourke, 1993. ISBN 0-86593-289-1. SERIES: Insect Discovery Library. SUBJECTS: Animals—Ants; Animals—Insects. RL B.

Various species of ants are shown in clear color photographs and discussed in facing text. The information is carefully presented and shows the life cycle of various ants as well as their predators and their prey. A brief book, this also includes a glossary and an index.

1843 *Dragonflies*. Photos. Rourke, 1993. ISBN 0-86593-287-5. SERIES: Insect Discovery Library. SUBJECTS: Animals—Dragonflies; Animals—Insects. RL B.

Rowan, James P. (cont.)

Dragonflies and damselflies are discussed in an interesting text alternating with full-page color photographs. The text offers information on several dragonflies and damselflies, their life cycle, habits, food, predators, and prey. This brief book also has a glossary and an index.

1844 *Grasshoppers*. Photos. Rourke, 1993. ISBN 0-86593-286-7. SERIES: Insect Discovery Library. SUBJECTS: Animals—Grasshoppers; Animals—Insects. RL B.
Using alternating pages of clear color photographs and a topically arranged text, the author provides young readers with solid information on the grasshopper, its growth and development, its relatives, predators, and prey, and its relationship to humans. An index and a glossary are appended.

1845 *Honeybees*. Photos. Rourke, 1993. ISBN 0-86593-290-5. SERIES: Insect Discovery Library. SUBJECTS: Animals—Bees; Animals—Insects. RL B.
Topically arranged text alternates with full page color photographs that help to make the book attractive to young readers. Interesting facts are included about the bees, their relatives, life cycle, jobs, and so on. The book also includes an index and an appendix.

1846 *I Can Be A Zookeeper*. Photos. Childrens Pr., 1985. ISBN 0-516-01889-2. SERIES: I Can Be. SUBJECTS: Animals; Careers; Zoos. RL B.
Keepers for mammals, reptiles, sea mammals, birds, and so on are shown in color photographs caring for their charges while the text discusses their responsibilities. Most of the pictures show animals in traditional caged situations. A brief glossary and an index are included.

1847 *Ladybugs*. Photos. Rourke, 1993. ISBN 0-86593-291-3. SERIES: Insect Discovery Library. SUBJECTS: Animals—Insects; Animals—Ladybugs. RL B.
The gardener's friend, the ladybug eats aphids, mealybugs, and scale insects. The clear color photographs alternate with interesting pages of text to offer readers a well-rounded look at a very helpful insect. Book includes a glossary and an index.

Rowland, Florence W.

1848 *Amish Boy*. Ill. by Dale Payson. Putnam, 1970, o.p. SERIES: See and Read. SUBJECTS: Amish—Fiction. RL B.
When lightning hits and destroys a barn, other Amish families come to help Jonathan's family build a new one. The text, a vehicle for information about the Amish, is readable but occasionally stilted, relying on the realistic pencil drawings to soften the tone.

1849 *Amish Wedding*. Ill. by Dale Payson. Putnam, 1971, o.p. SERIES: See and Read. SUBJECTS: Amish—Fiction; Marriage and wedding customs—Fiction. RL C.
Young Jonathan Lapp's oldest sister, Rebecca, is about to be married and it is through Jonathan's eyes that the reader sees Amish courtship and wedding customs. A good introduction to the Amish, the story has realistic charcoal pencil and wash pictures.

Roy, Ron

1850 *Awful Thursday*. Ill. by Lillian Hoban. Pantheon, 1979, o.p. SERIES: I Am Reading. SUBJECTS: Behavior—Responsible—Fiction; Emotions—Fear—Fiction. RL A.
Jack borrows a tape recorder from the school library. He puts it down, and a bus runs over it. Devastated, he cannot imagine how he can tell the librarian what happened and is afraid she will be very angry. Well written with some humorous moments, the story is illustrated with simple sketches.

1851 *Great Frog Swap*. Ill. by Victoria Chess. Pantheon, 1981, o.p. SUBJECTS: Animals—Frogs and toads—Fiction; Contests—Fiction. RL B.
Harriet defeats the neighborhood boys' best-laid plans and shady efforts at winning the frog-jumping contest. The boys' machinations are a bit convoluted but fascinating as they try to win. Illustrations are in shades of gray.

1852 *A Thousand Pails of Water*. Ill. by Vo-Dinh Mai. Knopf, 1978, o.p. SUBJECTS: Animals—Whales—Fiction; Japan—Fiction; Parent and child—Fiction. RL B.

Yukio does not like the fact that his father has to kill whales for a living when his friend's father can work in a market. Finding a whale stranded on the beach, Yukio tries to save it by pouring water over it. The quiet story has soft charcoal sketches that place it in Japan.

Royston, Angela

1853 *Birds*. Photos. Macmillan, 1992. ISBN 0-689-71644-3. SERIES: Eye Openers. SUBJECTS: Animals—Birds. RL C.
Colorful photographic silhouettes set against white pages and assisted by smaller descriptive paintings and a brief text offer young readers introductory information about eight birds. Included are the parrot, sparrow, kiwi, flamingo, and others. The 21-page book uses very heavy paper.

1854 *Cars*. Photos. Macmillan, 1991. ISBN 0-689-71517-X. SERIES: Eye Openers. SUBJECTS: Cars and trucks. RL C.
In 21 pages, eight varieties of cars, including sedan, jeep, sport, and racing, are shown in colorful photographic silhouettes. The text is brief and little more than a caption for the type of car.

1855 *The Cow*. Ill. by Bob Bampton. Watts, 1990. ISBN 0-531-19077-3. SERIES: Farm Animal Stories. SUBJECTS: Animals—Cows; Farm and country life. RL C.
A British farm is the home for this Holstein heifer who matures, has a calf, and becomes a milk cow. An overview of the farm animal's life, including some of the difficulties it has, this is brief and illustrated with realistic, colorful paintings. A list of other breeds and a glossary are added.

1856 *The Deer*. Ill. by Bernard Robinson. Warwick, 1988, o.p. SERIES: Animal Life Stories. SUBJECTS: Animals—Deer. RL C.
The life of a red deer fawn is told as a work of fiction as he grows into adulthood in the English forest. A two page addendum gives more information about the deer. Illustrations are in full color and detailed with occasional black and white drawings. A very short glossary is included.

1857 *Diggers and Dump Trucks*. Photos. Macmillan, 1991. ISBN 0-689-71516-1.

SERIES: Eye Openers. SUBJECTS: Cars and trucks. RL C.
Eight construction machines and trucks are given double-page spreads with illustrations featuring colorful photographic silhouettes. A brief text acts as a lengthy caption in this 21-page book with thick pages.

1858 *The Duck*. Ill. by Maurice Pledger and Bernard Robinson. Warwick, 1988, o.p. SERIES: Animal Life Stories. SUBJECTS: Animals—Ducks. RL B.
Courtship and rearing of young by mallard ducks are presented in a factual look at a year in a duck's life. The text introduces some of the dangers of life, differentiates between drakes and ducks, and is illustrated with full color, detailed, and realistic paintings.

1859 *The Fox*. Ill. by Bernard Robinson. Warwick, 1988, o.p. SERIES: Animal Life Stories. SUBJECTS: Animals—Foxes. RL B.
A young vixen leaves her mother and siblings to find her own habitat, mate, and to raise her cubs in this realistic account of a red fox's life. Lovely, full color paintings illustrate the story along with black and white sketches. The glossary seems inadequate for the somewhat difficult text.

1860 *The Frog*. Ill. by Bernard Robinson. Watts, 1989. o.p. SERIES: Animal Life Stories. SUBJECTS: Animals—Frogs and toads; Animals—Reptiles and amphibians. RL B.
Detailed, realistic paintings and a brief text follow frog mating, laying of eggs, and growth of tadpoles to frogs. Their life, the hazards they face, as well as their winter aestivation are included. Brief facts about other frogs and a glossary are at the end.

1861 *The Goat*. Ill. by Eric Robson. Watts, 1990. ISBN 0-531-19078-1. SERIES: Farm Animal Stories. SUBJECTS: Animals—Goats; Farm and country life. RL C.
Life for a nanny goat on a small farm is shown in watercolor illustrations and explained clearly in the text. The book follows her for a year as she produces two kids and then becomes a milk-goat. A list of other goats and a glossary are included.

Royston, Angela (cont.)

1862 *The Hedgehog*. Ill. by Maurice Pledger. Watts, 1989, o.p. SERIES: Animal Life Stories. SUBJECTS: Animals—Hedgehogs. RL B.
The European hedgehog's life is described in a brief text and realistic color pictures. The book follows a young female as she raises her young, meets predators, and continues her life. A glossary and additional facts are included.

1863 *The Hen*. Ill. by Dave Cook. Watts, 1990. ISBN 0-531-19079-X. SERIES: Farm Animal Stories. SUBJECTS: Animals—Chickens; Farm and country life. RL C.
A free-range Rhode Island Red chicken lives on a farm with other hens and rooster, lays eggs, and then hatches her own brood of chicks. The realistic look at life for chickens on small farms is illustrated with attractive watercolors. A list of other chickens and a glossary are appended.

1864 *Insects and Crawly Creatures*. Photos. Macmillan, 1992. ISBN 0-689-71645-1. SERIES: Eye Openers. SUBJECTS: Animals—Insects; Nature. RL B.
Double-spreads are dedicated to a snail, a spider, a butterfly, a bumblebee, a grasshopper, a wood ant, a ladybug, and a damselfly. Each is dominated by an oversize photo. Some small pastel drawings amplify and decorate the spreads, which include a few sentences about each insect.

1865 *Jungle Animals*. Photos. Macmillan, 1991. ISBN 0-689-71519-6. SERIES: Eye Openers. SUBJECTS: Animals—Jungle. RL C.
In colorful photographic silhouettes, eight animals are presented with the text acting as a lengthy caption to the picture. Pages are thick and sturdy and the book is 21 pages long.

1866 *The Mouse*. Ill. by Maurice Pledger. Watts, 1989, o.p. SERIES: Animal Life Stories. SUBJECTS: Animals—Mice. RL C.
The many litters she bears and the constant hazards she faces from predators and nature fill the life of the mouse. Illustrated with realistic paintings, the story is interesting and not sentimentalized. Also included are a list of other species of mice and a glossary.

1867 *The Otter*. Ill. by Bernard Robinson. Warwick, 1988, o.p. SERIES: Animal Life Stories. SUBJECTS: Animals—Otters. RL B.
The description of the life and habitat of a river otter is spare, nearly poetic, in this story that follows its travels along the river to the sea and back from fall to summer. The full color paintings and black and white drawings are realistic. Includes an addendum and short glossary.

1868 *The Penguin*. Ill. by Trevor Boyer. Warwick, 1988. ISBN 0-531-19042-0. SERIES: Animal Life Stories. SUBJECTS: Animals—Penguins. RL C.
The penguin's life on the ice and in the sea is described in a richly illustrated story about typical events in a year of a penguin—including the rearing of young. A two page section, "More about Penguins," defines some terms and clarifies differences among penguins. A glossary is included.

1869 *The Pig*. Ill. by Jim Channel. Watts, 1990. ISBN 0-531-19080-3. SERIES: Farm Animal Stories. SUBJECTS: Animals—Pigs; Farm and country life. RL C.
A female pig is followed as she grows, matures, has piglets, and weans them. Farm life for the outdoor pig is explained in text and watercolor pictures—although no mention of the butchering of pigs is made. Brief information on other breeds and a glossary are provided.

1870 *Planes*. Photos. Macmillan, 1992. ISBN 0-689-71564-1. SERIES: Eye Openers. SUBJECTS: Airplanes. RL B.
A small plane, a passenger plane, a fighter plane, and a helicopter are some of the planes featured in this brief, well-illustrated book. Text almost acts as a caption to the photographic silhouettes of planes and the small ink-and-wash pictures.

1871 *The Pony*. Ill. by Bob Bampton. Watts, 1990. ISBN 0-531-19081-1. SERIES: Farm Animal Stories. SUBJECTS: Animals—Horses; Farm and country life. RL C.
Readers learn about a British pony from shortly after its birth until it is over four years old and ready to be trained for riding. The brief but interesting text is accented with watercolor paintings. A list of other breeds of ponies and a glossary are appended.

1872 *The Sheep*. Ill. by Josephine Martin. Watts, 1990. 0-531-19082-X. SERIES: Farm Animal Stories. SUBJECTS: Animals—Sheep; Farm and country life. RL C.

A British farm in hilly country is the home for the Welsh Mountain Sheep described in this story. Readers follow her through a year, during which she has a lamb, is sheared, and heads back to the high hill country. Watercolors are used to illustrate this and other sheep. Glossary is provided.

1873 *The Squirrel*. Ill. by Maurice Pledger. Watts, 1989. o.p. SERIES: Animal Life Stories. SUBJECTS: Animals—Squirrels. RL C.

The life cycle of the red squirrel is shown through a female and her kittens. The way the animal builds its nest, prepares for and raises its young, and deals with some of its enemies are included. Additional information on squirrels and a glossary are at the end. Realistic watercolors accompany the text.

1874 *The Tiger*. Ill. by Graham Allen. Warwick, 1988. ISBN 0-531-19043-9. SERIES: Animal Life Stories. SUBJECTS: Animals—Tigers. RL B.

A female tiger is observed as she seeks a mate, has a litter, and, over a two year period, raises and trains her cubs. Realistic full color paintings and black and white sketches ably depict this largest member of the cat family. A two page addendum and short glossary are included.

1875 *Trucks*. Photos. Macmillan, 1991. ISBN 0-689-71405-X. SERIES: Eye Openers. SUBJECTS: Cars and trucks. RL B.

A fire engine, a tanker truck, a tow truck, and a snowplow are some of the vehicles featured here. The brief text extends well-chosen photographic silhouettes and ink-and-wash pictures. Paper is heavy.

1876 *The Whale*. Ill. by Jim Channel. Watts, 1989. o.p. SERIES: Animal Life Stories. SUBJECTS: Animals—Endangered; Animals—Whales. RL C.

Through the life story of one female blue whale, the endangered animal's patterns of feeding, travel and raising young are learned as well as some of the dangers (other than man) they face. Illustrated with detailed watercolors, the book also includes a glossary and facts on other whales.

Ruane, Joanna

1877 *Boats, Boats, Boats*. Ill. by Patti Boyd. Childrens Pr., 1990. ISBN 0-516-05351-5. SERIES: My First Reader. SUBJECTS: Boats and boating. RL A.

Colorful comic paintings and a 16-word vocabulary use repetition and rhyming to give an introduction to some kinds of boats without identifying them in any way other than their color or age. Upbeat format and simplicity of text will make this appropriate for the newest reader.

Rubin, Mark

1878 *The Orchestra*. Ill. by Alan Daniel. Firefly, pap., 1984. ISBN 0-920668-99-2. SUBJECTS: Music and musicians. RL C.

A very good introduction to music and musical instruments, this book clearly explains some aspects of composing, identifies the instruments of the orchestra and how they are played, and tells how they all work together. Illustrations are colorful and attractive, and the design is good.

Ruchlis, Hy

1879 *How a Rock Came to Be in a Fence on a Road near a Town*. Ill. by Mamoru Funai. Walker, 1973, o.p. SUBJECTS: Geology. RL B.

Formed from fossil sediments millions of years ago, a piece of gray limestone is now part of a fence. A clear, informative narrative follows the stone from its beginnings, through different geologic eras, to the stone fence. Illustrated with line drawings with aquamarine and gray washes.

Rudeen, Kenneth

1880 *Roberto Clemente*. Ill. by Frank Mullins. HarperCollins, 1974, o.p. SERIES: HarperCollins Biography. SUBJECTS: Biographies; Sports—Baseball. RL C.

A member of the Baseball Hall of Fame, Clemente worked hard to be a professional

Rudeen, Kenneth (cont.)

player. The book looks back on his life in Puerto Rico, his triumphs with the Pittsburgh Pirates, and his tragic death on a humanitarian mission to Nicaragua. Illustrated with impressionistic drawings.

Ruthstrom, Dorotha

1881 *The Big Kite Contest.* Ill. by Lillian Hoban. Pantheon, 1980, o.p. SERIES: I Am Reading. SUBJECTS: Kites and kite flying—Fiction; Siblings—Fiction. RL C.
Stephen is practicing for the kite contest when he trips and tears his prize kite. Unable to earn enough money to replace it, he gives up. Stephen's little sister repairs the kite and wins the contest with her brother's help. Illustrated with warm, sketchy drawings.

Ryder, Joanne

1882 *Fireflies.* Ill. by Don Bolognese. HarperCollins, 1977, o.p. SERIES: Science I Can Read. SUBJECTS: Animals—Fireflies. RL B.
A simple text tells how, after spending nearly two years underground as a glowworm, the firefly goes in search of a mate, using his special yellow light as a signal to attract a female. Detailed ink and colored wash illustrations.

1883 *First Grade Elves.* Ill. by Betsy Lewin. Troll, hb and pap., 1994. ISBN 0-8167-3010-5. SERIES: First Grade Is the Best! SUBJECTS: Friendship—Fiction; Holidays—Fiction; School stories. RL B.
Just before the holidays of Christmas, Hanukkah, and Kwanzaa, the first-graders in Miss Lee's class decide to become secret elves and do nice things for each other. Illustrated with cartoonlike line drawings, the book also has a snowflake craft at the end.

1884 *First Grade Ladybugs.* Ill. by Betsy Lewin. Troll, hb and pap., 1993. ISBN 0-8167-3006-7. SERIES: First Grade Is the Best! SUBJECTS: Gardening—Fiction; School stories. RL B.
The first-graders in Miss Lee's class work hard to create an outdoor garden. With the help of Gabe's grandmother, their garden flourishes

until the fourth-graders damage it. All ends well when things are patched up. Illustrations are cartoonlike ink drawings.

1885 *First Grade Valentines.* Ill. by Betsy Lewin. Troll, hb and pap., 1993. ISBN 0-8167-3004-0. SERIES: First Grade Is the Best! SUBJECTS: Holidays—Valentine's Day; School stories. RL B.
Miss Lee manages to not only keep the children in her class excited about Valentine's Day but to make the holiday an opportunity for learning as they count hearts, send cards to an elderly woman, and make valentines. Illustrated with line drawings, the book also includes an origami craft.

1886 *Hello, First Grade.* Ill. by Betsy Lewin. Troll, hb and pap., 1993. ISBN 0-8167-3008-3. SERIES: First Grade Is the Best! SUBJECTS: Animals—Rabbits—Fiction; School stories. RL B.
Miss Lee knows just how to make her new first-graders comfortable: She introduces them to her friendly lop-eared bunny, Martha. When they decide to do a quilt for First Grade Day, everyone paints Martha on a square. Cartoonlike line drawings and instructions for a paper bag puppet are included.

1887 *White Bear, Ice Bear.* Ill. by Michael Rothman. Morrow, 1989. ISBN 0-688-07174-0. SERIES: Just for a Day. SUBJECTS: Animals—Bears; Seasons—Winter; Weather—Snow. RL B.
A boy wakes up to a snow-covered world and, as he looks out at it, he is transformed into a polar bear. For a day he is a bear—living on the ice, hunting for food, and surviving the cold. Wintry, blue-toned landscapes and a well-paced, poetic text make his transformation believable.

Ryder, Joanne, and Feinburg, Harold S.

1888 *Snail in the Woods.* Ill. by Jo Polseno. HarperCollins, 1979, o.p. SERIES: Nature I Can Read. SUBJECTS: Animals—Snails. RL C.
A tiny white-lipped snail hatches and begins to grow and explore its environment. It faces many dangers, survives them, and finally is old enough to lay its own eggs. The story pro-

vides good information about the snail's life cycle and is illustrated in watercolors.

Rylant, Cynthia

1889 *Henry and Mudge: The First Book of Their Adventures*. Ill. by Suçie Stevenson. Macmillan, 1987. ISBN 0-689-71399-1. SERIES: Henry and Mudge. SUBJECTS: Friendship—Fiction; Pets—Dogs—Fiction. RL B.
Henry, an only child with no other children on his street to play with, is given a tiny puppy—Mudge—that grows into a very lovable 180-pound dog. Each chapter reinforces the close friendship that develops between the two. Illustrations are lively and colorful.

1890 *Henry and Mudge and the Bedtime Thumps: The Ninth Book of Their Adventures*. Ill. by Suçie Stevenson. Macmillan, 1991. ISBN 0-02-778006-6. SERIES: Henry and Mudge. SUBJECTS: Family life—Fiction; Grandparents—Fiction; Pets—Dogs—Fiction. RL B.
When Henry and his big dog, Mudge, go to the country to visit his grandmother, Mudge is just too large to stay in the house. Afraid in the strange house, Henry ends up sleeping with his pet on the porch. This childlike book has a very real story and appealing illustrations.

1891 *Henry and Mudge and the Careful Cousin: The Thirteenth Book of Their Adventures*. Ill. by Suçie Stevenson. Macmillan, 1994. ISBN 0-02-778021-X. SERIES: Henry and Mudge. SUBJECTS: Family life—Fiction; Pets—Dogs—Fiction. RL B.
Henry's cousin Annie is too neat and clean for Mudge and Henry. The little boy worries about spending a whole day with her until they start playing frisbee and Annie forgets about staying clean. Fun to read, this story effectively captures a moment in childhood. It is well illustrated.

1892 *Henry and Mudge and the Forever Sea: The Sixth Book of Their Adventures*. Ill. by Suçie Stevenson. Macmillan, 1989. ISBN 0-02-778007-4. SERIES: Henry and Mudge. SUBJECTS: Humorous stories; Pets—Dogs—Fiction; Seashore—Fiction. RL B.

Henry, his father, and their dog, Mudge, pack up the car for a day at the ocean. They spend the day playing in the waves, eating hot dogs and snow-cones, and building a sand castle. Their glorious day is illustrated with whimsical pen-and-ink and watercolor drawings.

1893 *Henry and Mudge and the Happy Cat: The Eighth Book of Their Adventures*. Ill. by Suçie Stevenson. Macmillan, hb and pap., 1990. ISBN 0-02-778008-2. SERIES: Henry and Mudge. SUBJECTS: Lost and found Possessions—Fiction; Pets—Cats—Fiction; Pets—Dogs—Fiction. RL B.
Though the cat they find looks a lot like mashed prunes, it is so friendly and happy that Henry and Mudge hope that they do not find its owner. Unfortunately, he does turn up, thrilled to have the cat back. Pictures and text are full of life and true to a young child's feelings.

1894 *Henry and Mudge and the Long Weekend: The Eleventh Book of Their Adventures*. Ill. by Suçie Stevenson. Macmillan, 1992. ISBN 0-02-778013-9. SERIES: Henry and Mudge. SUBJECTS: Family life—Fiction; Pets—Dogs—Fiction. RL B.
What starts out as a dismal, boring weekend is quickly changed into an exciting, fun-filled one when Henry's mother suggests they make the stove and refrigerator boxes into a castle. Delightful watercolor pictures show a close-knit family.

1895 *Henry and Mudge and the Wild Wind: The Twelfth Book of Their Adventures*. Ill. by Suçie Stevenson. Macmillan, 1993. ISBN 0-02-778014-7. SERIES: Henry and Mudge. SUBJECTS: Emotions—Fear—Fiction; Family life—Fiction; Pets—Dogs—Fiction. RL B.
When a summer storm strikes, Henry and Mudge are both afraid. It takes Henry's clever father to help the little boy overcome his fear and relax and have fun when the lights go out. The fear of thunderstorms is handled well in the text and in the watercolor illustrations.

1896 *Henry and Mudge Get the Cold Shivers: The Seventh Book of Their Adventures*. Ill. by Suçie Stevenson. Macmillan,

Rylant, Cynthia (cont.)

1989. ISBN 0-02-778011-2. SERIES: Henry and Mudge. SUBJECTS: Friendship—Fiction; Illness—Fiction; Pets—Dogs—Fiction. RL B.

No one expects Henry's huge dog, Mudge, to get sick and when he does it is a major operation to get him to the vet. With loving care, the big dog is soon well again. The simple text and free-flowing watercolor pictures capture the special relationship between a child and a dog.

1897 *Henry and Mudge in Puddle Trouble: The Second Book of Their Adventures.* Ill. by Suçie Stevenson. Bradbury, 1987. ISBN 0-02-778002-3. SERIES: Henry and Mudge. SUBJECTS: Humorous stories; Pets—Dogs—Fiction; Seasons—Spring—Fiction. RL B.

Henry and his big dog, Mudge, enjoy spring as they discover a beautiful blue flower and try not to pick it, play in a deep puddle, and become protectors of their neighbor's five new kittens. Full color washes with bold outlining make simple yet lively pictures for these gentle, funny stories.

1898 *Henry and Mudge in the Green Time: The Third Book of Their Adventures.* Ill. by Suçie Stevenson. Bradbury, 1987. ISBN 0-02-778003-1. SERIES: Henry and Mudge. SUBJECTS: Pets—Dogs—Fiction; Seasons—Summer—Fiction. RL B.

Henry shares a summer picnic with his lovable dog, gives Mudge a bath, and turns Mudge into a dragon in these delightful and imaginative adventures. Bright summery watercolors capture the warmth and liveliness of the devoted friends.

1899 *Henry and Mudge in the Sparkle Days: The Fifth Book of Their Adventures.* Ill. by Suçie Stevenson. Bradbury, 1988. ISBN 0-02-778005-8. SERIES: Henry and Mudge. SUBJECTS: Holidays—Christmas—Fiction; Pets—Dogs—Fiction; Seasons—Winter—Fiction. RL B.

After an almost interminable wait, snow finally falls and Henry and his big dog, Mudge, play in it, build forts, enjoy a special Christmas dinner, and share quiet and cozy moments at home or on special family walks. The well-written stories, helped by vibrant and colorful pictures, capture the best parts of childhood winters.

1900 *Henry and Mudge Take the Big Test: The Tenth Book of Their Adventures.* Ill. by Suçie Stevenson. Macmillan, 1991. ISBN 0-02778009-0. SERIES: Henry and Mudge. SUBJECTS: Humorous stories; Pet training—Fiction; Pets—Dogs—Fiction. RL B.

Henry is impressed when a very well-trained collie goes by. He wants Mudge to be just as smart and decides to take him to obedience school. His hard work pays off when Mudge does pass the final test. Sketchy ink and watercolor pictures illustrate the story.

1901 *Henry and Mudge under the Yellow Moon: The Fourth Book of Their Adventures.* Ill. by Suçie Stevenson. Bradbury, 1987. ISBN 0-02-778004-X. SERIES: Henry and Mudge. SUBJECTS: Pets—Dogs—Fiction; Seasons—Fall—Fiction. RL B.

With his dog, Mudge, beside him, Henry finds that fall is better than ever. The ghost stories are not as frightening, and Aunt Sally's dreaded visit is actually fun. One of a series, this book continues to maintain high-quality writing along with lively, warm, and childlike illustrations.

1902 *Mr. Putter and Tabby Bake the Cake.* Ill. by Arthur Howard. Harcourt, hb and pap., 1994. ISBN 0-15-200205-7. SERIES: Mr. Putter and Tabby. SUBJECTS: Cookery—Fiction; Friendship—Fiction; Holidays—Christmas—Fiction. RL B.

Mr. Putter enjoys giving Christmas presents and decides to bake a special cake for his friend and neighbor Mrs. Teaberry. Though he knows nothing about baking, he spends Christmas Eve baking and baking until he gets it right. The story is illustrated with gentle line-and-wash pictures.

1903 *Mr. Putter and Tabby Pour the Tea.* Ill. by Arthur Howard. Harcourt, hb and pap., 1994. ISBN 0-15-256255-9. SERIES: Mr. Putter and Tabby. SUBJECTS: Friendship—Fiction; Old age—Fiction; Pets—Cats—Fiction. RL B.

Though he spends his time doing things he enjoys, elderly Mr. Putter is lonely. A cat is what he needs and he finds the perfect companion in Tabby, an old cat that also enjoys flowers, food, and company. Humorous mixed-media illustrations capture the mood of the gentle story.

1904 *Mr. Putter and Tabby Walk the Dog.* Ill. by Arthur Howard. Harcourt, hb and pap., 1994. ISBN 0-15-256259-1. SERIES: Mr. Putter and Tabby. SUBJECTS: Old age—Fiction; Pets—Cats—Fiction; Pets—Dogs—Fiction. RL B.

When his neighbor is unable to walk her dog, Mr. Putter volunteers to walk Zeke for her. The determined little dog is a nightmare until Mr. Putter promises him a special treat and then all is well. Delightfully funny mixed-media illustrations reflect the quiet humor of the story.

S

Sabin, Louis

1905 *Birthday Surprise.* Ill. by John Magine. Troll, hb and pap., 1981. ISBN 0-89375-527-3. SERIES: Giant First-Start. SUBJECTS: Animals—Skunks—Fiction; Birthdays—Fiction; Self-esteem—Fiction. RL A.

Sammy, a skunk, is sure no one likes him or will remember his birthday. A huge box arrives with a birthday hat inside, and he feels more unhappy and goes to bed. Just then his many friends arrive to wish him a happy birthday. Pencil and marker drawings look hurried and too childlike.

Sadler, Marilyn J.

1906 *It's Not Easy Being a Bunny.* Ill. by Roger Bollen. Beginner, 1983. ISBN 0-394-96102-1. SERIES: I Can Read It All By Myself. SUBJECTS: Animals—Fiction; Animals—Rabbits—Fiction; Self-esteem—Fiction. RL B.

Tired of eating cooked carrots, having long ears, and being in a large family, P. J. Funnybunny tries being a variety of other animals. Finally he decides that being a bunny is just right. Full color comic-style pictures complement the brief, humorous story.

1907 *P. J. Funnybunny Camps Out.* Ill. by Roger Bollen. Random House, hb and pap., 1993. ISBN 0-679-93269-0. SERIES: Step into Reading. SUBJECTS: Animals—Rabbits—Fiction; Camps and camping—Fiction; Humorous stories. RL A.

P. J. and his best friends decide to go camping but refuse to allow his little sister and her friend to come. P. J. and his friends turn out to be inept campers and are easily scared by the two little girl animals. Very simple and brief text is paired with funny, cartoonlike pictures.

1908 *P. J. Funnybunny in the Great Tricycle Race.* Ill. by Roger Bollen. Western, 1988. ISBN 0-307-11745-6. SERIES: Golden Look-Look. SUBJECTS: Animals—Rabbits—Fiction; Bicycles and bicycling—Fiction; Humorous stories. RL A.

Against all odds P. J. and his family decide that he will win the Great Turtle Creek Tricycle Race. He practices hard and, despite a spill, manages to win the race. The silly cartoon style pictures in bold colors should appeal to many children.

1909 *The Very Bad Bunny.* Ill. by Roger Bollen. Beginner, 1984. ISBN 0-394-96861-1. SERIES: I Can Read It All By Myself. SUBJECTS: Animals—Rabbits—Fiction; Behavior—Fiction. RL B.

P. J.'s thoughtless behavior causes his family to think him a very bad bunny until cousin Binky arrives. Binky's intentionally nasty conduct leads them to change their opinion of P. J. Humorous, cartoonlike pictures in vibrant colors illustrate this very funny story.

Saintsing, David

1910 *The World of Butterflies.* Photos. Stevens, 1987. ISBN 1-55532-072-4. SERIES: Where Animals Live. SUBJECTS: Animals—Butterflies and moths. RL C.

The different stages in the development of butterflies are presented along with a discussion of their enemies and the way butterflies protect themselves. The text, color photographs, and food-chain diagram are all well done and accessible to young readers.

1911 *The World of Owls.* Photos. Stevens, 1988. ISBN 1-55532-301-4. SERIES: Where

Saintsing, David (cont.)

Animals Live. SUBJECTS: Animals—Owls. RL C.

The habitats, prey, anatomy, and life cycles of a variety of owls are carefully documented in color photos and clear text. Photos are arranged to reflect exactly what is being discussed in the text and arrows are used to match captions and photos. Excellent glossary clearly defines new terms. Adapted from Jennifer Coldrey's *The Owl in the Tree* (Gareth Stevens, 1988).

Saltzberg, Barney

1912 *What to Say to Clara*. Ill. by author. Atheneum, 1984, o.p. SUBJECTS: Behavior—Shyness—Fiction; School stories; Self-esteem—Fiction. RL B.

Otis wants to be his new classmate Clara's friend but cannot make up his mind how to do it. After much agonizing he decides to try the direct approach. He tries saying hello and it works! Ink line drawings shaded with dots illustrate this good story about overcoming shyness.

Sandin, Joan

1913 *The Long Way to a New Land*. Ill. by author. HarperCollins, 1981; pap., 1986. ISBN 0-06-025194-8. SERIES: I Can Read History. SUBJECTS: Emigration and immigration—Fiction; Sweden—Fiction; United States—Fiction. RL C.

A Swedish farm family reluctantly decides to leave their drought-stricken land and emigrate to the United States. Their journey across the Atlantic is harrowing but ends with hope in the United States. The moving story has detailed, realistic drawings.

1914 *The Long Way Westward*. Ill. by author. HarperCollins, hb and pap., 1989. ISBN 0-06-025206-5. SERIES: I Can Read Books. SUBJECTS: Emigration and immigration—Fiction; Historical Fiction; United States—History—Fiction. RL C.

Once Carl Erik's family arrives in America, they have to find their way to Minnesota, knowing little English and having little money. An excit-

ing sequel to *The Long Way to a New Land*, this is illustrated in full-color, realistic watercolors.

Saunders, Susan

1915 *Charles Rat's Picnic*. Ill. by Robert Byrd. Dutton, 1983, o.p. SUBJECTS: Animals—Armadillos—Fiction; Animals—Rats—Fiction; Picnics—Fiction. RL A.

Charles Rat, intent on doing things just right, ends up very wet and without dinner when he takes Miranda Armadillo on a picnic. Illustrated with carefully drawn pictures of a nattily attired rat and armadillo.

1916 *Puss in Boots*. Ill. by Elizabeth Miles. Scholastic, pap., 1989. ISBN 0-590-41888-2. SERIES: Easy-to-Read Folktale. SUBJECTS: Animals—Cats—Fiction; Folklore. RL C.

The story of the wondrous cat who cleverly gains his poor master a dukedom and a princess is faithfully retold with no feeling of abridgment or oversimplification. Illustrations are appealing pencil sketches with delicate watercolor washes.

1917 *Tyrone Goes to School*. Ill. by Steve Bjorkman. Dutton, 1992. ISBN 0-525-44981-7. SERIES: Speedsters. SUBJECTS: Pets—Dogs—Fiction; Pets—Training; School stories. RL C.

Robert and his dog, Tyrone, have a lot in common: Neither one of them pays attention when he should. After obedience class Robert thinks it will be impossible to teach his dog until his teacher shows him the perfect solution. Text is illustrated with sketchy line drawings.

Scarf, Maggi

1918 *Meet Benjamin Franklin*. Ill. by Harry Beckhoff. Random House, 1968, o.p. SERIES: Step-Up. SUBJECTS: Biographies; Inventors and inventions; United States—Revolution. RL B.

This biography of Benjamin Franklin is a complete history of his life. The writing is simple and clear with no fictionalized dialogue. Information on electricity is inaccurate, however, but it is a very small part of an otherwise good book. Illustrated with somewhat idealized colored drawings.

Scarry, Richard

1919 *Best Read-It-Yourself Book Ever*. Ill. by
author. Western, 1990. ISBN 0-307-16551-
5. SERIES: Golden Easy Reader. SUBJECTS:
Humorous stories. RL B.

Twelve stories previously published individually are combined to make a collection featuring
Scarry's well-known characters: Frances Fix-it,
Chief Hound, Smokey, Katie Kitty, and so on.
Though Scarry updated names of characters,
the ink-and-wash pictures might still be
thought "sexist."

1920 *Dr. Doctor*. Ill. by author. Western, 1988.
ISBN 0-307-11654-9. SERIES: Golden Easy
Reader. SUBJECTS: Doctors and nurses—
Fiction. RL B.

Popular with children, this contrived story features a husband-and-wife team of doctors
about to have their own family. Illustrations
are familiar Scarry characters done in cartoonlike watercolors. Mrs. Dr. Doctor is
dressed as a nurse, her title seeming to be a
last-minute addition.

1921 *Frances Fix-It*. Ill. by author. Western,
1988. ISBN 0-307-11655-7. SERIES: Golden
Easy Reader. SUBJECTS: Animals—
Fiction; Careers—Fiction; Humorous
stories. RL A.

No matter how simple or complex the job,
Frances is always able to fix it. The bunny is
able to repair TVs, ovens, cars, and so on.
Familiar Scarry characters in bright watercolors illustrate the brief, repetitive text.

Schade, Susan, and Buller, Jon

1922 *Railroad Toad*. Ill. by Jon Buller.
Random House, hb and pap., 1993. ISBN
0-679-93934-2. SERIES: Step into
Reading. SUBJECTS: Animals—Frogs and
toads—Fiction; Stories in rhyme;
Trains—Fiction. RL A.

A railroad enthusiast, Toad does not care
where he goes as long as it's on a train.
Through the smiling amphibian, readers catch
a comically painted but relatively realistic picture of the different cars of a passenger train.

1923 *Toad on the Road*. Ill. by Jon Buller.
Random House, hb and pap., 1992. ISBN

0-679-92689-5. SERIES: Step into
Reading. SUBJECTS: Animals—Frogs and
toads—Fiction; Cars—Fiction; Travel—
Fiction. RL A.

With great exuberance, Frog leaves driving
school behind and heads out onto the road,
picking up friends, stopping for gas, and just
enjoying driving. Comic and colorful illustrations add much to the very brief rhyming text.

Schecter, Ellen

1924 *The Boy Who Cried "Wolf!" Retold in
Rebus*. Ill. by Gary Chalk. Bantam,
1994. ISBN 0-553-09043-7. SERIES: Bank
Street Ready-to-Read. SUBJECTS: Fables;
Rebuses. RL B.

Accented with rebus drawings rather than told
with them, the story of the boy who lied once
too often is illustrated with paintings of leering
wolves and villagers in nineteenth-century garb.

Schick, Alice, and Schick, Joel

1925 *Just This Once*. Ill. by Alice Schick.
HarperCollins, 1978, o.p. SERIES: I-Like-
to-Read. SUBJECTS: Animals—Dogs—
Fiction; Cave dwellers—Fiction;
Historical fiction. RL C.

Og, Glok, and their children are the only ones
in their tribe not terrified by the friendly wolf.
Again and again they say "just this once" as
they pet and feed her. Ultimately they make
her a part of their tribe and the first domesti-
cated "dog." Realistic drawings of the prehistoric setting have a humorous look to them.

Schick, Eleanor

1926 *Home Alone*. Ill. by author. Dial, 1980.
ISBN 0-8037-4255-X. SERIES: Dial Easy-to-
Read. SUBJECTS: Latchkey children—
Fiction; Self-esteem—Fiction. RL B.

On his first day home alone after school, Andy
carefully follows the instructions his mother
and father gave him as he passes the time
waiting for them to come home. Carefully executed realistic colored pencil drawings illustrate this very common situation.

1927 *Joey on His Own*. Ill. by author. Dial,
1982. ISBN 0-8037-4302-5. SERIES: Dial

Schick, Eleanor (cont.)

Easy-to-Read. SUBJECTS: Behavior—
Responsible—Fiction; Shopping—
Fiction. RL B.

Joey's little sister is sick and he must go to the store for his mother. Walking past unsavory characters on the way, Joey finally makes it to the store and returns home with a new sense of responsibility. The sympathetic text has realistic colored pencil drawings.

1928 *Neighborhood Knight*. Ill. by author. Greenwillow, 1976, o.p. SERIES: Read-alone. SUBJECTS: Families, single parent—Fiction; Imagination—Fiction. RL B.

Since his father, the "king," has been gone a long time, the little boy pretends he is a courageous knight defending his mother and sister and their apartment "castle." Sensitively written and drawn, the story shows a small child dealing in the best way he can with anger and frustration.

1929 *Rainy Sunday*. Ill. by author. Dial, hb and pap., 1981. ISBN 0-8037-7369-2. SERIES: Dial Easy-to-Read. SUBJECTS: City and town life—Fiction; Family life—Fiction; Weather—Rain—Fiction. RL B.

Everything in the city looks gray and feels cold when a little girl wakes up. As she shares a quiet day with her mother and father, the day brightens with their pleasure in one another's company. The colored pencil illustrations are spare and as clearly defined as the activities the small family shares.

1930 *Summer at the Sea*. Ill. by author. Greenwillow, 1979, o.p. SERIES: Read-alone. SUBJECTS: Seashore—Fiction; Vacation—Fiction. RL B.

After an entire summer at the ocean spent meeting people, fishing, planting flowers, and enjoying almost every minute, it is hard for a little girl to return to her busy city life. The meticulous pencil and wash drawings are a perfect complement to the quiet text.

Schneider, Herman, and Schneider, Nina

1931 *Science Fun with a Flashlight*. Ill. by Harriet Sherman. McGraw-Hill, 1975, o.p. SUBJECTS: Science experiments; Shadows. RL B.

A clever text shows children how to have a good time experimenting with light and shadows. By using a flashlight they can discover color in light, how the angle of light affects shadows, and how color and light are reflected. The pictures are delightful.

Schulman, Janet

1932 *The Big Hello*. Ill. by Lillian Hoban. Greenwillow, 1976; Dell, pap., 1980. ISBN 0-688-80036-X. SERIES: Read-alone. SUBJECTS: Emotions—Fear—Fiction; Moving, household—Fiction; Toys—Dolls and dollhouses—Fiction. RL A.

A little girl comforts her doll as they fly to their new home in California. Once there the doll is lost but fortunately found by a child certain to be the little girl's hoped-for new friend. Pencil drawings help readers to empathize with the child's fear of the unknown.

1933 *Camp Kee Wee's Secret Weapon*. Ill. by Marylin Hafner. Greenwillow, 1979, o.p. SERIES: Read-alone. SUBJECTS: Camps and camping—Fiction; Sports—Softball—Fiction. RL B.

Forced to go to camp when she wants to stay home and play softball, Jill reluctantly goes but ends up loving it, especially when she becomes the pitcher on a softball team. Attractive colored pencil sketches of children are lively and fit Jill's varying moods.

1934 *The Great Big Dummy*. Ill. by Lillian Hoban. Greenwillow, 1979, o.p. SERIES: Read-alone. SUBJECTS: Emotions—Loneliness—Fiction; Friendship—Fiction; Imagination—Fiction. RL B.

When her friends are too busy to play with her, Anna decides to create a "sister" out of her clothes and play with her until her friends are free to play. The story and appealing pencil and wash drawings successfully present a child who is both imaginative and independent.

1935 *Jack the Bum and the Halloween Handout*. Ill. by James Stevenson. Greenwillow, 1977, o.p.; U.S. Committee for UNICEF, pap., 1977, o.p. SERIES: Read-alone. SUBJECTS: Holidays—Halloween—Fiction; Tramps—Fiction. RL A.

Wanting a cup of coffee, Jack the bum tries trick-or-treating and even using the word *UNICEF* as he goes door to door. Finally he follows children into a UNICEF party where he is the winner of $5.00, which he donates to UNICEF. Illustrated with humorous pencil and wash drawings.

1936 *Jack the Bum and the Haunted House.* Ill. by James Stevenson. Greenwillow, 1977, o.p. SERIES: Read-alone. SUBJECTS: Haunted houses—Fiction; Robbers and outlaws—Fiction; Tramps—Fiction. RL A.

With nowhere else to go during the cold weather, Jack takes up residence in a supposedly haunted house. Jack's determination to stay there results in his capturing a jewel thief. Humorous pencil and wash drawings show a kindly but resolute "tramp" resigned to his lot.

1937 *Jack the Bum and the UFO.* Ill. by James Stevenson. Greenwillow, 1978, o.p. SERIES: Read-alone. SUBJECTS: Tramps—Fiction; UFOs—Fiction. RL A.

When the children beg Jack the bum to stop a land developer from turning their forest and pond into a parking lot, Jack cleverly convinces the developer that the area is a haven for UFOs. The text combines humor with concern for the environment. Illustrated with comic pencil and wash sketches.

1938 *Jenny and the Tennis Nut.* Ill. by Marylin Hafner. Greenwillow, 1978, o.p.; Dell, pap., 1981. ISBN 0-440-44211-7. SERIES: Read-alone. SUBJECTS: Self-esteem—Fiction; Sports—Gymnastics—Fiction; Sports—Tennis—Fiction. RL B.

Insistent that Jenny be accomplished in at least one sport, her father tries to teach her his favorite—tennis—overlooking her obvious talent in gymnastics. Imaginative pencil drawings capture the enthusiasm that father and daughter give to their respective sports.

Schultz, Walter A.

1939 *Will and Orv.* Ill. by Janet Schultz. Carolrhoda, 1991. ISBN 0-87614-669-8. SERIES: On My Own Books. SUBJECTS: Aeronautics; Biography. RL B.

One of the five people who witnessed the Wright brothers' first flight, Johnny Moore is the one through whom the story of that historic event is told. A well-developed story line and good color-pencil drawings add appeal to an already fascinating story.

Schwartz, Alvin

1940 *All of Our Noses Are Here and Other Noodle Tales.* Ill. by Karen A. Weinhaus. HarperCollins, 1985; pap., 1987. ISBN 0-06-025288-X. SERIES: I Can Read Books. SUBJECTS: Folklore—United States; Humorous stories. RL B.

Anyone reading these five stories about the Brown family is sure to end up laughing. The Browns are typical noodles doing absolutely ridiculous things in total seriousness. The colored pencil and wash drawings give these silly folktales from around the world a special zany look.

1941 *Busy Buzzing Bumblebees and Other Tongue Twisters.* Ill. by Paul Meisel. HarperCollins, 1982. ISBN 0-06-025268-5. SERIES: I Can Read Books. SUBJECTS: Tongue twisters. RL C.

Children and adults will have a good time with 46 phrases that are guaranteed to twist and torment tongues. The brightly colored, humorous ink-and-wash paintings definitely add to the fun and to an understanding of the rhymes.

1942 *Ghosts! Ghostly Tales from Folklore.* Ill. by Victoria Chess. HarperCollins, hb and pap., 1991. ISBN 0-06-021796-0. SERIES: I Can Read Books. SUBJECTS: Folklore; Ghosts; Scary stories. RL B.

A wonderful collection of ghostly folktales sure to attract and hold the attention of young readers, this has Victoria Chess's delightfully spooky and rather zany illustrations to fill the book and lighten the stories.

1943 *I Saw You in the Bathtub and Other Folk Rhymes.* Ill. by Syd Hoff. HarperCollins, 1989., pap., ISBN 0-06-025298-7. SERIES: I Can Read Books. SUBJECTS: Folklore—United States; Humor; Poetry. RL B.

Included here are rhymes and chants that children in the United States say or sing at play. Readers will be familiar with most of

Schwartz, Alvin (cont.)

them and enjoy their familiarity. Hoff's comic ink and wash drawings are in his popular sketchy and very funny and attractive style.

1944 *In a Dark, Dark Room and Other Scary Stories*. Ill. by Dirk Zimmer. HarperCollins, 1984; pap., 1985. ISBN 0-06-025274-X. SERIES: I Can Read Books. SUBJECTS: Folklore; Ghost stories; Scary stories. RL A.

The seven short, scary stories and lyrics from spooky songs are perfect for young readers to learn and tell at camp or on Halloween. The detailed ink pictures have red and yellow accents that blend humor into somewhat scary pictures.

1945 *Ten Copycats in a Boat and Other Riddles*. Ill. by Marc Simont. HarperCollins, 1980; pap., 1985. ISBN 0-06-444076-1. SERIES: I Can Read Books. SUBJECTS: Jokes and riddles. RL B.

Familiar yet still funny jokes and riddles get two pages each—one for the joke or riddle and the other for the answer. The ink, watercolor, and colored pencil drawings capably extend the silliness.

1946 *There Is a Carrot in My Ear and Other Noodle Tales*. Ill. by Karen A. Weinhaus. HarperCollins, 1982; pap., 1986. ISBN 0-06-025234-0. SERIES: I Can Read Books. SUBJECTS: Folklore—United States; Humorous stories. RL B.

The Brown family are the noodles as they swim in a waterless pool, try to hatch a "mare's egg," or mistake long underwear for an intruder. The six stories offer children an opportunity to have fun with absolutely ridiculous characters and comic illustrations in red, yellow, and gray.

Scott, Geoffrey

1947 *Egyptian Boats*. Ill. by Nancy L. Carlson. Carolrhoda, 1981, o.p. SERIES: On My Own. SUBJECTS: Boats and boating; Egypt, ancient. RL B.

A vocabulary builder, this informative history of Egyptian watercraft describes different types and sizes of boats, how they were used, and for what purposes. It provides a brief

glance at the social structure of ancient Egypt. Illustrated with detailed, realistic ink drawings.

1948 *Labor Day*. Ill. by Cherie R. Wyman. Carolrhoda, 1982. ISBN 0-87614-178-5. SERIES: On My Own. SUBJECTS: Holidays—Labor Day. RL C.

A brief look at the first Labor Day celebration shows the difficult working conditions in the 1880s when the Central Labor Union and the Knights of Labor held the first Labor Day parade. The book, illustrated with romanticized pictures of workers, encourages pride in the labor movement.

1949 *Memorial Day*. Ill. by Peter E. Hanson. Carolrhoda, 1983. ISBN 0-87614-219-6. SERIES: On My Own. SUBJECTS: Holidays—Memorial Day. RL C.

The origin of Memorial Day is traced to just after the Civil War and the celebration by the northern states of Decoration Day. Carefully written and providing good historical information and context, this book is illustrated with semirealistic ink drawings of historical scenes.

Seibert, Patricia

1950 *Mush! Across Alaska in the World's Longest Sled-Dog Race*. Ill. by Jan Davey Ellis. Millbrook, 1992. ISBN 1-56294-705-2. SUBJECTS: Animals—Dogs; Animals—Dogs—Racing. RL C.

Framing the text or in double-page spreads, the illustrations look at the famous Alaskan Iditarod sled-dog race and give readers a sense of the terrain, the strength of the dogs, and the mushers' determination. A well-written text conveys the excitement of the 1,000-mile race.

Seixas, Judith S.

1951 *Alcohol: What It Is, What It Does*. Ill. by Tom Huffman. Greenwillow, 1977, o.p.; pap., 1981. ISBN 0-688-00462-8. SERIES: Read-alone. SUBJECTS: Drugs and drug abuse. RL B.

Much of the 56 pages is devoted to the nature of alcohol and its effect on the body and mind of the average person. One section also deals with alcoholism from the perspective of the alcoholic's family and stresses not taking the blame for another's drinking. Illustrated with comic ink sketches.

1952 *Allergies: What They Are, What They Do.* Ill. by Tom Huffman. Greenwillow, 1991. ISBN 0-688-09638-7. SERIES: Read-alone. SUBJECTS: Allergies. RL C.
The history, identification, and treatment of allergies are covered in this very thorough discussion of the subject. Also mentioned are a number of common allergens: food, dust mites, chemicals, plants, and so on. A light touch is given to the serious topic by pictures using two colors.

1953 *Drugs: What They Are, What They Do.* Ill. by Tom Huffman. Greenwillow, 1987. ISBN 0-688-07400-6. SERIES: Read-alone. SUBJECTS: Drugs and drug abuse. RL C.
How drugs affect a person's ability to think and act and the other dangers they present are discussed in this guide to psychoactive drugs. The book stresses that it is important for children not to try *any* drugs. It is effectively illustrated with comic drawings that add to the book's impact.

1954 *Junk Food: What It Is, What It Does.* Ill. by Tom Huffman. Greenwillow, 1984. ISBN 0-688-02560-9. SERIES: Read-alone. SUBJECTS: Food; Nutrition. RL C.
A useful guide to nutrition, this book encourages children to compare "junk" food to foods that are lower in calories, are good to eat, and provide more nutrients for growth and development. Clever ink sketches with orange accents accompany the well-written text.

1955 *Vitamins: What They Are, What They Do.* Ill. by Tom Huffman. Greenwillow, 1986. ISBN 0-688-06066-8. SERIES: Read-alone. SUBJECTS: Nutrition; Vitamins. RL C.
Children reading this book will learn what vitamins are, how they were discovered, why they are added to foods, who needs supplements, and more. A section on nutrition and an easy-to-use vitamin chart are also included. Two-color ink drawings of smiling fruit and vegetables highlight the text.

1956 *Water: What It Is, What It Does.* Ill. by Tom Huffman. Greenwillow, 1987. ISBN 0-688-06608-9. SERIES: Read-alone. SUBJECTS: Conservation; Pollution—Water; Water. RL C.
Using simple, straightforward language, the author discusses water's properties, its uses, and the abuses it suffers. With five interesting experiments, the text offers a relatively thorough examination of the subject. Illustrated with funny line drawings.

Selsam, Millicent E.

1957 *Benny's Animals and How He Put Them in Order.* Ill. by Arnold Lobel. HarperCollins, 1966, o.p. SERIES: Science I Can Read. SUBJECTS: Animals—Classification. RL A.
Benny's curiosity about how to classify his pictures of animals takes him, with his parents' encouragement, to the natural science museum. While there he learns about the way in which animals are classified. Sketchy ink and colored pencil drawings keep this story upbeat and entertaining.

1958 *Egg to Chick.* Rev. ed.; photos. Ill. by Barbara Wolff. HarperCollins, 1970; pap., 1987. ISBN 0-06-025290-1. SERIES: Science I Can Read. SUBJECTS: Animals—Reproduction. RL B.
The development of a chick embryo is examined from the day of conception until 21 days later when the chick hatches. Multicolored drawings alternate with black and white photographs to present an accurate portrayal of the growth of the embryo.

1959 *Greg's Microscope.* Ill. by Arnold Lobel. HarperCollins, 1963. ISBN 0-06-025296-0. SERIES: Science I Can Read. SUBJECTS: Microscopes. RL B.
Soon after Greg's father gives him a microscope, the whole family becomes involved in using it to learn about the things around them. A well-done introduction to the microscope, the book has charming and informative pictures that help to explain the use of this instrument.

1960 *Let's Get Turtles.* Ill. by Arnold Lobel. HarperCollins, 1965, o.p. SERIES: Science I Can Read. SUBJECTS: Animals—Turtles; Pets—Turtles. RL A.

Selsam, Millicent E. (cont.)

Two best friends, Billy and Jerry, agree to get the same kind of pet—a turtle. Once they have them they learn how to take care of them and what to feed them. The lively ink and wash drawings add to the appeal of the book.

1961 *More Potatoes!* Ill. by Ben Shecter. HarperCollins, 1972, o.p. SERIES: Science I Can Read. SUBJECTS: Farm and country life; Vegetables. RL B.

Curious about how the grocery store gets potatoes, Sue asks questions that lead her class to a trip to a warehouse and a farm. Through the illustrations and the text, readers will quickly learn that vegetables do not just appear on the shelves of supermarkets.

1962 *Plenty of Fish.* Ill. by Erik Blegvad. HarperCollins, 1960, o.p. SERIES: Science I Can Read. SUBJECTS: Animals—Fish; Pets—Fish. RL A.

Irrepressible Willy is determined to have goldfish but must be constantly reminded to stop and find out the proper way to care for them. Willy's father patiently explains the curious world of goldfish to him. Illustrated with ink drawings showing a middle-class British family.

1963 *Seeds and More Seeds.* Ill. by Tomi Ungerer. HarperCollins, 1959, o.p. SERIES: Science I Can Read. SUBJECTS: Plants—Seeds, roots, and bulbs. RL A.

With his father's encouragement, Benny explores why seeds grow. He plants a variety of things and watches as seeds grow while other things do not. The sketchy ink drawings show a turn-of-the-century father and son in an opulent setting investigating seeds.

1964 *Strange Creatures That Really Lived.* Ill. by Jennifer Dewey. Scholastic, 1987, o.p. SUBJECTS: Animals—Prehistoric. RL B.

Not all of the creatures described in Selsam's clear style and Dewey's colored pencil, sometimes fanciful, drawings are all that strange, but all are interesting. A useful chart on the last page lists the dinosaurs, ancient mammals, insects, and birds included in the book.

1965 *Terry and the Caterpillars.* Ill. by Arnold Lobel. HarperCollins, 1962, o.p. SERIES: Nature I Can Read. SUBJECTS: Animals—

Butterflies and moths; Animals—Caterpillars. RL A.

Terry finds three caterpillars and watches curiously as they eat, grow, spin cocoons, and months later become moths. The story is full of factual information and, with its detailed ink and wash pictures, continues to fascinate children.

1966 *Tony's Birds.* Ill. by Kurt Werth. HarperCollins, 1961, o.p. SERIES: Science I Can Read. SUBJECTS: Animals—Birds—Fiction. RL A.

An evening walk with his father leads Tony to an interest in birds. The well-developed relationship between father and son is the foundation of a story that introduces children to the rudiments of bird watching. The spare ink and wash sketches still appeal and do not appear dated.

1967 *Up, Down and Around: The Force of Gravity.* Ill. by Kenneth Dewey. Doubleday, 1977, o.p. SERIES: Chicago Museum of Science and Industry. SUBJECTS: Gravity. RL C.

A clearly written text accurately explains the fundamental concepts associated with gravity, using space travel and planetary systems as examples. Realistic but sketchy illustrations and diagrams do not add much to the text.

1968 *When an Animal Grows.* Ill. by John Kaufmann. HarperCollins, 1966, o.p. SERIES: Science I Can Read. SUBJECTS: Animals; Animals—Growth and development. RL B.

Four baby animals, two mammals and two birds, are contrasted from birth to independent living. A gorilla is compared with a lamb while a sparrow is compared with a mallard on alternating pages using different colors of ink for the text. Illustrated with gray watercolor paintings.

Selsam, Millicent E., and Hunt, Joyce

1969 *Animal Mixups.* Ill. by John Wallner. Macmillan, 1992, o.p. SUBJECTS: Animals. RL A.

Where an animal lives, the young it raises, the tail it has, are all part of this exercise in observation. Readers are encouraged to look at the pictures and think about what is wrong and what would be right in mismatched art and oddly made animals. Ink-defined watercolors are humorous.

1970 *A First Look at Animals with Horns*. Ill. by Harriett Springer. Walker, 1989. ISBN 0-8027-6872-5. SERIES: First Look At. SUBJECTS: Animals—Horned. RL B.
After identifying and defining "horns," animals with varying numbers of horns are then distinguished from one another. Accurate black and white pencil drawings accompany the simple text and work with it to help readers identify different varieties of animals by their characteristics.

1971 *A First Look at Animals without Backbones*. Ill. by Harriett Springer. Walker, 1976. ISBN 0-8027-6269-7. SERIES: First Look At. SUBJECTS: Animals—Invertebrates. RL C.
After differentiating between animals that have and do not have backbones, the book discusses a variety of invertebrates. Those covered include arthropods, echinoderms, mollusks, worms, coelenterates, sponges, and protozoa. Illustrated with detailed pencil drawings that help clarify the text.

1972 *A First Look at Bats*. Ill. by Harriett Springer. Walker, 1991. ISBN 0-8027-8135-7. SERIES: First Look At. SUBJECTS: Animals—Bats. RL B.
Using pencil drawings and a text intent on getting readers to carefully look at similarities and differences among bats, the authors discuss bats, their habits, their lives, and how to tell them apart. A map showing where bats live and an index are also in the book.

1973 *A First Look at Bird Nests*. Ill. by Harriett Springer. Walker, 1984. ISBN 0-8027-6565-3. SERIES: First Look At. SUBJECTS: Animals—Nests. RL C.
Basic information on the identification of nests of specific birds is offered. Also, an attempt is made to involve readers in identifying a nest, which is shown in detailed and realistic pencil drawings. Well researched, the book provides good information for school assignments or the satisfaction of curiosity.

1974 *A First Look at Birds*. Ill. by Harriett Springer. Walker, 1973. ISBN 0-8027-6164-X. SERIES: First Look At. SUBJECTS: Animals—Birds. RL B.
Children can learn a great deal about birds and their physical characteristics by reading this clearly written and factually accurate book. Intending to hone powers of observation, Selsam and Hunt ask readers to choose the correct illustration from among detailed pencil drawings.

1975 *A First Look at Caterpillars*. Ill. by Harriett Springer. Walker, 1988, o.p. SERIES: First Look At. SUBJECTS: Animals—Butterflies and moths; Animals—Caterpillars. RL B.
Children reading this are encouraged to use the information in the text to help them in examining the pictures of caterpillars, butterflies, and moths, and detecting differences among them. The book has detailed, realistic pencil drawings with green accents.

1976 *A First Look at Dinosaurs*. Ill. by Harriett Springer. Walker, 1982; Scholastic, pap. ISBN 0-8027-6456-8. SERIES: First Look At. SUBJECTS: Dinosaurs; Geology. RL C.
All kinds of dinosaurs are introduced and compared in the text and in the many detailed pencil drawings. Children are encouraged to match information in the text to pictures of dinosaurs. The book also includes some information on continental drift.

1977 *A First Look at Ducks, Geese and Swans*. Ill. by Harriett Springer. Walker, 1990. ISBN 0-8027-6975-6. SERIES: First Look At. SUBJECTS: Animals—Ducks; Animals—Geese; Animals—Swans. RL B.
A good introduction to the characteristics and differences of ducks, geese, and swans, this encourages young readers to look closely at these waterfowl, to note their differences and similarities. Carefully crafted pencil and wash pictures are essential to the text.

1978 *A First Look at Horses*. Ill. by Harriett Springer. Walker, 1981, o.p. SERIES: First Look At. SUBJECTS: Animals—Horses. RL B.
After a brief introduction to equine anatomy, several breeds of horses are mentioned and

**Selsam, Millicent E., and
Hunt, Joyce (cont.)**

compared. The book emphasizes the importance of recognizing observable external differences among and between the horses pictured in detailed pencil drawings. Horse fans should enjoy this one.

1979 *A First Look at Insects*. Ill. by Harriett Springer. Walker, 1974. ISBN 0-8027-6182-8. SERIES: First Look At. SUBJECTS: Animals—Insects. RL C.

Like others in the First Look At series, this book attempts to get readers to use the information in the well-written text to test their powers of observation. Here they are asked to distinguish detailed pencil drawings of particular insects from pictures of other animals and insects.

1980 *A First Look at Leaves*. Ill. by Harriett Springer. Walker, 1972. ISBN 0-8027-6118-6. SERIES: First Look At. SUBJECTS: Plants—Trees. RL C.

Like others in the First Look At series, this book asks the reader to scan the illustrations on a page and match an object (a leaf) to a description. It also presents useful information about leaves and their parts. Simple line drawings are very clear and sufficiently accurate for leaf identification.

1981 *A First Look at Owls, Eagles, and Other Hunters of the Sky*. Ill. by Harriett Springer. Walker, 1986. ISBN 0-8027-6642-0. SERIES: First Look At. SUBJECTS: Animals—Birds of Prey. RL C.

Owls, eagles, falcons, and other birds of prey are pictured in lovely, realistic drawings and are compared to facilitate identification. The book further challenges the reader to identify birds' pictures based on the facts presented in the text.

1982 *A First Look at Poisonous Snakes*. Ill. by Harriett Springer. Walker, 1987. ISBN 0-8027-6683-8. SERIES: First Look At. SUBJECTS: Animals—Snakes. RL C.

Encouraging children to notice the distinguishing marks and behavior of poisonous snakes, the book compares the snakes by body shape, especially head, and by type of fangs. Cobras, vipers, pit vipers, and sea snakes are contrasted. Illustrated with very detailed pencil drawings.

1983 *A First Look at Sharks*. Ill. by Harriett Springer. Walker, 1979. ISBN 0-8027-6373-1. SERIES: First Look At. SUBJECTS: Animals—Sharks. RL C.

Like other books in the First Look At series, this book presents its subject, sharks, in terms of classification characteristics. It encourages the reader to distinguish sharks from bony fishes and different sharks from one another. The black and white pencil drawings are detailed and realistic.

1984 *A First Look at Spiders*. Ill. by Harriett Springer. Walker, 1983, o.p. SERIES: First Look At. SUBJECTS: Animals—Spiders. RL C.

Children are prompted to examine detailed black and white pencil drawings to learn what distinguishes a spider from an insect, one spider from another, and one web from another. Children reading this will increase their observational skills rather than gaining in-depth knowledge.

1985 *A First Look at the World of Plants*. Ill. by Harriett Springer. Walker, 1978. ISBN 0-8027-6299-9. SERIES: First Look At. SUBJECTS: Plants. RL B.

This book gives its readers an opportunity to learn about plants in a variety of ways. It encourages children not only to read the text but to carefully examine the pencil and wash drawings for differences among fungi, gymnosperms, and other plants.

Seltzer, Meyer

1986 *Here Comes the Recycling Truck!* Photos by the author. Whitman, 1992. ISBN 0-8075-3235-5. SUBJECTS: Recycling. RL C.

Elisa, the driver of her community's recycling truck, is followed for a day and shown gathering glass, paper, cardboard, and cans. She takes everything to the recycling center and the text explains how recycled items are used. Clear photographs and text show the importance of her work.

Serventy, Vincent

1987 *Kangaroo*. Photos. Raintree, 1985; Scholastic, pap., 1987. ISBN 0-8172-2418-1. SERIES: Animals in the Wild. SUBJECTS: Animals—Kangaroos. RL B.

About five kinds of kangaroos are introduced in the brief text. Much of the book is devoted to following baby kangaroos from birth to the time that they are ready to leave the pouch. Good information is presented well, and the large full color photographs are delightful.

1988 *Koala*. Photos. Raintree, 1983; Scholastic, pap., 1987. ISBN 0-8172-2416-5. SERIES: Animals in the Wild. SUBJECTS: Animals—Koalas. RL B.

A full color photograph dominates each page with the brief text below it acting like a caption. The information ranges from the koala's diet and habitat to its young, its enemies, and current attempts by Australia to protect it. This appealing book is an Australian production.

1989 *Turtle and Tortoise*. Photos. Raintree, 1985; Scholastic, pap., 1987. ISBN 0-8172-2403-3. SERIES: Animals in the Wild. SUBJECTS: Animals—Turtles. RL C.

Good information and excellent full color photographs tell about the natural habitats (land, sea, and shore) and life cycle of turtles and tortoises. The photos dominate this book, and the text acts as captions.

Seuling, Barbara

1990 *Just Me*. Ill. by author. Harcourt, 1982, o.p. SERIES: Let Me Read. SUBJECTS: Imagination—Fiction. RL A.

Using odds and ends from around her home and a lot of imagination, a little girl tries being a horse, a dragon, and a robot but she always returns to being "just me." Ink and wash drawings are simple, uncluttered, and attractive.

Seuss, Dr.

1991 *Cat in the Hat*. Ill. by author. Random House, 1957. ISBN 0-394-90001-4. SERIES: I Can Read It All By Myself. SUBJECTS: Humorous stories; Stories in rhyme. RL A.

With nothing to do on a cold, rainy day, two children are roused from their lethargy by the Cat in the Hat, who promises lots of good fun. Seuss's cartoon drawings and rhymed text always attract young readers and listeners.

1992 *Cat in the Hat Comes Back*. Ill. by author. Random House, 1958. ISBN 0-394-90002-2. SERIES: I Can Read It All By Myself. SUBJECTS: Humorous stories; Stories in rhyme. RL B.

While Mother is gone, the children are busily working when the Cat in the Hat returns to create havoc and fun with his Little Cats A to Z. Seuss's absurdly funny drawings and text quickly capture the attention of young readers.

1993 *The Cat's Quizzer*. Ill. by author. Random House, 1976. ISBN 0-394-83296-5. SERIES: Beginner Books. SUBJECTS: Miscellanea; Tests. RL B.

A wild assortment of questions testing general knowledge is given the Seuss touch with zany illustrations and an offbeat tone. Children will be challenged to try their best at answering questions from natural science, history, and more. Answers are given at the end.

1994 *Foot Book*. Ill. by author. Random House, 1968. ISBN 0-394-90937-2. SERIES: Bright and Early. SUBJECTS: Human body—Feet—Fiction; Stories in rhyme. RL B.

The many varieties of feet and the many things they can do are amusingly described in words and lively colorful pictures in this humorous rhyming text with a total of 126 words.

1995 *Fox in Socks*. Ill. by author. Random House, 1965. ISBN 0-394-90038-3. SERIES: I Can Read It All By Myself. SUBJECTS: Humorous stories; Stories in rhyme; Tongue twisters. RL C.

Children who are about to read these wild tongue twisters are warned at the outset to take them slowly. Children will sympathize with poor Mr. Knox's attempts at tongue twisters and will enjoy his final victory over Fox. Typical zany Seuss creations illustrate the text.

1996 *Great Day for Up!* Ill. by Quentin Blake. Random House, 1974. ISBN 0-394-92913-6. SERIES: Bright and Early. SUBJECTS: Stories in rhyme. RL A.

This rousing, jubilant rhyme encourages everyone to get "up" in the morning—except for the narrator, who is sleeping in. The clever illustrations are lively, funny, and perfect for the rhyme.

Seuss, Dr. (cont.)

1997 *Green Eggs and Ham*. Ill. by author. Random House, 1960. ISBN 0-394-90016-2. SERIES: I Can Read It All By Myself. SUBJECTS: Food—Fiction; Nonsense; Stories in rhyme. RL A.
Sam-I-am relentlessly pursues a furry top-hatted creature trying every way he can think of to get the creature to eat green eggs and ham. The well-known, cleverly illustrated creatures and the silly rhyming text are perpetual favorites of young children.

1998 *Hop on Pop*. Ill. by author. Random House, 1963. ISBN 0-394-90029-4. SERIES: I Can Read It All By Myself. SUBJECTS: Stories in rhyme. RL A.
Introducing the very simplest of words, usually of one syllable, Seuss puts them into a nonsensical rhyming format with humorous results. His illustrations of outlandish "things" entice children into trying to read.

1999 *I Am Not Going to Get Up Today!* Ill. by James Stevenson. Random House, 1987. ISBN 0-394-99217-2. SERIES: I Can Read It All By Myself. SUBJECTS: Humorous stories; Sleep—Fiction; Stories in rhyme. RL B.
In a rhyming story, neighbors, police, newspapers, and television attempt to get a little boy out of bed, but he refuses to get up. Illustrations are done with full color wash and ink sketches in an amusing comic style.

2000 *I Can Read with My Eyes Shut!* Ill. by author. Random House, 1978. ISBN 0-394-93912-3. SERIES: I Can Read It All By Myself. SUBJECTS: Books and reading—Fiction; Stories in rhyme. RL B.
The Cat in the Hat gives children countless reasons for reading and learning while they involve themselves in a rousing, rhyming text. Seuss's typical free-form creatures are colorfully illustrated and will attract children.

2001 *Mister Brown Can Moo! Can You?* Ill. by author. Random House, 1970. ISBN 0-394-90622-5. SERIES: Bright and Early. SUBJECTS: Sound—Fiction; Stories in rhyme. RL C.
From the noises made by cows and owls to that of thunder, Mister Brown can imitate just about any sound. The humorous text and illus-trations encourage children not only to try making the sounds themselves but also to decode new words.

2002 *Oh, Say Can You Say?* Ill. by author. Random House, 1979. ISBN 0-394-94255-8. SERIES: I Can Read It All By Myself. SUBJECTS: Tongue twisters. RL B.
The cover warns children that the tongue twisters inside are terrible to try to read and to try not to stumble over. The text is longer than others by Seuss and more challenging. His comic drawings of imaginative creatures will encourage children to try these creative phrases.

2003 *Oh, the Thinks You Can Think!* Ill. by author. Random House, 1975. ISBN 0-394-93129-7. SERIES: I Can Read It All By Myself. SUBJECTS: Imagination—Fiction; Stories in rhyme. RL A.
Children reading this will be encouraged to think imaginatively and to enjoy playing with words. Seuss creates outlandish word and picture combinations that should spur children to try making up some of their own. The illustrations are full color, cartoonlike, and fun.

2004 *One Fish Two Fish Red Fish Blue Fish*. Ill. by author. Random House, 1960. ISBN 0-394-90013-8. SERIES: I Can Read It All By Myself. SUBJECTS: Humorous stories; Nonsense; Stories in rhyme. RL A.
Aided by a delightfully nonsensical rhyming text, two children explore the world of funny creatures. Seuss's silly story introduces children to wordplay and to an enjoyment of language. The illustrations are extremely entertaining.

2005 *There's a Wocket in My Pocket!* Ill. by author. Random House, 1974. ISBN 0-394-92920-9. SERIES: Bright and Early. SUBJECTS: Stories in rhyme. RL B.
Zany Seuss creations rhyming with the names of familiar items and common household objects are sure to inspire children to try to make up their own rhyming words. Typical Seuss illustrations.

Shaffer, Ann

2006 *The Camel Express*. Ill. by Robin Cole. Dillon, 1989, o.p. SERIES: It Really

Happened! SUBJECTS: Animals—Camels—Fiction; Historical fiction; Western stories. RL C.

When the pony express rider is hurt, Grandpa and Mary Claire ride Carlos, a camel set free by the army, nearly 35 miles through storms and great danger to the next post. Loosely based on events of the times, the adventure is fast paced and nicely illustrated with pencil drawings.

Shannon, George

2007 *The Gang and Mrs. Higgins.* Ill. by Andrew Vines. Greenwillow, 1981, o.p. SERIES: Read-alone. SUBJECTS: Frontier and pioneer life—Fiction; Robbers and outlaws—Fiction; Western stories. RL C.

The Andersons, the meanest gang in Kansas, try to rob kindly Mrs. Higgins of her gold. She tells them there is no gold, as she washes and washes clothes. They give up and leave, and she takes the gold out of the washtub. The humorous story is illustrated with comic, semirealistic pictures.

Shapiro, Irwin

2008 *Gretchen and the White Steed.* Ill. by Herman Vestal. Garrard, 1972, o.p. SERIES: Venture. SUBJECTS: Adventure stories; Animals—Horses—Fiction; Frontier and pioneer life—Fiction. RL B.

On the way to Texas with her big family, Gretchen is tied to their gentle mare when it wanders away with her. Lost on the prairie and surrounded by wild horses, the little girl is rescued by a wonderful white horse. Illustrated with detailed ink and wash drawings.

Shapp, Martha, and Shapp, Charles

2009 *Let's Find Out about Animals of Long Ago.* Ill. by Bette Davis. Watts, 1968, o.p. SERIES: Let's Find Out About. SUBJECTS: Animals—Prehistoric; Dinosaurs. RL B.

After being introduced to several dinosaurs and other prehistoric animals, the reader learns how fossils are made and what scientists do with the fossils and the information from them. The realistic illustrations are done in pencil and ink.

2010 *Let's Find Out about Babies.* Ill. by Jenny Williams. Watts, 1974, o.p. SERIES: Let's Find Out About. SUBJECTS: Animals—Reproduction. RL B.

From egg and sperm to birth, the development of animal and human babies is discussed without great detail and in general terms. The authors stress the importance of loving, supportive families for babies. The book has realistic, full color pictures.

2011 *Let's Find Out about Houses.* Rev. ed. Ill. by Tomie dePaola. Watts, 1975, o.p. SERIES: Let's Find Out About. SUBJECTS: Houses. RL B.

Houses from around the world, the material used to construct them, and the reasons for their particular kind of construction are briefly surveyed in the text and vibrant pencil and watercolor pictures.

2012 *Let's Find Out about the Moon.* Ill. by Brigitte Hartmann. Watts, 1975, o.p. SERIES: Let's Find Out About. SUBJECTS: Astronomy; Space travel. RL C.

In this book children learn of discoveries about the moon, how the moon's rotation affects the earth, and what the men who landed on the moon found there. The text is interesting and illustrated with detailed and informative pencil drawings.

2013 *Let's Find Out about Trees (Arbor Day).* Ill. by Allan Eitzen. Watts, 1970, o.p. SERIES: Let's Find Out About. SUBJECTS: Holidays—Arbor Day; Plants—Trees. RL B.

The emphasis here is on the importance of trees to everyday life with additional information—such as trees being the oldest and largest living things—briefly given. It does not include information on kinds of trees and their growth. Illustrated with spare pictures in gold, gray, and green.

Sharmat, Marjorie W.

2014 *Burton and Dudley.* Ill. by Barbara Cooney. Holiday House, 1975, o.p.; Avon, pap., 1977, o.p. SUBJECTS: Friendship—Fiction; Humorous stories; Walking—Fiction. RL A.

Sharmat, Marjorie W. (cont.)

Dudley Possum has to prod his quiet friend Burton into taking a walk with him, but it is Burton who revels in the outdoors and only reluctantly comes home, determined to walk all over the world. The well-done pen and ink drawings are detailed and clever and reflect the story's humor.

2015 *Griselda's New Year*. Ill. by Normand Chartier. Macmillan, 1979, o.p. SERIES: Ready-to-Read. SUBJECTS: Animals—Geese—Fiction; Holidays—New Year's Day—Fiction; Humorous stories. RL B.
Oblivious to the problems she is creating for her friends, Griselda Goose pushes forward with her New Year's resolution to make someone happy. The funny story is illustrated with detailed ink and wash drawings of semirealistic, humorous animals.

2016 *Little Devil Gets Sick*. Ill. by Marylin Hafner. Doubleday, 1980, o.p. SERIES: Reading On My Own. SUBJECTS: Devils—Fiction; Fantasy; Illness—Fiction. RL B.
When Little Devil wakes up with a terrible cold, he tries everything (hot spider soup, warm fires, nasty spells) to get rid of it. Only when he does a good deed does it go away. Illustrated with comical colored pencil drawings that are sure to appeal to children.

2017 *Mitchell Is Moving*. Ill. by Jose Aruego and Ariane Dewey. Macmillan, 1978; pap., 1985. ISBN 0-02-782410-1. SERIES: Ready-to-Read. SUBJECTS: Dinosaurs—Fiction; Friendship—Fiction; Moving, household—Fiction. RL B.
After 60 years of living in his house, dinosaur Mitchell decides to move. He has not counted on missing his good friend and neighbor Margo and is ecstatic when she follows and moves next to him. Simple, humorous drawings effectively illustrate this delightful story.

2018 *Mooch the Messy*. Ill. by Ben Shecter. HarperCollins, 1976, o.p. SERIES: I Can Read Books. SUBJECTS: Animals—Rats—Fiction; Parent and child—Fiction; Self-esteem—Fiction. RL B.
When his father comes to visit his hole, Mooch, a rat, tries to make him more comfortable by cleaning up. Though he enjoys the time with his father, Mooch is happy to be alone and messy again. Simple pencil and wash drawings illustrate this humorous story about self-acceptance.

2019 *Nate the Great*. Ill. by Marc Simont. Putnam, 1972; Dell, pap., 1977. ISBN 0-698-20627-4. SERIES: Break-of-Day. SUBJECTS: Mystery and detective stories. RL A.
Pancake-eating child detective Nate the Great is involved in solving mysteries for his friends. Using a "Dragnet" style speech pattern, Nate tells about his sleuthing. Expressive pencil and wash pictures showing Nate in a trench coat and deer-stalker cap are a perfect match to the text.

2020 *Nate the Great and the Boring Beach Bag*. Ill. by Marc Simont. Putnam, 1987. ISBN 0-698-20631-2. SERIES: Break-of-Day. SUBJECTS: Mystery and detective stories; Seashore—Fiction. RL A.
Even while swimming in the ocean, Nate is asked to help solve a mystery. This time it is Oliver's beach bag that is missing. The watercolor paintings place the well-known children from this series and their pets at a crowded beach in the summer.

2021 *Nate the Great and the Fishy Prize*. Ill. by Marc Simont. Putnam, 1985; Dell, pap., 1988. ISBN 0-440-40039-2. SERIES: Break-of-Day. SUBJECTS: Mystery and detective stories. RL A.
Rosamond asks Nate to find her prize tuna fish can for the smartest pet contest. After diligent detecting, Nate and his dog Sludge find it. Illustrated with amusing pencil and watercolor pictures.

2022 *Nate the Great and the Halloween Hunt*. Ill. by Marc Simont. Putnam, 1989. ISBN 0-698-20635-5. SERIES: Break-of-Day. SUBJECTS: Holidays—Halloween—Fiction; Mystery and detective stories. RL B.
At home with his dog, Sludge, on Halloween, Nate is asked to find Rosamund's black kitten, Little Hex. The search takes them out among trick-or-treaters, to a haunted house, and finally, after a pancake snack, to the solution. Funny text and suitably Halloweenish pictures work well together.

2023 *Nate the Great and the Lost List*. Ill. by Marc Simont. Putnam, 1975; Dell, pap., 1981. ISBN 0-698-20646-0. SERIES: Break-of-Day. SUBJECTS: Mystery and detective stories. RL A.
Taking a well-earned break from detecting, Nate reluctantly agrees to use his detective skills to help Claude find his missing grocery list. Short, choppy sentences are perfectly suited to reading aloud and the pencil and wash illustrations are expressive and humorous.

2024 *Nate the Great and the Missing Key*. Ill. by Marc Simont. Putnam, 1981; Dell, pap., 1982. ISBN 0-440-46191-X. SERIES: Break-of-Day. SUBJECTS: Mystery and detective stories. RL A.
Rosamond has put Annie's house key in a safe place leaving clues to its whereabouts in a poem. Annie turns to Nate for help and again he solves the case—just in time to go to Fang's birthday party. The pencil and wash drawings capture Nate and his friends perfectly.

2025 *Nate the Great and the Mushy Valentine*. Ill. by Marc Simont. Delacorte, 1994. ISBN 0-385-31166-4. SUBJECTS: Holidays—Valentine's Day—Fiction; Mystery and detective stories; Pets—Dogs—Fiction. RL C.
Nate the Great is determined to discover who sent his dog, Sludge, a valentine as well as who took Annie's valentine. After a few false leads, the young sleuth discovers the answers to both. This has all pictures in full color.

2026 *Nate the Great and the Phony Clue*. Ill. by Marc Simont. Putnam, 1977; Dell, pap., 1981. ISBN 0-440-46300-9. SERIES: Break-of-Day. SUBJECTS: Mystery and detective stories. RL A.
A strange piece of paper with "vita" on it leads Nate on a challenging hunt for the rest of the message. Adults and children will have fun reading aloud this text reminiscent of "Dragnet's" Joe Friday dialogue. Pencil and wash drawings ably capture the tongue-in-cheek humor.

2027 *Nate the Great and the Snowy Trail*. Ill. by Marc Simont. Putnam, 1982, o.p.; Dell, pap., 1984. ISBN 0-440-46276-2. SERIES: Break-of-Day. SUBJECTS: Mystery and detective stories. RL A.

Busy making a snow detective, Nate the Great and his dog are interrupted by Rosamund and her four cats. Rosamund wants Nate and his dog Sludge to find Nate's lost and very mysterious birthday present. Soft, humorous pencil and wash illustrations are delightful, as is the story.

2028 *Nate the Great and the Sticky Case*. Ill. by Marc Simont. Putnam, 1978, o.p.; Dell, pap., 1981. ISBN 0-440-46289-4. SERIES: Break-of-Day. SUBJECTS: Dinosaurs—Fiction; Mystery and detective stories. RL A.
After Claude asks him to find his missing stegosaurus stamp, Nate the Great begins searching for clues. During the search Nate learns a lot about the stegosaurus and of course finds the missing stamp. The illustrations, done in ink and wash, capture perfectly the detective and his friends.

2029 *Nate the Great and the Stolen Base*. Ill. by Marc Simont. Putnam, 1992. ISBN 0-698-20708-4. SERIES: Nate the Great Break-of-Day. SUBJECTS: Mystery and detective stories; Sports—Baseball—Fiction. RL B.
Nate's baseball team cannot practice because second base—Oliver's purple plastic octopus—is missing. As usual, Nate follows the clues and soon has the group playing ball again. Illustrated with Simont's usual delightful sketches with watercolor washes.

2030 *Nate the Great Goes Down in the Dumps*. Ill. by Marc Simont. Putnam, 1989. ISBN 0-698-20636-3. SERIES: Break-of-Day. SUBJECTS: Humorous stories; Mystery and detective stories. RL A.
When Rosamond cannot find her empty money box she turns to the inimitable Nate the Great for help. His search takes him to the garbage dump before he realizes just how to find the box. Lots of humor, a challenging mystery, and delightful pencil and wash pictures are sure to attract readers.

2031 *Nate the Great Goes Undercover*. Ill. by Marc Simont. Putnam, 1974; Dell, pap., 1978. ISBN 0-698-30547-7. SERIES: Break-of-Day. SUBJECTS: Mystery and detective stories. RL B.
Pesky Oliver insists that Nate find out who or what is getting into his garbage cans. Nate

Sharmat, Marjorie W. (cont.)

does a thorough job and uncovers the numerous culprits, including his own dog, Sludge. Charcoal, pencil, and wash pictures.

2032 *Nate the Great Stalks Stupidweed*. Ill. by Marc Simont. Putnam, 1986, o.p.; Dell, pap., 1989. ISBN 0-440-40150-X. SERIES: Break-of-Day. SUBJECTS: Mystery and detective stories. RL B.

Oliver goes to Nate for help in finding his newly adopted and lost weed. With his usual panache Nate recovers it while providing great reading fun. Pencil and watercolor pictures of the familiar cast of characters add to the book's appeal.

2033 *Scarlet Monster Lives Here*. Reissued ed. Ill. by Dennis Kendrick. HarperCollins, 1988. ISBN 0-06-025527-7. SERIES: I Can Read Books. SUBJECTS: Monsters—Fiction; Moving, household—Fiction; Neighbors—Fiction. RL C.

When Scarlet Monster moves into a new house, she tries hard to make it inviting to her new neighbors and cannot understand why none of them have come to meet her. The ink and wash drawings show a variety of gawky, nonthreatening monsters wanting to be liked by each other.

2034 *Sophie and Gussie*. Ill. by Lillian Hoban. Macmillan, 1973, o.p. SERIES: Ready-to-Read. SUBJECTS: Animals—Squirrels—Fiction; Friendship—Fiction. RL C.

Sophie and Gussie's friendship survives misunderstandings and hurt feelings as the two squirrels visit each other, plan a party, and share special moments. The quiet story is illustrated with sketchy ink and wash drawings that are a delight.

2035 *The Story of Bentley Beaver*. Ill. by Lillian Hoban. HarperCollins, 1984. ISBN 0-06-025513-7. SERIES: I Can Read Books. SUBJECTS: Animals—Beavers—Fiction; Family life—Fiction; Old age—Fiction. RL B.

From his birth to loving beaver parents to his quiet death, Bentley Beaver's journey through a long and happy life is gently and affectionately recalled. The sketchy, whimsical animal pictures add to the reader's appreciation of Bentley and his family.

2036 *The Trip and Other Sophie and Gussie Stories*. Ill. by Lillian Hoban. Macmillan, 1976, o.p. SERIES: Ready-to-Read. SUBJECTS: Animals—Squirrels—Fiction; Friendship—Fiction; Humorous stories. RL B.

Although close friends Sophie and Gussie, two squirrels, sometimes disagree, they share a special friendship that sees them through occasional difficulties and their own foolish behavior. The sketchy, lighthearted drawings are in pen with gray, green, and yellow washes.

2037 *The Trolls of Twelfth Street*. Ill. by Ben Shecter. Putnam, 1979, o.p. SERIES: Break-of-Day. SUBJECTS: Fantasy; Trolls—Fiction. RL B.

Eldred Troll's curiosity leads the Troll family from their safe and comfortable home beneath the Brooklyn Bridge up to the streets of New York City. Mistaking human rudeness for Troll good behavior gets them into difficulty. The charcoal drawings have a rough and hurried but fanciful look.

2038 *Uncle Boris and Maude*. Ill. by Sammis McLean. Doubleday, 1979, o.p. SERIES: Reading On My Own. SUBJECTS: Animals—Moles—Fiction; Behavior—Bored—Fiction. RL B.

Maude tries everything to rid Uncle Boris of his apparently incurable boredom until she becomes bored too. Then it is his turn to drag her out of the dumps. The illustrations, done with humorous ink and wash drawings, show two very pleasant moles.

2039 *Who's Afraid of Ernestine?* Ill. by Maxie Chambliss. Putnam, 1986, o.p. SERIES: Break-of-Day. SUBJECTS: Emotions—Fear—Fiction. RL B.

Afraid of Ernestine, Cecil imagines her as a vampire, a dragon lady, and a devil as he tries to escape her clutches. Finally the two children are forced to work together and Cecil discovers Ernestine is actually very nice. Illustrated with humorous ink and wash drawings.

Sharmat, Marjorie W., and Sharmat, Craig

2040 *Nate the Great and the Musical Note*. Ill. by Marc Simont. Putnam, 1990, o.p.; Dell, pap., 1991. ISBN 0-440-40466-5.

SERIES: Break-of-Day. SUBJECTS: Music and musicians—Fiction; Mystery and detective stories. RL C.

Rosamund leaves Pip a message from his mother—but she has put it into a secret code. Nate the Great has less than an hour to come up with the musical solution to Pip's message. The adventures of the young detective continue to be expertly illustrated in pencil and watercolors.

Sharmat, Marjorie W., and Weinman, Rosalind

2041 *Nate the Great and the Pillowcase*. Ill. by Marc Simont. Delacorte, 1993. ISBN 0-385-31051-X. SUBJECTS: Mystery and detective stories. RL B.

Nate the Great, detective, gets a telephone call at two o'clock in the morning from Rosamund. Big Hex, her cat, cannot sleep without his pillowcase; Nate must find it. In typical Nate fashion, the young detective gathers clues and solves the mystery. Expressive and colorful watercolors accompany the text.

Sharmat, Mitchell

2042 *Reddy Rattler and Easy Eagle*. Ill. by Marc Simont. Doubleday, 1979, o.p. SERIES: Reading On My Own. SUBJECTS: Animals—Eagles—Fiction; Animals—Snakes—Fiction; Self-esteem—Fiction. RL B.

Depressed because nobody seems to like him, Reddy Rattler is helped by his good friend Easy Eagle to find a new career as part of a desert rock band. The expressive ink, wash, and pencil drawings add humor and individualize the characters of the story.

Sharoff, Victor

2043 *The Heart of the Wood*. Ill. by Wallace Tripp. Putnam, 1971, o.p. SERIES: Break-of-Day. SUBJECTS: Historical fiction; Religion—Fiction; Wood carving—Fiction. RL C.

Isaac is torn between obeying the laws of Judaism and not carving animals and keeping his promise to carve a bowl with animals for the duke. The wood he finds enables him to obey the laws of his faith and keep his promise. Realistic ink and wash drawings place the story in medieval times.

Sharp, Paul

2044 *Paul the Pitcher*. Ill. by author. Childrens Pr., hb and pap., 1984. ISBN 0-516-02064-1. SERIES: Rookie Readers. SUBJECTS: Sports—Baseball—Fiction; Stories in rhyme. RL C.

Paul has great fun pitching, unless the batter gets a hit. He hopes that someday he will be a professional baseball player. The lively, rhyming text uses 38 words and has ink and wash action drawings.

Shaw, Evelyn

2045 *Alligator*. Ill. by Frances Zweifel. HarperCollins, 1972, o.p. SERIES: Science I Can Read. SUBJECTS: Animals—Alligators and crocodiles. RL B.

A female alligator makes a nest, lays eggs, guards them, is nearly killed by hunters, and survives to care for her young. A straightforward, unsentimental account of an interesting animal's life, this book is illustrated with realistic colored pencil drawings.

2046 *Elephant Seal Island*. Ill. by Cherryl Pape. HarperCollins, 1978, o.p. SERIES: Science I Can Read. SUBJECTS: Animals—Seals, elephant. RL C.

The behavior and life cycle of elephant seals are explored in this factual, descriptive look at a young bull's birth and growth. The well-done illustrations are detailed and realistic.

2047 *Fish Out of School*. Ill. by Ralph Carpentier. HarperCollins, 1970, o.p. SERIES: Science I Can Read Books. SUBJECTS: Animals—Fish. RL A.

Focusing on the plight of one fish separated from its school, the author uses a story format to explain how fish live and the dangers they face. Other fish are seen in the realistic watercolor paintings and identified as the little herring swims past them to join a new school.

2048 *A Nest of Wood Ducks*. Ill. by Cherryl Pape. HarperCollins, 1976, o.p. SERIES:

Shaw, Evelyn (cont.)

Nature I Can Read. SUBJECTS: Animals—Ducks. RL B.

Two wood ducks are followed from mating season to the hatching and raising of their ducklings. Solid factual information combines with clear, realistic full color pencil and watercolor pictures to present an interesting look at the wood duck.

2049 *Octopus*. Ill. by Ralph Carpentier. HarperCollins, 1971, o.p. SERIES: Science I Can Read. SUBJECTS: Animals—Octopi; Oceans and ocean life. RL B.

The life cycle and behavior of this eight-armed mollusk are discussed in such a way that the octopus seems less threatening and far more interesting than usually thought. The realistic illustrations add to the reader's knowledge and appreciation of the animal.

2050 *Sea Otters*. Ill. by Cherryl Pape. HarperCollins, 1980, o.p. SERIES: Nature I Can Read. SUBJECTS: Animals—Otters, sea. RL B.

Susan, a scientist, observes two sea otters, Garbo and her pup, Bo. Through Susan's eyes, children learn how this endangered mammal survives the cold Pacific waters, what it eats, and how Garbo trains Bo to be independent. Excellent realistic watercolor paintings.

Shecter, Ben

2051 *The Big Stew*. Ill. by author. HarperCollins, 1991. ISBN 0-06-025609-5. SUBJECTS: Cookery—Fiction; Witches—Fiction. RL A.

A couple get carried away adding things to their stew. They are transformed into witches as they add one strange thing after another. Then the stew explodes and all is back to normal. A minimal text counts on the sketchy yet colorful pictures to help tell the story.

2052 *Hester the Jester*. Ill. by author. HarperCollins, 1977, o.p. SERIES: Early I Can Read. SUBJECTS: Sex roles—Fiction. RL A.

A little girl tries being a jester, a knight, and a king and finally chooses just to be a little girl. The author's seriocomic pictures with ink cross-hatchings show a very self-confident child who manages to convince adults that she can be whatever she wishes.

Sheehan, Angela

2053 *The Duck*. Ill. by Maurice Pledger and Bernard Robinson. Warwick, 1976, o.p. SERIES: A First Look at Nature. SUBJECTS: Animals—Ducks. RL C.

This rather lengthy and detailed look at the courtship of mallards and the raising of their ducklings presents factual information in a story format. The very realistic full color paintings give a clear idea of what the mallard looks like. This book was first published in England.

Sheehan, Cilla

2054 *The Colors That I Am*. Ill. by Glen Elliott. Human Sciences, 1981. ISBN 0-89885-047-9. SUBJECTS: Concepts—Color; Emotions. RL B.

Intent on getting children to express their feelings, Sheehan chooses color as the vehicle for discussion. Emotions are related to colors. Each color is given a full page of text, the facing page contains an abstract painting. Conversational in tone, the text might stimulate discussion among children regarding their feelings.

Shefelman, Janice

2055 *A Mare for Young Wolf*. Ill. by Tom Shefelman. Random House, 1993. ISBN 0-679-83445-1. SERIES: Step into Reading. SUBJECTS: Native Americans—Fiction; Animals—Horses—Fiction. RL C.

When it is time for him to choose a horse, Young Wolf goes against tradition and asks for a beautiful and smart mare. Although he is laughed at for his choice, the horse and boy are ultimately redeemed when they warn the people of raiders. Colorful paintings depict Native Americans of the plains.

Sherrow, Victoria

2056 *Wilbur Waits*. Ill. by James Watts. HarperCollins, 1990, o.p. SUBJECTS: Birthdays—Fiction; Friendship—Fiction. RL B.

For his birthday Wilbur gets a sled, a kite, and a boat but the weather does not allow him to use any of them. Finally Wilbur discovers that playing with his friend is just as much fun anyway. Energetic colored pencil and wash pictures illustrate the story.

Shiefman, Vicky

2057 *M Is for Move.* Photos by Bill Miller. Dutton, 1981, o.p. SERIES: Smart Cat. SUBJECTS: English language—Verbs. RL A.
Schoolchildren are captured in lively black and white photos as they demonstrate the action of verbs. The children seem natural rather than posed in the well-done pictures. The arrangement of the text, which captions the photos using first a letter and then a verb, is not alphabetical.

Shortall, Leonard

2058 *Just-in-Time Joey.* Ill. by author. Morrow, 1973, o.p. SUBJECTS: Grandparents—Fiction; Plants—Trees—Fiction. RL B.
The diseased elm trees on Joey's grandmother's street are being marked with big yellow circles of paint and then cut down. As a prank, one of the boys in the neighborhood sprays Joey's grandmother's healthy tree and Joey is just in time to save it. Illustrated with detailed ink drawings.

2059 *Steve's First Pony Ride.* Ill. by author. Morrow, 1966, o.p. SUBJECTS: Animals—Horses—Fiction; Behavior—Responsible—Fiction; Farm and country life—Fiction. RL B.
Steve's neighbor Mr. Turner gets a horse and pony and allows the little boy to help him take care of them. When Steve discovers the animals missing one day, he finds them for Mr. Turner and earns the opportunity to ride the pony. The well-written story is illustrated with realistic paintings.

2060 *Tony's First Dive.* Ill. by author. Morrow, 1972, o.p. SUBJECTS: Emotions—Fear—Fiction; Self-esteem—Fiction; Sports—Swimming—Fiction. RL B.
Seeing that Tony is afraid of the water, one of the lifeguards at the beach gives him special lessons. He teaches Tony not only to swim but also to dive with a mask and flippers. A good story of overcoming fear and gaining self-esteem, it is illustrated with attractive ink drawings.

Showers, Paul

2061 *A Baby Starts to Grow.* Ill. by Rosalind Fry. HarperCollins, 1969, o.p. SERIES: Let's-Read-and-Find-Out. SUBJECTS: Human body—Reproduction. RL B.
Drawings of siblings, mothers, and babies combine with an upbeat text to present a limited picture of how a baby develops from fertilized ovum to birth. This book does not contain information on human sexuality. Illustrations are semirealistic.

2062 *A Drop of Blood.* Ill. by Don Madden. Rev. ed. HarperCollins, hb and pap., 1989. ISBN 0-690-04717-7. SERIES: Let's-Read-and-Find-Out Science Books. SUBJECTS: Human body—Blood. RL B.
Newly revised, this introduction to the study of human blood has been updated in both illustrations and text. The book contains information on white and red cells, platelets, and scab formation as well as how to use a flashlight to see the blood in your hands, cheeks, and ears.

2063 *Ears Are for Hearing.* Ill. by Holly Keller. Rev. ed. HarperCollins, 1990. ISBN 0-690-04718-5. SERIES: Let's-Read-and-Find-Out Science Books. SUBJECTS: Human body—Ears; Senses—Hearing. RL B.
Using a brief, clearly written text and simple, childlike ink-and-watercolor pictures, an explanation is given for the process of hearing. Text and pictures also depict and explain the parts of the ear and their functions.

2064 *How Many Teeth?* Ill. by True Kelley. Rev. ed. HarperCollins, 1991. ISBN 0-06-021633-6. SERIES: Let's-Read-and-Find-Out Science Books. SUBJECTS: Human body—Teeth. RL B.
Through Sam, his baby sister, parents, and friends, readers learn about teeth, the number that children and adults have, and how they are used. Rhyming verses are interspersed to

Showers, Paul (cont.)

reinforce information. The full-color illustrations attractively augment the text.

2065 *How You Talk*. Ill. by Megan Lloyd. Rev. ed. HarperCollins, 1992. ISBN 0-06-022767-2. SERIES: Let's-Read-and-Find-Out Science Books. SUBJECTS: Human body—Speech. RL B.

Using a conversational tone and a family situation, the book takes a look at how speech occurs, starting with babies and how they learn to make sounds. Lots of activities help to explain how particular sounds are made. Text is illustrated with lively pen-and-ink drawings with watercolors.

2066 *The Listening Walk*. Ill. by Aliki. New ed. HarperCollins, 1991. ISBN 0-06-021637-9. SUBJECTS: Senses—Hearing; Sound. RL B.

As a little girl, her father, and their dog take a walk they avoid talking and instead listen carefully. They hear a great many sounds: footsteps, sprinklers, bees, a baby crying, and more. Put into a new format, the illustrations are full color, energetic, and enticing.

2067 *Look at Your Eyes*. Ill. by True Kelley. Rev. ed. HarperCollins, hb and pap., 1992. ISBN 0-06-020188-6. SERIES: Let's-Read-and-Find-Out Science Books. SUBJECTS: Human body—Eyes. RL B.

A little boy uses his observation skills to see how his eyes work. He shows readers how to tell the ways in which eyes can move, how pupils enlarge or grow small, and how eyes are protected by eyebrows and eyelashes. Pen and ink and watercolor pictures add much to this well-done book.

2068 *Me and My Family Tree*. Ill. by Don Madden. HarperCollins, 1978, o.p. SERIES: Let's-Read-and-Find-Out. SUBJECTS: Heredity. RL B.

Parents, grandparents, and even great-great grandparents are seen as a part of a child's heritage in this overview of genetics. Gregor Mendel and his pioneering experiments in genetics are briefly mentioned and explained. The detailed Pentel drawings with orange and gold add appeal.

2069 *No Measles, No Mumps for Me*. Ill. by Harriett Barton. HarperCollins, 1980, o.p. SERIES: Let's-Read-and-Find-Out. SUBJECTS: Diseases; Vaccination. RL B.

A little boy tells how he will never have to get diseases like measles, mumps, and whooping cough because he has had the shots or drops that vaccinate him against them. The text and the simple, childlike pictures explain the way white cells act to fight bacteria and viruses.

2070 *Sleep Is for Everyone*. Ill. by Wendy Watson. HarperCollins, 1974. ISBN 0-690-01118-0. SERIES: Let's-Read-and-Find-Out. SUBJECTS: Human body—Sleep; Sleep. RL B.

After a discussion of the ways a variety of animals sleep, the reader is led into a look at why humans need sleep and what happens when they are deprived of it. The pictures are detailed ink and wash sketches that complement the subject very well.

2071 *What Happens to a Hamburger*. Rev. ed. Ill. by Anne Rockwell. HarperCollins, hb and pap., 1985. ISBN 0-690-04427-5. SERIES: Let's-Read-and-Find-Out. SUBJECTS: Human body—Digestion. RL C.

A simple, straightforward presentation is made of how digestion works. The book's diagrams and the simple observations that children are encouraged to make will help them to understand the digestive process. Attractive, full color illustrations supplement the text.

2072 *Where Does the Garbage Go?* Ill. by Randy Chewning. Rev. ed. HarperCollins, hb and pap., 1994. ISBN 0-06-021054-0. SERIES: Let's-Read-and-Find-Out Science Books. SUBJECTS: Conservation; Garbage and garbage disposal; Recycling. RL C.

At school a class is learning about garbage and its disposal, and the need for recycling. Readers learn about landfills, waste incinerators, and recycling plants. Very well written and supported with detailed ink-and-watercolor pictures, this book provides good general information.

2073 *You Can't Make a Move without Your Muscles*. Ill. by Harriett Barton. HarperCollins, 1982, o.p. SERIES: Let's-Read-and-Find-Out. SUBJECTS: Human body—Muscles. RL C.

As they learn about the kinds of muscles and their functions, children are encouraged to take part in activities that help them understand and feel how their muscles work. The text is illustrated with very simple childlike pictures, some in color.

2074 *Your Skin and Mine*. Ill. by Kathleen Kuchera. Rev. ed. HarperCollins, 1991. ISBN 0-06-022522-X. SERIES: Let's-Read-and-Find-Out Science Books. SUBJECTS: Human body—Skin. RL C.

A little boy discusses his skin and what it is made of, how it works to protect the body, and how melanin makes the color of skin and can help to prevent some burning from the sun. The updated text and full-color illustrations are even more appealing than in the first edition.

Showers, Paul, and Showers, Kay S.

2075 *Before You Were a Baby*. Ill. by Ingrid Fetz. HarperCollins, 1968, o.p. SERIES: Let's-Read-and-Find-Out Science Books. SUBJECTS: Human body—Reproduction. RL B.

Accurate but not explicit information on human reproduction is provided through a brief text and ink and colored pencil diagrams and drawings. Any children reading this may be inspired to seek more information from other books or from their parents.

Shub, Elizabeth

2076 *Clever Kate*. Ill. by Anita Lobel. Macmillan, 1973, o.p. SERIES: Ready-to-Read. SUBJECTS: Folklore—Germany; Humorous stories. RL B.

The farmer's bride is a kindhearted simpleton who lets peddlers steal their gold. Her foolishness ultimately helps her husband to retrieve it. A well-known humorous German folktale, this version maintains the wit and charm of the Grimms' original. The detailed ink and wash drawings have a folk look.

2077 *Seeing Is Believing*. Ill. by Rachel Isadora. Greenwillow, 1979, 1994. ISBN 0-688-13647-8. SUBJECTS: Folklore—England; Folklore—Ireland; Leprechauns. RL B.

New readers will be entranced by the new cover and larger format of these superb retellings of two folktales. In the first, Tom is tricked by a leprechaun; in the second, he makes his way home in spite of pixies. The detailed pen-and-ink drawings are sure to capture the attention of children.

2078 *The White Stallion*. Ill. by Rachel Isadora. Greenwillow, 1982; Bantam, pap., 1984. ISBN 0-688-01211-6. SERIES: Read-alone. SUBJECTS: Animals—Horses—Fiction; Frontier and pioneer life—Fiction; Western stories. RL B.

Gretchen's grandmother tells her how her great-great-grandmother Gretchen was rescued by a beautiful white stallion on her family's journey west in 1845. A lovely and exciting story, it is illustrated with remarkable ink drawings using cross-hatchings and pointillism.

Silverman, Maida

2079 *Dinosaur Babies*. Ill. by Carol Inouye. Simon & Schuster, 1988, pap., 1990. ISBN 0-671-69438-3. SUBJECTS: Animals—Prehistoric; Dinosaurs. RL C.

After a good introduction that attempts to differentiate between facts and speculation, Silverman presents theories about the behavior and rearing of the young of nine dinosaurs. The text is easily understood and interesting. Attractive detailed pictures do not always interpret the text well.

Silverman, Martin

2080 *My Tooth Is Loose!* Ill. by Amy Aitken. Viking, 1991. ISBN 0-670-83862-4. SERIES: Hello Reading! SUBJECTS: Human body—Teeth—Fiction. RL A.

Georgie has a loose tooth and does not know what to do. Each of his friends has advice that does nothing but scare him. Finally his mother advises that he just wait—and he does. The book, illustrated with watercolors, successfully captures the feelings of a timid child.

Simon, Norma

2081 *Why Am I Different?* Ill. by Dora Leder. Whitman, 1976. ISBN 0-8075-9074-6.

Simon, Norma (cont.)

SERIES: Concept Books. SUBJECTS: Families; Self-esteem. RL B.

The ways that children and their families can differ from each other are presented from many children's perspectives, one per page. The overriding theme of the book is that it is okay to be different—everyone is. The full-page drawings are in black and yellow.

Simon, Seymour

2082 *Finding Out with Your Senses*. Ill. by Emily A. McCully. McGraw-Hill, 1971, o.p. SERIES: Let's-Try-It-Out. SUBJECTS: Science experiments; Senses. RL C.

A thoughtful text calls attention to many things in daily life that are experienced through the senses. Very simple experiments also help readers to appreciate sight, touch, hearing, taste, and smell. Well written, it has attractive black, gray, and blue drawings.

2083 *The Smallest Dinosaurs*. Ill. by Anthony Rao. Crown, 1982, o.p. SUBJECTS: Dinosaurs. RL B.

Young readers are introduced to fossils and to seven kinds of small dinosaurs, ranging in size from about eight inches to that of a person. These dinosaurs may be the ancestors of present-day birds. Generally consistent with current scientific thought, the book is illustrated in three colors in a realistic way.

2084 *Soap Bubble Magic*. Ill. by Stella Ormai. Lothrop, 1985. ISBN 0-688-02685-0. SUBJECTS: Science experiments; Science experiments—Soap bubbles. RL C.

The "magic" of bubbles is explained in easily understood terms. Children are encouraged to experiment with soap and water to understand how surface tension and soap film can entrap air in a bubble. The realistic, three-color drawings are lively and enticing.

Sims, Lesley

2085 *Exploring Space*. Ill. by Jamie Medlin. Raintree, 1994. ISBN 0-8114-5507-6. SERIES: First Starts. SUBJECTS: Space travel. RL C.

A brief overview of space travel and the means by which man has attempted to explore space are included here. An attractive layout of color paintings and photographs augments the text. Glossary is included.

2086 *The Moon*. Ill. by Michael Lye. Raintree, 1994. ISBN 0-8114-5504-1. SERIES: First Starts. SUBJECTS: Astronomy; Space Travel. RL C.

A brief look at the moon as a satellite of the earth and also as the site for space travel and exploration, this book has an attractive format with a good blend of paintings and photographs. Index and glossary are included.

2087 *Planets*. Ill. by Nick Shewring. Raintree, 1994. ISBN 0-8114-5506-8. SERIES: First Starts. SUBJECTS: Astronomy; Space travel. RL C.

Basic facts about each of the planets in this solar system are presented along with the Big Bang theory for the creation of them. Good layout of paintings and photographs adds to the brief text. Index and glossary follow.

2088 *The Sun and Stars*. Ill. by Ian Thompson. Raintree, 1994. ISBN 0-8114-5505-X. SERIES: First Starts. SUBJECTS: Astronomy. RL C.

Stars, supernovas, light, galaxies, constellations, and so on are given brief explanatory comments. The book is attractively illustrated with color photographs and paintings. Index and glossary are included.

Singer, Bill

2089 *The Fox with Cold Feet*. Ill. by Dennis Kendrick. Parents Magazine Pr., 1980. ISBN 0-8368-0890-8. SERIES: Read Aloud Originals. SUBJECTS: Animals—Fiction; Animals—Foxes—Fiction; Humorous stories. RL B.

On a cold winter day, a sparrow tells fox that he needs boots to keep his feet warm. First sparrow, then beaver, then raccoon, trick fox into helping them in exchange for useless "boots." The silly story has broad enough humor to attract young readers. It is illustrated with heavily outlined paintings.

Sipiera, Paul P.

2090 *Globes*. Photos. Childrens Pr., 1991. ISBN
0-516-01124-3. SERIES: New True.
SUBJECTS: Concepts—Time; Globes. RL B.
The proof that the earth is round, the development of longitude and latitude, time zones, and much more are a part of this look at globes of all kinds. Text is illustrated with color photographs; a glossary and an index are appended.

2091 *I Can Be a Biologist*. Photos. Childrens
Pr., 1992. ISBN 0-516-01966-X. SERIES: I
Can Be. SUBJECTS: Biology and biologists;
Careers; Science and scientists. RL C.
The amount of education and hard work involved in becoming a biologist are weighed against the satisfaction of a career devoted to working with or for animals and humans. The color photographs show a variety of individuals and their work. The book has an index and a glossary.

2092 *I Can Be a Chemist*. Photos. Childrens
Pr., 1992. ISBN 0-516-01965-1. SERIES: I
Can Be. SUBJECTS: Careers; Chemistry
and chemists; Science and scientists. RL
C.
Biochemistry, pharmacy, and environmental chemistry are just a few of the fields in which an individual interested in chemistry can work. The great variety of occupations makes the area inviting. Illustrated with color photographs, the book also has a glossary and an index.

2093 *I Can Be a Geologist*. Photos. Childrens
Pr., 1986. ISBN 0-516-01897-3. SERIES: I
Can Be. SUBJECTS: Careers; Geology and
geologists; Science and scientists. RL C.
Using color photographs and large, well-spaced type, the author explains the training and work required of those entering the field of geology. The great diversity of work within the field is also explored. Index and glossary are included.

2094 *I Can Be a Physicist*. Photos. Childrens
Pr., 1991. ISBN 0-516-01964-3. SERIES: I
Can Be. SUBJECTS: Careers; Physics and
physicists; Science and scientists. RL C.
For individuals interested in science and mathematics, the study of physics is presented as a fascinating and exciting career area with great possibilities for making discoveries. Illustrated with color photographs, the book includes an index and a glossary.

2095 *I Can Be an Astronomer*. Photos.
Childrens Pr., 1986, o.p. SERIES: I Can
Be. SUBJECTS: Astronomy and
astronomers; Careers. RL C.
The many ways astronomers help mankind—through development of calendars, predicting eclipses, and so on—as well as the satisfaction of studying the stars and planets are part of this introductory look at astronomy as a career. Color photographs accent the text as do an index and a glossary.

2096 *I Can Be an Oceanographer*. Photos.
Childrens Pr., 1987. ISBN 0-516-01905-8.
SERIES: I Can Be. SUBJECTS: Careers;
Oceans and ocean life. RL C.
Measuring tides, observing animal life, studying minerals in the depths of the oceans—individuals interested in the sea have a great many careers to choose from. Color photographs supplement the useful text. Index and glossary are appended.

Siracusa, Catherine

2097 *Bingo, the Best Dog in the World*. Ill. by
Sidney Levitt. HarperCollins, 1991. ISBN
0-06-025812-8. SERIES: I Can Read
Books. SUBJECTS: Pets—Dogs—Fiction;
Siblings—Fiction. RL B.
Sam and her brother Stuart, wanting to give their dog a bath, trap her with too many dog treats. By the time they get her to the school dog show, Bingo has eaten so much that she just wants to sleep. Very childlike pen and ink drawings with watercolors add to the fun of the text.

2098 *The Giant Zucchini*. Ill. by author.
Hyperion, 1993. ISBN 1-56282-286-1.
SUBJECTS: Animals—Fiction; Fairs—
Fiction; Plants—Zucchini—Fiction.
RL B.
Two animal friends plant one giant zucchini seed and end up with one very tiny zucchini—until they start singing to it. Then it grows big enough to be guaranteed a prize at the fair, unless Humphrey Hog gets the better of them.

Siracusa, Catherine (cont.)

Illustrated with humorous cartoonlike paintings.

2099 *No Mail for Mitchell*. Ill. by author. Random House, hb and pap., 1990. ISBN 0-679-90476-X. SERIES: Step into Reading. SUBJECTS: Friendship—Fiction; Mail—Fiction. RL B.

Mitchell, a dog, is a good mailman to the animal community but he wishes someone would send him mail. When he gets sick and someone else has to deliver the mail, he gets his wish: a whole bag full of get-well notes. Well done pictures with child appeal illustrate the story.

2100 *The Parrot Problem*. Ill. by author. Hyperion, 1994. ISBN 1-56282-626-3. SUBJECTS: Animals—Birds—Fiction; Animals—Parrots—Fiction; Humorous stories. RL B.

While her aunt takes a nap, Gina takes her parrot, Pepperoni, outside, lets him out of the cage, and ends up chasing him through town as he creates one near disaster after another. The bright, attractive art uses a variety of media.

Sislowitz, Marcel

2101 *Look! How Your Eyes See*. Ill. by Jim Arnosky. Putnam, 1977, o.p. SERIES: Science Is What and Why. SUBJECTS: Human body—Eyes. RL B.

Detailed information is provided on the various parts of the eye with clear explanations of how each works. The section on eye care and visual problems suggests seeing an ophthalmologist for treatment. A page on eye care, a glossary, and a brief index are included. Amusing ink drawings help clarify the text.

Sitomer, Mindel, and Sitomer, Harry

2102 *Circles*. Ill. by George Giusti. HarperCollins, 1971, o.p. SERIES: Young Math. SUBJECTS: Mathematics. RL C.

Exercises using compass, ruler, and paper introduce the young reader to some of the terminology (radius, diameter) of circles and to many of their properties. Diagrams show the concepts and present a number of attractive geometric designs based on the circle.

Skoglund, Elizabeth

2103 *Harold's Dog Horace Is Scared of the Dark*. Ill. by Dale Bjorkman. Tyndale, pap., 1992. ISBN 0-8423-1047-9. SERIES: I Can Talk About It. SUBJECTS: Bible stories—Fiction; Emotions—Fears—Fiction; Pets—Dogs—Fiction. RL B.

When Harold and his dog go to visit his aunt and uncle at their oceanside home, he becomes fearful at night, hearing strange sounds and worrying. His aunt tells how to use his mental tape player to combat his fears. An afterword explains how a child can be shown ways to use this mental device to control fears. Illustrated with unpolished pencil drawings.

Skurzynski, Gloria

2104 *Honest Andrew*. Ill. by David Wiesner. Harcourt, 1980, o.p. SERIES: Let Me Read. SUBJECTS: Animals—Otters—Fiction; Behavior—Honest—Fiction; Behavior—Manners—Fiction. RL C.

Andrew, a young otter, tries hard to keep his word to his father and always tell the truth. Unfortunately, telling the truth can sometimes conflict with good manners and Andrew's honesty gets him into trouble. The humorous story is illustrated with skillful, realistic drawings.

Slater, Teddy

2105 *N-O Spells No!* Ill. by Meredith Johnson. Scholastic, pap., 1993. ISBN 0-590-44186-8. SERIES: Hello Reader! SUBJECTS: Behavior—Argumentative—Fiction; Parent and child—Fiction; Stories in rhyme. RL B.

Katie is determined to do the opposite of anything her mother suggests—even when her mother attempts to bribe her with ice cream and a puppy. Finally Mom learns the power of reverse psychology. The pictures show an obnoxious child exhibiting behavior much too young for her age. Illustrations are ink and watercolor.

2106 *The Wrong-Way Rabbit*. Ill. by Diane de Groat. Scholastic, pap., 1993. ISBN 0-590-45359-9. SERIES: Hello Reader! SUBJECTS: Animals—Rabbits—Fiction; Behavior—Fiction; Stories in rhyme. RL B.
Tibbar Jack does everything backward—counting, bathing with his clothes on, putting his socks on his ears, and so on. The silly rhyming story has obvious humor suited to young readers and is illustrated with comical watercolors.

Sleator, William

2107 *Once, Said Darlene*. Ill. by Steven Kellogg. Dutton, 1979, o.p. SERIES: Fat Cat. SUBJECTS: Behavior—Lying—Fiction; Fantasy; Friendship—Fiction. RL A.
When Darlene tells fantastic stories about the adventures she used to have, none of her friends but Peter believe her. It is his belief that frees her to return to her magic kingdom. Children will empathize with Darlene while enjoying the fanciful illustrations, in ink and wash.

2108 *That's Silly*. Ill. by Lawrence DiFiori. Dutton, 1981, o.p. SERIES: Smart Cat. SUBJECTS: Fantasy; Imagination—Fiction; Magic—Fiction. RL A.
More practical and analytical than Tom, Rachel thinks that his constant need to pretend is silly until the two children become involved with magic. Then imagination is essential to their survival. Pastel peach and gray washes with pencil and ink accent illustrate the story well.

Smath, Jerry

2109 *But No Elephants*. Ill. by author. Parents Magazine Pr., hb and pap., 1979. ISBN 0-8193-1007-7. SERIES: Read Aloud Originals. SUBJECTS: Animals—Elephants—Fiction; Animals—Fiction; Humorous stories. RL B.
Grandma Tildy buys one animal after another, making each welcome in her little house, and reluctantly agrees to take the elephant. When winter comes she is forced to bring it inside. Instead of creating a disaster, the elephant finds a way to get them all to a warmer climate. The story is illustrated with humorous paintings.

2110 *The Housekeeper's Dog*. Ill. by author. Parents Magazine Pr., 1980. ISBN 0-8368-0885-1. SUBJECTS: Behavior—Manners—Fiction; Behavior—Selfish—Fiction; Pets—Dogs—Fiction. RL B.
While the housekeeper is away on a brief vacation, her dog is at a dog-training school becoming a vain and arrogant semihuman. On her return she gets fed up with her dog's behavior and sends him away. He returns, happy to be just a dog again. The rollicking story is illustrated in full color.

2111 *Mystery at Camp Crump*. Ill. by author. Troll, hb and pap., 1994. ISBN 0-8167-3422-4. SERIES: Investigator. SUBJECTS: Animals—Alligators and crocodiles—Fiction; Mysteries; Puzzles—Fiction. RL C.
Investigator gets a letter from his nephew asking him to solve the mystery of the creature who is scaring him and his fellow campers. Mixed into the humorous watercolor pictures are puzzles that challenge readers' observation skills.

2112 *Pretzel and Pop's Closetful of Stories*. Ill. by author. Silver Burdett, 1991. ISBN 0-671-72232-8. SUBJECTS: Animals—Rabbits—Fiction; Family life—Fiction; Humorous stories. RL B.
When things pour out of their overstuffed closet, bunny Pretzel's father is reminded of stories about their family and friends. Longer than many books for beginning readers, this is divided into eight stories and illustrated with humorous watercolor pictures.

Smith, Janice Lee

2113 *Wizard and Wart*. Ill. by Paul Meisel. HarperCollins, 1994. ISBN 0-06-022960-8. SERIES: I Can Read Books. SUBJECTS: Magic—Fiction; Pets—Dogs—Fiction; Wizards—Fiction. RL B.
When Wizard and his dog, Wart, move into their new home, they are sure they will get plenty of customers for their magical problem solving. After advertising works, the twosome have more problems than they want to handle. Comical situations are illustrated with cartoonlike watercolors and ink.

Smith, Lucia

2114 *My Mom Got a Job*. Ill. by C. Christian Johanson. Holt, Rinehart, 1979, o.p. SUBJECTS: Family life—Fiction; Mothers, working—Fiction. RL B.

A little girl recalls the special times she and her mother shared before she went back to work. Then she tells about the special things she does instead that have become just as important. A good look at the pros and cons of having a working mother. The detailed ink drawings have pink accents.

Smith, Mary M.

2115 *Orla's Upside Down Day*. Ill. by Jan Lewis. Forest House, 1990. ISBN 1-878363-05-0. SERIES: Quality Time. SUBJECTS: Imaginative play—Fiction. RL A.

All day long Orla and her friend do everything upside-down and even inspire others to have fun doing it as well. The repetitive text and funny watercolor pictures should attract young readers.

Smith, Mavis

2116 *A Snake Mistake*. Ill. by author. Harper-Collins, pap., 1991. ISBN 0-06-107426-8. SERIES: Amazing Animal Reader SUBJECTS: Animals—Snakes; Farm and country life. RL B.

Meaning to fool his chickens into laying more eggs, a farmer puts light bulbs in their nests. The only one that is fooled is a pine snake, which swallows two of the bulbs. The kindly farmer rushes the snake to the vet. Cartoon illustrations in full color lighten this true story.

Smith, Susan M.

2117 *No One Should Have Six Cats*. Ill. by Judith Friedman. Follett, 1982, o.p. SERIES: Beginning to Read. SUBJECTS: Pets—Cats—Fiction. RL A.

David rescues one homeless cat after another until his mother says no one should have six cats. While David worries about which cat to give up, Mom, as kindhearted as her son, picks up another stray. The story and humor-

ous watercolor pictures depict a caring and responsible child.

Snell, Nigel

2118 *Nita's Gerbil*. Ill. by author. Childrens Pr., 1988, o.p. SERIES: First Pet Care Book. SUBJECTS: Pet care; Pets—Gerbils. RL C.

With her parents' support Nita gets two female gerbils and learns how to take care of them. Using just the right amount of information for young readers, this book realistically presents the rigors and joys of pet ownership. Illustrations are colorful cartoon pictures.

2119 *Roy's Puppy*. Ill. by author. Childrens Pr., 1988, o.p. SERIES: First Pet Care Book. SUBJECTS: Pet care; Pets—Dogs. RL C.

The fun and work of having and training a dog are seen in this good look at dog care. Though the book is directed to children, it emphasizes the importance of involving parents. Responsible pet ownership is stressed as well. Cartoon illustrations personalize and lighten the text.

2120 *Sam's Rabbit*. Ill. by author. Childrens Pr., 1988, o.p. SERIES: First Pet Care Book. SUBJECTS: Pet care; Pets—Rabbits. RL C.

Solid information on caring for a pet rabbit is shown using Sam's care of his pet, Bugsie, as an example. The book discusses building a hutch, keeping it clean, providing food, water, and salt, and being responsible in handling the animal. Colorful cartoon illustrations work well with the text.

Snow, Pegeen

2121 *Eat Your Peas, Louise!* Ill. by Mike Venezia. Childrens Pr., hb and pap., 1985. ISBN 0-516-02067-6. SERIES: Rookie Readers. SUBJECTS: Food—Fiction; Stories in rhyme. RL A.

Louise seems impervious to any attempts to convince her to eat her peas until her big brother finally says please. The rough, full color illustrations and brief rhyming text are vibrant and funny.

2122 *A Pet for Pat*. Ill. by Tom Dunnington. Childrens Pr., hb and pap., 1984. ISBN 0-

516-02049-8. SERIES: Rookie Readers. SUBJECTS: Pets—Dogs—Fiction; Stories in rhyme. RL A.

Pat's parents take her to the pound to choose a dog. Back home with her new pet, Pat introduces it to her friend. The rhyming story is short, uses very few words, and depends on the realistic full color paintings to help in its telling.

Solomon, Chuck

2123 *Our Little League*. Photos by author. Crown, 1988, o.p. SUBJECTS: Sports—Baseball. RL A.

The Little Mets, a little league baseball team from Brooklyn, practice batting and fielding, get pep talks, and play and win a game. Throughout the photo story the children (one girl is on the team) are encouraged to have fun. The color photographs are excellent and the text is good.

2124 *Our Soccer League*. Photos by author. Crown, 1988, o.p. SUBJECTS: Sports—Soccer. RL A.

While Solomon's text is not meant to "teach" soccer, his photostory of a game played by elementary school children does show what fun the game can be. Further, it presents in clear color photos a multiracial melting pot of boys and girls having a good time.

Sorrells, Dorothy

2125 *The Little Shell Hunter*. Ill. by Carol Rogers. Raintree, 1961, o.p. SUBJECTS: Shells. RL B.

Realistic three-color pictures of shells in their habitats are matched to a very brief, informative text. The shell pictures are all labeled and the text includes something about the live inhabitants of the shells and how they live.

Spanjian, Beth

2126 *Baby Duckbill*. Ill. by Karel Havlicek-Novosad. Western, 1990. ISBN 0-307-12600-5. SERIES: Golden Look-Look Nature Books. SUBJECTS: Dinosaurs. RL B.

Using a story format, the supposed life-style of a young duckbill dinosaur is presented. Fol-

lowing that is a page of information meant for an older reader or adult. It provides known facts about this dinosaur. Illustrations are detailed colored pencil drawings.

2127 *Baby Grizzly*. Ill. by John Butler. Childrens Pr., 1988, 1990. ISBN 0-307-12595-5. SERIES: Little Reader. SUBJECTS: Animals—Bears. RL C.

Two grizzly bear cubs share a summer day with their mother—fishing, playing, and learning to take care of themselves. The interesting story is short, has large print, and is illustrated with full color, realistic pictures. The text is followed by a page of facts about grizzlies.

2128 *Baby Raccoon*. Ill. by Eva Cellini. Childrens Pr., 1988, 1990. ISBN 0-307-12596-3. SERIES: Little Reader. SUBJECTS: Animals—Raccoons. RL C.

The text tells about a family of raccoons exploring their surroundings on a quiet summer night. The brief story is interesting, has large print, and is followed by a page of facts about raccoons. Realistic full color pictures.

2129 *Baby Stegosaurus*. Ill. by Alex Bloch. Western, 1990. ISBN 0-307-12601-3. SERIES: Golden Look-Look Nature Books. SUBJECTS: Dinosaurs. RL C.

After hatching, a baby stegosaurus joins its siblings in hunting for food. Hiding from a predator, they witness an adult stegosaurus defending itself. A page of more detailed information follows. It is geared to older children or adults. Illustrations are detailed watercolors.

2130 *Baby Triceratops*. Ill. by John Butler. Western, 1990. ISBN 0-307-12602-1. SERIES: Golden Look-Look Nature Books. SUBJECTS: Dinosaurs. RL C.

After hatching, the young triceratops stays in the nest until its mother decides to lead it out to forage and learn about danger. While the story supposes a family life for this dinosaur, the addendum gives basic known facts about the animal. Detailed watercolors illustrate the text.

2131 *Baby Wolf*. Ill. by Bob Travers. Childrens Pr., 1988, 1990. ISBN 0-307-12598-X. SERIES: Little Reader. SUBJECTS: Animals—Wolves. RL C.

Spanjian, Beth (cont.)

Baby Wolf is shown in the midst of his family practicing his hunting, playing, and learning from others. The brief text is followed by a page of facts about wolves and is illustrated with full color, realistic paintings.

Springstubb, Tricia

2132 *My Minnie Is a Jewel*. Ill. by Jim La Marche. Carolrhoda, 1980, o.p. SERIES: On My Own. SUBJECTS: Humorous stories; Marriage—Fiction. RL A.
Minnie is forever distracted and her cooking suffers because of it. To her husband, Henry, everything she does is just right. Strangers bet a casket of jewels that Henry will not like or eat the huge and ugly cake she baked and of course they lose. This humorous story is illustrated with detailed ink sketches.

Srivastava, Jane J.

2133 *Averages*. Ill. by Aliki. HarperCollins, 1975, o.p. SERIES: Young Math. SUBJECTS: Mathematics. RL C.
Clear, careful explanations paired with opportunities to try out concepts help children to gain an understanding of mean, mode, and arithmetic mean. Ink and pencil drawings aid in the communication of information.

Stadler, John

2134 *The Adventures of Snail at School*. Ill. by author. HarperCollins, 1993. ISBN 0-06-021041-9. SERIES: I Can Read Books. SUBJECTS: Animals—Snails—Fiction; Fantasy; School stories. RL B.
In three chapters, the diminutive snail eagerly volunteers to get things for his teacher. Each time he has adventures. A flood erupts from the drinking fountain, a fire extinguisher takes him to outer space, and musical instruments come to life in this humorous story with cartoonlike pictures.

2135 *Cat at Bat*. Ill. by author. Dutton, 1988. ISBN 0-525-44416-5. SERIES: Dutton Easy Reader. SUBJECTS: Animals—Fiction; Stories in rhyme. RL A.

Fourteen three-line, rhyming verses describe animals doing many different and very silly things. The humorous illustrations will help the beginning reader to decipher the nonsensical rhymes.

2136 *Cat Is Back at Bat*. Ill. by author. Dutton, 1991. ISBN 0-525-44762-8. SERIES: Dutton Easy Reader. SUBJECTS: Animals—Fiction; Stories in rhyme. RL A.
Short rhyming sentences describing silly circumstances, such as "A crab tries to grab a cab," are made funnier when accompanied by the zany watercolor illustrations.

2137 *Hooray for Snail!* Ill. by author. HarperCollins, 1984; pap., 1985. ISBN 0-690-04413-5. SUBJECTS: Animals—Snails—Fiction; Sports—Baseball—Fiction. RL A.
When Snail finally gets to bat, he hits the ball so hard it lands on the moon and bounces back. Snail barely makes it around the bases before the ball returns. Full color illustrations show comical animal teammates shouting encouragement to the tiny runner.

2138 *Snail Saves the Day*. Ill. by author. HarperCollins, 1985, o.p. SUBJECTS: Animals—Fiction; Sports—Football—Fiction. RL A.
When his team of small animals is pitted against a team of bears, hippos, and other large creatures, Snail oversleeps, making it to the stadium just in time to make a winning touchdown. Bright, comic illustrations and a very brief story make this appropriate for the beginning reader.

2139 *Three Cheers for Hippo!* Ill. by author. HarperCollins, 1987, o.p. SUBJECTS: Animals—Fiction; Humorous stories. RL A.
Hippo, who is teaching Cat, Dog, and Pig to parachute, must quickly rescue them before they are eaten by alligators. The book's extremely brief text relies on humorous pencil, ink, and watercolor pictures to help tell the story.

Stamper, Judith B.

2140 *What's It Like to Be a Bus Driver*. Ill. by T. R. Garcia. Troll, hb and pap., 1990.

ISBN 0-8167-1795-8. SERIES: What's It Like to Be a . . . . SUBJECTS: Buses; Careers. RL C.

The training, knowledge, and skill required of a bus driver and the daily routines he follows are included in an introductory look at this career. Illustrations are colorful cartoonlike pictures.

2141 *What's It Like to Be a Dentist.* Ill. by Dana Gustafson. Troll, hb and pap., 1990. 0-8167-1799-0. SERIES: What's It Like to Be a . . . . SUBJECTS: Careers; Dentists; Human body—Teeth. RL B.

A child's first visit to a dentist offers an opportunity to demonstrate the many tools used and the things done to keep teeth healthy. Very little career training information is provided. Simple Pentel and watercolor illustrations are used.

2142 *What's It Like to Be a Truck Driver.* Ill. by George Ulrich. Troll, hb and pap., 1989. ISBN 0-8167-1424-X. SERIES: What's It Like to Be a . . . . SUBJECTS: Careers; Trucks. RL C.

The kinds of trucks and the cargoes they carry, as well as the skill required of drivers, are discussed here. Also included are some trucking terms frequently used on CBs. Text is illustrated with ink drawings with color washes.

2143 *What's It Like to Be a Veterinarian.* Ill. by Marcy Dunn Ramsey. Troll, hb and pap., 1990. ISBN 0-8167-1817-2. SERIES: What's It Like to Be a . . . . SUBJECTS: Careers; Doctors and nurses; Pet care. RL C.

When Ben takes his sick puppy to the veterinarian, he asks her how to become a vet. Through Ben and other clients, readers learn what kind of work she does daily. Sketchy watercolors illustrate the story.

2144 *What's It Like to Be a Zoo Worker.* Ill. by Kathleen Garry-McCord. Troll, hb and pap., 1989. ISBN 0-8167-1440-1. SERIES: What's It Like to Be a . . . . SUBJECTS: Careers; Zoos. RL C.

To make today's modern zoo run smoothly, a great many well-trained people are needed. This book briefly introduces the staff and the kinds of work they do. Illustrations are very attractive colored pencil drawings.

Standiford, Natalie

2145 *The Best Little Monkeys in the World.* Ill. by Hilary Knight. Random House, hb and pap., 1987. ISBN 0-394-98616-4. SERIES: Step into Reading. SUBJECTS: Animals—Monkeys—Fiction; Baby-sitting—Fiction; Humorous stories. RL B.

Marvin and Mary are two mischievous little monkeys whose baby-sitter is so wrapped up in her telephone conversations that she is oblivious to the mess they are creating. The colorful pencil and wash pictures are full of unexpected details and add to the humor in this funny story.

2146 *The Bravest Dog Ever: The True Story of Balto.* Ill. by Donald Cook. Random House, hb and pap., 1989. ISBN 0-394-99695-X. SERIES: Step into Reading. SUBJECTS: Alaska—History; Animals—Dogs; Diseases. RL B.

When medicine is urgently needed to save the people of Nome from diphtheria, Balto, a sled dog, bravely leads his team over 53 miles through heavy snow and subzero weather to get the serum to them. Good illustrations help tell this true story.

2147 *The Headless Horseman.* Ill. by Donald Cook. Random House, 1992. ISBN 0-679-81241-5. SERIES: Step into Reading. SUBJECTS: Ghost stories; Legends—Fiction. RL C.

Ichabod Crane, the vain Sleepy Hollow schoolteacher, is certain that he will marry Katrina until the night he meets the headless horseman on his way home. Told with a sly humor, especially evident in the colorful pictures, the book is a good retelling of the classic story.

Stanek, Muriel

2148 *Left, Right, Left, Right!* Ill. by Lucy Hawkinson. Whitman, 1969, o.p. SERIES: Concept Books. SUBJECTS: Concepts—Left and right—Fiction; Self-esteem—Fiction. RL B.

Katie gets confused between left and right, turns in the wrong direction during a parade, and is humiliated. Her grandmother gives her a ring for her right hand and that solves her

Stanek, Muriel (cont.)

problem. A sensitive look at a problem faced by many children, it is illustrated in black and white and in color.

Stanovich, Betty Jo

2149 *Hedgehog Adventures*. Ill. by Chris L. Demarest. Lothrop, 1983, o.p. SUBJECTS: Animals—Hedgehogs—Fiction; Animals—Woodchucks—Fiction. RL B.
Exuberant Hedgehog takes his friend Woodchuck on three ill-fated adventures. Each time his spirits are revived by his kindly homebody friend Woodchuck. The gentle, expressive pencil drawings capture the pair's moods and the story's fun.

2150 *Hedgehog Surprises*. Ill. by Chris L. Demarest. Lothrop, 1984, o.p. SUBJECTS: Animals—Hedgehogs—Fiction; Animals— Woodchucks—Fiction; Birthdays—Fiction. RL B.
Excitable Hedgehog is saved from worry and a disastrous case of nerves by his friend Woodchuck as he tries to give Bear a perfect birthday party. Expressive colored pencil drawings are as humorous as the very funny story.

Staub, Frank

2151 *Mountain Goats*. Photos by the author. Lerner, 1994. ISBN 0-8225-3000-7. SERIES: Early Bird Nature Books. SUBJECTS: Animals—Mountain goats. RL C.
Well organized into chapters and attractively illustrated with carefully placed photographs, this introduction to the mountain goat makes interesting reading. The life cycle, enemies, and habitat of the animal are discussed.

Stevens, Bryna

2152 *Ben Franklin's Glass Armonica*. Ill. by Priscilla Kiedrowski. Carolrhoda, 1983, o.p.; Dell, pap., 1992. ISBN 0-440-40584-X. SERIES: On My Own. SUBJECTS: Biographies; Musical instruments; United States—History. RL B.
Ben Franklin hears someone perform a concert on crystal glasses and is so fascinated by the sound that he creates an armonica—an instrument played by rubbing one's fingertips over glass bowls on rods. Even Mozart composed for the armonica. Illustrated with realistic pencil drawings.

Stevens, Carla

2153 *Anna, Grandpa, and the Big Storm*. Ill. by Margot Tomes. Houghton Mifflin, 1982; Penguin, pap., 1986. ISBN 0-89919-066-9. SUBJECTS: Emergencies—Fiction; Grandparents—Fiction; Weather—Snow—Fiction. RL B.
Grandpa changes his mind about staying in New York City after helping Anna and other stranded passengers get back home during a terrible blizzard in the late 1800s. The exciting story is illustrated with detailed realistic pen and ink drawings.

2154 *Hooray for Pig!* Ill. by Rainey Bennett. Seabury, 1974, o.p. SUBJECTS: Animals—Pigs—Fiction; Emotions—Fear—Fiction; Sports—Swimming—Fiction. RL A.
Afraid of the water, Pig does not even want to try swimming until Otter patiently helps him begin to overcome his fear. A good handling of a common situation—it does not make fears magically disappear but shows how much work it takes. Illustrated with simple line drawings with washes.

2155 *Pig and the Blue Flag*. Ill. by Rainey Bennett. Seabury, 1977, o.p. SUBJECTS: Animals—Fiction; School stories; Self-esteem—Fiction. RL B.
Pig is so big and heavy that he never seems to do anything right in gym. Then Otter suggests they play Capture the Flag, and everyone is a winner. Children will empathize with Pig and be glad he finally succeeds. Illustrated with pen and ink drawings with soft blue and orange washes.

2156 *Sara and the Pinch*. Ill. by John Wallner. Houghton Mifflin, 1980, o.p. SUBJECTS: Behavior; School stories. RL B.
At school Sara is always determined to have things her own way and can be quite pesky when she does not. Reprimanded for pinching and sent into the hall, Sara is comforted by Mr. Zamatsky, the school custodian. Colored

pencil and wash pictures capture Sara's feisty, independent nature.

2157 *Your First Pet and How to Take Care of It*. Ill. by Lisl Weil. Macmillan, 1974, o.p. SERIES: Ready-to-Read. SUBJECTS: Pet care; Pets. RL B.

Good advice on the care and training of eight popular animals is offered to children about to select a pet. Not the usual overview of a subject found in most books for beginning readers, this is a substantial 120 pages of good information with help from sketchy ink drawings.

Stevens, Philippa J.

2158 *Bonk! Goes the Ball*. Ill. by Clovis Martin. Childrens Pr., 1990. ISBN 0-516-02061-7. SERIES: Rookie Readers. SUBJECTS: Sports—Soccer—Fiction. RL A.

A little girl does her best to play well in a game of soccer and finally makes a goal. Colorful watercolor illustrations add a light touch and help tell the very short story.

Stevenson, James

2159 *Clams Can't Sing*. Ill. by author. Greenwillow, 1980, o.p. SERIES: Read-alone. SUBJECTS: Animals—Mollusks—Fiction; Humorous stories; Seashore—Fiction. RL B.

The seashore animals confidently prepare for their concert and just as confidently tell Beatrice and Foster they are not in it because clams cannot sing. The two surprise everyone with a symphony for two clams. Hilarious text and drawings might get children to try to create their own music.

2160 *Fast Friends: Two Stories*. Ill. by author. Greenwillow, 1979, o.p. SERIES: Read-alone. SUBJECTS: Animals—Fiction; Friendship—Fiction; Self-esteem—Fiction. RL B.

The first story has Murry, a turtle, and Fred, a snail, get plenty of friends when they find a skateboard. In the second story Clem Turtle convinces Thomas Mouse to build a house to attract friends. In both stories the humorous characters come to accept themselves. Pictures are ink and wash.

2161 *The Mud Flat Olympics*. Ill. by author. Greenwillow, 1994. ISBN 0-688-12923-4. SUBJECTS: Animals—Fiction; Humorous stories; Olympics—Fiction. RL B.

The elephants, hippos, skunks, moles, and even snails of Mud Flat compete in their own special version of the Olympics. When the games are finished, everyone happily shares a picnic. The quiet but delightfully humorous stories are illustrated with droll ink-and-watercolor pictures.

2162 *Oh No, It's Waylon's Birthday!* Ill. by author. Greenwillow, 1989. ISBN 0-688-08235-1. SUBJECTS: Animals—Fiction; Birthdays—Fiction; Humorous stories. RL B.

In three different stories, an elephant has a very unusual two-hundred and forty-ninth birthday; a hippo discovers noise can be just right for sleeping; and penguins slip and slide to the water's edge—and into it. Delightful ink-and-watercolor wash paintings carry through on the fun.

2163 *Which One Is Whitney?* Ill. by author. Greenwillow, 1990. ISBN 0-688-09061-3. SUBJECTS: Animals—Dugongs—Fiction; Humorous stories. RL B.

Of Mrs. Dugong's five children, Whitney is the one who is not so noticeably polite, funny, friendly, or cheerful—or is he? In three short stories Whitney cleverly outsmarts his sea mammal family as well as overconfident fish. Illustrations are simply drawn, humorous ink-and-watercolor paintings.

2164 *Winston, Newton, Elton, and Ed*. Ill. by author. Greenwillow, 1978, o.p. SERIES: Read-alone. SUBJECTS: Animals—Penguins—Fiction; Animals—Walruses—Fiction; Sibling rivalry—Fiction. RL B.

In the first of two Antarctic stories, three little walrus brothers are so intent on upstaging each other that they lose their dinners. In the second, Ed, a penguin, is marooned on an ice floe, far from his friends. Deftly drawn humorous pictures accompany the two very funny stories.

Still, John

2165 *Amazing Beetles*. Photos. Knopf, 1991. ISBN 0-679-81519-8. SERIES: Eyewitness

Still, John (cont.)

Juniors. SUBJECTS: Animals—Beetles; Animals—Insects. RL C.

Clear photographic silhouettes of beetles, accompanied by small watercolor paintings of additional beetles, are supported by a brief text and much captioning. The very inviting book offers a good deal of information while giving the appearance of being a "browser." Index is included.

Stille, Darlene R.

2166 *The Greenhouse Effect*. Photos. Childrens Pr., 1990. ISBN 0-516-01106-5. SERIES: New True. SUBJECTS: Global warming. RL C.

A clear explanation of how the earth holds in heat and keeps it balanced is offered. Potential dangers of global warming are also shown, with their possible causes. Clear color photographs, a table of contents, an index, and a glossary are included.

2167 *The Ice Age*. Photos. Childrens Pr., 1990. ISBN 0-516-01107-3. SERIES: New True. SUBJECTS: History—Ice Age. RL C.

A carefully written text is accompanied by museum photographs and paintings depicting Ice Age humans and animals. Information about glacial epochs is interesting and presented in a manner that stresses the theoretical aspect of knowledge about the time. Index, table of contents, and glossary are included.

2168 *Soil Erosion and Pollution*. Photos. Childrens Pr., 1990. ISBN 0-516-01188-X. SERIES: New True. SUBJECTS: Pollution; Soil erosion. RL C.

Problems caused by farming, garbage dumps, toxic waste, and other sources of damage to the soil are looked at and discussed for possible effects they have in polluting land. Color photographs augment the text as do a table of contents, an index, and a glossary.

2169 *Water Pollution*. Photos. Childrens Pr., 1990. ISBN 0-516-01190-1. SERIES: New True. SUBJECTS: Pollution; Water. RL C.

The dangers of water pollution to life on earth are seen in the discussion of its effects on plankton, ground water, and so on. Color pho-

tographs extend the text. Also included are a table of contents, an index, and a glossary.

Stolz, Mary

2170 *Emmett's Pig*. Ill. by Garth Williams. HarperCollins, 1959. ISBN 0-06-025856-X. SERIES: I Can Read Books. SUBJECTS: Animals—Pigs—Fiction; Pets—Fiction. RL A.

More than anything else, city dweller Emmett wants to see a real pig. For his birthday Emmett's parents take him to a farm and he is given his own piglet—to be raised by the farmer. Soft pencil and wash drawings complement this quiet story of a dream fulfilled.

Stone, Lynn M.

2171 *African Buffalo*. Photos. Rourke, 1990. ISBN 0-86593-052-X. SERIES: African Animal Discovery Library. SUBJECTS: Animals—African buffalo. RL C.

Native to Kenya and Tanzania, the African buffalo lives in herds, is a plant eater, and is often prey to the lion. The life, habits and habitat, enemies, and so on of the animal are briefly explored through alternating pages of colored photographs and text. Index, table of contents, and glossary are included.

2172 *Alligators and Crocodiles*. Photos. Childrens Pr., 1989. ISBN 0-516-01170-7. SERIES: New True. SUBJECTS: Animals—Alligators and crocodiles; Animals—Endangered; Animals—Reptiles and amphibians. RL B.

With full-color photographs and a chapter format, the life-style, habits, physical characteristics (especially those differentiating between the alligator and crocodile), and relatives of these reptilians are all discussed. An index and glossary finish the book.

2173 *Antelopes*. Photos. Rourke, 1990. ISBN 0-86593-053-8. SERIES: African Animal Discovery Library. SUBJECTS: Animals—Antelopes. RL C.

Through a brief text, alternating pages with colored photographs, readers are given an overview of life for the 70 species of African antelopes. The book also includes a table of contents, an index, and a glossary.

2174 *Baboons*. Photos. Rourke, 1990. ISBN 0-86593-067-8. SERIES: Monkey Discovery Library. SUBJECTS: Animals—Baboons. RL C.
Readers are given an opportunity to learn about the general characteristics, habits, and habitat of the seven species of baboons in a brief book with text alternating with full-color photographs. The book also includes a table of contents, an index and a glossary.

2175 *Bats*. Photos. Rourke, 1993. ISBN 0-86593-293-X. SERIES: Discovery Library of Nighttime Animals. SUBJECTS: Animals—Bats; Animals—Endangered. RL C.
How bats locate things, where they live, and what they eat are some of the things discussed in this brief look at an unusual mammal. Color photographs alternate with the text and offer a good introduction to the many kinds of bats. Glossary and index are appended.

2176 *Bears*. Photos. Rourke, 1990. ISBN 0-86593-042-2. SERIES: North American Animal Discovery Library. SUBJECTS: Animals—Bears; Animals—Endangered. RL C.
A descriptive text alternates with pages of full color photographs to introduce general characteristics, habitat, and so on of bears such as the grizzly, polar, and black. The brief book also contains a table of contents, an index, and a glossary.

2177 *Bears*. Photos. Rourke, 1993. ISBN 0-86625-438-2. SERIES: Discovery Library of Predators. SUBJECTS: Animals—Bears. RL C.
Although only the polar bear is a full-time predator, other North American bears are at times predators as well. In alternating pages of text and color photographs, the habits, food, habitat, and so on of a selection of bears are introduced. Index and glossary are appended.

2178 *Beavers*. Photos. Rourke, 1990. ISBN 0-86593-041-4. SERIES: North American Animal Discovery Library. SUBJECTS: Animals—Beavers. RL B.

A very short book with alternating pages of text and rather muddied photographs, this shows beavers and their way of life, their environment, and their relationship to the world of people. An index and a glossary are appended.

2179 *Birds*. Photos. Rourke, 1993. ISBN 0-86625-440-4. SERIES: Discovery Library of Predators. SUBJECTS: Animals—Birds; Animals—Endangered. RL C.
The concentration here is on predator birds, especially hawks, eagles, and owls. There is also mention of egrets, herons, and pelicans. Their means of attacking and killing their prey and their status in the wild are also covered. Color photographs, a glossary, and an index add to the brief text.

2180 *Butterflies*. Photos. Rourke, 1993. ISBN 0-86593-288-3. SERIES: Discovery Library of Insects. SUBJECTS: Animals—Butterflies and moths; Animals—Endangered. RL C.
The development, food, and life cycle of the butterfly are introduced through alternating pages of colorful photographs and clear text. Many examples of butterfly species can be seen in the pictures. An index and a glossary are included.

2181 *Cheetahs*. Photos. Rourke, 1989. ISBN 0-86592-503-8. SERIES: Big Cats Discovery Library. SUBJECTS: Animals—Cats; Animals—Cheetahs. RL C.
An overview of the life, habitat, and enemies of the fastest mammal on earth, this look at the uncatlike cheetah uses alternating pages of topically arranged text and full-color photographs to present its information. Also included are an index, a glossary, and a table of contents.

2182 *Chickens*. Photos. Rourke, 1990. ISBN 0-86593-034-1. SERIES: Farm Animal Discovery Library. SUBJECTS: Animals—Chickens. RL C.
Here chickens, their habits, uses, and history, are introduced to readers via alternating pages of topically arranged text and full-color photographs. The book also includes an index, a table of contents, and a glossary.

2183 *Chimpanzees*. Photos. Rourke, 1990. ISBN 0-86593-064-3. SERIES: Monkey

Stone, Lynn M. (cont.)

Discovery Library. SUBJECTS: Animals—
Monkeys. RL C.
An overview of the life, habits, habitat, and so
on of the chimpanzee is supported by full col-
or photographs accenting the topically
arranged text. The book also contains an index
and a glossary as well as a table of contents.

2184 *Cougars*. Photos. Rourke, 1989. ISBN 0-
86592-505-4. SERIES: Big Cats Discovery
Library. SUBJECTS: Animals—Cats;
Animals—Cougars. RL C.
An animal of many names, the cougar is found
throughout North and South America. The animal's life-style, habits, habitat, and so on are
covered in a topically arranged text alternating
with color photos. The book also includes an
index, a glossary, and a table of contents.

2185 *Cows*. Photos. Rourke, 1990. ISBN 0-
86593-039-2. SERIES: Farm Animal
Discovery Library. SUBJECTS: Animals—
Cows; Farm and country life. RL C.
Not native to North America, the domestic
cow is an import from Europe and other parts
of the world. This brief book is topically
arranged and in alternating pages of text and
color photographs shows how cows are
raised, their uses, their great variety, and so
on. Index and glossary are included.

2186 *Crocodiles*. Photos. Rourke, 1990. ISBN
0-86593-060-0. SERIES: Australian
Animal Library. SUBJECTS: Animals—
Alligators and crocodiles; Animals—
Reptiles and amphibians. RL C.
Its relatives, way of living, habitat, and physical characteristics are subjects covered in this
brief look at the saltwater crocodile. Alternating pages of text and full-color photographs
are supported by an index, a glossary, and a
table of contents.

2187 *Deer*. Photos. Rourke, 1990. ISBN 0-
86593-043-0. SERIES: North American
Animal Discovery Library. SUBJECTS:
Animals—Deer. RL C.
The relatives, habitat, physical characteristics,
and so on of North American deer are
described in a brief text and shown in full-
page color photographs. The book also has an
index, a glossary, and a table of contents.

2188 *Dingoes*. Photos. Rourke, 1990. ISBN 0-
86593-057-0. SERIES: Australian Animal
Library. SUBJECTS: Animals—Dingoes;
Animals—Dogs. RL C.
A wild dog, the dingo is native to Australia and
roams throughout it. The animal's habits,
habitat, life cycle, and physical characteristics
are some of the topics covered in this introductory look at the dingo. Full-color photographs are often grainy and dull. Index and
glossary are included.

2189 *Ducks*. Photos. Rourke, 1990. ISBN 0-
86593-036-8. SERIES: Farm Animal
Discovery Library. SUBJECTS: Animals—
Ducks. RL C.
Though this concentrates most text on the
domestic duck, wild ducks such as the mallard
are also mentioned. The book discusses the
bird's physical characteristics, habits, habitat,
food, and so on. Text alternates with full-page
color photographs. Index, glossary, and table
of contents are included.

2190 *Eagles*. Photos. Rourke, 1989. ISBN 0-
86592-321-3. SERIES: Bird Discovery
Library. SUBJECTS: Animals—Eagles. RL C.
Stone introduces several species of eagles and
gives examples of their habitats, diet, nesting,
and relationship to humans without dwelling
on life cycles or any specifics. The color photographs are good. The brief book includes an
index and glossary.

2191 *Endangered Animals*. Photos. Childrens
Pr., hb and pap., 1984. ISBN 0-516-01724-
1. SERIES: New True. SUBJECTS: Animals—
Endangered. RL C.
Many of the world's endangered animals are
discussed. Stone stresses the role played by
humans as hunters, consumers, and farmers
in destroying wildlife. Animals are shown in
clear full color photographs.

2192 *Fish*. Photos. Rourke, 1993. ISBN 0-
86625-436-6. SERIES: Discovery Library
of Predators. SUBJECTS: Animals—Fish. RL
C.
The shark, lamprey, and muskellunge are a
few of the fish mentioned in this look at fish as
predators. The text is topically arranged and
alternates with full-page colored photographs.
Also included are an index, a table of contents,
and a limited glossary.

2193 *Flamingoes*. Photos. Rourke, 1993, ISBN 0-86593-283-2. SERIES: Discovery Library of Unusual Animals. SUBJECTS: Animals—Birds; Animals—Flamingoes. RL C.
Found throughout the world, the flamingo is known for its pink plumage, long neck, and large bill. The large bird also builds a most unusual chimney-shaped nest of mud. Information about the various types of flamingoes and their habits is accompanied by color photographs, an index, and a glossary.

2194 *Flying Squirrels*. Photos. Rourke, 1993. ISBN 0-86593-298-0. SERIES: Discovery Library of Nighttime Animals. SUBJECTS: Animals—Flying squirrels. RL C.
Unlike tree squirrels, the flying squirrel is nocturnal and is able to glide from tree to tree. Found throughout the world, the animal has membranes that stretch between its side legs and can be used to navigate as it glides. Lifestyle, habitat, and more are included, as are color photographs.

2195 *Frogs*. Photos. Rourke, 1993. ISBN 0-86593-279-4. SERIES: Discovery Library of Unusual Animals. SUBJECTS: Animals—Frogs and toads; Animals—Reptiles and amphibians. RL C.
Good color photographs alternate with topical pages of text to give readers an introduction to some of the many species of frogs found throughout the world. The book covers generally their life cycle, food, means of protection, and so on. It also includes an index and a glossary.

2196 *Gibbons*. Photos. Rourke, 1990. ISBN 0-86593-062-7. SERIES: Monkey Discovery Library. SUBJECTS: Animals—Gibbons; Animals—Endangered. RL C.
Endangered because of deforestation, gibbons are apes that live high in trees and have few enemies. Their physical characteristics, habits, habitat, and more are introduced via text and full-color photographs. Index, glossary, and table of contents are included.

2197 *Giraffes*. Photos. Rourke, 1990. ISBN 0-86593-050-3. SERIES: African Animal Discovery Library. SUBJECTS: Animals—Giraffes. RL C.
Living in areas south of the Sahara Desert, the giraffe is in danger of losing its habitat to

humans. In this introduction to the world's tallest animal, its habitat, relatives, physical characteristics, and so on are mentioned in a text that alternates pages with full-color photographs.

2198 *Gorillas*. Photos. Rourke, 1990. ISBN 0-86593-063-5. SERIES: Monkey Discovery Library. SUBJECTS: Animals—Endangered; Animals—Gorillas. RL C.
Gorillas are native to rain forest areas in Africa. The author describes this endangered animal's habitat, life cycle, food, and more. Page-length topical discussions are complemented with full-color photographs. The book also contains a table of contents, an index, and a glossary.

2199 *Hippopotamus*. Photos. Rourke, 1990. ISBN 0-86593-051-1. SERIES: African Animal Discovery Library. SUBJECTS: Animals—Hippopotami. RL C.
The life-style, habitat, predators of, and future hopes for the survival of the hippopotamus are explored in a brief, topically arranged text complemented by color photographs. The book is made more accessible by a table of contents, an index, and a glossary.

2200 *Horses*. Photos. Rourke, 1990. ISBN 0-86593-035-X. SERIES: Farm Animal Discovery Library. SUBJECTS: Animals—Horses. RL C.
Stone uses color photographs alternating with topical pages of text to give readers a glimpse of the history, uses, life, and habitat of a variety of horses. The brief book also contains a table of contents, an index, and a glossary.

2201 *Hyenas*. Photos. Rourke, 1990. ISBN 0-86593-049-X. SERIES: African Animal Discovery Library. SUBJECTS: Animals—Endangered; Animals—Hyenas. RL C.
As Stone explains, at least one species of hyena has become endangered due to loss of African habitat and too much hunting. In a topically arranged book, the author explains the physical characteristics, habitat, and life cycle of the hyena. Text is heavily illustrated with color photographs.

2202 *Jaguars*. Photos. Rourke, 1989. ISBN 0-86592-506-2. SERIES: Big Cats Discovery Library. SUBJECTS: Animals—Cats;

Stone, Lynn M. (cont.)

Animals—Endangered; Animals—
Jaguars. RL C.
Found most often in tropical forests, the
jaguar resembles the leopard but is larger and
stockier. Here readers can learn about the animal's habitat, food, life cycle, and so on. The
text is accompanied by many full color photographs, an index, a table of contents, and a
glossary.

2203 *Jellyfish*. Photos. Rourke, 1993. ISBN 0-
86593-284-0. SERIES: Unusual Animals.
SUBJECTS: Animals—Jellyfish. RL C.
The common kinds of jellyfish found throughout the world, their habits and habitats, their
prey and predators, and much more are
included in this brief book. Text alternates
with well-done full-page color photographs.
An index and a glossary are included.

2204 *Kangaroos*. Photos. Rourke, 1990. ISBN
0-86593-058-9. SERIES: Australian Animal
Library. SUBJECTS: Animals—Kangaroos;
Animals—Marsupials. RL C.
Variations in size and other characteristics
differentiate among the 54 species of kangaroos in Australia. Here the author provides
readers with introductory information on
physical characteristics, habitat, and much
more. The book is illustrated with many full-
color photographs.

2205 *Koalas*. Photos. Rourke, 1990. ISBN 0-
86593-055-4. SERIES: Australian Animal
Library. SUBJECTS: Animals—Koalas;
Animals—Marsupials. RL C.
Once nearly extinct from overhunting, the
koala now faces difficulties from loss of habitat—especially eucalyptus trees. The life cycle,
physical characteristics, habitat, and more are
explained with a brief, topical text and full-
color photographs. Index, table of contents,
and glossary are included.

2206 *Leopards*. Photos. Rourke, 1989. ISBN 0-
86592-502-X. SERIES: Big Cats Discovery
Library. SUBJECTS: Animals—Cats;
Animals—Leopards. RL C.
Similar to but smaller than the jaguar, the
leopard is found in Africa and Asia. Its characteristics, life cycle, habitat, and so on are
discussed in the brief text complemented by

full-color photographs. The book also has a
table of contents, an index, and a glossary.

2207 *Lions*. Photos. Rourke, 1989. ISBN 0-
86592-501-1. SERIES: Big Cats Discovery
Library. SUBJECTS: Animals—Cats;
Animals—Lions. RL C.
Found only in Africa and India, the lion now
faces diminishing habitat as land is used for
farming and populations of humans increase.
Stone offers readers brief information on the
lion's habitat, life cycle, food, and so on. Many
slightly fuzzy color photographs illustrate the
text. Index and glossary are included.

2208 *Moths*. Photos. Rourke, 1993. ISBN 0-
86593-297-2. SERIES: Discovery Library
of Nighttime Animals. SUBJECTS:
Animals—Butterflies and moths;
Animals—Insects. RL C.
Related to the butterfly, the moth is explained
here as usually being nocturnal and identifi-
able by its feathery antennae. Clear explanations of the moth's life cycle, habitat, and so on
alternate with pages of good color photographs. The book also includes an index and
a glossary.

2209 *Opossums*. Photos. Rourke, 1993. ISBN 0-
86593-295-6. SERIES: Discovery Library
of Nighttime Animals. SUBJECTS:
Animals—Marsupials; Animals—
Nocturnal; Animals—Opossum. RL C.
A relative of the Australian opossum and
North America's only marsupial, the Virginia
opossum now lives in a great part of the
United States. In alternating pages of full-
color photographs and topically arranged
text, the opossum's life and habits are surveyed. A very brief index and a glossary are
included.

2210 *Orangutans*. Photos. Rourke, 1990. ISBN
0-86593-065-1. SERIES: Monkey
Discovery Library. SUBJECTS: Animals—
Endangered; Animals—Orangutans.
RL C.
Hunting and loss of habitat have made the
orangutan of Borneo and Sumatra a rare pri-
mate. The shy animal's life cycle, habits, physical characteristics, and so on are described in
this brief, topically arranged book. Illustrated
with mediocre color photographs, the book
includes an index and a glossary.

2211 *Ostriches*. Photos. Rourke, 1989. ISBN 0-86592-323-X. SERIES: Bird Discovery Library. SUBJECTS: Animals—Ostriches. RL B.
A simple, clear text and excellent photos describe an ostrich's habitat, appearance, nesting, diet, and its predators. The book is small with only 18 pages of alternating text and photos.

2212 *Owls*. Photos. Rourke, 1989. ISBN 0-86592-326-4. SERIES: Bird Discovery Library. SUBJECTS: Animals—Owls. RL B.
Examples of several species and the characteristics, habitat, and prey of owls are presented in color photos and easily understood text. Although not a detailed study, this does provide good information in 18 pages of alternating text and photos.

2213 *Parrots*. Photos. Rourke, 1993. ISBN 0-86593-280-8. SERIES: Discovery Library of Unusual Animals. SUBJECTS: Animals—Birds; Animals—Endangered; Animals—Parrots. RL C.
Alternating pages of color photographs and topically arranged text give readers an introductory look at some of the many varieties of parrots—from the hyacinth Macaw to the budgerigar. Brief glossary and index are included.

2214 *Penguins*. Photos. Rourke, 1989. ISBN 0-86592-325-6. SERIES: Bird Discovery Library. SUBJECTS: Animals—Penguins. RL B.
Although information about the penguin's life cycle is not included, this book is nevertheless a nice introduction to penguin types, habitats, diets, and predators. The color photos are quite good.

2215 *Pigs*. Photos. Rourke, 1990. ISBN 0-86593-037-6. SERIES: Farm Animal Discovery Library. SUBJECTS: Animals—Pigs. RL C.
Although an intelligent animal, the pig is most useful as food and as leather for apparel. Stone describes the animal, how it is raised, its wild ancestors and more. Several of the color photographs show pigs in mud without indicating why the usually clean animal coats itself with mud.

2216 *Prairie Dogs*. Photos. Rourke, 1993. ISBN 0-86593-282-4. SERIES: Discovery Library of Unusual Animals. SUBJECTS: Animals—Endangered; Animals—Prairie dogs. RL C.
A relative of the squirrel, the very social prairie dog lives on the western prairie in underground "towns" with connecting tunnels. With their number decreasing, some kinds of prairie dogs are facing extinction. Illustrated with color photographs, the brief text also has a glossary and an index.

2217 *Puffins*. Photos. Rourke, 1993. ISBN 0-86593-281-6. SERIES: Discovery Library of Unusual Animals. SUBJECTS: Animals—Birds; Animals—Puffins. RL C.
Cousins of the auk, puffins have unusual markings that make them quite distinct. They also nest underground, spend their winters at sea, and dive for their food—fish. Initially the text is confusing about whether puffins actually fly. Color photographs complement the topically arranged text.

2218 *Raccoons*. Photos. Rourke, 1990. ISBN 0-86593-045-7. SERIES: North American Animal Discovery Library. SUBJECTS: Animals—Raccoons. RL C.
Common throughout North America, the raccoon is discussed in terms of life-style, habitat, food, and so on in a topically arranged text. Color photographs illustrate the book, which also includes an index, a table of contents, and a glossary.

2219 *Reptiles*. Photos. Rourke, 1993. ISBN 0-86625-437-4. SERIES: Discovery Library of Predators. SUBJECTS: Animals—Endangered; Animals—Reptiles and amphibians. RL C.
North American reptiles such as the alligator, rattlesnake, and snapping turtle are introduced as creatures that feed on other animals. Some of their habits and habitats are included in the topically arranged book, which has text alternating with colored photographs. Index and glossary are included.

2220 *Sea Turtles*. Photos. Rourke, 1993. ISBN 0-86593-296-4. SERIES: Discovery Library of Nighttime Animals. SUBJECTS: Animals—Endangered; Animals—Reptiles and amphibians; Animals—Sea turtles. RL C.

Stone, Lynn M. (cont.)

In a very brief topical text with alternating pages of photographs, the author discusses several kinds of sea turtles, their nesting, food, homing instinct, and so on. The book also has both a brief—and not always clear—glossary and an index.

2221 *Sheep*. Photos. Rourke, 1990. ISBN 0-86593-038-4. SERIES: Farm Animal Discovery Library. SUBJECTS: Animals—Sheep; Farm and country life. RL C.
Alternating pages of grainy color photographs and topically arranged text look at the many kinds of sheep found around the world but especially the domestic breeds found in Great Britain and the United States. The book also has a glossary of limited usefulness and an index.

2222 *Skunks*. Photos. Rourke, 1990. ISBN 0-86593-046-5. SERIES: North American Animal Discovery Library. SUBJECTS: Animals—Skunks. RL C.
The various kinds of skunks are discussed in a topically arranged text that alternates pages with grainy photographs that often seem of little importance to the subject. The text will be useful for children studying this common animal. Index and glossary are included.

2223 *Snow Monkeys*. Photos. Rourke, 1990. ISBN 0-86593-066-X. SERIES: Monkey Discovery Library. SUBJECTS: Animals—Endangered; Animals—Monkeys. RL C.
A very social animal, the snow monkey, a macaque, lives in northern Japan and is related to many other types of macaques throughout the world. Adequate color photographs alternate with brief, topically arranged pages of text. Index and mediocre glossary are included.

2224 *Tasmanian Devil*. Photos. Rourke, 1990. ISBN 0-86593-056-2. SERIES: Australian Animal Library. SUBJECTS: Animals—Marsupials; Animals—Tasmanian devils. RL B.
The Tasmanian devil is the size of a small dog. Here its habits, food, habitat, and relatives are looked into in a topically arranged book with alternating pages of grainy photographs and clearly written text. An easy-to-understand glossary and an index are included in the very brief book.

2225 *Tigers*. Photos. Rourke, 1989. ISBN 0-86592-504-6. SERIES: Big Cats Discovery Library. SUBJECTS: Animals—Cats; Animals—Endangered; Animals—Tigers. RL C.
Well written and interesting with a text slightly longer than others in this series, the story of the tiger, its habitat, endangerment, wild relatives, and its rearing of young are all covered in alternating pages of text and grainy photographs. Index and glossary are included.

2226 *Toads*. Photos. Rourke, 1993. ISBN 0-86593-294-8. SERIES: Discovery Library of Nighttime Animals. SUBJECTS: Animals—Frogs and toads; Animals—Reptiles and amphibians. RL B.
Good color photographs and a brief text are on alternating pages in this short book. The toad and its relatives, its habitat, its life cycle, and more are mentioned here. A glossary and an index follow the text.

2227 *Vultures*. Photos by author. Rourke, 1989. ISBN 0-86592-324-8. SERIES: Bird Discovery Library. SUBJECTS: Animals—Vultures. RL B.
An excellent text that gives an overview of the types of vultures, habitats, and diet. Explains why most vultures have no head feathers. Illustrated with color photos.

2228 *Wild Cats*. Photos. Rourke, 1993. ISBN 0-86625-441-2. SERIES: Discovery Library of Predators. SUBJECTS: Animals—Cats; Animals—Endangered. RL C.
Four of the North American wild cats—the lynx, cougar, jaguar, and bobcat—and their characteristics, habitat, food, and so on are explored in text and color photographs arranged topically. The book also includes an index, a glossary, and a table of contents.

2229 *Wolves*. Photos. Rourke, 1990. ISBN 0-86593-044-9. SERIES: North American Animal Discovery Library. SUBJECTS: Animals—Endangered; Animals—Wolves. RL C.
The habitat, characteristics, life-style, and so on of the North American gray wolf are discussed as is its relationship to humans. Illus-

trated with color photographs, the book also provides access to readers through a table of contents and an index. A glossary is also included.

2230 *Wombats*. Photos. Rourke, 1990. ISBN 0-86593-059-7. SERIES: Australian Animal Library. SUBJECTS: Animals—Marsupials; Animals—Wombats. RL C.

A plant eater, the wombat is discussed in terms of habits, characteristics, predators, and so on in a brief, topically arranged book that alternates text with full-color photographs. The straightforward book is accessed via an index and a table of contents. A glossary is included.

2231 *Zebras*. Photos. Rourke, 1990. ISBN 0-86593-048-1. SERIES: African Animal Discovery Library. SUBJECTS: Animals— Zebras. RL C.

The zebra is a herd animal similar to the horse. Here the life cycle, habitat, physical characteristics, and so on of the zebra are briefly looked at in a clearly written text, topically arranged, with alternating pages of rather grainy color photographs. The book also has a table of contents, an index, and a glossary.

Stone, Rosetta (pseud.)

2232 *Because a Little Bug Went Ka-Choo!* Ill. by Michael Frith. Beginner, 1975. ISBN 0-394-93130-0. SERIES: I Can Read It All By Myself. SUBJECTS: Humorous stories; Stories in rhyme. RL B.

A mere sneeze from a bug sets off a chain of events that results in a ship being airlifted into a circus parade. The silliness of this rhyming story is carried over into the zany full color pictures.

Storad, Conrad J.

2233 *Saguaro Cactus*. Photos by Paula Jansen. Lerner, 1994. ISBN 0-8225-3002-3. SERIES: Early Bird Nature Books. SUBJECTS: Plants—Cacti. RL C.

A good introduction not just to the saguaro but to cacti in general, this book handles most aspects of the saguaro's life cycle in a well-written text augmented by excellent color pho-

tographs. A glossary and an index add to the usefulness of the book.

Storm, Betsy

2234 *I Can Be an Interior Designer*. Photos. Childrens Pr., 1989. ISBN 0-516-01958-9. SERIES: I Can Be. SUBJECTS: Careers; Interior design. RL C.

The complexities of design work are shown in photographs and explained in the text. The amount of training, the interaction with clients, and the understanding of the effects of color are some of the things mentioned. The book also includes glossary and index.

Storr, Catherine

2235 *David and Goliath*. Ill. by Chris Molan. Raintree, 1985. ISBN 0-8172-1995-1. SERIES: People of the Bible. SUBJECTS: Bible stories. RL B.

A brief text and many colorful romanticized paintings tell the story of the shepherd David and how he came to slay the giant Goliath and lead the Israelites to victory. Included is a map showing the sites mentioned in the Old Testament story.

2236 *Noah and His Ark*. Ill. by Jim Russell. Raintree, 1982. ISBN 0-8172-1975-7. SERIES: People of the Bible. SUBJECTS: Bible stories. RL B.

The Old Testament story of Noah and the flood is retold in simple language with much dialogue. The detailed watercolor pictures set the story in biblical times. This might be useful for Sunday school classes as well as individual interest.

Suhr, Mandy

2237 *How I Breathe*. Ill. by Mike Gordon. Carolrhoda, 1992. ISBN 0-87614-736-8. SERIES: I'm Alive! SUBJECTS: Human body—Lungs; Human body— Respiration. RL B.

A child explains the importance of oxygen to her lungs and tells how her lungs work to help her muscles. Cartoon illustrations make this an enjoyable book and an additional section of

Suhr, Mandy (cont.)

ideas for parents reinforces the information found in the text.

2238 *I Am Growing*. Ill. by Mike Gordon. Carolrhoda, 1992. ISBN 0-87614-734-1. SERIES: I'm Alive. SUBJECTS: Animals— Growth and development; Growing-up; Human body. RL B.

A little boy explains how he grew from a baby to a toddler to a child old enough to read. He then talks about the food and exercise that keep him healthy. Comic ink drawings with color washes humorously extend the text.

2239 *I Can Move*. Ill. by Mike Gordon. Carolrhoda, 1992. ISBN 0-87614-735-X. SERIES: I'm Alive! SUBJECTS: Human body— Skeleton. RL B.

Cartoon illustrations and a short but lively text explain how it is that muscles help skeletons to move. The information is easily understood and interesting. A final page of activities and information for parents reinforces the text.

Sullivan, George

2240 *Willie Mays*. Ill. by David Brown. Putnam, 1973, o.p. SERIES: See and Read Beginning to Read Biography. SUBJECTS: African Americans; Biographies; Sports—Baseball. RL C.

The story of baseball great Willie Mays's beginnings and career is written very clearly and well. One of the leading home-run hitters of all time, Mays was also one of the first black athletes to integrate major-league baseball. Illustrated with black, white, and green line drawings.

Super, Gretchen

2241 *Drugs and Our World*. Ill. by Blanche Sims. Twenty-First Century, 1990. ISBN 0-8050-2888-9. SERIES: Drug-Free Kids. SUBJECTS: Behavior—Responsible; Drugs and drug abuse. RL B.

Stressing that each person is a part of a larger community and the world, the book shows how drugs can hurt or cause unhappiness to others. Not intent on providing information on drugs, this instead pushes personal responsibility. Attractive illustrations complement the text.

2242 *Family Traditions*. Ill. by Kees de Kiefte. Twenty-First Century, 1992. ISBN 0-8050-2218-X. SERIES: Your Family Album. SUBJECTS: Customs; Holidays. RL C.

Throughout the year and the world, families celebrate holidays in particular ways or establish traditions for themselves to share. Explanations of festivals, community holidays, and evolving traditions are given.

2243 *What Are Drugs?* Ill. by Blanche Sims. Twenty-First Century, 1990. ISBN 0-8050-2549-9. SERIES: Drug-Free Kids. SUBJECTS: Drugs. RL B.

After explaining how the body works and how to keep it healthy, Super tells how different drugs (alcohol, nicotine, marijuana, cocaine, and crack) work and how they hurt the body. The final chapter gives advice on what to do in the face of drugs. Humorous watercolor-and-ink paintings help to get the message across.

2244 *You Can Say "No" to Drugs*. Ill. by Blanche Sims. Twenty-First Century, 1990. ISBN 0-8050-2628-2. SERIES: Drug-Free Kids. SUBJECTS: Behavior—Responsible; Drugs and drug abuse. RL B.

Never saying that refusing drugs is easy, the author reminds readers that they have people they can turn to, even when peer pressure is very strong. The drugs mentioned here are alcohol, cigarettes, and marijuana. Illustrations are attractive pictures with child appeal.

Swallow, Su

2245 *Water*. Photos by Chris Fairclough. Watts, 1990. ISBN 0-531-14061-X. SERIES: Starting Points. SUBJECTS: Arts and crafts; Science experiments; Water. RL C.

Experiments, crafts, and art activities combine with a photographic overview of water in its many forms throughout the world to engage a child's interest. Also included is information on water customs in a variety of cultures.

Swanson, June

2246 *I Pledge Allegiance*. Ill. by Rick Hanson. Carolrhoda, 1990. ISBN 0-87614-393-1. SERIES: On My Own. SUBJECTS: Flags; History—United States. RL B.

More than just a stirring history of the creation of the pledge of allegiance, this book also explains what the words mean in relation to U.S. history and how saying the pledge grew in importance. Illustrated with expressive watercolors, the book is well done.

Swayne, Dick, and Savage, Peter

2247 *I Am a Farmer*. Photos by Dick Swayne. HarperCollins, 1978, o.p. SERIES: I-Like-To-Read. SUBJECTS: Careers; Farm and country life. RL B.
First published in Britain, this book shows a young girl (the farmer) as she leads the reader around her farm and discusses animals and chores. The text is interesting and offers some insights into farm life. Photographs are in full color.

2248 *I Am a Fisherman*. Photos by Dick Swayne. HarperCollins, 1978, o.p. SERIES: I-Like-To-Read. SUBJECTS: Careers; Fishing. RL C.
A short but lively text shows a young boy on a fishing expedition with four seasoned sailors. The climax of this British story comes when the child catches a flounder almost as large as he is. Illustrated with good full color photographs.

Szekeres, Cyndy

2249 *Things Bunny Sees*. Ill. by author. Western, 1990. ISBN 0-307-11591-7. SERIES: Golden Very Easy Reader. SUBJECTS: Animals—Rabbits—Fiction; Behavior—Curiosity—Fiction. RL A.
A very young bunny observes the world around him, noticing colors, the moon, and much more. The limited text is closely tied to the watercolor pictures, which make the story complete.

T

Tangborn, Wendell V.

2250 *Glaciers*. Rev. ed. Ill. by Marc Simont. HarperCollins, hb and pap., 1988. ISBN 0-690-04684-7. SERIES: Let's-Read-and-Find-Out. SUBJECTS: Geology. RL C.
Children will find this look at glaciers fascinating as they discover how they are made, how they move, and what happens to them as they travel. The pencil and watercolor illustrations make the book even more interesting and will add to a child's understanding of the information.

Tarcov, Edith H.

2251 *The Frog Prince*. Ill. by James Marshall. Scholastic, 1974, 1993. ISBN 0-590-46571-6. SERIES: Easy-to-Read Folktales. SUBJECTS: Animals—Frogs and toads; Folklore; Princes and princesses. RL B.
While playing with her ball, a princess accidentally knocks it into a well. When a frog retrieves it for her, she promises to share her life with him. Forced to keep her promise, the princess discovers the frog is really a prince. Comical ink and watercolor paintings are a delight.

Taylor, Kim

2252 *Frog*. Photos. Dutton, 1991. ISBN 0-525-67345-8. SERIES: See How They Grow. SUBJECTS: Animals—Frogs and toads. RL B.
Colorful photographic silhouettes set against white backgrounds and accompanied by a brief captioning text take readers from the hatching of a frog to its maturity. The frog, in this first-person account, discusses being an egg and a tadpole, and developing into a year-old frog. In 21 thick pages, the frog goes through seven stages.

Taylor, Sydney

2253 *The Dog Who Came to Dinner*. Ill. by John Johnson. Follett, 1966, o.p. SERIES: Beginning to Read. SUBJECTS: Animals—Dogs—Fiction; Moving, household—Fiction. RL B.
When a large dog comes into the Browns' home along with their new neighbors, each family assumes it belongs to the other. Both families are too polite to say anything when the dog misbehaves. The detailed illustrations are realistic yet humorous and are done in full color.

Terban, Marvin

2254 *In a Pickle and Other Funny Idioms*. Ill. by Giulio Maestro. Houghton Mifflin, hb and pap., 1983. ISBN 0-89919-153-3. SUBJECTS: English language—Idioms. RL C.
Every right-hand page of this book presents an idiom, its definition, an explanation for it, and its origin. Each left-hand page has a funny illustration of the idiom. Definitions and illustrations do a good job of clarifying idioms while being entertaining to readers.

Tether, Graham

2255 *The Hair Book*. Ill. by Roy McKie. Beginner, 1979, o.p. SERIES: Bright and Early. SUBJECTS: Animals—Fiction; Human body—Hair—Fiction; Stories in rhyme. RL C.
A whimsical rhyming text points out all kinds of hair on people and animals. Animals such as baboons do many kinds of things with hair—wash it, comb it, set and dry it, and even cut it. Illustrated with comic-style drawings in full color.

Thaler, Mike

2256 *Camp Rotten Time*. Ill. by Jared Lee. Troll, hb and pap., 1994. ISBN 0-8167-3024-5. SERIES: Funny Firsts. SUBJECTS: Camps and camping—Fiction; Humorous stories. RL C.
A little boy imagines all kinds of humorously frightening things happening at camp. Once there he helps another, bigger boy overcome his fears. Illustrations will be the big attractions in this book as they zanily portray the boy's far-out concerns.

2257 *Come and Play, Hippo*. Ill. by Maxie Chambliss. HarperCollins, 1991. ISBN 0-06-026176-5. SERIES: I Can Read Books. SUBJECTS: Animals—Fiction; Animals—Hippopotami—Fiction; Humorous stories. RL B.
In four chapters, Hippo and his friends share hilarious times playing an unusual game, being careful about Friday the thirteenth, trying to start a band, and watching for magic. The blend of funny text and humorous, brightly colored pictures will work well for readers.

2258 *Fang the Dentist*. Ill. by Jared Lee. Troll, hb and pap., 1994. ISBN 0-8167-3020-2. SERIES: Funny Firsts. SUBJECTS: Dentists—Fiction; Humorous stories. RL C.
Before his first visit to the dentist, a boy visualizes everything his relatives tell him—creating scary yet totally silly mental pictures of what he will encounter. Once there, Snarvey finds it almost fun. Illustrations are humorous ink and wash cartoonlike paintings.

2259 *Hippo Lemonade*. Ill. by Maxie Chambliss. HarperCollins, 1986, o.p. SERIES: I Can Read Books. SUBJECTS: Animals—Hippopotami—Fiction; Humorous stories. RL B.
Childlike Hippo wishes to be something else, sets up a lemonade stand in competition with Snake, gets scared telling spooky stories, and finally decides that being alone is all right but being with friends is better. Lively, humorous text and carefully drawn illustrations work well together.

2260 *It's Me, Hippo!* Ill. by Maxie Chambliss. HarperCollins, 1983, o.p. SERIES: I Can Read Books. SUBJECTS: Animals—Hippopotami—Fiction; Birthdays—Fiction; Humorous stories. RL A.
Whether he is trying to build a house, is feeling left out when everyone else is sick, is trying to paint a picture, or thinks his friends have forgotten his birthday, Hippo should appeal to young readers with his slapstick humor. Illustrated with peach and green humorous drawings.

2261 *My Cat Is Going to the Dogs*. Ill. by Jared Lee. Troll, hb and pap., 1994. ISBN 0-8167-3022-9. SERIES: Funny Firsts. SUBJECTS: Humorous stories; Pets—Cats—Fiction; Veterinarians—Fiction. RL C.
When Snarvey Gooper's cat seems tired all the time, his mom says they must take it to the vet. Snarvey imagines what the vet's office will be like in this very funny continuation of Snarvey's misunderstandings of familiar situations. Illustrations are humorous ink-and-wash paintings.

2262 *Pack 109*. Ill. by Normand Chartier. Dutton, 1988. ISBN 0-525-44393-2. SERIES: Dutton Easy Reader. SUBJECTS:

Animals—Fiction; Humorous stories; Scouts and scouting—Fiction. RL B.
The five scouts of Pack 109 are avid collectors of Merit Badges. In one of the stories in this book, the little woodland animals earn them even for unsuccessful attempts—cookies as hard as rocks are piled together to earn a rock-collecting badge. Good humor always reigns in these stories with delightful color illustrations.

2263 *There's a Hippopotamus under My Bed.* Ill. by Ray Cruz. Watts, 1977, o.p.; Avon, pap., 1978. ISBN 0-380-40238-6. SERIES: Easy-Read Story. SUBJECTS: Animals—Hippopotami—Fiction; Animals, zoo—Fiction; Humorous stories. RL A.
Followed home by a hippopotamus, the little boy lets it into his house. Because of its size the hippo creates disaster wherever it moves until zoo keepers finally arrive to claim it. The imaginative and funny story is illustrated with humorous ink and wash paintings.

Thomas, Art

2264 *Fishing Is for Me.* Photos by author. Lerner, 1980, o.p. SERIES: Sports for Me. SUBJECTS: Fishing. RL C.
Kevin takes the reader on his fishing trips for bluegill, bass, and trout. He explains about the kinds of equipment and bait and about the fishing techniques that are used. He also gives instructions on how to cast, set a hook, and cook fish. Illustrated with black and white photographs.

Thompson, Brenda, and Giesen, Rosemary

2265 *Pirates.* Ill. by Simon Stern and Rosemary Giesen. Lerner, 1977, o.p. SERIES: First Fact. SUBJECTS: Pirates. RL C.
The short text of this book briefly discusses pirates, the terrors of the sea, and provides information on some of the most famous pirates. Busy ink and watercolor pictures dominate the pages.

Thompson, Vivian

2266 *The Horse That Liked Sandwiches.* Ill. by Aliki. Putnam, 1962, o.p. SERIES: See and

Read. SUBJECTS: Animals—Horses—Fiction; Humorous stories. RL A.
While Tony is taking an afternoon nap, his horse Mario goes off in search of sandwiches. Poor Tony is left to deal with the angry and hungry people Mario has deprived of lunch. This humorous story has comic-style ink and wash illustrations that are lively and fun though somewhat dated.

Thomson, Pat

2267 *Can You Hear Me, Grandad?* Ill. by Jez Alborough. Delacorte, hb and pap., 1988. ISBN 0-385-29599-5. SERIES: Share-A-Story. SUBJECTS: Grandparents—Fiction; Humorous stories; Zoos—Fiction. RL A.
Silly Grandad feigns deafness, pretending to mis-hear everything his granddaughter tells him about a trip to the zoo. His twisting of her words and her reactions to it are hilarious. Meant to be read by an adult and child alternating pages, it is illustrated with expressive, humorous drawings and is delightful.

2268 *Good Girl Granny.* Ill. by Faith Jaques. Delacorte, 1987, o.p.; Dell, pap., 1988. ISBN 0-440-40026-0. SERIES: Share-A-Story. SUBJECTS: Behavior—Fiction; Grandparents—Fiction; Humorous stories. RL B.
In response to her grandchild's questions about her youth, Granny insists that in those days all children behaved well as she tells of one bit of mischief after another. Alternating pages for adult and child to read, good colorful illustrations, and great humor make this perfect for sharing.

2269 *My Friend Mr. Morris.* Ill. by Satoshi Kitamura. Delacorte, hb and pap., 1988. ISBN 0-385-29603-7. SERIES: Share-A-Story. SUBJECTS: Humorous stories; Nonsense; Shopping—Fiction. RL B.
A little boy's neighbor, Mr. Morris, looks through catalogs and muses about what he might buy: socks for his bed (bed socks), a can of food as a pet (pet food), and other silly but delightful nonsense. To be read by children and adults together, it is illustrated with watercolors.

Thomson, Pat (cont.)

2270 *One of Those Days*. Ill. by Bob Wilson. Delacorte, 1986, o.p.; Dell, pap., 1987. ISBN 0-440-46646-6. SERIES: Share-A-Story. SUBJECTS: Emotions—Frustrations—Fiction; Humorous stories; Parent and child—Fiction. RL B.
A little girl rushes home to tell Mom about her terrible day at school only to discover that her mother's day was far worse and far more humorous. Meant to be read alternately by adult and child, the book is delightfully silly and has colorful illustrations of people and settings.

2271 *Thank You for the Tadpole*. Ill. by Mary Rayner. Delacorte, hb and pap., 1988. ISBN 0-385-29604-5. SERIES: Share-A-Story. SUBJECTS: Birthdays—Fiction; Nonsense; Parent and child—Fiction. RL A.
Having asked his dad for an idea for Becky's birthday present, a little boy seriously considers all the silly things his father suggests. Meant to be shared by an adult and child reading alternate pages, this delightful story shows colorful pictures of a house-husband father and his son.

2272 *The Treasure Sock*. Ill. by Tony Ross. Delacorte, 1987, o.p.; Dell, pap., 1987. ISBN 0-440-48814-1. SERIES: Share-A-Story. SUBJECTS: Clothing—Fiction; Humorous stories; Parent and child—Fiction. RL B.
Holding up a very full sock, a little girl tells her mother about all the "treasures" she has found on her way home. Mother and daughter alternate pages and reactions to the frog, pig, key, rubber band, chewing gum, false teeth, perfume, and so on. Illustrated with outrageously funny pictures.

Thomson, Ruth

2273 *Creepy Crawlies*. Ill. by Dom Mansell. Macmillan, pap., 1991. ISBN 0-689-71489-0. SERIES: Aladdin Basics. SUBJECTS: Animals—Insects. RL C.
Caterpillars, ants, beetles, snails, and grasshoppers are some of the "creepy crawlies" introduced in this chatty book. Illustrations, done in watercolors, are spread throughout the pages giving the book a very busy look. An index and activities are appended.

Tobias, Tobi

2274 *Maria Tallchief*. Ill. by Michael Hampshire. HarperCollins, 1970, o.p. SERIES: HarperCollins Biography. SUBJECTS: Biographies; Dancing; Native Americans—Osage. RL C.
A member of the Osage tribe, Maria Tallchief begins dancing as a child, practices hard, has good teachers, and becomes a member of the Ballet Society of New York and a world-renowned ballerina. Well written and interesting, it is illustrated with realistic sketches.

2275 *Marian Anderson*. Ill. by Symeon Shimin. HarperCollins, 1972, o.p. SERIES: HarperCollins Biography. SUBJECTS: African Americans; Biographies; Music. RL B.
One of the world's great singers, Marian Anderson fought poverty and prejudice to get recognition for her talent. This inspiring biography covers her life until her retirement. The illustrations are realistic, lovely, and often moving pencil and wash pictures.

Tomchek, Ann Heinrichs

2276 *I Can Be a Chef*. Photos. Childrens Pr., 1985, o.p. SERIES: I Can Be. SUBJECTS: Careers; Cookery. RL C.
Chefs of all types are introduced as well as a bit of the history surrounding their careers. The rigors of the work are not overlooked nor is the training. The book is illustrated with color photographs and small watercolor pictures. Index. and glossary are included.

Tompert, Ann

2277 *Little Otter Remembers and Other Stories*. Ill. by John Wallner. Crown, 1977, o.p. SUBJECTS: Animals—Otters—Fiction; Parent and child—Fiction. RL B.
In three stories Little Otter tries hard to find something for his mother's birthday, attempts to remember where he put his pinecone, and wants to get his friends to a coasting party. With Mother Otter's support each story ends

happily. Illustrated with detailed colored pencil drawings.

2278 *Sue Patch and the Crazy Clocks*. Ill. by Rosekrans Hoffmans. Dial, 1989. ISBN 0-8037-0656-1. SERIES: Dial Easy-to-Read. SUBJECTS: Clocks—Fiction; Kings and queens—Fiction; Time—Fiction. RL B.
With no two clocks in his huge palace giving the same time, the King of Tango sends for Sue Patch and her bag of tricks. Detailed, humorous, yet zany and fantastic, the watercolor and pencil pictures extend the brief, often silly but satisfying story.

Towne, Peter

2279 *George Washington Carver*. Ill. by Elizia Moon. HarperCollins, 1975, o.p. SERIES: HarperCollins Biography. SUBJECTS: African Americans; Biographies; Science. RL B.
Born into slavery, George Washington Carver fights hard against bigotry and hatred to get an education. Although his research at Tuskegee Institute wins him fame, Carver has a social mission as well. Well written and interesting, this is illustrated with charcoal drawings.

Tremain, Ruthven

2280 *Teapot, Switcheroo, and Other Silly Word Games*. Ill. by author. Greenwillow, 1979, o.p. SERIES: Read-alone. SUBJECTS: Wordplay. RL B.
Spoonerisms, Pig Latin, Gotcha, palindromes, secret messages, and word scrambles are just some of the "games" that help children have fun with language. Ink and wash sketches are used to give hints to the answers, which can be found at the end of the book.

Trier, Carola S.

2281 *Exercise: What It Is, What It Does*. Ill. by Tom Huffman. Greenwillow, 1982, o.p. SERIES: Read-alone. SUBJECTS: Exercise; Physical fitness. RL B.
With the silly commentary of an omnipresent cat, this volume takes children through an assortment of exercises meant to promote good posture and strengthen the body. The

instructions and the exercises themselves invite participation. Humorous ink line drawings add to the fun.

Tripp, Valerie

2282 *Baby Koala Finds a Home*. Ill. by Sandra C. Kalthoff. Childrens Pr., 1987. ISBN 0-516-01577-X. SERIES: Just One More. SUBJECTS: Animals—Koalas—Fiction; Stories in rhyme. RL A.
A mother koala and her baby go from branch to branch in search of a place to stay. Each time they stop an animal forces them to move on. Then they find just the right place for them. Rhyming, repetitive text is paired with childlike paintings.

2283 *Happy, Happy Mother's Day!* Ill. by Sandra K. Martin. Childrens Pr., 1989. ISBN 0-516-01521-4. SERIES: Just One More. SUBJECTS: Animals—Fiction; Holidays—Mother's Day—Fiction. RL A.
As giraffe heads home to plant flower seeds for Mother's Day, she generously shares with the other animals. When she arrives at home, all she has is one seed but it proves its worth. A minimal text, with repetitive phrases, is illustrated with ink drawings with watercolor washes.

2284 *The Penguins Paint*. Ill. by Sandra Cox Kalthoff. Childrens Pr., 1987. ISBN 0-516-01567-2. SERIES: Just One More. SUBJECTS: Animals—Penguins—Fiction; Concepts—Color—Fiction; Stories in rhyme. RL A.
A family of penguins wants color in its life and goes to the new paint store to try first blue, then green, then yellow, and finally red. When they are done they have a rainbow. The rhyming verse moves well and the color reinforcement is good.

2285 *Sillyhen's Big Surprise*. Ill. by Sandra K. Martin. Childrens Pr., 1989. ISBN 0-516-01522-2. SERIES: Just One More. SUBJECTS: Animals—Chickens—Fiction; Stories in rhyme. RL A.
Thinking her house too small, Sillyhen asks for advice from the duck next door. She advises Sillyhen to invite a chicken to share it, and when it seems worse, suggests she adds another. A variant of a Jewish folktale, this is illustrated in watercolors and pen and ink.

Tripp, Valerie (cont.)

2286 *The Singing Dog.* Ill. by Sandra C. Kalthoff. Childrens Pr., 1986, o.p. SERIES: Just One More. SUBJECTS: Animals—Fiction; Contests—Fiction; Friendship—Fiction. RL A.

Dog offers rides to one animal after another as he travels to the music show. Each wants to win first prize and together they do. The rhyming text is illustrated with framed, rather muddied watercolors.

Troughton, Joanna

2287 *How Rabbit Stole the Fire: A North American Indian Folk Tale.* Ill. by author. Peter Bedrick, 1986. ISBN 0-87226-040-2. SERIES: Folk-tales of the World. SUBJECTS: Folklore—Native Americans. RL B.

Rabbit the mischief maker contrives a way to steal fire from the Sky People, entering their land with a special headdress that he sets ablaze. He runs back to his own land with the Sky People chasing him and passes the fire to animal after animal. Lavish illustrations capture the excitement of the tale.

Tusan, Stan

2288 *Who Will Be My Pet?* Ill. by Roy McKie. Western, 1992. ISBN 0-307-15972-8. SERIES: Golden Very Easy Reader. SUBJECTS: Pets—Fiction. RL A.

Each time a little boy gets, is given, or wins an animal, somehow it manages to get away from him. At story's end, they all manage to return—to the boy's surprise. Illustrated with bold, humorous drawings with watercolor washes, the very limited text works well.

V

Van Leeuwen, Jean

2289 *Amanda Pig and Her Big Brother Oliver.* Ill. by Ann Schweninger. Dial, hb and pap., 1982. ISBN 0-8037-0017-2. SERIES: Dial Easy-to-Read. SUBJECTS: Animals—

Pigs—Fiction; Family life—Fiction; Sibling rivalry—Fiction. RL A.

One of a series of books about a close-knit family of pigs with very human personality characteristics, this story takes Amanda and Oliver through five everyday events common to small children. The illustrations are soft and pastel colored.

2290 *Amanda Pig on Her Own.* Ill. by Ann Schweninger. Dial, 1991. ISBN 0-8037-0894-7. SERIES: Dial Easy-to-Read. SUBJECTS: Emotions—Loneliness—Fiction; Family life—Fiction; Siblings—Fiction. RL B.

When big brother Oliver goes to school, Amanda is left at home with mother. Slowly the little pig learns to enjoy doing things on her own and starts taking responsibility for herself. The four quiet chapters are illustrated with watercolors.

2291 *More Tales of Amanda Pig.* Ill. by Ann Schweninger. Dial, 1985; pap., 1988. ISBN 0-8037-0224-8. SERIES: Dial Easy-to-Read. SUBJECTS: Animals—Pigs—Fiction; Family life—Fiction. RL A.

Amanda Pig; her brother Oliver; their good-natured parents, aunt, uncle, and cousins; and assorted stuffed animals share a variety of adventures common to small children everywhere. The illustrations are done in soft watercolors and pencil that deftly capture a loving family.

2292 *More Tales of Oliver Pig.* Ill. by Arnold Lobel. Dial, hb and pap., 1981. ISBN 0-8037-8714-6. SERIES: Dial Easy-to-Read. SUBJECTS: Animals—Pigs—Fiction; Family life—Fiction; Siblings—Fiction. RL A.

From one spring to the next, Oliver shares gentle everyday adventures with his family. The stories are low key and quiet and present situations common to young children. The ink and wash illustrations capture the love, warmth, and frustrations of a very human family of pigs.

2293 *Oliver, Amanda, and Grandmother Pig.* Ill. by Ann Schweninger. Dial, 1987. ISBN 0-8037-0362-7. SERIES: Dial Easy-to-Read. SUBJECTS: Animals—Pigs—Fiction; Family life—Fiction; Grandparents—Fiction. RL A.

Initially disturbed by Grandmother's inability to bend over or read without her glasses, Oliver and Amanda soon begin to cherish the time they spend with her. A gem of a story of intergenerational understanding and love, it is supported by simple yet colorful pastel drawings.

2294 *Oliver and Amanda's Christmas.* Ill. by Ann Schweninger. Dial, 1989. ISBN 0-8037-0636-7. SERIES: Dial Easy-to-Read. SUBJECTS: Family life—Fiction; Holidays—Christmas—Fiction; Siblings—Fiction. RL B.

Oliver and Amanda get ready for Christmas by writing letters to Santa, making presents, helping to find a Christmas tree, and hanging their stockings. A quiet and gentle look at a family holiday too often commercialized, the story has soft, colored pencil illustrations.

2295 *Oliver and Amanda's Halloween.* Ill. by Ann Schweninger. Dial, 1992. ISBN 0-8037-1237-5. SERIES: Dial Easy-to-Read. SUBJECTS: Animals—Pigs—Fiction; Holidays—Halloween—Fiction; Siblings—Fiction. RL B.

In four short chapters illustrated with gentle yet often humorous colored pencil and watercolor drawings, the brother and sister pigs prepare for and then go out trick or treating. Amanda dislikes scary things, Oliver loves them, and their parents manage to balance things beautifully.

2296 *Oliver Pig at School.* Ill. by Ann Schweninger. Dial, 1990. ISBN 0-8037-0812-2. SERIES: Dial Easy-to-Read. SUBJECTS: Animals—Pigs—Fiction; School stories. RL B.

As he rides the bus for his first day of school, Oliver is not sure he wants to go. Once he meets his teacher and makes a new friend, Oliver decides school is fun. Van Leeuwen captures the feelings of small children well and the pencil and watercolor pictures add another dimension.

2297 *Tales of Amanda Pig.* Ill. by Ann Schweninger. Dial, hb and pap., 1983. ISBN 0-8037-8450-3. SERIES: Dial Easy-to-Read. SUBJECTS: Animals—Pigs—Fiction; Emotions—Fear—Fiction; Family life—Fiction. RL A.

The pig family's youngest member, Amanda, is the center of five gentle stories of everyday life with which children can identify. She faces fears, gains responsibility, and puts Mother to sleep by telling her a bedtime story. Pastel pictures add humor and warmth to a lovely book.

2298 *Tales of Oliver Pig.* Ill. by Arnold Lobel. Dial, hb and pap., 1979. ISBN 0-8037-8736-7. SERIES: Dial Easy-to-Read. SUBJECTS: Animals—Pigs—Fiction; Family life—Fiction; Sibling rivalry—Fiction. RL A.

Oliver is a part of a very loving family of pigs. He bakes cookies on cold wet days and does not always appreciate his little sister, Amanda. The four short chapters about Oliver's family are illustrated in ink and wash pictures that bring them all to life.

Van Woerkom, Dorothy

2299 *Abu Ali: Three Tales of the Middle East.* Ill. by Harold Berson. Macmillan, 1976, o.p. SERIES: Ready-to-Read. SUBJECTS: Folklore—Turkey; Humorous stories. RL A.

Abu Ali, which is Van Woerkom's name for the foolish Hodja of Turkish folklore, has trouble keeping track of nine donkeys, gets even with his friends who try to cheat him, and gets his own comeuppance. The delightfully funny stories are illustrated with whimsical ink sketches in full color.

2300 *Becky and the Bear.* Ill. by Margot Tomes. Putnam, 1975, o.p. SERIES: See and Read. SUBJECTS: Animals—Bears—Fiction; Behavior—Brave—Fiction; United States—Colonial period—Fiction. RL B.

With only corn and berries to eat, Becky and Granny hope that Ned and father will be bringing back meat. Left alone briefly, Becky bravely and cleverly captures a bear. Based on a true story set in colonial Maine. The illustrations are done with ink, wash, and silhouettes.

2301 *The Friends of Abu Ali: Three More Tales of the Middle East.* Ill. by Harold Berson. Macmillan, 1978, o.p. SERIES: Ready-to-Read. SUBJECTS: Folklore—Turkey; Humorous stories. RL B.

Van Woerkom, Dorothy (cont.)

The three stories of Abu Ali and his friends are ridiculously silly, like those in the Hodja stories from Turkey, and are sure to have children smiling at the men's antics. Illustrated with ink line drawings and watercolor washes.

2302 *Harry and Shellburt*. Ill. by Erick Ingraham. Macmillan, 1977, o.p. SERIES: Ready-to-Read. SUBJECTS: Animals—Rabbits—Fiction; Animals—Turtles—Fiction; Friendship—Fiction. RL A.

The title characters—Harry, a hare, and Shellburt, a tortoise—agree to rerun the race made famous by Aesop. Predictably, the tortoise wins but the two remain friends. The well-written and entertaining story has soft, detailed pencil drawings of realistic animals and settings.

2303 *Hidden Messages*. Ill. by Lynne Cherry. Crown, 1979, o.p. SUBJECTS: Animals—Communication; Science. RL B.

The experiments of Benjamin Franklin and other scientists lead to the discovery of pheromones, the odors particular to a species that provide them with a variety of nonverbal messages. The interesting narrative and realistic paintings combine to provide a good introduction to an unusual subject.

2304 *Meat Pies and Sausages*. Ill. by Joseph Low. Greenwillow, 1976, o.p. SERIES: Read-alone. SUBJECTS: Animals—Foxes—Fiction; Animals—Wolves—Fiction; Folklore. RL A.

Three stories based on Eastern European folklore pit Fox and Wolf against one another in their quest for food. Fox cleverly outwits Wolf, leading him into trouble with humans. The humorous stories are illustrated with ink and wash pictures with an Eastern European setting.

2305 *Old Devil Is Waiting: Three Folktales*. Ill. by Jan Brett. Harcourt, hb and pap., 1985. ISBN 0-15-257766-1. SERIES: Let Me Read. SUBJECTS: Folklore; Humorous stories. RL B.

In the first two tales devils try to get a clever glassblower and wicked landlord to go back with them to hell. In the third, the Old Devil himself is outwitted by a farmer's wife. The three humorous stories, based on folklore from around the world, are tied together by Old Devil and all are illustrated with detailed black and white pictures.

2306 *Sea Frog, City Frog*. Ill. by Jose Aruego and Ariane Dewey. Macmillan, 1975, o.p. SERIES: Ready-to-Read. SUBJECTS: Animals—Frogs and toads—Fiction; Folklore—Japan. RL A.

In this Japanese folktale, two frogs meet at the top of a high hill on their respective journeys to see the city and the sea. They help each other to stand up and see where they are going. Their eyes point backward and each believes where he is going is just like where he comes from. Humorous ink and wash drawings.

2307 *Tit for Tat*. Ill. by Douglas Florian. Greenwillow, 1977, o.p. SERIES: Read-alone. SUBJECTS: Behavior—Greedy—Fiction; Folklore—Latvia. RL A.

On a bitter winter night, a ragged stranger seeks shelter from a miser, who refuses him, and then from a kindly old woman, who helps him. Both are appropriately rewarded for their treatment of him. Based on a Latvian folktale, this is illustrated with stylized ink, wash, and pencil pictures.

Vaughn, Jenny, and Bailey, Donna

2308 *Greece*. Photos. Ill. by Gill Tomblin. Raintree, 1990. ISBN 0-8114-2551-7. SERIES: Where We Live. SUBJECTS: Greece. RL B.

A little girl introduces her country and village to readers, also explaining the work done in the area and the customs that people observe. The book ends with a look at Easter traditions. Illustrated with color photographs and detailed watercolors.

Vaughn, Jenny, and Barnard, Chris

2309 *Russia*. Ill. by Gill Tomblin. Raintree, 1990. ISBN 0-8114-2549-5. SERIES: Where We Live. SUBJECTS: Russia. RL B.

In a simple and brief introduction to Russian life, a child's eye view of the former Leningrad (now St. Petersburg) offers readers a look at the palaces and gardens, and winter and summer activities for children. Photographs and watercolors accompany the text.

Venezia, Mike

2310 *Da Vinci*. Ill. by author. Childrens Pr., 1989. ISBN 0-516-02275-X. SERIES: Getting to Know the World's Greatest Artists. SUBJECTS: Art and artists; Biography. RL C.
The combination of light-hearted cartoons and solid information about Leonardo da Vinci and his art make this enjoyable reading for children just learning about the world of art. Changes in composition and the use of light—contributions of da Vinci—are mentioned and shown in examples of his paintings.

2311 *Edward Hopper*. Ill. by author. Childrens Pr., 1989. ISBN 0-516-02277-6. SERIES: Getting to Know the World's Greatest Artists. SUBJECTS: Art and artists; Biography. RL C.
Using comical cartoon paintings and reproductions of many of Hopper's paintings and etchings, the author is able to make the study of this major American artist accessible to beginning readers.

2312 *Mary Cassatt*. Ill. by author. Childrens Pr., 1989. ISBN 0-516-02278-4. SERIES: Getting to Know the World's Greatest Artists. SUBJECTS: Art and artists; Biography. RL C.
Combining cartoonlike paintings with reproductions of Cassatt's art, the author cleverly introduces the artist's life and work. The illustrations comically bridge eras to help children understand important moments in her life.

2313 *Michelangelo*. Ill. by author. Childrens Pr., 1991. ISBN 0-516-02293-8. SERIES: Getting to Know the World's Greatest Artists. SUBJECTS: Art and artists; Biography. RL C.
As in his other books on famous artists, the author gives some information on the artist's childhood and schooling while concentrating on his great works. Cartoon art mixed with reproductions of Michelangelo's work lightens the book and makes it more accessible to youngsters.

2314 *Paul Gauguin*. Ill. by author. Childrens Pr., 1992. ISBN 0-516-02295-4. SERIES: Getting to Know the World's Greatest Artists. SUBJECTS: Art and artists; Biography. RL C.
Paul Gauguin's life before he discovered his talent as an artist and the changes he faced once he became a full-time painter are discussed here. Full of reproductions of Gauguin's art, that of his contemporaries, and cartoon commentaries on the time, the book has much to look at.

2315 *Paul Klee*. Ill. by author. Childrens Pr., 1991. ISBN 0-516-02294-6. SERIES: Getting to Know the World's Greatest Artists. SUBJECTS: Art and artists; Biography. RL C.
Through a careful combination of biography, cartoon drawings, reproductions of Klee's work, and commentary on his art, children are given a fascinating look at an unusual modern artist. Illustrated in full color with balloon-captioned cartoons and reprints of art.

2316 *Rembrandt*. Ill. by author. Childrens Pr., 1988. ISBN 0-516-02272-5. SERIES: Getting to Know the World's Greatest Artists. SUBJECTS: Art and artists; Biographies. RL C.
Through reproductions of his better-known paintings and humorous cartoon illustrations, the life and work of Rembrandt are presented so that young readers can understand his significance.

2317 *Van Gogh*. Ill. by author. Childrens Pr., 1988. ISBN 0-516-02274-1. SERIES: Getting to Know the World's Greatest Artists. SUBJECTS: Art and artists; Biographies. RL B.
A factual text presents an interesting picture of Van Gogh and his struggles as an artist. The reproductions of his work are carefully chosen to represent his genius.

Victor, Joan B.

2318 *Shells Are Skeletons*. Ill. by author. HarperCollins, 1977, o.p. SERIES: Let's-Read-and-Find-Out. SUBJECTS: Animals—Mollusks; Shells. RL C.
Carefully drawn pen-and-wash pictures of a variety of shells combine with the text to explain how shells and the mollusks they house grow, protect themselves, and eat.

Vinton, Iris

2319 *Look Out for Pirates*. Ill. by H. B. Vestal. Beginner, 1961. ISBN 0-394-90022-7. SERIES: I Can Read It All By Myself. SUBJECTS: Pirates—Fiction. RL B.

Pursued by pirates, Captain Jim's ship capsizes and his trunk of gold washes overboard. His men dive and retrieve the gold and Captain Jim finds a way to outwit the pirates. Though the sailors' use of diving gear seems odd, the story is popular. Illustrated with realistic paintings.

Voigt, Cynthia

2320 *Stories about Rosie*. Ill. by Dennis Kendrick. Atheneum, 1986, o.p. SUBJECTS: Humorous stories; Pets—Dogs—Fiction. RL A.

Rosie, a large, irrepressible spaniel, thinks Mommy, Daddy, Jessie, and Duff are meant to serve her. Rosie barks, runs, chases, and is always happy and excited in four humorous stories about her and her family. Color and ink sketches in a comic style capture Rosie's exuberance.

W

Waddell, Martin

2321 *The Tough Princess*. Ill. by Patrick Benson. Philomel, 1986, o.p. SUBJECTS: Fairy tales; Humorous stories; Sex roles—Fiction. RL C.

The king and queen want their daughter to marry a prince who will take care of them. Instead Princess Rosamund heads off on her rickety bicycle to fight monsters and rescue princes. The role reversals are splendid in this modern, humorous fairy tale as are the comic illustrations of feisty Rosamund.

2322 *We Love Them*. Ill. by Barbara Firth. Lothrop, 1990. ISBN 0-688-09331-0. SUBJECTS: Animals—Fiction; Farm and country life—Fiction; Pet care—Fiction. RL A.

On a snowy day two children and their dog find a nearly dead rabbit and bring it home.

The dog helps care for the rabbit and the two become friends. The dog dies and a puppy turns up to join the rabbit. Very short sentences and gentle pencil and watercolor pictures suit this quiet story.

Wagner, Ken, and Olson, Mary C., eds.

2323 *The Lion Who Couldn't Say No*. Ill. by Don Page. Golden, 1976, o.p.; pap., 1987. ISBN 0-307-03680-4. SERIES: Step Ahead Beginning Reader. SUBJECTS: Animals—Lions—Fiction; Behavior—Generous—Fiction; Humorous stories. RL A.

Leo the lion is so generous with the hair in his mane, allowing the birds to use it for nests, that he is soon almost bald. When nothing helps his hair grow back, the birds create a mane for him out of greenery. Comically illustrated in watercolors with attractive borders.

Wahl, Jan

2324 *Drakestail*. Ill. by Byron Barton. Greenwillow, 1978, o.p. SERIES: Read-alone. SUBJECTS: Animals—Ducks—Fiction; Folklore—France. RL A.

On his way to get his money from the king, Drakestail is joined by four friends who shrink and hop into his gizzard. They reappear just in time to save him from disaster. A marvelous retelling of a French folktale, it is illustrated in green, gold, and orange with black outlining.

2325 *The Teeny, Tiny Witches*. Ill. by Margot Tomes. Putnam, 1979, o.p. SUBJECTS: Witches—Fiction. RL C.

Too tiny to do much magic and always driven from their homes by animals, Ma, Pa, and Sam Witch finally find a little cottage with a friendly old mouse who welcomes them. The gentle and whimsical pen and ink drawings are carefully created with red and brown accents.

Wallace-Brodeur, Ruth

2326 *Stories from the Big Chair*. Ill. by Diane de Groat. Macmillan, 1989. ISBN 0-689-50481-0. SUBJECTS: Sibling rivalry—Fiction; Siblings—Fiction. RL A.

When Molly tells Mama she wishes she were an only child, Mama suggests she tell stories about it. Every night when Molly tells her story she finds that somehow her little sister appears in it in a positive role. This well-written and honest portrait of siblings has charming charcoal drawings.

Wandro, Mark, and Blank, Joani

2327 *My Daddy Is a Nurse*. Ill. by Irene Trivas. Addison-Wesley, 1981, o.p. SUBJECTS: Careers; Sex roles. RL C.
Ten fathers are seen in occupations usually associated with women, such as flight attendant, nurse, ballet dancer, preschool teacher, librarian, and telephone operator. The brief text is illustrated with black and white cartoon drawings.

Wang, Mary Lewis

2328 *The Good Witch: A Charles Perrault Tale Retold*. Ill. by Melodye Rosales. Childrens Pr., 1989. ISBN 0-516-02368-3. SERIES: Start-off Stories. SUBJECTS: Folklore—France; Sibling rivalry. RL A.
A very abbreviated version of a well-known folktale, the story of two sisters, one hardworking and generous, the other vain and selfish, is told more through the pictures than the text. In the story the good sister is rewarded with jewels while the bad sister receives snakes and toads.

Waters, John F.

2329 *Camels: Ships of the Desert*. Ill. by Reynold Ruffins. HarperCollins, 1974, o.p. SERIES: Let's-Read-and-Find-Out. SUBJECTS: Animals—Camels. RL C.
By comparing the camel's physiology to that of humans, Waters is able to explain the camel's suitability for desert life. He also does away with myths surrounding the animal's hump while presenting a very interesting and factual book. Pencil and wash pictures are well done.

2330 *Hungry Sharks*. Ill. by Ann Dalton. HarperCollins, 1973, o.p. SERIES: Let's-Read-and-Find-Out. SUBJECTS: Animals—Sharks. RL C.

The shark is a subject of perennial interest to children. Shark behavior and physiology is briefly explained without placing undue emphasis on its predatory nature. Expressive rather than realistic drawings suggest the shark, possibly making this book less attractive to many young readers.

2331 *A Jellyfish Is Not a Fish*. Ill. by Kazue Mizumura. HarperCollins, 1979, o.p. SERIES: Let's-Read-and-Find-Out. SUBJECTS: Animals—Jellyfish. RL B.
Found all over the world, jellyfish come in all sizes. Some are harmless while others, such as the sea wasp of Australia, are poisonous and deadly. Children will find the text and realistic watercolor paintings attractive.

Watson, Jane W.

2332 *The First Americans: Tribes of North America*. Ill. by Troy Howell. Pantheon, 1980, o.p. SERIES: I Am Reading. SUBJECTS: Native Americans. RL C.
A look at customs and life-styles among the Native Americans of the plains, eastern woodlands, far north, northwest coast, and the southwest places some emphasis on the role of children in these cultures. Black and white illustrations realistically depict the clothing, artifacts, and so on.

Watts, Barrie

2333 *Butterflies and Moths*. Photos. Watts, hb and pap., 1991. ISBN 0-531-14160-8. SERIES: Keeping Minibeasts. SUBJECTS: Animals—Butterflies and moths; Pet care. RL C.
Following a section providing basic information on butterflies and moths, instructions for capturing and keeping the insects are given. Good color photographs of the insects as well as the cage for keeping them make this a useful tool for the budding scientist. Index is appended.

2334 *Duck*. Photos. Dutton, 1991. ISBN 0-525-67346-6. SERIES: See How They Grow. SUBJECTS: Animals—Ducks; Animals—Growth and development. RL B.
Through color photographic silhouettes carefully placed on a white background and bor-

Watts, Barrie (cont.)

dered with sketches of the developing duck, children can observe a duckling from the time it hatches until it is full grown. The text is minimal, acting as appropriate captions to the photographs.

2335 *Honeybee*. Photos by Helen Senior. Silver Burdett, 1989. ISBN 0-382-24013-8. SERIES: Stopwatch. SUBJECTS: Animals—Bees; Animals—Insects. RL B.
Clear color photographs and black and white paintings depict the stages in the development of worker and queen bees. The text is succinct, easily understood, and an index is included.

2336 *Moth*. Photos. Silver Burdett, 1990. ISBN 0-382-24220-3. SERIES: Stopwatch. SUBJECTS: Animals—Butterflies and moths; Animals—Insects. RL B.
The growth and development of a moon moth is followed from the laying of an egg to its hatching from a cocoon and flying. The text and occasional descriptive drawings work with fine color photographs to clearly provide an explanation of the life of a moth.

2337 *Mouse*. Photos. Dutton, 1992. ISBN 0-525-67357-1. SERIES: See How They Grow. SUBJECTS: Animals—Growth and development; Animals—Mice. RL B.
Very well designed color photographic silhouettes are placed against a white background and framed with a watercolor border showing a mouse's development. The text, done in first person, tells about the things a mouse can do at each stage of development.

2338 *Potato*. Photos. Ill. by Helen Senior. Silver Burdett, 1988. ISBN 0-382-09528-6. SERIES: Stopwatch. SUBJECTS: Plants; Vegetables. RL B.
A straightforward, clearly written text takes the reader through the different stages of growth for the potato plant. The photographs, many of them cutaways of underground growth, and the line drawings work well with the text to explain the plant's life cycle.

2339 *Rabbit*. Photos. Dutton, 1991. ISBN 0-525-67356-3. SERIES: See How They Grow. SUBJECTS: Animals—Growth and development; Animals—Rabbits. RL B.

In seven stages, color photographic silhouettes set against a white background and accented with watercolor borders show the development of a white rabbit from birth to six weeks of age. The brief text is written in the first person as if told by the rabbit.

Webster, Vera

2340 *Weather Experiments*. Photos. Childrens Pr., 1982. ISBN 0-516-01662-8. SERIES: New True. SUBJECTS: Science experiments—Weather; Weather. RL B.
Simple experiments, none dangerous or requiring adult supervision, help children to learn about air pressure, measuring rainfall, and determining the difference in temperature between sun and shade areas. Clearly explained, experiments are illustrated with diagrams and full color photos.

Weiss, Ellen

2341 *Millicent Maybe*. Ill. by author. Watts, 1979, o.p.; Avon, pap., 1980, o.p. SERIES: Easy-Read Story. SUBJECTS: Behavior—Decisive—Fiction; Humorous stories. RL B.
Unable to make choices, Millicent fills her home with things she does not need. She buys a large number of parrots to make decisions for her. They lead her into more trouble and finally into taking responsibility for herself. This funny story is illustrated with humorous ink drawings with blue, yellow, and green.

Weiss, Leatie

2342 *Funny Feet!* Ill. by Ellen E. Weiss. Watts, 1978, o.p.; Avon, pap., 1984, o.p. SUBJECTS: Animals—Penguins—Fiction; Physically and mentally impaired—Fiction; Self-esteem—Fiction. RL B.
Priscilla Penguin is supposed to wear corrective shoes and take ballet lessons because she is pigeon-toed. She loves ballet lessons but not her klunky shoes. At her recital someone takes her ballet slippers but Priscilla soars with her clodhoppers. Illustrated with comic sketches.

2343 *Heather's Feathers*. Ill. by Ellen E. Weiss. Watts, 1976, o.p.; Avon, pap., 1978, o.p.

SERIES: Easy-Read Story. SUBJECTS: Animals—Birds—Fiction; Self-esteem—Fiction; Tooth fairy—Fiction. RL B.
The only bird in her class, Heather is happy and popular until her classmates start losing their teeth. Heather feels left out when they talk of the Tooth Fairy but when she starts molting she feels like one of the crowd again. Well written, this is illustrated with soft yet playful paintings.

Weiss, Nicki

2344 *Menj*. Ill. by author. Greenwillow, 1981, o.p. SERIES: Read-alone. SUBJECTS: Animals—Frogs and toads—Fiction; Sibling rivalry—Fiction. RL B.
To rile Francine, her older sister Norma uses the word Menj repeatedly and refuses to tell its meaning. Finally Francine wises up and ignores the teasing. This story about two frog sisters and the book's other similar stories are fun, recall the rivalry between children, and are delightfully illustrated with simple, homey pictures.

West, Colin

2345 *Monty, the Dog Who Wears Glasses*. Ill. by author. Dutton, 1990, o.p. SERIES: Speedsters. SUBJECTS: Animals—Dogs—Fiction; Humorous stories. RL C.
Monty's owner gives him lensless glasses hoping they will improve his behavior. In six short chapters illustrated with comical ink sketches, Monty causes mischief and induces laughter.

2346 *Shape Up, Monty!* Ill. by author. Dutton, 1990. ISBN 0-525-44777-6. SERIES: Speedsters. SUBJECTS: Animals—Dogs—Fiction; Humorous stories. RL C.
Monty is still clumsy and nearly always in trouble despite his lensless glasses, and his appetite and eavesdropping ways cause confusion. Illustrated with many line drawings that humorously break up the text.

Wheeler, Cindy

2347 *Bookstore Cat*. Ill. by author. Random House, hb and pap., 1994. ISBN 0-394-94109-8. SERIES: Step into Reading.

SUBJECTS: Animals—Birds—Fiction; Bookstores—Fiction; Pets—Cats—Fiction. RL B.
Mulligan, a black and white cat, spends his days watching over a bookstore. When a pigeon accidentally gets in, Mulligan jumps right into action, creating havoc everywhere, but finally getting rid of it. The humorous story and light watercolor pictures will attract readers.

Wheeler, M. J.

2348 *Fox Tales*. Ill. by Dana Gustafson. Carolrhoda, 1984, o.p. SERIES: On My Own. SUBJECTS: Animals—Foxes—Fiction; Folklore—India. RL A.
Based on folktales from India, these three stories have a fox outwitting a rascal of a farmer and a hungry tiger and being made foolish by his own ignorance. Well written and suitable for storytelling, the stories are illustrated with line drawings and watercolor pictures.

White, Laurence B.

2349 *Science Toys and Tricks*. Ill. by Marc Brown. Addison-Wesley, 1975; HarperCollins, pap., 1980. ISBN 0-201-08659-X. SUBJECTS: Science experiments. RL B.
Twenty-three very simple and enticing science activities or crafts introduce children to scientific principles without giving lengthy explanations. Pencil drawings are clear and should help children to duplicate the activities.

Wilder, Laura Ingalls

2350 *Dance at Grandpa's*. Ill. by Renee Graef. HarperCollins, 1994. ISBN 0-06-023878-X. SERIES: My First Little House Books. SUBJECTS: Dancing—Fiction; Family life—Fiction; Frontier and pioneer life—Fiction. RL B.
When Grandma and Grandpa have a party, Laura and her family all get dressed up and pile into the sleigh, traveling to Grandpa's. There they dance, eat, and enjoy seeing neighbors and friends. The warmth and honesty of the original stories are captured in the text and the pictures.

Wilder, Laura Ingalls (cont.)

2351 *Winter Days in the Big Woods: Adapted from the Little House Books.* Ill. by Renee Graef. HarperCollins, 1994. ISBN 0-06-023014-2. SERIES: My First Little House Books. SUBJECTS: Family life—Fiction; Frontier and pioneer life—Fiction; Seasons—Winter—Fiction. RL B.

Adapted from Wilder's *Little House in the Big Woods*, the brief text and warm pencil-and-watercolor pictures effectively capture the closeness of Laura's family as they do their chores and spend time together. The art is based on that of Garth Williams.

Wilkinson, Sylvia

2352 *I Can Be a Race Car Driver.* Photos. Childrens Pr., hb and pap., 1986, o.p. SERIES: I Can Be. SUBJECTS: Careers; Sports—Car racing. RL C.

Beginning with a picture dictionary, this survey of the world of car racing repeats dictionary entries in the margins as the words appear in the text. Facts on go-carts, cars, trucks, drivers, dangers, safety, and so on are included along with full color photos, a glossary, and an index.

Wilkinson, Valerie

2353 *Flies Are Fascinating.* Photos. Childrens Pr., 1994. ISBN 0-516-06020-1. SERIES: Rookie Read-About Science. SUBJECTS: Animals—Flies; Animals—Insects. RL B.

Flies of all kinds are very briefly introduced through a limited and slightly more difficult than expected text and supporting color photographs. The names of flies and their order have no pronunciation guide or glossary to help young readers.

Williams, John

2354 *The Life Cycle of a Swallow.* Ill. by Jackie Harland. Bookwright, 1989, o.p. SERIES: Life Cycles. SUBJECTS: Animals—Birds. RL B.

Realistically illustrated with full color paintings, the book clearly describes the major events in the swallows' breeding season and its habits, habitat, and diet. The book also includes an invitation to observe other birds. A glossary, index, bibliography, and table of contents are included.

2355 *The Life Cycle of a Tree.* Ill. by Jackie Harland. Bookwright, 1989, o.p. SERIES: Life Cycles. SUBJECTS: Plants—Trees. RL B.

A clear, simple text and accurate color paintings depict the stages in the development of a chestnut tree from buried nut to mature plant. With an emphasis on explanation in the text and pictures, this is an inviting science book with a glossary, bibliography, index, and table of contents.

Williamson, Stan

2356 *The No-Bark Dog.* Ill. by Tom O'Sullivan. Follett, hb and pap., 1962. ISBN 0-8136-5042-9. SERIES: Beginning to Read. SUBJECTS: Pets—Dogs—Fiction. RL A.

Everyone keeps asking Timothy why his new dog does not bark. His mother and father tell him to be patient but Timothy worries. Illustrated with full color realistic paintings, this is a quiet story with a humorous and satisfying ending.

Willner-Pardo, Gina

2357 *Natalie Spitzer's Turtles.* Ill. by Molly Delaney. Whitman, 1992. ISBN 0-8075-5515-0. SUBJECTS: Animals—Turtles—Fiction; Friendship—Fiction; School stories. RL C.

On the first day of second grade, Jess learns what it means to be left out when only she and Natalie Spitzer are not included in a new girl's games. Jess and Natalie become friends and Jess learns the importance of being herself. Longer than most readers, this has attractive watercolors.

Wilmer, Diane

2358 *Nuts about Nuts.* Ill. by Paul Dowling. Forest House, 1990. ISBN 1-878363-09-3. SERIES: Quality Time. SUBJECTS: Humorous stories; Plants—Trees—Fiction. RL B.

Mr. Conker loves fall because of the huge horse chestnut tree planted by his great-grandfather. The neighbors think he is bonkers because of his obsession with the tree's nuts but Mr. Conker does not care—he loves nuts. Illustrations are zany ink-and-wash pictures.

2359 *The Playground.* Ill. by Margaret Chamberlain. Forest House, 1986. ISBN 1-878363-10-7. SERIES: Quality Time. SUBJECTS: Friendship—Fiction; School stories. RL B.

Dan, the new boy at school, is reluctant to join in at recess. Then Jack decides to get his friends to include Dan in their fun. Upbeat and illustrated with childlike sketchy ink-and-watercolor pictures, this book has the potential for breaking barriers when used by a teacher with a class.

2360 *Zap Zero: The Delivery Man.* Ill. by Paul Dowling. Forest House, 1989. ISBN 1-878363-11-5. SERIES: Quality Time. SUBJECTS: Careers—Fiction; Noise—Fiction. RL B.

Zap, a London delivery man, is sent with a package to Scotland. As he rides his motorcycle north, the package starts making strange noises. Only when he gets to Scotland does he realize how perfect the noise is. Text is illustrated with sketchy, vibrant drawings with color washes.

Wilson, Beth

2361 *Martin Luther King, Jr.* Ill. by Floyd Sowell. Putnam, 1971, o.p. SERIES: See and Read Beginning to Read Biography. SUBJECTS: African Americans; Biographies. RL B.

Opening with King's funeral in 1968, the text looks back on King's life and especially notes the Montgomery bus boycott, his winning the Nobel Peace Prize, and his "I have a dream" speech. The writing style is good, giving a sense of the times. Illustrated with very effective sketches.

Wilson, Lynn

2362 *Sharks!* Ill. by Courtney Studios, Inc., staff. Putnam, hb and pap., 1992. ISBN 0-448-40301-3. SERIES: All Aboard. SUBJECTS: Animals—Sharks. RL C.

Detailed, realistic pictures help to explain the kinds of sharks, their size, habits, and differ-

ence from other fish. The text is clearly written, interesting, and full of unusual bits of information (e.g., a set of armor was found in a shark's stomach). It mentions the endangered status of the shark.

Winnick, Karen

2363 *Sandro's Dolphin.* Ill. by author. Lothrop, 1980, o.p. SUBJECTS: Animals—Dolphins—Fiction; Fishing—Fiction. RL B.

The mullet are becoming scarce and the fishermen in Sandro's village often come back with none at all. Young Sandro is befriended by a dolphin that seems to understand the village's problem and with other dolphins comes to the villagers' rescue. Illustrated with ink drawings with blue accents.

Wise, William

2364 *Booker T. Washington.* Ill. by Paul Frame. Putnam, 1968, o.p. SERIES: See and Read Beginning to Read Biography. SUBJECTS: African Americans; Biographies. RL A.

Born into slavery, Booker T. Washington does whatever is necessary to earn an education. He then begins a lifelong career as a teacher and educator at Tuskegee Institute. Well written and factual, the book does not overlook the controversy surrounding Washington. Illustrated with sketches.

2365 *Monsters of the Middle Ages.* Ill. by Tomie dePaola. Putnam, 1971, o.p. SERIES: See and Read. SUBJECTS: Mythical creatures. RL B.

The 14 fantastic creatures of medieval lore that are presented here are by no means all fearful monsters. They include a race of one-legged people, centaurs, unicorns, and giants, to mention a few. Entertainingly written, the book is fancifully illustrated in black line with red highlights.

Wiseman, Bernard

2366 *The Big Yellow School Bus.* Ill. by Ed Rodriguez. Disney, 1992. ISBN 1-56282-048-6. SERIES: Disney First Reader.

Wiseman, Bernard (cont.)

SUBJECTS: English language—Spelling—Fiction; Safety—Fiction; School stories. RL A.

Familiar Disney characters—Mickey, Goofy, Donald, Minnie, and Daisy—ride the school bus together. The text is divided into two chapters. The first features a humorous attempt by Mickey to get Goofy to put on his seat belt. The second has the group try arithmetic. Text is illustrated in Disney cartoon style.

2367 *Bobby and Boo*. Ill. by author. Holt, Rinehart, 1978, o.p. SUBJECTS: Humorous stories; Science fiction. RL A.

Bobby is playing spaceman when Boo arrives in a flying saucer. The amazing visitor spends the day with Bobby. He eats lunch, does tricks, and plays ball while Mom and Dad think he is the new boy on the street. Illustrated with heavily outlined, comic pictures in yellow and gray.

2368 *Christmas with Morris and Boris*. Ill. by author. Little, Brown, 1983; Scholastic, pap., 1986. ISBN 0-316-94855-1. SERIES: Morris and Boris. SUBJECTS: Animals—Fiction; Friendship—Fiction; Holidays—Christmas—Fiction. RL A.

Though infuriated by Morris's constant interruptions, Boris the bear still attempts to introduce the silly moose to Christmas and Santa Claus. Morris's misunderstandings and Boris's impatience are very funny, as are the heavily outlined brown, red, and green pictures.

2369 *Don't Make Fun!* Ill. by author. Houghton Mifflin, 1982, o.p. SUBJECTS: Animals—Pigs—Fiction; Behavior—Manners—Fiction. RL B.

The way Bobby, a boar, constantly makes fun with words irritates his father, but when obnoxious, ill-mannered relatives arrive, his parents rely on Bobby's special wit to drive them away. Funny drawings and a humorous text have readers rooting for Bobby.

2370 *Halloween with Morris and Boris*. Ill. by author. Dodd, Mead, 1975, o.p.; Scholastic, pap., 1986. ISBN 0-590-41498-4. SERIES: Morris and Boris. SUBJECTS: Animals—Fiction; Friendship—Fiction; Holidays—Halloween—Fiction. RL A.

Boris takes Morris on a Halloween adventure filled with costumes, trick-or-treating, a party, and their own brand of slapstick humor. Popular with many children, the silly but appealing characters and settings are illustrated in brown, orange, and blue.

2371 *Little New Kangaroo*. Ill. by Theresa Burns. Houghton Mifflin, 1993. ISBN 0-395-65362-2. SUBJECTS: Animals—Fiction; Animals—Kangaroos—Fiction; Australia—Fiction. RL A.

Baby Kangaroo invites four other Australian animals—a koala, a wombat, a bandicoot, and a platypus—to join him for a ride in his mother's pouch. The rhyming text is often awkward but the unusual animals and the humorous situation will appeal to readers.

2372 *The Lucky Runner*. Ill. by author. Garrard, 1979, o.p. SERIES: For Real. SUBJECTS: Sports—Running—Fiction; Superstitions—Fiction. RL A.

Buddy practices hard and is a good runner but he thinks he wins races because of his lucky socks. At the big track meet he accidentally puts on the wrong pair and still wins—reinforcing his coach's message about hard work, not luck, making winners. Illustrated in gray and coral.

2373 *Morris and Boris: Three Stories*. Ill. by author. Dodd, Mead, 1974, o.p.; Scholastic, pap., 1974, o.p. SUBJECTS: Animals—Fiction; Jokes and riddles—Fiction; Tongue twisters—Fiction. RL A.

Serious, impatient Boris the bear tries to get the good-natured but very dense Morris the moose to try riddles, tongue twisters, and games. Children will laugh at the pair's antics and enjoy the comical green and brown illustrations.

2374 *Morris and Boris at the Circus*. Ill. by author. HarperCollins, 1988. ISBN 0-06-026478-0. SERIES: I Can Read Books. SUBJECTS: Animals—Bears—Fiction; Animals—Moose—Fiction; Circuses—Fiction. RL A.

Ever-patient Boris the bear takes Morris the moose to the circus. When he sees no moose in the show, Morris joins in with predictably funny results. The text is illustrated in three colors with comical drawings.

2375 *Morris Goes to School.* Ill. by author. HarperCollins, 1970; pap., 1983. ISBN 0-06-026548-5. SERIES: I Can Read Books. SUBJECTS: Animals—Moose—Fiction; Humorous stories; School stories. RL A.

After going to the wrong store and being unable to count his money, Morris the moose decides he needs to go to school. At school, he has a great time and learns enough to read store names and count his change. Children will enjoy the funny story and the humorous illustrations.

2376 *Morris Has a Birthday Party!* Ill. by author. Little, Brown, 1983, o.p. SUBJECTS: Animals—Bears—Fiction; Animals—Moose—Fiction; Birthdays—Fiction. RL A.

Morris the moose knows nothing of birthdays until Boris the bear gives him a party. Morris's predictable misunderstandings of common words continue to plague poor, impatient Boris and entertain the reader. The comic-style illustrations are amusingly drawn in orange, green, and brown.

2377 *Morris Has a Cold.* Ill. by author. Dodd, Mead, 1978, o.p. SUBJECTS: Animals—Bears—Fiction; Animals—Moose—Fiction; Illness—Fiction. RL A.

Boris the bear nearly loses his patience when he tries to help literal-minded Morris the moose get over a cold. Everything Boris suggests is misinterpreted by the moose in this very silly and very funny story. The cartoon-style pictures capture the two characters well.

2378 *Morris Tells Boris Mother Moose Stories and Rhymes.* Ill. by author. Dodd, Mead, 1979, o.p.; Scholastic, pap., 1980, o.p. SUBJECTS: Animals—Bears—Fiction; Animals—Moose—Fiction; Sleep—Fiction. RL A.

Trying to help Boris the bear get to sleep, Morris the moose tells him other Moose stories. Boris's constant interruptions and his demands for changes in the stories are great fun for the reader. The two friends are comically illustrated in brown, black, and green.

2379 *Morris the Moose.* Rev. ed. Ill. by author. HarperCollins, 1989. pap., ISBN 0-06-026475-6. SERIES: Early I Can Read.

SUBJECTS: Animals—Moose—Fiction; Humorous stories. RL A.

When Morris the Moose meets a cow, he tries to convince her that she is a moose, too. Unsuccessful he asks two other "moose"—a cow and a deer—who turn out to be as silly as he is. New, more colorful illustrations as well as a revised text make this more attractive than the original.

2380 *Quick Quackers.* Ill. by author. Garrard, 1979, o.p. SERIES: Easy Venture. SUBJECTS: Animals—Ducks—Fiction; Animals—Parrots—Fiction; English language—Pronunciation—Fiction. RL A.

Polly, a parrot, cannot pronounce r so her request for a "quacker" brings on a trio of ducks. After much frustration and many hijinks, the ducks finally decipher her request and provide crackers. The simple story is illustrated with full color humorous paintings.

Wittman, Sally

2381 *Pelly and Peak.* Ill. by author. Harper-Collins, 1978, o.p. SERIES: I Can Read Books. SUBJECTS: Animals—Peacocks—Fiction; Animals—Pelicans—Fiction; Friendship—Fiction. RL A.

Sharing April Fool's Day jokes and fishing together are just two of the special things that Pelly Pelican and Peak Peacock do to bring smiles to young readers. Ink, colored pencil, and paint are used to create the simple, almost childlike illustrations.

2382 *Plenty of Pelly and Peak.* Ill. by author. HarperCollins, 1980, o.p. SERIES: I Can Read Books. SUBJECTS: Animals—Peacocks—Fiction; Animals—Pelicans—Fiction; Friendship—Fiction. RL B.

In four stories, Pelly Pelican and Peak Peacock try adopting an egg, learn the earth is round, help each other fly a kite, and lose a birthday—February 29th. The simple illustrations are done with ink, colored pencils, and paint and are appealing and humorous.

Wolcott, Patty

2383 *Beware of a Very Hungry Fox.* Ill. by Lucinda McQueen. Addison-Wesley,

Wolcott, Patty (cont.)

1975, o.p. SERIES: First Read-By-Myself. SUBJECTS: Animals—Chipmunks—Fiction; Animals—Foxes—Fiction; Behavior—Brave—Fiction. RL A.
Professing not to be afraid of a very hungry fox, the chipmunks change their minds when they see one and flee leaving the fox to eat crabapples. The very limited and repetitious text relies on the vibrant illustrations to create a sense of story.

2384 *The Cake Story*. Ill. by Lucinda McQueen. Addison-Wesley, 1974, o.p. SERIES: First Read-By-Myself. SUBJECTS: Animals—Fiction; Food—Fiction. RL A.
Bear excitedly announces to the other animals that he has baked a cake. While he naps they eat the entire cake, but they make another to replace it. The ten words in this story are constantly repeated and rely on the expressive and colorful pictures to actually create the story.

2385 *Eeeeeek!* Ill. by Ned Delaney. Random House, 1981, o.p. SERIES: 10-Word Readers. SUBJECTS: Animals—Fiction. RL A.
Using ten words, and relying on the brightly colored pictures to really tell the story, the author relates the tale of Lynx and his capture of Fox, Hare and Woodpecker. The captured three foil lynx's attempt to make them into stew.

2386 *The Forest Fire*. Ill. by Robert Binks. Addison-Wesley, 1974, o.p. SERIES: First Read-By-Myself. SUBJECTS: Animals—Fiction; Plants—Flowers—Fiction. RL B.
Using a ten-word text and much repetition, a story is told through colorful illustrations more than words. In the story animals mistake flame-colored flowers for a forest fire. Although the words are not all easy or familiar, the repetition may make them a part of a reading vocabulary.

2387 *I'm Going to New York to Visit the Queen*. Ill. by Blair Drawson. Addison-Wesley, 1974, o.p. SERIES: First Read-By-Myself. SUBJECTS: Boats and boating—Fiction; City and town life—Fiction. RL A.
Two little girls walk through New York City on their way to visit the queen—the *Queen Eliza-beth II* steamship. Full color pictures show well-known New York attractions and provide a brief tour of the ship. The ten-word text is repetitious and very dependent on the illustrations.

2388 *Pickle Pickle Pickle Juice*. Ill. by Blair Dawson. Random House, 1975, o.p. SERIES: 10-Word Readers. SUBJECTS: Food—Fiction. RL A.
Peter picks pickles until, with more than a million, they pop and form a pickle juice pond. Comical, brightly colored pictures give the story a medieval setting while being essential to the very brief text.

2389 *Pirates, Pirates Over the Salt, Salt Sea*. Ill. by Bill Morrison. Addison-Wesley, 1981, o.p. SERIES: First Read-By-Myself. SUBJECTS: Animals—Mice—Fiction; Animals—Whales—Fiction; Pirates—Fiction. RL A.
The ten words of this text are rearranged and repeated throughout. The text is popular with beginning readers and the repetition helps to introduce new words. The story, told in detailed and colorful drawings, is of a small sailboat of mice that are rescued from pirates by a friendly whale.

2390 *Super Sam and the Salad Garden*. Ill. by Marc Brown. Addison-Wesley, 1975, o.p. SERIES: First Read-By-Myself. SUBJECTS: Animals—Dogs—Fiction; Gardening—Fiction. RL A.
A boy and a girl plant a garden only to have it vandalized by other children. When Sam, a dog, is left in the yard, the next planting is safe and grows to be harvested. The ten-word text relies on the brightly colored pictures to tell the story.

2391 *Tunafish Sandwiches*. Ill. by Hans Zander. Random House, 1975, o.p. SERIES: 10-Word Readers. SUBJECTS: Animals—Fish—Fiction; Food chains—Fiction. RL A.
In a text that uses only ten words and relies almost totally on the brightly colored pictures, the child reader quickly sees how a food chain operates. Plants are eaten by small fish, small fish are eaten by larger fish, and so on up to the human predator.

2392 *Where Did That Naughty Little Hamster Go?* Ill. by Rosekrans Hoffman. Random House, 1974, o.p. SERIES: 10-Word Readers. SUBJECTS: Animals—Hamsters—Fiction; Lost and found possessions—Fiction; School stories. RL A.

In a classroom, children search for their hamster and finally find him, first in the dollhouse and then among their books. The intentionally limited text relies on the amusing watercolor pictures to tell the story.

Wolff, Barbara

2393 *Evening Gray, Morning Red: A Handbook of American Weather Wisdom.* Ill. by author. Macmillan, 1976, o.p. SERIES: Ready-to-Read. SUBJECTS: Folklore—Weather; Weather. RL C.

A potpourri of weather rhymes and lore is given historical context and meanings are explained. This interesting book is illustrated with detailed ink and colored wash pictures.

Wong, Herbert, and Vessel, Matthew

2394 *My Ladybug.* Ill. by Marie N. Bohlen. Addison-Wesley, 1969, o.p. SERIES: Science Series for the Young. SUBJECTS: Animals—Ladybugs. RL A.

The narrator of this investigation of ladybugs talks about what they look like, their diet, the different stages in their development, and how helpful they are to farmers. The illustrations are detailed and lovely, and demonstrate the many different varieties of ladybugs.

2395 *Plant Communities: Where Can Cattails Grow?* Ill. by Michael Eagle. Addison-Wesley, 1970, o.p. SERIES: Science Series for the Young. SUBJECTS: Plants. RL A.

By following cattail seeds into different natural areas, readers learn about various kinds of habitats and the plant life they support. Ink drawings are sometimes so full of things that it is difficult to distinguish the plants being discussed.

Wood, Audrey

2396 *The Horrible Holidays.* Ill. by Rosekrans Hoffman. Dial, 1988. ISBN 0-

8037-0544-1. SERIES: Dial Easy-to-Read. SUBJECTS: Family life—Fiction; Holidays—Christmas—Fiction; Holidays—Thanksgiving—Fiction. RL B.

Tormented by his horrible cousin Mert, Alf does not enjoy the holidays. Worse, when he tries to get even with her, he is the one punished. Funny and a very real view of just how horrible holidays can be (family fights, bickering children), this has humorous illustrations done in pencil and watercolors.

2397 *Three Sisters.* Ill. by Rosekrans Hoffman. Dial, 1986. ISBN 0-8037-0280-9. SERIES: Dial Easy-to-Read. SUBJECTS: Animals—Pigs—Fiction; Humorous stories; Siblings—Fiction. RL B.

Three exuberant porcine sisters unabashedly create their own version of French, anxiously await stardom for the dancing member of the trio, and finally confront Uncle George about his smelly cigars. The softly colored pictures have confident pigs creating inoffensive mischief.

2398 *Tugford Wanted to Be Bad.* Ill. by author. Harcourt, hb and pap., 1983. ISBN 0-15-291083-2. SERIES: Let Me Read. SUBJECTS: Animals—Mice—Fiction; Behavior—Fiction; Family life—Fiction. RL C.

Inspired by movie outlaws, Tugford, a mouse, takes a can full of shiny coins and buries it. When his father says his money is missing, Tugford mistakenly confesses to stealing it and promises to reform. The lush 1940s setting in the illustrations is perfect for Tugford's misadventure.

Wood, Tim

2399 *Out in Space.* Ill. by Tony Wells. Macmillan, pap., 1991. ISBN 0-689-71491-2. SERIES: Aladdin Basics. SUBJECTS: Astronomy and astronomers; Space travel. RL C.

On a trip into space, travelers land on the moon, pass the sun, stop at Mercury, and go on to see the other planets in this solar system. A light touch makes this fun to read. Illustrations are cartoonlike and dominate the book. An index is included.

Woodson, Jacqueline

2400 *Martin Luther King, Jr.* Ill. by Floyd
　　　 Cooper. Silver Burdett, 1990. ISBN 0-671-
　　　 69112-0. SERIES: Let's Celebrate. SUBJECTS:
　　　 African Americans; Biographies; Holi-
　　　 days—Martin Luther King, Jr., Day. RL B.
King is shown as a dynamic and forceful man
determined to bring about social change. The
text is very brief and jumps from event to
event. Full-color illustrations will draw readers into the biography.

Woodworth, Viki, comp.

2401 *Animal Jokes.* Ill. by Viki Woodworth.
　　　 Child's World, 1993. ISBN 0-89565-861-5.
　　　 SUBJECTS: Animals—Fiction; Jokes and
　　　 riddles. RL B.
Hippos, snakes, sheep, ocean creatures, dogs,
birds, mice, and cats are topics for worn and
forced jokes and riddles, with an occasional
winner. Wavy ink and watercolor pictures of
clothed animals adorn the pages. Jokes are in
dark type, answers are in standard type with
an unimaginative format.

2402 *Bug Riddles.* Ill. by Viki Woodworth.
　　　 Child's World, 1993. ISBN 0-89565-864-X.
　　　 SUBJECTS: Animals—Insects—Fiction;
　　　 Jokes and riddles. RL B.
Worn jokes are refitted or forcefully adapted
to fit the insect theme. Centipedes, spiders,
flies, caterpillars, ants, and other insects, the
topics of the poems, grace the illustrations in
wobbly ink sketches awash with violet, green,
brown, and orange.

Woolfitt, Gabrielle

2403 *Blue.* Photos. Carolrhoda, 1992. ISBN 0-
　　　 87614-704-X. SERIES: Colors. SUBJECTS:
　　　 Concepts—Colors. RL C.
Blue is looked at not just as a color but as what
it means in a culture and where the color is
found: music, art, religion, space, nature, and
so forth. Useful for discussion and for extending awareness of color, this is illustrated with
textbook-like arrangements of photographs.

2404 *Green.* Photos. Carolrhoda, 1992. ISBN 0-
　　　 87614-705-8. SERIES: Colors. SUBJECTS:
　　　 Concepts—Color. RL C.

Far beyond the color identification books
associated with younger children, this book
looks at how the word *green* is used as well as
things that are green or might have been. A
page of activities is included along with the
full color photographs.

2405 *Red.* Photos. Carolrhoda, 1992. ISBN 0-
　　　 87614-706-6. SERIES: Colors. SUBJECTS:
　　　 Concepts—Color. RL C.
Red is looked at in symbols, emotions, food,
nature, and more in a book designed to get
young readers to observe and think about the
color around them and its uses. Illustrated
with photographs and a few paintings, the
book also includes activities.

Worthylake, Mary M.

2406 *The Pomo.* Photos. Childrens Pr., 1994.
　　　 ISBN 0-516-01057-3. SERIES: New True.
　　　 SUBJECTS: Native Americans—Pomo. RL C.
Native to the area surrounding and south of
San Francisco, the Pomo were hunters and
gatherers who created beautiful baskets and
used "money" for trade. Interesting text is
accompanied by archival and modern-day
photographs.

Wright, David

2407 *Canada Is My Home.* Photos by the
　　　 author. Stevens, 1992. ISBN 0-8368-0846-
　　　 0. SERIES: My Home Country. SUBJECTS:
　　　 Canada; Family life—Canada. RL C.
An aspiring young gymnast, Rachel is moving
from an upper-middle-class Toronto area to
rural Nova Scotia. Photos and text combine to
present a picture of life in school, at practice,
and at home for an eleven-year-old girl.

2408 *Vietnam Is My Home.* Photos by Vu Viet
　　　 Dung. Stevens, 1993. ISBN 0-8368-0905-
　　　 X. SERIES: My Home Country. SUBJECTS:
　　　 Family life—Vietnam; Vietnam. RL C.
Eleven-year-old Chau is the focus of this look
at a child's life in Vietnam. Readers learn
about family life, school, work, play, and
more. Full-color photographs extend the text.
A section of additional facts about Vietnam, a
map, and an index complete the book, which
is adapted from Patricia Norland's *Children of
the World: Vietnam.*

Wright, J. B.

2409 *Dinosaurs*. Ill. by Gene Biggs. Western, 1991. ISBN 0-307-11464-3. SERIES: Star Reader. SUBJECTS: Dinosaurs. RL C.
Carefully written with an emphasis on the many different kinds of dinosaurs and their characteristics, this book also gives information on the discovery of the reptiles and their reconstruction. Colorful paintings and black and white sketches add information. A glossary is included.

Wright, Mildred W.

2410 *Henri Goes to the Mardi Gras*. Ill. by Syd Hoff. Putnam, 1970. SUBJECTS: Animals—Bears—Fiction; Holidays—Mardi Gras—Fiction; Humorous stories. RL C.
Looking for honey, Henri the bear leaves the swamp for New Orleans during Mardi Gras. Everyone thinks he is in costume and treats him to all kinds of food until Henri slips away, surprised that no one was afraid of him. The cartoon-style pictures in brown and blue fit this story well.

Wyler, Rose

2411 *Science Fun with Mud and Dirt*. Ill. by Pat Stewart. Messner, 1986; pap., 1987. ISBN 0-671-55569-3. SERIES: Science Fun. SUBJECTS: Science experiments. RL C.
From a brief narrative and easily performed experiments, children learn that the makeup of dirt determines what can be done with it and whether plants will grow in it. The realistic brown and rust drawings help to clarify the instructions and the narrative sections.

2412 *What Happens If . . . ? Science Experiments You Can Do by Yourself*. Ill. by Daniel Nevins. Walker, 1974, o.p. SUBJECTS: Science experiments. RL B.
A variety of simple experiments teach children about air pressure, chemical solutions, batteries, shadows, and the properties of ice cubes. The projects are interesting and the instructions easy to follow. The illustrations are sketchy but informative.

Wyler, Rose, and Ames, Gerald

2413 *Magic Secrets*. Ill. by Arthur Dorros. Rev. ed. HarperCollins, 1990. ISBN 0-06-026646-5. SERIES: I Can Read Books. SUBJECTS: Magic. RL B.
Children will enjoy trying the tricks included in this new edition. Instructions are clear and are helped by the watercolor paintings. Wyler and Ames even include ways to divert audience attention from the actual "magic" to make it seem more believable.

2414 *Prove It!* Ill. by Talivaldis Stubis. HarperCollins, 1963, o.p. SERIES: Science I Can Read. SUBJECTS: Science experiments. RL B.
By trying these very simple experiments, children at home or in the classroom can have fun learning the properties of water, air, sound, and magnets. The illustrations are simple and help to explain the procedures.

2415 *Spooky Tricks*. Ill. by S. D. Schindler. Newly illustrated ed. HarperCollins, 1968, 1994. ISBN 0-06-023025-8. SERIES: I Can Read Books. SUBJECTS: Magic. RL C.
For aspiring magicians, this sequel to *Magic Secrets* (see above) has more easy-to-do tricks that will need some practice but should be within the capabilities of seven- and eight-year-olds. Suitably spooky, brightly colored paintings of costumed characters maintain the ghostly ambience.

Y

Yenawine, Philip

2416 *Colors*. Ill. with art from the Museum of Modern Art. Delacorte, 1991. ISBN 0-385-30254-1. SUBJECTS: Art and artists; Concepts—Color. RL B.
Through depictions of art by well-known modern artists, young readers are shown how expressive art can be as they learn about how color is used.

2417 *Lines*. Ill. with art from the Museum of Modern Art. Delacorte, 1991. ISBN 0-385-

Yenawine, Philip (cont.)

30253-3. SUBJECTS: Art and artists; Concepts—Line. RL B.
Through a simple text and well-chosen examples of art, children are shown how to see "line" within a work of art. Some of the works included are by Picasso, Klee, and Van Gogh.

2418 *People*. Ill. with art from the Museum of Modern Art. Delacorte, 1993. ISBN 0-385-30901-5. SUBJECTS: Art and artists. RL B.
Portraits and group paintings by artists such as Degas, Cezanne, and Rivera are used as examples of how people are depicted in art and what the pictures tell about them.

2419 *Places*. Ill. with art from the Museum of Modern Art. Delacorte, 1993. ISBN 0-385-30900-7. SUBJECTS: Art and artists. RL B.
Real and imaginary places are looked at in the works of great artists like Thomas Hart Benton, Ben Shahn, and Jacob Lawrence. Children are encouraged to carefully observe the art to see what is happening in it.

2420 *Shapes*. Ill. with art from the Museum of Modern Art. Delacorte, 1991. ISBN 0-385-30255-X. SUBJECTS: Art and artists; Concepts—Shapes. RL B.
Observing shapes used in paintings by artists such as Gauguin, Mondrian, and Dali, children are shown how shapes are used to create interesting effects and to represent objects.

2421 *Stories*. Ill. with art from the Museum of Modern Art. Delacorte, 1991. ISBN 0-385-30256-8. SUBJECTS: Art and artists. RL B.
Yenawine shows children how to imaginatively look at a work of art and pick out the story it is telling. Examples used include work by Magritte, Miro, and Wyeth.

Yolen, Jane

2422 *Commander Toad and the Big Black Hole*. Ill. by Bruce Degen. Putnam, hb and pap., 1983. ISBN 0-698-30741-0. SERIES: Break-of-Day. SUBJECTS: Animals—Frogs and toads—Fiction; Humorous stories; Science fiction. RL C.
What appears to be a black hole is actually an extraterrestrial toad whose long pink tongue has taken hold of Commander Toad's ship, *Star Warts*. The brave and bright commander ingeniously finds a way to free it. The story and the pencil drawings of the zany crew are delightfully funny.

2423 *Commander Toad and the Dis-Asteroid*. Ill. by Bruce Degen. Putnam, hb and pap., 1985. ISBN 0-698-30744-5. SERIES: Break-of-Day. SUBJECTS: Animals—Frogs and toads—Fiction; Humorous stories; Science fiction. RL C.
Heroic Commander Toad leads his crew on a rescue mission after receiving a cryptic message about bad beans. The droll, mock science fiction story is accompanied by carefully drawn, comic illustrations.

2424 *Commander Toad and the Intergalactic Spy*. Ill. by Bruce Degen. Putnam, hb and pap., 1986. ISBN 0-698-20623-1. SERIES: Break-of-Day. SUBJECTS: Animals—Frogs and toads—Fiction; Humorous stories; Science fiction. RL C.
The crew of the spaceship *Star Warts* is sent to the planet Eden to pick up Space Fleet's most famous spy (0007 1/2), a master of disguise who happens to be Commander Toad's cousin. The commander has great difficulty finding him in this funny spoof illustrated with pencil drawings.

2425 *Commander Toad and the Planet of the Grapes*. Ill. by Bruce Degen. Putnam, hb and pap., 1982. ISBN 0-698-30736-4. SERIES: Break-of-Day. SUBJECTS: Animals—Frogs and toads—Fiction; Humorous stories; Science fiction. RL C.
In a hilarious parody of "Star Trek," Commander Toad takes his bored and tired crew to a planet where purple grapes mysteriously engulf them. Good old Doc Peeper finds a way to free them all. The carefully drawn illustrations are done in pencil and have a zany humor of their own.

2426 *Commander Toad and the Space Pirates*. Ill. by Bruce Degen. Putnam, hb and pap., 1987. ISBN 0-698-30749-6. SERIES: Break-of-Day. SUBJECTS: Animals—Frogs and toads—Fiction; Pirates—Fiction; Science fiction. RL C.
After a long journey taking them where no spaceship has ever gone before, the crew of

the *Star Warts* is tired and bored. They are caught off guard by a shipload of pirate salamanders who try to take over the ship. A terrific parody of "Star Trek," this farce is illustrated in pencil.

2427 *The Giants' Farm*. Ill. by Tomie dePaola. Seabury, 1977, o.p. SUBJECTS: Farm and country life—Fiction; Giants—Fiction; Humorous stories. RL B.
Five giants, very different in size and temperament, decide to build a farm and live together on it. In five chapters the work and fun they share help them to care about each other and become a family. Muted pencil drawings are well matched to the story. A recipe for candy is also included.

2428 *The Giants Go Camping*. Ill. by Tomie dePaola. Seabury, 1979, o.p. SUBJECTS: Camps and camping—Fiction; Giants—Fiction; Humorous stories. RL B.
The five friendly giants of Fe-Fi-Fo Farm decide to go camping together and have a much better time than any of them expected. Huge Grizzle adopts a bear as his dog; they fish, play, and do not want to go home. The delightful story is illustrated with amusing multicolored drawings.

2429 *Sleeping Ugly*. Ill. by Diane Stanley. Putnam, pap., 1981. ISBN 0-698-20617-7. SERIES: Break-of-Day. SUBJECTS: Behavior—Manners—Fiction; Fairy tales; Humorous stories. RL B.
A wise fairy is forced to put herself and kindly Plain Jane under a sleeping spell to stop the nasty antics of Princess Miserella. Years later a prince, wise to the ways of princesses, finds them and kisses the first two, but lets Princess Miserella, the "lying princess" sleep. Delightful, humorous text and illustrations.

2430 *Spider Jane on the Move*. Ill. by Stefen Bernath. Putnam, 1980, o.p. SERIES: Break-of-Day. SUBJECTS: Animals—Spiders—Fiction; Moving, household—Fiction. RL C.
Argumentative Spider Jane is helped by her ever-faithful friend Bluebottle Burt to make a new web, have a party, and finally relax. The pictures are slightly humorous and appropriate to the story.

York, Carol B.

2431 *The Midnight Ghost*. Ill. by Charles Robinson. Putnam, 1973, o.p. SERIES: Break-of-Day. SUBJECTS: Humorous stories; Mystery and detective stories. RL C.
With his new detective kit, Andrew determines to solve the mystery of a ghost that appears around midnight and leaves clues and gifts. Realistic pencil drawings capture the humor and suspense of the story.

Young, Robert

2432 *Christopher Columbus and His Voyage to the New World*. Ill. by Arvis Stewart. Silver Burdett, 1990. ISBN 0-671-69110-4. SERIES: Let's Celebrate. SUBJECTS: Biographies; Explorers and exploration. RL B.
As a boy in Italy, Columbus is shown longing to sail. The book follows him to Portugal where he is educated, through a long search for backers, and finally to his sighting of the New World in 1492. A good look at the man and the time, this is illustrated in color.

Z

Zarins, Joyce A.

2433 *Toasted Bagels*. Ill. by author. Putnam, 1988, o.p. SERIES: Break-of-Day. SUBJECTS: Animals—Fiction; Bakers and baking—Fiction; Friendship—Fiction. RL B.
Pleased at how his bagels have turned out, P. C. invites his animal friends for a special treat. Instead of attending a party, they all battle a fire in the bakery. The gentle and satisfying story is illustrated with cartoonlike ink and watercolor and black and white pictures.

Zemach, Harve, and Zemach, Kaethe

2434 *The Princess and Froggie*. Ill. by Margot Zemach. Farrar, Straus, 1975; pap., 1992. ISBN 0-374-46011-6. SUBJECTS: Animals—Frogs and toads—Fiction; Fantasy; Humorous stories. RL A.

**Zemach, Harve, and
Zemach, Kaethe (cont.)**

In each of three stories, when things seem to be going poorly for the little princess, Froggie appears to save the day and earn himself a lollipop. The princess appears as a rather disheveled and very likable child and Froggie as comic and appealing in the lively pictures.

Ziefert, Harriet

2435 *Andy Toots His Horn.* Ill. by Sanford Hoffman. Viking, 1988, o.p.; Puffin, pap., 1988. ISBN 0-14-050813-9. SERIES: Hello Reading! SUBJECTS: Family life— Fiction; Noise—Fiction. RL A.
Andy gets out his horn and starts making noise until other family members complain. Frustrated, he leaves and toots his horn outside until his family misses him. The very brief text has large print and is illustrated with humorous, childlike paintings in full color.

2436 *The Best Castle Ever.* Ill. by Carol Nicklaus. Random House, pap., 1989, o.p. SERIES: Pictureback Reader. SUBJECTS: Animals—Cats—Fiction; Sandcastles— Fiction; Seashore—Fiction. RL A.
Three cats help build a sandcastle, each adding a special feature. Each of them tries to take credit for how good it is, causing some shoving, which knocks it down. The three decide to work together to build another. A slim paperback, this has colorful, cartoonlike paintings.

2437 *The Big Birthday Box.* Ill. by Laura Rader. Random House, pap., 1989, o.p. SERIES: Pictureback Reader. SUBJECTS: Animals—Mice—Fiction; Birthdays— Fiction. RL A.
A little mouse wakes up to her fifth birthday and a special present from her grandmother— a bicycle. With a very brief text and reinforcing repetition of words, the easy story is accompanied by watercolor pictures and bound in a stapled paperback binding.

2438 *Can You Play?* Ill. by Mavis Smith. Random House, pap., 1989. ISBN 0-394-82001-0. SERIES: Pictureback Reader. SUBJECTS: Friendship—Fiction; Pets— Dogs—Fiction. RL A.

When Jon cannot play, Jessie decides to play with her dog and teach it some new tricks. Jon finally comes to play and it is his turn to be taught. Brief text is helped by lively, cartoon-like color illustrations.

2439 *Car Trip for Mole and Mouse.* Ill. by David Prebenna. Viking, 1991. ISBN 0-670-83858-6. SERIES: Hello Reading! SUBJECTS: Animals—Mice—Fiction; Animals—Moles—Fiction; Travel— Fiction. RL A.
Friends Mole and Mouse decide to take a trip to a flea market. Mole drives as Mouse very cautiously reads a map and very slowly gives directions. Text is illustrated with pencil sketches with watercolor washes.

2440 *Cat Games.* Ill. by Claire Schumacher. Viking, 1988, o.p.; Puffin, pap., 1988. ISBN 0-14-050809-0. SERIES: Hello Reading! SUBJECTS: Animals—Cats— Fiction; Games—Fiction. RL A.
Pat and Matt, two cats, play a game of hide-and-seek in a tree in Chapter 1. In Chapter 2 they chase each other until a friendly dog intrudes on their game. The text is very brief and repetitive, is in large type, and is easy enough for beginners. Simple but engaging color pictures.

2441 *A Clean House for Mole and Mouse.* Ill. by David Prebenna. Viking, hb and pap.,1988. ISBN 0-670-82032-6. SERIES: Hello Reading! SUBJECTS: Animals—Mice—Fiction; Animals— Moles—Fiction; Cleanliness—Fiction. RL B.
Mole and Mouse work hard to clean their home and then, not wanting to dirty it, go outside to shower, nap, and eat. The very brief and humorous story has large print and is illustrated with comical pencil and wash pictures in full color.

2442 *Dancing.* Ill. by Laura Rader. HarperCollins, pap., 1991, o.p. SERIES: Stickerbook Reader. SUBJECTS: Animals— Fiction; Dancing—Fiction. RL A.
Little animals are shown in watercolors going through various dance exercises—usually with great exuberance. Heavy pages in a paperback format and a minimal text gear this to very beginning readers. They and their parents will

enjoy the reusable stickers, which reinforce word knowledge.

2443 *A Dozen Dogs: A Read-and-Count Story*. Ill. by Carol Nicklaus. Random House, hb and pap., 1985. ISBN 0-394-96935-9. SERIES: Step into Reading. SUBJECTS: Animals—Dogs—Fiction; Concepts—Numbers—Fiction. RL A.
The story starts with a dozen dogs cavorting on the beach, but their number changes as they swim, dive, fish, or play. Children will want to count them as they read the simple text. The illustrations are done in full color and tell more of a story than does the very brief text.

2444 *Dr. Cat*. Ill. by Suzy Mandel. Viking, 1989. ISBN 0-14-050985-2. SERIES: Hello Reading! SUBJECTS: Doctors and nurses—Fiction. RL B.
Patient Dr. Cat cleverly finds ways to gain the trust of two kittens. A very brief text is illustrated with humorous yet reassuring pictures done in bold shapes with good clear contrasts.

2445 *Follow Me!* Ill. by Laura Rader. Viking, 1990. ISBN 0-670-83197-2. SERIES: Hello Reading! SUBJECTS: Animals—Dogs—Fiction; Shopping—Fiction. RL A.
Lee, a young dog, joins his mother on a shopping trip for a baby gift. When the elevator closes without him, the resourceful pup uses his reading skills to find his mother. A very brief text with much repetition, illustrated with watercolor pictures.

2446 *Good Luck Bad Luck*. Ill. by Lillie James. Viking, 1991. ISBN 0-670-84275-3. SERIES: Hello Reading! SUBJECTS: Superstitions. RL A.
Stepping on cracks in the sidewalk, walking under ladders, finding a four-leaf clover, and seeing the new moon over your shoulder are some of the superstitions mentioned and illustrated with pencil and watercolor.

2447 *Goody New Shoes*. Ill. by Laura Rader. Viking, 1991. ISBN 0-670-83859-4. SERIES: Hello Reading! SUBJECTS: Animals—Pigs—Fiction; Shopping—Fiction. RL A.
Daddy pig takes his two young children for haircuts and shoes. At the end of the day, he takes them to a bookstore, where each buys a book. Illustrated with lively watercolors.

2448 *Halloween Parade*. Ill. by Lillie James. Viking, 1992. ISBN 0-670-84568-X. SERIES: Hello Reading! SUBJECTS: Holidays—Halloween—Fiction; School stories. RL A.
Allie is very busy preparing for Halloween and her school's holiday costume parade. The spirited and very simple text catches the fun of Halloween with few words and lively pencil and watercolor pictures.

2449 *Harry Gets Ready for School*. Ill. by Mavis Smith. Viking, 1991. ISBN 0-670-83861-6. SERIES: Hello Reading! SUBJECTS: Animals—Hippopotami—Fiction; School stories. RL A.
Harry the hippo gets ready for school by shopping for clothes, going to the doctor, getting a haircut, and more. He experiences the nervousness that most children do but quickly makes friends on the first day. Text is attractively illustrated.

2450 *Harry Goes to Fun Land*. Ill. by Mavis Smith. Viking, 1989. ISBN 0-670-82664-2. SERIES: Hello Reading! SUBJECTS: Amusement parks—Fiction; Animals—Hippopotami—Fiction; Grandparents—Fiction. RL A.
Little hippo Harry goes with his grandfather to an amusement park. Each time he takes a ride, he reassures himself that he is not scared—yet when Grandpa is gone for a long time, Harry really has to convince himself he is not afraid. Attractive, colorful paintings accompany the text.

2451 *Harry Takes a Bath*. Ill. by Mavis Smith. Viking, hb and pap., 1987. ISBN 0-670-81721-X. SERIES: Hello Reading! SUBJECTS: Animals—Hippopotami—Fiction; Bathing—Fiction. RL A.
Hippopotamus Harry gathers his things and heads for the bathroom for a good cleanup and some fun. Afterward the bathroom is a mess and Harry cleans it up. The very limited vocabulary and large type with clearly drawn, colorful illustrations are good for a child just starting to read.

2452 *How Big Is Big?* Ill. by Andrea Baruffi. Viking, 1989, o.p.; Puffin, pap., 1989. ISBN 0-14-050983-6. SERIES: Hello Reading! SUBJECTS: Concepts—Size. RL A.

Ziefert, Harriet (cont.)

Each double page spread uses comparisons to show the relative nature of size. An example would be a picture showing an elephant larger than a man and another showing a man larger than a baby elephant. Text is easy to understand and well illustrated.

2453 *I Hate Boots*. Ill. by Laura Rader. HarperCollins, pap., 1991. ISBN 0-06-107423-3. SERIES: Stickerbook Reader. SUBJECTS: Animals—Pigs—Fiction; Weather—Snow—Fiction. RL A.

A little pig says she hates each article of clothing her mother insists she wear before going out into the snow. Once outside she appreciates them. Illustrated with childlike watercolor paintings, the heavy paper pages and the reusable stickers should have both child and parent appeal.

2454 *Jason's Bus Ride*. Ill. by Simms Taback. Viking, hb and pap., 1987. ISBN 0-670-81718-X. SERIES: Hello Reading! SUBJECTS: Buses—Fiction; Emergencies—Fiction. RL A.

Jason gets on the bus expecting an uneventful ride. Instead he becomes a hero when he is the only one able to get a dog to move out of the path of the bus. The bold, full color pictures are marvelous, offering a variety of perspectives of the bus and its riders.

2455 *Later, Rover*. Ill. by David Jacobson. Viking, 1991. ISBN 0-670-83863-2. SERIES: Hello Reading! SUBJECTS: Behavior—Bored; Pets—Dogs—Fiction. RL A.

Again and again Andy asks his busy parents and sister to play with him and the answer is always "Later, Andy." Finally Andy begins tossing a stick for the dog. When he tires of the game, it is Andy's turn to say "Later, Rover." Text is illustrated with cartoonlike full color paintings.

2456 *Let's Trade*. Ill. by Mary Morgan. Viking, 1989, o.p.; Puffin, pap., 1989. ISBN 0-14-050982-8. SERIES: Hello Reading! SUBJECTS: Picnics—Fiction; Siblings—Fiction. RL A.

Meg, Sam, and Jo take their lunches and go to the park for a picnic. Once there they begin trading each other for what they want to eat and then what they need to play ball. Realistic situations are handled well in text and in the full-color illustrations.

2457 *Mike and Tony: Best Friends*. Ill. by Catherine Siracusa. Viking, 1987; Puffin, pap., 1994. ISBN 0-14-050744-2. SERIES: Hello Reading! SUBJECTS: Friendship—Fiction. RL B.

Mike and Tony do everything together—walk to school, ride bikes, play on the same team. They even spend Friday nights at one or the other's home until they have a fight that takes some effort to settle. The vibrant full-color pictures are a good match to the story of a common situation.

2458 *Move Over*. Ill. by Laura Rader. HarperCollins, pap., 1991. ISBN 0-06-107421-7. SERIES: Stickerbook Readers. SUBJECTS: Boats and boating—Fiction; Friendship—Fiction; Humorous stories. RL A.

Five friends start out in an inflatable boat and one after another other animals ask to be let in. When the number climbs to ten, they sink. Heavy paper pages, reusable stickers, humorous illustrations in full color, and repetitive lines will all be attractive to children.

2459 *My Apple Tree*. Ill. by Laura Rader. HarperCollins, pap., 1991. ISBN 0-06-107420-9. SERIES: Stickerbook Readers. SUBJECTS: Food—Fiction; Seasons—Fiction; Trees—Fiction. RL A.

A little dog tells how his tree looks through the year and how much he loves it and its apples. Gentle and childlike watercolors support and extend the text. Reusable word stickers reinforce the vocabulary for new readers and the heavy pages guarantee a long life for this paperback.

2460 *A New House for Mole and Mouse*. Ill. by David Prebenna. Viking, hb and pap., 1987. ISBN 0-670-81720-1. SERIES: Hello Reading! SUBJECTS: Animals—Mice—Fiction; Animals—Moles—Fiction; Moving, household—Fiction. RL B.

Mouse and Mole move into a new house and excitedly try everything out. Pastel pictures of the two friendly little animals and their very cozy home accompany the short but interesting story.

2461 *Nicky Upstairs and Down*. Ill. by Richard Brown. Viking, hb and pap., 1987. ISBN 0-670-81717-1. SERIES: Hello Reading! SUBJECTS: Animals—Cats—Fiction; Pets—Cats—Fiction. RL A.

Nicky, a kitten, and his mother are pets in a household with an upstairs and a downstairs. Nicky runs from floor to floor when his mother calls until he decides he wants to stay in the middle. The pictures to this very brief story are bright and childlike; the cats have expressive faces.

2462 *No More TV Sleepy Dog*. Ill. by Norman Gorbaty. Random House, pap., 1989. ISBN 0-394-81996-9. SERIES: Pictureback Reader. SUBJECTS: Animals—Dogs—Fiction; Bedtime—Fiction. RL A.

Just as small children do, a puppy begs to stay up later and tries one delaying tactic after another. He finally falls asleep after being read a story. Using very few words and with good reinforcement of the message from the simply drawn humorous pictures, the story will succeed with readers.

2463 *Penny Goes to the Movies*. Ill. by Laura Rader. Viking, 1990, o.p.; Puffin, pap., 1990. ISBN 0-14-054225-6. SERIES: Hello Reading! SUBJECTS: Animals—Pigs—Fiction; Movies—Fiction. RL A.

On a rainy afternoon, a little pig and her mother decide to go to a movie. Shortly after it begins, the little pig notices a space child in the theater but everyone hushes her. The pictures and very brief text combine to make this warm story with a twist easy to read.

2464 *Please Let It Snow*. Ill. by Amy Aitken. Viking, 1989, o.p.; Puffin, pap., 1989. ISBN 0-14-050981-X. SERIES: Hello Reading! SUBJECTS: Weather—Snow—Fiction. RL A.

With all kinds of new clothes for snow, a little boy anxiously awaits the first snowfall. Day after day he watches for snow until finally he gives up and—of course—it snows. The very brief text works well with the colorful yet simply drawn illustrations.

2465 *The Prince Has a Boo-boo!* Ill. by R. W. Alley. Random House, pap., 1989. ISBN 0-394-81999-3. SERIES: Pictureback Reader. SUBJECTS: Injuries—Fiction; Kings and queens—Fiction; Princes and princesses—Fiction. RL A.

When the little prince bumps his head, everyone in the castle gets involved in helping him. Lively, humorous watercolor pictures help tell the story. Cutout vocabulary cards are useful for reinforcing vocabulary. This is a good purchase for the home collection.

2466 *The Prince's Tooth Is Loose*. Ill. by R. W. Alley. Random House, pap., 1990. ISBN 0-394-84840-3. SERIES: Pictureback Reader. SUBJECTS: Human body—Teeth—Fiction; Humorous stories; Princes and princesses—Fiction. RL A.

When the young prince has a loose tooth, the whole court jumps into action to find an apple for him to bite into. Humorous watercolor pictures extend the repetitive text. The vocabulary cards make this book attractive for home purchase and use.

2467 *Sam and Lucy*. Ill. by Claire Schumacher. HarperCollins, 1992. ISBN 0-06-026913-8. SUBJECTS: Animals—Dogs—Fiction; Animals—Reproduction—Fiction. RL B.

Sam, a gray terrier, decides to wander away from home and meets Lucy, a tan poodle. They play, mate, and ultimately have four puppies. Hardly likely to instill responsible pet ownership habits, the story is nevertheless well done with colorful pictures with much child appeal.

2468 *Say Good Night!* Ill. by Catherine Siracusa. Viking, hb and pap., 1988. ISBN 0-670-81722-8. SERIES: Hello Reading! SUBJECTS: Morning—Fiction; Night—Fiction; Sleep—Fiction. RL A.

A little girl has to be convinced that night and morning are "good." Her parents oblige, and she goes to sleep and gets up happily. The very short text is accompanied by simple, colorful, and attractive pictures.

2469 *The Small Potatoes and the Snowball Fight*. Ill. by Richard Brown. Dell, pap., 1986, o.p. SERIES: Small Potatoes. SUBJECTS: Clubs—Fiction; Friendship—Fiction; Weather—Snow—Fiction. RL C.

After the first heavy snowfall, the Small Potatoes Club gets together to play. They build a tunnel in a drift, cause an accident throwing snowballs, and, after cocoa and donuts, end

Ziefert, Harriet (cont.)

up making snow people. Illustrated with cartoonlike ink drawings, the stories are fun.

2470 *The Small Potatoes' Busy Beach Day*. Ill. by Richard Brown. Dell, pap., 1986, o.p. SERIES: Small Potatoes. SUBJECTS: Clubs—Fiction; Friendship—Fiction; Seashore—Fiction. RL C.

The members and Molly's dog spend the day at the seashore collecting shells, swimming, playing games, and having a good time. Illustrated with black and white pictures, the good natured stories are just right for readers almost ready for chapter books.

2471 *The Small Potatoes Club*. Ill. by Richard Brown. Dell, pap., 1984. ISBN 0-440-48034-5. SERIES: Small Potatoes. SUBJECTS: Clubs—Fiction; Friendship—Fiction. RL C.

Six friends and one's dog, Spot, get together to build a clubhouse, play soccer, visit the museum, and generally have fun together. A good introduction to longer chapter books, this is illustrated with cartoonlike ink drawings.

2472 *So Hungry!* Ill. by Carol Nicklaus. Random House, hb and pap., 1987. ISBN 0-394-99127-3. SERIES: Step into Reading. SUBJECTS: Animals—Lions—Fiction; Food—Fiction. RL B.

Hungry and unable to find cookies, Kate and Lewis, lions, decide to make great big sandwiches and race to finish them. With a very limited and repetitive but not necessarily easy vocabulary, the bold, full color cartoonlike illustrations carry the story.

2473 *So Sick!* Ill. by Carol Nicklaus. Random House, hb and pap., 1985. ISBN 0-394-97580-4. SERIES: Step into Reading. SUBJECTS: Animals—Lions—Fiction; Illness—Fiction. RL A.

After finally getting well, Lewis, a lion, plays doctor with his friend Angel. When Angel eats too many cookies in spite of Lewis's warnings, he gets sick. Full color pictures of "cute" animals accompany a very brief, bold-type text.

2474 *Sometimes I Share*. Ill. by Carol Nicklaus. HarperCollins, pap., 1991, o.p. SERIES: Stickerbook Readers.

SUBJECTS: Behavior—Selfish—Fiction; Behavior—Sharing—Fiction; Sibling rivalry—Fiction. RL A.

A little girl honestly mentions how sometimes she does share with her little brother but other times she does not want to and then she becomes selfish. Lively charcoal pencil drawings have colorful washes. Heavy pages guarantee little tearing and the reusable stickers reinforce word knowledge.

2475 *Stitches*. Ill. by Amy Aitken. Viking, 1990, o.p.; Puffin, pap., 1993. ISBN 0-14-036553-2. SERIES: Hello Reading! SUBJECTS: Accidents—Fiction; Doctors and nurses—Fiction. RL A.

When Jon falls off his bike, he cuts his head, is taken to the doctor, and has six stitches. Although far from happy during the ordeal, Jon proudly shows off his bandage and tells his story of the stitches. Easy to read the book has colorful illustrations.

2476 *Strike Four!* Ill. by Mavis Smith. Viking, 1988, o.p. SERIES: Hello Reading! SUBJECTS: Behavior—Bored—Fiction; Family life—Fiction; Sports—Baseball—Fiction. RL A.

With nothing to do, Debbie tries tossing her ball in the house until she is told to do it elsewhere. She finally takes her ball and bat outside and practices hitting—until she breaks a window. A good, brief story and simple, colorful pictures combine to create an easy yet appealing book.

2477 *Surprise!* Ill. by Mary Morgan. Viking, 1988. ISBN 0-670-82036-9. SERIES: Hello Reading! SUBJECTS: Birthdays—Fiction; Families—Fiction; Mothers—Fiction. RL B.

Three young children get up very early and quietly prepare a breakfast tray of juice and cookies for their mother on her birthday. The text is very brief, relying on the pictures of the excited children and their rambunctious cat to help tell the story.

2478 *Take My Picture!* Ill. by Amy Aitken. HarperCollins, 1991. ISBN 0-06-107424-1. SERIES: Stickerbook Reader. SUBJECTS: Photography and photographers—Fiction; Sibling rivalry—Fiction; Zoos—Fiction. RL A.

When they visit the zoo, a little boy's older sister takes lots of pictures of the animals but none of him until the very end of their visit. Humorous watercolor pictures extend the brief text. Heavy pages and reusable word stickers should have appeal for home purchase.

2479 *Tim and Jim Take Off*. Ill. by Suzy Mandel. Viking, 1990, o.p. SERIES: Hello Reading! SUBJECTS: Airplanes—Fiction; Airports—Fiction. RL A.

Two kitten brothers are taken to the airport for their flight to visit their grandparents. At the airport and on the plane, they see and do the things that all passengers do. A good introduction to flying for young travelers, this has colorful illustrations.

2480 *Under the Water*. Ill. by Suzy Mandel. Viking, 1990, o.p.; Puffin, pap., 1993. ISBN 0-14-036535-4. SERIES: Hello Reading! SUBJECTS: Oceans and ocean life; Sports—Snorkeling. RL B.

Readers are introduced to life in the ocean and a snorkeler's view of it. Expressive mixed-media pictures show a variety of ocean fish and plants. Good advice is also given for would-be snorkelers.

2481 *Wait for Us!* Ill. by Amy Aitken. Random House, pap., 1989, o.p. SERIES: Pictureback Reader. SUBJECTS: Cumulative tales; Sports—Running—Fiction. RL A.

As Jenny and her dog Buffy run, they attract a crowd of other children—no one knowing where Jenny is heading. When they arrive, they all excitedly scream for ice cream. Very limited vocabulary effectively works with colorful pictures to give a sense of story.

2482 *The Wheels on the Bus*. Ill. by Andrea Baruffi. Random House, pap., 1990. ISBN 0-394-84870-5. SERIES: Pictureback Reader. SUBJECTS: Buses—Fiction; Music and musicians—Fiction. RL A.

The repetitive children's song "The Wheels on the Bus" is illustrated with appropriate pencil and watercolor pictures. Though the music is not included, the song is familiar enough and the rhythm catchy enough to get children singing. Vocabulary cards make this a useful home purchase.

2483 *When the TV Broke*. Ill. by Mavis Smith. Viking, 1989, o.p.; Puffin, pap., 1993. ISBN 0-14-036540-0. SERIES: Hello Reading! SUBJECTS: Television—Fiction. RL A.

When the TV breaks, Jeffrey finds a whole world of things to do with his time. When it returns, the little boy is too busy playing to be bothered. Simple color-pencil and watercolor pictures and a very short text are combined effectively.

2484 *Wish for a Fish*. Ill. by Argus Childers. Random House, pap., 1989, o.p. SERIES: Pictureback Reader. SUBJECTS: Sports—Fishing—Fiction. RL A.

A little boy is determined to catch the biggest fish in the lake. Instead he manages to catch an umbrella, a swimsuit, a tube, and finally a very feisty minnow. A repetitive and very brief text is supported by humorous and colorful pictures.

Ziefert, Harriet, and Ziefert, Jon

2485 *The Small Potatoes and the Birthday Party*. Ill. by Richard Brown. Dell, pap., 1985. ISBN 0-440-48035-3. SERIES: Small Potatoes. SUBJECTS: Birthdays—Fiction; Clubs—Fiction; Friendship—Fiction. RL C.

The members of the Small Potatoes Club decide to surprise Molly's dog, Spot, with a birthday party while adding a porch onto their clubhouse. They buy Spot his own Pet, a guinea pig, and end the day with a ball game. The book's line drawings and chapters make it appear harder than it is.

2486 *The Small Potatoes and the Magic Show*. Ill. by Richard Brown. Dell, pap., 1984, o.p. SERIES: Small Potatoes. SUBJECTS: Clubs—Fiction; Friendship—Fiction; Magic—Fiction. RL C.

The members of the club spend the day having a picnic, playing games, and coming up with a password for their club. When it is time to think about making money, they decide on a magic show. The show is a success. The book is illustrated with cartoonlike pictures.

2487 *The Small Potatoes and the Sleep-Over*. Ill. by Richard Brown. Dell, pap., 1985,

Ziefert, Harriet, and Ziefert, Jon (cont.)

o.p. SERIES: Small Potatoes. SUBJECTS: Camps and camping—Fiction; Clubs—Fiction; Friendship—Fiction. RL C.

The six members of the club and Molly's dog, Spot, camp out in the clubhouse. They play games, use a telescope to look at the sky, almost tell scary stories, and wake up the next day very tired. Black-and-white line drawings add to the fun and make this seem geared to older readers.

Ziegler, Sandra

2488 *Understanding*. Ill. by Jenny Williams. Child's World, 1989. ISBN 0-89565-452-0. SERIES: What Is It? SUBJECTS: Behavior—Understanding—Fiction. RL B.

A middle child demonstrates to readers the many ways to show understanding to family and friends and how to treat them as she would like to be treated. Meant to reinforce positive patterns of behavior, this brief text is nicely illustrated with pencil sketches and watercolors.

Ziner, Feenie, and Thompson, Elizabeth

2489 *Time*. Photos. Childrens Pr., hb and pap., 1982. ISBN 0-516-41651-0. SERIES: New True. SUBJECTS: Concepts—Time. RL A.

In the first part of this book, the reader learns that long before modern-day clocks were invented, people measured time using shadow sticks, sundials, candles, and ropes. The second part of the book describes how to tell time with modern-day clocks. Full color photos, a glossary, and an index are included.

Zinnemann-Hope, Pam

2490 *Time for Bed, Ned*. Ill. by Kady MacDonald Denton. Macmillan, 1986, o.p. SUBJECTS: Bedtime—Fiction. RL A.

With difficulty, a patient mother corrals a toddler for bath and bed. This preprimer has warm watercolor washes, which include the family pets.

Zion, Gene

2491 *Harry and the Lady Next Door*. Ill. by Margaret B. Graham. HarperCollins, hb and pap., 1960. ISBN 0-06-026852-2. SERIES: I Can Read Books. SUBJECTS: Humorous stories; Music—Fiction; Pets—Dogs—Fiction. RL A.

Harry, a white dog with black spots, tries one thing after another to get the lady next door to stop her terrible high-pitched singing. A popular picture-book character, Harry is familiar to most children. This good story is combined with simple humorous pictures.

Zoehfeld, Kathleen W.

2492 *What Lives in a Shell?* Ill. by Helen K. Davie. HarperCollins, hb and pap., 1994. ISBN 0-06-022998-5. SERIES: Let's-Read-and-Find-Out Science Books. SUBJECTS: Animals—Snails; Shells. RL B.

With most of its focus on snails and shells found in the sea, this book provides good information about animals living in shells as well as fine realistic watercolor pictures of animals and their shells. Factual information is presented in an interesting and attractive manner.

Zoo Animals

2493 *Zoo Animals*. Photos. Macmillan, 1991. ISBN 0-689-71406-8. SERIES: Eye Openers. SUBJECTS: Animals; Zoos. RL B.

In 21 pages of heavy paper featuring photographic silhouettes of zoo animals, the elephant, camel, zebra, parrot, and four other animals are highlighted. The design of the book is enticing and the text offers basic information on the habits and life of the animals.

Zweifel, Frances W.

2494 *Bony*. Ill. by Whitney Darrow, Jr. HarperCollins, 1977, o.p. SERIES: I Can Read Books. SUBJECTS: Animals—Squirrels—Fiction; Pets—Wild animals—Fiction. RL B.

Kim rescues an orphaned baby squirrel, names her Bony, and raises her in his home. Finally grown and behaving like the wild animal she is, Bony is reintroduced to the wild. Whimsical pencil drawings add humor to a situation that does not always end so happily.

2495 *Pickle in the Middle and Other Easy Snacks*. Ill. by author. HarperCollins, 1979, o.p. SERIES: I Can Read Books. SUBJECTS: Cookery. RL C.

Without having to cook, children can use this recipe book to create 26 snacks. The instructions occasionally call for expensive items like sweetened condensed milk or dates. Many of the recipes are very sweet but most are nutritious. Appealing illustrations help to explain the instructions.

SUBJECT INDEX

Subject heads are to nonfiction works unless designated with the word "Fiction." To make this index easier to use, "Fiction" cross-references can refer to both fiction and nonfiction headings. When a cross-reference does not have the label "Fiction," that cross-reference applies solely to nonfiction works. *Note*: Numerals refer to entry numbers, not page numbers.

Birds—Fiction

BIRTHDAYS

BIRTHDAYS—Fiction

Carlson, Nancy
The Perfect Family, 346
Christensen, Nancy
Good Night, Little Kitten, 401
Claverie, Jean
The Picnic, 419
Conway, Lisa
I Like Ketchup Sandwiches, 453
Cresswell, Helen
The Weather Cat, 474
Dauer, Rosamund
Bullfrog Grows Up, 488
Grindley, Sally, ed.
A Day with Alice and Sam. Ten Stories and a Picture Dictionary, 755
Himmelman, John
The Day-Off Machine, 843
Hooks, William H.
Where's Lulu?, 925
Hutchins, Pat
The Best Train Set Ever, 955
Impey, Rose, and Knox, Jolyne
Desperate for a Dog, 958
Jensen, Patricia
The Mess, 979
Kessler, Ethel, and Kessler, Leonard
Stan the Hot Dog Man, 1019
Kessler, Leonard
Are We Lost, Daddy?, 1022
Krensky, Stephen
Lionel-at-Large, 1074
Lionel in the Spring, 1075
Kuskin, Karla
Soap Soup, 1089
Manushkin, Fran
The Perfect Christmas Picture, 1283
Mayer, Mercer
Little Critter's Read-It-Yourself Storybook: Six Funny Easy-to-Read Stories, 1346
Minarik, Else H.
Father Bear Comes Home, 1382
Little Bear, 1384
Moncure, Jane B.
Caring for My Baby Sister, 1398

Monjo, F. N.
The One Bad Thing about Father, 1429
Moore, Lilian
Junk Day on Juniper Street and Other Easy-to-Read Stories, 1435
Nixon, Joan L.
Muffie Mouse and the Busy Birthday, 1491
Power, Barbara
I Wish Laura's Mommy Was My Mommy, 1701
Rice, Eve
Mr. Brimble's Hobby and Other Stories, 1749
Papa's Lemonade and Other Stories, 1751
Rockwell, Anne, and Rockwell, Harlow
Blackout, 1811
Rylant, Cynthia
Henry and Mudge and the Bedtime Thumps: The Ninth Book of Their Adventures, 1890
Henry and Mudge and the Careful Cousin: The Thirteenth Book of Their Adventures, 1891
Henry and Mudge and the Long Weekend: The Eleventh Book of Their Adventures, 1894
Henry and Mudge and the Wild Wind: The Twelfth Book of Their Adventures, 1895
Schick, Eleanor
Rainy Sunday, 1929
Sharmat, Marjorie W.
The Story of Bentley Beaver, 2035
Smath, Jerry
Pretzel and Pop's Closetful of Stories, 2112
Smith, Lucia
My Mom Got a Job, 2114
Van Leeuwen, Jean
Amanda Pig and Her Big Brother Oliver, 2289
Amanda Pig on Her Own, 2290
More Tales of Amanda Pig, 2291
More Tales of Oliver Pig, 2292

Oliver, Amanda, and Grandmother Pig, 2293
Oliver and Amanda's Christmas, 2294
Tales of Amanda Pig, 2297
Tales of Oliver Pig, 2298
Wilder, Laura Ingalls
Dance at Grandpa's, 2350
Winter Days in the Big Woods: Adapted from the Little House Books, 2351
Wood, Audrey
The Horrible Holidays, 2396
Tugford Wanted to Be Bad, 2398
Ziefert, Harriet
Andy Toots His Horn, 2435
Strike Four!, 2476

FAMILY LIFE—Vietnam

Wright, David
Vietnam Is My Home, 2408

FANTASY

Buller, Jon, and Schade, Susan
Mike and the Magic Cookies, 289
Yo! It's Captain Yo-Yo, 292
Donnelly, Liza
Dinosaur Beach, 552
Hamilton, Virginia M.
Jahdu, 770
Hasler, Eveline
Winter Magic, 785
Komaiko, Leah
Earl's Too Cool for Me, 1063
Marshall, Edward
Troll Country, 1297
Minarik, Else H.
Little Bear's Friend, 1385
Moncure, Jane B.
The Magic Moon Machine, 1412
A Wish-For Dinosaur, 1424
Mozelle, Shirley
Zack's Alligator, 1452
Murdocca, Sal
Take Me to the Moon!, 1460
Nixon, Joan L.
Bigfoot Makes a Movie, 1489

FOLKLORE—Netherlands

Evans, Katherine
Maid and Her Pail of Milk, 591
The Man, the Boy, and the Donkey, 592

FOLKLORE—Peru

Alexander, Ellen
Llama and the Great Flood: A Folktale from Peru, 15

FOLKLORE—Russia

Cole, Joanna
Bony-Legs, 435
Dolch, Edward W., and Dolch, Marguerite P.
Stories from Old Russia, 546
Ginsburg, Mirra
The Night It Rained Pancakes, 699
Jameson, Cynthia
The House of Five Bears, 971
Winter Hut, 972
Littledale, Freya
The Snow Child, 1156

FOLKLORE—Spain

Rockwell, Anne
The Bump in the Night, 1801

FOLKLORE—Turkey

Evans, Katherine
Camel in the Tent, 590
Van Woerkom, Dorothy
Abu Ali: Three Tales of the Middle East, 2299
The Friends of Abu Ali: Three More Tales of the Middle East, 2301

FOLKLORE—United States

Bang, Molly G.
Wiley and the Hairy Man: Adapted from an American Folktale, 102

Blassingame, Wyatt
How Davy Crockett Got a Bearskin Coat, 192
Pecos Bill and the Wonderful Clothesline Snake, 193
Pecos Bill Catches a Hidebehind, 194
Gilchrist, Theo E.
Halfway Up the Mountain, 697
Hayward, Linda
Hello, House!, 806
Kumin, Maxine W.
Paul Bunyan, 1084
Rockwell, Anne
Thump Thump Thump!, 1806
Schwartz, Alvin
All of Our Noses Are Here and Other Noodle Tales, 1940
I Saw You in the Bathtub and Other Folk Rhymes, 1943
There Is a Carrot in My Ear and Other Noodle Tales, 1946

FOLKLORE—Weather

Wolff, Barbara
Evening Gray, Morning Red: A Handbook of American Weather Wisdom, 2393

FOOD

Aliki
Corn Is Maize: The Gift of the Indians, 28
Milk: From Cow to Carton, 37
Lillegard, Dee
I Can Be a Baker, 1146
Moncure, Jane B.
What Was It Before It Was Bread?, 1423
Pillar, Marjorie
Pizza Man, 1649
Robbins, Ken
Make Me a Peanut Butter Sandwich and a Glass of Milk, 1779

Seixas, Judith S.
Junk Food: What It Is, What It Does, 1954

FOOD CHAINS—Fiction

Wolcott, Patty
Tunafish Sandwiches, 2391

FOOD—Fiction

Krasilovsky, Phyllis
The Man Who Cooked for Himself, 1067
McDaniel, Becky B.
Larry and the Cookie, 1209
Namm, Diane
Little Bear, 1476
Nobens, C. A.
The Happy Baker, 1495
Seuss, Dr.
Green Eggs and Ham, 1997
Snow, Pegeen
Eat Your Peas, Louise!, 2121
Wolcott, Patty
The Cake Story, 2384
Pickle Pickle Pickle Juice, 2388
Ziefert, Harriet
My Apple Tree, 2459
So Hungry!, 2472

Football—Fiction

SEE Sports—Football—Fiction

FORESTRY AND FOREST RANGERS

Pearce, Q. L., and Pearce, W. J.
In the Forest, 1603
Pellowski, Michael J.
What's It Like to Be a Forest Ranger, 1607

FOSSILS

Aliki
Dinosaur Bones, 30
Fossils Tell of Long Ago, 32

Rinkoff, Barbara
Guess What Rocks Do,
1775
Ruchlis, Hy
*How a Rock Came to Be in
a Fence on a Road near a
Town,* 1879
Selsam, Millicent E., and
Hunt, Joyce
A First Look at Dinosaurs,
1976
Sipiera, Paul P.
I Can Be a Geologist, 2093
Tangborn, Wendell V.
Glaciers, 2250

GHOST STORIES

Ahlberg, Allan
The Ghost Train, 11
Alexander, Sue
*More Witch, Goblin, and
Ghost Stories,* 18
*Witch, Goblin, and Ghost
Are Back,* 20
*Witch, Goblin, and Ghost
in the Haunted Woods,*
21
*Witch, Goblin, and Some-
times Ghost: Six Read-
Alone Stories,* 22
Allen, Laura J.
*Rollo and Tweedy and the
Ghost at Dougal Castle,*
47
Alley, Robert
Ghost in Dobb's Diner, 51
Baker, Barbara
All-by-Herself, 82
Benchley, Nathaniel
A Ghost Named Fred, 126
Berenstain, Stan, and Beren-
stain, Jan
*Berenstain Bears and the
Ghost of the Forest,* 148
Berry, Steve
*The Boy Who Wouldn't
Speak,* 180
Coville, Bruce, and Coville,
Katherine
The Foolish Giant, 465
Gage, Wilson
Mrs. Gaddy and the Ghost,
669
My Stars, It's Mrs. Gaddy!,
670

Glendinning, Sally
*Jimmy and Joe Find a
Ghost,* 703
Holl, Adelaide
George the Gentle Giant,
906
Levitt, Sidney
Mighty Movers, 1133
O'Connor, Jane
The Teeny Tiny Woman,
1512
Patterson, Lillie
*Haunted Houses on Hal-
loween,* 1598
Peters, Sharon
The Goofy Ghost, 1620
Quackenbush, Robert
*Sheriff Sally Gopher and
the Haunted Dance Hall,*
1730
Rockwell, Anne
*A Bear, a Bobcat, and Three
Ghosts,* 1798
The Bump in the Night,
1801
Schwartz, Alvin
*Ghosts! Ghostly Tales from
Folklore,* 1942
*In a Dark, Dark Room and
Other Scary Stories,* 1944
Standiford, Natalie
The Headless Horseman,
2147
Yolen, Jane
The Giants' Farm, 2427
The Giants Go Camping,
2428

**GIFTS AND GIFT-GIVING—
Fiction**

Numeroff, Laura J.
The Ugliest Sweater, 1503
Gelman, Rita G.
Hey, Kid!, 677

GLOBAL WARMING

Stille, Darlene R.
The Greenhouse Effect,
2166

GLOBES

Sipiera, Paul P.
Globes, 2090

Goats—Fiction

SEE Animals—Goats—Fiction

Gophers—Fiction

SEE Animals—Gophers—
Fiction

Gorillas—Fiction

SEE Animals—Gorillas—
Fiction

GRANDPARENTS—Fiction

Baker, Barbara
Staying with Grandmother,
81
Brenner, Barbara
Beef Stew, 259
Calmenson, Stephanie
*Marigold and Grandma on
the Town,* 321
Cazet, Denys
Saturday, 372
Eugenie, and Olson, Mary C.,
reteller
Kittens for Keeps, 588
Fernandes, Kim
Visiting Granny, 602
Goldman, Susan
*Grandma Is Somebody Spe-
cial,* 708
Keller, Beverly
*Don't Throw Another One,
Dover,* 1005
Lapp, Eleanor J.
*The Mice Came in Early
This Year,* 1100
Lexau, Joan M.
I Hate Red Rover, 1141
McCully, Emily Arnold
The Grandma Mix-Up,
1204
Grandmas at the Lake,
1205
Minarik, Else H.
A Kiss for Little Bear, 1383
Little Bear's Visit, 1386
Neasi, Barbara
Listen to Me, 1478
Numeroff, Laura J.
*Does Grandma Have an
Elmo Elephant Jungle
Kit?,* 1502

Johnson, Crockett
Picture for Harold's Room,
985
Kotzwinkle, William
*Up the Alley with Jack and
Joe*, 1065
Krensky, Stephen
Lionel and Louise, 1073
McClintock, Mike
What Have I Got?, 1200
Paterson, Katherine
*The Smallest Cow in the
World*, 1596
Pearson, Susan
Monday I Was an Alligator,
1605
Roche, P. K.
*Webster and Arnold and the
Giant Box*, 1796
Schick, Eleanor
Neighborhood Knight, 1928
Schulman, Janet
The Great Big Dummy,
1934
Seuling, Barbara
Just Me, 1990
Seuss, Dr.
*Oh, the Thinks You Can
Think!*, 2003
Sleator, William
That's Silly, 2108

IMAGINATIVE PLAY—Fiction

Moses, Amy
I Am an Explorer, 1450
Mozelle, Shirley
Zack's Alligator, 1452
*Zack's Alligator Goes to
School*, 1453
Smith, Mary M.
Orla's Upside Down Day,
2115

Immigration

SEE Emigration and Immi-
gration

INDIA

Greene, Carol
*Indira Nehru Gandhi: Ruler
of India*, 731

INDIA—Fiction

SEE ALSO Folklore—India

Bang, Betsy
Cucumber Stem, 99
Tuntuni the Tailor Bird, 100
Barr, Catherine
Gingercat's Catch, 105
Firmin, Peter
Basil Brush in the Jungle,
610

INJURIES—Fiction

Ziefert, Harriet
The Prince Has a Boo-boo!,
2465

Insects—Fiction

SEE Animals—Insects—
Fiction

INTERIOR DESIGN

Storm, Betsy
*I Can Be an Interior
Designer*, 2234

INVENTORS AND INVENTIONS

Martin, Patricia M.
Thomas Alva Edison, 1312
Radford, Ruby
Robert Fulton, 1738
Scarf, Maggi
Meet Benjamin Franklin,
1918

INVENTORS AND INVENTIONS—Fiction

Corbett, Scott
Boy Who Walked on Air,
461
Firmin, Peter
*Basil Brush and the Wind-
mills*, 606
Himmelman, John
The Day-Off Machine, 843
Great Leaf Blast-Off, 844

IRELAND

Kessel, Joyce K.
St. Patrick's Day, 1014

ISLANDS

May, Julian
These Islands Are Alive,
1343

ITALY

Bailey, Donna
Italy, 77

JAPAN—Fiction

Roy, Ron
A Thousand Pails of Water,
1852

Jealousy—Fiction

SEE Emotions—Jealousy—
Fiction

JOKES AND RIDDLES

Adler, David A.
*The Carsick Zebra and
Other Animal Riddles*, 3
*The Twisted Witch and
Other Spooky Riddles*, 8
Ball, Jacqueline A.
*What Can It Be? Riddles
About the Senses*, 96
Bishop, Ann
Merry-Go-Riddle, 185
Cerf, Bennett A.
*Bennett Cerf's Book of Ani-
mal Riddles*, 375
*Bennett Cerf's Book of
Laughs*, 376
*Bennett Cerf's Book of Rid-
dles*, 377
More Riddles, 378
Cole, Joanna
Get Well, Clown-Arounds!,
437
Degen, Bruce
*The Little Witch and the
Riddle*, 497
Elkin, Benjamin
*Big Jump and Other
Stories*, 577
Fleischman, Sid
Kate's Secret Riddle Book,
623
Hall, Katy, and Eisenberg,
Lisa
Buggy Riddles, 760

Ostriches—Fiction

SEE Animals—Ostriches—
Fiction

Otters—Fiction

SEE Animals—Otters—
Fiction

Owls—Fiction

SEE Animals—Owls—Fiction

PANAMA—Fiction

Palacios, Argentina
*A Christmas Surprise for
Chabelita*, 1549

PARADES—Fiction

Carrick, Carol
*The Longest Float in the
Parade*, 351
Kroll, Steven
The Goat Parade, 1079

PARENT AND CHILD

Clinton, Patrick
I Can Be a Father, 424
Fitz-Gerald, Christine
I Can Be a Mother, 622

PARENT AND CHILD—Fiction

Eastman, Philip D.
Are You My Mother?, 565
Greenwood, Pamela D.
I Found Mouse, 747
Hurd, Edith T.
Johnny Lion's Bad Day, 944
Marzollo, Jean
Amy Goes Fishing, 1314
Cannonball Chris, 1315
Mooser, Stephen, and Oliver,
Lin
Tad and Dad, 1442
Palacios, Argentina
*A Christmas Surprise for
Chabelita*, 1549
Parish, Peggy
No More Monsters for Me!,
1579
Porte, Barbara Ann
Harry's Mom, 1676

Quinlan, Patricia
Anna's Red Sled, 1736
Roy, Ron
A Thousand Pails of Water,
1852
Sharmat, Marjorie W.
Mooch the Messy, 2018
Slater, Teddy
N-O Spells No!, 2105
Thomson, Pat
One of Those Days, 2270
Thank You for the Tadpole,
2271
The Treasure Sock, 2272
Tompert, Ann
*Little Otter Remembers and
Other Stories*, 2277

PARENTS, WORKING—Fiction

Adams, Florence
Mushy Eggs, 2
Claverie, Jean
Working, 421

PARTIES—Fiction

Allard, Harry
*There's a Party at Mona's
Tonight*, 45
Claverie, Jean
The Party, 418
Park, W. B.
The Costume Party, 1588
Porte, Barbara Ann
Harry's Birthday, 1674
Prager, Annabelle
*The Spooky Halloween
Party*, 1702
The Surprise Party, 1703

Parrots—Fiction

SEE Animals—Parrots—
Fiction

PEACE—Fiction

Lattimore, Deborah N.
*The Flame of Peace: A Tale
of the Aztecs*, 1104

Peacocks—Fiction

SEE Animals—Peacocks—
Fiction

Pelicans—Fiction

SEE Animals—Pelicans—
Fiction

Penguins—Fiction

SEE Animals—Penguins—
Fiction

PET CARE

Anders, Rebecca
Dolly the Donkey, 58
Lorito the Parrot, 59
Winslow the Hamster, 60
Conklin, Gladys
I Caught a Lizard, 452
dePaola, Tomie
The Kids' Cat Book, 529
Landshoff, Ursula
Cats Are Good Company,
1096
Okay, Good Dog, 1097
Moncure, Jane B.
Caring for My Kitty, 1401
Snell, Nigel
Nita's Gerbil, 2118
Roy's Puppy, 2119
Sam's Rabbit, 2120
Stamper, Judith B.
*What's It Like to Be a Vet-
erinarian*, 2143
Stevens, Carla
*Your First Pet and How to
Take Care of It*, 2157
Watts, Barrie
Butterflies and Moths, 2333

PET CARE—Fiction

McArthur, Nancy
Pickled Peppers, 1195
Pape, Donna L.
*Mrs. Twitter the Animal Sit-
ter*, 1560
Pilkey, Dav
*Dragon's Fat Cat: Dragon's
Fourth Tale*, 1645
Waddell, Martin
We Love Them, 2322

PETS

Anders, Rebecca
Dolly the Donkey, 58
Lorito the Parrot, 59

Shrews—Fiction

SEE Animals—Shrews—
Fiction

Shyness—Fiction

SEE Behavior—Shyness—
Fiction

SIBLING RIVALRY—Fiction

Boegehold, Betty
Three to Get Ready, 204
Brenner, Barbara
Nicky's Sister, 263
Byars, Betsy
The Seven Treasure Hunts,
315
Carley, Wayne
Puppy Love, 329
Chorao, Kay
*Ups and Downs with Oink
and Pearl*, 400
Jensen, Patsy
Monster Party, 980
Keller, Beverly
*Don't Throw Another One,
Dover*, 1005
Leech, Jay, and Spencer,
Zane
Bright Fawn and Me, 1116
Mayer, Mercer
*Little Critter's Read-It-Your-
self Storybook: Six Funny
Easy-to-Read Stories*,
1346
McDaniel, Becky B.
Katie Can, 1206
McNulty, Faith
*The Elephant Who Couldn't
Forget*, 1261
Minarik, Else H.
No Fighting, No Biting!,
1387
O'Connor, Jane
Lulu and the Witch Baby,
1507
Olson, Mary C., ed.
This Room Is Mine!, 1521
Pickett, Anola
Old Enough for Magic,
1643
Roche, P. K.
*Webster and Arnold and the
Giant Box*, 1796

Stevenson, James
*Winston, Newton, Elton,
and Ed*, 2164
Van Leeuwen, Jean
*Amanda Pig and Her Big
Brother Oliver*, 2289
Tales of Oliver Pig, 2298
Wallace-Brodeur, Ruth
Stories from the Big Chair,
2326
Wang, Mary Lewis
*The Good Witch: A Charles
Perrault Tale Retold*, 2328
Weiss, Nicki
Menj, 2344
Ziefert, Harriet
Sometimes I Share, 2474
Take My Picture!, 2478

SIBLINGS—Fiction

Boegehold, Betty
Three to Get Ready, 204
Bonsall, Crosby
*The Day I Had to Play with
My Sister*, 213
Brenner, Barbara
*Rosa & Marco and the
Three Wishes*, 265
Bronin, Andrew
*Gus and Buster Work
Things Out*, 274
Brown, Marc
D.W. Thinks Big, 278
Buller, Jon, and Schade,
Susan
The Video Kids, 291
Byars, Betsy
*The Golly Sisters Ride
Again*, 313
Calmenson, Stephanie
The Little Witch Sisters,
320
Carlson, Nancy
Harriet and Walt, 337
The Perfect Family, 346
Castiglia, Julie
Jill the Pill, 369
Chorao, Kay
Oink and Pearl, 399
Cocca-Leffler, Maryann
What a Pest!, 427
de Saint Mars, Dominique
*Lily Fights with Her Broth-
er*, 532
Galbraith, Kathryn O.
Roommates, 672

Glaser, Linda
*Keep Your Socks On,
Albert!*, 701
Heilbroner, Joan
*The Happy Birthday
Present*, 812
Hoban, Lillian
Arthur's Camp-out, 857
Arthur's Funny Money, 859
Arthur's Honey Bear, 861
Arthur's Pen Pal, 863
Arthur's Prize Reader, 864
Holl, Adelaide
*Small Bear and the Secret
Surprise*, 909
Hooks, William H.
Mr. Baseball, 923
Mr. Monster, 924
Hutchins, Hazel
And You Can Be the Cat,
954
Jewell, Nancy
Two Silly Trolls, 984
Krensky, Stephen
Lionel and Louise, 1073
Lawrence, James
Binky Brothers, Detectives,
1112
Lexau, Joan M.
*Finders Keepers, Losers
Weepers*, 1140
The Rooftop Mystery, 1143
McDaniel, Becky B.
Katie Couldn't, 1207
Katie Did It, 1208
Mallett, Anne
Here Comes Tagalong, 1278
Marshall, Edward
Four on the Shore, 1290
Moncure, Jane B.
Caring for My Baby Sister,
1398
Oneal, Zibby
Maude and Walter, 1522
Pape, Donna L.
Snowman for Sale, 1561
Pearson, Susan
Molly Moves Out, 1604
Petersen, P. J.
The Fireplug Is First Base,
1630
Ruthstrom, Dorotha
The Big Kite Contest, 1881
Siracusa, Catherine
*Bingo, the Best Dog in the
World*, 2097

TITLE INDEX

Note: Numerals refer to entry numbers, not page numbers.

Aaron and the Green Mountain Boys (Gauch, Patricia L.), 675

ABC Pigs Go to Market (DeLage, Ida), 499

About Monkeys in Trees (Porter, Wesley), 1678

Abu Ali: Three Tales of the Middle East (Van Woerkom, Dorothy), 2299

Ace Dragon Ltd. (Hoban, Russell), 873

Addie Meets Max (Robins, Joan), 1781

Addie Runs Away (Robins, Joan), 1782

Addie's Bad Day (Robins, Joan), 1783

The Adventures of Mole and Troll (Johnston, Tony), 991

The Adventures of Snail at School (Stadler, John), 2134

Adventures with a Ball (Milgrom, Harry), 1367

Adventures with a Cardboard Tube (Milgrom, Harry), 1368

Adventures with a Party Plate (Milgrom, Harry), 1369

Adventures with a Straw (Milgrom, Harry), 1370

Adventures with a String (Milgrom, Harry), 1371

Aesop's Stories (Dolch, Edward W., and Dolch, Marguerite P.), 539

African Buffalo (Stone, Lynn M.), 2171

After the Dinosaurs (Berenstain, Stan, and Berenstain, Jan), 141

Air (Richardson, Joy), 1752

Airplanes (Petersen, David L.), 1623

Airports (Petersen, David L.), 1624

Albert the Albatross (Hoff, Syd), 878

Alcohol: What It Is, What It Does (Seixas, Judith S.), 1951

All Aboard Overnight: A Book of Compound Words (Maestro, Betsy), 1270

All about Whales (Patent, Dorothy H.), 1594

All-by-Herself (Baker, Barbara), 82

All of Our Noses Are Here and Other Noodle Tales (Schwartz, Alvin), 1940

All Pigs Are Beautiful (King-Smith, Dick), 1042

Allergies: What They Are, What They Do (Seixas, Judith S.), 1952

Alligator (Shaw, Evelyn), 2045

Alligators and Crocodiles (Stone, Lynn M.), 2172

Alligators (Martin, Louise), 1304

The Almost Awful Play (Giff, Patricia R.), 691

Almost Goodbye (Cresswell, Helen, and Brown, Judy), 475

Always Wondering: Some Favorite Poems of Aileen Fisher (Fisher, Aileen), 616

Amanda Pig and Her Big Brother Oliver (Van Leeuwen, Jean), 2289

Amanda Pig on Her Own (Van Leeuwen, Jean), 2290

Amazing Beetles (Still, John), 2165

Amazing Otters (Brownell, M. Barbara), 282

The Amazing the Incredible Super Dog (Bonsall, Crosby), 207

Amelia Bedelia and the Baby (Parish, Peggy), 1564

Amelia Bedelia and the Surprise Shower (Parish, Peggy), 1565

Amelia Bedelia Goes Camping (Parish, Peggy), 1566

Amelia Bedelia Helps Out (Parish, Peggy), 1567

Amelia Bedelia (Parish, Peggy), 1563

Amelia Bedelia's Family Album (Parish, Peggy), 1568

Amish Boy (Rowland, Florence W.), 1848

Amish Wedding (Rowland, Florence W.), 1849

Amy for Short (Numeroff, Laura J.), 1500

Amy Goes Fishing (Marzollo, Jean), 1314

Anatosaurus (Riehecky, Janet), 1766

And I Mean It, Stanley (Bonsall, Crosby), 208

And You Can Be the Cat (Hutchins, Hazel), 954

Andy Toots His Horn (Ziefert, Harriet), 2435

Animal Camouflage: Hide-and-Seek Animals (McDonnell, Janet), 1212

Animal Clowns (McGoldrick, Jane R.), 1218

Animal Cracks (Quackenbush, Robert), 1715

Reddy Rattler and Easy Eagle (Sharmat, Mitchell), 2042

Redwoods Are the Tallest Trees in the World (Adler, David A.), 7

Rembrandt (Venezia, Mike), 2316

Reptiles (Markert, Jenny), 1288

Reptiles (Stone, Lynn M.), 2219

Reptiles Do the Strangest Things (Hornblow, Leonora, and Hornblow, Arthur), 934

Rhinoceros (Martin, Louise), 1307

Ricky, Rocky, and Ringo Count on Pizza (Kunnas, Mauri), 1088

Ring around Duffy (Hearn, Emily), 807

The River (Jeunesse, Gallimard, and Bour, Laura), 982

A Robber! A Robber! (Brandenberg, Franz), 237

The Robber of Featherbed Lane (Holding, James), 904

Robert Fulton (Radford, Ruby), 1738

Robert the Rose Horse (Heilbroner, Joan), 813

Roberto Clemente (Mercer, Charles), 1356

Roberto Clemente (Rudeen, Kenneth), 1880

Robert's Robot (Granowsky, Alvin; Tweedt, Joy A.; and Tweedt, Craig L.), 716

Robin of Bray (Marzollo, Jean, and Marzollo, Claudio), 1325

The Robot Birthday (Bunting, Eve), 295

Rocks and Soil (Richardson, Joy), 1754

Rollo and Tweedy and the Ghost at Dougal Castle (Allen, Laura J.), 47

Ronald Morgan Goes to Bat (Giff, Patricia R.), 693

The Rooftop Mystery (Lexau, Joan M.), 1143

Roommates (Galbraith, Kathryn O.), 672

Rosa & Marco and the Three Wishes (Brenner, Barbara), 265

Rosie's Mouse (Mayer, Gina, and Mayer, Mercer), 1344

Row, Row, Row Your Boat (Oppenheim, Joanne), 1530

Roy's Puppy (Snell, Nigel), 2119

Ruff Leaves Home (Carter, Anne), 358

Rugs Have Naps (But Never Take Them) (Klasky, Charles), 1051

Run to the Rainbow (Hillert, Margaret), 838

Running Owl the Hunter (Benchley, Nathaniel), 129

Russia (Vaughn, Jenny, and Barnard, Chris), 2309

Rutherford T. Finds 21B (Rinkoff, Barbara), 1778

Ruthie's Rude Friends (Marzollo, Jean, and Marzollo, Claudio), 1326

Sad Song, Happy Song (Miklowitz, Gloria), 1362

Saguaro Cactus (Storad, Conrad J.), 2233

Sailor's Book (Agell, Charlotte), 9

Sam and Lucy (Ziefert, Harriet), 2467

Sam and the Firefly (Eastman, Philip D.), 568

Sam the Minuteman (Benchley, Nathaniel), 130

Sam's Rabbit (Snell, Nigel), 2120

Sammy the Seal (Hoff, Syd), 894

Sammy's Mommy Has Cancer (Kohlenberg, Sherry), 1061

Samuel Clemens (Daugherty, Charles M.), 489

Sandbox Betty (Petrie, Catherine), 1633

Sandpipers (Hurd, Edith T.), 951

Sandro's Dolphin (Winnick, Karen), 2363

Sara and the Pinch (Stevens, Carla), 2156

Sarah's Unicorn (Coville, Bruce, and Coville, Katherine), 466

Satchel Paige: The Best Arm in Baseball (McKissack, Patricia, and McKissack, Fredrick), 1251

Saturday (Cazet, Denys), 372

Saving the Forests: A Rabbit's Story (Riehecky, Janet), 1772

Say Good Night! (Ziefert, Harriet), 2468

Scarlet Monster Lives Here (Sharmat, Marjorie W.), 2033

The Science Book of Light (Ardley, Neil), 64

Science Fun with a Flashlight (Schneider, Herman, and Schneider, Nina), 1931

Science Fun with Mud and Dirt (Wyler, Rose), 2411

Science Toys and Tricks (White, Laurence B.), 2349

Scruffy (Parish, Peggy), 1582

Scurry's Treasure (Carter, Anne), 359

Sea Frog, City Frog (Van Woerkom, Dorothy), 2306

Sea Otters (Shaw, Evelyn), 2050

Sea Shells (Cooper, Jason), 459

Sea Turtles (Stone, Lynn M.), 2220

Seahorse (Morris, Robert), 1449

Seals (Martin, Louise), 1308

Seashore (Pluckrose, Henry), 1659

The Seasons (Milburn, Constance), 1363

The Seasons (Richardson, Joy), 1755

Second Car in Town (Bourne, Miriam A.), 223

The Secret of Foghorn Island (Hayes, Geoffrey), 804

Secret Three (Myrick, Mildred), 1474

Secrets of the Mummies (Milton, Joyce), 1379

Seeds and More Seeds (Selsam, Millicent E.), 1963

Seeing Is Believing (Shub, Elizabeth), 2077

Sequoya (Gleiter, Jan, and Thompson, Kathleen), 702

The Seven Treasure Hunts (Byars, Betsy), 315

Several Tricks of Edgar Dolphin (Benchley, Nathaniel), 131

ILLUSTRATOR INDEX

Note: Numerals refer to entry numbers, not page numbers.

Abel, Simone
I Can Add, 957

Abolafia, Yossi
Buffy and Albert, 1670
Harry Gets an Uncle, 1672
Harry in Trouble, 1673
Harry's Birthday, 1674
Harry's Dog, 1675
Harry's Mom, 1676
Harry's Visit, 1677
Leo and Emily's Zoo, 235
What I Did Last Summer,
1711

Adams, Lynn
Kitty's First Airplane Trip,
595

Agell, Charlotte
Sailor's Book, 9

Aitken, Amy
My Tooth Is Loose!, 2080
Please Let It Snow, 2464
Stitches, 2475
Take My Picture!, 2478
Wait for Us!, 2481

Alborough, Jez
*Can You Hear Me,
Grandad?*, 2267

Alexander, Ellen
Fireflies in the Night, 795
*Llama and the Great Flood:
A Folktale from Peru*, 15

Aliki
At Mary Bloom's, 26
*Aunt Nina and Her
Nephews and Nieces*, 230
Averages, 2133
Communication, 27
*Corn Is Maize: The Gift of
the Indians*, 28

Digging Up Dinosaurs, 29
Dinosaur Bones, 30
Dinosaurs Are Different, 31
Everyone Ready?, 231
Fossils Tell of Long Ago, 32
*The Horse That Liked Sand-
wiches*, 2266
How a Book Is Made, 33
I'm Growing, 34
*The King's Day: Louis XIV
of France*, 35
*Leo and Emily and the
Dragon*, 233
Leo and Emily's Big Ideas,
234
The Listening Walk, 2066
*Long-Lost Coelacanth and
Other Living Fossils*, 36
Milk: From Cow to Carton,
37
My Feet, 38
My Hands, 39
My Visit to the Aquarium,
40
My Visit to the Dinosaurs,
41
Nice New Neighbors, 236
A Robber! A Robber!, 237
Six New Students, 238
Story of Johnny Appleseed,
42
*This Is the House Where
Jack Lives*, 814
*A Weed Is a Flower: The
Life of George Washing-
ton Carver*, 43
What Can You Make of It?,
239
*Wild and Woolly Mam-
moths*, 44

Allen, Elizabeth
Who Is Who?, 1232

Allen, Graham
The Tiger, 1874

Allen, Joan
Tiny Bear Goes to the Fair,
1172

Allen, Laura J.
Ghost in Dobbs Diner, 51
Ottie and the Star, 46
*Rollo and Tweedy and the
Ghost at Dougal Castle*,
47
Where Is Freddy?, 48

Alley, R. W.
The Ball Game, 1544
Buck-Buck the Chicken,
572
The Little Witch Sisters,
320
The Prince Has a Boo-boo!,
2465
The Prince's Tooth Is Loose,
2466
The Teeny Tiny Woman,
1512
Where's Lulu?, 925
*Who Put the Pepper in the
Pot?*, 448

Almquist, Don
Spring Is Like the Morning,
473

Aloise, Frank
*Bob Bodden and the Seago-
ing Farm*, 426
Hello, Year!, 962
I Know a Plumber, 480
*Poems about Fur and
Feather Friends*, 966
*Poetry for Space Enthusi-
asts*, 969

READABILITY INDEX

Titles have been categorized by range of difficulty for beginning readers: low (Reading Level A), middle (Reading Level B), and high (Reading Level C). Using the criteria established for including a title (see Preface) and relying on our experience and judgment, rather than strict adherence to readability levels, allowed for inclusion of books such as *The Berenstains' B Book*, which tested beyond the first and second grade levels. *Note:* Numerals refer to entry numbers, not page numbers.

READING LEVEL B (cont.)

Henry and Mudge in Puddle Trouble: The Second Book of Their Adventures, 1897

Henry and Mudge in the Green Time: The Third Book of Their Adventures, 1898

Henry and Mudge in the Sparkle Days: The Fifth Book of Their Adventures, 1899

Henry and Mudge Take the Big Test: The Tenth Book of Their Adventures, 1900

Henry and Mudge: The First Book of Their Adventures, 1889

Henry and Mudge under the Yellow Moon: The Fourth Book of Their Adventures, 1901

Mr. Putter and Tabby Bake the Cake, 1902

Mr. Putter and Tabby Pour the Tea, 1903

Mr. Putter and Tabby Walk the Dog, 1904

Sadler, Marilyn J.
It's Not Easy Being a Bunny, 1906
The Very Bad Bunny, 1909

Saltzberg, Barney
What to Say to Clara, 1912

Scarf, Maggi
Meet Benjamin Franklin, 1918

Scarry, Richard
Best Read-It-Yourself Book Ever, 1919
Dr. Doctor, 1920

Schecter, Ellen
The Boy Who Cried "Wolf!" Retold in Rebus, 1924

Schick, Eleanor
Home Alone, 1926
Joey on His Own, 1927
Neighborhood Knight, 1928
Rainy Sunday, 1929
Summer at the Sea, 1930

Schneider, Herman, and Schneider, Nina
Science Fun with a Flashlight, 1931

Schulman, Janet
Camp Kee Wee's Secret Weapon, 1933
The Great Big Dummy, 1934
Jenny and the Tennis Nut, 1938

Schultz, Walter A.
Will and Orv, 1939

Schwartz, Alvin
All of Our Noses Are Here and Other Noodle Tales, 1940
Ghosts! Ghostly Tales from Folklore, 1942
I Saw You in the Bathtub and Other Folk Rhymes, 1943
Ten Copycats in a Boat and Other Riddles, 1945
There Is a Carrot in My Ear and Other Noodle Tales, 1946

Scott, Geoffrey
Egyptian Boats, 1947

Seixas, Judith S.
Alcohol: What It Is, What It Does, 1951

Selsam, Millicent E.
Egg to Chick, 1958
Greg's Microscope, 1959
More Potatoes!, 1961
Strange Creatures That Really Lived, 1964
When an Animal Grows, 1968

Selsam, Millicent E., and Hunt, Joyce
A First Look at Animals with Horns, 1970
A First Look at Bats, 1972
A First Look at Birds, 1974
A First Look at Caterpillars, 1975
A First Look at Ducks, Geese and Swans, 1977
A First Look at Horses, 1978
A First Look at the World of Plants, 1985

Serventy, Vincent
Kangaroo, 1987
Koala, 1988

Seuss, Dr.
Cat in the Hat Comes Back, 1992
The Cat's Quizzer, 1993
Foot Book, 1994

I Am Not Going to Get Up Today!, 1999
I Can Read with My Eyes Shut!, 2000
Oh, Say Can You Say?, 2002
There's a Wocket in My Pocket!, 2005

Shapiro, Irwin
Gretchen and the White Steed, 2008

Shapp, Martha, and Shapp, Charles
Let's Find Out about Animals of Long Ago, 2009
Let's Find Out about Babies, 2010
Let's Find Out about Houses, 2011
Let's Find Out about Trees (Arbor Day), 2013

Sharmat, Marjorie W.
Griselda's New Year, 2015
Little Devil Gets Sick, 2016
Mitchell Is Moving, 2017
Mooch the Messy, 2018
Nate the Great and the Halloween Hunt, 2022
Nate the Great and the Stolen Base, 2029
Nate the Great Goes Undercover, 2031
Nate the Great Stalks Stupidweed, 2032
The Story of Bentley Beaver, 2035
The Trip and Other Sophie and Gussie Stories, 2036
The Trolls of Twelfth Street, 2037
Uncle Boris and Maude, 2038
Who's Afraid of Ernestine?, 2039

Sharmat, Marjorie W., and Weinman, Rosalind
Nate the Great and the Pillowcase, 2041

Sharmat, Mitchell
Reddy Rattler and Easy Eagle, 2042

Shaw, Evelyn
Alligator, 2045
A Nest of Wood Ducks, 2048
Octopus, 2049
Sea Otters, 2050

SERIES INDEX

Under each series title entries are arranged by author, then title and entry number. No distinction has been made where publishers share the same series title.

About Me

de Saint Mars, Dominique
Lily Fights with Her Brother, 532
Max Is Shy, 533

African Animal Discovery Library

Stone, Lynn M.
African Buffalo, 2171
Antelopes, 2173
Giraffes, 2197
Hippopotamus, 2199
Hyenas, 2201
Zebras, 2231

Aladdin Basics

Thomson, Ruth
Creepy Crawlies, 2273
Wood, Tim
Out in Space, 2399

All Aboard Books

Ashrose, Cara
The Very First Americans, 73
Demuth, Patricia
Inside Your Busy Body, 524
Wilson, Lynn
Sharks!, 2362

All Aboard Reading

Buller, Jon, and Schade, Susan
Mike and the Magic Cookies, 289
The Video Kids, 291
Yo! It's Captain Yo-Yo, 292
Cocca-Leffler, Maryann
What a Pest!, 427
Cole, Joanna
You Can't Smell a Flower with Your Ear! All About Your Five Senses, 449
Demuth, Patricia
Snakes, 525
Herman, Gail
Double Header, 825
What a Hungry Puppy!, 826
Milton, Joyce
Bats: Creatures of the Night, 1377
O'Connor, Jane
EEK! Stories to Make You Shriek, 1506

All about you

McNamara, Louise G., and Litchfield, Ada B.
Your Busy Brain, 1258
Your Living Bones, 1259

Amazing Animal Reader

Smith, Mavis
A Snake Mistake, 2116

American Folktales

Blassingame, Wyatt
Pecos Bill and the Wonderful Clothesline Snake, 193
Pecos Bill Catches a Hidebehind, 194

Animal Friends

Anders, Rebecca
Dolly the Donkey, 58
Lorito the Parrot, 59
Winslow the Hamster, 60
Johnson, Sylvia A.
Elephants around the World, 988
Lions of Africa, 989
Penney and Pete the Lambs, 990

Animal Life Stories

Royston, Angela
The Deer, 1856
The Duck, 1858
The Fox, 1859
The Frog, 1860
The Hedgehog, 1862
The Mouse, 1866
The Otter, 1867
The Penguin, 1868
The Squirrel, 1873
The Tiger, 1874
The Whale, 1876

Easy-Read Fact

Lowery, Barbara
Mammals, 1180

Easy-Read Story

Fleischman, Sid
Kate's Secret Riddle Book,
623
Gelman, Rita G.
Hey, Kid!, 677
Gibbons, Gail
*The Magnificent Morris
Mouse Clubhouse*, 682
Mooser, Stephen
*Funnyman and the Penny
Dodo*, 1438
Funnyman's First Case,
1439
*The Ghost with the Hal-
loween Hiccups*, 1440
Newman, Alyse
It's Me, Claudia!, 1480
Nicklaus, Carol
Harry the Hider, 1485
Numeroff, Laura J.
Beatrice Doesn't Want To,
1501
The Ugliest Sweater, 1503
Quackenbush, Robert
No Mouse for Me, 1727
Ross, Dave, and Wilson,
Jeanne
Mr. Terwilliger's Secret,
1828
Thaler, Mike
*There's a Hippopotamus
under My Bed*, 2263
Weiss, Ellen
Millicent Maybe, 2341
Weiss, Leatie
Heather's Feathers, 2343

Easy Readers

Mayer, Mercer
This Is My Friend, 1347

Easy Reading

Klasky, Charles
*Rugs Have Naps (But
Never Take Them)*, 1051

Easy-to-Read Folktale

Saunders, Susan
Puss in Boots, 1916
Tarcov, Edith H.
The Frog Prince, 2251

Easy Venture

Carley, Wayne
*Percy the Parrot Yelled
Quiet!*, 328
Jacobs, Leland B.
Teeny-Tiny, 970
Latham, Jean L.
*What Tabbit the Rabbit
Found*, 1103
McInnes, John
*Have You Ever Seen a
Monster?*, 1221
Leo Lion Paints It Red,
1223
Pape, Donna L.
The Big White Thing, 1553
Wiseman, Bernard
Quick Quackers, 2380

Eye Openers

Royston, Angela
Birds, 1853
Cars, 1854
Diggers and Dump Trucks,
1857
*Insects and Crawly Crea-
tures*, 1864
Jungle Animals, 1865
Planes, 1870
Trucks, 1875
Zoo Animals, 2493

Eyewitness

Still, John
Amazing Beetles, 2165

Famous Animal Stories

Denzel, Justin
*Jumbo: Giant Circus Ele-
phant*, 527
Hall, Lynn
*Captain: Canada's Flying
Pony*, 765

Farm Animal Discovery Library

Stone, Lynn M.
Chickens, 2182
Cows, 2185
Ducks, 2189
Horses, 2200
Pigs, 2215
Sheep, 2221

Farm Animal Stories

Royston, Angela
The Cow, 1855
The Goat, 1861
The Hen, 1863
The Pig, 1869
The Pony, 1871
The Sheep, 1872

Fast Start

Berenstain, Michael
*Michael Berenstain's Hop,
Waddle, Swim!*, 138
*Michael Berenstain's When
I Grow Up Oh, the
Things I Can Be!*, 139

Fat Cat

Lexau, Joan M.
I Hate Red Rover, 1141
Sleator, William
Once, Said Darlene, 2107

Field Trip Mysteries

Binnamin, Vivian
*The Case of the Planetari-
um Puzzle*, 183
*The Case of the Snoring
Stegosaurus*, 184

First Discovery Book

Jeunesse, Gallimard
Castles, 981
Jeunesse, Gallimard, and
Bour, Laura
The River, 982
Jeunesse, Gallimard;
Delafosse, Claude; and
Valat, Pierre-Marie
*The Camera: Snapshots,
Movies, Videos, and Car-
toons*, 983

Nicky Upstairs and Down,
2461
Penny Goes to the Movies,
2463
Please Let It Snow, 2464
Say Good Night!, 2468
Stitches, 2475
Strike Four!, 2476
Surprise!, 2477
Tim and Jim Take Off, 2479
Under the Water, 2480
When the TV Broke, 2483

Helpful Betty

Morgan, Michaela
Helpful Betty Solves a Mystery, 1443
Helpful Betty to the Rescue,
1444

Henry and Mudge

Rylant, Cynthia
Henry and Mudge: The First Book of Their Adventures, 1889
Henry and Mudge and the Bedtime Thumps: The Ninth Book of Their Adventures, 1890
Henry and Mudge and the Careful Cousin: The Thirteenth Book of Their Adventures, 1891
Henry and Mudge and the Forever Sea: The Sixth Book of Their Adventures, 1892
Henry and Mudge and the Happy Cat: The Eighth Book of Their Adventures, 1893
Henry and Mudge and the Long Weekend: The Eleventh Book of Their Adventures, 1894
Henry and Mudge and the Wild Wind: The Twelfth Book of Their Adventures, 1895
Henry and Mudge Get the Cold Shivers: The Seventh Book of Their Adventures, 1896
Henry and Mudge in Puddle Trouble: The Second

Book of Their Adventures, 1897
Henry and Mudge in the Green Time: The Third Book of Their Adventures, 1898
Henry and Mudge in the Sparkle Days: The Fifth Book of Their Adventures, 1899
Henry and Mudge Take the Big Test: The Tenth Book of Their Adventures, 1900
Henry and Mudge under the Yellow Moon: The Fourth Book of Their Adventures, 1901

Hide-and-Seek Science Book

Brenner, Barbara, and Chardiet, Bernice
Where's That Insect?, 267

Holiday

Graves, Charles P.
Fourth of July, 718

How Animals Grow!

Burton, Jane
Fancy the Fox, 300

How Your Pet Grows!

Caper the Kid, 297
Chester the Chick, 298
Dabble the Duckling, 299
Freckles the Rabbit, 301
Jack the Puppy, 303

I Am Reading

Alexander, Sue
More Witch, Goblin, and Ghost Stories, 18
Seymour the Prince, 19
Witch, Goblin, and Ghost Are Back, 20
Witch, Goblin, and Ghost in the Haunted Woods, 21
Witch, Goblin, and Sometimes Ghost: Six Read-Alone Stories, 22

Klein, Monica
Backyard Basketball Superstar, 1054
Little Wild Chimpanzee, 1359
Little Wild Elephant, 1360
Little Wild Lion Cub, 1361
Prager, Annabelle
The Spooky Halloween Party, 1702
Ross, Pat
M and M and the Bad News Babies, 1831
M and M and the Big Bag, 1832
M and M and the Haunted House Game, 1834
Meet M and M, 1838
Roy, Ron
Awful Thursday, 1850
Ruthstrom, Dorotha
The Big Kite Contest, 1881
Watson, Jane W.
The First Americans: Tribes of North America, 2332

I Can Be

Beckman, Beatrice
I Can Be a Teacher, 119
Behrens, June
I Can Be a Truck Driver, 121
I Can Be an Astronaut, 122
Clinton, Patrick
I Can Be a Father, 424
Fitz-Gerald, Christine
I Can Be a Mother, 622
Greene, Carol
I Can Be a Football Player, 729
Lillegard, Dee
I Can Be a Baker, 1146
Martin, Claire
I Can Be a Weather Forecaster, 1302
Matthias, Catherine
I Can Be a Police Officer, 1336
Osinski, Christine
I Can Be a Photographer, 1541
Pickering, Robert
I Can Be an Archaeologist, 1642
Rowan, James P.
I Can Be A Zookeeper, 1846